Service
ETIQUETTE

Service ETIQUETTE

FIFTH EDITION

Cherlynn Conetsco and Anna Hart

NAVAL INSTITUTE PRESS
Annapolis, Maryland

Naval Institute Press
291 Wood Road
Annapolis, MD 21402

ISBN: 978-1-61251-449-9 (eBook)

Library of Congress Cataloging-in-Publication Data
Conetsco, Cherlynn.
  Service etiquette / Cherlynn Conetsco and Anna Hart. — 5th ed.
    p. cm.
  Rev. ed. of: Service etiquette / Oretha D. Swartz. 4th ed. 1988.
  Includes bibliographical references and index.
  ISBN 978-1-59114-357-4 (alk. paper)
  1. United States—Armed Forces—Military life. 2. Etiquette—United States. I. Hart,
Anna. II. Swartz, Oretha D. Service etiquette. III. Title.
  U766.C56 2009
  355.1'3360973—dc22
                                2009027764

Printed in the United States of America on acid-free paper

25 24 23 22 21 20 19   17 16 15 14 13 12 11

Photos: Sharon Connolly, of Connolly Creations, freelance photographer residing in Fairfax
Station, Virginia. She has received several Photographer of the Year awards from the Vienna
Photographic Society. She has also participated in juried exhibits with the Meadowlark Nature
Photography Expo. www.connollycreations.com

For David, Carla, Chrissy, and other world citizens

CONTENTS

Foreword   ix

Acknowledgments   xiii

Introduction   xv

Section I. United States Military and Government   1

  1 *Military and Government Protocol*   3

  2 *Military Honors and Official Government Ceremonies*   20

  3 *Hosting High-Profile Visits*   34

  4 *Organizing a Dining In and Dining Out*   57

  5 *The Fallen Comrade Table Observance*   81

  6 *The Military Funeral*   88

  7 *Flag Etiquette*   103

  8 *Order of Precedence and Military Forms of Address*   120

Section II. Military Weddings   139

  9 *Military Wedding Etiquette*   141

  10 *Military Wedding Invitations, Announcements, and Replies*   165

Section III. Communications Etiquette   185

  11 *Invitations*   187

  12 *Correspondence and Stationery Essentials*   200

  13 *Abbreviations in Social Correspondence*   221

  14 *Personal Electronics Etiquette*   223

  15 *Civilian Forms of Address*   238

Section IV. Good Manners and Civility   255

  16 *Place Settings, Table Manners, and Service Styles*   257

  17 *Family Dining, Buffets, and Formal In-Home Meals*   276

  18 *Official Business Functions, Cocktails, and Receptions*   286

  19 *Introductions, Conversations, and Farewells*   301

  20 *Toasts*   314

  21 *Guest and Visitor Civility*   324

  22 *Appropriate Attire*   335

  23 *Seating Plans*   394

Section V. International Considerations   419

  24 *International Travel*   421

  25 *International Protocol and Civility*   436

  26 *International Guest and Host Duties*   458

  27 *Manners at the Global Dinner Table*   480

  28 *Communal Platter Dining*   488

  29 *Chopstick Protocol*   496

  30 *Food and Drink Preferences of Various Religious Groups*   509

  Index   513

Foreword

*T*his book contains important lessons about life in uniform.

There is no denying that all of us must function in an increasingly diverse and interconnected world, rich with cultural differences, customs, traditions, mores, and courtesies too many to remember—but that's not why I want you to read this book.

The lessons in this book are not so much a recipe for professional success as they are fundamental guidelines to ensure our actions are perceived and received in the manner in which they were intended.

Simply put, we should acknowledge those around us, treating them with appropriate respect and dignity—not because it will help us succeed, but because it's the right thing to do.

This book is about doing the right thing.

It offers all of us, from different backgrounds, different interest levels, different responsibilities, a better understanding of each other, and what is expected of us in unfamiliar circumstances—a tall order for one word: etiquette.

Gone are the days when it was enough to recognize the basic customs and courtesies of our own Service. We now live in an Age of Information, in which our actions—intended or otherwise—are transmitted through cyberspace and viewed and interpreted by friends and enemies around the globe. Our actions have a profound impact on others—shouldn't it be the impact we want?

The authors are superbly equipped to teach us the rules for appropriate behavior in nearly every circumstance. Between them, Anna Hart and Cherlynn Conetsco have more than a half-century of hands-on experience in guiding both service personnel and civilians toward new levels of self-confidence as they master the basics of social interaction. Anna and Cherlynn not only have updated the venerable

4th Edition of Service Etiquette; they have added an international dimension, as well.

Actions really do speak louder than words. This book will help our actions—and our words—match our best intentions.

PETER PACE, USNA '67
General, USMC (Ret.)

16th Chairman of the
Joint Chiefs of Staff

EDUCATION AND COACHING

Executive education and coaching is recommended for the proper application of *Service Etiquette* materials and ancillary information. The authors are available to provide coaching services to private individuals, business, government, military, and diplomatic entities; domestically and internationally.

Contact the International Association of Protocol Consultants® and Officers™ at www.ChoosingCivility.org. IAPC is a non-profit 501(c)6 alliance dedicated to higher-level learning in protocol, etiquette, and civility.

Acknowledgments

We thank our immediate and extended family members (especially David Michael Conetsco, Carla Anne Hart, and Christine Hart Connolly) for their patience throughout the writing of this book, and the following friends and colleagues at the Naval Institute Press:

Susan Corrado, Editorial Manager
Tom Cutler, Director of Professional Publishing
Chris Gamboa-Onrubia, Director of Design and Production Services
Judy Heise, Publicist
Janis Jorgenson, Photo Archivist
George Keating, Director of Sales and Marketing
Jehanne Moharram, Copy Editor
Marla Traweek, Production Editor

We thank Colonel John G. Miller, United States Marine Corps (Retired), former Deputy Director of Marine Corps History, for reviewing the manuscript with regard to military history, traditions, and ceremonies.

We would also like to thank the following people listed in alphabetical order:

Jay Ackerman Photography
Colonel E. West Anderson, United States Air Force
Teresa Babb, Program Manager, Joint Military Attaché School
Eileen Beall
Julie Bellonte, National Geographic Global Entertainment
Margaret J. Bowen, Director of Social Development, United States
    Coast Guard Academy
Ensign Amanda Burney, United States Navy
Edward Buxton Photography
Lieutenant Cameron Collier, United States Navy

Daniel Connolly

Sharon Connolly, Fine Art Photography

Colonel Katie Haddock, USMC (Ret.)

Eric and Carol Hammersen, former military diplomats

William P. Herbert, Cadet, United States Military Academy, West Point

Ron Hunter (Army Reserves), Uniformed Services Almanac

Kim Kaplan, Neiman Marcus, Washington, D.C.

Maria F. Kress, MS, CCC-SLP, Professional Speech Associates

Lieutenant Junior Grade Joshua Larson, United States Navy

Alinda Lewris, founder and CEO, International Association
    of Protocol Consultants and Officers

Commander Aidan Logan, CHC, U.S. Navy Deputy Chaplain,
    2d Marine Division

Jeffrey D. Mainwaring, Cadet, United States Military Academy, West Point

Ensign Seth J. Marcusa, U.S. Navy

Captain Peter W. McGeory, CHC, U.S. Navy, Command Chaplain, U.S.
    Naval Academy

Mikaela and Stuart Meredith, U.S. Agency for International Development

Lieutenant Junior Grade and Mrs. Gavin Morrison

Anne Ojalehto

Colonel George Ojalehto, United States Air Force (Retired)

Bernard B. Quibilan, Command Master Chief, United States Navy (Retired)

Captain and Mrs. Stephen Ray

Chris Sharman, Personal Touch, Nordstrom, Tysons Corner, McLean, VA

John and Laura Sheehan

Karen Sheehan

Peggy Sheehan

Ginny Sniegon, Department of Defense

Miriam Stanicic, MA, professional interpreter and translator; member,
    American Translators Association

Justine Sterling

Stephen Vanilio, Book Arts

Religious Program Specialist Third Class De'Angelo Wynn,
    United States Navy

Introduction

Service Etiquette turns fifty this year, and in this edition our focus is inclusive for all government employees—whether they are entry-level or seasoned civilians, military officers, or enlisted—as well as the business professionals who serve them. Corporate executives, directors, and public managers in particular will appreciate our guidance through the maze of social and official interactions.

We live in an interconnected world of commerce and diplomacy. Excellent manners are the keys for fostering cooperative work and personal interactions across borders. The United States by itself is composed of layers of ethnicities who must work together, often in high-stress situations with global repercussions. Decision makers are scrutinized daily for the expected nobler conduct of leaders. They and their staffs must be prepared to face increased international media coverage at public (and private) social functions, more frequent press conferences, and accountability to a populace increasingly armed with small personal devices that will record—and transmit around the planet—their every social misstep.

From family dining rooms to international arenas, from host and guest duties to finessing high-profile visits, we designed this professional reference to instill new levels of competence in worldwide protocol, etiquette, and civility.

Whether you are the supporting business or the public servant, no matter your career length or cultural origins, we coach readers with a practical, concise "how to" book. No one should waste valuable energy worrying about personal social polish in lieu of focusing on professional duties. Regardless of work environment, your most successful strategy will be the deliberate use of the modus operandi we present in *Service Etiquette*, Fifth Edition.

Your authors,
CHERLYNN CONETSCO
ANNA HART

Section 1

UNITED STATES MILITARY
AND GOVERNMENT

CHAPTER 1

Military and Government Protocol

*Y*ou will find that relying on protocol, etiquette, and civility offers you both weapon and shield to help get things done in a professional manner. It is good sense to protect yourself by learning the traditions and conforming to the customs of a particular setting in the government or military. It is easier to exert influence with both groups if you use polite titles of respect in speech and writing, observe hierarchy, dress appropriately, and exercise restraint in verbal and body language. Roughly half of military officers have postgraduate degrees. More than 50 percent of federal employees work in professional, management, business, and financial occupations, compared with 29 percent in the private sector, according to the nonprofit organization Partnership for Public Service. Technical competence is valued, of course, but so are social and diplomacy skills—these earn promotions and respect, whether you are a private citizen, government civilian, or in the Armed Forces.

AT EASE KEY POINTS

- ✂ Write your bio summaries.
- ✂ Make office calls within first week of new assignments.
- ✂ Take subordinates to meetings to foster their development.

To some people, military civility is an oxymoron. They assume that wearing Kevlar vests and camouflage to commute, eating MREs (Meals Ready to Eat) in the field, or keeping weapons and ammo in your desk drawer hardly require formal manners. But Armed Forces personnel know better. They are easily identifiable public figures, drawing all eyes when in uniform. Everyone notices, for instance, that national ceremonies are always more memorable when dignified Service members perform military honors. Military bearing and command presence are

3

taught and reinforced with regulations because body language broadcasts plenty about an individual without the need for words.

Many Americans have no direct interaction with the military, and have developed some unfortunate notions. A Marine officer tells about rooming with a private citizen, who confessed his prejudice after several weeks. He thought his military roommate would want to jog everywhere, be combative, rude, crude, and otherwise "not play well with others." He was happy to overcome his bias and praise the Marine's good manners.

If you are a private citizen, the first thing to know about the U.S. uniformed Services is that there are seven of them, each with its own culture: the Army, Marine Corps, Navy, Air Force, Coast Guard, Commissioned Corps of the Public Health Service, and National Oceanic and Atmospheric Administration Corps. Executives in the military are called officers. Staff members in uniform are referred to as enlisted and non-commissioned officers. The everyday business of most Service members is administration and managing, not fighting. They routinely download and work with all kinds of data, imagery, and information from such mysterious sources as reconnaissance satellites. Government civilians and military members are engineers, scientists, accountants, computer specialists, criminal investigators, protocol experts, and air traffic controllers, among other specialized vocations.

REAL MEN

Men who succeed and are admired in present-day culture must demonstrate that they have opted for finesse, sympathetic awareness, and self-control. Fighting, swaggering, overeating, and drinking have all gone out of style. One result of the technological revolution has been to remove the requirements that "real men" should show themselves to be rough, tough, and overbearing: one does not need to be physically powerful in order to control the instruments of technology.

—Margaret Visser, *The Rituals of Dinner*

Luckily, military protocol includes tailor-made courtesies and customs perfect for times of peace and prosperity (indeed, business etiquette is modeled on military protocol) that also help maintain discipline and morale in times of conflict and hardship. For instance, responsibility toward others increases with rank. Royalty refers to this delicate balancing act of leading with humility as noblesse oblige. This chapter concerns activities where your best civility and good manners are expected, not acts of bravery. The topics are visiting a military reservation, attending meetings or discussions with government officials, making formal office calls, and handling letters of introduction.

VISITING A MILITARY RESERVATION

Civilians unfamiliar with military reservations are sometimes surprised to find them like small towns, with their own shopping areas, post offices, gas stations, and chapels. Fences or walls surround military reservations and there are guards/sentries. Security entry requirements vary, but at the least you must show some form of picture identification. Sometimes a resident or employee must act as sponsor before you can gain entry. If you are driving, all paperwork pertaining to the vehicle (license, registration, inspections, insurance) must be current. Allow extra time to get through security procedures and to find your location.

Unique Sights and Sounds

On military installations, you see unique behaviors and hear uncommon sounds. Bugle calls over loudspeakers alert troops to particular times and events, to which uniformed personnel respond even if they are in conversation with you. Cannons fire during ceremonies. People may be marching or jogging in formation on roadways. The vehicle speed limit is commonly 25 miles per hour or less to accommodate this. Do not pass troop formations until you are signaled to do so.

Q: When the bugle plays at my military installation workplace, what should I do as a civilian?

A: Bugle "retreats" announce that the American flag is being lowered. If you are outside, stop what you are doing, stand and face the sound (or flag if visible) as a sign of respect, placing your right hand over your heart if you are a citizen. When driving on most installations it is customary to stop right in the road during the ceremony. Military personnel in uniform will step out of their cars and salute until the last note sounds; civilians merely sit patiently. Proceed on your way when the music ends.

Military training includes immersion in the culture and values required by the particular Service component. These are reinforced daily, beginning with the clothes worn. Service personnel wear uniforms and headgear with insignia that indicate their affiliation and achievements at a glance. Rank devices appear on collars, shoulder boards, and lower coat sleeves. There are rules and regulations governing how and when to wear which uniforms. For example, "covers" (hats, caps, headgear) must be removed when entering buildings and put on before going outdoors. Some people find such group behavior intimidating. A new military spouse visiting the Pentagon for the first time reported in amazement, *"Do you know that there are separate corridors by color? In one hallway, everyone was dressed in green, over there they were all in white, and as we kept walking, it turned to blue uniforms. You start dressing these people in the same clothes and they all start acting alike."* The military men and women you meet will have been practicing correct bearing for years. It will only aid your cause if you also pay attention to professional grooming and stand tall during visits with them.

The American flag is displayed at numerous locations on every military installation and is always accorded proper respect. Those in uniform come to attention and salute each other and the flag at appropriate times. You may also notice international flags or foreign anthems if you visit a government installation during official visits or ceremonies. If so, remember that it is expected courtesy to respect them (see Chapter 7: Flag Etiquette).

Meals at a Military Dining Facility

In the places where Service personnel dine, meet, and lounge (the wardroom, mess hall, Officers' Club, NCO Club, etc.) proper behavior is expected. Service personnel do not loiter in a military dining area during working hours.

If you are the invitee, be punctual. Lunch periods may be short, and all diners could be required to take their seats at the same time. At an academy or during other training situations, Service personnel might remain standing directly behind their chairs until the senior officer tells them to sit. The guest normally sits at the right of the senior military member present. Food may already be on the table. Do not touch anything while you wait to be seated. If you are late joining a group, apologize to the senior member. At the conclusion of the meal, the senior member must dismiss the others or rise first, then all are free to depart. If you must leave before the termination of the meal, make your apologies to him or her.

If it is not a training situation, the same protocol is observed, except that it will be less obvious. Personnel will not stand behind their chairs, but will wait in an anteroom or lobby until all in their party have arrived—just as the entire group must be present before being led to their seats in a fine restaurant. The conversation may turn to the topic of discussion fairly quickly at "working lunches," especially if the meal period is a short one. At military clubs, just as in civilian clubs, the member is required to pay the bill.

If you are the military member and want guests to join you for a meal in a base dining venue with other uniformed personnel, give your guests at least two days' notice—more if possible, especially if they are invited to discuss a certain topic. Invitations may be verbal, e-mail, or hard copy. Invitations to high-level officials need to go through your chain of command. Meet your guests at the dining facility door, if not escorting them from another location. Walk them to their seats and offer to assist the encumbered: *"May I help with your chair?"*

Plan seating so that the most important guest is to the right of the table host and the others are seated among the table's military members (civilians may enjoy the novelty of being seated beside someone in uniform). See that your guests are served first. Your table skills will be highly visible—review other chapters for guidance on host demeanor, guest-of-honor behavior, and negotiating the meal— especially if most meals in your base dining venue could be described as devoured rather than savored. Thank your guests for joining you and escort them to the facility door or back to the meeting location after the meal.

Military Jargon

As with any organization, there is a specialized vocabulary, with each Service and government office having its own jargon not casually understood by others. You will hear most people talk using initials and acronyms; indeed, they use abbreviations so often that they forget that they are not the words they stand for (as TV is used for television). It is easy to make the wrong assumption when you are used to another definition. For instance, JFTR means "just for the record" to many people, but if you are associated with the Department of Defense (DOD), it stands for Joint Federal Travel Regulation. If you do not understand a command's language, do not hesitate to ask for clarification. As a rule, in written communications military and government abbreviations are spelled out completely the first time they are used, with their abbreviations in parentheses immediately following for use thereafter, for example: Headquarters, United States Army, Europe, and Seventh Army (HQ USAREUR/7A), Defense Attaché (DATT), or Department of Defense Intelligence Information System (DODIIS).

MEETINGS AND BRIEFINGS

Whether public servant or military, "stateside" or abroad, personnel assigned to U.S. government locations operate collegially in support of government policies. They are often hosts for meetings and conferences among decision-makers such as American flag rank (0–7 and above) officers, congressional representatives, Senior Executive Service (SES) officials, high-ranking foreign military officers and diplomats, and international business executives.

Military and government workplace locations and conditions vary. They may be on board ship, in city high-rise cubicles, inside trailers or tents in the field, in substandard buildings, or in former palaces. They are guarded with security check-points. When you make an appointment to visit them, an office aide, protocol officer, or administrative assistant will provide information regarding identification to bring, where to park, visit authorization requirements (such as theatre/area clearances or visas needed), how much time you will have, etc. Plan for a short meeting and keep to the agenda, with your "bottom line up front."

Be prepared to provide more than the names of those attending meetings with foreign dignitaries, government leaders, important political figures, and the like. Besides biographies and photos, security offices may require birth dates, social security numbers or government security clearances, home and office addresses, and phone numbers.

Turn off cell phones and other personal assistance devices before you arrive in the outer office or reception area. Generally, the higher the rank or government position, the more likely the executive will be accustomed to formality.

Your Biographical Sketch

High-level officials often request background information on the personnel they will meet. If you do not already have one, write a brief one-paragraph personal biography (bio), and a full-page version to provide via e-mail when the staffs of SES civilians or flag-rank military officers request them. Junior personnel should *not* forward a bio unless the senior person in their party sends one at the same time, or theirs is specifically requested. A bio is an abbreviated curriculum vitae. It contains full name, current title/position, security clearance level (if applicable), brief work/assignment history, formal education, accomplishments such as publi-cations, area(s) of expertise, and an optional (short) personal ending with place of residence, affiliations, hobbies, interests, or influences, such as: "*Colonel Miller is married with twin high-school boys. He and his wife, Susan, have lived in Bay Ridge since 1999. He enjoys a quiet round of golf and a noisy game of racquetball.*" Include a recent digital photo (head and shoulders).

You will find your bio will serve many purposes—as an introduction before your next presentation in front of a group, to provide before the receipt of an award, for social profiles (Web pages, newsletters), or for applications to organiza-tions. Save each submission separately, titled with recipient's name (e.g., Alumni Magazine, Re-election School Board, Commander of military unit) so that it is easier to choose a version to update next time. Always re-read your bio before sending to be sure that it is targeted to the particular audience.

When someone requests your bio, ask for his or hers in return. Check Web sites for published biographies first, but if necessary, call their office aides, protocol officers, or administrative assistants, as bios can be easily forwarded via e-mail.

Self-Introductions

As with your bio, you will need several versions of a self-introduction. Practice them all.

At official meetings, when an aide introduces you, pause for a moment to allow the introductions to be completed and for the official to offer a handshake. If you introduce yourself, step forward, extend your hand, and greet the official by title and name, before saying your own name and position: *"Good morning, General Scowcroft, I am Carol Hammersen, Office of Human Resources."* Do not say your rank or grade unless asked.

Rank is already prominent on military uniforms or is discerned from your position title or your presence at a particular meeting. If it is important that those you meet learn of your prominence immediately, have an accompanying associate, or the official's own protocol aide or administrative assistant, introduce you to the senior principal (host) at the start of your meeting: *"Sir, allow me to introduce Doctor Teresa Babb."* When a title is mentioned in introductions, its use implies that the person should always be addressed and introduced to others by that title.

Within your own organization, add your section location/name only if necessary. Save your job title for strangers from outside your unit or organization when you need an "elevator statement" or "party prologue." See the discussion in Chapter 19: Introductions, Conversations and Farewells on delivering these pleasant synopses, as well as the exceptions to including a rank, grade, or title when saying your own name.

CONFERENCE ROOM DISCUSSIONS

When you are invited into a conference room, places at the end of a conference table closest to the door are normally for the senior hosting official or meeting chairperson. Do not sit there, even if told, *"Sit anywhere."* In a meeting room with many host occupants, everyone stands to be introduced and remains standing until the entering visitors are invited to sit. If you are at a conference table with several new faces and business cards have just been exchanged, place their cards in front of you in the seating order for quick reference during the meeting so that you can address participants respectfully by honorific and name.

If the conference table does not accommodate everyone, the lowest-ranking persons ring the room in chairs against the wall. Participants wait for the senior host to sit down before taking a seat. On busy days, however, deputies may request that everyone be seated because the senior officer or executive has not yet returned from a previous meeting and will walk in last. Business proceeds immediately upon his or her arrival announcement, *"Keep your seats,"* with nods sufficing for handshakes. All attendees everywhere stand when upper-level government officials, such as ambassadors, enter a room. At internal staff meetings, junior military personnel will stand for commanding officers. Have an assistant ask the staffs of foreign nationals ahead of time what protocol will be expected of visiting Americans at their specific meetings.

If you bring folders or papers, personally hand them (global citizens use only their right hands to avoid offense) to meeting participants; do not shove or push items across a conference or coffee table. Unless you have been told to bring a brown bag lunch with you, do not bring any food—candy bar, gum, or water included. Keep comments germane to the subject. Listen carefully during the meeting and resist the temptation to do all the talking, even if you are selling a service. Be respectful, courteous, and do not interrupt others. Refrain from excessive movement or whispered asides with colleagues. As author Ambrose Bierce wrote, *"In the code of military etiquette, silence and fixity are forms of deference."*

Make every effort to wrap up your discussion before the stated departure time. Express appreciation for the time spent before departing, and if the host does not, you can summarize what was agreed to or requested. Attending staff members take notes on all requests and agreements during the visit and should be prepared to do the recap, if asked. In the outer office or with the secretary, junior staff members should also confirm names and addresses for sending any additional information requested. A handwritten thank-you note from the visiting senior principal to the senior hosting official (outside your own organization) should be sent within two working days.

When you are hosting a conference room meeting, seat people by precedence and direct them to their places (see Chapter 23: Seating Plans). Record the participant list and your precedence determination in your computer event file for future reference, including the correct pronunciation of names.

Pre-position notepads and pens at each place, and water pitchers and glasses (or coffee or tea) between every other person if your meeting length is longer than one hour. If the meeting lasts longer than four hours, provide a meal (breakfast, lunch, dinner). For instance, many high-profile visits are maximized by having briefings continue over a hosted lunch. If you provide food, all menus should be coordinated ahead of time: with visitors because of allergies and religious preferences; with headquarters because of authorized meal rates and reimbursement regulations.

Q: How should a mixed meeting with U.S. and international military and government civilians be conducted? I was appalled that my boss put his feet on his desk facing foreign colleagues, an officer chewed her pen when she wasn't clicking/twirling it, and a civilian drank a "big gulp" kept on the floor beside the chair.

A: A conference room should be booked or the meeting held in a seating area so that a desk is not between persons. Dress should be consistent with office standards—leaning toward more formal if you are the chair, if outside visitors are present, or if high-ranking persons are invited—even on "Casual Fridays." If you are the chair, plan the agenda and seating arrangements beforehand, open by introducing yourself and others, and direct the proceedings: *"Good afternoon, I am Trent Samples, chair today. With us are (names in protocol order). The meeting agenda is before you. Our first order of business is . . ."* Sit up straight and keep your feet flat on the floor. Address people by honorific and last name, look at them when they talk, and do not interrupt. When it is your turn, speak to the point briefly and respectfully, avoiding slang words, acronyms, and sports terminology. These rules are for every meeting, but especially when many cultures are represented.

Office Calls

Office calls serve four main purposes: introductions, farewells, formal diplomatic occasions, and conducting private in-office business. The focus here is on meeting senior officials (executives), but the procedures are readily adaptable to any manager level and may provide guidelines for holding calls in your own office.

Introductory Calls
Courtesy calls to introduce new personnel to their own superiors and various secondary managers are normally arranged by an individual's predecessor or immediate supervisor, who most often escorts the employee around for the first couple of days. However, if they have not been arranged, please remember that introductory calls on workplace section heads and colleagues are mandatory civility; make appointments to introduce yourself, if necessary. Such calls should occur (or at least be scheduled) within the first week of work, if not mandated sooner. For example, when an officer reports for duty on board ship, he or she calls on the commanding officer within forty-eight hours. Internal workplace calls last ten

minutes or less, unless a formal briefing or staff meeting has been planned (usually to accommodate a group of newcomers). Various office managers will in turn escort the newcomer around their spaces to explain internal working relationships and make further staff introductions. Office calls do not include spouses.

Strive to make a good first impression and communicate your desire to do a first-rate job. Your new co-workers or counterparts can be either the biggest help or the greatest hindrance in getting your objectives accomplished. A little sincere respect and attention to civility goes a long way, especially in isolated locations or among small American contingents. A military officer in Honduras wrote: *"I wish I had known to 'kiss the ring' upon arrival. The (American civilian colleague) felt insulted because I did not make it a point to have an office call. My fault, but I hit the ground running and consequently suffered when it came time to work with this individual. He was so miffed that he actually went out of his way to hinder me."*

Business cards are not normally exchanged within your own workplace, as all employees will have access to names, e-mail addresses, and company phone numbers. If the office call is to acquaint you with people in the community "outside the gates," provide business cards only if they have the new position and contact information. Otherwise, take the other person's card and send a thank-you-for-welcoming-me note with your complete contact information below your signature. The more people you meet, the more likely you are to be comfortable and successful in a new job. Your predecessor or supervisor will advise you on local practices. On diplomatic duty, for instance, calls both on internal colleagues and counterparts in the community are normally done in precedence order.

An American official newly arrived to a foreign location should make an appointment for an office call with host country counterparts as well as American colleagues. Delays in initial contact with host nationals could be seen as a slight if the American is high-ranking, which might strain country-to-country relations. The most acceptable times for international calls are mid-morning and late afternoon—avoiding the lunch hour. Notice during your courtesy visits to host nationals whether refreshments are served. When it comes time for you to host the locals in your office, please reciprocate in the same manner. Ask about area practices each time you are reassigned. If counterpart calls are expected, obtain beforehand the bios of the senior military officers or government civilians you will be meeting. An invitation to a change-of-command ceremony and reception is not a substitute for an official call.

Farewell Calls

When you are departing a work situation, the procedure is basically the same. Make an appointment with your commanding officer or senior executive and various favorite colleagues to say farewell and inform them of new contact numbers and addresses. Sometimes your farewell call is the same one in which you introduce your successor. Expect to give an exit briefing or verbal after-action report to immediate supervisors, personnel, and security officials. Be formal during final briefings as you communicate your experiences of office harmony, teamwork, and efficiency. Be constructive and professional; you may work with these people again. Even if you cannot wait to see the building in your rearview mirror for the last time, you can thankfully state that your experiences have prepared you for your next position. It will further enhance your professional reputation if you write a short note (hard copy, not e-mail) of farewell to key individuals, perhaps with an offer to be of service after departure. A brief note can even be jotted on the back of a card (see Chapter 12: Correspondence and Stationery Essentials).

Diplomatic Calls

Diplomatic representatives and military officials pay formal office calls on specific occasions such as the death of a national figure, patriotic holidays, or to deliver demarches (formal statements of displeasure). These calls may entail signing a book of condolence, participating in a large event with media coverage, or a simple private exchange (still using formal language). No government or military person should take spontaneous action on such occasions. Obtain guidance from the Department of State or U.S. embassies at overseas locations, but the rest of this section will undoubtedly apply.

Private In-Office Visits

Those who host in-office meetings normally have enough space to accommodate a seating area with two armchairs or a sofa (in addition to or instead of a conference table and chairs) so that they do not have to sit behind a desk like a school principal. Arrive punctually (five minutes early). Be respectful to aides and secretaries. Either they will knock on the official's door or you will be directed to do so. Wait until told to enter. The senior person in your party enters the meeting room first and is introduced first. A well-mannered executive greets you at his door or moves toward you as you enter.

Be very courteous. Remain standing until invited to sit. If not directed, ask where to sit and move to that position, but then wait until the official begins to sit down before taking your chair. Just as in a private home, the right side of a couch (the sofa's own right) is normally the honored seat, so defer to the highest ranking. The hosting official normally takes a chair perpendicular to or facing the senior visitor. Watch your body language; keep feet on the floor. If you must, cross ankles but not legs because that looks too casual and shows the bottom of your shoe.

Bring only the minimum of briefing papers. Never bring your coffee cup. Keep to the meeting agenda and stay both on topic and on time.

If the host official asked for you to visit, he or she will bring the meeting to a close by summarizing what was covered and what actions have been planned. He or she escorts you out of the office to the elevator or lobby door, or hands you over to an assistant guide, especially if security is an issue.

If you initiated the call and the host executive stands and thanks you for your visit, the meeting is over, even if you were mid-sentence and only there for five minutes. Accept the dismissal graciously, stand and say thank you for his or her time, and depart. In the outer office with an aide you can determine if it is worthwhile to reschedule. Be sure to write a thank-you note the next day, especially if the meeting was outside your own organization.

Planning for an Official Call

Senior officials have busy agendas, sometimes scheduled as tightly as every fifteen minutes. For business meetings with them, be sure to clarify in writing the date and time, the discussion topic(s), and whether or not there will be any ceremonies such as official gift exchanges or media photographs (see Chapter 3: Hosting High-Profile Visits). Be sure that you know precisely which location you are traveling to, as many executives have more than one office.

Prior to a business discussion in an official's office, brief your entourage on the agreed-upon talking points—and, sometimes just as important, what topics to avoid. Go over the etiquette to observe during the office call, such as seating precedence, exchanging business cards, signing a guest book, official gift-exchanges, etc. Determine who will answer any questions or do particular negotiating.

Upon entering the meeting room, you may be introduced as the leader, but it is your duty to properly introduce all others accompanying you. State the host official's name first, and then your colleagues in protocol order, for example: "*Admiral Jones, may I introduce my colleagues, Ms. Fran McConville, our Director of Public Affairs* [pause for handshake] *and Ms. Olga Hrycaj, Vice President for Business Development.*"

Typically, the senior person will offer a handshake first. When introducing a military person in his or her official capacity, use the full rank, as it is written. Thereafter, the rank may be shortened during conversation: Lieutenant Colonel James Martin becomes simply "Colonel Martin;" Major General Leoma Short becomes "General Short," etc. Service personnel call each other by rank and last name. Junior military say "Sir" or "Ma'am" as terms of respect to every member who outranks them. Civilian employees under military supervisors also adopt this polite language, but visitors are not expected to employ anything but ranks and last names. Keep in mind that the American businessperson's custom of using a first name immediately after initial introductions will be extremely irritating to senior military, government officials with titles, and foreign nationals. Especially if you are, for example, a young engineer who says "*Hi, Bob*" to a military officer older than yourself; it will make him clench his jaw and yearn to "lock your heels" (make you stand at attention while he rebukes your manners). You will have lost credibility from the first moment.

Allow senior principals to do the talking; accompanying staff take notes (see Chapter 25: International Protocol and Civility for information regarding interpreters). Only when specifically addressed by one of the principals should junior personnel volunteer comments. Team members are there to gain practical experience in procedure and decorum and to serve as information resources, if needed. Do not surprise your team with topics not previously agreed upon once the meeting is under way. Follow your superior's lead in public—never disagree with him or her in front of outsiders.

Everyone likes to know where their own "rank" fits in the hierarchy. See a comparison of government grades in the chart, United States Military Rank and Federal Government Grade Equivalency, at the end of this chapter.

LETTERS OF INTRODUCTION

A letter of introduction can be useful in business as well as in social matters. If a friend writes a hard-copy letter of introduction for you (perhaps to a contact in an overseas location), it is considered poor form for you to present it in person and expect the receiver to see you immediately. Enclose it instead in a handwritten note of your own asking for a telephone appointment or an office call. Provide your contact information if your friend has not enclosed cards (see below). Send the whole package by mail or messenger.

If you want to *recommend someone as a potential friend, or possibly for employment,* write a letter of introduction for him or her. You may send it via e-mail (be sure to copy the person being introduced and include his or her contact information) or prepare a handwritten or typed letter. Give the letter to your friend unsealed. He or she will want to read it, but may also have to fold it again to enclose inside his or her own note. Write a few simple sentences, such as:

Dear Anna,

A good friend of mine, John Smith, will be in Paris the week of April 5, and I want very much for him to get acquainted with you. He is reading a paper at the Medical Center and will be doing research there for a month.

John is a fine person, a very good doctor, and a specialist in his field. As a speech therapist, you have much in common with him. I do hope that you can find time to get together.

Warmly,
Robert Decatur

One advantage of a hard-copy letter of introduction is that you can enclose your friend's business or social card with your own personal card, writing on it in this manner:

Introducing John Smith

Robert Edward Decatur

Major General
United States Air Force

If you do not have a social card, you may mention that you are enclosing your friend's card alone, or use your business card. Draw a slash through your name, write lowercase "n.b." on the front, and write your message on the back. Diplomats accomplish colleague introductions by writing "p.p." in lowercase at the bottom left-hand corner of their social cards (see Chapter 13: Abbreviations in Social Correspondence).

If you receive an e-mail or hard-copy letter of introduction, immediately (or as soon as possible) contact the person being introduced. Arrange a phone appointment and talk several minutes with the stranger. If you are favorably impressed and time permits, you may invite him or her to call on you at your office or to join you for lunch or drinks. However, a letter of introduction does not commit the receiver to anything beyond a phone call.

Self-Introduction Letters

You may wish to write your own letter of introduction. Decide how you will send your letter: hard copy via the post office, transmitted as a facsimile, written as an e-mail (see Chapter 14: Personal Electronics Etiquette), or sent as an e-mail attachment. The higher the rank or status of the recipient, the more formal your correspondence should be and the longer the lead-time for requesting an appointment. Two weeks' advance time is normally sufficient. Type it in business-letter configuration, but do not use government or company letterhead unless it is official business.

The following guide encourages your own style and wording:

(heading)	Include the date on one line, double space and continue with the recipient's full formal address, as it would appear on an envelope.
(salutation)	Be respectful. Use the correct honorific and surname with a colon, *Dear Senator Byrd:*
(paragraph 1)	Open immediately with the purpose of your letter, something similar to, *"Please accept this letter as a personal introduction"* and your goal in writing it, *"I am requesting a photo opportunity with our state's favorite senator"* or *"I am hoping for the opportunity of a short office call or telephone appointment to discuss our mutual interest in . . ."*
(paragraph 2)	Introduce yourself very briefly (see section above, Your Biographical Sketch). Offer to provide a more complete biography if the recipient desires, or provide a Web site where your bio appears.
(paragraph 3)	Give your availability dates—*"During the month of April, I will be on temporary assignment to Washington,"* your e-mail address, and when your phone numbers are valid: *"After this date I am in transit but may be reached by cell phone."*
(paragraph 4)	Offer applicable assistance; for example, is there anything you can bring with you or do for an overseas recipient while you are still in the United States? Thank the recipient for his or her kind consideration of your request.
(closing)	Be formal in tone, using either *Very respectfully,* or *Sincerely,* with a comma. Do not enclose your business card in a self-generated communication. Instead, leave room to sign your name in ink above a complete signature block:

Your full name
Title and agency or affiliation (possibly including a Web site)
Your addresses: street and/or e-mail
Applicable phone numbers: residence, cell, business

United States Military Rank and Federal Government Grade Equivalency Chart

Military Rank	Civil Service General Schedule (GS)	Foreign Service	Diplomatic Title
O-10 General or Admiral	SES-6 (Senior Exec Service)	Career Ambassador (CA)	Ambassador Chief of Mission (COM)
O-9 Lieutenant General or Vice Admiral	SES-6 & 5	Career Minister (CM)	Ambassador or Minister
O-8 Major General or Rear Admiral (Upper Half)	SES-5 & 4; GS-18, 17, or 16 (General Service)	Minister Counselor (MC)	Minister-Counselor or Counselor of Embassy
O-7 Brigadier General or Rear Admiral (Lower Half)	SES-4; GS-18, 17, or 16	Counselor (OC)	Minister-Counselor or Counselor of Embassy
O-6 Colonel or Captain	GS-15 & 14	FP-1 (Foreign Service Professional)	First Secretary; perhaps a Deputy Chief of Mission
O-5 Lieutenant Colonel or Commander	GS-14 & 13	FP-2	First Secretary; perhaps a Chief of Section
O-4 Major or Lieutenant Commander	GS-12	FP-3	Second Secretary; perhaps a Desk Officer
O-3 Captain or Lieutenant (Junior Officer/Entry-level Officer)	GS-11 & 10	FP-4 or JO-4 or ELO-4	Second Secretary; perhaps a Deputy Chief of Section
O-2 First Lieutenant or Lieutenant Junior Grade or W-4 & W-3 Chief Warrant Officer	GS-09 & 08 / ELO-5/6	FP-5/6 or JO-5/6 or	Third Secretary
O-1 2nd Lieutenant or Ensign or W-2 & W-1 Warrant Officer or E-9, E-8, E-7 Enlisted, Non-Commissioned Officer (NCO)	GS-07 & 06	FP-6/7 or JO-6/7 or ELO-6/7 or FS-7 (Foreign Service Specialist)	Third Secretary

Military Rank		Civil Service General Schedule (GS)	Foreign Service	Diplomatic Title
E-7	Enlisted (NCO)	GS-06	FS-8	Staff
E-6, E-5	Enlisted (NCO)	GS-05	FS-9	Staff
E-4	Enlisted (NCO)	GS-04	FS-10	Staff

Table is for general comparisons only, based on military rank and federal civilian relationships established for the Geneva Convention, SES-Flag Level protocols, the fifteen grades of the Civil Service, and the ten grades of the Foreign Service. Exact equations depend not only on rank, but on variable factors such as time in grade and position occupied.

CHAPTER 2

Military Honors and
Official Government Ceremonies

Ceremonies provide public acknowledgment and celebration of an official event in an individual's life. All military and government ceremonies must be planned and executed in a formal and dignified manner. They may be held at any time of day, indoors or outdoors, and are best viewed as continuations of the working day. They may be arranged for observation only, or include a reception afterward, perhaps for a change of command, an exhibition, or the observance of a country's national day. Alternatively, receptions may precede an official event, such as a building dedication, ribbon cutting, or parade.

The nominal host is the person being honored. However, a presiding official administers ceremonies. For retirements, promotions, and awards, that official is normally the first appropriate person in the honoree's chain of command (officer or senior civilian) who is higher in rank or grade to the honoree. Enlisted members and lower-grade civilians (GS-6, FS-8, and below) do not officiate. The honoree may invite an outside person to officiate after coordinating with the supervisor.

AT EASE KEY POINTS

- ✂ Develop generic ceremony checklists.
- ✂ Rehearse all ceremony participants.
- ✂ Print programs to cue participants.

The format of a ceremony is flexible, according to the preferences of the honoree; for instance, clergy may be invited to give an invocation. A guest speaker may be invited to speak at retirements, national days, and memorial commemorations. Honorees may elect to speak briefly to acknowledge the event and to thank the many individuals who contributed to their success and supported them.

Whenever appropriate, including music (live or recorded) during a ceremony is a military and government tradition.

Generic Sequence of Events

The following sequence includes the typical elements appropriate to official ceremonies. Adjust as desired and relevant.

Office Call
The official party (ceremony host, honoree, special guests, family) gathers in the presiding official's office to await their cue to proceed to the ceremony. This may be the time to review upcoming events so that everyone knows his or her part.

Opening Narration
Loudspeaker or Master of Ceremonies (MC) explanation of event as audience gathers. The MC may sit on the official party's platform, but off to the side. Give him or her a separate lectern.

Musical Honors
A band or recording may play an appropriate *arrival fanfare* while the official party is in motion, for example, as the honoree mounts a stage. When the official party is in position at their chairs, appropriate musical honors (i.e., "Ruffles and Flourishes" for uniformed general officers and above) are rendered once. Honors are not played while the official party is walking or if the presiding official is an SES civilian. Outdoors, when musical honors are rendered, Service members in uniform face and salute the person being honored. Veterans who are present but not in uniform may also salute. The honoree returns the salute. The *national anthem* may be played or sung during "posting the colors" (positioning the flags). The appropriate *Service song* may be played at the conclusion of the ceremony as an audience departs.

Family and Special Guests Escorted
Uniformed personnel are chosen as ushers to escort family and special guests to their reserved seats. They introduce themselves to the guests. If applicable, they remind uniformed personnel to stay "covered." Escorts automatically offer their right or left arms to females and walk sedately. Males usually follow the escort. Escorts should be prepared to assist guests with disabilities. People with wheelchairs and guide dogs are seated at the ends of rows.

Q: A female officer escorted me to my seat at a military ceremony and as I am also
      female, I did not take her arm. Was I right?

A: Feel free to take her arm, if offered. Escorting is gender neutral. Escorts offer their arms
      to females as a matter of courtesy, and as a service to anyone who might appreciate it.

Entrance of the Official Party

They arrive in protocol order to stand or to be seated before an audience. Audience
members face the honoree, who is on the stage.

Posting of the Colors

Flags may be positioned before the ceremony if space or time is limited. Escorting is suspended for the duration of a color guard ceremony (see Chapter 7: Flag
Etiquette).

Invocation

Clergy may be invited at the honoree's discretion.

Opening Remarks and Recognition

A presiding officer or MC reads official orders or citations, administers oaths, presents awards or decorations, or pins on medals or insignia.

Certificates, Letters, Special Presentations

When an individual retires from the government or military, the government pays
for a certificate that will serve as a tangible reminder of public service and a token
of appreciation for the retiree's contributions to the particular Service, department, or agency. A plaque or other item may also be presented, but if so, the honoree's co-workers or the person receiving it pays for it. Similarly, if a certificate or
letter of appreciation is presented to the spouse, the government does not fund
further spouse tributes, such as flowers.

Official Pictures

Concurrent with recognition or presentations, if an official photographer is available, a record of the ceremony makes a nice souvenir.

Honoree Remarks

All remarks are kept as brief as possible—five minutes or less—because many may
speak. Escorts and others assisting are standing throughout the ceremony, and for

as much as one hour prior to its commencement. Outdoor ceremonies may be hot or chilly, creating guest discomfort.

Personal Flags
At promotion or retirement ceremonies for general officers or high-ranking civilians, the furling and unfurling of the honoree's personal colors is appropriate. Do not case personal flags in view of the audience at any ceremony except the conclusion of funerals, as that is symbolic of death. Personal colors are displayed with the national and Service flags (if applicable), and may be moved to the reception (if held) and displayed behind a receiving line.

Closing Remarks or Dismissal
A presiding officer or MC announces the conclusion of the event and directs participants to any further activities.

Departure Receiving Line
If no reception will follow, or not all in the audience are invited, the honoree stands in a convenient location to shake hands and receive congratulations.

Reception, Luncheon, or Dinner
Optional and funded by the honoree.

GENERIC CEREMONY CHECKLIST

There are many details involved with arranging military honors and official ceremonies. These are among the more important:

- Reserve location for ceremony (and reception, if applicable).
- Arrange music and flag honors.
- Send invitations. A general message can be posted online in the workplace wherever appropriate, cordially inviting all interested personnel and their spouses to attend. If invitations are forwarded electronically (the norm), written "hard copies" will still be needed for the guest speaker and high-ranking participants outside the command. Invite them telephonically and send "to remind" cards. Maintain an R.s.v.p. list.
- Provide honoree bio to presiding official.
- Provide words to pertinent citation, oath, award, etc. to the reader.

- Construct a sequence of events for printed programs (souvenirs). Civilian guests need notes on when to stand, and explanations of Service customs.

- Review all aspects of the ceremony with honoree, presiding official, MC or reader, escorts, chaplain, honor guard, band leader, protocol officer, etc.

- Provide schedules to everyone involved, including secretaries, aides, executive officers, guest speaker, and spouse.

- Reserve and label seats for the honoree's family, guests, and any officials in the grades of military 0-6, civilian GS-14 or FP-1, or above.

- Assign escorts for family and guests.

- Ensure all assets (flags, award, podium, microphones) are in place.

- Brief official party (include spouses) just prior to the ceremony, so that everyone knows what protocol actions are expected of them.

ARRIVAL CEREMONIES

See Chapter 3: Hosting High-Profile Visits

AWARD CEREMONIES AND PRESENTATION OF MEDALS

An award ceremony provides an opportunity for the entire group to share in the accomplishments of one of its members. Commanders and supervisors must ensure the presentation method reflects the significance of the particular award or medal. If several individuals are being presented medals or awards at the same time, a combined ceremony can be planned with all the attendant components. Specific rules apply to the sequential presentation of medals or awards, based first on the precedence of the decoration (highest first), then on the rank of the recipient (most senior first). Precedence lists of medals and awards are listed in Service regulations or civilian personnel manuals.

However, due to the brevity of a ceremony where only one individual receives an award or medal, many military units make single presentations during commander's call; civilian government organizations present them during staff meetings. Flags are posted beforehand and music is not played. The recipient is called forward to stand beside the commander or supervisor; both face the rest of the group. If military, the commander or assistant announces, *"Attention to orders."* Civilians say something such as, *"Please stand and join me for an award presentation."* Everyone in attendance stands at attention and faces the principals.

An assistant reads the citation, after which the principals face each other. For medals, the commander affixes the decoration on the individual's uniform. For awards, the supervisor or commander presents the certificate (in a folder or frame) along with a handshake and personal congratulations. If a photographer is present, the principals pause both at affixing the medal and at the handshake to allow two pictures of each transaction. The uniformed recipient salutes the commander, and the commander returns it. At the meeting chair's discretion, recipients are offered an opportunity to say a few words, after which applause concludes the ceremony and the commander's call or staff meeting proceeds.

Special Decoration Ceremony

Decoration ceremonies formally recognize Service members for meritorious service, outstanding achievement, or heroism. When possible, the commander personally and formally presents the decoration at the earliest possible date after approval of the decoration. All military participants (including retired members, if they choose) and military attendees wear the uniform specified by the presiding officer. Although decoration ceremonies may differ slightly from one Service to another, they normally proceed as in the preceding paragraph.

BUILDING DEDICATIONS, RIBBON CUTTINGS, OR GROUNDBREAKINGS

To recognize the beginning, completion, or grand opening of a new building or facility, special ceremonies are sometimes held with all appropriate formality. Entrance of the official party and official pictures are especially important during these events as photos or video are normally provided to the media or posted online.

CANNON AND GUN SALUTES

Gun salutes began in the days when it took a long time to reload. By firing all artillery, the ship, fort, or battery was rendered vulnerable and no threat to a Very Important Person (VIP). The highest international salute is twenty-one guns, used primarily as a greeting. The U.S. version began as equal to the original number of states (thirteen) in the Union and increased every time a state was added; after twenty-six states the U.S. agreed to the international standard of twenty-one guns in August 1875. Twenty-one-gun salutes are reserved for the President, ex-President, and President-elect (and fired at noon on the day of their funerals), and for a friendly nation's chief of state or head of government, members of its reigning royal family, and its national flag. Lesser gun salutes are rendered to other military and civilian leaders of this and other nations. The salutes (always in odd numbers) are based on protocol rank. To honor deceased Service personnel, a firing party performs the 3-volley gun salute (see Chapter 6: The Military Funeral).

CHANGES OF COMMAND

Unit members witness their new leader assume the responsibility and trust associated with the position of commanding officer. The ceremony itself may be executed in a conference room, auditorium, or on a parade field. If conducted on a military parade field, several marks of respect are incorporated. (If held in an aircraft hangar, that is considered outdoors for purposes of saluting and wearing headgear.) Events may include a full parade of personnel *passing in review* or an *inspection of troops*. Everyone stands during the playing of the national anthem, "Ruffles and Flourishes," and the Service song during the reading of orders (promotion, retirement, or change of command), during award presentations, and as the official party arrives and departs stage right (if possible). They arrive in inverse order of precedence with the senior entering last, except that the relieved officer generally precedes the officer assuming command, even if the latter is junior.

Military members salute during "Ruffles and Flourishes" and the General's or Admiral's March. Veterans who are present but not in uniform may also render the military salute. Civilians (men and women) stand and place their hands over their hearts as the colors pass in review. See Chapter 23: Seating Plans, for dais seating order.

Formal Guidon Exchange

The guidon (regimental flag) may be passed during a change of command ceremony as a symbolic gesture of authority being transferred from one commanding officer to the next. As viewed from the audience, from left to right, the presiding officer, outgoing commander, and incoming commander stand side by side. A fourth participant, the guidon bearer, stands behind and between the presiding officer and outgoing commander. The guidon bearer gives a subdued command, "*Officers, center*" and the presiding officer turns to the left while the two commanders execute a right face. The outgoing commander salutes the presiding officer, saying "*Sir (or Ma'am), I relinquish command.*" The presiding officer returns the salute. The outgoing commander takes the guidon from the bearer, holding the flag staff angled away from the audience and presents it to the presiding officer. The outgoing commander takes a step to the right, two steps back, and a step to the left. Simultaneously, the incoming commander takes two steps forward, taking the outgoing commander's place. The presiding officer presents the guidon to the incoming commander, who receives it, pauses a moment, and passes it back to the guidon bearer. The incoming commander salutes the presiding officer, saying, "*Sir* (or *Ma'am*), *I assume command.*" The presiding officer returns the salute. The guidon bearer gives a subdued command, "*Officers, post*" and all three officers face the parade field.

DOCUMENT SIGNINGS

This ceremony involves the principals involved in the agreement contents. Principals ratify two copies of a document by signing them before an audience (of contributors from both sides and possibly the media). Good pens and penholders are souvenirs after signing important documents. Documents are presented in (paper or imitation leather) folders with a seal of the applicable department, the Great Seal of the United States (if appropriate), and perhaps red, white and blue streamers.

The setting's features are important during this primarily visual event, with a nice-looking table large enough for the two signatories. For agreements between countries, same-size national flags are displayed. Full-size flags of each country are placed behind the seated principals, and miniatures are placed on the tabletop. A staff photographer or videographer should record the moment. A podium with a public address system may be needed for remarks. Speak slowly and clearly, emphasizing consonants, especially if another language is involved.

FALLEN COMRADE OBSERVANCE
(also known as POW/MIA Recognition, Two-Bell Ceremony,
or Missing Man Table and Honors)
See Chapter 5: The Fallen Comrade Table Observance.

FLAG RETIREMENT (CREMATION) CEREMONIES
See Chapter 7: Flag Etiquette.

FUNERALS

See Chapter 6: The Military Funeral

U.S. HONORS CEREMONIES

The intent of honors is to extend formal military courtesy to a distinguished person because of his or her high-ranking official position. In general, honors ceremonies are reserved for the President, Vice President, statutory civilian and military officials of the Department of Defense, and general or flag officers of the military in the United States. Appropriate honors are rendered also to international government and military dignitaries occupying positions at the highest levels (regardless of personal rank) and on occasions when such ceremonies promote international goodwill.

Honors are accorded an individual rather than a group. A delegation is honored in the person of the senior or ranking member. Honors are extended only to the distinguished person him or herself and not to his or her personal representatives.

The national flag of a foreign civilian official or the personal flag of a foreign military officer (if available) is flown during their honors ceremonies. Service bands play the foreign honoree's national anthem followed immediately by the U.S. anthem. Civilians and those not in uniform stand erect with right hands over their hearts for the American flag and national anthem, or with both hands at their sides for a foreign anthem. Uniformed persons (and veterans not in uniform, if they choose) salute the American flag and national anthem. Uniformed persons also salute a foreign flag or anthem (this is coordinated with commanders).

Honors do not occur at night (between retreat and reveille), on Sundays, or on national holidays (except Armed Forces Day, third Saturday in May; and Independence Day, July 4). A distinguished official arriving at night, for instance, is normally honored during daylight the next day, as desired. The President of the United States is the exception: upon arrival at a military installation, the President is accorded full honors, no matter the time of day.

Full Honors

A military formation of troops gives the proper gun tribute to honor an individual VIP. During gun salutes, military personnel in uniform stand at attention and salute. Veterans who are present but not in uniform may also salute, if they desire. If on a parade field, the honoree may "inspect the troops"—walking past the first row with the commanding officer, perhaps stopping to speak with one or two people. The hosting official and the honoree depart the field or ceremony before any audience members are dismissed.

Honor Cordon

The prescribed numbers of military troops align themselves side by side to form two columns creating a passageway through which the honoree (sometimes a casket) passes. A host may escort the honoree; dignitaries walk at the host's right side through a cordon to the reception area.

PARADE REVIEWS

See Chapter 7: Flag Etiquette.

PROMOTIONS, FROCKINGS, AND RE-ENLISTMENTS

Promotion and re-enlistment ceremonies are typically held indoors. All Service members present come to attention and hold their positions throughout the reading and pinning on of new insignia. The oath is recited by the presiding officer and repeated by the promotee. Group promotions are sometimes performed; if so, individuals are promoted in descending rank order and oaths recited simultaneously.

The word "frock" (once referring to the woolen jersey worn by sailors) is used as a verb in the military to refer to the official authorization for an officer to assume the title and all privileges of the next rank immediately. He or she will not, however, receive the corresponding increase in pay of that rank, but must wait on the bureaucratic process of selection. This action is taken so that the officer can carry out subsequent duties. If the military member will be supervising someone of higher rank than him or herself at the next command, for instance, without frocking it would prove difficult.

Officer Promotion Orders

Attention to Orders:
The President of the United States, acting upon the recommendation of the Secretary of the [Service], has placed special trust and confidence in the patriotism, integrity, and abilities of [previous grade and name]. In view of these special qualities and [his/her] demonstrated potential to serve in the higher grade, [previous grade and name] *is promoted to the grade of** [new grade], United States [Service], effective this day, [date]. By order of the Secretary of the [Service].

*Note: If the officer is being frocked, the following wording replaces the italicized text: "*is authorized to assume the grade of . . .*"

Officer Oath of Office:
I, [name], having been appointed a [new grade], in the United States [Service] do solemnly swear [or affirm] that I will support and defend the Constitution of the United States against all enemies, foreign and domestic; that I will bear true faith and allegiance to the same; that I take this obligation freely, without any mental reservation or purpose of evasion; and that I will well and faithfully discharge the duties of the office upon which I am about to enter, so help me God.

Enlisted Promotion Orders

Attention to Orders:
[Previous grade and name] is promoted to the permanent grade of [rank], effective [date] with a date of rank of [date]. For the Commander, Signed [name].

Enlisted Oath of Office:
I, [name], do solemnly swear [or affirm] that I will support and defend the constitution of the United States against all enemies, foreign and domestic; that I will bear true faith and allegiance to the same; and that I will obey the orders of the President of the United States and the orders of the officers appointed over me, according to regulations and the Uniform Code of Military Justice, so help me God.

Re-enlistees and promotees may request any commissioned officer (active duty, reserve, guard, or retired) of the United States to be the administering officer. The ceremony may be conducted in any location that lends dignity to the event, with the national flag always as a backdrop for the participants. Their immediate families should be invited and other guests encouraged. Principals wear an authorized uniform for the ceremony, except if the administering officer is retired, when his uniform is optional.

Reveille and Retreat

See Chapter 7: Flag Etiquette.

Silent Drill Platoons

These performances by selected Service members are carried out without verbal commands. For example, the Silent Drill Platoon is a part of Company A at Marine Barracks, Washington, D.C. They perform in ceremonies during the summer months at the Iwo Jima Memorial, located in Arlington, Virginia, on Tuesdays and at the Marine Barracks on Fridays.

NAVY VESSELS AND CEREMONIES

During the construction and fitting out of a ship, there are three ceremonial occasions authorized by Congress: the keel laying, the christening launch, and the commissioning. The construction of a large warship takes about three years from keel-laying to launching. The Secretary of the Navy, upon the recommendation of the Chief of Naval Operations, chooses the name of a ship long before launching, but a ship does not receive her name until she is christened in a ceremony that is partly religious. "Sponsors" are the females who do the christening.

Boarding a Naval Vessel

The senior official always boards the ship first. No matter the vessel size and regardless of a military visitor's rank, it is protocol to face the quarterdeck (the seat of authority and the place nearest the U.S. flag, called an *ensign* when flown from ships and boats) and salute as soon as the ladder or gangway is cleared. Veterans not in uniform may also render the hand salute to the ensign, if they desire. Civilians remove their hats to pay respect and stand at attention facing the ensign for a brief moment with the right hand over the heart (non-citizens may bow slightly or nod). Immediately thereafter, military visitors salute (civilians nod to) the Officer of the Deck (OOD) regardless of his or her rank, saying, "*Request permission to come aboard.*" The OOD returns the salute and grants permission. The captain of the ship and any flag rank officers on board will be waiting nearby until this time-honored ceremony is complete before greeting visiting dignitaries.

The Ship's Captain

Guests attending any function on board a navy ship must remember to address the ship's commanding officer as "Captain" regardless of his or her rank. A lieutenant commander (O-5 pay grade), for example, would still be called "Captain."

Side Boys and Tending the Side

Side boys attend official visitors who come on board or depart from large naval vessels (and smaller ones during formal ceremonies such as changes of command). "Tending the side" of a naval vessel with side boys originated long ago when officers from other ships were invited to dinner or conferences at sea. Sometimes the sea was rough enough that visitors were hoisted aboard in boatswain's chairs. The boatswain (warrant officer or noncommissioned officer in charge of ship's maintenance and equipment) used his call (whistle) to pipe the order "hoist away" and "vast heaving." Members of the crew did the hoisting, and from the aid they rendered evolved the custom of having a certain number of men always in attendance when high-ranking visitors come on board. The Navy has extended this distinct nautical courtesy to military, diplomatic, and consular officers, as well as to dignitaries of the legislative and executive departments of the U.S. federal government.

If visitors approach the ship by boat, junior personnel sit forward with the senior sitting aft. The senior disembarks first, the junior last. The boatswain pipes when the boat comes alongside the ship and again when the visitor's head reaches the level of the deck. This "piping aboard" alerts the side boys, who salute the ranking officer or government official as he or she boards the ship first.

Q: What do I do when going on board a ship where "side boys" render honors to my husband?

A: If you precede him, move "smartly" when you hear the piping begin because he must salute as he steps on deck, before it ends. Otherwise, stand aside (not between the saluters) and pause. You will be directed where to proceed. When walking on deck, the place of honor is outboard. Follow behind if there is not room beside your husband and another officer. If the latter is the case, often you will have your own escort.

Shipboard Etiquette

The ship's command post is the bridge when under way (unless in a combat environment) or the quarterdeck while at anchor. High-ranking visitors are usually escorted there upon arrival (the place of honor is outboard when pacing the deck). All personnel remove covers (headgear) in respect when passing through the crew's spaces at meal times, when entering sickbay, and for worship services, funerals, and other religious ceremonies (even if they are in the open on deck). All personnel uncover when passing through the Captain's or Admiral's spaces. Warrants and junior officers remove covers in the wardroom.

Officer Wardroom Etiquette

While the ship is under way, officers may be required to wait for the Commanding Officer (CO) before seating themselves for daily meals in the wardroom (officers' mess hall). If the CO is busy or running late, usually the senior officer in the wardroom at the time will call and get permission to start the meal. Officers must request permission from the most senior officer present to join late or depart the mess.

Occasionally there may be formal, sit-down dinners for all officers to eat together. Dress will be uniform of the day, such as working khakis. This meal may include the tradition of "passing the buck." The buck is a small item, such as a brass lantern, that is passed from person to person. The senior ensign (O-1 pay grade) chooses a topic to discuss during the meal and passes the buck to an officer of his or her choice. That officer tells a story concerning the topic before passing the buck to another officer. This process is repeated throughout the meal and generally ends with the CO receiving the buck and closing out the meal with a final anecdote.

Disembarking a Naval Vessel
Junior military personnel leave a ship first, saluting the OOD and requesting permission to depart. When permission is granted, they face the ensign, salute, and disembark. As on arrival, civilians remove their hats to pay respect and stand at attention facing the ensign for a brief moment with the right hand over the heart (non-citizens may bow or nod). The senior official always departs the ship last, and is piped over the side. By custom, the corpse of any naval officer is also piped over the side if sent ashore for burial.

WREATH LAYINGS

Every country has its own customs. Military personnel overseas generally need only concern themselves with turning up in the proper uniform at the proper time in the proper place for guidance by protocol officers. In the United States, ceremony officials at the monument location, such as the Tomb of the Unknowns at Arlington National Cemetery, control the procedure. Often, the uniformed person will simply assist someone in the physical placement of a flower wreath, most likely mounted on a wire stand. For instance, two Service members together, or one helping a government dignitary, will lift the stand and walk forward in a slow, dignified manner to place it as briefed by the protocol officer. The military personnel will then stand near any civilian principals for other aspects of the ceremony. If given the choice, keep the U.S. dignitary on the honored right side (the audience's left) at all times. If you are the invited dignitary, prepare appropriate comments for a short speech, which may be broadcast.

CHAPTER 3

Hosting High-Profile Visits

*V*ery Important Persons (VIPs) and Distinguished Visitors (DVs) often travel. Every field—education, science, business, law, medicine, engineering, computers, government and politics, and the military— has renowned dignitaries or senior officials who benefit from professional exchanges. Because of his or her position, achievements, or significant status, everything is carefully planned for the VIP/DV (these terms are used interchangeably here), from travel and accommodations to counterpart appointments to hospitality and socializing opportunities. There are protocol offices and foreign liaison offices at each major government and military headquarters or command. They make excellent resources when action officers and mid-level managers have specific questions, but they do not plan details outside their organizations.

AT EASE KEY POINTS

- ❧ Develop sample VIP agendas.
- ❧ Draft toast, gift presentation, and gift acceptance language.
- ❧ Greet DVs at first entry point: flight line, shipside, curbside, facility door.
- ❧ Keep VIPs on right side (seating, walking, standing), in front and outboard (ships), backseat curbside (cars), and left rear in aircraft.
- ❧ Rank precedes through doorways, boards and disembarks ship first.
- ❧ Rank takes the stage last, enters last and disembarks first from cars and aircraft.

International VIP visits to American government and military locations require advance coordination and approval through the highest U.S. official channels, such as the Department of State and the Joint Chiefs of Staff. The country's embassy in Washington, D.C., will also be involved. The offices work together in hopes of promoting favorable relations between the two countries. One or more "aides" will accompany international DVs. Frequently, they are high-ranking officials destined for future positions of authority in their countries, who form lasting impressions about the U.S. based on their experience as members of a visiting party. Treat them with all courtesy together or separate from the VIP.

Visit locations and levels of classified discussions for internationals are agreed to in writing. Local requirements regarding classified materials are coordinated with the Foreign Disclosure Office, Special Security Office (SSO), or other security managers. They review potential briefings to help determine the level of classification and even help with simplifying them for foreigners by pointing out acronyms or abbreviations to be eliminated.

There are other parameters to follow, such as regulations for using public funds. If your department or agency requests an official visit (or the U.S. government directs you to host one), yours is considered the benefiting entity; therefore, the government will pay for certain things. For example, the military consults Department of Defense Directive 7250.13, *Official Representation Funds*, for policy on hosting, such as:

> Generally, such events are hosted and official courtesies extended for civilian or military dignitaries and officials of foreign governments, senior U.S. Government officials, dignitaries and senior officials of State and local governments, and other distinguished and prominent citizens who have made a substantial contribution to the nation or the Department of Defense (DOD), and members of the news media on certain occasions. . . . Official courtesies may include the cost of luncheons, dinners, receptions, mementos, and participation expenses at DOD-sponsored events. Other expenses may be approved with specific justification. . . . [Mementos should be] of little intrinsic value, such as coins, paperweights, lapel pins, and plaques. . . . Under no circumstances may mementos for visiting DOD officials be purchased with Operation and Maintenance (O&M) funds, or with Morale, Welfare, and Recreation (MWR) funds.

The proper source of funds is often the visiting individual. Your unit or its assigned escorts should not feel obligated to spend personal money to host VIPs—they have their own travel budgets. Provide per-head costs and ask for credit card numbers for planned event expenses (refer to them as hospitality fees) or to reserve personal desires such as tours, interpreters, etc. Alternatively, provide points of contact so that visitors can arrange and pay for their own personal services. Be very clear in communications about who is responsible for what expenses. VIPs often travel with team members, aides, personal staffs, and family members. Everyone in the entourage requires support, but not necessarily at the same level. For instance, the VIP may stay in a suite, the staff in regular hotel rooms. The DV gets a car; the entourage may be transported by bus or van.

Readers who are at the right hand of prominent individuals, or managers required to assist with visits, will benefit from contingency planning for hosting VIPs/DVs. See Chapter 23: Seating Plans, and Chapter 25: International Protocol and Civility, for more particulars. Make plans with alternatives to stay at the forefront of circumstances and maintain the prestige of the military or government office you support. The following suggestions will get you started on issues that might arise:

DUTY-FREE ENTRY INTO THE UNITED STATES

Certain high-ranking international officials (chiefs of state, heads of government, cabinet members, and senior government personnel, including military and diplomatic) and distinguished foreign visitors (their immediate family members, members of royal families, religious dignitaries, and sometimes world-renowned business tycoons, entertainment celebrities, athletic heroes, and academic leaders) are eligible to enter the United States duty-free. Check eligibility with your headquarters' foreign liaison office to help arrange "expedited port clearance" with the U.S. Department of State's Chief of Protocol (www.state.gov/s/cpr). Customs and immigration officials, money exchanges, security (police escorts), are also alerted as appropriate.

SECURITY ISSUES

Security is a prime concern for any visiting VIP, in terms of both physical safety and privacy. Use short-term classification markings (declassify one week after the event concludes) to control visit information. Coordinate possible scenarios with installation security officials ahead of time so that you are prepared to send restriction notices. Leaders will agree to most anything if coordinated in advance. For example, if customs searches with magnetometers are required when international planes arrive, they must be notified or it could be misconstrued as personally insulting. Camera phones may be prohibited, but no one wants theirs confiscated, so warn them in advance to leave them behind when visiting government facilities. If a high-profile leader's protective detail insists on accompanying their principal and carrying weapons at all times, or the DV brings an entourage that includes an unexpected media representative, you will be relieved to be able to quote from policy that was forwarded during the planning stages. When notified of a visit, do a threat assessment regarding the VIP's safety, and whether the visit will affect U.S. military and government Force Protection Conditions (FPCON). Such details may affect everything from the arrival location, transportation route and vehicles, the hotel and other local venues to be utilized, the government meeting location, and the size of gatherings.

WELCOME PACKETS

Develop a generic welcome packet to be further tailored depending on the delegation. Acquire bio information (name and position, picture, business and e-mail addresses for thank-yous) on prominent people that VIPs will likely meet so that they can function even with jet lag. For U.S. locations, provide brochures on the local historic and natural wonder sites, along with a few maps (city and military installation). Include a list of key points of contact. If you are posted in an overseas location visited by American VIPs, it is helpful to include a one-page overview with the country name, world map location, flag, main religions, list of current government leaders, and the currency name and exchange rate. Particular attention should be given to a section on local courtesies and social mores, such as greeting phrases in the official language(s), behavior toward ethnic groups (regarding perhaps giving alms to the poor or sensitivities to picture taking), appropriate street dress, tipping customs and amounts, etc. One or two short paragraphs about the current political landscape, the economic situation, and local military infrastructure can be prepared for inclusion, as needed; however, most DVs will consider themselves regional experts. Draft a note of welcome for the host to personalize (handwriting is best) and offer small gift ideas for the VIP's hotel room, such as local sweets or mixed nuts.

LOCAL MEALS AND TOASTING

Most visits will include a local meal or two at a restaurant or in the home of the hosting official. Sometimes a working breakfast or lunch with military troops is requested. If the DV or delegation is making several stops, try to coordinate the probable menus so that not every host takes the VIPs out for seafood, for instance. Consider restaurants with themes or menus unique to your geographic area, taking into consideration any dietary restrictions. Choose typical regional restaurants based on easy access, private rooms, service hours, good food, and accommodating staff. Preplan appropriate menus and cultivate a relationship with owners or headwaiters so that it is easy to set up what you need. When planning an evening for international visitors, smaller gatherings are better than large cocktail parties. Since it is such an intimate honor to be asked into a private home, internationals in particular are impressed by such invitations. If an in-home event will require catering, have several reliable providers in mind and double-check cancellation policies.

Since at least one meal is likely to be a dinner with local dignitaries, draft several suitable toasts for senior American officials to deliver if you are in an international setting (include a phonetic rendering of the favored local toasting words). Any such toast you provide should not be your own favorite. Formal and ceremonial toasts follow strict protocol (see Chapter 20: Toasts), and VIPs may reference policy matters in them. However, it is common to exchange short beverage tributes at the individual table level or between dinner partners, and your help with these will impress your VIP and encourage friendly relations between communities or countries.

Utilizing Staff

Promote the intellectual, cultural, ethnic, and linguistic diversity of your colleagues (military or civilian) by employing staff as interpreters, escorts, or tour guides. There are always restrictions on the number of individuals a VIP can meet because of time constraints, language capabilities, office sizes, etc. Wise leaders expose as many on their staffs as possible so that they gain hands-on experience in process and protocol. VIPs rate a local car or limousine and driver, with an official escort to all meetings, seminars, office calls, and tourist sites. The entourage, if not accompanying the VIP for official purposes, is also provided a separate group tour guide. The guide could even be a volunteer spouse. Otherwise, compile a list of professional tour guides, commercial tour bus/local sightseeing businesses, and interpreters.

Accommodating Desires

VIPs/DVs often need your advice on where to go and who to see. Combine their desires with your own requirements and everyone will be happy. Escort them somewhere you also need to visit. Arrange meetings with officials you must cultivate for professional reasons. Local officials are usually flattered by dignitary visits. Improve your organization's relationships with community leaders by using the VIP as a reason to entertain. People will come to a social event honoring a DV, even if they have not yet met the host.

Accommodate the desires of an international group for shopping; always anticipate a request to stop at the military exchange and commissary, as well as local malls. Besides museums and historic sites, consider taking internationals to a working farm, ranch, or local manufacturing plant as an example of free enterprise. Careful planning will make the visit rewarding for both sides.

CHRONICLE VISITS

Any time you have distinguished, important, or world-renowned dignitaries at your location, always chronicle their visits to the fullest extent possible. Arrange to videotape or audio record the event for your archives, as well as for streaming on the organization Web site. Arrange it well in advance of the event, develop release forms, and gain signatures of participants. The twenty-first century will see increasing reliance on video records of events, but do not neglect a written article or report; assign at least one note-taker and writer. Via your own Web site and in-house publication, post the upcoming event on the calendar. Afterward, post a summation or synopsis. Consider sending articles to local or national newspapers and magazines, or to your professional association's publication, to highlight your office and enhance its standing. Always coordinate contacts with the Public Affairs Office (PAO) in government and military circles before dealing with any public media.

Photogenic Backgrounds and Photo Ops
Determine photogenic backgrounds symbolic of your organization or its location for official photographs. Flags and emblems such as seals, crests, or logos create an attractive setting or backdrop indoors; outside, military or applicable equipment in front of natural scenery emphasize your locale. Brainstorm what transactions (contracts being signed, fine points of daily work in progress, annual meeting visited) could "tell a story" and if signed releases are needed before publishing. Arrange photo opportunities with the VIP for organization personnel who may be thrilled with the opportunity to have a souvenir of the visit (and feel rewarded for their support efforts). Know how to schedule staff photographers or where the office digital cameras are located. For facility tours, keep the dignitaries on the right of the hosting official, open doors and allow DVs to pass through first, and otherwise strictly observe protocol, *especially* if there will be a record in video or still photography.

The media may expect to observe, including international news services if the VIP is foreign. The PAO will either organize your dealings with the media or give advice. For visual media, principals are usually positioned more formally in front of your chosen backdrops, perhaps seated in armchairs and chatting (proviso sound off), standing and shaking hands, or accepting a commemorative item (do not duplicate something given previously). Limit the number of other individuals in the picture—the media will do close-ups anyway. Delegations may bring their own spokespersons for dealing with news services. Even so, they should check with the hosts regarding content.

GIFT CEREMONIES

Draft proper presentation language and acceptance speeches for gift ceremonies. (Do the same kind of brainstorming for possible award presentations.) The formality of the public ritual and wording are likely to be more important than the actual items exchanged. Read Chapter 25: International Protocol and Civility for more on international gift-giving and official gift presentations, such as the importance of accepting items with both hands. Research your headquarters' policy on gift exchanges and protocol requirements. For instance, the protocol or foreign liaison office may caution against initiating an unprecedented gift exchange because of the escalation repercussions. VIP gift exchanges should be carefully coordinated and mutually agreed to well ahead of time for this reason. Most gifts to VIPs are given for a particular purpose, such as to recognize past support, to cultivate relationships toward future goodwill, or to symbolize the influence (politically, financially, or socially) of governments or individuals.

Develop a list of gift ideas in different price ranges, some appropriate purchase avenues, and lead-time requirements. Locate the nearest engraver to discuss prices and the time needed from order to delivery. Affix engraved plates onto gifts (best in a discreet location) at the last possible moment in case a visitor's plans change. (In that case, save the unsullied gift for another purpose.) Since VIPs will be departing your location, consider offering the following verbally or on a card inside the gift box: *"We are pleased to package this item in protective wrap for travel, if you desire."* Finally, keep a gift record of what was given, who gave it to whom and why, and the date presented. It will prove a very useful document.

PRIVATE INTERACTIONS BETWEEN PRINCIPALS

Senior principals may desire a private discussion after a group meeting. Devise ways to create one-on-one time without being obvious. Take the visitor's entourage members out of the meeting room for a tour of the facility. Create a scenario where the host official invites the senior visiting principal to step away, perhaps to view a historic object or work of art in his office, or a view of the city from a balcony. The respective staffs should work on cultivating their own friendships during such times.

EDUCATING VISIT PARTICIPANTS

It may be necessary to educate VIPs and their staffs about your mission. For instance, be prepared to correct blatant civilian misconceptions concerning the military lifestyle, such as that the military does not pay taxes, does not vote, gets free food at the commissary, or receives overtime pay. Escorts are often seen as speaking for their superiors, so they should be briefed about how to respond diplomatically on local matters that may arise. The PAO will help hosting personnel realize that, if it is consistent with their own agendas, outsiders will quote escorts as "credible inside sources."

LETTERS OF APPRECIATION

It is important to send letters of appreciation following official visits, especially if gifts were exchanged. Determine what level in the organization should send formal thank-you notes on letterhead to a visiting delegation hierarchy, as well as to personnel who support visits. Draft sample language for your files. In addition to the formal organization's letters of appreciation, handwritten notes sent to the VIP from the escort will be well received, especially if providing some requested follow-up information. Thank-you notes are mailed or hand-delivered alone; they are not included with other correspondence.

GREETERS AND ESCORTS

When dignitaries travel to or from government or military installations, they are often assigned one or more U.S. military officers or civilian officials as escorts. Escorts are responsible for such things as liaison between principals and support players (action officials, drivers, hotel employees), coordinating access to military exchanges, commissaries, or hospitals (if privileges are authorized), facilitating with financial matters, and even interpreting.

Escorts are chosen based on the probability that they will be able to nurture relationships between the principals, alleviate social stress for the visitor(s), and ably represent the military or government in public. Often junior personnel are simply informed that their collateral (secondary or parallel) duty will be supporting one or more visits. Everyone can hone leadership skills to great advantage if willing to volunteer in these roles. Doing so enhances sophistication and will sometimes aid in acquiring a future assignment.

Hosts, greeters, and escorts must be warm and gracious. Exhibiting civility is important. If official guests feel at ease and comfortable with individuals, they are likely to have more confidence in your organization.

Escort Contact with VIP/DV Office

As an escort, call the DV's office to introduce yourself to the administrative aide, executive officer, deputy, or other assistant. Indicate your availability to support the DV and the home office. Ensure you have the phonetic pronunciation and correct spelling of the VIP's name. Request the biography and picture (aids in recognizing him or her on arrival). E-mail a list of appropriate questions regarding lodging preferences, dietary or customs restrictions, degree of desired interaction with the local populace, and publicity/press conferences to solicit or avoid (work with your PAO). Determine whether the spouse will accompany, or if the VIP is bringing other officials or support personnel, such as interpreters or bodyguards.

Consult your own office superiors for specific briefings and meetings that will produce a productive visit from your hosting organization's point of view. If security clearances need passing, or classified material carried by the VIP will need storage, the Foreign Disclosure Office or SSO will need to coordinate directly with the VIP office. If the DV is a congressperson, coordinate the visit with your Service's Legislative Liaison personnel.

There will be changes . . . there are always changes; handle them professionally. Just prior to the visit, call the VIP office again to confirm flight numbers as well as arrival and departure times. A commercial airline arrival may be changed to military transport or vice versa just one day prior to the visit. If the DV's office calls you with a change, make sure you inform others working on the visit, as the update may affect everything from who will greet to seating charts. Provide your own office and the VIP/DV office with the final itinerary and your phone number in case of emergencies.

Planning for VIP/DV Visits

Include escorts in all visit events (alongside a foreign principal if interpreting), be they briefings, tours, or social functions. Escorts should be co-located with VIPs/DVs, staying at the same hotel or military guest quarters with them, in case of after-hours emergencies. Escorts may need to communicate on secure telephones or have access to computers and copiers. They should carry a current list of emergency phone numbers, such as the nearest hospital, dentist, and the PAO who is available after hours.

The hallmark of a true professional is being able to act efficiently and gracefully in the role of escort or greeter. Both roles require a personal emphasis on socially correct and gracious civility. Familiarity with the local area is important. Language capability and knowledge of an international visitor's culture would be important for a foreign DV.

High-ranking visitors and hosts may read the plans beforehand or get briefings, but they will still expect to be reminded or guided in the moment by a trustworthy person. If you are a local greeter or escort, rehearse the day before the expected VIP arrival. If the DVs are of sufficient status, an advance party from their end may be present to accompany you on the walk-through. For example, U.S. Government VIPs in descending protocol order include POTUS (President of the United States), CODELs (Congressional Delegations, both Senate and House of Representatives), and GODELs (Governor Delegations from any state or territory) who often send advance parties that include security officials and media representatives. NODELs (Non-official Delegations) and NGOs (Non-Governmental Organizations) are private persons, interest groups, boards, societies, teams, volunteers, foundations, commissions, etc. Delegations are referred to by their ranking principal's name, as in CODEL Clinton.

During the dry run, walk the precise routes. Know exactly which facility entrance doors will be used, where the car or limousine will stop, and who will open car doors. At a hotel for example, the door attendant opens car doors and a valet attendant provides a ticket to the guest before parking a car. Before you leave the greeting area, the greeter/escort or assistant takes the ticket and determines exactly how to call for the vehicle's return. Similarly, at a restaurant, get the door attendant or valet parking phone number and ask management for parking validation stamps. At a secure government location, entry must be pre-arranged and gate guards apprised of license tag numbers and all passenger names. Taxis cannot wait for extended times on a military reservation. Government drivers need a place to park and wait, and again, make sure to get their cell phone numbers to call them back at the conclusion of a function or meeting.

A building's security manager can be of great help for such things as expediting DV passage though security checkpoints, and "locking out" an elevator for exclusive VIP use or programming it so that it will not stop on extraneous floors. Walk the emergency stairwell steps also, as sometimes entry cannot be gained from them back into the main part of the building.

> Q: I was asked to escort my university president from the lobby of a downtown hotel to his seat upstairs for a conference. What is the proper way to do this?
>
> A: Get details such as whether he is a guest speaker, if parking is validated, if you are on call throughout the conference, and so on. Be in position at the hotel entrance (verify exact door if there is more than one) fifteen minutes before he is expected. Know your precise route (e.g., which elevator bank and room door to use). Greet the president curbside and introduce yourself (*"Good morning, Dr. Connolly. I am Maria Kress, your escort."*) Take the valet ticket, if appropriate. Offer a restroom stop. Escort all the way to the VIP seat, usually in the front row. Stand by to reverse the procedure at the end of a short conference. For an all-day or multiday event where you are not assigned for the duration, wait until the first break to return a validated parking ticket, asking if there is anything else required before you depart.

Where to Meet

Meet VIPs at the closest points possible to their arrival point in your city or location: planeside, on the train platform, dockside (see Chapter 1: Military and Government Protocol), or at the entrance to the hotel or temporary quarters if they arrive by automobile. If the visit host cannot meet the VIP/DV, the greeter must be a spokesperson of appropriate rank or status to deliver the host's welcome. You may also greet VIPs at a front security gate or building curbside as their car pulls up for a social function. If met initially at a building curbside, it is very important that as the car door is opened, the ranking VIP is the first person publicly greeted (review Chapter 25: International Protocol and Civility on proper seating in a limousine).

Proper Introductions

Whether escorting high-ranking individuals to a meeting or assisting at social events, it is usually necessary for a greeter to introduce him- or herself. Stand and remain standing until all introductions are complete. Use appropriate time of day greeting, correct honorific, and precedence sequence in introductions:

> *"Good afternoon, Senator Lowe, I am Sandra Eaton, your escort this afternoon."*
>
> *"Mrs. Dean, my name is Sondra Jones. My husband helped arrange this conference. May I show you to the reception area?"*

Introduce any accompanying colleague in the same manner (honored name first, then colleague's full name). The generally accepted phrases are *"Allow me to introduce"* or *"May I introduce."*

As you introduce yourself (or are introduced), assume a dignified posture facing each new person in turn, make smiling eye contact, wait for the introduction to be complete, respond with *"How do you do?"* and shake hands. See further discussions in Chapter 19: Introductions, Conversations, and Farewells, and Chapter 1: Military and Government Protocol.

VIP Walking Briefs

Be prepared to provide a very brief (two-minute) "executive summary" of upcoming activities to the DV. Explain what is about to happen or offer a few key insights, especially when asked. Perhaps give a general overview of how the meeting room is configured and who will be there, or explain that you are escorting the VIP to an anteroom where he or she will wait until introduced before walking to the podium for a speech. If the VIP is dining, it is very gracious to provide a 3x5 card with a diagram of the tablemates' names (or position it at the VIP's place setting if it does not seem appropriate to hand it over in person). Be prepared to act efficiently and gracefully. Lead your VIP along the quickest route to the event location, but offer a restroom opportunity, *"Do you need to freshen up* (or *wash your hands*)*?"* Do not make negative comments about anything (i.e., the elevator wait, the hotel employees). Do not talk constantly.

It is helpful to have two people escort high-ranking VIPs, so that one can lead by staying a few steps in front (clearing the path, opening doors, pushing elevator buttons), and another can walk beside the DV, keeping him or her to the right. The DV naturally looks at the left shoulder of the lead escort to know when and where to move. If there is a problem, one escort can handle it while the other stays with the VIP. If the DV drops anything, the escort bends and picks it up. If the VIP opens a gift in front of an audience, he or she hands it to the escort afterward. Escorts deal with umbrellas, coats, etc.

Do not leave VIPs alone—the purpose of an escort is to take them where they must be. Escort them all the way to their chairs or be sure they know exactly where to sit, according to protocol rules of precedence. Open the doors and usher DVs in after an audience or group is seated. The public needs to respond to principals acting in a confident manner as they proceed with their duties.

Seating a VIP on a Stage

Your boss hosting on his or her own turf may not wish to accompany you on the dry run the day before an important meeting. If that is the case, he or she should be briefed along with the VIPs, out of public sight and immediately before "showtime," especially if there are updates or changes—using that as an excuse for the combined briefing, as necessary. A good supervisor will encourage such a moment,

as it accomplishes such things as introductions behind the scenes and lining dignitaries up in the correct protocol order to walk onto a stage before a live audience
or television cameras. (See Chapter 23: Seating Plans.)

Q: How do I question a conference panel from the audience? Do I stand? Do I remain
standing?

A: Raise your hand. When called on, rise from your seat to direct attention to your question. Speak in a projecting voice. If you are handed a microphone, hold it firmly under
your chin because it will transmit all movements or bumps. If there is a microphone
stand, walk to it and maintain a constant distance, about 5–7 inches (15–20 cm)
without touching it. Speak in a normal voice *over* microphones to eliminate unwanted
breath effects. Greet the panel (*"Good afternoon"*), introduce yourself with position
title if the audience does not know you (*"Bill Hart, Marine Corps Headquarters"*),
direct your question (*"My question is for Dr. Short"*), ask the question, and remain
standing while it is answered. Say thank you and sit down.

Escorts for a Guest Speaker

If the DV is a guest speaker at a conference, escorts offer to keep time by suggest-
ing a 5-minute and 1-minute warning from the back of the room. This signal can
be as simple as standing up. Escorts also offer to record all audience questions for
the VIP's future use. Before the speech, ensure that a glass of water is available
at the podium and determine if lecterns or microphones can be height-adjusted.
For persons who are physically challenged, make sure that there is a stool or that
the podium is sturdy enough to lean on. If it cannot be done out of sight, turn the
speaker's back to the audience and help put on a lapel microphone. Clip the unit
to a waistband and hook the microphone to men's ties, or a convenient side of
women's lapels or necklines.

DEVELOPING A VIP VISIT AGENDA

Everyone performs best with a carefully planned and published itinerary. For
example, a schedule helps everyone involved select (or pack) appropriate clothes.
Detailed agendas are necessary for all visits, but especially for high-profile ones.
The papers will be used to coordinate between the hosts and visitors, so date and
number each draft version and label them *Draft 1, 2,* etc., and only the last version as *Final.* Avoid major changes after going final. Announcing a major schedule change to a VIP or members of a delegation when they arrive at the airport is

psychologically devastating. On arrival, visitors are usually tired and this kind of distraction reduces their ability to feel good about being there.

Provide agendas for everyone in a delegation upon arrival, even if the information was sent electronically beforehand. A folder may be handed out in a control room at check-in, or placed in hotel rooms (positioned attractively in a prominent location so that it will not be overlooked). Include *annotated* participant lists for local meetings and seating plans for dinners. Just a list of names is useless. Separate the list into at least two sections—"Visiting Delegation" and "Hosting Organization"—with correct honorifics and ranks, full names (include pronunciation guides, as needed), and positions or titles. For example:

Colonel Abdullah Saed Al Mansoori [ab-*DOO*-lah sah-*EED* ahl man-*SOOR*-ee]

Commander, Royal Bahrain Navy

Include everyone in such a list by name or specialty: spouses, action officers, escorts, interpreters, accompanying bodyguards, public affairs personnel, drivers, etc. Event times should use the 24-hour clock with "dress requirements" based on planned events. Include details such as vehicle/motorcade assignments, and escort information (who will meet them when and where). Escorts or action officers need further annotated schedules with detailed reminders on their responsibilities, such as:

Day, Location, Time	Greeter	VIP
Fri, curbside, 0945	General Jerrod Brown	Vice Admiral David Moore
Comments: Greet at curbside, escort into auditorium, make formal introduction. VADM wants timing to be such that he walks right to podium for his speech at 1000.		
Fri, curbside, 1200	Ms. Nicole Rasmussen	Ms. Carla Moore
Comments: She has waived spouse tour but desires escort on arrival and your company during hotel luncheon. She will eat only a salad & fruit; confirm with headwaiter.		

Do not fill every minute on the agenda. VIPs may be coming from or going to another site, especially likely if yours is an overseas location. Their schedules are full of activities at every stop. You can help keep a DV at his or her peak if you allow sufficient quiet time after arrival, especially if he or she will attend a critical meeting or an evening program the first day. If a flight delay of one hour would ruin your planned schedule, then reconsider and make the first appointment a courtesy call or something else that can be canceled without consequence, if needed. It is also a major scheduling flaw to program too little time between the last daytime

UNCLASSIFIED// FOR OFFICIAL USE ONLY
(printed top and bottom of every page, along with any safety caveats)
Sample Itinerary for Delegation Name or Rank-Name-Service-Position of VIP/DV

DAY ONE
Attire: Civilian Business Suit *(always provide dress requirements)*

Schedules of Events *(be as specific as possible; use 24-hour clock)*

1600   U.S. Host Names *(include spouses if delegation brings spouses)* proceed to airport via motorcade (list vehicles and necessary escorts).

1630   Greet at planeside, welcome refreshments in airport VIP lounge *(delaying tactic so baggage can be located and loaded into luggage vehicle)*.

1700   Motorcade departs for drive-by past local monuments/sites of interest *(listed as place holder to be cut short or eliminated if time constraints dictate)*.

1745   Party welcomed at hotel door by Mr. Secondary Host *(perhaps a host country representative or hotel manager)* for escort to hospitality/control room *(preregister DVs; keys in a control room eliminate standing in lobby. Guests enjoy drinks while waiting for luggage to be delivered to their rooms)*. Evening at leisure *(provide points of interest and restaurants within walking distance)*.

DAY TWO
Attire: Military Service Dress / Civilian Business Suit

Breakfast at leisure in hotel

0900   Official party (spouses have their own separate schedule) met in lobby by U.S. host for escort to meetings with local officials.

0920   Arrive at meeting location to meet (Admirals, Generals, Ministers, Prime Minister, Provincial Council, Judges, Mayors, whomever appropriate; coordinate any gift exchanges).

1230   Lunch (at meeting venue or local restaurant) hosted by __ (name).

1400   Depart for briefings on local political aspects/military conditions (such meetings would exclude nonessential personnel).

1415   Arrive Conference Location via Gate 3. Met by __ (include all POC information here or attached—full names, positions, office & e-mail addresses, phones).

1830   Dinner hosted by U.S. official (schedule on first evening if delegation is foreign and would benefit from relationship development before business).

DAY THREE
Attire: Civilian Casual

Special requests accommodated. *Labor Secretaries and business people want to talk to locals about free enterprise. Humanitarians and health professionals like to visit orphanages or hospitals. Celebrities and those with no prior military experience like to ride in a tank or enjoy a meal with the troops.*

UNCLASSIFIED//FOR OFFICIAL USE ONLY *(top and bottom of every page)*

Use large fonts and single sided pages for itineraries. Reduce to pocket size for escorts.

appointment and an evening event. Allow a minimum of one hour to freshen up and change clothes or rest.

If you are in an unsafe area or VIPs arrive during times of crisis, all visit papers should have a caveat similar to this at the top:

All logistics, visits, and meetings are subject to security assessments and intelligence reports. YOUR SAFETY COMES FIRST.

VIP/DV FLIGHT-LINE ARRIVALS

Whether VIPs arrive in a private jet, a military aircraft, or a commercial plane, security concerns might preclude a planeside welcome. Military ceremonies are not performed at commercial airports, train stations, or ports. If dignitaries are greeted planeside, the host and two or three others welcome them on the tarmac as they deplane and escort them to another location. For international arrivals, someone must be prepared to collect passports, baggage-claim tickets, and luggage for the entire delegation and clear them through customs. Coordinate customs procedures with local airport officials beforehand. Often there is a lounge where VIPs can wait while this is accomplished.

If the DV arrives on a military aircraft, coordinate early with Base Operations and the protocol office. Ensure a welcome message is displayed on the appropriate base marquee. Determine where the nearest restrooms are located. Request permission for vehicles to drive onto the flight line where the aircraft will park (have them point out the exact location) thirty minutes prior to aircraft arrival. The driver of the DV vehicle should position it close to the yellow line or red carpet. (Disposable earplugs are available at Base Ops.) For delegations, consider the wisdom of having an additional escort and vehicle present for the unexpected. Uniformed greeters and escorts salute the aircraft as it makes its final turn into its parking spot. Once the aircraft comes to a complete stop, the salute is dropped. (Salutes are also rendered as the aircraft starts rolling until it makes its first turn for departure.)

If a planeside ceremony is conducted at a military location, it may entail media, local civilian officials, a band, and perhaps some type of honor cordon or ceremony. Provide diagrams and a detailed sequence of events to all parties involved. VIPs do not like surprises and they hate not knowing where the cameras are, or who is greeting them. DVs deplane first (unless the senior is also the pilot). A "red carpet receiving line" (which may be painted on the tarmac) starts at the door or steps of the plane with the highest-ranking greeter/host. Ensure that the line is at least two paces from the steps. *"I can't tell you how many times*

I've seen someone crowd the stairs and force the arriving DV to shift concentration from completing the final step to that of 'greeting' and the DV falls or stumbles," reports an Air Force navigator.

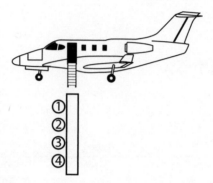

When you travel on board the personal aircraft of a high-ranking flag officer or the corporate jet of an executive, unless instructed otherwise, you board first and fasten your seatbelt ready for takeoff before the senior ranking official arrives. DVs board an aircraft last and will not wait for you. If not instructed where to sit, avoid the VIP seat or section—the left rear, which allows the DV to see the greeting party outside the window. Do not put packages, coats, or any articles in that section or seat. To acknowledge flag rank officers, detachable plates displaying stars appropriate to the highest rank aboard may mark the aircraft.

VIP/DV Motorcades

DV delegations may be loaded into cars at planeside and driven to the meeting venue. Bios with pictures are important, because you may need to identify them within the first two minutes in order to direct them to the proper cars, perhaps sorting them by clearance access for the first meeting. In a precarious forward area, your main concern may be to get people safely into military vehicles and on toward the secure headquarters. The convoy or motorcade could consist of "hard" (protective armor) vehicles for the VIPs, regular vehicles for the protocol officers, lead and trail security HUMVs with 50-caliber guns, and APACHE helicopter gunships flying overhead . . . but probably not that often. VIPs/DVs are accustomed to seeing and being seen. It may be politic, therefore, to display the insignia of the highest-ranking passenger (general and admiral ranks, civilian leaders of state and federal governments, foreign dignitaries) on the principal's (lead) automobile in either flag or license plate form. If no flag or plate is available for a foreign dignitary, a U.S. military flag and plate equivalent to the foreigner's grade may be displayed. (Do not, however, use individual U.S. position flags, such as Service secretaries or chiefs of staff.)

Assign escorts for each vehicle, brief them on how to seat principals, and make sure that they have (and review) the same visit folder that the delegation will receive, with participant lists, schedules, seating plans, etc., so that they can answer questions. Do not forget that the crew on private planes also needs transportation and may be required to stay longer to secure the aircraft. If there is a separate vehicle for luggage, visitors need not wait for their bags to be loaded, but do not let the motorcade pull away until you account for all the people. The car with the host and ranking visitor departs first; the rest follow, senior to junior ranking, with the baggage vans last. This precedence order can be modified to suit the local security situation. For example, the use of lead and trail security vehicles ensure that outside cars do not interfere with the motorcade. In addition, an arrangement with local police for traffic control at busy intersections may be a good idea.

If the government is not providing transportation, work with the VIP's office to help them assemble their own appropriate rental cars (with a reliable firm that meets requirements such as vehicles with GPS units, proper van height restrictions for parking garages, drivers with background checks, and emergency backup cars in case there is a problem). Arrange for access passes, as needed, to allow rental cars onto military or government grounds. Reserve parking spaces, as necessary, at the lodging and meeting locations.

VIP Hotel Arrivals

Choose a hotel that is convenient for your purposes, perhaps near the military or government facility where numerous classified discussions will be held, or because it has an auditorium, break-out conference rooms, informal meeting places, and a good dining room to eliminate time-consuming movement from building to building. If the delegation is free in the evenings, hotels located in metropolitan areas offer restaurant and amusement options. Of course, always consider security issues when choosing lodging. The highest-ranking VIPs require the greatest protections. Venues may need to comply with such things as parking barriers, access restrictions (metal detectors and scanners), and a review of their procedures for evacuation and verifying the credentials of their employees and vendors. Your unit security office can coordinate with the local police, Homeland Security, Secret Service, the FBI, Department of Defense, or the State Department's Diplomatic Security Service, as appropriate.

To avoid creating a scene in the lobby, and as another level of security, pre-register all guests and keep rooms co-located. Arrange for a hospitality room for handing out keys and other front-desk transactions such as exchanging money (if overseas). Consider retaining this room after its service as an initial welcome reception area (provide drinks and bottled water), and turn it into a visit control room, especially if the hotel is willing to provide it free of charge for a large entourage or very high-ranking VIP. If you reserve a two-room suite for this purpose, keep it on the same floor as the delegation; the escort or office staffer can sleep in the suite's bedroom to be on-call during evening hours. Keep extra visit folders and agendas there (someone is sure to need another copy), and the all important "key points of contact" list with phone numbers. The extra space is also useful for storing supplies and for holding or collecting luggage and purchases, especially if it is guarded twenty-four hours a day.

Walk the ranking VIP to his or her room. Give the DV your escort card/business card with your cell phone number, or show where the information is in the visit folder. Keep your cell phone fully charged (carry a car adapter and an extra battery) and use a hands-free earpiece during the visit. Before you depart, discuss any requirements with the DV and agree on the next meeting point. Every time an escort greets the VIP, he or she should ask if there is any additional support needed, as circumstances may change from day to day.

VIP/DV Spouse Itineraries

Government and military family members are generally prohibited from travel in government aircraft and vehicles. For spouses to be authorized government transportation, the travel must be an official obligation ("for the good of the service or government"), and the spouse must actually participate in the event requiring the government transportation. High visibility means high responsibility. Invitational travel orders are issued to spouses as the authorizing mechanism, but only the highest levels may approve spouse travel, and only then on a case-by-case basis. In the DOD, the authorization comes from the Secretary of Defense, Service Secretaries, Principal Under Secretaries, appropriate four-star officers, and certain three-star general officers in designated overseas areas, as authorized by the Joint Federal Travel Regulation (JFTR).

When a VIP spouse does travel with his or her military or government sponsor under invitational travel orders, offer a separate itinerary for periods when the principal must be briefed alone. Since spouses are instantly credible as speaking for the VIP, however, do include them in (unclassified) briefings before sending them out separately into the local community. If the dignitary is given a stag luncheon, it is considerate to honor the spouse with a luncheon or tea hosted by one or several hosting officials' spouses, which may include notable local citizenry.

Assign a dedicated person to escort the VIP spouse when not with the principal. This escort should be a government employee. Invite and encourage hosting officials' spouses to greet (and bid farewell to) the visitors at the airport and to tour with them. However, if the local spouses cannot accommodate volunteering, this must be respected. If the VIP spouse is escorted by a local volunteer spouse, fully support the nonemployee with a car and driver.

You may have two weeks' or less notice of the arrival of VIPs/DVs. If you do not have one already, develop now a generic Plan A (half-day itinerary), Plan B (one-day itinerary), and Plan C (two-day itinerary) of local sights and experiences that can be tailored to heighten the importance of the specific spouse.

When visits are announced, the hosting office should request permission for the volunteer escort or project officer to correspond directly with the VIP spouse via e-mail without the screening confusion of the two offices. When contact is established, options for the spouse schedule should be sent for approval, following privacy laws (protect personal data and travel plans) and Force Protection Conditions.

Start by determining the VIP spouse's interests, expectations, and whether this is a first visit to your location. Focus on the local area (easy travel radius) to search out activities that may be of interest to him or her personally, such as visiting businesses or arranging luncheons with local notable citizens, especially if they are the same national heritage as the visitor. The most interesting aspect of an overseas location may be to witness the cultural view of appropriate roles for men, women, and children; or the rigid societal separation of the elite and poor. Spouses may desire personal interactions with those they see. Include whatever the local residents would want them to experience or more fully understand. If you are near a large military installation, consider stops at spouse employment assistance programs, schools, and medical facilities.

Strive to adhere to the times indicated in the itinerary. Do not cut into the "free time" of spouses without consulting them. Set aside ample time for coffee/tea breaks, to rest or exercise, and for bargain shopping. Between the daytime and evening events there must be enough time to rest, shower, change clothes, and travel from point to point—a minimum of an hour and a half on spouse schedules. Make sure the VIP spouse has the escort's cell phone number. Escorts walk the DV spouse all the way to the hotel room door and wait until the spouse dismisses them. Offer to get ice or call room service for foreign spouses; proficiency in a second language can decrease with fatigue.

The same protocol applies to both VIP and spouse. If the U.S. government has paid for the spouse to accompany the principal, everyone's expectations are great. Primarily, spouses are judged on appearance, manners, immediate reactions, and speech. The more confident they appear, the more successful the visit, so provide all reasonable assistance. In order to function, they must know dress (and shoe) requirements; address people by name and title; prepare for delivering remarks or toasts; and send thank-you notes after any hospitality extended. Cut down spouse confusion by providing cue cards with pictures of those they will meet, with full names and addresses for follow-up communication (include host and escort information also). DV spouses are often considered goodwill ambassadors, and there may be local requests for photo opportunities or gift presentations if the VIP is of sufficient stature. Make it easier to succeed by offering suggestions about what to say or give in return (perhaps carry a small memento or two for emergency presentations). Record who, what, where, and when on paper so that you will be able to annotate photographs before forwarding them to the DVs.

Finally, promote acknowledgment of local staff by requesting a group picture of the VIP spouse with the hosting unit spouses, for instance. The honor of being included in an important event will not be forgotten, photos make good souvenirs, and pictures can be used for in-house publications.

SAMPLE SPOUSE SCHEDULE
Choice of Activity for Your Free Afternoon

All options are available but no VIP arrangements have been made.

1. Visit a popular spa, frequented by foreigners and locals. Good massages, exercise room and track, swimming pool (hot & cold), hair and manicure services.
2. Shop for souvenirs. The local (woodworking, linens, copper, brass, pottery, paintings, jewelry, whatever) are especially popular with visitors.
3. Return to your room for free time alone.
4. Tour local site (craft or art museum, botanical garden, historic site, etc.)
5. Eat at a popular restaurant to taste regional cuisine.
6. A whim of your own we might be able to arrange.

VIP/DV DEPARTURES

It is just as important to bid a proper farewell to a VIP/DV at the conclusion of a visit, as it is to greet them. Hosts or appropriate representatives stay with the dignitary until he or she departs, until they "see the tail lights." As a one-time function is about to end, call for the driver, then escort the dignitary all the way back to the waiting car or taxi. Shake hands when you say goodbye and promise to send any follow-on communication (such as audience questions asked a guest speaker, or gift presenter names and addresses for thank-you notes). Stay at curbside until the vehicle pulls away.

For a delegation flying out, put on the schedule that there will be a "pre-departure bag pick-up." Schedule it for about an hour before the leave-taking. The baggage van or truck will move more slowly than cars, and may need to depart even earlier. If you have a very, very important person (VVIP) or two, their luggage can be carried in the trunks of the cars they will be using, especially if their rooms have been under constant guard. You may wish to suggest that the delegation order a boxed meal from the hotel, depending on the flight length and airline service. Boxed meals should be delivered to the cars fifteen minutes before the delegates are seated (again in protocol order).

The host or an appropriately high-ranking designate travels with the VIP/DV to the airport and there bids farewell. If official photos were taken by the hosting organization, a digital album can be presented in the car, which can end the visit on a positive note. The car with the host and ranking visitor departs first; the rest follow, senior to junior ranking. As with arrivals, you may request local security support (motorcycle escorts) to return to the airport. Stay until the aircraft lifts off and call the VIP/DV office to inform them of the departure and expected arrival time at the next destination.

AFTER ACTIONS

Escorts or project officers may be required to write an official, detailed after-action report. If so, do not be critical of the VIP/DV or the entourage, because your report could be widely distributed. Make a genuine effort to record any lessons learned, perhaps in a separate document (a continuity folder) kept with the database of visit information. If your office does not have such a database, start one immediately.

Each visit should be a new document entry in your database, listed by VIP last name, organization, and visit month and year as the title. Databases are as complete as possible, with the DV's full name (and nickname plus spouse name, as applicable), bios and pictures, military or government rank/grade or equivalency title, nationality, and lists of accompanying persons. Include other key information such as who in the community (flag officers, business executives, local officials) met with the delegation members, and the hotel location. Keep careful records of official expenditures, what mementos were received and presented, the menus served (with personal preferences and dietary restrictions), the precedence lists and seating charts, any special needs, and most important of all, what worked well during the visit and your recommendations for making the next one better.

Finally, you are not done until you say "thank you" both officially and personally. Normally, only the host, project officer, escort, and the head of protocol will receive a note from the VIP/DV. That leaves the hosting office to recognize—by name, in writing—the efforts of everyone else who worked on the visit.

CHAPTER 4

Organizing a Dining In and Dining Out

ormal dinners in the company of military fellows are among the oldest of Service traditions. No family members or "non-official" guests are invited to a Dining In. If the function includes personal, nonbusiness guests or family members, it is termed a Dining Out (see last section). A guest speaker, if invited, should be distinguished or outstanding in his or her field so that the speech is the highlight of the evening. Any *official* guests—U.S. civil servants, military leaders, officials of civic or philanthropic organizations, prominent foreign nationals, persons of renown—are guests of the members as a whole; their expenses are shared. Invite civic leaders occasionally as a good way to enhance relations with civilian neighbors.

AT EASE KEY POINTS

- ✂ Prepare a relevant toast and justification for it.
- ✂ Arrive punctually. Greet president, guest of honor, others.
- ✂ Wait for president before sitting, eating, or drinking.
- ✂ Request permission to report an offense or propose a toast.
- ✂ Do not rest decanters on table until everyone's glass is charged.

Seasoned participants delight in the order of events and in introducing neophytes to the atmosphere of dignity, protocol, and esprit de corps of a Dining In. Conversation is general during dinner, with members showing off their best dining styles (read Chapter 16: Place Settings, Table Manners, and Serving Styles) to avoid fines themselves while delivering flamboyant or impertinent reports of their peers' minor transgressions in civility, bearing, or table manners. Permission to toast or report misbehavior must always be sought from the presiding officer (the president) or his or her designate (the vice president), or the informer himself risks a penalty. Some gregarious individuals deliberately violate rules so they will be singled out for fines or penalties, practicing witty and imaginative justification rebuttals (which will probably only earn more censure). The in-jokes that result are amusing and build camaraderie.

Formal toasts are an important part of a Dining In and always honor guests and the chain of command. Toasts begin with the president's welcome and continue at dessert or the separate port wine course. It is better to schedule the majority of toasts after food has been consumed, as toasts may be many in number. Provide underage or non-drinking participants with a nonalcoholic beverage so that they may also drink toasts.

By first asking permission of the president, anyone may leave after the meal if important duties the following day preclude a late evening. "Duty" is an accepted excuse for not following the prevailing etiquette practice of waiting for the ranking person to depart a social event before taking leave. The senior officer is usually not inclined to depart quickly anyway, but to stay on and enjoy the ingenuity and comradeship of a Dining In. Even if the president or guest of honor departs early, the evening usually continues with singing, parlor games, feats of skill, or dancing.

Preparation

The commanding officer of the unit (or a designate) is president of a Dining In or Dining Out and chooses its purpose or main focus. He or she selects which optional ceremonies to include (too many will actually detract from an evening's success), limiting the formal program to no more than two and a half hours, especially if informal entertainment will follow.

The president decides the date, time, and location for the evening, arranges for a guest speaker and the chaplain (as desired), decides which office staff (officer, enlisted, and civilian personnel inclusive) to invite, appoints various committees, and selects the vice president (always a military junior, though not necessarily the lowest ranking). The president ensures that protocol is observed throughout the evening and is the final arbiter for violations and toasts, but may delegate those duties to the vice president, as desired.

The vice president is also a key player for the occasion, making reservations, arranging for the color guard and musicians (or recorded music), coordinating all committees, and directing activities during the event. A printed program will add a professional touch and aid in keeping time. It also serves as a souvenir of the occasion. Program agendas normally include the toasts and proper responses, biographical sketches and photos of the guest speaker and commander, the menu, the "Rules" (see Member Points of Order below), the words to the Service song (if sung), and a brief description of all activities. A band, for instance, needs a full program agenda in order to choose appropriate music. (It is kind to provide musicians with dinner, if possible, especially if they are requested to play sets throughout the evening. During a break, they may go to another part of the facility to eat; their meal need not be the same as the Dining In.)

The vice president is the first to arrive at cocktails, sounds the dinner chimes, proposes or seconds toasts as directed or delegated by the president, perhaps calms unruliness or maintains a list of offenders, and otherwise keeps the party moving. The vice president has great latitude in how the proceedings are conducted, and is always the last to depart.

Committees may include:

- *Table Preparation* (ordering food, seating arrangements and seating chart, Fallen Comrade Observance, place cards, place settings, and menu cards)

- *Decorations* (national or organizational colors behind receiving line and the president's chair, centerpieces, displays of unit trophies [recently polished], photographs or paintings)

- *Sponsorship* (collecting money, paying food and bar charges)

- *Protocol* (issuing invitations and tracking R.s.v.p.s; printing programs, preparing Fallen Table scripts; drafting the president's thank-you letters to speaker and key players)

- *VIP Courtesies* (providing advance agendas, arranging transportation, greeting, escorting, etc.). See Chapter 1: Military and Government Protocol for guidance.

- *Order of Events* (public address system, handing out awards, positioning the gavel and chimes, organizing and cueing wait staff, and the photographer). Brief the photographer beforehand so that he or she will not detract from ceremonies or activities; provide the program agenda and request the specific photographs desired. Photographs (for example, of couples at a Dining Out) may be staged before or after the event.

Invitations
Since a Dining In is a formal occasion, formal wording is used, with invitations extended in the name of the hosting organization (full name spelled out), even on electronically transmitted (e-mail) invitations. If they are computer-generated for those within the unit, wording the second line *"requests the honor of your presence"* negates the need to personalize with individual names. Extend invitations at least two weeks prior to the event for members, up to one month for others. Unless fully

hosted by the Unit fund, indicate whether the event is no-host (members pay for all food and drink, splitting the honored guest[s] expenses), or partially hosted (individuals pay their own bar tabs). All invited unit personnel are expected to attend unless duty prevents it; R.s.v.p. within forty-eight hours.

If the event is held at a well-known location, for instance the Officer's Club on base, the street address may be omitted. Include separate times for cocktails and dinner, especially if they are in separate areas, as in the sample invitations below.

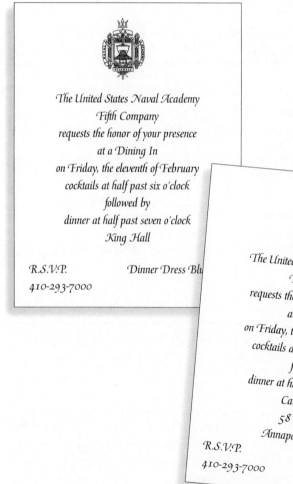

The dress must be stated on the invitation, for example, *Dinner Dress Blue* (Coast Guard) or *Mess Dress* (Air Force), which conforms to civilian *Formal* (Black Tie/tuxedo). If desired, further event-specific guidance can be given: "appropriate dress uniform for foreign cadets," "with miniature medals," "no name tags," etc. (See Chapter 22: Appropriate Attire, for uniform charts.)

The hosting unit's hierarchy must be notified and approval obtained before an invitation is extended to a high-ranking military officer, government official, or other dignitary, including if the guest is asked to be the evening's speaker. If desired, a memento may be presented to the guest speaker. Send a "hard-copy" *p.m. card* to anyone outside the hosting unit who accepted an e-mail or telephone invitation (see Chapter 11: Invitations), without meal cost information, using the more traditional *"requests the honor of the presence of"* followed by the guest's name. Issue an invitation to speak as far in advance as possible and include a precise speech requirement—for instance, "twenty minutes on the history of . . ." Have an alternate speaker in mind if your first choice is unavailable. Provide an advance copy of the program agenda to other support personnel (guest speaker, chaplain, bandleader, color guard leader) as well as to the head office. If an important foreign dignitary has accepted, it may be prudent to invite his U.S. counterpart or associate, another guest who speaks his language, or arrange for an interpreter. See Chapter 25: International Protocol and Civility, for more information.

HISTORY OF THE SMOKING LAMP

On board wooden ships there was always the chance of fire, so naval safety measures restricted smoking to the forecastle or the area directly surrounding the galley. An oil lamp was mounted there that allowed seamen to get a light for their pipes. If it was unlit, everyone knew that meant, "No smoking permitted at this time."

The illustration caught on during hazardous land operations, before drills, or during refueling when open flame was unsafe. The simple announcement *"The smoking lamp is out,"* conveyed the danger.

Before offering cigars and cigarettes at a venue permitting public smoking, such as a cigar bar or an international location, the president of wardroom dinners, mess nights, or dinings in might still call, *"Light the smoking lamp."*

The Dinner Menu and Service

Good food should be served formally, in several courses as budget allows, ending with a savory (e.g., cheese) or a less-sweet dessert (such as fruit or bitter chocolate) because a sugary confection spoils the taste of port, traditionally used for toasting after the meal. Table wines may accompany the meal, as appropriate. Pouring the first wine may be ceremonial or it may already be in glasses before guests walk into the dining room, and thereafter replenished by servers. Guests who are underage must be provided an alternative beverage. Those who do not drink alcohol should notify the wait staff or caterer before wine is poured, which is more considerate than ignoring filled glasses. Otherwise, a simple hand motion or touch to the glass rim with your first two fingertips lets servers approaching with wine know not to fill (or refill) your glass.

Full wait staff cooperation is necessary in order to support traditional ceremonies at a Dining In. Along with identifying the ranking guest of honor to be served first at each table, servers will need the ceremonies and their supporting roles explained in detail (for instance a rum punch procession to the head table). If there is a band, the courses and table service can help cue the music, or vice versa. For instance, musicians might play "The Roast Beef of Old England" if the main course (which can be any meat choice nowadays, but in times past was usually prime rib) is presented for the president's approval.

> Q: An Academy classmate died recently and our Company Dining In is scheduled in two weeks. Should we set up an empty small table and chair like we do for the POW table?
>
> A: Although the death of your colleague was a tragedy, the ceremony you speak of is strictly for Combat Comrades. An empty seat at your event could cast too much of a dark cloud on proceedings. Perhaps your company officer would consider two to three sentences *"in memory of,"* with a picture of your classmate on the printed agenda. A prayer or a moment of silence for the deceased can be said by an attending clergy before the formal toasts (*be sure to request this from the chaplain ahead of time*). Either of these choices is in keeping with the established and time-honored sequence of events at Dinings In.

Each course begins with the wait staff serving the ranking guest of honor at the president's table and continues to the right, *not* serving according to rank. A second server may proceed concurrently in the other direction, if desired. Multiple tables may be served in tandem after service has begun at the president's table, beginning with each table's ranking guest. The table host is always served last. See that the vice president is served immediately after the ranking guest of honor. Duties and activities will take up so much of the vice president's time that there will be no time to eat unless he or she is served early.

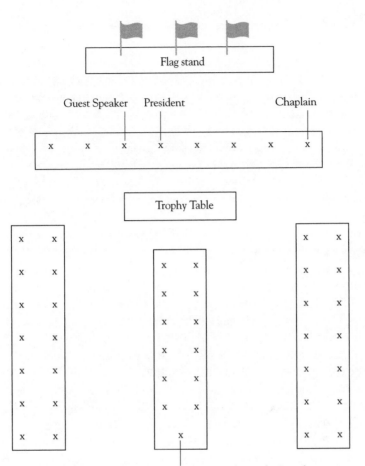

Possible Vice President location to remain facing the President

Seating and Table Arrangements

Table arrangements suit the room configuration and size of the gathering. Wherever the president is seated, he or she is the focal point and any flags must be positioned at his or her back, preferably against a wall.

For *small gatherings*, the president sits at the head of a banquet table (or at the center of a long side) with the ranking guest of honor, usually the speaker, seated at his or her right and the second-ranking guest on the left. The vice president may sit directly opposite the president, with the third-ranking guest at his or her right and the fourth-ranking on the left. If only two tables are needed, they are placed side-by-side with the president and vice president each hosting one at opposite ends from each other, because the vice president and the president must face each other when speaking. Members are seated according to rank.

For large gatherings, the president, speaker, and honored guests may be seated at a head table facing multiple smaller tables, so that everyone can see them and vice versa. Strive for even numbers of head table seats so that persons may pair off for conversation, with event co-hosts at the ends so that guests do not feel marginalized. Because of directing responsibilities, the vice president is never seated at the head table. The vice president sits as the single occupant of a small table across the banquet room directly facing the president, or in another suitable area (note position of the vice president in the table illustration). The other tables may be round, square, or rectangular in any stand-alone formation, or oblongs may be placed against each end of the head table in a modified "E" or "U" shape, but no one is ever seated at a head table facing the principals, or on the short ends of a head table. Designate appropriate unit co-hosts and guests of honor for each separate table.

Guests are assigned to a specific table or to a designated seat at a specific table. Post one or two seating diagrams in the cocktail area but not too near the entrances because people will block the passage as they check their seat locations. Alternatively, *You Are Seated At* (YASA) cards may be displayed for pick-up to assist members in finding their tables. Place cards are always used on the head table or one long banquet table or the president's table, but are not strictly necessary at subordinate tables as long as table guests of honor are seated at the right of co-hosts. Co-hosts may be directed to escort their guests of honor into the dining room first in order to ensure this. There should be no vacant seats at a formal dinner. In the event of last-minute cancellations, the entire place setting is removed from the table. (See Chapter 23: Seating Plans.)

Q: I know that a female guest of honor is seated to the right of her male host, and a male guest of honor is to the right of his hostess. How do I follow this rule for a Top Table with the host in the middle?

A: Head Table seating is based on rank order, not gender. First, plan on even numbers so that everyone has a conversation partner. Guest speakers should be close to the podium for easy access. Regardless of gender, the host (H) is positioned in the middle with the guest of honor (GH) on the right; the second ranking guest is on the H's left. At a Dining Out with spouses present, the GH spouse will on the H's left. The H spouse will be on the GH's right. When one married couple is honored (a wedding or anniversary party), seat them beside each other at the center of a head table with the female to the male's right. Finally, it is considered refined to have event co-hosts anchor the ends of a head table.

Comprehensive Sample Sequence
of Appropriate Events

The evening is divided into formal and informal sessions. Any pre- and post-dinner activities are relaxed, with opportunities to make connections in a congenial atmosphere. Smoking is permitted during informal portions, but only if a smoking lamp is lighted during the formal gathering.

Hour

1845–1900 Committees, president, and vice president are in place early, seeing to their duties, but not less than fifteen minutes prior to stated start time. The guest of honor (speaker) and anyone else in a receiving line is also requested to arrive early (fifteen minutes or more, depending on parking situations) to be greeted by the president at the facility entry door and escorted to the venue. (Escorting VIP information is in Chapter 1: Military and Government Protocol.) Vice president positions the receiving line with facilitators and photographer in proper places. (See Chapter 18: Official Business Functions, Cocktails, and Receptions, for detailed receiving line instructions and diagram.)

1900 Members and guests arrive precisely on time. Punctuality is mandatory. Vice president sets cocktails or reception in motion (opens lounge door). Members go by the receiving line (if existing), giving their names correctly. If there is no receiving line, members greet president first, and then pay respects to distinguished visitor(s) and guest(s). All members of the sponsoring unit are responsible for showing warm, gracious hospitality by greeting each guest (specific escorts may be assigned), introducing them, and seating them properly (see Chapter 17: Family Dining, Buffets, and Formal In-Home Meals). Members watch for vice president direction and facilitate passing any last-minute changes, as necessary.

1925 Check seating chart/pick up YASA cards. Make a lavatory stop, as necessary before dinner chimes/mess call. Finish your drink; do not take it into the dining room.

1935 Vice president sounds chimes (if available), or commands *Officers' Call*, or signals band (if available) to play an appropriate march to close pre-dinner cocktails. Chimes are used solely by vice president to signal participant movement from one location to another. Attendees file into dining room. Head table occupants wait until others are seated, then enter formally in one of these ways:

- President leads, escorting guest of honor on his or her right. Others pair up, with head table co-hosts escorting official guests.
- A line forms in seating order and all file in together. This choice is preferred if the platform is too narrow for easy movement behind people and chairs.
- President and guest of honor enter last after everyone is assembled and waiting.

Once the head table is in place, "Ruffles and Flourishes" and the "General's March" are played if a general officer is present. All members stand at attention during "Ruffles and Flourishes."

Optional Fife or Drum Procession: A single drummer or fifer may lead a procession of participants into and around the dining area to open the formal part of the evening. Put table names or numbers on stands beside the centerpieces, the print large enough to be easily read. If the group is large, the vice president or committee head will direct traffic by working the room during cocktails with the seating chart on a tray:

> Committee head: *"Tables* V & W, *please enter the dining room directly behind the Fifer [or Drummer]. Tables* X & Y, *please wait to enter the dining room until signaled. Table* Z, *please go in last, right before the head table."*

Attendees drop out of the procession as they reach their tables. Fifer or drummer leads procession in counter order to the traffic directions, that is, in such a manner that attendees nearest him don't all drop away immediately—perhaps circling the periphery before walking through a center aisle. Fifer/drummer may go back to the entry door to collect head table occupants for a procession of their own, proceeding directly to table without touring the room.

1935 Find your seat and remain standing behind the chair. President calls gathering to order by rapping with a gavel (if available). The gavel is used solely by president to gain attendees' attention. Depending on the local unit's rules, multiple raps (two or three) of the gavel require immediate and full attention; a single rap punctuates president's orders.

1940 President raps once and requests colors to be posted (if there is a color guard).

Optional Color Guard Presentation: As flags are carried in, a bugler may sound "To the Colors" or the national anthem may be played. Color guard places flags in their stands behind president and departs. There is no protocol requirement that the colors, once posted, must be retired, so the color guard may be dismissed after this duty, unless a retiring ceremony is desired. Flags may need to be moved from their receiving line location. This ceremony is only recommended if trained personnel are available, otherwise the flags are in place before dining room doors open. See Chapter 7: Flag Etiquette, for more color guard information.

Optional Sword Ceremony: A sheathed sword is brought to the president, who removes the sword from its scabbard and places it in front of his or her place setting at the front of the head table, saying words similar to, *"This is the appropriate time for warriors to lay aside their arms to enjoy the fellowship and camaraderie of companions. Dinings In trace their beginnings to Viking formal celebrations of great battles and heroes' feats of bravery. King Arthur's Knights of the Round Table carried out a form of Dining In during the sixth century. George Washington's Continental Army practiced Dinings In during the eighteenth century. I welcome you to our twenty-first century version of the military Dining In."*

1950 President welcomes attendees and introduces chaplain for the invocation (if clergy is present). President always proposes the initial toast (see Typical Toasting Order below), followed by vice president's opening toasts. President raps once and requests all to be seated. After this point no one may enter or leave without first requesting president's permission. President remains standing to make a proper self-introduction (see Opening Toasts below) and formally introduce head table (if guests are present) and all other distinguished visitors, remembering to introduce vice president. If guests are at every table, president may instead introduce each member co-host (in protocol order) with the request that they introduce their table's guests. Direct this option beforehand so that proper introductions can be practiced by co-hosts (see Chapter 19: Introductions, Conversations, and Farewells). Guests briefly rise when announced and resume seats. Do not applaud. When all are introduced, vice president rises to propose a toast encompassing all visitors.

2000 Dinner service begins; dignified dinner music may accompany. If guests are foreign, remember that pork or beef may be problematic (see Chapter 30: Food and Drink Preferences of Various Religious Groups). Serve American food, but consider rice if the guest cultures do not regard meals complete without it. Do not begin eating any course until all at your table are served and table host lifts his or her fork.

Optional Wine Pouring Ceremony: A wine decanter may be handed to the president and to each table host. The president immediately passes it to the guest of honor with instructions, *"Please serve yourself and pass the decanter on."* Each table host follows the president's lead. Wine is passed hand to hand, left to right (counterclockwise) until all glasses are filled, never letting the decanter touch the table until it returns to the table host. When a decanter becomes empty, the person affected holds it aloft to be exchanged for a full one by the server. Never pass an empty decanter. Servers pour a nonalcoholic beverage into the wine glasses of those who prefer that option. When all glasses are charged with either wine or alternate beverage and president has placed his decanter on the head table, all members and guests are ready for toasts. This ceremony is too time-consuming for large groups.

Optional Punch Bowl or Grog Ceremony: A Master of the Punch (or Grog) may be appointed when this ritual is a unit tradition. The punch is prepared ceremonially before attendees. The Master selects one assistant for each recipe ingredient. As each assistant adds an ingredient to the bowl, he or she makes suitable remarks: *"We begin at the birth of the Nation. The favorite wine of General George Washington was Madeira. Indeed, it was the wine chosen to toast the signing of our Declaration of Independence. We add Madeira today in tribute to the first Commander in Chief."* Ingredient remarks are limited only by imagination: Ice can represent friendly Academy rivalries at winter football games, seltzer's effervescence epitomizes sparkling personalities, red punch may represent blood shed in defense, champagne is excellent because, *"In victory we deserve it, in defeat we need it"*—a quote attributed to both Napoleon and Winston Churchill.

> Master: *"Mr. President, the punch [or grog] is prepared. Who shall pass judgment?"*
>
> President: *"Mr. [or Ms.] Vice, will you taste the punch?"*
>
> Vice President: *"Yes, Mr. [or Ms.] President."* (tastes) *"Sir [or Ma'am], this punch has been prepared correctly and is fit for human consumption."* (Vice presidents have been known to rhapsodize with an original poem.)
>
> President: *"Thank you, Mr. [or Ms.] Vice. Master of the Punch [or grog], please see that everyone receives a fair share."*

Optional Penalty Grog Bowl: Grog may be reserved for penalties, depending on inventiveness of ingredients. If so, the contents should be nonalcoholic so that individuals who do not consume alcoholic beverages may participate. When directed to the grog bowl, the individual proceeds there immediately. The violator is not permitted to talk during the following process. Upon arriving at the grog bowl, the violator does an about-face and salutes the president, then turns to the bowl and fills a cup. When the cup is full, the violator executes another about-face and toasts, *"To the Members,"* before drinking the entire contents without pause. When finished, the humbly penalized person inverts the cup over his or her head to show that it is empty, disposes of the cup, salutes the president once more, and returns to his or her seat. If a member has the temerity, even the president and guest speaker may be charged with a violation. However, before leaving the head table, the president must appoint another to assume command until he or she returns.

Optional Parading the Beef: When time for the entrée (meat) course, the chef or server may ceremoniously present it to the president (or vice president), who tastes it and declares it fit for human consumption, with compliments to the chef. This ceremony is similar to showing off the Thanksgiving turkey before it is taken back to the kitchen and carved.

Member Points of Order: Rules preserve a unit's unique traditions and ensure proper conduct, as well as promote levity. Make them available to every member and guest, usually on the back of the program agenda. Late arrival, carrying a cocktail drink to the table, beginning a course without regard for the table host, failure to toast, not laughing at the guest of honor's joke, pounding on the table, not abiding by uniform regulations, or using foul language are all considered rules violations. Some units write their rules in a mischievous fashion, such as "Do not leave while the Dining In is convened. Military protocol overrides all calls of nature," or "Clip-on bow ties at an obvious list are not tolerated. Members riding at a comparable list will be forgiven."

Points of order are raised during dinner, but do not conflict with formal toasting times. Any member wishing to report an infraction of the rules must first request permission. On being recognized, he or she will briefly present rationale for chastising a colleague. Subtle sarcasm, irony, and humor are much admired:

Informer (stands): *"Mr. President, I have a point of order."*

President: *"*[Rank and name] *is recognized. What is your report?"*

Informer: *"I deeply regret to report that* [rank and name] *has committed an outrageous and grievous uniform violation. Wearing a tiara tonight only confirms that she is a legend in her own mind, but it brings dishonor to us before our guests."*

President: *"*[Rank and name of accused], *what is your defense?"*

Accused (stands): *"Mr. President,* [informer's rank and name] *continues to commit social and fashion faux pas because he has no friends to correct him. First, being a tattletale is not worthy of an officer. Second, it is obvious to anyone not inebriated that this is a tasteful headband."*

President: *"*[Rank and name of accused], *your diamond-studded headband is indeed a lovely fashion statement, but I deem it a uniform violation. Since it appears that money is no object to you, you are hereby fined twenty-five cents in the form of a quarter from my home state of Ohio. If you do not produce said state quarter, your fine will be fifty cents."* (Raps once with the gavel.) *"Please pay the Vice President."*

President (or vice president if designated) imposes punishments or fines suitable to the offense. They are inventive but not excessive: less than a dollar fine, orders to consume a glass of grog (especially if concocted with dubious ingredients), push-ups or marching the room's perimeter, forfeiture of dessert, or performances for the pleasure of those assembled such as singing, whistling, reciting, even arm-wrestling.

2035   Schedule a distinctive break during a Dining In between the entrée and dessert and toasting. It is appropriate for the party to recess while the table is cleared before the port wine ceremony. President raps once (or more times) with the gavel (chimes may also be sounded) and announces the length of time for the recess. Members stand quietly until head table occupants depart the room; they then retire to the bar where coffee may be offered (if not to be served at table), go to a smoking anteroom (modern option as fewer venues allow smokers—see Smoking Lamp alternative below), or visit the lavatory, as desired.

2100   Recess is over. Vice president sounds chimes and attendees return to their chairs and remain standing while the head table files in as at the beginning. President raps once and requests all to be seated. Dessert or port wine course is served, as appropriate.

Optional Port Wine Ceremony: This is the most usual ceremony included at a Dining In. Runners or placemats are encouraged instead of tablecloths to facilitate the removal of everything (except candelabras, centerpieces, and port glasses) after dinner. Decanters of port are then set before each table host. Follow the procedure explained in optional wine-pouring ceremony above for charging glasses. Formal toasts are always proposed with the port wine, if served. The last toast with port is *"Bottoms Up."* Remember to provide for non-drinkers.

Optional Rum Punch Ceremony: Variation of Punch Bowl or Grog Ceremony, but this punch is usually prepared ahead of time and the drinking of it ends the evening. Vice president personally and ceremonially serves the rum punch to the head table. The punch bowl used for the presentation must be small enough to be easily carried and held by a server while vice president ladles from it. Instruct wait staff to position punch cups or glasses for each place at the head table, but position two at president's place:

President: *"Mr. [or Ms.] Vice, the Rum Punch."*

A drum roll may be played while vice president serves punch to guest of honor first, then the rest of the head table, ending with president, after which president serves the vice president. Wait staff then ladles punch (or delivers full cups from the kitchen) to the remaining attendees. The last rum punch toast is "Bottoms Up." Remember to provide for nondrinkers.

Optional Smoking Lamp: If appropriate to the venue, the ceremony occurs while members are at table drinking port or rum punch. The smoking lamp can be lighted following toasts, if preferred. Since public smoking is prohibited in many locations, this ritual survives mainly in the field or fleet, usually with cigars, either passed by wait staff or provided on the tables. Ashtrays must also be provided; wait staff can bring them in when the port or punch is served.

President: *"Mr. [or Ms.] Vice, light the smoking lamp."*

Vice President (to the accompaniment of drum rolls, if available) illuminates the smoking lamp (an oil or kerosene lantern, a large [3-inch/7.62-centimeter] diameter white candle covered with a hurricane globe, or an antique-looking electric lamp) situated on a side table where attendees can see it. Vice president carries a large table lighter (previously positioned beside the smoking lamp) to president, who uses it to light the tobacco, as desired, of guest of honor on the right, then the second ranking guest's on the left, and finally his or her own. Vice president stands by to take the lighter from president and strike it for other head table guests, lighting his or her own tobacco last.

President: *"Ladies and Gentlemen, the smoking lamp is lighted. You may smoke, if desired."* Smokers around the room may use their own lighters or the head table lighter may be handed along.

Port is not for the very young, the vain and the active. It is the comfort of age and the companion of the scholar and the philosopher.

—Evelyn Waugh (1903–1966), British novelist

Formal Toasts, Member Toasts, and Violation Tally: President stands, calls for silence with one rap of the gavel, and directs a series of formal toasts. (See Typical Toasting Order, next section.) After formal toasts, any member who wishes to initiate another toast will stand and address the president. On being recognized, member will briefly present justification for desiring such a toast, ending with the words of the proposed toast. If president deems the proposal justified, he or she will second it or will direct vice president to second the toast in the same manner as formal toasts (*"To the __"*). When president judges that informal toasting should cease, he or she raps two or three times with the gavel before calling for vice president to read a formal tally of offenders and any customs or traditions dishonored during the evening. If violations have not been dealt with as they occurred (considered much more enjoyable), president or vice president (if delegated) assesses fines as necessary.

2120   President (or an appropriate designate) rises to introduce after-dinner proceedings. If there is an Award Presentation (participants rehearsed beforehand), a Hail and Farewell acknowledgment, or a skit, they must be short enough not to detract from the next event, the guest speaker (or do not invite). See especially Chapter 5: The Fallen Comrade Table Observance. President introduces the guest speaker, whose twenty-minute address is always the highlight of the evening with no other formal events following, except final toasts and benediction.

2145   President presents memento to guest speaker, if desired. If dignitary is foreign, especially if there will be a photographic record, make sure to present the gift with both hands. Vice president immediately toasts speaker.

2150   President raps once and calls for all to stand for final toasts, followed by the benediction, if clergy is present. Immediately after the benediction, president raps once again and commands, *"Retire the colors"* (if desired). President renders two or three raps of the gavel (chimes may also be sounded) to adjourn the Dining In:

> President: *"Ladies and Gentlemen, please join me in the* [bar or another room]. *The formal portion of the evening is concluded, but informal activities continue* [as desired]."

All remain standing as president escorts out guests at his or her table. Vice president immediately follows. Table co-hosts escort their ranking guests immediately after, and finally the remaining attendees depart the dining room.

In some cases, dancing may follow a Dining In if the venue can accommodate it. Otherwise, the remainder of the evening may be spent more or less as impulse and ingenuity suggest. The purpose of these gatherings is to engender camaraderie in all present. The universal after-dinner activity is conversation, and members again have the opportunity to introduce themselves to the evening's guests. Singing is always in order, and by this time, many members are often pleasantly surprised to discover how uninhibitedly they can produce harmony.

Typical Toasting Order

Formal toasts are a prime feature of Dinings In. Print toasting order and correct replies in every guest's program agenda; if not printed, the person giving the toast must supply the appropriate responses as needed, such as *"Please reply 'Hear, Hear,'"* or *"Please reply 'To the Corps,'"* or whatever is fitting. *Formal* toasts are the traditional way to honor a country, organization, or position (not necessarily the incumbent).

Q: I am underage. If wine is already poured at my place, aren't I obligated to sip when there is a toast so I won't call attention to myself?

A: Under no circumstances should you drink alcohol until you are of age. Besides the health and legal aspects, you are being scrutinized for role-model behavior (especially as a class leader, midshipman, or cadet). Feel free to toast with any other beverage in front of you, or simply hold aloft the wine goblet by its stem in your right hand throughout the toast. Join your voice with others and set your glass down immediately with a smile at the conclusion so that you do not appear to disagree with the sentiments expressed. Nondrinkers of age do the same thing, adding a motion toward their lips, but underage persons who add this motion might look as if they were about to drink, except being caught in the act prevented their sipping.

Q: The budget allows for only one glass of wine per person at our Dining In. What are your suggestions?

A: Skip the Wine Pouring Ceremony. Servers are adept at pouring measured amounts so all share equally. Choose house wine instead of bottles. Some guests will not drink wine; instruct servers to ask, *"Wine or sparkling cider (iced tea, etc.)?"* before pouring, to eliminate waste.

Opening Toasts

As dinner begins, after optional elements color guard and national anthem:

President (before seating attendees): *"Welcome to* [organization, academy class, ship's name, battalion, wing, or regiment, etc.] *Dining In. I am* [first and last name*], *president this evening. Please consult your program for the order of this evening's events. At this time it is my pleasure to ask* [attending clergy] *to give the invocation."*

* Never introduce yourself by including a rank, grade, or title with your own name, except to someone who will repeat it to another (an announcer at a receiving line, an assistant in an outer office, someone answering the telephone or entry buzzer, etc.), or to a child or service provider.

After a blessing, president may toast the colors, then perform the sword ceremony, or vice versa. This is always the first toast.

> President (lift glass by stem in right hand at shoulder height): *"To the National Flag of the United States of America."*
>
> Attendees (lift glasses by stem in right hand and say together):*"To the Colors."*
>
> All drink and return their glasses to the table.

President may now call for toasts to heads of government or chiefs of state. Consumption of alcoholic beverages may be considered offensive by some foreign guests; consider fruit juice for opening toasts (orange juice is clearly identifiable if there will be pictures). Guests of honor might not drink, but would have no objection if others toast with alcohol. Toasts always follow protocol order, the sovereign or leader of the ranking foreign guest present followed by immediate subsequent toasts honoring any additional foreign guests' sovereigns. See Chapter 20: Toasts, for correct ritual phrases. Lacking foreign guests, president may call for a toast recognizing the guest of honor's Service (if from another military branch). After these toasts, the band plays a stanza of the pertinent national anthems, or "Ruffles and Flourishes" for a U.S. flag officer. The senior foreign (or visiting Service branch) guest should reciprocate immediately with a toast to the U.S. President or the Service chief of the hosting organization. Therefore, always coordinate with said individual(s) ahead of time.

Sample Opening Sovereign Toasts

All present drink to all rulers and countries. President calls attendees to stand and proposes the first foreign sovereign toast:

> President (lifts glass aloft by stem in right hand, looks at guest of honor): *"I have the honor to propose a toast to the Prime Minister* [or other title] *of* [guest's country]*."*

Or president may call on vice president for a less formal version of the toast by saying:

> *"Mr.* [or *Ms.*] *Vice, the Prime Minister* [or other title] *of* [guest's country]*."*
>
> Vice President (lifts glass aloft by stem in right hand, looks at guest of honor): *"Ladies and Gentlemen, to the Prime Minister."*
>
> All Attendees (lift glasses by stem in right hand and say together): *"To the Prime Minister."*

Everyone drinks and returns glasses to the table but remains standing for the appropriate foreign national anthem, if there is a band.

Guest of Honor (after his anthem, lifts glass aloft by stem in right hand, looks at president): *"Thank you. It is my great honor to propose a toast to the President of the United States."*

All Attendees (lift glasses by stem in right hand and say together): *"To the President."*

All drink and return glasses to the table but remain standing for "The Star Spangled Banner," if there is a band. If no foreign guests attend, president may propose a toast to the U.S. Commander in Chief (after the colors toast) or recognize a member to do so before any guest Service toasts are proposed (see Member Toasts below).

Sample Opening Service Toasts

President calling for toast (stands, holds glass by stem in right hand, waist level): *"Mr. [or Ms.] Vice, the Secretary of the United States* [Army, Marine Corps, Navy, Air Force, Coast Guard, Public Health Service, or National Oceanic and Atmospheric Administration]."

Vice President seconds (stands, lifts glass by stem in right hand, shoulder high): *"Ladies and Gentlemen, the Secretary of the* [appropriate Service]."

All Attendees (stand and lift glasses by stem in right hands and say together): *"To the Secretary of the* [appropriate Service]."

Vice President initiating toast (stands, lifts glass by stem in right hand shoulder high): *"Mr. [or Ms.] President, I propose a toast to the Chief of Staff* [or Commandant] *of the* [appropriate Service]."

All Attendees (stand and lift glasses by stem in right hands and say together): *"To the Chief of Staff* [or Commandant]."

The band, if available, plays the appropriate song after any guest Service toast, after the first hosting Service toast, and after the final unit toast of the evening:

"The Army Goes Rolling Along" is the official song of the U.S. Army

"The Marines' Hymn" is the official song of the U.S. Marine Corps

"Anchors Aweigh" is the official song of the U.S. Navy

"The U.S. Air Force" is the official song of the U.S. Air Force

"Semper Paratus" is the official song of the U.S. Coast Guard

"Forward with NOAA" is the official song of the U.S. National Oceanic and Atmospheric Administration Corps

"The Public Health Service March" is the official song of the U.S. Commissioned Corps of the Public Health Service

Everyone follows president's direction whether to sit down when the music ends or remain standing for the next round.

Sample Welcome Guests Toast

If no foreign sovereigns or outside Services are to be toasted, president may seat attendees for dinner after the colors toast and proceed directly to guest introductions, holding all command hierarchy toasts together during the dessert or port wine course.

> President (remains standing): *"Please be seated. It is my pleasure to introduce the head table* [or guest(s) of honor]: ___, ___, ___ [gives honorifics and full names]."
>
> Vice President (stands, lifts glass by stem in right hand, shoulder high): *"Ladies and Gentlemen, to our distinguished guest*[s]."
>
> Members: (stand and lift glasses by stem in right hand and say together): *"Hear, Hear."* Only members rise to toast. During this corporate toast all guests remain seated with a smile while they are toasted; they do not drink to themselves.
>
> President: *"Please be seated for dinner."*

Command Hierarchy Toasts

Hierarchy toasts may begin during the welcome segment and continue during dessert, or may commence at dessert or port wine course. President may give a formal toast or may call for one to be seconded by the vice president; vice president may initiate a toast, or various members may be recognized to propose toasts. If time is a consideration, or alcohol consumption a concern, not all command toasts are necessary. Designate those responsible for formal toasts in advance; toasting proceeds down the chain of command:

> Commander in Chief, President of the United States
>> *Not always included:*
>> Secretary of Defense [for Army, Marine Corps, Navy, and Air Force]; or
>> Secretary of Homeland Security [for Coast Guard]; or
>> Secretary of Commerce [for National Oceanic and Atmospheric Administration Corps (NOAA)]; or
>> Secretary of Health & Human Services [for Public Health Service (PHS)]
>> Secretary of the (Army, Marine Corps, Navy, Air Force, Coast Guard); or
>> Under Secretary of Commerce for Oceans and Atmosphere; or
>> Deputy Secretary of Health & Human Services
> Chief of Staff of the Army; or
>> Commandant of the Marine Corps; or
>> Chief of Naval Operations; or

Chief of Staff of the Air Force; or

Commandant of the Coast Guard; or

Director of the NOAA Corps; or

Assistant Secretary for the Commissioned Corps of the PHS (sometimes this is the Surgeon General)

Parent Service or Agency

Unit commander; and finally, the unit's personnel

Member Toasts

Any member will stand and state, *"Request to be recognized"* before proposing a toast. Toasts may welcome a newcomer, salute a departing one, recognize unit accomplishments, honor a co-worker who has died, or flatter the presiding officer, as desired. When recognized (by rank and name) the member justifies his or her toast (usually only for informal, non-hierarchy ones). Vice president solicits a ruling from president or takes appropriate action if empowered to judge the toast worthy. Here is an example from a member of the U.S. Army Sergeants Major Academy designated to propose a hierarchy toast:

SGM Doe (standing): *"Mr. Vice, request to be recognized."*

Mr. Vice: *"SGM Doe has the floor. What is the nature of your request?"*

SGM Doe: *"Mr. Vice, I would like to propose a toast."*

Mr. Vice: *"SGM Doe, what is the nature of your toast?"*

SGM Doe: *"Mr. Vice, in keeping with this most auspicious and centuries-old Service ceremony, I would like us to keep another long-standing tradition, that the first toast of the evening be to honor the Commander in Chief, the President."*

Mr. Vice: *"SGM Doe, I find your toast most appropriate. Please propose your toast."*

SGM Doe: *"Fellow Noncommissioned Officers, I propose a toast to the Commander in Chief, the President of the United States."*

All: *"To the President."*

Final Toasts

After any guest speaker presentation, attendees will applaud. Guest speaker will also be honored immediately with a toast.

Vice President (stands with port glass or punch cup in right hand, shoulder high): *"Ladies and Gentlemen, to our distinguished speaker."*

Members (rise with glasses or cups and say together): *"To our speaker."*

Concluding Service toasts are *"Bottoms Up"* for the port wine or rum punch. When president calls for one or both of these toasts, participants charge their glasses immediately, as necessary.

> President: *"Mr. [or Ms.] Vice, The [Parent Service]."*
>
> Vice President (stands with port glass or punch cup and makes an appropriate toast): *"Ladies and Gentlemen, 'Take courage then, seize the fortune that awaits you and drink together: Long live the United States and success to the* [Army, Marine Corps, Navy, Air Force, Coast Guard, Public Health Service, or National Oceanic and Atmospheric Administration].'"
>
> Members (rise with glasses or cups in right hands and say together): *"The [Service]."*
>
> All drain the entire glass or cup and remain standing while the band, if available, plays the Service song.
>
> President: *"Mr. [or Ms.] Vice, The [local Organization; e.g., academy class, ship, battalion, wing, regiment, unit]."*
>
> Vice President (stands with port glass or punch cup): *"Ladies and Gentlemen, the [Organization]."*
>
> Members (rise with glasses or cups in right hand and say together): *"The [Organization]."*
>
> All drain the entire glass or cup and remain standing for the fallen comrades' toast (if proposed), the benediction (if offered), or retiring the colors (if performed).

If the Fallen Comrade Table Observance (see full script in Chapter 5) is not part of proceedings, missing compatriots may be recognized with the last toast of the evening, just before the benediction and retiring of the colors. As in the observance, this toast may be performed with water, if desired (be sure water glasses are on the table and charged).

> President: *"Our final toast will be with water instead of wine. As we solemnly toast, please keep silent."* (Lifts water glass shoulder-high.) *"To our comrades killed in action, missing in action, or prisoners of war."* All drink and keep a moment of silence.

Not all of the events described here can occur in one evening! Adapt the sequence of events, the toasting order, and other aspects of the occasion to meet the command's situation in regard to purpose of the celebration, uniform, menu and alcohol, room arrangement, available support personnel, after-dinner activities, etc. Enjoy participating in a long-standing military ritual of unity.

Q: I was eager to have my wife with me for the first time at a recent Dining Out, but it was done so poorly that she said, *"I will not go to another one."* What is the current guidance for hosting these events?

A: When an organization desires to share military traditions with those not familiar with them, it has a duty to make the experience an enriching one. The presiding officer is in charge of ensuring that Dining Out customs are maintained.

Q: We would like to invite a prominent retired flag officer to speak at our Dining Out for around 150 people. How do we do that? Also, should we have nameplates at the tables?

A: Contact your Head (hosting) Office to request approval and protocol guidance (regarding the invitation, appropriate service flag, etc.). Only after approval do you extend the invitation. When the flag officer accepts, be sure to ask if there are any special needs (food restrictions, disability access, audiovisual support). Keep your chain of command informed as plans proceed. Post a seating diagram at a minimum, using table names (famous military leaders, battles, ships, spaceships, patriotic holidays, whatever is appropriate) instead of numbers so no one feels they are last in hierarchy. Individual place cards will reduce confusion even more.

DINING OUT

If the evening includes non-business guests or family members, it is termed a Dining Out. Personal guests may only be invited with the permission of the Dining Out presiding officer, the president. (If a member's friends or family members are senior in rank to the president, they might more properly be considered "official guests" and invited to a Dining In, especially if they can be induced to speak.) Personal guests are not seated at the head table. As with a Dining In, the most important consideration is to choose a venue within means, as bar tabs and dinner costs of personal guests are paid by the member who invites them. Further considerations are a private room and willing participation of wait staff during the selected ceremonies.

For the benefit of guests, after introducing himself the president gives a few words about the history of the evening, such as: *"Since our country's inception we have continued a very old tradition of restricted banquets, called Dinings In. They trace their beginnings to formal Viking celebrations of great battles and brave heroes. The custom soon spread to early monasteries, universities, and to King Arthur's Knights of the Round Table. The British spread Dinings In worldwide, particularly to Canada, Australia, and colonial America, where George Washington's Continental Army enjoyed them. When we include guests and family members, our event is called a Dining Out. We are pleased that you are witnessing the continuing saga."*

The president will also remember to properly introduce clergy providing the invocation (if present), vice president, and honored guests in protocol order (members may be recognized to introduce their own guests).

A Dining Out is conducted with the same formality as a Dining In, focusing less on "offenses and fines" and more on providing an inside look at time-honored military customs. Including the Fallen Comrade Table Observance would serve this goal in an especially poignant fashion, as it educates civilian guests about the sacrifices of their country's guardians. Another fine tribute is to include a historic rundown of major battles fought by the parent Service or unit. If this tribute is desired, selected members from different points around the room rise from their seats one at a time and in a strong voice name one battle each after the president's appropriate introductory remarks: *"Ladies and Gentlemen, it is traditional to pay homage to the courage and sacrifices of our comrades who have distinguished themselves throughout history. For the courageous we name their battles."* If desired, a gong or ship's bell may be rung to punctuate each recitation. Members proclaiming battles remain standing in respect until all are named. The president then asks all to rise and drink with him, with words similar to, *"Honored guests, ladies and gentlemen, please stand and toast those in whose shadow we serve with pride. To the valor of our comrades who have died that we may all live in peace."*

Members who have invited companions to join them are responsible for their visitors. Guests will naturally have questions about suitable behavior and will turn to their hosts to guide them, so it is wise to be familiar with the evening's program and seating plan. Members stay with their guests throughout the event, introducing them during cocktails, escorting them to the correct table, and seating them properly. Guests and spouses are seated at the same table as their military hosts, if possible, but not necessarily beside them. Spouses of military personnel, for instance, are often seated across from their mates. If there is a Dining Out head table, the president's spouse is seated to the right of the guest of honor, and the guest of honor's spouse is seated to the left of the president.

CHAPTER 5

The Fallen Comrade Table Observance

*A*ppropriate to set up during any Dining In, this solemn observance is also an especially moving tribute during a Dining Out. It both honors fellow Service members and educates civilian guests about the sacrifices of their country's guardians. Near patriotic holidays would be a fine time to consider this ceremony, also called POW/MIA Recognition, Two-Bell Ceremony, or Missing Man Table and Honors Ceremony.

AT EASE KEY POINTS

- Decide which optional portions to include; collect all props.
- Copy appropriate portions of script and print 3x5 cards.
- Recruit two readers; rehearse the script.

PREPARATION

As part of organizing a Dining In, a small round or square table should be located in a place of honor where most guests can see it as they enter or while seated during the meal. Decide if you will only honor your own Service branch (one place setting), or whether you will set a place to represent all: Army, Marine Corps, Navy, Air Force, and Coast Guard. (*Optional if appropriate*: Include civilians and the other two uniformed Services, the National Oceanic and Atmospheric Administration Corps and the Commissioned Corps of the Public Health Service.) If service personnel from other branches are invited, it is easy to ask if you may borrow their hats for the duration of your event to complete multiple place settings. Otherwise, arrange to borrow headgear from appropriate friends and colleagues ahead of time.

Copy the full script for Reader #1. Print 3x5 cards with the President's Toast and the final lines for Reader #2, using a large, bold font that is easy to read from tabletop height. Guests will be watching and listening closely; choose two dignified military members to read the script unsmiling, with clear voices. If read near the beginning of the evening this observance sets a formal, solemn tone and guests can reflect on the sacrifices throughout the night. If read near the end of the proceedings, it serves as an especially fine capstone. Guests may walk up to inspect the table both before and after the meal, so Reader #2 should leave it in good order.

Request that the caterer provide a display table with a white table cloth, set for one (or more) using dinner and bread plate(s), wine goblet(s), and the minimum of silverware (one fork and knife). Also request that they have on hand wedges of lemon and salt. In most cases caterers will also be able to supply the black napkin(s), the candle and something to light it, and the rose. Be sure the caterer understands that all participants need water at their place settings to participate in the silent toast. Advise the caterer regarding the timing of the observance so servers can top off glasses as necessary.

SILENT TOASTS

An old British Royal Navy tradition, the "Immortal Memory" toast, honoring their war hero Admiral Lord Nelson, is always made standing in total silence.

At the Royal Military College of Canada (RMC), members silently raise their glasses and sip the traditional toast, "To absent comrades" for those who have died or fallen in combat.

In the United States, when honoring the September 11, 2001, terrorism victims, participants observe or toast during a moment of silence.

Here is a complete list of necessary items:

One *Display Table* with *White Tablecloth* and one (or more) low-backed *Chair(s)*

One *Dinner Plate* for each place setting (large enough to accommodate hats; or use only covers placed between silverware)

One *Cover, Dress Cap or Beret* (or one for each military Service and one for civilians)

One (or more) stemmed *Wine or Water Goblet(s)*

One (or more) *Bread plate(s)*

One (or more) set(s) of *Silverware* (one fork and knife each is sufficient)

Lemon wedges (enough for all bread plates)

Salt (enough for all bread plates)

One (or more) *Black Napkin(s)* in simple upright fold that will not fall apart when lifted

One (white or yellow) *Candle* with a *Yellow Ribbon* tied around its holder

Matches or Lighter to light the candle

One (red or pink) long-stemmed *Rose* with a *Red Ribbon* tied around its bud vase or stem (florist can insert it into a "bud" water reservoir to prevent wilting)

One *Bible*

Any or all of these optional items help fill in a table set for one:

A *Sword* or *Saber* situated under the lone hat now positioned opposite the one-person place setting instead of on top of the plate.

Dress Uniform *Gloves*

A *Purple Heart* medal

Blank *ID Tags* on chain

Unit Coin

Miniature *Table Flags*: U.S. national, specific Service, or POW/MIA, as desired

Well before guests enter the room, a facilitator should finalize the display. Turn the wine glass(es) upside down, and place a wedge of lemon and some salt on each bread plate. Place the hat(s) atop the dinner plate(s). Tie the ribbons around the rose and candle. Nearest the side most easily reached by Reader #2, position the rose, the bible, the candle, and matches/lighter. If preferred, the candle can be lit now instead of during the ceremony. Give the 3x5 card with President's Toast to him for reference. Give the 3x5 card with last "*Remember, Remember . . .*" remark to Reader #2 to hide discreetly under a plate on the display table so that guests cannot see it but it can be retrieved easily. Position the script on the lectern or give it to Reader #1.

Optional procession: At the beginning of the observance, uniformed honor guards can ceremonially deliver covers to each place setting. Make sure there is enough room around the table for the team to walk. In silence, the appropriate number of individuals enter the room in correct precedence order (Army, Marine Corps, Navy, Air Force, Coast Guard, civilian), holding the covers at waist level with hat bills facing forward. Upon reaching the table, the team circles once, and on the second circuit halts when the hosting Service's cover is correctly positioned so that Reader #2 can stand behind it facing the audience. The honor guard leader quietly calls only loud enough for the team members to hear, "*Ready, Face*" and the team faces the table. The leader starts the movement and all bearers follow suit, sliding their right hands slowly around the front of the bill until their hands touch. Team members drop left hands after right hands turn the hats around 180 degrees. Bills now face away from the table. Each bearer positions his hat on top of (or in the place of) the dinner plate. Leader calls, *"Present, Arms"* and team members perform a three-second present and a three-second order. Leader calls *"Ready, Face"* and the honor guard performs a right face, waits one count, and then steps off without swinging their arms to exit the room.

SCRIPT

Reader #1 (standing in front of the room, at a podium with microphone, if needed) *"As you entered the dining room this evening you may have noticed a small table in a place of honor. It is set for one military member [or set to represent each of the military Services]. This table is our way of recognizing the fact that members of our profession of arms (and American civilians who served with them) are absent from our midst. Missing in Action (MIA) is the official designation when the fate of the person is not known. If it is determined that the enemy has captured him or her, then the official designation is changed to* Prisoner of War (POW). *We call them 'comrades.' They are unable to be with us this evening, but we remember their sacrifice."*

Reader #2 moves to a side of the table facing the audience in order to indicate or hold aloft each item as it is mentioned and to speak solemnly after Reader #1 reads. Reader #2 returns each item to its exact previous position so table remains orderly.

Reader #1: *"The* Table *is small, symbolizing the frailty of one prisoner alone against his oppressors. The* Tablecloth *is white, symbolizing the purity of their motives in answering our country's call to arms."*

Reader #2: (gestures to indicate table and makes direct eye contact with several people in the room) *"REMEMBER!"*

Reader #1: *"The* Chair(s) *is [are] empty—they are missing. The* Hat(s) *represent no specific soldier, sailor, marine, or airman (or civilian) but all personnel who are not here with us."*

Reader #2: (lifts a hat or two as Reader #1 speaks so that guests can see; makes eye contact with guests in another section of room) *"REMEMBER!"*

Reader #1: *"The* Bible *represents faith in a higher power, our comrades' pledge to a country whose national motto is* 'In God we trust,' *and our never-ending prayers and concern for them."*

Reader #2: (holds the Bible aloft and continues to choose new people to make eye contact with around the room) *"REMEMBER!"*

Reader #1: *"The* Napkin *is black, the American color for mourning."*
Reader #2: (lifts napkin and makes eye contact with different guests)
"REMEMBER!"

Reader #1: *"The single* Rose *displayed in a vase [or lying on the table] reminds us of the hearts of loved ones who keep faith awaiting the return of our comrades-in-arms. The* Red Ribbon *tied so prominently around the rose bears witness to their unyielding determination to demand a proper accounting."*
Reader #2: (holds up vase or long stemmed rose and continues to make eye contact with new people) *"REMEMBER!"*

Reader #1: *"A single* Candle *flame represents an eternal flame for their sacrifices. It is tied with a* Yellow Ribbon *to symbolize the everlasting hope for a joyous reunion with those yet unaccounted for. Yellow ribbons have been worn upon the lapels of contemporary Americans since the Iranian Hostage Crisis of 1979."*
Reader #2: (may light the candle at this point, hold it aloft, and then continue to focus eye contact on guests not yet receiving attention) *"REMEMBER!"*

Reader #1: *"The slice of* Lemon *on the bread plate reminds us of their bitter fate. There is also* Salt, *symbolic of the tears endured by the missing and their loved ones."*
Reader #2: (lifts & slightly tilts bread plate toward audience—no need to touch lemon or salt—and continues singling out some guests for eye contact) *"REMEMBER!"*

OPTIONAL ITEMS, if included, are explained before the wine glass:

Reader #1: *"The oldest symbol and award given to members of the U.S. military graces this table. It is a heart-shaped medal bordered in gold with a profile of General George Washington and his coat of arms. It hangs from a purple ribbon, and we call it the Purple Heart. It is the first American order ever established. President Washington, in 1782, approved the phrase, 'Let it be known that he who wears the military order of the Purple Heart has given of his blood in the defense of his homeland and shall forever be revered by his fellow countrymen.'"*

If appropriate, especially if the guest of honor or speaker has earned it: *"The medal tonight belongs to [name] at [table], awarded after [conflict]."*

Reader #2: (holds up medal) *"REMEMBER!"*

Reader #1: *"A set of blank* Identification Tags *represent the unknown fallen whose faces and names have been lost to us. The tags could bear names representing any creed, ethnic group, or color, for our Nation always has and will continue to value as full citizens immigrants from around the world. Many of them volunteer to defend their new homeland."*
Reader #2: (holds up ID tags) *"REMEMBER!"*

Reader #1: "*A long-standing military tradition is to issue* Unit Coins, *directing members always to carry them, ready to be produced whenever called for by peers. We delight in catching each other without our coins, often extracting a round of drinks in forward areas. This [military unit] coin has on it [physical description].*"
Reader #2: (holds up Unit Coin) "REMEMBER!"

Reader #1: "*The* Sword *represents the hard-fought battle—wounds given and received, and the ebb of life sacrificed for others.*"
Reader #2: (holds sword blade flat across both palms, not brandished) "REMEMBER!"

Reader #1: "*Flags have been flown in every battle the United States has fought, including our civil war. This [Army, Marine Corps, Navy, Air Force, Coast Guard] Flag(s) represents the entire Service. The Stars and Stripes represent the entire nation. In our vocation, we see flags every day. They are living symbols of our heritage, present achievements, and future readiness.*" If POW/MIA flag is used: "*Our fallen comrades also have a flag. I quote from the United States Code, Title 36, Chapter 10, Section §189: 'The National League of Families POW/MIA flag is hereby recognized officially and designated as the symbol of our Nation's concern and commitment to resolving as fully as possible the fates of Americans still [held] prisoner, missing and unaccounted for in Southeast Asia, thus ending the uncertainty for their families and the Nation.'*"
Reader #2: (stands two-flag holder on flat palm of one hand, steadying it with the other hand as it is held chest high, or holds two flags in separate holders, one in each hand) "REMEMBER!"

Reader #1: "*The* Wine Glass *is inverted. Our distinguished comrades cannot toast us this night or join in our festivities.*"
Reader #2: (sweeps room with eye contact; does not touch the glass. Looks down to read the previously concealed 3x5 card with these words) "*Remember, Remember their sacrifices, you who served with them and called them comrades, and you who witness our observance. Let us also remember Service personnel and civil servants currently in harm's way, for all of us depend upon their skill and aid in protecting our American freedoms.*" (As President begins silent toast inconspicuously removes card so that those taking a closer look at the table later do not see it.)
Reader #1: (quietly) "*Remember.*" (Readers #1 and #2 stay quietly in place)

President of the Mess (or person other than whoever read the above script, after a silent moment rises to conclude the observance): "*Honored guests, ladies and gentlemen, we will now toast with water instead of wine. Wine is unavailable to prisoners and water is a luxury. As we solemnly toast,* please keep silent. *Now, please stand and join me.*" (President lifts his or her water glass shoulder high and waits for everyone to raise their own water glasses):"*To our comrades killed in action, missing in action, or prisoners of war.*" (President leads in sipping water.)

President of the Mess:
(if observance is at the beginning of the meal or before guest speaker)
   "This concludes our Fallen Comrade Observance. Please be seated."
(if observance is at the end of the meal)
   "This concludes our Fallen Comrade Observance. Please feel free to take a closer look at the table on your way to join me in the [bar or another room]. Now remain standing as the [head table or guests of honor] depart." (President escorts out honored guests. Table co-hosts escort their ranking guests immediately after.)

ONE MORE ROLL

by U.S. service members in North Vietnam prisoner-of-war camps

We toast our hearty comrades who have fallen from the skies,
And were gently caught by God's own hands to be with him on high,
To dwell among the soaring clouds they've known so well before,
From victory roll to tail chase at heaven's very door.
And as we fly among them, we're sure to hear their plea,
Take care, my friend, watch your six, and do one more roll for me.

CHAPTER 6

The Military Funeral

*H*umans have a deep-seated need for rituals to mark the most profound moments of our lives, and all major world religions—Buddhism, Christianity, Hinduism, Islam, and Judaism—have ceremonies to help us at the time of death. United States, formal procedures for military funerals are based on long-standing customs and traditions that demonstrate the nation's recognition of the debt it owes for the service and sacrifice of members of the Armed Forces. A military funeral is authorized for personnel who die on active duty, honorably discharged veterans, and military retirees. When requested by the next of kin, a military funeral ceremony includes, at a minimum, a two-person active duty uniformed Honors Detail (one of whom is from the parent Service of the deceased), a U.S. flag draping the casket, a ceremonial folding of the U.S. flag and presentation to the next of kin, and a bugler sounding "Taps." In addition, there may be a rifle squad to fire three volleys, military pallbearers, and honorary pallbearers. For U.S. dignitaries and higher ranks, honors such as a cannon salute, a color guard, a military band, and a caisson may be part of the military funeral.

AT EASE KEY POINTS

Basic elements of all military funerals:

- ✂ Flag-draped casket.
- ✂ Bugler sounding "Taps".
- ✂ Flag-folding ceremony.
- ✂ Presentation of the flag.

Additional honors:

- ✂ Rifle squad volleys.
- ✂ Canon salute.
- ✂ Caisson.
- ✂ Color guard.
- ✂ Military band.

The military aspect of a funeral starts when the escort (the Honors Detail) first receives the remains. Before that, the body bearers conduct the remains wherever necessary. In general, the escort receives the body at the designated place (home of the deceased, mortuary, railroad station, chapel or house of worship, cemetery gates) and conducts it to the place of services and to the gravesite.

The leader (senior active duty Service representative) of an Honors Detail coordinates all arrangements for the military ceremony with the funeral director or clergy. The Honors Detail Leader will ensure that the honors to be performed, in accordance with the next of kin's request, have been made clear to immediate family members attending before the funeral begins (first respectfully deferring to the clergy or funeral director to make the explanation), and that the order of events is understood. The Honors Leader coordinates all elements and commands all military personnel: active duty Armed Forces personnel, retired members, bugler, firing party, honorary pallbearers, color guard, and veterans' organization members (e.g., Veterans of Foreign Wars, the American Legion) during the military honors portion of the funeral. The Honors Leader gives detailed information (such as the uniform to be worn, whether they will uncover or salute and when) to the pallbearers in advance of the funeral.

SAMPLE SEQUENCE OF MILITARY HONORS

Each military Service, and different commands within them, has one or more funeral protocol manuals posted online for reference. There may be differences in the sequence of events, distinctions between active duty and veterans' ceremonies, variations in the positioning of personnel during the graveside ceremony and so on, but all seek to pay dignified respect and gratitude to those who have faithfully defended our nation. What the family and other mourners will always remember is the honor cortege in uniform, the precise folding of the flag, the haunting notes of "Taps," and the sharp rifle volleys of respect over the grave of a fallen comrade—no matter the protocol order.

When the chapel, funeral home, or graveside committal service is concluded (whichever is the final civilian observance), the clergy or funeral director steps aside and asks the mourners to stand for the rendering of military honors. The Honors Leader then assumes a position at the head of the casket or grave and directs the military honors participants.

The National Anthem

If there is a band, the national anthem may be played. As always, uniformed personnel (and veterans who choose to, even if not in uniform) render a salute as it begins and hold it throughout, but instead of facing the music, it is appropriate to face the casket. Civilians (and military members in civilian dress) stand at attention and pledge with their right hands over their hearts. Civilian men wearing hats remove them with their right hands and hold them over their hearts. Those saluting during the anthem stand ready to salute again because the anthem will be immediately followed by a 3-volley salute.

Q: Grandmother wants me to wear my Academy uniform for grandfather's civilian funeral. Is this appropriate?

A: We extend our sympathy as you grieve for your grandfather. Wearing your seasonal Service Dress uniform will add solemnity and dignity, thus honoring your grandfather. Be aware that all eyes are drawn to uniforms in a civilian gathering; proper decorum and dignity at all times is a must.

Q: This weekend I will attend a funeral for a close family friend. When I was accepted last year to the Academy he gave me his officer's sword from his commissioning sixty years ago. Is it OK for me to wear that sword to his Catholic funeral?

A: We are sorry for your loss. It is not appropriate to carry a sword to the funeral, nor is it considered part of your Academy student uniform. When writing your condolence note to the family, mention how meaningful the gift was to you, along with how your friend touched your life. In the future when you have an opportunity to wear or display the sword, write again and tell the family how his legacy continues.

Q: An Academy classmate passed away this weekend. The Class Officers would like to send flowers and a gift to his family. Do you have any suggestions?

A: We commend your leadership actions in response to this time of sadness. Ask the florist to use ribbons in your Service colors, with a card reading "From the Class of 20__." An appropriate gift might be the Academy prayer, framed with a brass plate, "In memory of__." Individual condolence cards to his parents should include sincere recollections of friendship. Since there are several of you, it would be thoughtful to send cards one at a time over several months to let the family know that you continue to think of them.

The 3-Volley Salute

Generally, uniformed personnel who die (military or police active duty, honorably discharged veterans, and retirees) are entitled to three rifle-volley salutes as part of their funeral, subject to availability of rifle squad teams. The rifle squad can consist of any number, but usually three to seven members. The Honors Leader calls all honors participants to *"Present arms,"* and commands the squad to fire their weapons in unison, for a total of three volleys. (Artillery or musketry volleys are not a 21-gun salute, which is done with cannons. See Cannon Salute below.) The firing party is usually positioned in view of the family, about fifty feet (fifteen meters) from the grave with their muzzles pointed over the casket of the honored deceased during the graveside committal. Alternatively, the three-rifle volley may be performed outside the military chapel with the rifle squad typically positioned near the front entrance ready for their cue from the Honors Leader. City ordinances usually prohibit firing at local houses of worship.

The tradition of three volleys comes from an old battlefield custom. The two warring sides would cease hostilities in order to clear their dead from the battle ground. Firing three volleys meant that the dead had been properly cared for and the side was ready to resume battle. Military personnel salute facing the casket from the first volley to the last.

Taps

Playing "Taps" at a military funeral signifies that the departed has entered the final sleep with full confidence in his readiness to respond to his maker's reveille. It is widely considered the most poignant moment of a military funeral. Again, instead of facing the music, it is appropriate to face the casket. One bugler is placed at the gravesite in view of the family, approximately thirty yards (twenty-seven meters) from the grave. Military personnel salute from the first note until the last note fades, when the Honors Leader calls all honors participants to "*Order arms*" and the clergy or funeral director requests mourners to be seated for the folding of the flag.

The American history of "Taps" began during the Civil War, when Union Army Captain Robert Ellicombe discovered the body of his son on the battlefield. The boy had been studying music in the South and without telling his father had enlisted in the Confederate Army. In his uniform pocket was a series of musical notes composing a haunting melody. The Union captain buried his Confederate Army son with a lone bugler playing the notes of "Taps." See the text box for evocative words written by General Daniel Butterfield in Charles City, Virginia, July 1862.

The entire U.S. military has only about five hundred buglers. About 1,800 veterans pass away each day. In an attempt to meet the demand, the Services began issuing a standard bugle that has a special electronic device which looks like a trumpet mute, but fits snugly deep inside the bugle and plays a high-quality rendition of "Taps" (www.ceremonialbugle.com). Immediately following "Taps," the U.S. flag is folded.

Everyone attending the funeral service stands during the anthem, the 3-volley salute, and "Taps." They sit down at the conclusion of military honors (if there are seats).

TAPS

Day is done. Gone the sun, From the lakes,
From the hills, From the skies, All is well.
Safely rest. God is nigh.

Fading light, Dims the sight. And a star,
Gems the sky, Gleaming bright. From afar,
Drawing nigh, Falls the night.

Thanks and praise, For our days, 'Neath the sun,
'Neath the stars, 'Neath the sky. As we go,
This we know: God is nigh.

Flag Folding and Presentation

The flag is folded immediately after the sounding of "Taps." The body bearers may have been holding the flag at "pall" (waist level, stretched taut and kept even at all points) over the coffin, but if not, any combination of Honors Detail participants can fold it. The flag is folded in half, long sides together, with the blue field underneath facing the casket, and then folded again. Starting at the foot end it is folded into a triangle and that shape maintained as it is folded all the way up, the last bit tucked in so as to end with the blue field on both sides of the triangle. The flag detail sometimes slips three shell casings from the volley salute into the folded flag at this time. Each casing represents one volley. The folded flag is passed to the Honors Leader who takes it with the right hand supporting the bottom and the left hand on top and waits until the bearer salutes the flag. The Honors Leader then presents it to the next of kin. Each military Service has published traditional wording to help Honors Leaders at this time, similar to these: *"On behalf of the President of the United States, a grateful nation, and a proud* [Service], *this flag is presented as a token of our appreciation for the honorable and faithful service rendered by your loved one to* [his or her] *country."* After presenting the flag, the Honors Leader offers condolences to other family mourners seated in the front row. If the Honors Leader is not from the parent Service of the deceased, that representative also offers condolences immediately following.

Once condolences have been offered, the Honors Leader will direct the Honors Detail participants to return to the cortege arrival point or release them. They may choose to remain in place until the family departs or return quietly to their own vehicles.

A U.S. national flag covers the casket or accompanies an urn to symbolize the service of the deceased to our nation. Flags are provided free by the Veterans

Administration (www.va.gov) and may be requested using Form 21-2008, *Application for United States Flag for Burial Purposes* (www.vba.va.gov/pubs/forms/VBA21-2008.pdf). The completed form (eligibility requirements and flag folding instructions are on the back) is taken to any U.S. post office, which is then authorized to hand out a flag.

COLOR GUARDS

A color guard detail may consist of three to eight Service members. When a Joint Armed Forces Color Guard cannot be formed, the senior member of the senior military Service in the color guard will carry the national colors (U.S. flag). Soldiers, when present, will carry the colors since the Army is the senior Service.

A Joint Armed Forces Color Guard includes representatives from as many Military Services as possible in accordance with Department of Defense Directive 1005.8 (reference (t), as in the photo in Chapter 7: Flag Etiquette.

DUTIES OF PALLBEARERS

Body bearers, also called active pallbearers, carry a casket whenever it is moved. Six or eight body bearers are normally needed to carry a casket. For a military funeral they are uniformed personnel. In addition to the body bearers, honorary pallbearers (in even numbers), form a cordon when the casket is moved and walk to the cemetery alongside or behind the hearse (or caisson). Honorary pallbearers have no other duties except following the direction of the Honors Leader to render appropriate honors to the deceased. Usually six or eight honorary pallbearers are designated by the family of the deceased from among close friends, acquaintances, or extended family members currently serving in uniform (including academy students). At the request of the family, the commanding officer will appoint honorary pallbearers. Pallbearers remain silent throughout.

The body bearers are positioned near wherever the hearse will stop and the casket will be moved. They position themselves so they can easily follow the funeral director's signal to withdraw the casket from the hearse, carry it into and from the chapel, transfer it to a caisson, and position it at the grave.

The Honors Leader directs military participants to "*Attention*" and "*Present arms*" as the body bearers carry the casket to the grave, then "*Order arms*" after the casket has been placed on the lowering device. The Honors Leader may instruct body bearers to hold the flag at pall or to move off as a group and stand in formation at "*Parade Rest*" for the committal.

Q: My grandfather's obituary says that full military honors will be rendered at the cemetery this weekend. I have never even attended a military funeral, but I will be a uniformed pallbearer. If I am carrying the casket, how do I salute?

A: Please accept our condolences on the death of your grandfather. A military representative will have been appointed to guide all uniformed personnel according to a protocol guide. This Honors Detail Leader will give the guidance you need, so make contact as soon as possible. Expect that after you help position the casket at graveside, you will face it and salute during the 3-volleys and "Taps" at a minimum. You may also help fold the flag.

Q: My little sister was killed in Iraq. Her interment is at a national cemetery with full honors. I will be escorting her remains from Dover. What is the proper uniform for my escort duties and the service? What do my civilian family members do during the gun salute and "Taps"?

A: You have our deepest sympathy over the loss of your sister. Service Dress Blue is an all-occasion uniform suitable for her funeral and your escort duties. If you desire more formality, Full Dress Blue allows you to incorporate full medals, ribbons, and gloves. A mourning band is also appropriate. Civilians stand at attention and render respect by placing right hands over their hearts whenever the military salutes. Veterans who are present but not in uniform may also render the military salute, if they choose. Civilian men wearing hats remove and hold them over their hearts. It may help comfort your family if you share the words penned to "Taps."

The Casket

A casket is carried foot first, except that of a clergyman, which is carried head-first. U.S. flags over military caskets are placed so that the blue field is at the head and over the left shoulder of the deceased to symbolize service to the nation. The casket is draped before it arrives for services and remains draped until the flag is folded graveside. The cap and sword of the deceased are never displayed atop a flag-draped casket (nothing touches the flag). Caskets are transported to the cemetery in a hearse or caisson.

Funeral with Military Chapel Service

Before the service begins, the funeral escort is formed outside facing the chapel. The band forms on the flank toward the direction of march. Chapel ushers ensure that a sufficient number of seats on the right front of the chapel are reserved for the immediate family, who are seated before the casket or urn is taken in. The two front pews on the left are reserved for honorary pallbearers, as needed. If body bearers are used to carry the casket or urn into position inside the chapel, seats are reserved for them at the rear of the chapel.

The conveyance bearing the casket or urn to the chapel arrives a short time before the hour set for the service. The escort outside is called to attention and the Honors Leader salutes as the conveyance arrives. When all is in readiness to move the casket or urn into the chapel, the Honors Leader brings the escort to *"Present arms."* At the first note of the hymn, the casket or urn is removed from the conveyance by the body bearers and carried between the ranks of honorary pallbearers, if any, into the chapel. The escort is brought to *"Order arms"* and then given *"At ease"* when the casket or urn is in position.

At the conclusion of the chapel service, the chaplain leads in exiting the chapel, followed by any honorary pallbearers, then the body bearers carrying the casket or urn. The honorary pallbearers form an aisle from the entrance of the chapel to the conveyance (caisson or hearse) and uncover or salute as directed by the Honors Leader as the casket passes. The rifle team can fire as the procession moves from the military chapel to the cemetery, rather than at graveside, if desired.

CREMATION

Hinduism, Jainism, and Buddhism mandate cremation. In other religions, it is either optional or preferred. For all phases of the military funeral where the receptacle containing cremated remains (cremains) is carried by hand, one uniformed body bearer will be designated to do so. Four men detailed as U.S. flag bearers will follow the receptacle whenever it is carried: into and from the chapel or the conveyance (hearse or caisson), or from the conveyance to the columbarium. The folded U.S. flag* is carried by the leading flag bearer on the right (the flag's own right). When the receptacle is placed on a stand or rostrum in the chapel or funeral home, or in the conveyance, the folded flag is placed beside it. An urn is never placed atop the Stars and Stripes. Honorary escorts may serve in the same manner as honorary pallbearers.

At the columbarium, the body bearer positions the urn on the stand and the flag bearers unfold the flag, holding it taut over the remains. Military honors are the same as the Graveside Service below.

---

* If a caisson is used that is equipped with a casket container for the cremains receptacle, an open flag is laid upon the container as prescribed for a casket and folded at the interment site.

Graveside Service Only

The body bearers may form at or near the entrance to the cemetery in order to escort the casket or urn to the grave or columbarium. Alternatively, the body bearers may join the bugler, firing party, and color guard already in their graveside positions before the arrival of the remains. The body bearers position the casket or urn as directed by the funeral director or the Honors Leader, who may call for a salute when it is in place. After the committal service, the Honors Leader gives the appropriate orders to commence military honors: the rifle squad fires three volleys, the bugler sounds "Taps" immediately upon completion of the last volley, the flag is folded, and the flag is presented to the next of kin with a formal statement (see Flag Folding and Presentation above).

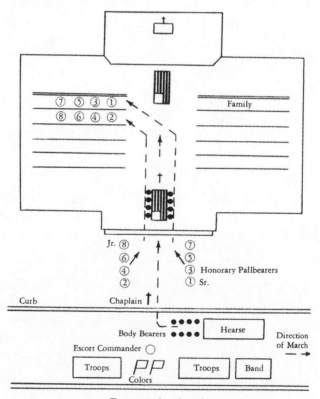

Entering the chapel

CANNON SALUTE

The funeral of a flag or general officer (active or retired) taking place at or near a military installation may be honored with minute guns (cannon fire; see Chapter 2: Military Honors and Official Government Ceremonies) at noon on the day of the funeral. Gun salutes (always in odd numbers) are based on the protocol rank of the deceased. If the funeral is held at a military chapel, the cannon salute may be fired immediately after the benediction, followed by the 3-Volley Salute above.

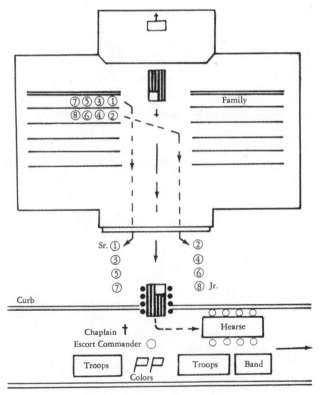

Leaving the chapel

Aviation Participation

When there is aviation participation in a military funeral, it may be timed so that the airplanes appear over the procession while the remains are being taken to the grave, or more usually, to coincide with the ending of the graveside service. As the aircraft pass overhead, it is customary for one plane to break out of the formation to symbolize the "missing member." When the funeral is that of an aviator, the aircraft may also fly in a normal tactical formation less one aircraft, indicating the vacancy resulting from the loss of the deceased.

Fraternal or Patriotic Organizations

A fraternal or military organization of which the deceased was a member may take part in the funeral service with the consent of the deceased's immediate family. When the ritual is military or semi-military, the rites begin immediately upon the conclusion of the military service. If the ritual contains some of the same elements as the military honors (the volley and "Taps"), the military participates at the appropriate time.

Burial at Sea

During burial at sea, the ship is stopped, if practical, and the ensign (national flag) displayed at half-mast from the beginning of the funeral service until the body has been committed to the deep. The senior officer present may stipulate further display of the ensign at half-mast, according to circumstances. Funeral honors are not rendered between sunset and sunrise. When it is necessary to bury the dead at night, such funeral services as are practical take place.

If there is no chaplain or cleric available, the commanding officer on board ship, or a designated representative, conducts the funeral service. There are normally six pallbearers and six body bearers. The pallbearers are the same grade or rating as the deceased, if possible.

The casket is covered with the national ensign, so placed that the union is at the head and over the left shoulder of the deceased. The ensign is removed from the casket before it is committed to the deep. Persons in the naval Services salute when the body is carried past them, while the body is being committed to the deep, during the firing of three rifle volleys, and the sounding of "Taps."

Boats taking part in a funeral procession display the ensign at half-mast. If the deceased was a flag or general officer, or at the time of death the deceased was a unit commander or a commanding officer of a ship, his or her flag (or command pennant or commission pennant) is draped in mourning and displayed at half-mast from a staff in the bow of the boat carrying the body.

MEMORIAL SERVICE HONORS

Upon the request of the next of kin, memorial services may be held for uniformed personnel whose remains have been declared non-recoverable. An honor guard and color guard arrive before the next of kin. Only one color bearer waits in the rear of the chapel or house of worship while the next of kin arrives and is seated. At the exact time set for the services to begin, the color bearer carries the folded U.S. national flag down the center aisle to the altar. He or she places it on the rostrum (where it remains throughout the ceremony) and retires to the wall at the left front of the congregation. For the remainder of the services, he or she stands at attention, facing inward. If requested by the next of kin, a military chaplain conducts the services. Otherwise, the family's own clergy presides.

The honor guard, with color guard on the left, forms outside the building exit to be used by the departing next of kin. They remain at ease outside during the services. When "Taps" is sounded, they come to attention.

At the conclusion of services, the bugler sounds "Taps" from the vestibule or other room separate from the congregation. The military chaplain or the officer in charge presents the national flag to the next of kin (see Flag Folding and Presentation above). The military representative (chaplain or officer in charge) not presenting the flag also speaks to the next of kin. The officer in charge escorts the next of kin from the church or chapel. The senior color bearer calls the honor guard and color guard to attention when the next of kin appears. As the next of kin approaches to within six paces, the leader orders *"Present arms,"* and this order is retained until the leader gives *"Order arms"* after the next of kin has departed the vicinity.

Great harm has been done to us. We have suffered great loss. And in our grief and anger we have found our mission and our moment.

—President George W. Bush, September 2001

SPECIAL MILITARY FUNERALS

Special military funerals are held for the following dignitaries:
Commander in Chief
Secretary of Defense
Deputy and former Secretary of Defense
Secretaries of the Army, Navy, and Air Force
Chairman, Joint Chiefs of Staff
Five-Star Generals and Admirals
Chiefs of Staff of the Army and Air Force
Chief of Naval Operations
Commandants of the Marine Corps and Coast Guard
Other personages specifically designated by the Secretary of Defense
Foreign military personnel when designated by the President

When the death of a dignitary occurs in Washington, D.C., the remains are moved to a selected place of repose attended by an honor guard composed of members of all the armed Services. When death occurs outside the city and the remains are transported to Washington for final honors, they are met at the point of arrival by a joint honor guard and escorted to the place of repose.

After three days, the dignitary's remains are escorted from the place of repose to the Arlington National Cemetery Amphitheater, the Washington National Cathedral, or the house of worship where the funeral service will be held. When burial is to be outside the nation's capital, the remains are escorted to the point of departure, where honors are rendered. Honors may also be rendered upon arrival at the burial location and at graveside services.

If there is a caisson: The Honors Leader supervises the transfer of the casket from the hearse to the caisson, usually at the cemetery entrance. While the casket is being transferred, the military escort is brought to *"Present arms."* Family and friends remain in their cars during the casket transfer. When transfer is complete, mourners follow the caisson in a march to the grave site.

When burial is to be outside Washington, the remains are escorted to the point of departure, where honors are accorded.

Death of Diplomatic, Consular, or Foreign Officials

On the death in a foreign place of a diplomatic or consular representative of the United States, the senior military officer present shall arrange for uniformed military participation in any local funeral ceremonies, as circumstances and the expressed wishes of the family warrant. When the body of a deceased American official is received or leaves a military aircraft or ship, the same honors are rendered as for deceased Armed Forces personnel.

Upon receiving official notice of the death or funeral of a foreign official or senior member of a foreign armed service from a country recognized by the United States, visits of condolence are made by local American Service members as international courtesy demands. The senior officer present (or higher authority) may direct uniformed military participation in the funeral ceremonies, as circumstances warrant.

Additional Protocol Notes

1. **Funeral Attire.** Civilians wear subdued colors. Mourning bands may be worn by the family or friends, if desired (see #2). Females limit the amount of bare skin and jewelry; international customs may dictate no bright lipstick. Dark sunglasses sometimes substitute for veils. Rarely are military funerals postponed because of bad weather. All attendees should be prepared to wear appropriate inclement weather apparel—that is, darkest available overcoat, raincoat, scarf, and so on. Attending military personnel wear the seasonal Service Dress uniform with an optional mourning band. For Navy personnel in summer whites, an alternate choice is Service Dress Blues (an all-occasion, all-year appropriate uniform) because it is more somber and professional-looking with the tie. Pallbearers at a military funeral must be in uniform with gloves. For full honor funerals, all uniformed personnel may wear gloves, ribbons, and medals.

2. **Mourning Bands.** Official military funeral escorts normally wear mourning bands. Officers wear the band on the left sleeve; enlisted personnel wear it on the right sleeve of the outer garment, halfway between the shoulder and elbow. The mourning band is a strip of black crepe three inches (7.62 centimeters) wide and long enough to fit around the arm. Personnel wearing the sword may knot a three-inch wide by twenty-inch (7.62 x 50.8 centimeters) long piece of black crepe in the middle at the base of the sword hilt in lieu of the sleeve band.

3. **Cemetery etiquette.** This includes speaking quietly, refraining from stepping on graves, and not intruding on mourners at any graveside by staring. If driving, do not play the car stereo loudly; do not cut in front of (or hinder in any way) the funeral vehicle procession.

4. **Terminology.** The *gravesite* is the section of the cemetery where the funeral ceremony takes place; *graveside* is the area immediately surrounding a burial plot or columbarium niche.

5. **Honorariums.** The military Honors Detail is never given a fee for services. Chaplains on active duty are also public servants and do not accept payment for military funeral services, but a donation to the chapel discretionary fund is appreciated, as is a note of appreciation afterward from a family member. There may be a charge for using a military chapel. Civilian clerics do customarily receive a fee for their time; place it in an envelope with a note and hand it over before the services.

6. **Saluting.** Uniformed personnel (and veterans not in uniform if they desire) salute whenever the casket or urn is moved: from the hearse, from the house of worship, from a caisson, and to the interment site. They salute when the national anthem is played, volleys are fired, and when "Taps" is sounded.

7. **Half Staff or Mourning Flags.** Hoist the colors to the peak of the flagpole or staff, and then lower it halfway. Before the flag is retired, raise it again to the peak. Where flags cannot be flown at half-staff, they should carry a black streamer from the spearhead halfway down the flag. The U.S. flag is never dipped at a funeral, but a unit or battalion flag may be dipped when appropriate.

8. **Personal Flags.** A flag bearer carries the personal colors of a deceased flag rank military officer or civilian dignitary and marches in front of his or her hearse or caisson. If the deceased was a unit commander or ship's captain, the command or commission pennant will also be carried. During or after the ceremony, the honor guard will furl and case the personal colors in full view of attendees, signifying death. The vehicle flags of attending general officers are encased beforehand as a sign of respect at the funeral service of another flag rank officer.

CHAPTER 7

Flag Etiquette

*E*very American citizen should know the history of the U.S. national flag, how to display it, how to show it respect, and proper disposal methods. Military personnel need to be experts on flags because others will not hesitate to ask them flag etiquette questions.

AT EASE KEY POINTS

U.S. flag protocol can be complicated, but generally:

- ⚘ It is considered a living thing and never dips to any person or thing.
- ⚘ Keep it always to its own far right hanging aloft and free.
- ⚘ Keep its staff in front of any other flag's staff when crossed.
- ⚘ Other flags can be the same size, but never larger.
- ⚘ Civilian citizens stand with right hands over hearts. Military personnel in uniforms salute. Veterans not in uniform may also salute, if desired.

HISTORY OF THE U.S. FLAG

With the onset of the American Revolution each of the thirteen colonies created at least one flag; many colonies had several versions. The flags were symbolic of the struggle for independence and carried such symbols as a tree, anchor, rattlesnake, or beaver with mottos such as "HOPE," "LIBERTY," "AN APPEAL TO HEAVEN," or "DON'T TREAD ON ME." Each regiment had its own colors, and the naval vessels and privateers fitted out by each colony flew distinctive flags.

Eventually, standardization became necessary. On December 2, 1775, the Continental Congress approved the design of a flag that was first hoisted on board the *Alfred* by Lieutenant John Paul Jones. It consisted of thirteen red and white stripes and, on a canton, the British Union Jack with its crosses of St. George and St. Andrew.

On January 1, 1776, the day the Continental Army came into being, these flags were displayed in the lines of the colonial forces besieging Boston. This famous flag has been called the Continental flag and, later, the Grand Union flag. After the Declaration of Independence, continued use of the British Union Jack became inappropriate, and a new flag was created. The first Act of Congress establishing the Stars and Stripes on June 14, 1777, ordained the present arrangement of red and white stripes and a union of blue with thirteen white stars representing "a new constellation." The Continental Army adopted a design in which the thirteen stars were arranged in a circle so that no colony would take precedence. Both stripes and stars continued to be added as the nation grew. By May 1, 1795, the flag had fifteen stars and fifteen stripes. This flag flew over Fort McHenry on the occasion of its bombardment by a British fleet and inspired Francis Scott Key to write "The Star-Spangled Banner."

Realizing that the flag would soon become unwieldy, Captain Samuel C. Reid, U.S. Navy, who commanded the *General Armstrong* during the War of 1812, suggested to Congress that the stripes be fixed at thirteen to represent the founding colonies, and that only stars be added for new states. His suggestion became the text of a resolution by Congress, effective April 18, 1818, whereby the flag should contain thirteen alternate red and white stripes representing the original states, with a new star added to the blue field for each new state on July 4 following its admission date to the Union. During the Civil War the flag had thirty-three, thirty-four, and thirty-five stars; no stars were removed even though eleven states seceded. During World War I, World War II, and the Korean War there were forty-eight stars. With the admission of Alaska and Hawaii in 1959, our flag now carries fifty stars.

HOW TO DISPLAY THE U.S. FLAG

A code of display adopted by Congress on June 22, 1942, states: *"It is the universal custom to display the flag only from sunrise to sunset on buildings and on stationary flagstaffs in the open. However, the flag may be displayed at night upon special occasions when it is desired to produce a patriotic effect."* The flag of the United States of America must be properly illuminated during hours of darkness. The flag is raised and lowered by hand. Do not raise the flag while it is folded or rolled. Unfurl it and hoist it quickly to the top of the staff. When lowering it, however, do so slowly and with dignity. The national flag is never *carried* flat or horizontally or half-staff.

When displayed in the chancel or on a platform in a house of worship, the national flag should be placed on a staff at the clergy's right, and all other flags at the left. If displayed in the body of the religious gathering, the flag should be at the congregation's right as they face the clergy.

When the flag is displayed from a flagpole projecting horizontally or at any angle from a window sill, balcony, or front of a building, the union (blue field of stars) of the flag should go toward the peak of the staff. When the flag is suspended over a sidewalk from a rope, extending from house to pole at the edge of the sidewalk, it should be hoisted out from the building, toward the pole, union first.

When hung over the middle of a street or hall corridor, the flag should be suspended vertically, with the union to the north in an east-west street or corridor, or to the east in a street or corridor going north-south. If there is only one entrance to a building lobby, suspend the flag near the center of the lobby with the union to observers' left as they enter. If there are two entrances, follow the street directions above. If there are entrances in more than two directions, the union should be to the east. When painted or displayed on an aircraft or vehicle, the union is toward the front of the conveyance.

When displayed with another flag from crossed staffs, the U.S. flagstaff should always be in front of the staff of the other flag, pointing to the left as viewed by the audience. This keeps the U.S. flag on its own far right (also called the heraldic right). Use flags of the same size and the same material in a display; do not mix outdoor flags with indoor flags. Drape all flags in the same manner so that the bottom tips are all in the same location.

When the flag is displayed in a manner other than by being flown from a staff, it should be flat against a wall either horizontally or vertically, indoors or out; the union should be uppermost and to the flag's own right—that is, to the observer's left. When displayed in a window, the flag should be situated in the same way, with the union to the observer's left as seen from the street.

In the United States or in any parade of U.S. troops (see The Parade Review below), when carried in a procession with another flag or flags, the U.S. Stars and Stripes should have the place of honor at its own far right; or, when there is a line of other flags, our national flag may be *in front of* the center of that line.

When the flag is used at the unveiling of a statue or monument, it never covers the object to be unveiled. It is displayed on a flagpole, staff, or hung aloft to enhance the ceremony.

When flags of states, cities, or localities, or pennants of societies are flown on the same halyard with the flag of the United States, the national flag should always be at the peak. When the flags are flown from adjacent staffs, the flag of the United States should be hoisted first and lowered last.

At official dinners or receptions, it is customary (but not necessary) to display flags either centered behind the head table or behind the receiving line.

U.S. Flag Order of Precedence and Bunting

The proper protocol order for flags on U.S. property, from the audience perspective is, left to right:

- The U.S. national flag
- Other country flags follow ours in English alphabetical order (see International Flag Etiquette below)
- The presidential flag (if present)
- States (host state first, then appropriate others in order of admission to the union) or territory or protectorate flags
- Military Services (Army first, then Marine Corps, Navy, Air Force, and Coast Guard, followed by other uniformed Service flags [such as National Guard or Merchant Marine])
- Event host organization flag (such as military command, university, hotel, or unit)
- Personal flags (for example, presiding generals, admirals, or leaders of societies)

Flags may be flown from a single staff, observing protocol order. For instance, the correct flagpole order (from the top down) for these three would be: U.S. flag, Missing in Action/Prisoner of War flag, Virginia state flag.

The flag of the United States of America should be at the center and at the highest point of the group when a number of flags of U.S. states or localities, organizations, or pennants of societies are grouped and displayed from staffs. No foreign flags or pennants may be placed above the flag of the United States or to its right on U.S. ground or property. Place the U.S. flagstaff atop a box or platform, if necessary, to give it additional height.

When festoons, rosettes, or drapes of patriotic colors are desired, *never* use the flag itself. Bunting is available in broad stripes of blue, white, and red. Hang bunting so that the blue is at the top, white in the middle, and red at the bottom.

Ordering Flags for Special Ceremonies

If you would like a U.S. flag that has flown over the nation's capitol (Congress) contact your congressional representative. If you would like a state flag that has flown over your state capitol building, contact your governor. Typically, there are modest "at cost" charges for these flags. They come with certificates stating the date the flag was flown, at what official's request, and for what reason—for example, the retirement of a Service member.

MINIATURE FLAGS

Miniature flags are attractive when displayed in stands behind guest books, on tables during document-signing ceremonies, or centered on head tables during events honoring several countries. Place them in correct protocol order as the majority of viewers see them, left to right. Alternatively, if the stand is a circular one, or the display is a centerpiece, the U.S. flag, as host, is in the center position surrounded by other country flags.

Small U.S. flags carried by individuals are not saluted.

FLAG DESIGNATIONS

When the flag is carried by dismounted military units it is known as the *colors*. When flown from ships and boats, the flag is an *ensign*. When carried by tank, car, truck, or on horseback, the flag is the *standard*.

DIPPING THE U.S. FLAG

The U.S. national flag is not dipped to any person or thing, with one exception. When any ship under U.S. registry, or the registry of a nation diplomatically recognized by the United States, salutes a ship of the U.S. Navy by dipping its ensign, the formal greeting is answered dip-for-dip. Unit colors, state flags, and organizational or institutional flags can be dipped as a mark of honor. It is not meant as disrespect to anyone or any country that the American national flag is not dipped; it is intended to preserve it as a symbol of national dignity.

U.S. MILITARY FUNERALS

If a Service member dies while on active duty, the flag for the funeral ceremonies is provided by the Service to which he or she belonged. For an honorably discharged veteran, the flag is provided by the Veterans Administration, Washington, D.C. (www.va.gov), and may be procured from the nearest post office using

Form 21-2008, *Application for United States Flag for Burial Purposes* (www.vba. va.gov/pubs/forms/VBA21-2008.pdf).

When the U.S. flag is used at a military funeral it may cover a closed urn or casket with the union (blue field) at the head and over the left shoulder of the deceased, but a cremation receptacle or urn may not sit atop a flag-draped surface. The flag is never lowered into a grave, or placed in a columbarium, or committed to the deep during burial at sea.

Military personnel salute during the passing of a military funeral procession, to honor the deceased and because of the U.S. flag over the casket or urn. When attending a military funeral, uniformed Service members (and veterans who choose to, even if not in uniform) salute whenever the casket or urn (and flag) is moved: from the hearse, from the house of worship, from a caisson, and to the interment site. (See Chapter 6: The Military Funeral for more information.)

HALF-STAFF AND MOURNING

The custom of lowering a flag comes from the old military practice of "striking the colors" in time of war as a sign of submission. As early as 1627 it was done as a symbol of corporate mourning; it is never an individual expression of grief. "Half-staff" means lowering the flag to one-half the distance between the top and the bottom of the flagpole. When flown at half-staff, the U.S. flag should first be raised to the top for an instant, and then lowered to the half-staff position; before being lowered for the day, it should again be raised to the peak. On Memorial Day, the U.S. flag is displayed at half-staff until noon, but then hoisted to the top of the staff for the rest of the day. Where U.S. flags cannot be flown at half-staff, they should have a black streamer from the spearhead halfway down the flag; if hung horizontally or perpendicularly, they bear a black bunting border of appropriate width.

By order of the President, the U.S. national flag shall be flown at half-staff upon the death of principal figures of the government as a mark of respect to their memory. In the event of the death of other officials or foreign dignitaries, the flag is to be displayed at half-staff according to presidential instructions or orders. Section 5 of Presidential Proclamation 3044 delegates to the heads of agencies and departments the authority to lower flags within their jurisdiction to half-staff. If you are advising anyone establishing local guidelines, remind them that when flags are ordered to half-staff, a precedent is being established that must be followed every time identical circumstances arise in the future.

Q: How long are national flags to fly at half-staff for President Gerald Ford's death? Also our representative is very elderly and in ill health; how long for congressmen?

A: Consult www.WhiteHouse.gov under News/Proclamations as the need arises. The U.S. flag is flown at half-staff thirty days from the death of the President or a former President; ten days from the death of a Vice President, Chief Justice (active or retired), or the Speaker of the House; from the day of death until interment of an Associate Justice of the Supreme Court, a Secretary of an executive or military department, a former Vice President, or the governor of a state, territory, or possession; and on the day of death and the following day for a Member of Congress. Flags are normally flown at half-staff until sunset on the day of interment for other dignitaries.

U.S.-Approved Flag Customs

Religious Pennants. All uniformed Services have precise regulations regarding the display of the national flag—when, where, and how—that may at times differ from the laws governing the use of the flag as mentioned above. It is the custom at all bases, posts, and stations to raise the flag every morning at eight o'clock and to lower it at sunset or retreat. However, when naval vessels are entering or leaving port, the flag is flown prior to 0800 and after sunset. Also, one Navy flag may be flown above the Stars and Stripes—the Church Pennant, a dark blue cross on a white background. Code signal books of the Navy, which date back to the early 1860s, state: "The Church Pennant will be hoisted immediately above the ensign at the peak or flagstaff at the time of commencing and kept hoisted during the continuance of divine service on board all vessels of the Navy."

Individual Rank Flags. Civilian dignitaries of the federal and state governments, flag and general officer ranks, and military chaplains are entitled to individual flags that indicate their title or grade. These official flags may be displayed in their offices (and in the case of a chaplain at the place of divine worship) and miniature versions may be flown from official automobiles on staffs fixed firmly to the chassis or fender (high enough so that the flag does not touch the car). Army and Marine Corps general officer flags are red fields with white stars; Air Force and Navy flags have a blue background. The national flag is always displayed on the vehicle's right fender. Remember, no flag or pennant is ever displayed on the heraldic right of the flag of the United States of America.

Dates for U.S. Flag Display

The national flag may be displayed each and every day when the weather permits, especially on *national holidays*, the *birthdays of states* (dates of admission to the Union), and on *state holidays*. The flag should also be displayed on *birthdays of the United States, uniformed Services*: **Army,** June 14 (1775); **Marine Corps,** November 10 (1775); **Navy,** October 13 (1775); **Air Force,** September 18 (1947); **Coast Guard,** January 28 (1915); **Public Health Service,** January 4 (1889); and **National Oceanic and Atmospheric Administration Corps,** May 22 (1917); and on the *birthdays of the National Guard,* December 13 (1636) *and the Merchant Marine,* June 12 (1775).

Disposal of U.S. Flag

At all times, every precaution should be taken to prevent our nation's flag from becoming soiled. It should not be allowed to touch the ground or floor, nor brush against objects, nor have any objects set upon it. A flag should be dry-cleaned, not washed. When it is worn out, the national flag should be respectfully "retired" by cremation. Many American Legion posts offer this service. Boy Scouts, Girl Scouts, and similar patriotic young people's groups may be happy for an opportunity to hold a training session regarding flag disposal (retirement), especially near Flag Day, June 14.

Flag Retirement (Cremation) Ceremony

The United States Flag Code, Title 4, Chapter 1, states: *"The flag, when it is in such condition that it is no longer a fitting emblem of display, should be destroyed in a dignified way, preferably by burning."* A formal ceremony is not required. However, when one is desired, the National Flag Foundation has provided the following suggestions for conducting one.

The ceremony is conducted out-of-doors, preferably in conjunction with a campfire program, and it should be very special. Only one flag is used for the service. If more flags have been collected, a corporate, government, or military incinerator or furnace can usually be found for incinerating them.

The ceremony involves two color guards, the regular one for the flag currently in use and a special guard for the flag to be cremated. Just before sunset, the flag that has been flying all day is retired in the normal ceremonial procedure for that location or group. The special color guard moves front and center. The presiding official (leader) presents them with the flag selected for its final tribute and subsequent cremation. The leader instructs, *"Hoist the colors."*

When the flag is secured at the top of the pole, the leader says, *"This flag has served its nation well and long. It has worn to a condition in which it should no longer be used to represent the nation. It represents all of the flags collected and being retired from service today. The honor we show here for this one flag, we are showing for all of the flags, even those not physically present."*

The leader calls the group to attention for the final tribute, orders a salute, and leads them in the Pledge of Allegiance, after which the flag is retired by the color guard who slowly and ceremoniously lowers it, respectfully folding it in the customary triangle, and handing it to the leader. The group is dismissed to re-assemble at the site of the cremation ceremony.

PLEDGE OF ALLEGIANCE
U.S. Flag Code, June 22, 1942

I pledge allegiance to the Flag of the United States of America and to the
Republic for which it stands, one Nation, under God, indivisible, with liberty
and justice for all.

It is important that the fire be sizable, preferably having burned down to a bed of red-hot coals (to avoid bits of the flag being carried off by a roaring fire) and sufficient in intensity to ensure the complete burning of the flag. The leader hands the folded tri-corner flag to the special color guard, who open and refold it into a coffin-shaped rectangle. *Optional:* One approved custom is to cut the union (blue field) from the flag, so that there are two pieces, which no longer form a flag.

The leader calls the group to attention as the color guard come forward and place the flag (or the two pieces) onto the fire. All briskly salute. After the salute, but while still at attention, the leader conducts a respectful memorial service as the flag burns. The National Flag Foundation recommends singing "God Bless America," followed by an inspiring message of the flag's meaning, followed by the Pledge of Allegiance, and then silence while the flag is burned so that nothing left is recognizable. The leader dismisses observers, who depart silently in single file. The leader and the color guard remain until the flag is completely consumed and the fire can be safely extinguished. The ashes are buried with dignity.

Honors to the U.S. Flag
and National Anthem

Reveille is the morning ceremony that raises the U.S. national flag (the colors) for the day's activities. *Retreat* is the evening ceremony that lowers the colors from the day's activities and puts it away for safekeeping. These ceremonial honors are performed every day. During inclement weather, a smaller "storm flag" or all-weather flag is flown. On special occasions a larger-than-normal "holiday flag" may be flown. Military members conducting the ceremonies wear their Service dress uniform with cover (hat, cap, beret, headgear). Military attendees at reveille and retreat wear the uniform of the day unless ordered otherwise by the installation commander.

PATRIOTIC MUSIC

The national anthem is *The Star-Spangled Banner*
by Francis Scott Key

The national march is *The Stars and Stripes Forever*
by John Philip Sousa

Reveille and Retreat Ceremonies

The installation commander decides what bugle call or music is played for the ceremonies. When a bugler or band is not present, recorded music is broadcast. Reveille is played for approximately twenty seconds while the flag is raised quickly to the top of the flagpole. During retreat, the flag is lowered slowly and ceremoniously, reaching the bottom at the last note of the bugle call (normally "To the Colors") or music (the national anthem).

Outdoors during reveille, all individuals (regardless of nationality) stand quietly, facing the flag, if one is present; otherwise, they face the direction of the music. All dismounted uniformed personnel (and veterans who are present but not in uniform, should they wish) come to attention facing the flag and salute until the last note of music.

Indoors during retreat ceremonies and whenever and wherever the national anthem is played, all individuals (regardless of nationality) stand quietly, facing the flag, if one is present; otherwise, they face the direction of the music. Military personnel stand at attention but do not salute, unless covered or under arms.

Citizen civilians and military members in civilian clothes place their right hands over their hearts. Male citizens in civilian dress remove their hats or caps and hold them with their right hands over their hearts. Courtesies are not necessary if the national anthem is heard over the Internet, radio, or television.

Outdoors during retreat and whenever and wherever the national anthem is played:

- Uniformed personnel *in formation* begin at *"Parade rest,"* then are brought to *"Attention"* and *"Present arms"* at the first note, and *"Order arms"* at the conclusion. At the first note, all dismounted uniformed personnel *not in formation* come to attention facing the flag and salute until the last note of music. Veterans who are present but not in uniform may also render the military salute. All other civilians (regardless of nationality) stand quietly, facing the flag, if visible; otherwise, they turn toward the music. Citizen civilians and military members in civilian clothes place their right hands over their hearts. Males in civilian dress remove their hats or caps and hold them with their right hands over their hearts.

- Vehicles in motion on military installations during retreat should be brought to a halt. Uniformed military personnel riding in a passenger car step out of the vehicle (or dismount a motorcycle) and salute if practical; otherwise, they may remain seated at attention. Tank or armored car commanders salute from the vehicle.

- A Navy boat under way within sight or hearing of the retreat ceremony either lies to or proceeds at the slowest safe speed. The boat officer (or, in his absence, the coxswain) stands and salutes, except when dangerous to do so. All other persons in the boat remain seated or standing, and do not salute.

FOREIGN FLAGS AND ANTHEMS

Treat a national flag as the historical record of its nation and as a strong symbol of sovereignty. American civilians can be very casual about our flag, even printing portions (red and white stripes and white stars on a blue field) onto paper plates and napkins, which are discarded negligently. Some people continue talking or eating (e.g., at ballgames) when our national anthem is played. Such actions will be construed as dishonoring by other nationalities if done to their national symbols. Show respect to the national anthem and flag (and religious symbol) of any and all friendly countries. Highest honors to the national flag and anthem of any friendly country are rendered by all branches of the Armed Forces in uniform during *official* occasions (the commanding officer should issue a program of events so that military personnel know when to salute). All other men and women stand quietly facing the foreign flag on a flagpole or as it passes by, or face forward during the foreign country's anthem music.

When the United States is host, international anthems are usually followed, without pause, by our own anthem, "The Star-Spangled Banner." If you are working with a band, the national anthems of foreign visitors are played in protocol order, beginning with the guest of honor's country, followed by any others in English alphabetical order. When two or more foreign anthems are played, the U.S. national anthem is played following the sequence. Courtesy requires that anthems be played with great dignity.

The positioning of a flag display indoors is arbitrary and based on the best location for the event, with the protocol order proceeding left to right (like reading this page) as viewed by the audience. For instance, an American colonel in Virginia is hosting a reception with four foreign guests of honor and wants to place their flags behind his receiving line. If he were serving overseas, the local diplomatic order of precedence might be more appropriate for the guests of honor, their flags, and country anthems if played. However, since he is in Virginia, the five flags are placed in descending English alphabetical order by country name *after* his and the ranking guest of honor's flag. His flag display is: U.S. (farthest right from its own perspective, or first in line because our host is American), Zimbabwe (his ranking guest), France, Ghana, and Qatar flags. Since pictures will be taken at our example event, the receiving line is placed on the *left* of the guest entrance so that

---

Q: We have our Murrah Building (Oklahoma) Bombing Anniversary here in April and plan to fly foreign flags at a dedication in honor of foreign attendees we are recognizing with an award. How should they be flown?

A: According to U.S. Code, Title 4, Sections 1–10, when flags of two or more nations are displayed in peacetime they should be approximately equal in size and flown from separate staffs of the same height. The protocol order is always the same: host, guest of honor, and others in descending precedence order. The U.S. flag is always on its own far right (first on the left as viewed), the ranking guest's flag next, followed by others in English alphabetical order by country name.

Q: We want to fly a foreign flag to honor a citizen of that country. How do we fly it with our U.S. flag?

A: Both flags should be the same size and displayed on the same level. Cross the flagstaffs with the U.S. staff in front or display them in stands keeping the foreign flag on the U.S. flag's own left. On no occasion should any flag usurp our flag's place of honor on ground or property owned by the United States.

the flags are directly behind their representatives. No matter the placement and flow of the receiving line, however, the flag of the United States will be at the far right (its own right or the observer's left). See below, International Flag Etiquette, for more information.

THE PARADE REVIEW

In the United States, its possessions, or in any parade of U.S. troops, the Stars and Stripes has the place of honor at its own far right when carried in a procession with another flag or flags. When there is a marching line of other flags, our national flag may also be *in front of* the center of that line.

While a parade is in progress, those attending stand quietly facing the troops. A review (or honors ceremony), if desired, may be held during a parade. Troops are ceremoniously marched onto the field, and a person of distinction is on hand to take the review as an honor. Certain formalities are followed. Using a *Service Academy Parade* as our example, they are:

- A senior government official, or one or more officers, or retiring senior professors might be asked to take the review. The honored guest(s) and spouse(s) are invited by the superintendent's formal invitation both to review and for the reception that follows in his quarters.

- Other invited guests also sit in the superintendent's section on the parade ground and attend the reception. All uniformed personnel under the canopy are considered to be in the ceremonial party, and salute accordingly. Veterans who are present but not in uniform may also render the military salute, if they choose. The general public may attend the parade and sit in the stands.

- After the cadets or midshipmen have marched, by company or squadron, onto the parade ground—each company with its own colors following after the color guard—the Brigade or Corps or Wing Commander gives the *"Order arms"* and *"Parade rest."*

- The reviewing individuals will have already walked forward with the superintendent and taken a position facing the regimental officers on the field. An announcer will make appropriate remarks about the honored guest. The Brigade or Corps or Wing Commander brings the companies to attention and announces, *"Sir* (or *Madame*), *the Brigade of Midshipmen* (or *Corps of Cadets* or *Cadet Wing*)."* The superintendent (or commanding officer) gives the *"Pass in review"* command and, as each company marches by, their own flag is momentarily dipped in salute to the honored guest(s) and others under the canopy in the stands. (Remember, the U.S. national flag is never dipped.) Salutes are returned by the reviewing party.

- Everyone stands silently and respectfully during a review. Uniformed personnel salute the national flag; veterans who are present but not in uniform may also salute; other citizens not in uniform face the flag, their right hand (with or without a hat) over their hearts.

OTHER HONORS

To colors. Military personnel in uniform passing an uncased (unfurled) flag salute at a distance of six paces and hold the salute until they have passed six paces beyond it. Similarly, when an uncased color itself is moving past, military personnel salute when it is six paces away and hold the salute until it has passed six paces beyond. Veterans who are present but not in uniform may also render the military salute, if they choose.

Personal honors. When personal honors are rendered, uniformed military personnel salute at the first note of the music and hold the salute until the completion of the ruffles, flourishes, and march.

Gun salutes. When a gun salute is rendered, military personnel being saluted and other persons in the ceremonial party render the hand salute throughout the firing sequence. Others in the vicinity of the ceremonial party stand at attention. A gun salute to the national flag requires no individual action.

COLOR GUARD CEREMONY

A color guard ceremony honors the nation and is designed to establish a patriotic mood to open the formal portion of a civic, military, or governmental event. It consists of U.S. military personnel in uniform marching in formation carrying the national and military Service flags, and the playing of the national anthem (or a recitation of the Pledge of Allegiance for nonmilitary functions). The ceremony is about fifteen minutes in duration. A color guard detail may consist of three to eight Service members. When a Joint Armed Forces Color Guard cannot be formed, the senior member of the senior military Service in the color guard will carry the national colors, followed by the organizational colors in descending order of precedence. Soldiers, when present, will carry the national flag because the Army is the senior Service.

Eight-Member Color Guard (United States Naval Institute Photo Archives)

Three-Member Color Guard (United States Naval Institute Photo Archives)

A Joint Armed Forces Color Guard includes representatives from as many military Services as possible in accordance with Department of Defense Directive 1005.8 (reference [t]). A full color guard is as follows, left to right as viewed: Two Army members carry flags; the senior carries the U.S. flag, the other stands next bearing the Army flag. Continuing in order are one each Marine Corps, Navy, Air Force, and Coast Guard members carrying their Service colors. One Army and one Marine Corps rifleman act as escorts, "book ending" or "bracketing" the others, Army on the left, Marine on the right.

Posting the Colors

The officer in charge places the color guard in a column formation, the colors at the carry slings, the escorts at right shoulder arms; and upon the command "*Post the colors*," the file advances at half-step to the proper location. "*Mark time*" order is given, "*Halt*" is commanded, and the color guard is then faced toward the audience or flag stands. "*Present arms*" is ordered and the color bearers either hold position throughout the music, or are commanded to "*Post the colors*" (insert the staffs into flag stands). To depart, the color guard is commanded "*Right shoulder arms*" and faced toward the left if possible and marched to the nearest exit. There is no protocol requirement that the colors, once posted, must be retired, so the color guard may be dismissed after this duty, if desired.

Retiring the Colors

When flags are in flag stands, the officer in charge moves the color guard (in reverse order) to retire (remove) the colors. The file is halted and commanded "*Present arms*." The guard secures the colors in carry slings, receives the order, "*Right shoulder arms*"** and marches at half-step to the nearest exit, with the first escort and then the colors of the United States leading. When out of sight, the colors are cased.

UN FLAG REGULATIONS

The United Nations (UN) flag code prescribes:

The UN flag is normally displayed only on buildings and on stationary flagstaffs from sunrise to sunset. It should not be displayed on days when the weather is inclement. The UN flag should never be carried flat or horizontal, but always aloft. It should never be used as a drapery of any sort, festooned, drawn back, or up in folds, but always falling free. The UN flag may be displayed on all national and official holidays, on United Nations Day, October 24, and at any official event honoring the United Nations. On no occasion may any flag displayed with it be larger than the UN flag. The UN flag may be displayed on either side of any flag without being considered subordinate to any other flag.

UN flag etiquette ensures that no one country's flag has precedence over another country's flag. Member states' flags are assigned a flagpole outside the United Nations Headquarters in English alphabetical order, north to south. All flags are displayed on the same level and are approximately equal in size.

INTERNATIONAL FLAG ETIQUETTE

International usage forbids displaying the flag of one nation above that of another nation in time of peace. At all times, national flags displayed with flags of other nations should be flown from separate staffs of the same height, with the flags approximately equal in size. If any flags have fringes or tassels, the same decorations should appear on all the other flags.

In a line of flags, the host nation's flag normally appears at the far left (its own right, also called the heraldic right side). Alternatively, it may be situated in a center position if higher than, or in front of, all other flags. This is especially appropriate when there are an odd number of flagpoles. A foreign host flag is sometimes flown on both ends of a line of flags (depending on local country protocol). When displayed on crossed staffs, the host nation's flag is displayed on the pole in front of and pointing to the left of the other flag's staff, as viewed.

The flags of sovereign nations are displayed in alphabetical order of the host's language. Countries without alphabets rank order flags based on the number of lines in the pictogram of the nation's name.

National flags take precedence over provinces, states, or territories, which take precedence over corporate flags, or flags of individuals. A national flag can be flown from the top of the same flagpole as any other flag, except another national flag. For example, a single flagpole may hold (from top to bottom) a national flag, state flag, and university flag.

CHAPTER 8

Order of Precedence and Military Forms of Address

*H*ierarchy is observable everywhere; humans appreciate order. For example, we observe the importance of individuals so that everyone will recognize who is in charge, who is an honored guest, and who has held comparable positions longest ("first among equals").

Respect is strictly formalized across all military Services, government systems, and formal religions. It is easy to determine who ranks higher in most official systems because rank order lists are in the public domain, as is the length of time the incumbents have served in their positions. Other enterprises are no less interested in who is most important or more entitled to respect: Hollywood studios rate actors based on successful movies; sports heroes are recognized based on their physical ability and the latest games won.

In the corporate world, precedence is not a matter of public record because businesspersons rate themselves based on wealth and influence, yet companies normally closely guard their employees' wage scales. Organization charts are usually available online, so ascertaining internal hierarchy is not difficult. However, between companies, similar job titles may or may not help you determine precedence. In corporate venues, business cards must be relied upon to convey names and personal rank, since this information is not conspicuous (no uniforms or public access to salaries).

AT EASE KEY POINTS

- ❖ Order of precedence is most important in military hierarchies, government systems, and formal religions.
- ❖ Formally places persons and flags; the higher, the more privileges granted.
- ❖ Useful for introductions, seating, parades, lists of names, and assigning quarters or transportation.

U.S. federal government civilians (sometimes called public or civil servants) have clearly delineated positions determined by election or appointment to an office, and the length of time served. Government Order of Precedence depends on an individual's pay grade within the United States and on the rules established by the 1815 Congress of Vienna if they are serving as diplomatic envoys. Pay grade charts for all federal government personnel (civilian and military) are available online.

Q: The 1948 Universal Declaration of Human Rights adopted by the United Nations states that all people are born free and equal in dignity and rights. Why then should some people be accorded more respect than others?

A: Respect in society is based on position. We all hold many positions at the same time, and are therefore honored at different levels in different arenas. We prefer children to obey their parents and respect elders. We want students to value their teachers in school. Lawyers honor judges in the courtroom. Etiquette and civility expand the notion of dignity to include the principles of kindness and consideration for others, no matter YOUR rank. We are especially respectful of government officials, persons with disabilities, the very young, and the very old.

The Grade Equivalency Chart at the end of Chapter 1: Military and Government Protocol is helpful to compare U.S. military, civil service, and foreign service rankings with each other for precedence purposes. In some countries, government or military Service is considered more prestigious than private business; in others, the opposite is true, so there is no reliable way to compare across borders, except within the diplomatic world. The Department of State determines precedence among foreign representatives accredited to the United States on the official Diplomatic Order of Precedence list. Every other country maintains its own list. (See Chapter 25: International Protocol and Civility for more on diplomatic protocol and precedence.)

GOVERNMENT ORDER OF PRECEDENCE

The President of the United States determines precedence for U.S. government officials and the Department of State maintains the President's official Order of Precedence lists, which they strive to keep current. Across the entire government system, great numbers of people come and go, new positions are established, others are abolished, and leadership changes the status ranking of departments.

Because of these difficulties and other considerations, an official order of precedence is never distributed by the Department of State.

Military Order of Precedence is easy to understand, because it is readily observable and follows strict written guidelines. Rank and the date of attainment are the basis for precedence in all armed forces, both here and in foreign countries. Age and gender are not considerations. For the insignia of military ranks, see the chart at the end of Chapter 22: Appropriate Attire.

Many Web sites post very long Order of Precedence lists, but there is very little consistency or commonality among them after the first thirty or so entries. When there are conflicts, defer to the lists of the responsible entities (e.g., the Department of Defense list for military officials, the Department of State list for foreign diplomats, the particular states to rank governors or members of the House of Representatives, etc.). The Office of the Secretary of Defense's (OSD) Protocol Office maintains the official Department of Defense (DOD) Order of Precedence list.

RANK MEETS IMMOVABLE OBJECT

A naval captain spotted a light rapidly closing with his battleship one stormy night. He ordered a signal light flashed, "Alter your course ten degrees south." A moment later came the reply, "Alter your course ten degrees north." Determined that the other vessel steer clear, the officer ordered a new signal, "Alter course ten degrees. I am the Captain." The response came back, "Alter your course ten degrees. I am Seaman Third Class Jones." The infuriated captain seized the light himself to signal: "Alter course, I am a battleship." The reply winked in, "Alter your course, I am a lighthouse."

RANK MEETS IMMOVABLE MAN

The Air Force lieutenant general's driver was leaning against a Pentagon wall talking to another man. When his superior walked out, the driver snapped to attention but the other slouching man just watched. The lieutenant general addressed him, "Son, do you know who I am?" The idle man admitted that he did not, so the general enlightened him with his rank and title. The unimpressed man replied, "I don't give a [expletive deleted], I work for the phone company."

Visitor Codes

Very Important Person/Distinguished Visitor Codes (VIP/DV) were established to determine what military honors to render officials, such as the number of gun salutes or the number of persons in an honor cordon.

The following DOD list incorporates the seven U.S. uniformed Services: Army, Marine Corps, Navy, Air Force, Coast Guard, Commissioned Corps of the

Public Health Service (PHS), and National Oceanic and Atmospheric Administration (NOAA) Corps. Within a group listed together on a line under a Code, precedence is by date of appointment.

Q: I must "recognize" guests of honor. Whose name do I say first, the U.S. Secretary of Transportation or the Chinese ambassador to the United States?

A: For a U.S.-hosted event it is proper to recognize the foreign dignitary first: *"Ladies and Gentlemen, we are honored to have with us this evening His Excellency, the Ambassador of the People's Republic of China and our Secretary of Transportation."* You'll be happy to know that you need not say names if they are difficult to pronounce, as it is the position that must be formally recognized, not the individual serving (the successor will be equally important). However, if you use one name, be consistent and say all names the same way. A guest is introduced to his host in a receiving line, *"[American leader/host], may I present His Excellency, the Ambassador of . . ."*

Q: As a 1982 graduate of the Naval Academy, I was taught to address only the most senior officer of any group by rank or, if the entire group was the same rank, O-6s for example, as "Captains." A POD (Plan of the Day) note stated that all seniors refer to groups of juniors as "gentlemen." Does this still hold true?

A: All-male audiences (even senior military ones) are increasingly rare. When addressing remarks to groups or audiences, whether ranks are higher or lower than the speaker's, first recognize the host or highest-ranking person present, followed by any others deserving special recognition—prominent individual, major group category, reason for the gathering—in protocol order, and finally end with an all-encompassing phrase. **Military example:** *"Good afternoon, Mr. President, Admiral Roughead, distinguished guests, members of the press, and men and women of the Newport News Shipyard. Welcome to the christening launch of . . ."* **University example:** *"Good afternoon, Dean Boggs, parents, distinguished faculty and staff of the XYZ School of Business, ladies and gentlemen. Welcome to the graduation of Class 2010."*

VIP/DV CODE 1

President of the United States, Commander in Chief

VIP/DV CODE 2 (FOUR-STAR EQUIVALENT)

Vice President of the United States
Secretary of Defense
Deputy Secretary of Defense
Secretary of the Army

Secretary of the Navy

Secretary of the Air Force

Secretary of Commerce (NOAA Corps)

Secretary of Health and Human Services (Commissioned Corps of the PHS)

Secretary of Homeland Security (Coast Guard)

Chairman, Joint Chiefs of Staff

Under Secretary of Defense for Acquisition (precedes Service Secretaries
only on Acquisition matters)

Under Secretary of Defense for Policy

Comptroller and Chief Financial Officer

Under Secretary of Defense for Personnel and Readiness

Retired Chairman of the Joint Chiefs of Staff

Vice Chairman of the Joint Chiefs of Staff

Chiefs of Services

Commanders in Chief of Unified and Specified Commands of the
four-star grade

Retired Vice Chairman of the Joint Chiefs of Staff

Retired Chiefs of Services

Retired Commanders in Chief of Unified and Specified Commands of the
four-star grade

Principal Deputy Under Secretary of Defense for Acquisition

VIP/DV CODE 3 (FOUR-STAR EQUIVALENT)

Principal Deputy Under Secretary of Defense for Policy

Director of Defense Research and Engineering

Assistant Secretaries of Defense, DOD General Counsel, DOD Inspector
General, and Director of Operational Test and Evaluation

Judges on Court of Military Appeals

Under Secretaries of the Army, Navy, and Air Force

Vice Chiefs of the Army and Air Force

Vice Chief of Naval Operations, Assistant Commandant of the Marine
Corps, and Vice Commandant of the Coast Guard

Assistant Secretaries and General Counsels of the Army, Navy, and Air Force

Five-Star Generals and Admirals

Generals and Admirals (four-star)

Retired Generals and Admirals (four-star)

Special Assistants to the Secretary of Defense

Special Assistants to the Deputy Secretary of Defense

Assistants to the Secretary of Defense

Director, OSD Administration and Management
Director, OSD Program Analysis and Evaluation

VIP/DV CODE 4 (THREE-STAR EQUIVALENT)

Directors of Defense Agencies

Deputy Under Secretaries of Defense (non-statutory), Deputy Directors of Defense Research and Engineering, Principal Deputy Assistant Secretaries of Defense, DOD Principal Deputy General Counsel, DOD Deputy Inspector General, DOD Principal Deputy Comptroller, and Director of Defense Procurement

Administrative Assistants of the Army, Navy, and Air Force

Lieutenant Generals and Vice Admirals (three-star)

Retired Lieutenant Generals and Vice Admirals (three-star)

Principal Deputy Assistant Secretaries and Principal Deputy General Counsels of the Army, Navy, and Air Force

Deputy Assistant Secretaries of Defense, DOD Deputy General Counsels, Secretary of Defense Representatives to International Negotiations, Deputy Comptrollers, and Assistant Inspectors General

Deputy Under Secretaries of the Army, Navy, and Air Force

Members of Secretary of Defense Boards

Senior Enlisted Advisers (Sergeant Major of the Army; Master Chief Petty Officer of the Navy; Chief Master Sergeant of the Air Force; Sergeant Major of the Marine Corps; and Master Chief Petty Officer of the Coast Guard)

Auditor Generals of the Army, Navy and Air Force

VIP/DV CODE 5 (TWO-STAR EQUIVALENT)

Major Generals and Rear Admirals of the Upper Half (two-star)

Deputy Assistant Secretaries and Deputy General Counsels of the Army, Navy, and Air Force

Retired Major Generals/Rear Admirals (Upper Half)

Surgeon General and Deputy Surgeon General

OSD Historian

VIP/DV CODE 6 (ONE-STAR EQUIVALENT)

Brigadier Generals and Rear Admirals of the Lower Half (one-star)

Assistant Surgeon General (Public Health Service)

Assistant Deputy Under Secretaries and Principal Directors

Retired Brigadier Generals and Rear Admirals (Lower Half)

Parade Formation Order of Precedence

The following is the order of precedence, as established by Department of Defense Directive 1005.8, for members of the armed forces when in formation and for flags displayed together:

1. Cadets, United States Military Academy
2. Midshipmen, United States Naval Academy
3. Cadets, United States Air Force Academy
4. Cadets, United States Coast Guard Academy
5. Midshipmen, United States Merchant Marine Academy
6. United States Army
7. United States Marine Corps
8. United States Navy
9. United States Air Force
10. United States Coast Guard
11. Army National Guard of the United States
12. Army Reserves
13. Marine Corps Reserve
14. Naval Reserve
15. Air National Guard of the United States
16. Air Force Reserve
17. Coast Guard Reserve
18. Other training organizations of the Army, Marine Corps, Navy, Air Force, and Coast Guard, in that order.

During any period when the Coast Guard operates as part of the Navy, the Cadets of the Coast Guard Academy, the United States Coast Guard, and the Coast Guard Reserve take precedence respectively after the Midshipmen of the Naval Academy, the United States Navy, and the Naval Reserve.

Flag Order of Precedence

See Chapter 7: Flag Etiquette

Seating Order of Precedence

See Chapter 23: Seating Plans

MILITARY RANK CHARTS

Regular active duty personnel outrank Guard and Reserve personnel on extended active duty of the same rank. Guard officers precede Reserve officers on extended active duty. Retired military officers retain their rank and take precedence with, but after, regular active duty Reserve and Guard personnel of the same rank. Guard and Reserve personnel not on extended active duty follow regular active duty personnel.

Regular active duty rank charts follow. Use the **Ranks** column for formal envelope correspondence—on a line by itself if necessary, followed by the full name on the second line. Always strive to spell out complete rank on formal place cards also, but if necessary, use the Abbreviation column.

The **Abbreviation** column is for everyday military business envelopes and lists, for example, SA *Vincent Patton, USCG* or *Col. Henry Arnold, USAF.*

Use the **Salutation (Dear)** column (and surname) for letters, invitation cards, and YASA cards, for example: *Dear Lieutenant Jones:* instead of First Lieutenant; or *Dear Sergeant Smith* instead of First Sergeant.

Use the **Address** column when speaking to someone directly, for example, *"Good morning, Seaman Burdette"* or *"Good morning, General Takacs."* For formal introductions, use full rank, for example, *Vice Admiral Moore* not *Admiral Moore.* For casual or family place cards, the full name or just the first name may be used.

Q: Is it true that when an officer has been selected for promotion I should use "Select" or "Promotable" or initials "S" or "P" after their printed names?

A: No. Like most things, new rank honorifics and insignia must wait on the fact to become official. Selectees are not placed above others in the same rank and grade. For example, a Brigadier General selectee is still a Colonel, even though she understandably wants others to know that she is on the list for the next difficult-to-attain rank. You may be thinking of the word "frock." For the good of the Service, a person is sometimes granted the title and all privileges and courtesies (such as seating precedence) of the next higher rank (except for the corresponding increase in pay, which always waits on the bureaucratic process). "Frocking" occurs when it is essential to the officer's maximum effectiveness; for instance he or she may need to command a staff of ranks as high as his current rank, or will be assigned to an international position normally occupied by the higher rank (see DOD Directive 1334.2).

Q: What is a "Lower Half" Admiral?

A: The Navy refers to both O-7s and O-8s as "Rear Admirals." Technically, the O-7 is a Rear Admiral (Lower Half) and the O-8 is a Rear Admiral (Upper Half). When writing or speaking of them, both are *"Rear Admiral,"* when speaking to them, say *"Admiral."*

NAVY

Pay Grade	Ranks	Abbreviations	Salutations (Dear Admiral:) and Introductions	Direct Address
O-10	Admiral	ADM	Admiral	Admiral
O-9	Vice Admiral	VADM	Admiral	Admiral
O-8	Rear Admiral (Upper Half)	RADM	Admiral	Admiral
O-7	Rear Admiral (Lower Half)	RDML	Admiral	Admiral
O-6	Captain	CAPT	Captain	Captain
O-5	Commander	CDR	Commander	Commander
O-4	Lieutenant Commander	LCDR	Commander	Commander
O-3	Lieutenant	LT	Lieutenant	Lieutenant
O-2	Lieutenant (Junior Grade)	LTJG	Lieutenant	Lieutenant
O-1	Ensign	ENS	Ensign	Ensign
W-5	Chief Warrant Officer	CWO5	Chief Warrant Officer	Warrants are usually addressed by their specialty; as in "Boatswain," "Gunner," etc.
W-4	Chief Warrant Officer	CWO4	Chief Warrant Officer	
W-3	Chief Warrant Officer	CWO3	Chief Warrant Officer	
W-2	Chief Warrant Officer	CWO2	Chief Warrant Officer	
W-1	Not Currently in use			

NAVY

Pay Grade	Ranks	Abbreviations	Salutations (Dear Admiral:) and Introductions	Direct Address
E-9	Master Chief Petty Officer of the Navy	MCPON	MCPON	MCPON (pronounced "mick-pon")
"	Fleet Master Chief Petty Officer	FLTCM	Fleet Master Chief	Fleet
"	Force Master Chief Petty Officer	FORCM	Force Master Chief	Force
"	CNO-Directed Command Master Chief Petty Officer	CNOCM	CNO-Directed Command Master Chief	Master Chief
"	Command Master Chief Petty Officer	CMDCM	Command Master Chief	Master Chief
"	Master Chief Petty Officer	MCPO*	Master Chief	Master Chief
E-8	Senior Chief Petty Officer	SCPO*	Senior Chief	Senior
E-7	Chief Petty Officer	CPO*	Chief	Chief
E-6	Petty Officer First Class	PO1*	Petty Officer	Petty Officer
E-5	Petty Officer Second Class	PO2*	Petty Officer	Petty Officer
E-4	Petty Officer Third Class	PO3*	Petty Officer	Petty Officer
E-3	Seaman (or Airman, Fireman, Constructionman, Hospitalman,)	SN (or AN, FN, CN, HN)	Seaman (or Airman, Fireman, Constructionman, Hospitalman,)	Seaman (or Airman, Fireman, Constructionman, Hospitalman,)
E-2	Seaman Apprentice (or Airman Apprentice, Fireman Apprentice, etc.)	SA (or AA, FA, CA, HA)	Seaman (or Airman, Fireman, Constructionman, Hospitalman,)	Seaman (or Airman, Fireman, Constructionman, Hospitalman,)
E-1	Seaman Recruit (or Airman Recruit, Fireman Recruit, etc.)	SR (or AR, FR, CR, HR)	Seaman (or Airman, Fireman, Constructionman, Hospitalman,)	Seaman (or Airman, Fireman, Constructionman, Hospitalman,)

* Rating abbreviations (e.g., BMC or QM2, etc.) are used more often than CPO, PO2, etc.

MARINE CORPS

Pay Grade	Ranks	Abbreviations	Salutations (Dear Major:) and Introductions	Direct Address
O-10	General	Gen	General	General
O-9	Lieutenant General	LtGen	General	General
O-8	Major General	MajGen	General	General
O-7	Brigadier General	BGen	General	General
O-6	Colonel	Col	Colonel	Colonel
O-5	Lieutenant Colonel	LtCol	Colonel	Colonel
O-4	Major	Maj	Major	Major
O-3	Captain	Capt	Captain	Captain
O-2	First Lieutenant	1stLt	Lieutenant	Lieutenant
O-1	Second Lieutenant	2ndLt	Lieutenant	Lieutenant
W-5	Chief Warrant Officer	CWO5	Chief Warrant Officer	Chief Warrant Officer (Gunner)
W-4	Chief Warrant Officer	CWO4	Chief Warrant Officer	Chief Warrant Officer (Gunner)
W-3	Chief Warrant Officer	CWO3	Chief Warrant Officer	Chief Warrant Officer (Gunner)
W-2	Chief Warrant Officer	CWO2	Chief Warrant Officer	Chief Warrant Officer (Gunner)
W-1	Warrant Officer	WO	Warrant Officer	Warrant Officer (Gunner)

MARINE CORPS

Pay Grade	Ranks	Abbreviations	Salutations (Dear Major:) and Introductions	Direct Address
E-9	Sergeant Major of the Marine Corps	SgtMaj	Sergeant Major	Sergeant Major
"	Sergeant Major	SgtMaj	Sergeant Major	Sergeant Major
"	Master Gunnery Sergeant	MGySgt	Master Gunnery Sergeant	Master Gunnery Sergeant (Master Guns)
E-8	Master Sergeant	MSgt	Master Sergeant	Master Sergeant (Top)
"	First Sergeant	1stSgt	First Sergeant	First Sergeant
E-7	Gunnery Sergeant	GySgt	Gunnery Sergeant	Gunnery Sergeant (Gunny)
E-6	Staff Sergeant	SSgt	Staff Sergeant	Staff Sergeant
E-5	Sergeant	Sgt	Sergeant	Sergeant
E-4	Corporal	Cpl	Corporal	Corporal
E-3	Lance Corporal	LCpl	Lance Corporal	Lance Corporal
E-2	Private First Class	PFC	Private First Class	Private First Class (PFC)
E-1	Private	Pvt	Private	Private

Note: Addresses in parentheses are used informally.

COAST GUARD

Pay Grade	Ranks (and Rates)	Abbreviations	Salutations (Dear Ensign:) and Introductions	Direct Address
O-10	Admiral	ADM	Admiral	Admiral
O-9	Vice Admiral	VADM	Admiral	Admiral
O-8	Rear Admiral (Upper Half)	RADM	Admiral	Admiral
O-7	Rear Admiral (Lower Half)	RDML	Admiral	Admiral
O-6	Captain	CAPT	Captain	Captain
O-5	Commander	CDR	Commander	Commander
O-4	Lieutenant Commander	LCDR	Commander	Commander
O-3	Lieutenant	LT	Lieutenant	Lieutenant
O-2	Lieutenant (Junior Grade)	LTJG	Lieutenant	Lieutenant
O-1	Ensign	ENS	Ensign	Ensign
W-4	Chief Warrant Officer	CWO4	Chief Warrant Officer	Warrants are usually addressed by their specialty; as in "Boatswain," "Gunner," etc.
W-3	Chief Warrant Officer	CWO3	Chief Warrant Officer	
W-2	Chief Warrant Officer	CWO2	Chief Warrant Officer	
W-1	Warrant Officer	Not currently in use		

COAST GUARD

Pay Grade	Ranks (and Rates)	Abbreviations	Salutations (Dear Ensign:) and Introductions	Direct Address
E-9	Master Chief Petty Officer of the Coast Guard	MCPOCG	MCPOCGN	MCPOCG (pronounced "mick-pog")
"	Area Command Master Chief Petty Officer	CMC	Master Chief	Master Chief
"	Command Master Chief Petty Officer	CMC	Master Chief	Master Chief
"	Master Chief Petty Officer	MCPO*	Master Chief	Master Chief
E-8	Command Senior Chief Petty Officer	CSC	Master Chief	Master Chief
"	Senior Chief Petty Officer	SCPO*	Senior Chief	Senior
E-7	Command Chief Petty Officer	CC	Chief	Chief
"	Chief Petty Officer	CPO*	Chief	Chief
E-6	Petty Officer First Class	PO1*	Petty Officer	Petty Officer
E-5	Petty Officer Second Class	PO2*	Petty Officer	Petty Officer
E-4	Petty Officer Third Class	PO3*	Petty Officer	Petty Officer
E-3	Seaman (or Airman or Fireman)	SN (or AN or FN)	Seaman (or Airman or Fireman)	Seaman (or Airman or Fireman)
E-2	Seaman Apprentice (or Airman Apprentice or Fireman Apprentice)	SA (or AA or FA)	Seaman (or Airman or Fireman)	Seaman (or Airman or Fireman)
E-1	Seaman Recruit (or Airman Recruit, Fireman Recruit, etc.)	SR (AR or FR)	Seaman (or Airman or Fireman)	Seaman (or Airman or Fireman)

* Rating abbreviations, such as BMC or QM2, etc., are used more often than CPO, PO2, etc.

ARMY

Pay Grade	Ranks	Abbreviations	Salutations (Dear Sergeant:) and Introductions	Direct Address
O-11	General of the Army	GEN	Not currently in use	
O-10	General	GEN	General	General
O-9	Lieutenant General	LTG	General	General
O-8	Major General	MG	General	General
O-7	Brigadier General	BG	General	General
O-6	Colonel	COL	Colonel	Colonel
O-5	Lieutenant Colonel	LTC	Colonel	Colonel
O-4	Major	MAJ	Major	Major
O-3	Captain	CPT	Captain	Captain
O-2	First Lieutenant	1LT	Lieutenant	Lieutenant
O-1	Second Lieutenant	2LT	Lieutenant	Lieutenant
W-5	Chief Warrant Officer	CW5	Chief Warrant Officer	Mister
W-4	Chief Warrant Officer	CW4	Chief Warrant Officer	Mister
W-3	Chief Warrant Officer	CW3	Chief Warrant Officer	Mister
W-2	Chief Warrant Officer	CW2	Chief Warrant Officer	Mister
W-1	Warrant Officer	WO1	Warrant Officer	Mister

ARMY

Pay Grade	Ranks	Abbreviations	Salutations (Dear Sergeant:) and Introductions	Direct Address
E-9	Sergeant Major of the Army	SMA	Sergeant Major	Sergeant Major
"	Command Sergeant Major	CSM	Sergeant Major	Sergeant Major
"	Sergeant Major	SGM	Sergeant Major	Sergeant Major
E-8	Master Sergeant	MSG	Master Sergeant	Master Sergeant
"	First Sergeant	1SG	First Sergeant	First Sergeant
E-7	Platoon Sergeant	PSG	Sergeant	Sergeant
"	Sergeant First Class	SFC	Sergeant	Sergeant
E-6	Staff Sergeant	SSG	Sergeant	Sergeant
E-5	Sergeant	SGT	Sergeant	Sergeant
E-4	Corporal	CPL	Corporal	Corporal
"	Specialist	SP4	Specialist	Specialist
E-3	Private First Class	PFC	Private	Private
E-2	Private Second Class	PV2	Private	Private
E-1	Private	PVT	Private	Private

AIR FORCE

Pay Grade	Ranks	Abbreviations	Salutations (Dear Airman:) and Introductions	Direct Address
O-11	General of the Air Force	Not currently in use		
O-10	General	Gen	General	General
O-9	Lieutenant General	Lt Gen	General	General
O-8	Major General	Maj Gen	General	General
O-7	Brigadier General	Brig Gen	General	General
O-6	Colonel	Col	Colonel	Colonel
O-5	Lieutenant Colonel	Lt Col	Colonel	Colonel
O-4	Major	Maj	Major	Major
O-3	Captain	Capt	Captain	Captain
O-2	First Lieutenant	1st Lt	Lieutenant	Lieutenant
O-1	Second Lieutenant	2d Lt	Lieutenant	Lieutenant

There are no warrants in the Air Force

Pay Grade	Ranks	Abbreviations	Salutations (Dear Airman:) and Introductions	Direct Address
E-9	Chief Master Sergeant of the Air Force	CMSAF	Chief Master Sergeant of the Air Force	Chief
"	Chief Master Sergeant	CMSgt	Chief Master Sergeant	Chief
E-8	Senior Master Sergeant	SMSgt	Senior Master Sergeant	Sergeant
E-7	Master Sergeant	MSgt	Master Sergeant	Sergeant

AIR FORCE

Pay Grade	Ranks	Abbreviations	Salutations (Dear Airman:) and Introductions	Direct Address
E-6	Technical Sergeant	TSgt	Technical Sergeant	Sergeant
E-5	Staff Sergeant	SSgt	Staff Sergeant	Sergeant
E-4	Senior Airman	SrA	Senior Airman	Airman
E-3	Airman First Class	A1C	Airman First Class	Airman
E-2	Airman	Amn	Airman	Airman
E-1	Airman Basic	AB	Airman Basic	Airman

Section 2

MILITARY WEDDINGS

CHAPTER 9

Military Wedding Etiquette

At least one of the bridal couple must be an active or retired member of a U.S. Service in order to incorporate military traditions into their wedding. Many books and magazines are devoted exclusively to weddings, for instance *Emily Post's Wedding Etiquette, Fifth Edition* and *Emily Post's Wedding Planner, Fourth Edition*, both by Peggy Post. The following pages focus only on the important military protocol and etiquette aspects of your special event, whether held at a military location or in a civilian setting.

AT EASE KEY POINTS

Military weddings are unique:

- ⚘ Ranks are included on invitations.
- ⚘ Dress uniforms lend dignity.
- ⚘ Military venue and VIPs require security measures.
- ⚘ A sword arch or honor cordon salutes the newlyweds.
- ⚘ A saber may be used to cut the wedding cake.

UNIQUE ELEMENTS OF MILITARY WEDDINGS

A military wedding is like other weddings; the ceremony is not a military ceremony but a religious one. However, various elements make the day unique because the bride, groom, or both are serving their country in uniform. The wedding may be held on an armed forces facility with entry security requirements, such as a military chapel, club, or museum. The bride and groom may have an arch of swords or honor cordon. Their cake-cutting ceremony may be performed with a dress uniform sword or saber. Finally, Distinguished Visitors (DVs) or Very Important

Persons (VIPs) in the government may attend their festivities, necessitating coordination with protocol and security offices.

Civilian guests will probably be intrigued with the pageantry of life in your Service, so consider incorporating a few theme possibilities. Wedding cake figurines in military uniforms and Service-themed centerpieces are available. The groom's cake could be decorated with his Service seal, or in camouflage, or designed in an appropriate shape (e.g., an anchor for the Navy). Military backdrops such as a flag array, beautiful monuments, or impressive base, station, or post entry gates can give a sense of place to enhance wedding pictures. If the couple have served or are serving in exotic locations, those assignments might suggest wedding décor, particularly flowers and food choices. At the reception along with dance music, the applicable Service song, a march, or regimental music could be incorporated. The U.S. and appropriate Service flags may be centered behind a receiving line.

None of these elements is mandatory—not all military members prefer to have a military wedding—but including even some aspects can be a wonderful way to demonstrate pride in your chosen career. You have an opportunity to impress guests with your patriotism and to enhance the reputation or public image of the uniformed Services at the same time. Everyone can be a civilian, but not everyone can serve his or her country in uniform.

FORMALITY AND SCHEDULING CONSIDERATIONS

Your first decision will be what type of wedding will suit your personality and lifestyle: large or small, formal or informal, day or evening. Compare your desires to the size of your budget, and whether or not parents are contributing. The couple should give every consideration to the suggestions of their parents and others taking part, however, the decisions are primarily theirs. A great deal of sensitive discussion may be needed to determine how much planning each parent wants to do (or can accomplish long-distance) and how many decisions will be relegated to them. Family traditions are just as important as military customs, however, a military wedding of necessity must be scheduled "at the convenience of the Service" during leave or when a change of orders gives the couple an opportunity to travel to a new duty station in conjunction with their honeymoon. If orders are changed, the wedding may be affected. Many military members receive short notice of an unscheduled deployment. If a large formal wedding is a family tradition, or substantial financial deposits are required months in advance, the couple would be wise to consider purchasing wedding insurance.

The second decision will be the date and location for the wedding, which can be made as soon as the military leave is approved or the arrival date at the new assignment is determined via orders. Weddings are important enough occasions to warrant contacting people on your wedding list to ask them to "save the date" if their presence is desired. This may be done by e-mail or telephone call for informal weddings, or by letter or printed message for more formal events.

If vows will be exchanged at a military location, get in touch with the venue immediately to find out their applicable policies and directives. Also, contact your favorite minister, rabbi, priest, imam, or civil celebrant (Justice of the Peace) as soon as you can to start coordinating their counsel and availability.

MILITARY CLERGY

Clergy can advise the couple about such local legal requirements as blood tests, obtaining the marriage license, and signing the Marriage Register. Although military chaplains officiate at ceremonies held in the chapel to which they are assigned, a celebrant of the couple's choosing may assist at the military chapel if this is acceptable to the chaplain and is arranged beforehand. The military chaplain, like any clergy, is bound by ordination vows to uphold the laws and regulations of a particular denomination regarding marriage. Service chaplains are of many faiths, and as commissioned officers, they are subject to transfer. Therefore, what was customary in a chapel last year may not be valid this year.

Chaplains on active duty are paid by the Service they represent, but a donation to the chapel religious offering fund is essential. Any assisting civilian clergyman may require an honorarium. The bridegroom contacts all clergy concerned to determine donation amounts and clergy honorariums, which he pays. Before the ceremony, the best man hands fees to the individuals (in a sealed envelope with a brief note from the groom). Remember that donation checks are written out to a house of worship; fees are written directly to clergy by name. When a wedding is held in a private home the rules are similar, except if the officiating person is a high-ranking friend of the family's, such as a judge or a mayor, consider sending a nice gift later instead of a fee with your note of thanks.

INVITATIONS

See Chapter 10: Military Wedding Invitations.

Dress Equivalents

At a military wedding, the formality of the event determines the uniform worn, as do seasonal military regulations. Military attendants who wear uniforms must match the uniform choice of the bride or groom. Civilian attendants also conform to the level of formality chosen, for instance, if the bride or groom wears *Evening Dress "B"* (Marine Corps) or *Blue Evening* (Army) a civilian wears the equivalent *Formal* (Black Tie or tuxedo). If, however, the bride or groom wears *Service Dress Blue* (Navy), the civilian equivalent is *Informal* (dark, conservative business suit with tie). See Chapter 22: Appropriate Attire for more equivalents listings.

Dress information is not normally printed on a formal wedding invitation; guests judge what to wear by the time of day and location of your ceremony. Morning and early afternoon weddings usually require *Informal* but an evening wedding may require *Formal* attire for guests. Some active duty or retired military guests may wish to wear their uniforms. The engaged couple's parents, the bride, and the groom must all be prepared to answer questions regarding appropriate guest attire.

Depending on the Service and uniform choice, the bride or groom may think to wear his or her dress sword or saber. This is not advisable. Traditionally, weapons are banned inside a religious sanctuary as they are considered discordant at the very least. A sword should not be worn between the couple either, as it symbolizes division; to keep the groom's blade to the outside affects the side that the bride stands on, which in turn affects where attendants and guests are situated. Traditionally, a bride stands to the groom's left while being married, so that she is on the honored right side when they turn and face the congregation after the ceremony. Finally, all sword (or saber) bearers must also wear white gloves as part of the uniform; that will make it difficult for the bride, groom, and best man to handle the ring or rings. Ushers (greeters and escorts), who may also be serving in the arch or honor cordon, may wear white gloves throughout the ceremony without swords, but not swords without gloves.

Military Bride Dress Options

An armed forces bride, her Service attendants, or a military mother may wear uniforms, but many military brides prefer a wedding gown for this religious ceremony, and having any Service bridesmaids in dresses. Military mothers usually also select civilian clothing. If a bride chooses to wear her uniform, she may still carry a bridal bouquet or prayer book with flowers. But remember, boutonnieres and corsages are for civilian clothes; only military decorations are authorized for uniforms, never flowers. The bridegroom dresses in accordance with the type of gown or uniform his bride will be wearing.

The Rehearsal

Rehearsals are for the express purpose of emphasizing to key players that the wedding will place an emphasis on their conduct. The wedding party should be doubly conscious of being socially correct and gracious because all eyes will be upon them. Practicing the performance helps participants gain confidence in their personal demeanor and starring roles. Be sure to have ushers practice greeting and escorting any invited VIPs/DVs to their seats. Although not necessary during the rehearsal itself, the bride and groom must practice wielding the sword together for the cake-cutting ceremony, and they must see to it that the arch or honor cordon participants also train if these ceremonies will be part of their military wedding.

The bridegroom's family traditionally hosts the rehearsal dinner. This meal can be casual or formal, luncheon or dinner, whatever is appropriate following the rehearsal. The father of the bridegroom may propose a toast to the couple (see Toasts below).

Wedding Party Arrival and Departure Logistics

Some military locations allow horse-drawn carriages for a bride's arrival at the chapel and for the departure of a newly married couple. Commercial limousines are often hired for wedding parties. Privately owned automobiles decorated with "Just Married" signs are quite popular. Regardless of the conveyance chosen, you must provide information to the security office or front gate for access by all drivers and passengers without military access.

Coordinate early, request written confirmation of access and the names of security personnel you speak with, keep lists of the security information provided, and be sure to double-check the day before the wedding.

Distinguished Visitors (DVs)/ Very Important Persons (VIPs)

High-ranking government or military officials may be attending your military wedding. If so, there will be special greeting and seating requirements, and perhaps security issues for you to consider. Many eyes watch VIPs; they should never be placed in an awkward situation. Discuss requirements for high-ranking individuals with their aides, and be aware of the following:

1. High-ranking officials may have a bodyguard or Secret Service person accompanying him or her, which could affect your seating plans. Traditionally,

VIPs/DVs are given seats within the reserved area directly behind the immediate families at the wedding service, and at parents' tables as guests of honor for meals. They may require line of sight with bodyguards and their backs to a wall.

2. A commanding officer may indicate a desire to propose a toast in your honor at a dinner (or reception) and will require a detailed agenda of events focusing on the correct sequence for prayers, toasts, and so on. Even though you will brief everyone ahead of time, it is wise to print a card with this information to be placed beside every DV's plate, your plate, and the place settings of other key persons, including bodyguards.

3. A person in the public domain may attract the attention of the media. Reporters can be denied entry and "kept outside the gates" on a military installation, but coordinate the VIP entry and exit so that it will not conflict with the focus on your own arrival and departure. Every military installation has a Public Affairs Office (PAO) for help dealing with the media.

4. VIPs often request information regarding other invited guests. Be prepared to provide detailed information on where a VIP will be seated during the wedding and at dinner, the names of any seatmates, and their relationship to the bridal couple. For everyone's peace of mind when important guests are attending, use place cards at seated meals and print pew cards for them.

Enclose pew cards in invitations to close family members and friends who are sure to attend and send to other guests, such as VIPs, after their acceptance. Cards are handed to ushers, "Mr. and Mrs. Daniel Connolly, Pew #2." At the very least, brief ushers on your chapel seating plan and inform VIPs of their reserved seats behind or beside immediate family members.

WEDDINGS AT SERVICE ACADEMY CHAPELS

So many young couples wish to marry following graduation from the Service academies that their chapels are used here for discussing military weddings. The points raised may easily be adapted to weddings on military installations elsewhere.

Obtain permission for academy chapel use from the chaplain's office as soon as possible in order to secure the desired date and hour for your wedding. Although there is no formal charge at the time of the reservation, a donation may be expected just before the wedding. When a donation is made by check, it is *not* written to the officiating chaplain, but to a chapel's "Offering" or "General" fund. Most Service academies have more than one chapel. At the Air Force Academy

Cadet Chapel, for example, there are Protestant, Catholic, and Jewish chapels located on two separate levels, each having its own entrance. Services can be held simultaneously without interfering with one another.

Rice, confetti, and birdseed are prohibited inside or outside academy chapels. Wedding receptions are never held in the chapels and no arrangements for them are made by chapel staff. Each chapel has its own regulations concerning photographers and videographers. Rooms for last-minute preparation are available for the bride and groom and their attendants, but there are no dressing rooms for either group.

Academy Chapel Music

Wedding ceremonies are religious ceremonies. The music varies: traditional hymns or contemporary popular music, depending on the policies of the military venues. Organists play wedding music from the library of sacred music available in that chapel.

The couple selects their music after consultation with the music director. It is customary but by no means obligatory for the bridal chorus from Wagner's *Lohengrin* and the wedding march from Mendelssohn's *Midsummer Night's Dream* to be played for the processional and recessional. Less traditional music may be played, but the organist or music director must approve variations beforehand. No matter how modern the couple may be, some contemporary music is unsuitable for what should be a dignified occasion.

The organist and soloist may charge flat fees, or fees may be broken down for the rehearsal and the wedding. It is not necessary for them to attend the wedding rehearsal. The maid or matron of honor may give their fees to them in a sealed envelope with a brief thank you note from the bride at the house of worship prior to the wedding. The bride's family or the person in charge of the wedding expenses pays music fees.

Academy Chapel Flowers and Decorations

These elements are considered important enhancements to the exchange of vows. Rules for decorating military chapels vary throughout the nation, with most having a policy of only one to two flower arrangements at the altar. You may transport the altar flowers to your reception location, but be sure to plan who will do this task and arrange with them ahead of time. If you plan to give your flowers away, coordinate the desire with the chapel or reception site. They may have a suggestion for who could most benefit or enjoy them, perhaps the military base hospital or post school.

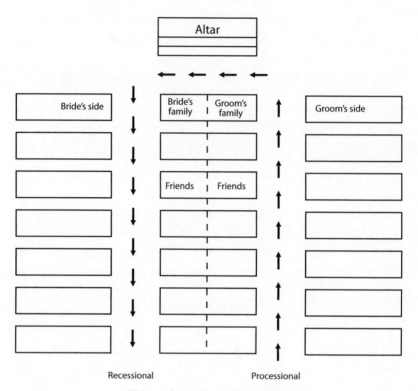

House of worship with two aisles

Academy Chapel Reserved Pews

Some chapels and places of worship do not have a single central aisle, but have two aisles. You may select one aisle and plan the wedding as though that were the only one, or you may use one aisle for the processional and the other aisle for the recessional. The bride's family is traditionally seated in reserved front pews on the left side of a center aisle (or on the left half of a center section) as you face the altar. The bridegroom's family is seated in reserved front pews on the right side of a center aisle (or on the right half of a center section). If the parents are divorced and remarried, mothers sit in the front rows of the proper side with their families and fathers sit in the second rows with their families. At very large weddings, friends of the bride sit at the far left, the groom's friends at the far right, as well as behind the families in the center section. Reserved pews are frequently the only ones decorated, perhaps with bows, or ribbons with a single flower and greenery, or sprays of flowers at the aisle ends.

Protocol rankings on this day belong primarily to the bridal party, their parents and family members. However, the commanding officer(s) of the bride and groom and their spouse(s) are often invited to sit in a reserved front pew if the parents are unable to attend. When the parents are in attendance, commanding officers may instead be seated behind the immediate families within the reserved areas along with any invited flag rank officers and official DVs/VIPs, but guests with military ranks are otherwise not accommodated at wedding ceremonies. Guests who arrive first are given the choice aisle seats; later arrivals take the inner seats, no matter their military or government ranks.

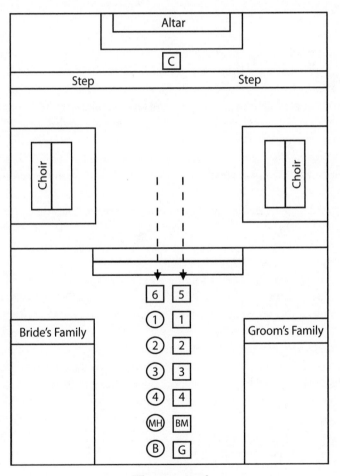

The recessional

Eligibility to Reserve Academy Chapel

Those eligible to be married in any of the Service academy chapels are graduates (active or retired), or one of the following: a dependent; military members (officer or enlisted) assigned to the academy complex, or his or her dependents; a faculty or staff member (active or retired) or his or her dependents who regularly attend that chapel's services.

THE ARCH OF SWORDS OR HONOR GUARD CORDON

The arch of swords (Coast Guard, Marine Corps, and Navy) or arch of sabers (Air Force and Army) or honor guard cordon (without swords or sabers) is one of the most colorful and photographed features of a military wedding. The tradition is an elegant symbol of the newlywed couple's journey together into military life.

Only military personnel in dress uniform, including gloves, participate in the arch of swords (or sabers). Six personnel usually perform the ceremony (three on each side), although more or fewer may take part. These servicemen or servicewomen can be bridal party attendants, family members, ushers, personnel "borrowed" from a nearby installation, active duty, retired, one or more Service branches, or any combination. The military member being married selects participants for this ritual and appoints an officer in charge to rehearse them. Arch participants who are also wedding attendants do not need complementary counterparts, for instance, the number of civilian dress bridesmaids need not correspond to the number of military groomsmen/ushers, especially if more of the latter are needed for the arch.

Military swords (sabers) are usually borrowed for the purpose of the arch. Swords may be signed out from a military chaplain, a local color guard or drill team, a military museum, or perhaps an ROTC unit. Active duty enlisted personnel and non-commissioned officers (NCOs) may need to obtain a waiver from the bridal couple's command before signing out swords. Reserve and National Guard personnel follow the same regulations as their Service (i.e., *Army* National Guard, *Air* National Guard, *Naval* Reserve). If swords cannot be obtained, uniformed personnel can still form an honor guard cordon and render courtesy hand salutes to the newlyweds. An honor cordon is also in Service dress uniform, with gloves.

There are two locations or times an arch ceremony (or honor cordon) may be formed: immediately following wedding on the walkway as the couple departs, or at the reception before the cake-cutting ceremony (optional).

(Edward Buxton, Buxton Photography)

Q: We want the old-fashioned country church bells to be rung after our wedding ceremony as we are passing under the sword arch. What do you think?

A: With advance clergy or celebrant permission and coordination, this would be a
charming blend of military and religious tradition.

Q: At my summer military wedding what should the one civilian groomsman (my
brother) wear? The military will be in Service Dress Whites. Can he be in the
sword arch?

A: Your uniform's civilian equivalent is a conservative business suit and tie. Your brother
can wear a boutonniere in bridal colors. Civilians cannot carry military weapons. Only
personnel in dress uniform with gloves are authorized to participate in an arch of
swords (or sabers).

Formation outside a Religious Sanctuary

Invited guests wait for direction following the vows. The newlyweds are the first
to leave the chancel, with the bride on the right arm of the groom. The maid or
matron of honor and the best man walk out together immediately afterward, followed by the bridesmaids and groomsmen. Additional ushers (numbers 5 and 6
in Illustration, The recessional) then escort the bride's mother first, the groom's
mother next, followed by the fathers and chaplain, all in a continuous recessional.
Usually guests depart as seated, from front to rear.

The newlyweds go immediately to an anteroom or any secluded area after
reaching the narthex or foyer and await notification that the arch is ready. As
parents depart, an usher clearly and courteously makes the following request of
the guests: "*Please assemble on the walkway outside to observe the arch of swords* [or
honor guard cordon]." Another attendant will be reserving space immediately
outside the sanctuary doors for the arch formation, as needed, by directing guests
farther along. Civilian ushers and bridesmaids may flank both sides of the outer
sanctuary doors and either step back unobtrusively to allow the arch or honor cordon center stage, or they form an adjunct leading to the honor corridor. Civilian
attendants stand at attention if they are nearby when military participants are
called to order—they may be in the background of pictures.

Honor guard swords (sabers) are left in a convenient side room until after
a religious ceremony when service members collect them in preparation for
the arch. Arch or honor cordon participants face each other in equal numbers.
Customarily, six or eight uniformed service members perform the ceremony.

Introduction of Newly Married Couple

When the honor guard is in position, the best man notifies the bride and groom that the observance can proceed. The officer in charge is normally positioned on the left side (the couples' right as they exit) closest to the sanctuary doors. The newlyweds pause at the first uniformed pair and the clergy or best man introduces them properly, "*Ladies and gentlemen,*

[Rank and Mrs. Joint Last Name] *for military male and female civilian*; or

[Mr. Last Name and Rank & Bride's Last Name] *for military female and male civilian*; or

[Rank Last Name] and [Rank Last Name] *if both are military.*"

The officer in charge of the arch then commands, "*Draw swords* [or *bridge swords* or *arch sabers*]" according to his particular Service drill manual. Each arch participant moves in one continuous motion (saber bearers rotate the right arm clockwise so that the cutting edge is on top), and points the tip at fully extended right arm's length upwards and toward the facing partner's. The arch must be wide enough for newlyweds to pass comfortably underneath. The newlyweds, *and only they may do so*, walk under the arch—moving slowly to accommodate picture taking—and pause at the end.

Conclusion of Sword Arch Ceremony

The last two service members cross their weapons in front of the newlyweds just below waist level to halt them for another (optional) tradition, the *Welcome Swat*, considered good luck and a symbolic pledge of loyalty to the couple from their new military family. This step is omitted if both bride and groom are in the military. The honor guard nearest the civilian half of the couple may gently "swat" the behind of the previously nonmilitary newlywed with the sword and say, "*Welcome to the Marine Corps* [or appropriate branch]." The bride and groom may kiss before exiting. The newlyweds turn together to watch the honor guard conclude.

After the bride and groom pass under the arch the officer in charge commands, "*Return swords* [or *carry sabers*]." Sword bearers return swords to scabbards until only three or four inches (7.62–10.16 centimeters) of their length remain; the final length to travel is completed in unison with a single click. Bearers may receive a command to face away from the chapel or house of worship and toward the newlyweds. The military groom or military bride (if in uniform) salutes the honor guard performance in thanks.

When swords are returned to scabbards and salutes completed, the ceremony is finished. Bridal attendants may lead the applause and bubble blowing (or butterfly release or flower petal throwing, if permitted) as the newlyweds enter the vehicle that will take them to the reception.

Wedding Receptions

A wedding reception may be held in any preferred location—a home or garden, a military NCO club, a hotel, or a meeting room in a house of worship. A "reception" is designed to be rather more formal than a simple party in order to honor a specific occasion or persons (such as newlyweds). Receptions normally last for two or more hours and the time frame is given on the invitation (for instance four to six o'clock). "Reception" means "receiving line": guests formally greet the honored people (the newlyweds and their parents for weddings). Military wedding receiving lines often incorporate the U.S., Service, and unit flags behind them, creating another distinctive feature.

Q: Our wedding will be followed by a seated dinner. Can we socialize when hors d'oeuvres are passed beforehand? If so, how are we officially announced at dinner? There will be no receiving line. Also, do we use Christian names and what about titles on place cards?

A: Drinks and appetizers occupy guests while newlyweds have pictures taken. Upon your arrival the event immediately proceeds. Socialize very briefly if desired, but do not eat or drink as dining room doors will open quickly; all guests take their seats before the wedding party enters. The announcer gives status and names ("Father of the bride, Mr. John Doe," etc.) as each pauses at the door before entering. The newlyweds enter last and together. A segment of the wedding march may herald your walk to the table. Seat the bride correctly as all eyes will be on you. Place cards may be formal with honorifics or ranks and surnames, or informal with first and last names, but be consistent throughout. VIPs may be identified by position only, as in *Governor of Ohio*.

Receiving Line or Announcer?

Instead of a receiving line, some couples prefer that a Master of Ceremonies (MC) or Disk Jockey (DJ) announce them to the assembled guests (*"For the first time anywhere, please welcome . . ."*) as they make a fashionably late arrival at the beginning of the reception or seated dinner. The announced newlyweds must then make every effort to circulate or visit all tables to speak to each guest. Far better and easier on the couple is a receiving line to ensure that all guests have a personal moment to congratulate them, after which everyone sits down.

The one who gives the reception is considered the host and welcomes guests first in a receiving line. The mother of the bride, for instance, might stand just inside the door of the reception room with the groom's mother next to her. (The fathers of the bride and groom may stand with the mothers for a brief time, but usually they stand a few steps off the end of the line to mix with and direct the guests.) The bride's mother greets arriving guests and introduces them to the groom's mother; then each guest moves on to greet the maid (or matron) of honor and perhaps a couple of bridesmaids. The bride and groom are next, always beside each other with *the bride always on the groom's right*. Next in order are any remaining bridesmaids. (All bridal attendants may be positioned after the newlyweds, if desired, but placing some before the couple creates a space so that mothers can speak to guests without distraction.) If a flower girl stands in the line for a while (she usually is age seven or younger), she is on the groom's left. Since she is very young, she need not be in the line at all, or only for a short time. When sisters are bridesmaids, the older sister precedes the younger. The line remains intact until all guests have been greeted, after which the receivers sit down. The best man and ushers *never* stand in the receiving line. The best man stays near the groom, however, ready to help in any way, while the ushers act as unofficial hosts. (See Chapter 18: Official Business Functions, Cocktails, and Receptions, for Receiving Lines illustrations.)

Guests approaching a receiving line wait for the host to extend a hand before introducing themselves by saying something like, *"I'm John Smith, Mrs. Jones. Such a lovely wedding."* Guests do not linger, even it they are longtime friends. When greeting the newly married couple, offer *best wishes* to the bride and *congratulations* to the groom.

Food and Beverage

Receptions always extend hospitality to guests with food and drink. The fare may feature favorite family heritage foods and beverages or the local cuisine of the couple's first military assignment together. Only a small number of bistro tables and some chairs are provided for stand-up affairs, as the point is to mingle while you munch. Stand-up affairs may have finger food passed on trays or displayed in stations around the room. Full buffet meals need chairs at tables for every guest to sit down at the same time. Also, remember that you will need tables for last-minute wedding gifts, for uniform hats, and for the guest book. Open seating for casual buffets is acceptable, but remember to reserve seats for the bridal party and the parents. More appropriate for weddings is carefully developing a full seating arrangement.

Q: We're doing two receptions, a 1:00 PM dessert reception for all guests after the
     wedding and a private dinner for family and out of town guests at 6:00 PM. There
     will be a different wedding cake at each reception. Do we cut both with a sword?
     When should we do the receiving line, throw the bouquet, and make toasts?

A: Form the receiving line at the first reception so that all guests may shake hands and
     congratulate you. A buffet tea with a wedding cake at the center of the table would
     conveniently permit nonalcoholic beverages and at least one non-sweet (cheese, fruit,
     tea sandwich). Cutting the cake with a sword is part of what makes a "military" wed-
     ding and we recommend that you do so for both cakes, unless you will change out
     of uniform for the private dinner. Toasts are appropriate at both receptions, as long
     as they are not duplicates. Throwing the bouquet is more suitable during the dessert
     reception.

Head Tables

The bridal pair sits beside each other at the center of a head table with the female
to the right of the male, together with all wedding attendants, minus young flower
girls and ring bearers. Consider seating only an even number of people (so all have
a conversation partner), alternating male and female, and chivalrously anchoring
the ends with males.

Seating Arrangements

If there is no head table the newly married couple and attendants still sit together
at one table, with their parents at another. If all parents are at the same long table,
the bride's mother is placed as hostess and the bridegroom's father is on her right
as the ranking male guest. At the other end (or on the opposite side) of the long
table the bride's father sits with the groom's mother on his right in the place of
honor. The priest, minister, or rabbi (and any clergy spouse), plus other close
relatives and VIPs round out the parents' table. Alternatively, parents can split
by family unit: the groom's family at one table and the bride's family at another.
Separate tables are particularly helpful when there are multiple sets of parents. A
combination of square, rectangle, and round tables can be advantageous and create more visual interest in a room. If there are uniformed guests, try to seat them at
different tables so that many civilian guests enjoy their company and perhaps the
novelty of being with someone in the military. Seating charts are posted for large
affairs, and place cards are used.

Q: We will not have drinks at our wedding as our minister and some family members prefer no alcohol. We will have water and iced tea at dinner, but we want toasts. Is champagne the only correct beverage for toasts?

A: No. Sparkling juice in champagne flutes is also festive. If you do not want an additional beverage service, serve the iced tea in stemmed glasses and use that for toasting.

Q: We know that toasting can sometimes get out of hand, and only want our best man and maid of honor to toast us. Is this acceptable? We really don't want anyone to just say whatever they want.

A: Celebratory toasts can be made to the bride and groom by anyone, including the couple's parents or a superior officer. We gather that would be fine; you are really only worried about high spirits among your friends. A printed program listing official toast order may limit other toasts, as may a videographer working the room, asking guests at each table to say a few words . . . that you can edit later, as desired.

TOASTS

The bridal couple accepts all toasts in their honor by smiling and remaining seated even if others rise. They do not drink to themselves. Toasts at an *engagement party* traditionally begin with the father of the engaged woman proposing a toast to his daughter, saying words to this effect, *"To my daughter, Melissa, and my future son-in-law, Paul Leighton. Let's drink to their happiness."* In the same way as the engagement party, the father of the engaged man opens toasting at the *rehearsal dinner* by calling for attention and raising his glass, saying words such as, *"I would like you to join me in welcoming a new member to our family. To Paul's fiancée, Melissa Sloan."*

Most toasts to the couple normally occur at their *wedding reception*, when toasters in the bridal party will rise one at a time in a predetermined order (perhaps printed in a program agenda, even if only for the bridal party and parents). The best man's toast is first. Toasters raise glasses by the stem in the right hand and formally introduce themselves by full name (not honorific; see Chapter 19: Introductions, Conversations, and Farewells) and role at the wedding before delivering a *very brief* toast, for example, the best man might say: *"I am William Smith, Paul's best man. Please join me in a toast to the bride and groom. Melissa and Paul, congratulations and best wishes."* A slightly longer toast might be, *"Good afternoon, ladies and gentlemen. I am Sandy Eaton, maid of honor. Please join me in a toast to my best friend and her new husband. To Melissa and Paul: may you laugh every week, celebrate every month, and reminisce each year on your anniversary."* When the bridegroom makes a toast to his bride he might say, *"I want you to join me in this toast to Melissa, who has just made me the happiest man in the world."* The groom may also propose a toast to the bride's parents. Traditionally, the bride remains seated and smiling and does not return any toasts on her wedding day. Following the bridal party's formal toasts, any guest may also toast the newlyweds, the bridal party, or the parents, but there should not be too many toasts. Again, it bears repeating: honorees do not drink to themselves in America.

CAKE-CUTTING CEREMONY

At a military wedding reception, it is traditional for the first slice of wedding cake to be cut with a sword (or saber) and shared between the newlyweds. The groom's cake, if present, is not cut with a sword. The sword arch or honor cordon may form at this time if the reception room is large enough (performed in the same manner as at the wedding venue or in lieu of it). They form an aisle leading to the wedding cake so that most spectators have a good view of the bride and groom walking. The newlyweds move slowly to allow more snapshots, and position themselves as decided previously with their photographer or videographer for another exceptionally photogenic moment.

With the bride on his left, the groom presents the sword to her by laying it over his left forearm, cutting edge away from the body, hilt toward the bride. The bride unhurriedly takes the sword; the groom rests his right hand over hers on the sword's hilt and places his left arm around her as they ceremonially cut the first piece of cake together, pausing graciously for photos. It is much easier on the couple if they cut a corner or small section with one stroke rather than trying to cut a wedge shape. The sword is then handed to one caterer to be cleaned while another server puts the cut slice onto a plate and hands the bride and groom one fork each. The bride lifts the plate and carefully gives the groom a small bite. She continues to hold the plate while he does the same for her. Picture taking complete, they step away and allow the caterer (or server) to distribute the cake to guests. Do not engage in any uncivil behavior such as mashing cake onto one another's faces during what should be a tender moment symbolizing that each will henceforth serve the other with respect. Some cultures include another generous and respectful action—the bride and groom carry slices of cake to their new parents-in-law (or other family elders) before returning to their seats.

If the sword (saber) is worn as part of the bride's or groom's uniform and drawn just prior to use, remember that gloves must also be worn. Instead, clean it and pre-position it unsheathed as part of the cake display. A military sword (saber) is never decorated, as a civilian cake knife might be with ribbons and flowers. Enlisted couples without an enlisted uniform sword (saber) may borrow one from a family member or colleague for the cake cutting ceremony, if desired.

GIFTS

Gifts for wedding attendants may have a military or patriotic theme, if desired. Pewter or silver mugs may be presented to ushers with their monograms (initials) engraved. By tradition, uniformed personnel have these mugs engraved with the geographic location of each new assignment throughout a military career. Civilians can use them as simple souvenirs or the basis for a collection. Bridesmaids often receive matching jewelry (necklace, bracelet, earrings) that they wear during the wedding.

Table favors, if given, are not expensive. There is normally one for each person or two coordinating items alternated so that each couple has a set. They might be suggested by your future military assignment, or be memorable for another reason. One couple assigned in the Far East gave souvenir chopsticks and personalized fortune cookies. Another gave airplane-size bottles of Scotch whiskey tied with plaid ribbon reflecting their family clan in Scotland.

A wedding gift registry at one to three favorite nationwide stores with mail-order capability is appropriate for a new military couple, especially if they are relocating for a new assignment in another state.

A wedding gift for your new spouse is also traditional. If military orders are expected to separate you soon, perhaps a small sentimental object would make a wonderful take-along keepsake.

THANK-YOU NOTES

It takes time to write thank-you notes, which all couples must do when they receive wedding presents. Notes are always handwritten, not e-mailed, with a mention of the specific gift, not just "thank you for a lovely present." Either the bride or the groom may write; thank-you notes are signed *only by the person writing*.

Such a note might read:

Dear Mrs. Smith,

It was thoughtful of you and Colonel Smith to send us such a beautiful picture. The temple rubbing will hang over our fireplace mantel. Thank you very much.

Very sincerely,
Jane Doe

For a belated present you might write:

Dear Aunt Martha,

Cheri and I are delighted with your check. It has helped us decorate our new military quarters. We bought a painting of the nation's capital where we met, and when you feel better we hope that you will come and see it. Thank you very much.

With love,
Dave

Gift Log or Registry

Thank-you notes for wedding presents *must* be written. If the givers can find the time to shop for the present, wrap it, and send it, then the couple can find time to say thank you in writing (not using ordinary "thank you" cards). A gift log is a good way to keep account of who gives you what wedding gifts, and it can be expanded for future presents as well, such as holiday or house warming gifts received. Create your computer file with headings like this as gifts arrive:

Sender's Article/Item	Sent By	Address	Date Rec'd	Thank you Sent on
Silver spoons (2)	Dr. & Mrs. G.W. Doe	1130 Conn. Ave. Washington, DC	7/15	8/10

Thank-you notes may be written as wedding gifts are received and mailed after the honeymoon during the first two months. If you wait longer than three months, the sender will either question whether their gift was received or begin to doubt your upbringing.

Q: How long do I have to send out my wedding thank-you cards? I have been very lax.

A: Ideally, you should handwrite thank-you notes throughout the pre-wedding period as you receive gifts. This allows you to focus on the specifics of each gift and giver. Mail them after the wedding or honeymoon. People want to hear from you personally, within two months, but remember, it is never too late to be gracious. Write your notes now, no matter how late.

Q: Are general officers seated within the ribbon pews at military weddings?

A: As a courtesy, the commanding officer(s) of the bride or groom, flag rank officers, and civilian government dignitaries (and any spouses) are invited to sit with or directly behind immediate family members within reserved areas. Very high-ranking dignitaries may be honored with assigned seats, but most are seated in the order they arrive.

OFFICIAL MARRIED STATUS

Advance military permission is not required for marriages between citizens in the United States. However, if a military member is stationed overseas and marrying a local or third-country foreign national, prior approval from the commanding officer must be obtained and marriage planning is best started several months in advance. The foreign person must complete military forms, such as filling out a U.S. security background investigation, and might also need to pass a standard medical exam. Counseling may be required by the local religious denomination; a civil ceremony could also be required in order to obtain a valid marriage certificate. The intended may need a name change on a passport. Finally, local language documents must be submitted to the U.S. Embassy for translation in order to obtain a visa before entry into the United States.

It is mandatory that service members notify their personnel departments concerning their married status. The new spouse will need a dependent identification card for base or post entry and enrollment in the Defense Eligibility Enrollment Reporting System (DEERS) for medical care. The military allowance for housing will need to be changed to "with dependent." Marriage before a Permanent Change of Station (PCS) move means that military orders must be written to include the relocation of the new spouse and additional household goods.

Rank, Mrs., or Ms.

The military bride may choose to take the last name of her husband, or she may legally retain her maiden name professionally; Lieutenant Smith is now also known socially as Mrs. Doe, the wife of (for instance) John Doe, Esquire. The military wife can, if she chooses, add her new husband's last name to her own maiden name, for example, Staff Sergeant Jane Smith-Doe, USAF. The civilian professional may prefer to be known as Doctor or Ms. Paula Mayer (her previous name), but socially in military circles she is also Mrs. Boggs, the wife of Captain Randall Boggs, USMC.

When a female service member marries, she must notify her personnel department of the marriage and her name choice. The Chief of Personnel acknowledges any change of name in writing. A notification might be as simple as an e-mail:

Subject: Notification of Marriage
From: Lieutenant Jane J. SMITH, USN
To: Chief of Naval Personnel
cc: Commanding Officer
Attachment: PDF of marriage certificate

1. *In accordance with regulations, the Chief of Naval Personnel is hereby notified of my marriage. See attached certificate.*
2. *No name change in my official records will be necessary. I will retain Jane Joyce Smith as my professional name.*
     OR
2. *Request that my name be changed in the official records from Jane Joyce Smith to JANE SMITH-DOE, effective immediately.*
3. *Please acknowledge receipt.*

    JANE J. SMITH*
    Official telephone number
    Official e-mail address
    Military location address

* The new name should not be used on any official forms until the personnel office has acknowledged receipt.

Q: I kept my name after marriage for professional reasons. I want to use it on luncheon invitations to my husband's military colleagues' spouses. Do I refer to
myself as "Mrs. Jane Doe"?

A: Traditionally, using "Mrs." with a first name signifies a divorcée. To avoid this mis-
perception, your formal invitation might read: "Ms. Jane Doe, wife of Captain John
Smith, requests the pleasure of your company. . . ." An informal invitation might say:
"Jane Doe invites you to lunch in her home on . . ." with your address as "The John
Smith Residence" to give people a clue to who you are. However, "Mrs. John Smith"
or "Ms. Jane Doe Smith" on your invitation is correct, even though you have kept
your maiden name. It is fine to use both versions of your name for different arenas; it
is not an illegal alias; it does not devalue your maiden name; it does not diminish your
professional significance.

Q: How do I address a formal wedding invitation to a LTJG? How do we list the RDML
minister's name in a formal wedding program? Where do the commas go?
What is the proper way to list the groomsmen and swordsmen?

A: Strive to spell out complete honorifics and full names on formal articles such as wedding invitations, envelopes, and programs. Commas go after a name, before Service
designations on a program (e.g., Officiant: Rear Admiral James Donovan, Chaplain
Corps, United States Navy) but no commas are part of the rank/name on a social
envelope, except with the suffix "Junior" (e.g., Lieutenant Junior Grade John Paul
Jones, Jr.). List participants by descending grade within categories (all groom's attendants first, then sword arch participants), abbreviating military ranks if space is limited. However, be consistent. Use all abbreviations or spell out completely; do not mix
styles.

WHAT TO CALL IN-LAWS

When you marry into a family, the dilemma arises: What do I call the in-laws?
While dating, you have undoubtedly addressed the parents as "Mr.," "Mrs.,"
"Colonel," or "Sergeant," and so on, to show respect, if not warmth. End the
worry. Ask each set of parents to write an "in-law letter" welcoming the prospective son- or daughter-in-law. Besides saying what they would like to be called, they
might include the "best advice anyone ever gave me for a happy marriage," what
holidays they hope the newlyweds will spend with them, how often they hope visits will be exchanged, and how long the ideal visit should last. Letters of welcome
are best handwritten.

THE MILITARY LIFESTYLE

The authors are pleased to welcome you to your new life together. We were military spouses for many years and know firsthand that the lifestyle is challenging but rewarding.

Probably the first thing you will do after marrying is relocate. Any move is work, taking enormous amounts of time and energy. Most of us value a supportive family, a fulfilling job, a network of friends, and a comfortable house. Losing any one of these is a traumatic event; losing all of them at once can lead to resentment. As one of us wailed after an international move, *"Yes, I love you and promised to follow you to the ends of the earth, but I didn't mean it literally! Do you realize that you are the only person I know in this entire country!?!"*

Moving can be exciting, confusing, exhausting, and isolating—pretty much in that order. Your family memories will include moving vans, hotel rooms, airplanes, military bases, and many diverse, warm-hearted friends because other military folks become like relatives. Everyone is far from home.

Spouses especially make significant personal, career, and financial sacrifices to support a military lifestyle. Military spouses have a professional association and non-profit advocacy group of their own. For those new to military issues, check out the *National Military Family Association* (www.NMFA.org). This volunteer, non-profit organization provides extensive information online and via newsletters and fact sheets. NMFA represents all seven uniformed Services' family members and their unique interests before Congress.

CHAPTER 10

Military Wedding Invitations, Announcements, and Replies

*M*ilitary wedding invitations deserve special attention. Order any tasteful invitation style that appeals to you and corresponds to the type of wedding you are having, but for military weddings remember to include full ranks held by the bride or groom and parents (if applicable). Order wedding invitations *at least three months* in advance of the wedding date. The bride's family mails them *six to eight weeks* before the wedding day in order to give out-of-town guests time to prepare and enough time to finalize preparations (developing seating charts and menu cards, writing place cards, meeting caterers' deadlines, etc.) once R.s.v.p.s are received.

For military weddings held in the same location as the couple's place of work, it is nice to invite their commanding officers (and spouses), both to the wedding ceremony and to the reception if the budget allows.

AT EASE KEY POINTS

- Style of invitation offers glimpse of wedding ambience.
- Traditional wording is best; contemporary words are acceptable.
- Informal invitations can be handwritten, e-mailed, or telephoned.
- Use no abbreviations on outer envelopes.
- Weigh the mailings; "postage due" detracts from first impression.

TRADITIONAL WEDDING INVITATIONS

The traditional wedding invitation is engraved on white or ivory vellum or kid-finish paper. One version may be a double sheet, about 5½ by 7½ inches (14 by 19 centimeters), which is folded and enclosed in an inner envelope; another may be a smaller invitation, about 4½ by 6 inches (11.43 by 15.24 centimeters) in size, which is not folded and is placed sideways in a mailing envelope.

Although traditional black engraving is beautiful, a good quality flat printing or *thermography* (raised printing) is less expensive. There are many lettering styles to choose from, but shaded Roman, antique Roman, and script are always in good taste. Some lettering styles may look too harsh in black against white paper; dark gray ink may be preferable.

Avoid abbreviations, initials, and Arabic numerals whenever possible in wedding invitations. However, Roman numerals may denote a second or third

Dr. and Mrs. Bryan Thomas Burney

request the honor of your presence

at the marriage of their daughter

Amanda Jane Burney

Ensign, United States Navy

to

John Carl Ross

Ensign, United States Navy

on Saturday, the thirtieth of August

two thousand and nine

at half past four o'clock

Castleton United Methodist Church

7160 Shadeland Avenue

Indianapolis, Indiana

Traditional Formal Wedding Invitation

generation: John Paul Truxtun II or III. The designation "Junior'" applies to the next in direct line of descent. The numbers "II" and so on indicate the sequence in the use of the name. A man usually does not continue to add "Junior" or "Jr." after his name following the death of his father, but he may if his mother is still living.

When invitations have double envelopes, the *inner* one has the guest's honorific and last name written on it in black or dark blue ink, for example, "Doctor and Mrs. Smith." The tissue protecting the engraving on the invitation is not removed before placing the invitation into the envelope.

SERVICE RANK

When the bride or groom is a member of the armed forces, the rank always goes before the name with the branch of Service beneath:

Staff Sergeant Elizabeth Anne Doe
United States Marine Corps

Reserve personnel may use their ranks on wedding invitations or announcements only while *on active duty*, adding "Reserve:"

Captain John (or Jane) Doe
United States Army Reserve

Commissioned officers of the rank of commander (O-5) and higher in the Navy and Coast Guard, and of captain (O-3) and up in the Army, Air Force, and Marine Corps, use their titles before their names on formal invitations they issue:

Colonel John (or Jane) Doe
United States Air Force

Junior grade personnel place the rank and branch of Service beneath their full names on formal invitations they issue. Spell out all grades completely—a wedding invitation is formal:

John (or Jane) Doe
Lieutenant Commander, United States Navy

Retired personnel of the ranks O-5 and above often keep their titles in civilian life and use them to issue wedding invitations. If the parent is single, divorced, or widowed the Service branch and "Retired" may be used as in example #6 under Variations in Wordings on page 172.

If one parent is retired military and the other is civilian, their joint names do not appear any differently than if the parent were still active duty. Rank is used as the appellation but no mention of the Service branch or "Retired" is listed after their names, to prevent inclusion of the civilian spouse in the military designation:

Commander Jane Doe and Mr. John Doe

or

Captain and Mrs. John Doe

Q: My fiancée's father is a doctor, mine is retired Navy. We want to respect them both as we marry. How do we word our wedding invitations?

A: Do not use "Retired" after your parents' combined names, which would falsely include your mother in the military designation. One version might read:

Dr. and Mrs. Daniel John Connolly
and
Commander and Mrs. Earl Leslie Blair
request the honor of your presence
at the marriage uniting their children . . .

THE GUEST LIST

The groom sends a list of his friends' names and addresses to his mother, who in turn will send his list with her own to the mother of the bride. If his mother is deceased, he will send the complete family list to the mother of the bride. To separate guests who are not all invited to the reception or breakfast following the wedding, an "R" for reception and "C" for ceremony can be used by the names. The bride's mother keeps an alphabetical checklist for acceptances and regrets.

ISSUING WEDDING INVITATIONS

Remember to send invitations to the bridegroom's parents and to members of the bride's immediate family and the bridal party also, even though they "know all about it." These invitations are often treasured mementos; the year should always be stated on them. If the parents of the bride are deceased, the invitations are issued by a close or older relative, or she sends them herself. In the case of divorced parents, they are usually issued in the name of the one with whom the bride has been living.

Guest Reply Cards and Other Invitation Inserts

As principals at the event, the bride and groom will be vitally concerned with whether or not guests plan to attend. Their wedding may be the very first event where they truly appreciate the importance of R.s.v.p.s! The home address of the bride's family is usually engraved on the reception or wedding breakfast card, so that replies will be sent to that address and *not* to the place of the wedding. There is a correct way to place extra items in the wedding invitation envelope:

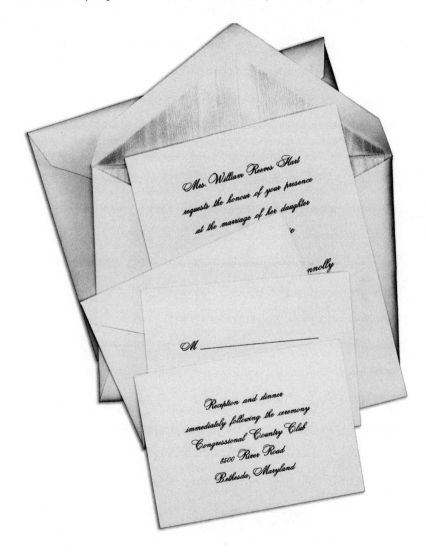

Although it is still correct for replies to be handwritten, the changing times have brought acceptance of reply cards. Small self-addressed and stamped envelopes with reply cards are included in the invitation to make it convenient for guests to respond promptly. If desired, add a line such as: *The favor of a reply is requested before the twentieth of April.* Invitations to some weddings are announced by the clergy as including the entire congregation; these do not require a reply.

Other inserts might be maps, pre-arranged guest information, and security entry requirements with the base or post front gate telephone number. A courtesy note will give unfamiliar civilians an idea of what to expect regarding security on a military installation (see Chapter 1: Military and Government Protocol).

ADDRESSING ENVELOPES

A formal engraved wedding invitation has two envelopes: the outside, gummed, which bears the full name and address of the guest or guests, and the inside, ungummed, envelope, which has only the honorific and the surname and holds the invitation or announcement. The inside envelope is faced toward the back of the outside envelope when inserted, so that the names will be face-up when the envelope is opened. All envelopes are addressed by hand, in black or dark blue ink. Order extra envelopes to allow for mistakes.

Wedding invitations are always sent to a married couple, even though you know only one or the other. The outside envelope will be fully addressed without abbreviations, initials, or commas between city and state if they are on separate lines:

Indented (staggered):

Lieutenant General and Mrs. John Pershing
  Quarters 2
    Fort Myer
      Virginia 22211

Centered:

Chief Warrant Officer Carla Jones and Mr. Jones
Quarters 25AL, Jackson Avenue
Fort Myer, Virginia 22211

The inner envelope is addressed with shortened rank: *Airman and Mrs. Vance Miller.*

Adult members of the family, such as a grandmother or mother-in-law, receive separate invitations. You may write the name or names of teenage children of the family directly under the parents' names on both envelopes. Or, when the children are underage, simply write: *Susan, Mary, and John* on the inside envelope under the parents' names.

When addressing a letter to a boy of twelve or under, use the word "Master," as in *Master Luke Michaels*. After age thirteen, he is addressed as "Mr." A man is "Mr." unless he has a title or rank. "Messrs." is the French plural of "Mister" and may be used to jointly address brothers but not a father and son.

A young girl is addressed *Elizabeth Doe* until she reaches her teens, when she is addressed as "Miss." A married woman is "Mrs." unless she has a title or rank. When you do not know the title of a woman college-age or older, write "Ms."

A widow may keep her husband's name, as in *Mrs. James Martin*, or she may be known by her own name, *Ms. Patricia Martin*. A divorcée may keep the last name of her former husband, especially if she has children, but usually adds her given name and maiden name, *Mrs. Patricia Samples Martin*. The more traditional form of using only surnames for both the widow and divorcée, as in *Mrs. Samples Martin*, is also correct.

When a spouse's Service rank or civilian title exceeds that of the person you know better, see Official Invitations for Ranking Spouses in Chapter 11: Invitations.

Q: How do I address my wedding invitation envelopes? My first cousin Brad married a doctor. My aunt is a widow.

A: Family members take precedence over in-laws for family events. The outer envelope for your cousin would read, *Mr. Bradley Lowe and Dr. Leslie Lowe*, each on a separate line if preferred. For your aunt there are two options. It is traditional etiquette to use her deceased husband's name, *Mrs. Elmer Arnie Davis*; however, many longtime widows prefer the honorific "Ms." with their own names: *Ms. Minnie Mae Davis*. For the inner envelopes, write *Bradley and Leslie* and *Aunt Minnie* or if you are not close, then *Mr. Lowe and Dr. Lowe*, and *Ms. Davis*.

Return Address

The option of an *embossed* return address on the back flap of the wedding invitation envelope may be considered, but for the sake of legibility, *raised printing* is better. The return address lets a person know where to send written R.s.v.p.s or wedding gifts. Also, if the invited person moved without leaving a forwarding address, the invitation can be returned.

Variations in Wordings

There are many variations in the wording of invitations:

1. When the bride's parents are deceased and a relative is sending the invitations:

Mr. George Oliver Smith
requests the honor of your presence
at the marriage of his sister
Mary Martha

When there are no close relatives, or if she is an orphan, the bride may send out her own invitations, with the wording as follows:

The honor of your presence
is requested at the marriage of
Miss Mary Martha Smith
to
Donald James Adams

2. When the bride's parents are divorced and the mother has not remarried, she uses her former husband's name (which is her child's name) with her maiden surname, for example, Mrs. Susan Brown Smith. When the divorce is "friendly," and both names are on the invitation, the mother's name appears first:

Mrs. Susan Brown Smith
and
Commander John James Smith
United States Navy, Retired
request the honor of your presence
at the marriage of their daughter

When the bride's parents are separated but not divorced, the fact of the separation is frequently ignored, and the invitations are engraved in the customary form.

3. When the mother has remarried and is widowed or divorced from her second husband, her name is placed first on the invitation, with the bride's father's name on the following line (when agreeable to all parties). Regardless of the number of times the parents have remarried, the bride is still *their* daughter:

Mrs. Julia Fern Doe
and Commander Peter James Smith
United States Navy, Retired

request the honor of your presence
at the marriage of their daughter

4. When the bride's father is dead, or her parents are divorced, and her mother
has remarried:

Colonel and Mrs. Paul Lewis Dorn
request the honor of your presence
at the marriage of her* daughter
Mary Martha Smith

5. Or the invitations may be issued in the mother's name only:

Mrs. Paul Lewis Dorn
requests the honor of your presence
at the marriage of her daughter
Katherine Mia Smith

6. Or issued in the father's name only:

Colonel Paul Lewis Dorn
United States Air Force, Retired
requests the honor of your presence
at the marriage of his daughter

7. If the bride's mother is dead and the father has married again, the form usually is:

Commander and Mrs. John James Smith
request the honor of your presence
at the marriage of his* daughter
Mary Martha

When a widow or widower who has not remarried is issuing the invitations,
her or his name appears alone.

* When the relationship between the stepparent and the bride is close, their
would be used instead of his or her in examples 4 and 7.

8. When a young widow is to be remarried, her previous married surname is
proper if she has not returned to her maiden name, and the form is:

Brigadier General and Mrs. David John Slotta
request the honor of your presence
at the marriage of their daughter

Amber Lynn Adams
to
Second Lieutenant Donald James Varndell
United States Air Force
on Saturday, the fourth of June
Two thousand and eleven
at seven o'clock
Randolph Air Force Base Chapel
Texas

When an older widow gives her own wedding, it is usually informal, and handwritten invitations are sent. But when engraved or printed invitations are used, the traditional form for a widow who kept her husband's name is:

The honor of your presence is requested
at the marriage of Mrs. Donald James Adams
to
Jack Edward Mosier

These forms may also be used by a divorcée who kept the last name of her former husband, except that her given name and maiden name are usually added: Mrs. Martha Smith Adams. The more traditional form, Mrs. Smith Adams, is also correct.

Q: On our wedding invitations Ella's and my name will be in a larger font than the rest of the invitation. I fear that "Ensign, United States Navy" under my name in a smaller font won't look right. Is rank really necessary?

A: If it is a military wedding, rank and Service are both important to acknowledge, as you will be in uniform. If the event is strictly civilian then rank is not required; however, you have earned the designation and we encourage it. Talk to the stationer about aesthetics.

---

9. When the bride-elect is adopted, there is no need to mention this fact. When her name is different or the family desires, both the engagement announcement and the wedding invitation could use the words "adopted daughter."

Weddings Given by Both Sets of Parents

Less customary but becoming more frequent today is the wedding that is given by both sets of parents. The wedding invitations are issued in the names of both sets of parents, and the reception is given jointly (and paid for jointly). You may wish to follow the customary wording on Jewish wedding invitations, which show that two families are uniting, with the groom's parents' names just below the bride's parents' and the word "and" used instead of "to" between the bride and groom's names, as in:

REVEREND AND MRS. BRUCE BOWERS

AND

MRS. KATHY DIRCKX

MR. ALBERT J. LARSON

REQUEST THE HONOUR OF YOUR PRESENCE

AT THE MARRIAGE OF THEIR CHILDREN

Molly Katherine

AND

Joshua John Larson
Ensign, United States Navy

ON SATURDAY, THE NINETEENTH OF AUGUST

TWO THOUSAND AND SIX

AT ONE O'CLOCK IN THE AFTERNOON

WORLD'S FAIR PAVILLION

FOREST PARK

ST. LOUIS, MISSOURI

Contemporary Formal Wedding Invitation

RECEPTION INVITATIONS

There are several ways of extending an invitation for a wedding reception. If the wedding takes place in the morning or early afternoon—but no later than one o'clock—a *wedding breakfast* card is enclosed. A small card about 3 by 4 inches (7.62 by 10.16 centimeters), engraved on the same type of paper as the wedding invitation, is included along with the invitation. There is no crest or coat of arms on the card, and the protecting tissue (when provided) is not removed before mailing. The phrase "pleasure of your company" is used, since this is now a social occasion:

> Colonel and Mrs. John Randall Smith
> request the pleasure of your company
> at the Wedding Breakfast
> following the ceremony
> at
> Dogwood Hills
> Arlington, Virginia
> R.s.v.p.

If the wedding is to be in the late afternoon or evening, a *reception invitation* card may be enclosed with the wedding invitation:

Please join us for the reception
immediately following the ceremony
at the Geist Club House
12549 Old Stone Drive
Indianapolis, IN 46236

DINNER AND DANCE

AT FIVE-THIRTY IN THE EVENING

GATEWAY CENTER

ONE GATEWAY DRIVE

COLLINSVILLE, ILLINOIS

Reception Invitation Cards

Or the reception information may be included as part of the wedding invitation when *all* guests are invited to *both* the wedding and reception. The information is added following the name and address of the house of worship:

and reception afterwards at
Dogwood Hills
Arlington, Virginia
R.s.v.p.

When the wedding will be private and only close friends and relatives invited, but a large reception will be held, the wedding invitation could be oral, e-mailed, or handwritten, but the reception invitations could be printed similar to the traditional wedding invitation:

Lieutenant General and Mrs. John Wilson Doe
request the pleasure of your company
at the Wedding Reception
of their daughter
Captain Karla Anne Doe
United States Marine Corps
and
Mr. James Lee Smith
Saturday, the ninth of January
Two thousand and eleven
at half after four o'clock
Quarters One
Marine Corps Base
Quantico, Virginia

LETTERS OF INVITATION AND REPLIES

A small gathering, including an informal wedding, does not require printed invitations. The host may e-mail or telephone the relatives and friends who are invited, providing brief but full information. The host (normally mother of the bride for weddings) may write short notes of invitation in the first person on the first page of single or folded cream-colored or white stationery, or on correspondence cards, if preferred. Such informal wedding invitations are sent on short notice, for instance, when a change of orders is imminent:

Dear Fern,

Janet is being married to Second Lieutenant John Curtis LeMay, who graduated from the Air Force Academy last week.

The wedding will take place in our quarters, A-4, U.S. Marine Corps Base, Quantico, Virginia on Thursday the sixteenth of June at four-thirty. We do hope you will be with us and stay for the reception afterwards.

As ever,
Martha Vance

Wednesday, the first

WRITTEN ACCEPTANCES AND REFUSALS

When you are invited to any event, the invitation *must* be answered within two days of receipt at the latest. Replies to invitations are made in the same manner they were extended, for example, by returning a reply card, by telephone or e-mail, or by writing a letter.

The writer of an informal letter signs with his or her full name, without title or any other information. Write replies on conservative white or cream stationery or a correspondence card with matching envelope. Address your reply to the person who issued the invitation. A written acceptance to the invitation in the previous paragraph might read:

Saturday

Dear Martha,

I am very happy about your daughter's forthcoming marriage to John LeMay, and I am especially pleased to be in the States and able to attend. I look forward to being with you at the reception also.

Sincerely,
Fern Doe

A handwritten acceptance or regret may be required if a reply card is not provided with a *formal invitation*, or there is no contact information printed under an R.s.v.p. Reply in longhand in the third person and always re-state the date and hour. If you use a personalized correspondence card, the first line, your name, might already be printed, so you start with *"and Mrs. [or Mr.] Last Name"* (if applicable) and continue, with lines centered:

Mr. and Mrs. Aaron Woodyard
accept with pleasure
the kind invitation of
Colonel and Mrs. Ryan
for
Monday, the sixth of June
at four o'clock

A formal dinner or luncheon invitation to a married couple must be refused when either one or the other cannot accept. The rule here is: both or neither, unless the hosts insist that one attending is fine. When a refusal is for an invitation from a close friend, the reason is frequently added in the second and third lines, such as *"regret that absence from the city prevents their accepting"*:

> Lieutenant and Mrs. Walter Allen
> regret that they are unable to accept
> the kind invitation of
> Colonel and Mrs. Heuser
> on Monday, the sixth of June

CHILDREN AS GUESTS

An invitation to a wedding is only for those persons whose names are written on the envelopes, unless the envelope reads "and guest" or "and family." Parents with older children whose names *are* on the envelope and who will attend the wedding do *not* bring their baby or small child to the house of worship or the reception (unless they are informed that a nursery has been made available). Invitations are sent out early enough for parents to make arrangements for a baby sitter. The wedding is one of the most important days in the bridal couple's life, and their wishes must be respected. Do not put them on the spot by asking if you may bring the baby along, even if the bride is your sister or the groom is your best friend. If you do ask, do not be offended when they say no.

WEDDING PROGRAMS AND MENU CARDS

Wedding programs and menu cards complete your wedding. They complement the style you have chosen, whether traditional or modern. Templates are available online to make your own, or you can order them from the same stationer who does your invitations. They are usually retained by family members as souvenirs.

Programs introduce the clergy and wedding party, provide the order of events, list ceremony music, and describe the significance of traditions or rituals. For instance, many Christian Orthodox brides and grooms circle the altar symbolizing their first steps together as husband and wife. In another Christian denomination there may be a memorial or unity candle, readings or prayers, and a ring ceremony. Jewish weddings are conducted under a canopy called the *chuppah* and the groom breaks a glass at the conclusion. During Indian and Hawaiian weddings, the bride and groom exchange garlands of flowers. Any of these details could be explained, especially if some guests are of another faith or culture, and for the benefit of following generations.

Menu cards typically include the date and location of the meal at the bottom after the listing of food (each course centered on a separate line). For weddings, a design element or quote may also be included, but more important is that the couple is honored by seeing, for the first time, their joint names in print:

> *To celebrate the marriage of*
> *Captain and Mrs.*
> *Daniel John Connolly*
>
> ⌒
>
> *Wedding Dinner*

MARRIAGE ANNOUNCEMENTS

Marriage announcements are mailed *after* a wedding takes place to those who were not invited to the nuptials, or to all friends and acquaintances following a ceremony when no guests were invited.

Engraved or printed marriage announcements are issued on the same type of paper used for wedding invitations. The announcements are sent by the bride's parents or by the person designated. In wedding announcements, the name of the house of worship may or may not be included, and the hour of the wedding is not specified:

> Captain and Mrs. John Jones Smith
> have the honor of announcing
> the marriage of their daughter
> Mary Ann
> to
> Mr. George Carl Wilson
> on Saturday, the fourth of June
> Two thousand and eleven
> Treasure Island Chapel
> San Francisco, California

The couple may announce their own marriage. When a civil ceremony was held, only the name of the city or town is mentioned:

Miss Jane Ellen Doe

and

William John Smith, Junior

Ensign, United States Coast Guard

announce their marriage

on Saturday, the fourth of June

Two thousand and eleven

at Mystic, Connecticut

RECALLING INVITATIONS

Because of major illness, a change of orders, or a change of mind in the case of weddings, invitations may have to be recalled after they have been issued. Notices must then be sent to all those who received invitations. The best form for recalling the wedding invitation is:

Dr. and Mrs. William Smith

announce that the marriage of their daughter

Mary Ellen

to

Ensign John Lee Jones

will not take place

When the wedding invitation is recalled because of a bereavement in the family, the engraved or printed card may state the reason:

Dr. and Mrs. William Smith

regret exceedingly

that because of the recent death of

the father of Ensign Jones

the invitations to the marriage of their daughter

Mary Ellen

to

Ensign John Lee Jones

must be recalled

or

Mrs. William Smith
regrets that the death of Dr. Smith
obliges her to recall the invitations
to the wedding of her daughter

The recalling of invitations in case of a death in the immediate family does not always mean that a wedding may not take place. If the families agree, a very quiet ceremony may be held on the original day of the wedding, but with no guests other than members of the families and perhaps only one attendant each for the bride and groom.

Postponing the Wedding

When it is necessary to postpone a wedding, a form similar to this may be followed:

Captain and Mrs. John Jones Smith
announce that the marriage of their daughter
Mary Ann
to
Mr. George Carl Wilson
has been postponed from
Saturday, the fourth of June
until
Saturday, the twenty-fifth of June
Two thousand and eleven
at four o'clock
Treasure Island Chapel
San Francisco, California

At-Home or Change of Address Cards

When you want friends to know your new address and will be living there long enough to make change of address cards worthwhile, at-home cards may be enclosed in the same envelope with the wedding announcement. The cards are the same color as the wedding announcement and perhaps 3 by 4 inches (about 7.5 x 10 centimeters). One form is:

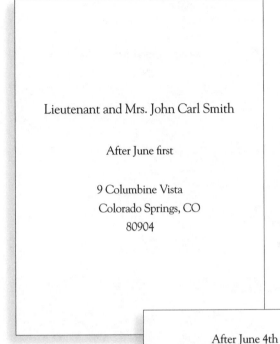

Lieutenant and Mrs. John Carl Smith

After June first

9 Columbine Vista
Colorado Springs, CO
80904

Or smaller cards, about the size of a personal or business card, may be used:

After June 4th
9 Columbine Vista
Colorado Springs, Colorado
80904

At-Home Card (Change of Address Card)

WEDDING ANNIVERSARIES

For announcements or invitations to celebrate wedding anniversaries, the year
of the wedding and the current year are customarily printed or engraved at the
top. The couple's initials, monogram, or coat of arms may also be used in gold,
silver, black, or dark blue ink. Such invitations may be sent out by the couple or
by their children:

1960   *2010*

Major General and Mrs. John James Smith
request the pleasure of the company of
Colonel and Mrs. George Ballou

on the fiftieth anniversary
of their marriage
on Friday evening, May the sixth
Two thousand and eleven
from seven until nine o'clock
The Broadmoor
Colorado Springs, Colorado

or

1962–2012
Captain and Mrs. John Paul Jones
At Home
Friday, the sixth of May
from five until seven o'clock
237 Mountain View Road
Colorado Springs, Colorado

Section 3

COMMUNICATIONS ETIQUETTE

CHAPTER 11

Invitations

*T*he issuance of invitations, as well as their acknowledgment, follows international protocol. Invitations the world over use the same format to allow both guest and host to meet their obligations with maximum advantage and minimum effort.

Invitations may be extended by telephone, via e-mail, by handwritten note, by the partially printed fill-in invitation, or with fully printed information. Those receiving invitations answer promptly in the same manner as the invitation, except when alternate direction is given (e.g., e-mail invitations may request reply via Web site).

AT EASE KEY POINTS

- ✄ Follow internationally recognized word order.
- ✄ Acknowledge rank or position on official invitations.
- ✄ Avoid initials and abbreviations.
- ✄ Answer invitations within forty-eight hours.
- ✄ Use correct dress terms: *Formal, Informal,* or *Casual.*

An invitation's style is the first indication that guests have about the ambience of the occasion. *Hand Calligraphy* and *Engraving* are the most expensive choices and are therefore reserved for the most formal events. *Thermography* (raised printing) is perfectly acceptable. Many prefer flat printing. White and ecru (cream) are classic paper colors that are well received internationally, as is black ink.

Partially engraved (or thermography or printed) fill-in invitations use a template of information that does not change, allowing space for handwriting (in black ink) the variables: guest name, event, time, and date (see illustration). This flexible and cost-effective option allows hosts to order large quantities to keep in stock.

Invitations can be printed with a home computer on a variety of papers, in your choice of colors and font. Invitations can also be written completely in longhand (see Handwritten Invitations below).

Fill-in Invitation and Envelope

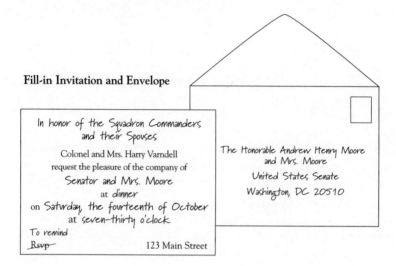

In honor of the Squadron Commanders
and their Spouses

Colonel and Mrs. Harry Varndell
request the pleasure of the company of
Senator and Mrs. Moore
at dinner
on Saturday, the fourteenth of October
at seven-thirty o'clock

To remind

~~Rsvp~~   123 Main Street

The Honorable Andrew Henry Moore
and Mrs. Moore
United States Senate
Washington, DC 20510

INTERNATIONAL INVITATION COMPONENTS

The following components are always in the same internationally recognized order. A formal invitation reads like a sentence, in the third person, with each line centered and beginning with a lower-case letter after the first line (except for proper names). All words and numbers, except those in the address and phone number, are written out. The following are keyed to the numbered lines in the Invitation Components illustration:

1. **Symbol:** A small symbol may be centered at the top of the invitation. A family crest or coat of arms is usually embossed without color on wedding and other important invitations. A military Service, religious denomination, or other official seal may be engraved in gold or silver, as appropriate. An admiral's or general's flag or an organization logo may be printed in color. If there are two hosts, the senior host's emblem is on its own far right (heraldic right)—the left as the viewer reads the invitation.

2. **Host Line:** Spell out the full name of the organization or the person or persons issuing invitations, such as "The Joint Military Attaché School" or "Master Sergeant and Mrs. John Jones." An invitation may carry the names of several

hosts or sponsors of the event. If the function is held at the home of one of the hosts, that name is written first; if at a commercial location, the senior ranking name is first, or to the left if side-by-side. Abbreviations, including initials, are avoided, unless the initials are always used, as in "Lieutenant C. S. Lewis."

3. **Request Line:** The verb is singular or plural depending on the number of hosts. Appropriate forms include *"request the honor of the presence of"* (most formal), *"requests the pleasure of the company of," "requests the honor of your presence," "request the pleasure of your company"* or *"cordially invites you"* (least formal). Different nationalities use other formal phrases, such as the hosts *"confer on themselves the honor of inviting."*

4. **Invited Guest Line:** If *"your presence"* or *"your company"* is used, it negates the need to enter individual names. If not, another line is needed. Only the conversational honorific and surname (*"General and Mrs. Doe"*) of guests goes on the invitation itself—the complete names appear on the mailing envelopes (*"Lieutenant General and Mrs. John Doe"*). However, sometimes international officials are possessive of their complete titles, so it might be politic to spell out the entire honorific again on the invitation as well as its envelope. This can be verified through their office staffs.

5. **Event Line:** Do not capitalize common terms such as lunch, dinner, or cocktails. A specific occasion such as Thanksgiving Dinner, or Change of Command Ceremony are capitalized. Details such as "reception on board ship" are not capitalized, but the ship's name appears in the address line.

6. **In Honor of Line:** Additional information may be added above or below the event line. An alternate *"in honor of"* location is above the host line. For partially printed fill-in invitations, the line may be handwritten across the top above the seal. *"To meet"* or *"To introduce"* is for new arrivals and houseguests. *"In recognition of"* or *"To celebrate"* or *"To bid farewell"* and similar phrases are entirely appropriate.

7. **Date Line:** The day, date, and month are spelled out, but the present year is assumed. *"Monday, the first of June"* or *"Friday, September twenty-second"* are both acceptable forms. The year will be included in circumstances that require extreme advance planning, such as a future Olympiad, or when the card is likely to be retained as a souvenir—for example, a wedding invitation. When the year is included, it is spelled out immediately beneath the date, as in *"Two thousand and twelve."* The Date Line may be written in numerals for international guests in the military style, because the day-month-year order is in general use worldwide: *Tuesday, 14 August 2012.*

8. **Time Line:** The hour is spelled out. Instead of *"four-thirty," "half past"* or *"half after"* may be used. For receptions (or any limited duration event), the "from–to" time is given, as in *"six until eight."* The numeric 24-hour clock times may be employed overseas as they are used universally outside the United States.

Q: Do I use regular time (7:30 PM) on an invitation instead of military time (1930)?

A: In the United States, we clarify the 12-hour clock with before noon/ante meridiem (AM) and after noon/post meridiem (PM) designations. Even so, these designations are not needed on an invitation, as it is rare that people would misunderstand dinner time to mean 7:30 AM. Therefore, in the United States, write out *seven-thirty* for formal invitations. When serving abroad, use the 24-hour numerals and enjoy the fact that the locals don't consider it "military" at all, but part of a world citizen's basic knowledge repertoire.

Q: Can I put "R.s.v.p. by e-mail" on my invitation or do I have to give a phone number?

A: Do not write "by e-mail;" simply print the e-mail address underneath.

---

9. **Location Lines:** If the event is held at a major hotel or well-known local venue, the street address may be omitted when the location follows the Time Line. An alternate address location, particularly for home addresses, is in the lower right corner.

10. **Reply Request Line:** "R.s.v.p." the French abbreviation for *"répondez s'il vous plait"* meaning "please reply," always goes on the bottom left-hand corner. Other languages may use different words, for example, the German equivalent is *U.A.w.g.* (*"Um Antwort wird gebeten"* or "response requested") but the location is the same. Include the name of a contact person and any preferred response method: phone number, e-mail address, or Web site. A time limit (*"by the fifteenth"* or *"before November first by enclosed card"*) may be added, as desired.

11. **Dress Line:** "Dress" or "attire" is never written—the only three terms used on a proper invitation are *Formal, Informal,* or *Casual*. You will see international translations for these terms and any number of host-invented categories—such as "dress smartly" or "sporty outfits" in an effort to clarify their wishes—that only manage to confuse guests. See more in Dress Terms on Invitations, in Chapter 22: Appropriate Attire,.

12. **Additional Information Line:** More information may be included such as, *"Cameras not permitted,"* or *"Parking on West Street."* Separate small cards may

be enclosed, such as reply cards with menu selections, seating or parking information cards, or security passes: *"Must present this card for admittance."*

(**1.** Optional Seal)

2. *Colonel and Mrs. Aaron Woodyard*

3. *request the pleasure of the company of*

4. *Major and Mrs. Heuser*

5. *at a reception*

6. *in honor of the Squadron Commanders and their Spouses*

7. *on Saturday, the fourteenth of October*

8. *at seven to nine o'clock*

9. *The Hangar Club Terrace*
17 Golf Club Road

10. *R.s.v.p.*
202.555.1212
Ms. Leighton
12. Photo I.D. required   (**11.** alternate)

11. Informal
(**9.** alternate)
(**12.** alternate)

Invitation Components

Reply Cards

A response card with a pre-addressed and stamped envelope (or a postcard) may accompany invitations to facilitate the R.s.v.p. Reply cards should be of the same stock as the invitations and at least 3½ by 5 inches (approximately 8 by 13 centimeters) to be an acceptable size for traditional U.S. mail service.

Modern hosts must make it as convenient for guests as possible because of the social decline in formal, handwritten replies. Replying in writing has always been "correct"—and is still the proper way to respond to a formal invitation without a phone number or e-mail address. To give the recipient a sense of urgency, a line on the reply card such as, *"The favor of a reply is requested before September thirtieth"* is often added. For large functions, number or code the reply cards, as some invited guests will not write their names legibly.

Addressing Envelopes

See Chapter 12: Correspondence and Stationery Essentials

Official Invitations for Ranking Spouses

For an *official social event* inviting a married couple, each with a Service rank or government civilian title, one will probably exceed the rank of the other. The envelope is addressed first to the person you know better, with no abbreviations for formal occasions. The important thing to remember is that rank is always recognized on official invitations, second line or not:

> *Major Carla Anne Smith, United States Marine Corps* (wife retained maiden name)
> *and Commander John Earl Doe, United States Coast Guard* (her husband's name)
> (Use her office address, since she is the principal guest you are inviting)

On the invitation inside, write *"Major Smith and Commander Doe."* If they were the same rank and name and Service, it would be, *"The Captains John Doe,"* and inside, *"The Captains Doe."*

Or another sample:

> *Colonel John Doe, United States Army*
> *The Honorable Janet Doe* (female is a congressional representative)
> (his office address)

On the invitation inside, write *"Colonel Doe and The Honorable Doe."* It is the name and office address of the person the host knows better that takes precedence for official invitations.

For *social (non-official)* invitations, married couples are normally addressed jointly as Senior Rank and Mrs. (or Mr.). In the first example, it could be *"Commander and Mrs. John Doe"* (Major Smith is still Mrs. Doe socially); in the second example, *"The Honorable and Mr. Doe"* (in the United States we still do not refer to the male spouse as "Mr. Female's first name"). If worried that the individuals are sensitive about the matter, alternatives would be, "Commander Doe and Major Smith," and "The Honorable Doe and Colonel Doe," keeping the highest rank listed first on joint social invitations.

CHINESE INVITATION, circa 1800s

Respectfully, and with goblet in hand, I await the light of your countenance on the sixth day of the 1st moon at midday.

HANDWRITTEN INVITATIONS

Handwritten invitations are usually reserved for small social gatherings involving no more than twenty to thirty people. Casual invitations may be issued on a flat correspondence card or a fold-over informal card with abbreviated wording:

Cocktails-Buffet
Wednesday, June ninth
1800–2030 [or 6:00–8:30]
R.s.v.p.
301.555.1212

LETTERS OF INVITATION

When you have more than one event to invite guests to, letter invitations are particularly effective (see Chapter 10: Military Wedding Invitations, Announcements and Replies for an example). Invitation letters may be typed for business, listing perhaps a series of offsite or conference functions, such as an opening ceremony, an awards banquet, and a closing happy hour in a hospitality suite. When inviting a VIP guest to attend your function, send a letter explaining the event and the importance you attach to the VIP's patronage.

Q: We want to invite a bishop to speak to our brigade at the Academy. Who sends the invitation?

A: Before a high-visibility speaker is invited, the request must go to the school's head office, protocol section, for two reasons. First, you need their approval and support with your letter of invitation—they will help coordinate with the VIP's protocol office. Second, the senior in your chain of command should be present for high-ranking VIP guests and plans may need altering in order to accommodate your event. After approval, the invitation may be extended via telephone, e-mail, or fax (bypassing mail-room security screening delays) to determine the bishop's availability. When verbally accepted, please send a "To remind" card in a correctly addressed envelope.

Postponing or Advancing Invitations

If the event must be postponed or advanced with short notice, notify invitees by telephone. Otherwise, an announcement to that effect would follow the same form as the original invitation, with complete information:

Because of the
imminent departure of
the Chief of Staff of the Army
the reception in honor of
General and Mrs. Galida
will be advanced from
Thursday evening, the twentieth of June
to
Friday evening, the fourteenth of June
at nine o'clock
Grand Ballroom, Mayflower Hotel
R.s.v.p.

Recalling an Invitation

It is better to postpone than to cancel an invitation once you have extended it, but a formal invitation may be recalled when unavoidable circumstances warrant. When the occasion was to have been small and the guests would know the reason for the withdrawing of the invitation—such as a bereavement or a serious accident—no reason need be stated:

The invitations of
Colonel and Mrs. George Ojalehto
for Saturday, the fifteenth of May
are recalled

But when it is an official occasion involving guests who might not know the circumstances, the reason for recalling the invitation would be stated:

General and Mrs. Daniel Connolly
regret exceedingly
that because of the recent death of
Admiral Doe
the invitations to the reception in honor of
The Secretary of Defense and Mrs. Gates
must be recalled

GUEST OF HONOR

In extending an invitation to someone to be your guest of honor, you may say, "*I would like so much to give a dinner for you* [and your wife/husband] *on either Thursday,*

Q: If I deliver invitations to Academy classmates before we graduate, but my wedding is after graduation, should I address them to Midshipman John Doe, or to Ensign John Doe?

A: It only seems confusing because the wedding invitations were ordered with your commissioned rank (the proper honorific for your marriage date), but invitations are always addressed with the title or rank that the recipient holds on the day you send them. You are not responsible for future changes.

Q: Is it more appropriate wording to "request the honor" or "the pleasure" of someone's company? Which is better: USMC Candidates of the USNA Class of 2014, or USMC Candidates, USNA class 2014?

A: The word "honor" is considered more formal for official ceremonies. If the party celebrates the graduates (or candidates) as guests of honor, you may handwrite "*In honor of . . .*" across the very top of the invitation or have it printed immediately before or after the event line. If the USMC Candidates are hosting the event, the first three lines of the invitation might read:

The United States Marine Candidates of Class 2014
United States Naval Academy
request the honor of your company

*the third of October, or Saturday, the twelfth, at eight o'clock. I want to ask some friends
to meet you, and hope very much that you are free on one of those evenings."*

When inviting guests over the telephone, do not use the phrase "in honor of,"
as this phrase is used only on written invitations. The host may say instead, *"We
are giving a dinner for Senator and Mrs. Jones on . . ."*

WHITE HOUSE INVITATIONS

An invitation to the White House must be answered promptly—no later than
twenty-four hours after its arrival. These invitations are an honor not to be missed.
An invitation from the White House or from your own Chief of Mission while on
embassy duty takes precedence over all other invitations. Accept unless you are
ill, have official duty that keeps or takes you a distance away, or there is a death in
your family. Reply as to any other invitation—in the same way that it was extended
or as directed. The White House may call by phone before sending a *p.m.* (see "To
Remind" cards below). For proper dress and conduct at the White House see the
end of Chapter 18: Official Business Functions, Cocktails, and Receptions.

The President and Mrs. Bush
request the pleasure of your company at a
Valentine's Dinner
to be held at
The White House
on Thursday, February 14, 2008
at seven o'clock

Black Tie   East Entrance

CHANGING YOUR ANSWER

When circumstances change after you have regretted an invitation and you find that you can go to the occasion after all, immediately phone the host to explain your change of plans. If the occasion has a flexible guest list, such as a cocktail party or a reception, you will very likely be told to come ahead. But if another guest has been invited in your place for a seated meal, they may not be able to accommodate you.

After accepting a formal invitation, you are committed to the occasion. Let your hosts know immediately if an emergency (serious illness, a family death, a job transfer, or official duty) precludes your attendance. A matter of hours either way can make all the difference when hosts are dealing with caterers or ordering food and supplies.

It is perfectly acceptable to withdraw your acceptance if the President of the United States or your ambassador at an American Embassy posting requests your presence. Handwrite or email your host:

> Captain and Mrs. Michael Conetsco
> regret that because of an invitation
> to the White House
> they must withdraw from
> General and Mr. Hart's dinner
> on the third of May

TELEPHONE AND FACE-TO-FACE INVITATIONS

Telephone and in-person invitations are often issued for smaller, immediate occasions, including lunches, morning coffees and teas, after-work cocktails, and movie dates or dinners out. Invitations by card—usually the fill-in kind—are for occasions when the hosts plan ahead for food and service, such as cocktail parties and holiday receptions, family events such as christenings, open houses, and in-home dinners.

It is quite correct, however, to issue even formal or official invitations by telephone. The White House and embassies use this method often, sending *p.m.* (To Remind) cards if the invitation is accepted. In offices, an aide or assistant often calls for his or her superior. In tendering telephone invitations, provide complete information:

> *"This is Mrs. Slotta, administrative assistant. Mr. and Mrs. Christopher Morris wish to invite Senator and Mrs. Boggs to dinner on Saturday, October fourteenth at eight o'clock. The dinner will be at their residence in McLean, Virginia, and the attire is Informal. Will you please R.s.v.p.? My phone number is 703.555.1212."*

or

"This is Cadet Katherine Boggs. The Class of 2012 requests the pleasure of your company at a dance on Saturday, the sixteenth of September from seven-thirty until ten o'clock. The dance is being held at the Academy Alumni Hall and the attire is Informal. Will you check your calendar and call us back? The phone number is 555.1212."

An everyday social invitation given face-to-face may be stated in a simple manner: *"John and I are having a few friends in to supper on Saturday at seven; we hope that you and Bill can join us. It will be informal."* By telephone, a casual social invitation is also simple: *"This is Julia Vance. Could you and Sergeant King have supper with us next Saturday at seven?"* Whether extended in person or on the telephone, you must allow the guest to call you back with their response. Some will accept or refuse immediately, but some will need to check with significant others and their calendars.

"To Remind" Cards

To confirm particulars for those guests who have accepted a verbal invitation, particularly guests of honor or VIPs, formal reminder cards are sent. The format is identical to an invitation except you draw a line through the "R.s.v.p." (if printed) and write in above it the lower case initials, *"p.m."* (see Chapter 13: Abbreviations in Social Correspondence) or the words *"To Remind."*

For informal occasions when printed invitations were not mailed, a personal or joint card may be sent shortly before the occasion with a sentence: *"To remind you—Thursday 12th, 7:00."*

No acknowledgment is necessary upon receipt of To Remind cards.

E-mail Invitations

See Chapter 14: Personal Electronics Etiquette.

"Hold the Date" Cards

If the date for an important function is firm, but not yet all the details, you can notify guests to "mark their calendars" or "save the date" by sending cards, notes, or e-mails as early as six months in advance. This allows out-of-town invitees especially to make tentative travel arrangements. Telephone calls to busy executives and officials or their administrative aides can also be used to alert them of upcoming invitations so that they can "protect the time" on their schedules until your invitation is received.

GUEST DUTIES

An officer wrote about American disregard for proprieties from overseas: *"Employees and their families need to be made aware of the importance of R.s.v.p.s and sending thank-you notes. Many apparently are not aware or simply don't care. Such a lack of simple social graces is appalling. Too many of our senior officials still lack polish and reflect negatively not only on themselves, but on our government, and the U.S. population in general."*

Invitations must be answered within forty-eight hours. R.s.v.p. is mandatory etiquette for guests. When acknowledging an invitation via phone to a third party, guests refer to themselves by their full names, *"Staff Sergeant and Mrs. Harold Fields accept the kind invitation"* but refer to hosts by last names only, *"of Captain Baker."* Guests accepting repeat the information concerning time, date, and place so any misunderstanding can be corrected, and then write it on a calendar or enter it into their personal digital assistant (PDA).

Without a mail-back card or other response method for very formal engraved invitations, handwritten replies are required. Guests write their acceptance or regret in the third person on quality white or cream-colored stationery paper (single or double sheets with matching envelopes) or on a correspondence card. If less formal invitations were extended in the first person, they are answered in kind. See Chapter 10: Military Wedding Invitations, Announcements, and Replies, under Letters of Invitation and Replies, for sample guest responses in the first and third person.

CHAPTER 12

Correspondence and Stationery Essentials

veryone needs personal stationery for identification (business or social cards) and for writing (correspondence cards or informals). These items support your good manners and lend presence to your professional career. The U.S. government does not provide them nor are they reimbursable. Government letterhead is supplied for official business, but is illegal for personal use. For instance, to write a letter of congratulations on official letterhead would mean that the entire military unit or government agency is offering the sentiment.

AT EASE KEY POINTS

- ⚬ Request personalized correspondence cards when asked for gift ideas (provide correct samples).
- ⚬ Social/Calling cards need name in classic font. Use as gift enclosures, interim business cards, and for exchanging contact information.
- ⚬ Write thank-you notes for courtesies extended.

Modern stationery is available in a variety of colors and styles for paper or card stock, borders, and typeface. Be conservative in your choices as you begin acquiring essentials. You will need some versatile enough to use for formal occasions (writing to superiors) and solemn reasons (notes of sympathy). Consider classic blue or black ink on white or ecru paper because these colors are well received internationally and it is easy to match with your fountain or ballpoint pen.

Each piece of social correspondence (except business cards) should come with matching envelopes. If you do not have personal writing items already, desirable items are stationery paper or blank informals or correspondence cards, all sold in packages. Avoid purchasing "theme" commercial stationery, if it could be misconstrued as juvenile, but branching out into colored cardstock, ink, envelope liners, and so on is acceptable after the conservative basics have been obtained.

Printing Styles

Engraving is the most expensive printing choice, used primarily for seals and such. It requires specialized machinery and metal plates to incise the surface of the card stock. *Photo-engraving* is the modern version used for lettering. *Thermography* is an imitation that results in a raised image above the surface of the card stock to simulate the feel of engraving. *Flat printing* is ink on paper, similar to what you see on this page. Engravers and stationers are generally qualified to advise concerning type choice and size, paper quality, and similar matters.

Flags, Insignia, Seals, Coats of Arms

If desired, admirals and generals may buy stationery embossed or printed with their flags in color for official use. Military attachés of any rank may purchase invitations and cards embossed with their Service seal in gold or silver. All other military insignia are normally printed or embossed without color. Service seals are not used by spouses. If spouses are also in the military, they order their own stationery items.

A family coat of arms (or crest) may be embossed or printed on personal stationery items, traditionally without color. They are the exclusive property of male members of a family unless the female has applied for her own heraldic symbol.

Suffixes

When a man's name is the same as that of his living father he adds *Junior* spelled out in full and separated from his name by a comma. If the line is too long, it may be abbreviated as *Jr.* (the only time an abbreviation is proper on a card unless the initial is your name—such as J. Paul Getty). A comma is always used between the surname and suffix, except for roman numerals, as in *Walter Delaney James III*. The Roman numeral II is used to identify a young man who was named after another living relative, such as a grandfather or uncle.

Usually Junior and II are dropped following the death of the senior, but a man may decide to keep the suffix for business purposes, or if his widowed mother kept her husband's name and lives in the same city, he may prefer to retain it for postal reasons.

MD, PhD, JD, or Esq., and other professional suffixes, such as certifications, follow the name when appropriate, separated by a comma:

Russell Walsh Anderson, PhD   Carla Hart, CPO

MILITARY TITLES AND RANK

Senior officer ranks normally precede the centered names, followed by the Service designation on all of their cards. Senior ranks are O-5 and above (Commander through Admiral) in the Sea Services; and O-4 and above (Major through General) in the Army, Air Force, and Marines.

General Brent Scowcroft
United States Marine Corps

Junior officers (O-3 and below, Warrant Officers, and Non-commissioned Officers) place the rank and Service beneath the name, separated by a comma if on the same line.

Curtis LeMay
Captain, United States Air Force

Reserve and Retired

The card of a reserve officer on active duty places the word *Reserve* at the end of the Service affiliation:

Leslie Denise Lowe
Lieutenant Junior Grade
United States Naval Reserve

All regular and reserve personnel who retire because of age or physical disability, including those on the temporary disability retired list, use the word *Retired* on the same line or below the Service affiliation if they retain their military title:

General John Pershing
United States Army Retired

There are restrictions in referring to yourself as a retired military person in connection with commercial enterprises when such use, intentionally or not, gives rise to any appearance of sanction, endorsement, sponsorship, or approval by any Service department or the Department of Defense. Be especially mindful regarding your Service affiliation when making public appearances outside of this country (check with the appropriate overseas commander).

Socially, retired military officers who have retained their ranks may continue to be addressed with no mention of the retired status necessary, as in: *Colonel (and Mrs.) John Doe*.

In official correspondence, however, the retired status is always acknowledged with the name (not the spouse's), as in: *Captain John D. Doe, USCG Retired (or USCGR Retired)*. If the couple were addressed jointly, it would read: *Captain John D. Doe, USCG Retired and Mrs. Doe*.

BUSINESS CARDS

Business cards are printed on white or a very light cream-colored, glazed or unglazed bristol board of medium or light weight. The lettering is usually black. If cards are engraved, the engraver will give you the engraving plate so that additional cards can be made up at any time thereafter, from any equipped stationer. Order only the number of cards that you anticipate using within a year; when you advance in position or rank you cannot use outdated cards.

Sophisticated leaders practice multicultural awareness and use clear lettering on their business (and social) cards instead of italic, Old English, or unusual fonts, because nonnative English speakers find plain letters easier to read. Business cards include your full name; rank, title, and position; office or company designation; a logo, seal, or slogan; street, e-mail, and Web site addresses; office telephone, cell phone, and fax numbers. That is a lot of information to crowd onto a 3.5 by 2 inch (approximately 9 by 5 centimeters) piece of bristol board. Aesthetically it can be difficult to arrange, but worth the effort to make it visually appealing because the card represents you. Choose only *essential* information; a simple card has more presence than one with multiple seals and every address and phone number you possess.

Center your full name on cards, larger or bolder than other information. Drop any reference to a middle name entirely rather than use an initial. Honorifics (Mr., Mrs., Ms., Dr., Judge, Senator, etc.) are not used before a name, with the exception of senior ranking military officers on attaché duty and ambassadors. Another exception to giving yourself an honorific may be advisable if a female working with internationals is often mistaken for a male because of her first name. In that case, use Ms. on your business cards:

Ms. Shelby Smith Jones   Ms. Milo Walker

The exchange of business cards is, of course, common during the workday. Business cards are handed to newly met persons and attached to documents. Cards are scanned into a computer file system, organized in a Rolodex, or a leather folder. Business cards serve as references for creating client and guest lists and, in private, notes are jotted on them to serve as a memory jogger. The exchange of business cards in another country may follow a ritual. See Chapter 25: International Protocol and Civility.

> Q: Thank goodness I took your advice and made myself "student cards" on the computer! I was ready for a group of business people at a recent party. My dilemma: how do I pass my card with my right hand and shake hands with my right hand at the same time?!
>
> A: Congratulations for being aware that many cultures find left hands objectionable. When meeting a new group of people, immediately shake hands with everyone as you introduce yourself. Then, if business cards are exchanged, you will be ready. Keep your own cards in a designated pocket and put the ones you receive in another pocket so that you will never be embarrassed by giving out someone else's card by mistake, as you move from group to group.

Diplomatic Attaché Cards

The business cards of all military officers attached to a diplomatic mission are traditionally white or ecru and engraved. If desired, the cards may have a gold or silver Service seal. After the name and Service lines, the third line is the position, such as Defense and Army Attaché, Naval Attaché and Naval Attaché for Air, Assistant Air Attaché, Defense and Army Liaison Officer, or Coast Guard Attaché. A last centered line is the diplomatic post, such as, "Embassy of the United States of America." The accreditation city is engraved in the lower right corner, and the office phone number or e-mail, if provided, is on the lower left.

U.S. attachés sometimes find it convenient to have two sets of cards, one in English, the other in the language of the host country—as in Colonel Hammersen's card example below—or a card in English on one side and in the local language on the back (of the same quality as the front lest insult be taken).

Martha Ella Adkins

United States Navy
Defense and Naval Attaché
Embassy of the United States of America

Wellington

Leslie Earl Blair

Assistant Air Attaché
Embassy of the United States of America

522-1776 Ext:2622   Manila

Oberst i.G. Frederick P. A. Hammersen

Verteidigungs-und Heeresattaché
Botscharf der Vereinigten Staaten von Amerika

Tel. (49) 30-8305-2463   10117 Berlin
Fax (49) 30-8305-2479   Neustädtische Kirchetraße4

Attaché Cards

SOCIAL CARDS

In the early 1900s, young American gentlemen agonized over the appropriate number of cards to leave in silver trays located on tables near the doors of homes they visited. Whatever you call them—social cards, calling cards, or visiting cards—this tradition is making its last formal stand in the diplomatic corps.

Now that personal digital assistants (PDAs) such as computer phones are ubiquitous, professionally printed social cards are most often used as gift enclosures or as bearers of short messages. If you feel the need to order them, make sure that you get some matching envelopes. Social cards are also useful when exchanging contact information with new friends (perhaps just met at a party) so that you do not need to find a scrap of paper or write on a napkin, or resort to using your business cards, which of course, are for occupational transactions. Social cards can also come in handy when you are between jobs or have no reason to possess a business card.

Today it is convenient to buy card sets that include small cards with envelopes, variously termed gift enclosures or information cards. This modern version of the social card has your name centered in the upper third of the card, leaving more room for messages below. They may be used in place of the more traditional calling card. If you are ever in a position to "leave cards," remember that they are not handed to anyone, but placed on a table near the front door (in a dish or tray, if provided) without an envelope.

It is not necessary to include rank or Service affiliation on social (calling) cards because that limits their shelf life due to promotions. If you do feel the necessity, order the smallest amount possible (First, Second and junior grade Lieutenants may all use "Lieutenant"). All military personnel may place the rank in the lower right corner of a social card above the Service designation. Staff Corps designations, if desired, properly appear before the Service affiliation wherever it is located.

David Andrew Skarpetowski, Jr.

Lieutenant
Medical Corps
United States Navy Reserve

Junior Officer Social Card

An alternative appropriate for students and temporary positions is make-your-own computer-generated cards. Commercial card stock is available that comes pre-perforated with ten business-sized cards on a page, each about 3.5 inches by 2 inches (approximately 9 by 5 centimeters), ready to be printed as the need arises. Since this is an economical choice, your contact information and rank are easy to update. They are, of necessity, thin enough to go through your printer; therefore, they do not make the same statement as professional card stock. The same format is used; the name is larger or bold and centered.

John Paul Jones
Midshipman
United States Naval Academy

410-555-1212 cell   P.O. Box 123
M00000@usna.edu   Annapolis, MD 21402

Computer-generated Academy Student Card

Q: We are ordering calling cards and announcements for our son's graduation. The announcements will be mailed from our home, but whose name should be on the return address label? Where should his new rank go on his calling card?

A: Your name or the address alone is appropriate on return labels, which may be affixed on the top left or on the back flap. Social (also known as calling) cards have full names (avoid initials) centered on them—no contact information, which is added as needed—so that they will never be out of date. His new rank, if you insist, goes in the lower right-hand corner above his Service designation on social cards, but consider how short a time he will retain the initial rank.

CONVEYING MESSAGES

Diplomats handwrite codified messages in French on their cards. If you receive a diplomat's card with mysterious initials, look them up in Chapter 13: Abbreviations in Social Correspondence.

Your social or business card makes a good delivery conveyance when attached to the front of a forwarded article, magazine, or document sent to a friend. Write a short message on the front, or if there is not room, draw a slash through your entire name, and write "n.b." (*nota bene*)—meaning "take note"—on one of the left front corners. Both automatically prompt the viewer to turn it over and read your handwritten message on the back, perhaps, *"Thought you might enjoy this international protocol information."* You might strike through the print and write your nickname above a lined-out legal name on the front or write your first initial after a handwritten message, but do not rewrite a printed name. You may write your telephone number or e-mail address on social cards when inviting special individuals to get in touch with you, but ordering cards with this perishable information makes them useless if contact information changes.

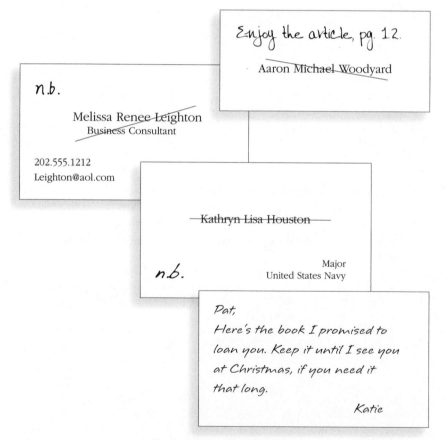

Cards with handwritten notes

CIVILIAN OFFICIALS

The Service Secretaries and Under Secretaries, although not members of the President's Cabinet, use only titles on social cards just as Cabinet members do, for instance, *The Secretary of the Navy*. An Assistant Secretary's or Under Secretary's card must carry the name with the title beneath since there is more than one person with the same title.

Civilian cards do not have honorific prefixes (see discussion in Business Cards above), except for "Ambassador," which may precede the name.

JOINT SOCIAL CARDS

Because wives sometimes retain maiden names upon marriage, or have ranks and titles of their own, or attend functions alone, purchase joint cards only *after* individual cards, as joint versions may not be used as often. A married couple's individual social cards match in color, style, and print type (engraving, thermography, or flat printing). The spouse of an official whose social card reads only by title (for example, *The Secretary of State*) uses a full name on his or her own social cards, as in *William Jefferson Clinton*.

A joint social card for married couples makes reference to both persons in the center, usually listing the husband first. Government service is never indicated on the joint card, and neither is retired or active status. Just as with individual cards, joint cards are useful for extending or confirming informal invitations from the couple (*"See you for lunch Tuesday"*) and are frequently enclosed with host gifts when both are invited (remember to order some matching envelopes). Unless the couple's address is permanent, omit it and pencil it in as the cards are used, if providing the address is important. Here are some variations:

> For military husband and civilian wife [Rank and Mrs. Joint Name]:
> *Rear Admiral and Mrs. John Paul Jones II*

> For military wife and civilian husband [Rank Wife's Name and Mr. Name]:
> *Colonel Jane Doe and Mr. John Doe*

> For civilian husband with a title [Honorific and Name] and [Rank and Name]:
> *Senator John Doe and Captain Jane Smith* or *Doctor John and Major Jane Doe*

> If both are military [Rank Name] and [Rank Name]:
> In the same Service: *Major John and Lieutenant Jane Doe*
> When their rank and Service are the same: *Majors John and Jane Doe*
> When each is in a different Service, or when one is non-commissioned or a civilian, one person may forgo his or her title and accept that of the spouse:
> *Sergeant and Mrs. John Doe* or *Doctor and Mrs. John Doe*

CORRESPONDENCE CARDS

When your finances allow, purchase personalized correspondence cards. They will become one of your favorite stationery essentials. They are flat, good quality card stock about the same size as an invitation, 4.5 inches by 6.5 inches (approximately 11 by 16 centimeters). They may have a monogram or your full name (without initials or nicknames) printed in a bold, classic font, centered across the top, with a border or not, as preferred. Your address can be pre-printed on the back flap of the accompanying envelopes.

Correspondence cards are just large enough for a short handwritten message, such as thank-yous, congratulations, condolences, informal invitations, or other social communications. Write on them with the same pen ink color as your printed name, the border, or monogram. On social notes, spell out the day-date in the lower left corner and sign with an appropriate closing (e.g., *Sincerely, Very Respectfully, Warmly*, etc.) using only your first initial or nickname if your full name is centered across the top. For invitations, your printed name serves as the host line and "*R.s.v.p.*" is written in the lower left corner with phone number or e-mail (see Chapter 11: Invitations).

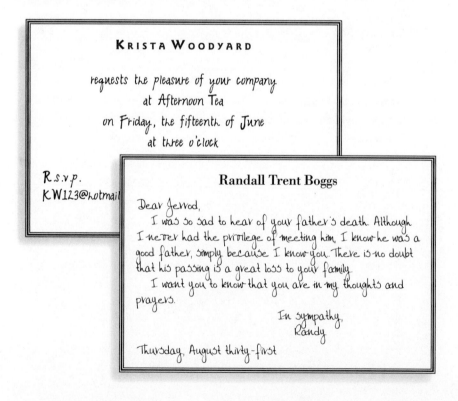

KRISTA WOODYARD

requests the pleasure of your company
at Afternoon Tea
on Friday, the fifteenth of June
at three o'clock

R.s.v.p.
KW123@hotmail

Randall Trent Boggs

Dear Jerrod,
   I was so sad to hear of your father's death. Although I never had the privilege of meeting him, I know he was a good father, simply because I know you. There is no doubt that his passing is a great loss to your family.
   I want you to know that you are in my thoughts and prayers.

In sympathy,
Randy

Thursday, August thirty-first

You may purchase separate *business* correspondence cards with additional information following the full name, if desired, but remember that the cards are then only suitable for business colleagues or clients:

Kennedy Renee Doe, Major, U.S. Army
Patricia Anne Boggs, ASID

INFORMALS

These traditional small fold-over cards, approximately 3.5 inches by 5 inches (about 9 by 13 centimeters) can be ordered with your full name (or joint names for married couples), Service crest or insignia (business purposes), or monogram, embossed or printed in the center of the front. You will not need them if you have the more contemporary correspondence cards. Insert them into their matching envelopes so that the front faces the recipient when it is opened. Write a short note or informal invitation inside below the fold. If you run out of room, continue writing on "page 2" above the fold, and on "page 3," which is on the back of the card.

Dear Sondra,

I look forward to seeing you on Tuesday the seventh. My flight lands at two o'clock. Thank you for volunteering to pick me up!

Debbie

Deborah Ann Morris

Informal Card

HOW TO WRITE

Being able to express yourself clearly in social communication is as essential as your business writing and speaking. The important thing for social notes is to take pen in hand, as the extra effort to send something handwritten is respected and valued. If you cannot write well in cursive, then print your social notes. You will be surprised at how a bit of forethought improves matters. First, draft what you want to say (on the computer if that is easier for you; save it for future reference). Double-check your draft for errors in spelling, grammar, and punctuation. Put a darkly lined paper underneath a piece of stationery or a thin informal. It will show through and keep your writing level. Or position an index card or straight edge over correspondence cards (this works for invitations and place cards also) and practice writing along it, then remove the straight edge to add the "tails" of letters. Write your final copy with a good pen, making sure your ink matches any printing or border, if possible. Sign cards pre-printed with your full name by signing your nickname or a bold initial. If your stationery has a monogram, sign your full name legibly.

In written correspondence, a senior sends his "compliments" to a junior; the junior sends his "respects" to the senior. The senior may "call" attention, but the junior many only "invite it." A senior writing to a junior may subscribe it "Respectfully," but a junior writing to a senior closes with "Very Respectfully."

Q: I was bowled over recently when the mayor of Miami wrote to me by hand. His handwriting made his message easy to understand. I have terrible penmanship. I need to write him back. What should I do?

A: Since you have probably been using a keyboard since third or fourth grade, it is no wonder that cursive is a weak point for you. But handwritten notes, as you have noticed, continue to make an excellent impression, building better and more personal relationships. The key here is to pick up a pen—*hand print* your social correspondence.

Q: I have worked for many prominent politicians and I know that even a guy is more respectable when he has good handwriting. I would really like to improve. Even my signature is just squiggles. Do you know a few resources for refining my cursive?

A: Congratulations on recognizing the benefits of good handwriting. Perhaps because of junk mail, an envelope addressed in cursive arrests our attention. There are cursive guides and practice sheets to download from the Internet, but simply writing a couple of sentences every day will soon end your print days. Sit up straight, hold the pen without tension between the tips of thumb and forefinger, the other fingers curled under. Neatness counts. Form letters regular in shape and size; do not press hard. Cursive is much harder to forge than printing, hence signatures on documents. The hardest signatures to counterfeit are the neat ones, so practicing cursive may improve your signature *and* protect your credit.

SOCIAL AND PERSONAL LETTERS

A social or personal letter or note follows basic rules. A long letter has the date at the upper right hand corner of the page. The date may also be written near the left-hand margin but slightly below the signature, for instance, on a correspondence card or one-page letter. The more formal the letter, the fewer the abbreviations (for example, spell out the month). The envelope address may use the indented or centered form, as desired.

The basic parts of a social or personal letter are:

(date top right)	June 10, 2011 (*civilian form*) 10 June 2011 (*international & military form*)
No inside address	
(salutation with comma)	Dear Mary, *or* My dear Mary, *or* Dear Mary Jones,
(body)	Indent paragraphs. One paragraph may be sufficient for a brief note. Avoid overuse of the pronoun "I." For the complementary closing, make it even with the date. Directly underneath it or slightly to the right, sign your name. In letters to a relative or intimate friend, the closing would probably be "Affectionately," or "Love."
(closing with comma)	Sincerely, *or* Sincerely yours,
(signature, no title or rank)	John Smith *or* John *First name is fine for friends and family.* *Otherwise, please write your name in full unless printed on top of your stationery.*
(alternate date location, lower left, two spaces lower than the signature)	Saturday, the tenth of June (*formal*) *or* "June tenth" or "Saturday" (*briefer, informal*)

VERY PERSONAL LETTERS

Certain types of informal letters may be typed in an e-mail, *but others must be written by hand.* It is obligatory to write thank-you notes by hand, as well as letters of congratulation, condolence, and "welcome to the family" letters to prospective sons- or daughters-in-law. Invitations to small weddings (and replies to them), engagement announcements, and birth announcements may be handwritten. Answers to very formal invitations without R.s.v.p. contact information are always handwritten.

A wise individual observes certain rules in writing letters, blogs, e-mails, or anything else: Never state anything that can be used against you. Be careful of making direct promises or of stating familiarities. Never write anything that might damage another's reputation or cause harm in any way. Do not write angry or abusive letters. If you must write a letter of complaint, wait several hours or overnight, and then reread the letter to see if you really want to mail it.

Letters of Apology
Even the best of us may need to write a letter of regret or a request for forgiveness. Brief and sincere handwritten notes of explanation are always advisable when you are unable to keep an appointment or your promise, when there has been some misunderstanding, or when you have hurt someone.

Thank You Notes
A short note of appreciation should be handwritten within forty-eight hours after you have received any kindness, whether a gift, or a party in your honor, or a favor. The benefits are enormous. Recipients admire these grace notes and never forget that you were the one who recognized what they did and made them feel valued. Failing to acknowledge benefactors makes them feel less than important and they will not forget that either, nor will they be disposed to favor you again.

When you have been a houseguest, the thank-you is sometimes called a "bread-and-butter" note. Since the envelope and note are usually (but not always) addressed to the wife after you have been in a couple's home, mention her husband in the body of the note (and your own spouse also, if appropriate).

It is easy to be a leader in this area. Stop thinking that a phone call is sufficient, forego the e-mail, find your favorite pen and your personalized correspondence card (or a piece of stationery), name the courtesy or item, say something personal about it, and emphasize your enjoyment. The person writing signs the correspondence without courtesy titles (i.e., *Nicholas*, not *Mr. Ryan*). Three sentences and you are done:

Dear Megan,

Thank you for including me at your lovely brunch. I will not soon forget that wonderful meal topped with strawberry daiquiris. It was a pleasure to meet your husband and to get to know your daughter.

> *My best wishes to you ,*
> *Cheri Smith*

Dear Mr. Allen,

I enjoyed meeting you at this year's Leadership Conference. I will put into practice immediately some of your suggestions for working as a civilian in a military environment. I hope we will meet again at the next conference, if not before.

Sincerely,
Cheri Smith

For a bridal couple's thank-you notes, see Chapter 9: Military Wedding Etiquette.

Q: It's been a week since I had lunch at the home of my school's dean. Isn't it too late to write a thank-you note? I don't think any of the other students who went wrote one. Can I send an e-mail?

A: A true leader knows that it is never too late to say thank you, regardless of peers' actions. Respect the host for including you and write today. Please resist the temptation to cite excuses for your tardiness. People with a fine motor skills disability do not control pens well enough to form letters on a page and may use e-mail, but if you can handwrite your note, be it cursive or printed, it will be considered much more personal and you will be favorably remembered. Manners demonstrate potential.

Letters of Condolence

One of the most difficult letters to write is a letter of condolence—but no letter is more appreciated than the one expressing sympathy at a time of sorrow. Respect, affection, and friendship are the motives for writing such letters. A letter of condolence is addressed to the spouse or closest family member, and references to other members of the family are made in the body of the letter. Always be careful of your choice of words in a message following a death that resulted from an accident, suicide, or any catastrophe. Write a few simple sentences expressing sympathy, offering a kind remembrance, encouragement, or a desire to help.

Dear Mrs. Smith,

I have just heard of Dan's fatal accident, and I want you to know that you have my deepest sympathy. Our friendship began at the Academy and continued through the years.

I am being transferred next month and plan to stop over in Atlanta en route. At that time, I want to call on you and, if possible, be of some service.

My deepest sympathy,
John Jones

Replies to Sympathy Messages

The individual to whom they were addressed personally acknowledges letters, cards, and other messages of condolence, as well as floral tributes, charity contributions, and such gifts as food for the family. This very brief reply of thanks is handwritten and mailed within six weeks after the message (or flowers or contribution) was received—earlier, if possible. A sentence or two will be enough, particularly in cases of ill health or extreme grief. In these cases, it is permissible for another member of the family to write the note:

> Dear Mrs. Kennedy,
>
> Thank you so much for your kind expression of sympathy.
>
> > Sincerely,
> > Luke Jones

To a longtime friend, a more personal note might read:

> Dear Mary,
>
> Your very kind letter gave me great comfort. Thank you so much for the roses, and for writing. I will call you and Bill as soon as I can.
>
> > Very sincerely,
> > Andy

In order for the bereaved to acknowledge accurately the messages of condolence, the flowers, and so on, a list must be compiled. A close friend or a member of the bereaved family should volunteer to do this. When services take place at a funeral home, a member of the staff will collect the cards left for the family.

Mourning Cards

It is correct to send engraved or printed cards of acknowledgment in response to expressions of condolence when in the hundreds or thousands. For example:

> Secretary of the Air Force and Mrs. Doe
> acknowledge with grateful appreciation
> your kind expression of sympathy

GREETING CARDS

Holiday cards are sent to close friends and acquaintances you cannot greet personally or see often. Usually, holiday cards are not sent within a Service activity or government office. Exceptions anywhere are shut-ins.

Envelopes for holiday cards are always addressed to both husband and wife, even if you know only one or the other. A card without the sending family's names pre-printed is signed at the bottom of the greeting. The person who knows the addressee best signs his or her name first. When cards are printed with names, the husband's name is typically listed before the wife's, but either way is correct. When the names of several members of a sending family are listed on the card, the father's name is printed first, then the mother's, then children. Sign above or below the printed names. Alternatively, you may sign or have the cards printed as: "The John Smiths."

In addressing the envelope to a family, you may write "The Alexander Eatons" rather than "Mr. and Mrs. Alexander Eaton and family."

Many people observe Christmas and Easter as national rather than religious holidays and send out secular cards. You may find generic "Season's Greetings" cards useful when you have many friends of different faiths. They can be used for Christmas, Hanukkah, Eid al Fitr (the three-day celebration at the end of Ramadan), and other occasions. or you can buy New Year's cards, since everyone celebrates the beginning of a new year, even if it occurs on their calendar on a date other than January 1, such as the Chinese New Year.

Birthday cards are usually appreciated as an indication of your thoughtfulness. "Turning the decade" (ages ending with zero) are considered especially important birthday years for some nationalities. Others celebrate their "name day"—the birthday of the saint that they are named after.

LETTERS OF REFERENCE

When you are asked to write a letter of reference—for example, for someone leaving military or public service, or your place of employment—you will want to write an honest, straightforward account of that person's ability and character. It is important that the letter be fair both to the future employer and to the employee.

A letter of reference, or any letter written to an unknown reader, needs neither salutation nor closing. The letter is a statement of fact, and is attested to by the signature. However, the phrase "To Whom It May Concern" may be used if you wish, as may "Dear Sir or Madam." When you know to whom the letter will be addressed, use that person's honorific and name.

Letters of reference are always dated and usually typewritten, but may be written by hand. The general points covered in the typical letter are:

- The name of the employee
- The length of his or her employment

- The nature of his or her work—and competence
- Comments on the employee's honesty, character, and loyalty
- Comments on the employee's ability to get along with others
- The reasons he or she is leaving the Service or business; an expression of your regret at losing the employee, if such is the case
- Your willingness to answer any further questions, and an expression of your confidence in the employee, as appropriate

When you know a person has been unsatisfactory in his or her work, or when the person has a questionable reputation, you are under no obligation to give any reference at all. However, you may feel pressured to write in some circumstances, for instance, on behalf of household help during an overseas tour of duty. Many times, there are local laws regarding termination if you "fire" someone. In such cases, you might find it prudent to have ready a letter such as the following, along with a statement the person signs as to dates of employment with you and receipt of all pay due, including any severance pay:

> This is a statement of services [*do not say "recommendation letter"*] provided by [name] from [date] to [date]. [He/She] is conscientious when under supervision. I have found [name] to have a pleasing personality, especially when serving our guests. It may be to your advantage to demonstrate preferred methods of cleaning during your probation period. [He/She] came to my home [number] of days a week/ month and was most often very prompt.

LETTERS OF INTRODUCTION

See Chapter 1: Military and Government Protocol.

LETTERS OF INVITATION

See Chapter 11: Invitations.

BIRTH AND ADOPTION ANNOUNCEMENTS

The announcement of a new baby is made soon after the birth. Usually, fill-in greeting cards are chosen. Handwritten notes are always appropriate alternatives. Social cards, a more expensive option, frequently join the parents' joint card and a small baby's name card, perhaps attached by a pink or blue ribbon, or edged in pink or blue.

Birth or Adoption Card

The baby's card may have the birth date printed on it, but if the accompanying note conveys the birth information, extra baby's cards may be ordered for use throughout childhood, to enclose with birthday party gifts and so on. In the case of twins, both names can appear on the same smaller card, if desired; when the twins are not the same sex, the ribbon bows may be of both colors.

Parents usually make public in the very beginning the fact of their adoption of a child. If the baby cards described above are not appropriate, announcement cards could be worded in this manner:

Lieutenant and Mrs. John Doe
have the pleasure of announcing the adoption of
Mary Jane, age two years

ADDRESSING ENVELOPES

Flat sheets of paper are folded, written side in, before inserting into envelopes. Invitations and folded cards are inserted printed side up so that when removed they face the recipient. See Chapter 10: Military Wedding Invitations, Announcements, and Replies for an illustration on inserting additional items such as maps and for writing honorifics for young persons and widows.

Regardless of the contents' formality, envelopes are properly addressed with the recipient's title/military rank/honorific, full name, and address centered on the face of a mailing envelope, in block style (business), or staggered, or each line centered (social). All social correspondence is best addressed by hand in black ink, but formal invitations *must* be. However, with the advancement of technology, there are now attractive computer-generated address labels, more appropriate for the largest gatherings.

Official business correspondence envelopes may be typed and may use the abbreviated form of the rank, but social correspondence envelopes spell the rank in full unless the social envelope is too small to accommodate everything. Then it is permissible to abbreviate the rank: RADM, LtCol, CWO, CMSAF, and so on (see Chapter 8: Order of Precedence and Military Forms of Address), but the recipient's full name is always written.

You may write only the honorific and name, such as "Ms. Smith," on a small social or business card envelope before enclosing it in a larger envelope for mailing (rectangular and light-colored). The U.S. Postal Service levies a surcharge on non-standard letter mail because it jams their letter-sorting machinery.

If you are extending an *official* invitation to a couple, both of whom are in the military, the first person listed is the principal being invited, with the spouse information (regardless of rank) following: *Major Jane Doe and Colonel John Doe*, on separate lines if desired. The office address of the principal person is used. *Socially*, this same couple could receive envelopes addressed to *Colonel and Mrs. John Doe* at their home address.

Your own name need not appear with your return address, which is written in the top left corner of the envelope (business and informal) or pre-printed on the back flap (formal and social).

CHAPTER 13

Abbreviations in Social Correspondence

*F*rench abbreviations facilitate social correspondence. You are undoubtedly familiar with the first three below, which are common in American contemporary life.

n.b. (*nota bene*)	Take note. Calls attention to a written message on the back of a card.
p.m. (*pour mémoire*)	To remind. Used in place of **R.s.v.p.** when an invitation has been accepted verbally.
R.s.v.p. (*répondez s'il vous plaît*)	Please reply. Written on the bottom left corner of invitations above a phone number or e-mail address. First letter is capitalized.

If you ever receive a diplomat's social card with mysterious initials, look them up on the list below. These six abbreviations are handwritten in lower case at the bottom left-hand (or top left-hand) corner of social cards. They are written in pencil if the card is delivered in person; in ink if sent by messenger.

p.c. (*pour condoléances*)	Condolence. Expresses sympathy at a death or anniversary of a national figure's death.
p.f. (*pour féliciter*)	Congratulations. For instance, on national patriotic days or birthdays.
p.f.n.a. (*Nouvel An*)	Extends New Year's greetings.
p.p. (*pour presenter*)	To present or introduce. Used on the card of a senior official or predecessor who is accompanying a subordinate or successor. In return for a "**p.p.**" card, one's own card is given to the person who was introduced.

p.p.c. (*pour prendre congé*)

To take leave from diplomatic post. For example, to notify friends and colleagues of one's departure in lieu of goodbye calls in person or via telephone.

p.r. (*pour remercier*)

To thank for a gift or a courtesy received. One may send this in response to "**p.f.**" and "**p.c.**" cards.

CHAPTER 14

Personal Electronics Etiquette

*T*he written word over the World Wide Web (Internet) will remain the easiest way to send and receive information even though video phones may surpass electronic mail (e-mail) for maintaining personal contact in the future. The Internet has not been viewed as a formal medium, but people are beginning to realize it is so much *more* public that it is vital to present ourselves graciously every time we access any web forum. E-mail, personal digital assistants (PDAs), text phones, and other electronics for written material as well as telephone, voice mail, and video phones for verbal communications are not temporary. Data records of our bad behavior or opinionated word choices can be stored (and retrieved) indefinitely. E-mails and blogs (short for Web Log journal) are not private or anonymous; they are retained on multiple computer hard drives and servers to be read by anyone, anywhere. E-mails are not secure; anyone's personal information can be obtained by persons wanting to abuse it.

AT EASE KEY POINTS

- Keep cell phone conversations and texting private activities.
- Say *"excuse me"* before quickly checking a text message or call.
- Do not write disparaging e-mails or record negative voice/video messages.
- Restrict dissemination of personal information, especially travel plans and location.
- Give name and number slowly at the beginning *and* end when leaving voice mails.

The challenge is to set personal and professional standards of decorum and security no matter the modern technology employed. The goals are to be more formal than previously thought necessary (a reputation is never lost by being *too* respectful or private) and to be more vigilant (do not write or say anything that can be misconstrued or taken out of context, and censor bad language).

ELECTRONIC MAIL

E-mail is most suitable for transmitting straightforward information in text, image, or sound bites, and for requesting or confirming facts, figures, and details. Such clear-cut data are rarely misunderstood. It is only when human emotions get involved that computer text can be a disadvantage. Sophisticated, well-mannered people are sometimes surprised that their messages are misconstrued.

The reason e-mail is not good for expressing emotions is that words are dashed off quickly in the manner that they might be spoken, but the receiver has no way to monitor your facial expressions or tone of voice for respect or humor or annoyance. This will change when video phones come into popular use because they will give the feeling of being face-to-face, returning people to real-time interactions.

Offense can also be taken precisely *because* e-mail is considered a quick, informal medium, even if you have spent an hour polishing your words. For example, expressing sympathy over a death should always be by handwritten note, because the time and attention it takes to generate and mail correspondence is well understood and therefore valued in a way that e-mail never will be appreciated.

"Electroniquette" is an elision of *Electronic* communications and *Etiquette;* "Netiquette" is an elision of *Internet* and *Etiquette.* The public is coming to understand with such words that it is worth including social niceties to eliminate friction. Some have resorted to abbreviations in personal correspondence, such as "LOL" meaning Laugh Out Loud, or "emoticons" (for *emotion* and *icons,* referring to inserts such as smiley faces) in order to say "*please accept my previous statements non-critically.*" These are not appropriate for business e-mails. What is appropriate are the traditional polite words such as *please* and *thank you,* and consideration of others' feelings.

Good workplace e-mail manners mean responding as soon as possible (hopefully within one business day) and setting up an *out of office* automatic reply if you will be gone for several days, notifying readers of the date you will return to work and perhaps including the name of another who will handle requests in the meantime. When waiting on a response to business e-mails, after three days you may recontact the person. Be aware that there are different networks that affect the receipt of your message. Sometimes the networks are incompatible, with firewalls or standalone protocols that limit interface. For instance, the government's NIPRNET (nonsecure Internet protocol router network) and SIPRNET (secret Internet protocol router network) do not "talk" with each other because security regulations dictate that information can go up in classification, but never back down.

Good business etiquette in cyberspace means to convey the same respectful tenor online as speaking in person or writing more traditional paper memorandums, notes, and letters. This is especially important when conveying strong disagreement. Electronic text should not always substitute for voice-to-voice (telephone calls are better for important or time-sensitive personal news, dating rapport, and apologies) or face-to-face interactions (arguments, reprimands, or workplace disputes; political or religious opinions should be delivered in person). If you are upset or angry when generating business e-mail, those emotions will inform your writing. Draft how you feel in a regular document page, not on the reply e-mail screen, because it is too easy to hit "send" by mistake. Let the words rest overnight or wait for a *minimum* of two hours without looking at the draft. You will be amazed at how much the tone needs to be revised. If you do not think change is necessary in a strongly worded e-mail, ask a third-party colleague to read it. At the very least, before pressing "send" read it out loud in order to imagine how the recipient will accept it. Even after the cooling-off period and the review, take a deep breath and decide if you really want your comments published in eternal cyberspace.

Q: I have sent repeated e-mails (once a month) to another person where I work but have not received an answer or acknowledgment. What should I do? How quickly do work e-mails need to be answered?

A: First, call to verify that the address is correct. If not, resend. Otherwise, give your business colleague the opportunity to explain over the phone. Perhaps you requested no action or did not ask a question. Hundreds of e-mails arrive in some inboxes daily; "info" messages are not answered. Business e-mails should be answered as soon as possible. If you have not received a reply within three business days, you may resend.

Q: When is it appropriate to text your co-workers or boss, instead of using e-mail?

A: Most offices welcome and encourage rapid response over formality, but if you are a new employee, double-check office etiquette. The level of formality for replying to messages should be matched, if possible. Return phone calls, reply to e-mails, and text back. If you must text a reply to a high-ranking superior's e-mail or a client's phone call, explain that you are on extended absence from your office, and that your interim reply will be followed up with a more complete e-mail or phone call later. Also, keep in mind that there may be security restrictions against portable devices in some workplaces; personnel there may not discover your quick message until they leave work.

A formal business e-mail can employ the same polite communication components that have rendered respect on paper for hundreds of years. Even such an efficient medium requires courtesy.

E-Mail Outline

From: An e-mail address containing a personal name (Name@business.com) should be written by that individual. Electronic mail is expected to be immediate and efficient. Make responses within twenty-four to forty-eight hours, if possible.

Subject Line: Along with the From: address, a meaningful subject line helps the business reader determine whether or not to open your e-mail. Make it as precise as possible with some formality—never "Hi" or impolite words—or risk the busy recipient deleting it as junk mail.

cc: Use "carbon copy" only if the copied persons will know why you included them. Repliers will hit "Reply All" at least half the time.

Bcc: "Blind carbon copy" can shorten the screen space needed to view an e-mail and will also protect others' addresses—an important privacy and security issue. For long lists of recipients, put your own address in the To: box and all others in Bcc: or use the "mail merge" feature in your word processing software to create a separate personalized message for each recipient—always a polished option. One caveat: it could appear a bit devious in situations where total transparency is wiser (would anyone be annoyed to see a particular name on your list?), so be careful that you are not using Bcc as a way of withholding information.

Priority: Do not mark every message as urgent or no one will pay attention when you need it.

Classification: In the government and military Services and for contractors who support them on their secure networks, it is required to put the highest classification levels used within the message on the top and bottom of e-mails and in the subject line.

Receipt Requested: You can determine whether the person addressed actually opened the message by selecting this function.

Reply All: It is better to respond only to the person who wrote instead of replying to everyone, especially when not advancing more than, "Roger that," "I agree," or "Thanks." When answering business e-mails, include the original at the bottom of your message (choose "Reply," instead of "Write" or "New Mail") so that the recipient can check for context as necessary to avoid misunderstanding.

Fwd: Do not forward anything that will reflect discredit on the originator or a third party. Do not forward pictures, videos, urban legend virus warnings, or *"you must share this great information"* chain letters to or from workplace computers. If you would not waste the paper to print them and an envelope and stamp to mail them, then just delete them.

Open with an address block for *new* business correspondence using whatever information you have from the initial query. The complete information may be valuable months from now, plus it gives the addressee an opportunity to correct inaccurate data. If the header block showing date sent and e-mail address will not be stored with the document file, include it in this block also.

(date)
Contact Name
Title, Agency or Company
Address, phone, facsimile number
(e-mail address)

Use polite salutations and respectful honorifics with a colon:
Good Morning (rank or courtesy title and surname):
Dear (full name—without Mr. or Ms. if gender is not readily identifiable):
Dear Sir or Madam: (for unknown persons)
Hello Colleagues: or Ladies and Gentlemen: (for multiple persons)

Write concise sentences in active voice. Keep paragraphs short. If your e-mail is more than one screen in length, consider writing it as a letter attachment to a forwarding e-mail. Formal legal documents (contracts, hirings, terminations, and other serious issues) should only be sent as formal letterhead attachments. Long messages are hard to read on handheld devices. Warn recipients in the transmitting e-mail if attachments are large files.

State action requests or conclusions immediately, followed by rationale, or open with an expansion of the subject line used in the mail header, such as *"The following answers are provided in the same order as your e-mail request,* [subject]." If you save the main point for the end of a communication, you risk the reader not reading that far, especially if it is a long, tightly written message.

Use bullet points or numbers with blank lines between them for easy reading:

1. **Style.** IF I WRITE ALL UPPERCASE IT IS READ AS SHOUTING. if i write all lowercase you understand that i am lazy. Write plain text e-mails unless you know that the recipient can receive Rich Text (formatting codes such as **bold** or *italic*) or HTML (HyperText Markup Language, a Web page layout) messages, especially when communicating internationally.

2. **Language.** Keep words gender-neutral and business-focused without slang (no sports or hunting references) or vulgar language. Emoticons, jokes, and so on do not belong in business e-mails either. When non-English speakers are addressees, do not use abbreviations such as For Your Information (FYI), or As Soon As Possible (ASAP). To avoid confusion, all military, government, or business acronyms and abbreviations should be spelled out completely with their abbreviations in parentheses immediately following their first use, as the examples in the preceding sentence. Thereafter the abbreviation is fine until the next new e-mail. For instance, Central Illinois Aerospace, Culinary Institute of America, Cleveland Institute of Art, and Central Intelligence Agency are all very widely known by "CIA."

3. **Templates** are valuable for frequently repeated responses such as directions to your office, security requirements, Web site contact information, or your personal or office business expertise explanation. Appropriate information can then be copied and pasted quickly.

4. **Re-read e-mails** *after* using spell check or grammar check, which are no substitutes for human eyes; especially verify names and honorifics and correct punctuation. If you cut and paste be sure that the font, type size, and formatting are consistent throughout. Send important e-mails to yourself or a colleague first to double-check this.

5. **Reconfirm or clarify** all dates, times, amounts, follow-up action requirements, and so on to avoid misunderstanding.

Close courteously:
Warm regards,
Very respectfully,
All the best,
Sincerely,

Develop a signature block:
Your full name (carefully considering whether fancy fonts or colors suit your image)

Title, Agency or Company
Street Address, phone, facsimile number
E-mail address, Web site address

End with liability caveats in a smaller font, such as one or more similar to these:

IMPORTANT: This message and any attachments are intended only for the individual or entity to which it is addressed. Information herein is privileged and confidential. If the reader is not the intended recipient, you are hereby notified that any dissemination, distribution, or copying of this communication is strictly prohibited. If you have received this message in error, please accept our apologies and notify sender immediately by replying and then deleting the e-mail completely from your system.

DISCLAIMER: E-mails are not guaranteed to be secure or error-free as information could be intercepted, corrupted, lost, destroyed, arrive late or incomplete, or contain viruses. The sender therefore cannot be held liable for any data tampering, loss of confidentiality, or damage from any transmitted virus.

WARNING: Copyright [date]. All rights reserved. All e-mails are subject to review by Legal Counsel.

NOTE: If you are providing information in response to a request from us, it may be published on our Web site at [address] or otherwise disseminated to our clients. Providing information will signify your consent to this. If you require further information on this policy, please see our Web site.

NOTICE: Employees are expressly required not to make defamatory, vulgar, or profane statements, or any sexist or racially discriminating comments. Employees are expressly forbidden from forwarding any such e-mails or other comments that are offensive or disrespectful. No responsibility is accepted by [organization] for personal e-mails or e-mails unconnected with the [company's or clients'] business.

ATTENTION CLIENTS: We guard your account and tax identification numbers, etc. If you receive any e-mail purporting to be from us that asks you to provide sensitive data, please contact us immediately to confirm its validity.

THINK GREEN: Please consider the environment before printing this e-mail.

SECURITY

Most readers will know the importance of safeguarding financial information like Social Security, bank account, credit or charge card numbers. It is also wise to protect personal information as sensitive. A simple, friendly web transmission, *"We are at the beach till Sunday but the neighbor knows where our key is hidden to check on Fluffy all week till Missy is dropped off after Girl Scout camp Friday"* discloses far too much to paparazzi, demonstrators, terrorists, or common criminals, depending on the family's situation. Do not view the web as secure; personal information may be intercepted or abused at any time. At the very least, always make it a point to protect your own and others' travel and location information.

Representatives of the U.S. government and those working with them are trained to use paragraph classification markings even within secure channels to indicate information that should be protected, along with declassification dates. As the example in the preceding paragraph shows, however, even unclassified information may need safeguarding. If printing out e-mails from military members, for example, handle them as "personal and confidential" because they could contain names, organization information, troop movement plans, and other data subject to compromise. Shred all such printed e-mails before throwing them away; they should never be put in a recycling container. In Chapter 25: International Protocol and Civility, under Written Faux Pas, read about safeguarding personal data as required by the United States Privacy Act of 1974 and how other countries and their citizens may not provide similar protections.

E-MAIL INVITATIONS

Formal invitations are better sent hard copy by mail or hand-delivered, but *Informal* and *Casual* ones may be sent via e-mail as an efficient and economical medium for the host to invite guests and track their responses. E-mail is most appropriate for in-house invitations. The time-tested format (see Chapter 11: Invitations) should always be used because it utilizes respectful language and all pertinent information is included in internationally accepted locations. Mailed invitations may include an e-mail address for responses or an event Web site for more information.

An electronic invitation can be written, centered, in the e-mail body but should also be attached as a separate document (in case one or the other version cannot be read), perhaps developed as a simple text box of how it would appear on card stock, even including an organization seal. Hosts may want to make their computer invitation more personal by typing in each person's name as invitee.

Guests nowadays expect to interact with electronic invitations: by clicking on the *R.s.v.p.* to give their response, viewing the *Address* for a map view, selecting the *Dress* requirements to read what the host is wearing, or other relevant buttons such as a list of who has already accepted or to choose from entrée options. Invitees must respond to electronic invitations with the same sense of duty as to "hard-copy" requests—that means to answer within forty-eight hours.

Hosts will certainly check often to tally responses. Thankfully, it is perfectly polite to give a deadline as some invitees will be lacking in courtesy and will put off answering, knowing that a simple last-second keystroke is easy to accomplish.

CELL PHONE POLLUTION

Unwanted and unnecessary, so much of everyday noise is a form of pollution stressing us, fatiguing us, and interfering with our ability to think, reflect, and decide. We must realize that silence and tranquility, especially in urban public spaces, are precious endangered resources that need respect and protection.

— P. M. Forni

CELL PHONE ETIQUETTE

It is a rare person these days who has not been placed in the position of unwilling voyeur, forced to listen to one-sided conversations, often with embarrassing personal information, gossip, or coarse language from someone talking in public on a cell phone. Socially proper behavior requires a minimum level of personal restraint. Talking on a cell phone or texting while ignoring others is rude, if they would otherwise have your attention. Some individuals, however, view themselves as entitled, "free" to do whatever they want while at the same time expecting others to limit any actions that impact them (I will talk loudly on my cell phone but you should not). Adults act as if others cannot hear them giving details of their surgeries, marital spats, or revenge on co-workers. Young people, much more self-conscious, usually prefer to text in an attempt to keep their exchanges private from adults.

Americans have absorbed, as part of the culture, an appreciation of a three-foot "bubble" of physical area around individuals (arm's length) and will arrange themselves to accommodate each others' bubbles when space allows, reducing their chance of touching or annoying a stranger. Self-absorbed cell phone "addicts" who do not care where they are or whom they may be bothering have caused the American public to recognize the necessity of extending the paradigm—that a stranger's bubble includes his aural airspace, which should be respected just as much as his physical space. Mannerly individuals can aid this evolution by modeling good cell phone etiquette in public:

- **Hold the cell phone in your left hand if you must talk in public.** Similar to holding a drink in the left hand at cocktail parties, this frees your right hand for handshaking and other interactions, such as opening doors for others, or saluting if in uniform. Military personnel may use cell phones in public, following all the courtesy rules in this section. If you need to salute, say, *"Excuse me"* (without explanation) to the caller, drop the left hand with the phone to your side, stand at attention, and render tribute. When the salute is complete and the other Service member has passed by, return to your call and explain.

- **Turn off the cell phone** where the focus should be on another's voice (during speeches, lectures, or in theaters for example); where silence and hushed voices are the respectful norm (such as libraries, hospitals, funeral homes, or cemeteries); or in any public spaces when seated in a crowd. In darkened rooms (during PowerPoint presentations or movies), even the lights from electronic devices can be distracting.

Q: We were both using PDAs at a working breakfast, so that's okay. . . . Right?

A: We reluctantly refrain from censuring your multitasking *if* you were recording meeting notes or sending quick questions in hopes of immediate feedback to facilitate your existing discussion, *and* your texting did not last throughout the entire breakfast meeting. It is similar to using a notepad and paper. Just as you do not pass notes instead of talking directly, do not slight those present in favor of electronic interactions. At least you were not talking loudly on a cell phone or working on a laptop next to the pancakes.

Q: When is it appropriate to use a cell phone at the table? I was invited to lunch and my friend took three calls and made one, none of which sounded like an emergency.

A: Your friend's behavior devalued your presence. It is never polite to ignore others. If waiting for an emergency call during a meal or any public event, set phone on vibrate and warn companions. Never put phones on the table. Excuse yourself and step out of the room to take *only* the expected call (check the number display), keep it short, and apologize when you return.

Q: If I am dining with a client and receive an extremely important e-mail or text message that requires immediate response, what are my options?

A: See the answers above. Otherwise, keep your phone and PDA turned off or risk losing the client, who should be your most important business while you are together.

- **Set the cell phone to silent or vibrate** (there is a reason it is called "manner mode") if you cannot bear to turn it off during a religious service, at dinner, during a board meeting, and so on. Unless you are on duty or on call (forced to be available twenty-four hours a day), there is no reason to disturb a public gathering. If waiting for an emergency call, let your companions know. Keep the phone in your lap or an accessible pocket. Excuse yourself and leave the room for a *short* conversation if necessary, and thank others for their understanding when you return.

- **Say *"Excuse me"*** to the room at large if your phone rings in a public place (for example, in the waiting room of a car repair shop), walk away (outside if necessary), and talk quietly. It is the responsibility of the person answering a cell phone to be considerate.

- **Do not get irritated when a physically present person responds** to your phone comment or question, especially if you use a small hands-free earpiece. These devices can make cell phone callers appear mentally absent, talking to themselves. A raised hand to your ear or a dangling cord is hard enough to see, but without them there is no clue that you are connected to something other than your imagination. If you make eye contact with a person in front of you while on the phone, you exacerbate the problem. You are the one who should apologize.

- **Do not try to continue business as usual** while talking on a cell phone. Stop shopping or delay going through a checkout line until your call is finished. Wait until you have flushed, washed your hands, and exited the restroom before answering the phone. Do not talk (or text) on the phone when your attention should be on driving.

- **Choose standard ring tones** for business cell phones, or be very sure that your personalized choice does not give us the impression that you hate something or someone based on the words in the selected song.

- **Do not confront rude cell phone users** who act as if no one can hear their loud conversations in a public place. Doing so is in itself rude and the confronted person may lash out. Report it to someone in authority instead (restaurant receptionist, theatre manager, waiting room attendant) and ask them to intercede.

Business Telephone Etiquette

When answering the business phone, identify yourself professionally with the name of the organization and your own, *"XYZ Company, Sondra Takacs."* If at another's desk, give their name, *"Sondra Takacs' office, Sandy Eaton speaking."*

When calling others, ask if it's a good time to talk before launching into a long conversation. Suggest another convenient time if they ask to call back.

If you must put a customer or client on hold during a business call, make sure to check back with them after about twenty seconds, so that they know they have not been forgotten.

Program an office phone so that incoming calls go to voice mail if you are not there to answer it. Silence your cell phone or put it on vibrate if you leave it in your cubicle unattended.

INTERRUPTIONS

The person you are currently speaking to has precedence and deserves your focused attention. Do not multitask—it is an unnecessary distraction. Except for an emergency or an urgent incoming communication, do not interrupt a present meeting or phone conversation. Today's technology records messages from others; check them later. Even asking permission is a rude disruption and immediately indicates that someone else is more important.

If you know ahead of time that you truly must answer a phone (text message, new call, or call waiting) or a knock on your door, let those you are with (or talking to by phone) know that you might be interrupted and why. Answer all interruptions quickly, state that you will get back to the interrupter as soon as possible (give a time period), and return to the meeting or conversation with an apology for the disruption.

Do not text message (or talk on a cell phone) when your attention should be on your driving. Such behavior crosses the line from rude to dangerous and may be unlawful.

Q: What should I do if my cell phone rings in the presence of a VIP, or during a meeting or another time when all cell phones and pagers should have been turned off?

A: Apologize for the interruption; everyone makes mistakes. Turn the phone off immediately; do *not* answer it. Return your attention to where it should be.

Q: Is it appropriate to check my PDA for messages on my phone during lulls at a meeting?

A: During a formal break when everyone is moving you may step away to check messages. Do not check them while the meeting is in session. Do not send lengthy messages. Focus on the business at hand.

TEXT MESSAGES

Just as talking on a cell phone, texting is a private activity. Sending and receiving messages is rude when in the company of others because it excludes them. Only for truly vital reasons would you explain *at the beginning of a conversation or meeting* the nature of an emergency and that an urgent incoming message is pending. Say, *"Excuse me"* before quickly checking a received text message. If your reply cannot wait, apologize, step away to a private area, answer as quickly as possible, and apologize again when you return.

Personal Digital Assistant (PDA) lights are distracting in darkened rooms, as are any clicking keyboard sounds or electronic audio in a quiet room. Do not text message during a meeting unless others know that you are simply requesting vital information so that the discussion can proceed.

CALLER ID

You do not have to call someone by name just because your phone offers caller identification, but customer expectations in your area may require it. Even pizza delivery services use this technology for personalized service. After the "hello/greeting" exchange identifies a caller as male or female, your next comment may incorporate caller ID recognition with an honorific, as in, *"Mrs. Smith,"* especially for regular callers.

LEAVING VOICE MAIL

Organize your thoughts before calling someone in case you get a recording. Listen to the entire message for notice of an extended absence, changes in hours, or phone number that might affect your decision to leave a voice mail. Speak clearly and start with your full name, organization, and phone number. Include the day/date, time zone (if different), and a brief message. Repeat your name and number slowly at the end, and give several good times to call back (*"I'm at my desk every morning between 8:00 and 10:00"*). Say thank you before ending the call. If given the option to review what you have just recorded, use it. You will probably choose to re-record more succinctly after listening. Never leave negative messages on voice mail; these conversations should be dealt with person-to-person, not via recordings.

If you leave a message with an informal or casual *verbal* invitation, do it correctly (see Chapter 11: Invitations) and follow up with a live person later to be sure the message was received. Check your own voice mail frequently if you are compiling many invitation R.s.v.p.s, lest your allotted space fills up.

IMPROVE YOUR PHONE STYLE

Are you aware of how you sound when people listen to you on the phone? Call yourself and leave a message using your normal rate of speed and manner while pretending that you are answering a routine call. Play it back to critique how you sound to others. Is your standard way of greeting, the company name, and your name clearly understood? Does your voice seem distracted or abrupt? Deliberately *smile* during your next conversation to improve your voice quality. Some people keep a mirror nearby to help their phone interactions. Try *closing your eyes* to limit distractions if you need to improve your focus during conversations.

CALLING FOR SERVICE OR HELP

If calling for service or information, ask to whom you are speaking. Note the name, date, and time. State your own name before explaining your problem or requesting a department. If the person you are speaking with asks you to leave a message with him or her for another, ask for your request to be repeated (your name and contact information) for accuracy and thank them by name. Knowing that you have jotted down an "accountable" name helps ensure that your issue receives proper attention.

SPEAKERPHONES

Avoid speakerphones outside of scheduled conference calls. If you must use them, make sure all parties know that others are listening. Make introductions of all parties clearly. If you are being introduced via speakerphone, greet each other party with, "*Hello,*" "*Good afternoon,*" or repeat the other's name as a courtesy response.

CONFERENCE CALLS

Organized by appointment in advance, conference calls are one way to include people who are not all able to be at a meeting location at the same time. Organizers should be aware that speakerphones will pick up background noises; eliminate as many as possible from the meeting room. Do not allow "sidebar" conversations between physically present participants because those on the phones will hear confusing smatterings. Keep conversation focused on the business at hand so that all can participate. Callers-in should also pick a quiet location; landlines are preferable to cell phones. Every time you speak from a distant location, identify yourself because disembodied voices can sound similar over speakerphones.

CHAPTER 15

Civilian Forms of Address

*T*he information here is good for basic education and general background, but always confirm a high-ranking guest's information with his or her office before sending written communications or addressing them publicly.

Military personnel and those who work with them can tell at a glance how to properly address persons in the uniformed services because they wear rank, insignia, and medals as part of their uniforms (see the charts at the end of Chapter 8: Order of Precedence and Military Forms of Address).

FEDERAL, STATE, AND LOCAL DIGNITARIES

The salutation of a letter to the President is *Dear Mr. President*. The closing is *Respectfully yours*, or *Very respectfully*.

In writing to all other American officials, the salutation is by title and surname, as in *Justice Sotomayor* and the closing is *Sincerely, Sincerely yours*, or *Very truly yours*. Spouses of American officials without titles of their own are addressed and introduced as *Mr.* or *Mrs.* and the surname. In the following list, the *official* form precedes the *social* form. When only one is given, it is appropriate for both occasions.

The Honorable is the preferred form for addressing most American officials in office or retired. It is always written out in an address on the line above and aligned with the name. The phrase is always used with the full name, but *never* with any other title (*The Honorable Admiral Jones* and *The Honorable Mr. Jones* are both incorrect).

When writing to a foreign head of state, ambassador, or senior church official, it is proper to use *His/Her Excellency*. Exceptions are in the British Commonwealth where the preference is *The Right Honourable*; or if the head of government is royalty it is *Your Royal Highness*.

In public group addresses (to audiences, when toasting or welcoming guests, during media-covered speeches), recognize the host or highest-ranking person present first, followed by any others deserving special recognition—such as a prominent individual or a group of like persons present—*in protocol order*, and end with an all-encompassing phrase. For example, Dianne Feinstein, senator from California, welcomed dignitaries during President Barack Obama's inauguration on January 20, 2009, by saying: *"President and Vice President, President-Elect and Vice President-Elect, Ladies and Gentlemen."*

Only by special invitation or circumstances of long-standing friendship or family relationship would you address high-ranking officials by their first names, even in private. Upon occasion, a senior may ask a junior to call him or her by first name socially—because the senior respects the junior's propriety *not* to use such familiarity in official conversation.

FEDERAL, STATE, AND LOCAL DIGNITARIES

WRITTEN ADDRESS	SPOKEN ADDRESS	INTRODUCTIONS
The President		
The President The White House Washington, District of Columbia* *Social:* The President and Mrs. (or Mr.) Doe The White House Washington, D.C.*	Mr. (or Madam) President	The President of the United States *Abroad, add:* of America or The President or President Doe

*Formally written *District of Columbia,* although the abbreviation D.C. is used on general correspondence, as in the remainder of this chapter.

WRITTEN ADDRESS	SPOKEN ADDRESS	INTRODUCTIONS
The President's Spouse		
Mrs. John Doe (President's name) or Mr. James Doe (own name) The White House Washington, D.C.	Mrs. Doe Mr. Doe	Mrs. Doe Mr. Doe
The Vice President		
The Vice President United States Senate Washington, D.C. *Social:* The Vice President and Mrs. (or Mr.) Doe (home address)	Mr. (or Madam) Vice President or Mr. (or Ms.) Doe*	The Vice President of the United States *Abroad, add:* of America or The Vice President or Vice President Doe

*In continued conversation, Mr. (or Ms.) Doe is used

Written Address	Spoken Address	Introductions
The Vice President's Spouse		
Mrs. John (or Mr. James) Doe (home address)	Mrs. (or Mr.) Doe	Mrs. (or Mr.) Doe
The Supreme Court		
CHIEF JUSTICE		
The Chief Justice of the Supreme Court Washington, D.C. *Social:* The Chief Justice and Mrs. (or Mr.) Doe (home address)	Mr. (or Ms.) Chief Justice or Mr. (or Ms.) Doe	The Honorable John (or Jane) Doe, Chief Justice of the Supreme Court of the United States *Abroad, add:* of America or The Chief Justice or Chief Justice Doe
ASSOCIATE JUSTICE		
Justice John (Jane) Doe The Supreme Court Washington, D.C. *Social:* Justice John (Jane) Doe and Mrs. (Mr.) Doe (home address)	Mr. (Madame) Justice or Justice Doe	The Honorable John (Jane) Doe, Associate Justice of the Supreme Court of the United States *Abroad, add:* of America or Justice Doe
Cabinet Officers*		
The Honorable John (Jane) Doe Secretary of ___ Washington, D.C. *Social:* The Secretary of ___ and Mrs. (Mr.) Doe (home address)	Mr. (Madam) Secretary or Secretary Doe or Mr. (Ms.) Doe	The Honorable John (or Jane) Doe, Secretary of ___ of the United States *Abroad, add:* of America or The Secretary of ___

Written Address	Spoken Address	Introductions

Cabinet Officers* continued

Written Address	Spoken Address	Introductions
The Honorable John (Jane) Doe Attorney General Washington, D.C.	Mr. (Madam) Attorney General or Mr. (Ms.) Doe	The Honorable John (Jane) Doe, Attorney General or The Attorney General

SECRETARY OF DEFENSE, AND OF THE ARMY, NAVY, AND AIR FORCE
(UNDER SECRETARY AND ASSISTANT SECRETARY)

Written Address	Spoken Address	Introductions
The Honorable John (Jane) Doe Secretary of___ Washington, D.C. *Social:* The Secretary of___ and Mrs. (Mr.) Doe (home address)	Mr. (Madam) Secretary or Secretary Doe or Mr. (Ms.) Doe	The Honorable John (Jane) Doe, Secretary of ___ or The Secretary of___

*All cabinet officers except the Attorney General and the Postmaster General use the title of *Secretary*. Although the Service secretaries do not have cabinet rank, they may be addressed and introduced as Mr. or *Madam Secretary, The Secretary of the Army*, etc. The Secretary of Defense does have cabinet rank.

Former President of the United States

Written Address	Spoken Address	Introductions
The Honorable John (Jane) Doe City, State, Zip	Mr. (Ms.) Doe (or any prior title, such as military)	The Honorable John (Jane) Doe, the former President of the United States

The Assistant to the President

Written Address	Spoken Address	Introductions
The Honorable John (Jane) Doe Assistant to the President The White House Washington, D.C.	Mr. (Ms.) Doe	The Honorable John (Jane) Doe, Assistant to the President of the United States or The Assistant to the President, Mr. John (Ms. Jane) Doe

Written Address	Spoken Address	Introductions
The Assistant to the President continued		
Social:		
The Honorable John (Jane) Doe and Mrs. (Mr.) Doe (home address)		
The Special Assistant to the President with Military Rank		
Major General John (Jane) Doe, U.S. Army	General Doe	The Special Assistant to the President, Major General John (Jane) Doe, United States Army
Special Assistant to the President		
The White House		
Washington, D.C.		
Social:		
Major General and Mrs. John Doe or Major General Jane Doe and Mr. Doe (home address)		
Diplomatic (The Department of State maintains embassy mail addresses.)		
AMERICAN AMBASSADOR		
The Honorable John Quincy Doe	Mr. Ambassador	The Honorable John Doe,
Ambassador	*If on leave:* Mr. Doe	Ambassador of the United States of America
Embassy of the United States	*Or with military rank:* General Doe	*(When not at his post, the name of the country of*
of America		*accreditation must be added:* to Greece)
Athens, Greece		

Note: When a woman is U.S. ambassador or minister, the word *Madam* is substituted for Mr. in the spoken address, or if the diplomat prefers, address her as *Ambassador Doe* or *Minister Doe.*

Written Address	Spoken Address	Introductions
Diplomatic *continued*		
AMERICAN AMBASSADOR continued		
Social:	Mr. Ambassador	Mr. John Doe, Ambassador of the United States of America (*when no foreign nationals are present:* American Ambassador . . . to Greece)
The Ambassador of the United States of America and Mrs. Doe		
Embassy of the United States of America		
Athens, Greece		*or*
Not at his post:		Ambassador Doe, United States of America
The Honorable John Quincy Doe and Mrs. Doe (home address)		
AMERICAN MINISTER		
The Honorable John Quincy Doe	Mr. Minister or Mr. Doe	The Honorable John Doe, Minister, of the United States of America . . . to Ireland
Minister, Embassy of the United States of America		
Dublin, Ireland		
Social:		Mr. John Doe, Minister of the United States of America (*when no foreign nationals are present:* American Minister . . . to Ireland) or Minister Doe, United States of America
The Minister of the United States of America and Mrs. Doe		
American Legation		
Dublin, Ireland		
AMERICAN CHARGÉ D'AFFAIRES		
The Honorable (*if Minister rank*) John (Jane) Doe	Mr. (Ms.) Doe	Mr. John (Ms. Jane) Doe, the Chargé d'Affaires of the United States of America . . . to France
Chargé d'Affaires ad interim		
Embassy of the United States of America		
Paris, France		

Written Address	Spoken Address	Introductions
Diplomatic *continued*		
AMERICAN CHARGÉ D'AFFAIRES continued		
Social:		
The Chargé d'Affaires of the United States of America and Mrs. (Mr.) John Doe		
FOREIGN AMBASSADOR		
His (Her) Excellency John Doe (no prefix unless titled: Sir, Count, Lord, etc.) The Ambassador of Ireland The Embassy of Ireland	Your Excellency or Mr. (Madam) Ambassador	His (Her) Excellency, the Honorable John (Jane) Doe, Ambassador Extraordinary & Plenipotentiary of Ireland or The Ambassador of Ireland
Social:		
His (Her) Excellency The Ambassador of Ireland and Mrs. (Mr.) John Doe The Embassy of Ireland		
United States Congress		
THE SENATE (or State Senator, with appropriate State address)		
The Honorable John (Jane) Doe United States Senate Washington, D.C.	Senator Doe or Senator	Senator Doe *or formal:* The Honorable John (Jane) Doe, Senator from Oklahoma
Social:		
Senator and Mrs. (Mr.) Doe (home address)		

Written Address	Spoken Address	Introductions
United States Congress continued		
THE HOUSE OF REPRESENTATIVES		
THE SPEAKER OF THE HOUSE		
The Honorable John (Jane) Doe Speaker of the House of Representatives The Capitol Washington, D.C. *Social:* The Speaker of the House of Representatives and Mrs. (Mr.) Doe (home address)	Mr. (or Madam) Speaker or Mr. (Ms.) Doe	The Honorable John (Jane) Doe, Speaker of the House of Representatives or The Speaker
STATE REPRESENTATIVES		
The Honorable John (Jane) Doe House of Representatives Washington, D.C. *Social:* The Honorable and Mrs. (Mr.) Doe (home address)	Congressman Doe or Mr. (Ms.) Doe	The Honorable John (Jane) Doe, Representative from (Florida) or Congressman Doe or Mr. (Ms.) Doe

Note: The prefix *Representative* is never used as a title in correspondence. *Congressman* or *Congresswoman* is widely used in informal introductions by the Representatives themselves and by others when introducing them.

Written Address	Spoken Address	Introductions
State and City Officials		
GOVERNOR		
The Honorable John (Jane) Doe Governor of __ City, State, Zip *Social:* The Governor and Mrs. (Mr.) Doe *or outside the state:* The Governor of __ and Mrs. (Mr.) Doe or His (Her) Excellency* the Governor and Mrs. (Mr.) Doe (home address)	Governor Doe or Governor	The Honorable John (Jane) Doe, Governor of the state of __ or Governor Doe or The Governor
*Many states give their Governor the title *Excellency*, but the Department of State uses only the term *Governor*.		
MAYOR		
The Honorable John (Jane) Doe Mayor of __ City, State, Zip *Social:* The Honorable and Mrs. (Mr.) Doe or Mayor and Mrs. (Mr.) Doe (home address)	Mayor Doe or Mr. (Madame) Mayor	The Honorable John (Jane) Doe, Mayor of __ or the city of__ or Mayor Doe

WRITTEN ADDRESS	SPOKEN ADDRESS	INTRODUCTIONS
State and City Officials continued		
JUDGE		
The Honorable John (Jane) Doe Judge of District Court (or other court) City, State, Zip *Social:*	Judge Doe	The Honorable John (Jane) Doe, Judge of the District Court or Judge Doe
The Honorable and Mrs. (Mr.) Doe or Judge and Mrs. (Mr.) Doe (home address)		
Head of a Federal Agency		
The Honorable John (Jane) Doe Director of (name of agency) Washington, D.C. *Social:*	Mr. (Ms.) Doe	The Honorable John (Jane) Doe, Director of (name of agency) or Mr. (Ms.) Doe
The Honorable and Mrs. (Mr.) Doe or Mr. and Mrs. John Doe (home address)		

Religious Dignitaries

Forms of address for persons holding ecclesiastical titles vary according to the religion, the country, and the house of worship. Please verify the correct local usage with their business offices. For instance, initials of the order or theology degrees such as STD (Sacrae Theologiae Doctor) may follow a name in an address. The preferred salutation of a letter might be *Your All Holiness*, or *My Lord Bishop*, or *Dear Imam*, used as a sign of respect whether or not you are a member of that religion. The preferred letter closing for the congregation might be *Faithfully yours*, or *Your humble servant*. However, any person may open a letter *Dear* [title and surname], and close with *Sincerely*, or *Respectfully*, without fear of offense.

RELIGIOUS DIGNITARIES

WRITTEN ADDRESS	SPOKEN ADDRESS	INTRODUCTIONS
Buddhist		
His Eminence or His Holiness (name) _ Temple	Venerable or Rinpoche or Reverend or Your Eminence	His Eminence or His Holiness, the Abbot (or Lama) of _
Roman Catholic		
CARDINAL		
His Eminence (name) Archbishop of _	Your Eminence	His Eminence or Cardinal (name) or His Eminence, Cardinal (name)
ARCHBISHOP OR BISHOP		
His Excellency The Most Reverend (name and degree) Archbishop Archbishop (or Bishop) of _	Archbishop (or Bishop) Doe	Archbishop (or Bishop) or His Excellency, The Most Reverend (name) of _, or His Excellency, The Archbishop of _
PRIEST ADDRESSED AS "FATHER"		
The Reverend (name and degree)	Father	Father (name) or The Reverend (name)
MOTHER SUPERIOR		
The Reverend Mother (name and order initials), The Convent of _	Reverend Mother	The Reverend Mother

Written Address	Spoken Address	Introductions
Hindu		
The Guru Maharaj or Swamiji (name) _ Temple	Swamiji or Pandit or Pujari	The Swamiji (name) Guru Maharaj, the Priest of _Temple
Islam		
The Imam (name) _ Mosque or Islamic Center	Imam (name)	The Imam of the _ Mosque or Islamic Center
Jewish Faith		
RABBI		
Rabbi (name) _ Synagogue or Temple	Rabbi or Rabbi (name) or *with scholastic degree:* Dr. (name)	Rabbi (name), of the _ Congregation (or Temple)
CANTOR		
Cantor (name) _ Synagogue or Temple	Cantor (name)	Cantor (name), of the _ Congregation (or Temple)
Mormon		
Mr. (name) President of _ Temple	Mr. (name)	Mr. (name), the President of _ Temple

Written Address	Spoken Address	Introductions
Protestant Faiths		
ANGLICAN or EPISCOPAL PRESIDING BISHOP		
The Most Reverend (name and degree), Presiding Bishop of __	Bishop (name)	Bishop (name) or The Most Reverend (name), Presiding Bishop of __
ANGLICAN or EPISCOPAL BISHOP		
The Right Reverend (name and degree), Bishop of __	Bishop (name)	Bishop (name) or The Right Reverend (name), Bishop of __
ANGLICAN or EPISCOPAL DEAN OR CANON		
The Very Reverend (name and degree), Cathedral or Seminary	Dean (name) or Canon (name) or Dr. (name)	The Very Reverend (name), Dean (or Canon) of __ (a cathedral or seminary)
CLERGY WITH A DOCTORATE		
The Reverend Dr. John (Jane) Doe	Dr. Doe or *Reverend Doe	Dr. Doe, the Minister (or Pastor) of __ Church or The Reverend Dr. Doe
CLERGY WITH NO DOCTORATE		
The Reverend John (Jane) Doe	Mr. (Ms.) Doe or Sir or Ma'am or *Reverend Doe	The Reverend Doe, the Minister (or Pastor) of __ Church

*Reverend is an adjective, not a noun, but it is used frequently to address Protestant clergy.

Various Individuals

Written Address	Spoken Address	Introductions
Professor		
Professor (or Associate Professor or Assistant Professor) John (Jane) Doe	Mr. (Ms.) Doe or Professor Doe	Professor Doe
Medical Doctor		
Dr. John (Jane) Doe, PhD (or MD or D.D.S. [dentist])	Dr. Doe	Dr. Doe
Divorcée		
Mrs. Jane Doe or Mrs. Smith Doe *(the maiden surname or given name may be followed by the ex-husband's name)*	Mrs. Doe or Ms. Doe	Mrs. Doe or Ms. Doe
Widow		
Ms. Anna Doe or Mrs. John Doe *(the same as when her husband was alive, if she desires)*	Mrs. Doe or Ms. Doe	Mrs. Doe or Ms. Doe

Section 4

Good Manners and Civility

CHAPTER 16

Place Settings, Table Manners, and Service Styles

*O*ur dining skills are often the competence people assess to judge our sophistication in other areas. Many times you are evaluated over meals—during job interviews, when introduced to a new family circle, during multinational representational functions, while negotiating business—for clues about your upbringing, training, and personal awareness. If you are not confident of your table manners, your valuable energy is wasted worrying about performance instead of focusing on the business at hand. The desirable attitude at even the most formal occasion is *relaxed competence.*

AT EASE KEY POINTS

- ✁ Master an all-purpose toast.
- ✁ Pocket a handkerchief or tissue to cover a cough or sneeze.
- ✁ Keep eyeglasses, purse, PDA, keys, etc., off the dining table.
- ✁ Polish international table manners; rest wrists on the table edge.
- ✁ Wait for host to start every course before eating or drinking.

Being competent in dining skills means having the assurance that you can manage any dining situation, be it a meal at a luxurious restaurant, in a private home, at an embassy function, or during a military Dining In. No one is born knowing how to cope with full place settings or food and wine presented in courses by wait staff. The good news is that these highly visible skills can be mastered as easily as other attributes crucial to your professional success.

The first things to master at "knife and fork school" are all of the components of an individual *table cover* (one formal place setting, page 263). All societies that eat with silverware have table manners derivative of the formal place setting presented in this chapter. Become so familiar with the positions of silverware, goblets, and so on that even without a menu card you will be able to tell what courses will be served.

Good hosts help guests negotiate formal meals by providing place cards and menu cards and by leading each course as a role model. Do not eat bread or take a drink, do not even place the napkin on your lap until someone in charge of the event indicates that the meal has begun. Hosts do this by picking up their own napkins, utensils, or goblets as a signal that it is the correct time for guests to do the same. Sometimes there will be a blessing or prayer, a formal welcome, a toast, or remarks before the meal begins. Your host may say grace (see Chapter 17: Family Dining, Buffets, and Formal In-Home Meals) or invite an ordained cleric from among your guests to give a benediction at public gatherings. Remain seated during prayers unless asked by the host or clergy to rise.

SIMPLE TABLE RULES

The following may seem elementary, but they are listed here because people break these basic rules all the time.

- Do not slump, but do not sit "at attention" either. Do not lean back to balance on the back chair legs. Avoid fully extending legs under the table and do not twist feet around chair legs.

- Keep elbows close to your sides when eating or cutting food to stay out of your dinner partner's space. Resting wrists or fingertips on the table edge between courses is appropriate, but elbows are not allowed. You may momentarily place forearms on the table if you do not turn your back on a dinner partner. Remain attentive to servers so that they need not interrupt your conversation in order to serve.

- If something is out of reach, do not rise out of your seat to obtain it; ask for it to be passed. Say "*Please*" when asking for something and "*Thank you*" when you receive it. International author Roger Axtell (*Dos and Taboos* series) reminds us that overseas people offer and receive using *both* hands in appreciation of generosity (read more in Chapter 27: Manners at the Global Dinner Table). However, you may reach for anything conveniently at hand without bothering your dinner partner, as long as you do not reach across another guest.

- Avoid such unattractive eating habits as smacking your lips or piling overly large mouthfuls of food high on your fork. Do *not* talk with food in your mouth, make noises while eating or swallowing, chew food with your mouth open, or blow on hot liquids to cool them. Never lick your fingers—use a napkin.

- After using silverware, never put it back down on the table—rest it on the plate. This means that not even handles touch the table once you have lifted the item. Do not put your knife to your lips or into your mouth.

- Do not play with the food (or with table utensils). Do not rearrange the place setting to suit yourself. Do not turn over your goblet or put a place card over the glass to indicate that you do not want wine.

Menu Cards

Menu cards are useful for letting guests at table know what food is being served, the number of courses, and to brag about the wine vintages. For informal meals, they can be composed and printed with a home computer. Otherwise, they may be written by hand or engraved by the same stationer who does your invitations, with black ink on heavy white or cream-colored flat card stock (sometimes with gilded or silvered beveled edges, and perhaps embossed at the top center with the host's flag, insignia, seal, crest, or coat of arms). They range in size but usually are no more than 9 inches high by 6 inches wide (about 23 by 15 centimeters). On a formal table, they are placed on top of a napkin that is centered on the service plate, or in a holder directly above each place setting. Sometimes menu cards are folded, which allows more information to be conveyed on the cover and inside on the left side, such as a tribute to a guest of honor or event explanation.

If "Anniversary Dinner" or "New Year's Luncheon" or other description is not used, the word *Menu* is at the top followed by each course listed separately. The first letter of each course description is capitalized and each line is centered, separated from the others by a blank line or symbol. List only the main courses and wines; bread, relishes, jellies, candy, and coffee are not normally mentioned.

Dated menu cards are considered souvenirs, especially those that include an "in honor of" or "to celebrate" line, or those from an annual event. If a host often serves the same "signature" meal, menu cards without dates (but perhaps personalized with a design element or quote) can be placed in picture frames for repeated use. These would not be souvenirs. Place them between every two guests; the hosts do not need them if frames are in short supply.

Place Cards

Place cards are used, as desired, at any seated meal to direct guests to a specific chair at a particular table without confusion, and to help diners identify one another.

Seating plans are worked out ahead of time by the host according to protocol (see Chapter 23: Seating Plans). Place cards are designed to stand by themselves in a folded position tent-style or with side "wings" folded back, or as a flat card to insert into a holder. They match the menu cards at formal and official meals and sit centered just above the dessert spoon and fork or on top (or tucked into a fold) of the napkin. Informal settings may have them leaning against a goblet stem or in creative locations such as between the tines of the dessert fork.

The face of place cards is usually about 2 inches by 3 inches (approximately 5 by 7.5 centimeters). The flag of an admiral or general, the seal of a ship or an embassy, or a family crest may be embossed or stamped in the top center or the upper-left corner of place cards. Spouses hosting alone do not use these emblems unless they themselves are the authorized person. A calligrapher or person with nice penmanship handwrites honorifics and surnames, or position titles alone, in the center or lower half of the card face in black or dark blue ink. Try to make the letters large enough to be read by those on either side of the individual and write on both sides of the tent-style card so that strangers across the table can also read them. Only titles are used for very senior dignitaries, for example, *The Duke of Edinburgh* because everyone is supposed to know that his name is Prince Philip, husband of Queen Elizabeth II; or *The Secretary of the Army*, and so on.

For official functions, always strive to spell out the full rank on place cards: *Lieutenant Colonel Allen* or *Chief Warrant Officer Moore*. On informal occasions, the "conversational" form or "salutation" name is used: *Chief Trent, Ms. Boggs*, or *Alinda*. If two people have the same names, then full names are necessary at even casual affairs, for instance: *Amber Slotta* and *Katie Slotta* (instead of *Ms. Slotta*), or *Ryan Worley* and *Ryan Woodyard*.

Napkin Etiquette at Knife and Fork Meals

The first table napkins were used exclusively in the palaces of kings and princes, and from the early part of the fifteenth century they were trimmed in lace and intricate embroidery. Later, in the seventeenth century, napkins became an important decorative element in table setting. They were folded and pleated to represent flowers, birds, sailing ships, bishop hats—there were supposed to be four hundred ways of folding napkins. Today, only a few simple methods of napkin folding are still published. Napkin folds that stand upright enhance tables at seated buffets. Placed between the silverware of each place setting they contribute to a finished look even though plates are waiting at the buffet line for guests to fill. At a seated dinner, napkins are usually folded flat and placed to the left of the cover (beside the forks). Napkins are sometimes centered on the service plate, perhaps with the place card or menu card resting on top or inserted in a fold.

Once the host lifts his or her napkin, place yours on your lap by lifting it with your left hand and unfolding it *under* the table. Dinner napkins are best kept folded in half with the fold toward the body. Wipe your fingers inside between the folds to keep the napkin clean next to your clothes. Luncheon napkins are smaller and may be unfolded completely. The napkin remains on your lap until needed to lightly dab the corners of your mouth or pat your lips (for instance, before taking a sip of beverage so that you do not smear the glass).

In an emergency, your napkin may be held in front of your mouth to mask the removal of something objectionable, but a more discreet method is described in the Question and Answer on this page. Do not wrinkle your napkin unnecessarily. It is very rude to blow or wipe your nose with a napkin. If you must cough or sneeze, turn away from the table and use your handkerchief or tissue as unobtrusively as possible (always carry them, especially if you experience rhinorrhea—drippy nose—when you eat). Although sometimes it is necessary for government and military representatives to attend an official function even when they are ill, whenever possible stay home and do not spread germs.

Q: What do I do if I get a piece of gristle in my mouth that I can't swallow? How do I handle spinach or something stuck in my teeth?

A: Be discreet. Chew an objectionable piece of food as small as possible, remove it the way it went in (on fork tines), and hide it beside other food on your plate. Fish bones should be removed between the index finger and thumb, as they are too small for the unobtrusive fork method. Often, if you take a drink and swish gently or keep eating, a piece of food clinging to your teeth will come unstuck. If needed, excuse yourself briefly and go to the restroom for major repairs.

Q: Should I wear my tongue stud to an interview luncheon? I notice that food, especially pasta and bread, gets caught on it when I eat.

A: Follow your intuition and remove the stud so that you will not worry about the interviewer's reaction or what is served for lunch.

Napkin Rest and Finished Positions

Be sure to visit the restroom, if necessary, before sitting down for a formal meal, which may last more than two hours. Never leave a meal in progress (except for emergencies). When a sip of water does not help a fit of coughing, it may be better to leave the table momentarily. Upon returning, murmur *"Sorry"* to the table host, or in the general direction of the host at a long banquet table. Apologizing at length or acting embarrassed will only draw attention to an incident that is best ignored.

During long award dinners, it may be necessary to depart a table briefly during the dessert or coffee course. Time your departure and return between speeches. The "Rest" position for napkins is on the seat of your chair. This alerts servers that you will be returning and not to disturb your place setting, although sometimes wait staff at Sunday brunch buffets, for example, are directed to refold your napkin and place it back on the table while you are gone. If you consider the napkin and silverware "private property" while eating, it might violate your personal space to have them touched by the server.

When finished eating, do not push back your plate—leave it alone. As soon as the host places his or her napkin on the table and prepares to rise, return yours to the table also. The "Finished" position for napkins is on the left side of your plate—or in the center of your place setting area if all dishes have been removed. Lift your napkin from the middle with your left index finger and thumb just as you stand to leave, not before. The napkin automatically arranges itself into soft folds as you lay it down; do not re-fold it. This position indicates to the wait staff that you will not return. Never discard a napkin on top of a plate. Paper napkins at table are left as neatly as possible in the same locations as cloth napkins; do not crush or roll them into a ball. The only exception to this rule is during a picnic or in a fast-food restaurant when all tableware is disposable—paper plates, plastic knives and forks, plastic cups, paper napkins—and you gather everything together to dispose of it yourself.

WESTERN TABLE TRADITIONS

The modern-day use of table silver goes back to AD 1100, when the wife of an Italian nobleman introduced the two-tined fork into table usage in Venice because she did not like to pick up meat with her fingers. The use of forks spread slowly, even in Italy where they had the blessing of nobility. Complete acceptance of the fork came only with the Renaissance, which also ushered in the use of the table knife to displace the common hunting knife which every freeman carried at all times on his belt and was accustomed to use when eating.

France and England were slower in accepting table silver, and it was not until the mid-1600s that English craftsmen commenced the manufacture of silver table knives and forks, followed by spoons. It fell to the gentry who could afford the expensive pieces to formulate the table manners of the land. It is from them that Americans inherited table manners.

Flatware (silverware) should be as easy and familiar to use as any mechanical device considered important to your career. Practice every day, at every meal, until manners "at table" become easy and automatic; poor manners at home will invariably mean poor manners in public.

One complete table cover is pictured below. Flatware is lined up on the left and right sides of the plate in the order that courses will be presented: appetizer, soup, fish, entrée, and salad for a formal dinner. There is also an individual butter spreader on the bread plate (upper left side of the place setting), and a dessert spoon and fork positioned directly above the plate. Alternatively, dessert silverware (or flatware for additional courses, such as cheese) will be provided when that course is served. Sorbet, fingerbowls, fruit, and demitasse coffee or tea are presented with their proper accoutrements as they are served. As a guest, if you drop utensils, do not pick them up. Say, *"Excuse me"* and ask the server (or the host, if he or she has not noticed your mishap) for what you need. Do not apologize; the less the incident is noticed, the better.

The Complete Table Cover

Wait for your host to begin eating and then pick up the utensil(s) on the outside, farthest from your plate. Once you have lifted silverware, never let it touch the table again. Upon completion of each course, the wait staff will remove that course's flatware with your plate or bowl. This leaves the next piece of silverware in the outside position, ready to be used.

GOBLETS

Wine is the traditional beverage served at formal meals. Goblets are placed in order of usage (and size) to match the courses: sherry, wine(s), water, and champagne flute. The water glass is the largest goblet at the tip of your entrée knife and remains on the table even if wine glasses are removed with each course. Although wine may already be poured, you do not have to drink it. The only time it is necessary for a nondrinker to pick up a full wine glass is during toasts (see Guest Demeanor below). To indicate "no, thank you" to servers approaching with a bottle, simply touch the rim of the glass with your right index and middle fingers held close together, or motion with your hand.

BREAD AND BUTTER PLATE

Bread is not always served and butter may only be provided at breakfast. However, if bread and butter is part of the meal, the bread may be pre-served on your own bread plate (above the forks) when you sit down, or directly on the tablecloth, or hidden in a napkin fold. It may be in a basket ready to be passed by guests counterclockwise (to the right). A small butter spreader (sometimes called a butter knife) is positioned across the top of each individual bread plate at a formal meal, with the handle at the right, the blade facing the table edge. Individual butter spreaders are used to take butter from the butter plate only if there is no butter-serving utensil.

Do not cut breads with a knife. Bread and rolls are broken in half by hand first, and then into individual one-bite pieces with the fingers. Put butter, jams, or condiments onto your bread plate with their serving utensils, then use your own spreader to apply them to a single morsel of bread right before eating it all in one bite, setting the butter spreader back on your bread plate between bites. An exception is hot breads. If you prefer, cut the hot biscuit, cornbread, or roll in half, place a small pat of butter inside, and wait patiently for it to melt before proceeding as above to eat a bite at a time. Bread may be used to get the last of your sauce or gravy, as desired, but drop a single bite onto your plate, then use your fork to eat it.

APPETIZER FORK

The short and slim appetizer fork, also called a seafood or oyster fork, is the only fork placed at the right of a cover, on the outside of the soupspoon. Sometimes the seafood fork is set at an angle with its tines positioned in the bowl of the soupspoon, with its handle aiming toward the table edge along the outside of the spoon handle. The standard rest and finished positions for all small pieces of silverware is the same: place them on the service plate supporting the bowl or item they accompany, on the right side. Never leave an implement sticking upright from a bowl because either you or the server could collide with it.

THE SOUP COURSE

The smallest glass on page 263 is for sherry to accompany the soup course, an old English custom. The French did not see the necessity for a beverage during this course, since broth is liquid already. Indeed, soup served in a cup or bowl with handles may be drunk; otherwise, eat soup by dipping your spoon into the bowl away from you. Touch the back rim of your soup bowl or plate with the bottom of your spoon to encourage any drips to fall before lifting it to your lips. You may tilt a soup bowl or plate away from you to eat the last spoonful. Soupspoons can be very large, especially overseas; sip from the side instead of putting the entire spoon into your mouth. The proper rest and finished positions for soupspoons depends on the depth of the bowl or soup plate. A soup plate is shallow; push your spoon further into the middle to indicate that you are finished. If the soup is served in a bowl, the spoon would stick up high enough to bump if left in it; place it instead on the right of the service plate supporting the bowl.

SPOONS AND SERVING UTENSILS

The iced beverage (iced tea) spoon is long-handled. After stirring, remove it and lay it on the small service plate that should be under the glass. However, if no such plate has been provided, and if this is not an informal meal where you could rest the spoon on your butter or luncheon plate, then leave it in the glass and drink by holding the handle against the far side with your index finger. This is awkward, but correct. Demitasse (coffee) spoons are only about 4 inches (10 centimeters) long and used with small cups of after-dinner coffee. As with teaspoons served with regular-sized cups of coffee or tea, remove the spoon from a cup after stirring and before drinking. Return it to the right side of the saucer behind the cup handle. Never lay used utensils on the table.

If diners are helping themselves, serving forks and spoons are returned to the serving platter or the vegetable dish. These pieces are larger than eating utensils, and the spoon may be pierced to permit liquids to drain from such vegetables as peas and corn. If servers are holding a platter for you, it will be on your left side; pick up the fork in your left hand, the spoon in your right. Portions are usually pre-cut, but if not, use the serving spoon to cut some—poached salmon, for example. Be sensitive about how much you take; you are never invited to a formal meal because you are hungry. Pierce or steady the food portion with the fork, slip the spoon under it, transfer the food to your plate with both utensils, then use the spoon to help remove the fork, if necessary, or to reposition the portion on your plate. Replace the serving utensils on the platter parallel and close together, ready for the next guest to help him or herself.

THE FISH COURSE

The second smallest glass on page 263 is for white wine, which accompanies the Fish Course. Goblets are meant for diners to hold by the stem while drinking. For white wine, this helps to preserve the chill; for all goblets, it eliminates fingerprints so that you can enjoy the sight of the liquid. Fish may be served cut into steaks or *filets* (meaning "without bones") or served whole with the head on. Fish knives with a special shape for gently de-boning a whole fish were not invented until the 1800s. Before that, the aristocracy ate with two forks to help lift out bones. If you are presented an accompanying sauce to serve yourself, spoon it *below* or *alongside* the fish (or any other course), not on top.

If you are served a whole fish, secure the fish on the plate with your fish fork, and with the tip of the fish knife slit it from head to tail at the belly. Flip up the top filet and eat it. Dab a single bite into the sauce, as desired. You may also wish to pierce the lemon wedge with your fork several times and squeeze over the fish, cupping with the other hand to prevent squirting your neighbor. After the top filet is eaten, cut off the head if the fish is large, then insert the tip of the knife under the backbone at the tail end and lift out the whole skeleton. Lay skeleton and bones on the side of your plate. Eat the bottom filet. Fish bones can be very small; if you are caught with any in your mouth, remove them with your thumb and forefinger and place on the rim of your plate. See discussion under Knife and Fork Manners below for the proper rest and finished positions.

THE SORBET COURSE

Following a fish course, sorbet (frozen juice) may be served with its own tiny spoon. You need not eat it all; it is a palate cleanser (also called an *intermezzo*) before the entrée, just as a simple green leaf salad serves as a palate cleanser before dessert. The rest and finished position for the small sorbet spoon is back on the right side of the service plate, behind the sorbet glass or bowl where you found it.

THE MAIN COURSE

The second largest stemmed glass on page 263 traditionally holds red wine to accompany the red meat that was usually served as the entrée or main course. Today it can be another white wine depending on contemporary menus. Do not take a drink of any wine served until your host does. He or she may wish to talk about the special vintage chosen in your honor, or to propose a toast before anyone takes a sip. Also, please review the paragraph above on manipulating serving forks and spoons. When you serve yourself, entrée portions go in the middle of your plate, accompanying vegetables go above, and any sauce is spooned below the entrée (imagine creating a smiley face). The largest knife and fork at your place setting is used to eat this course. Proper rest and finished positions are discussed under Knife and Fork Manners below.

THE SALAD COURSE

Salad is considered "unfriendly" to wine. The high acid level of vinaigrette wreaks havoc on your taste buds when followed by wine; therefore, water is the beverage that goes with the separate salad course. The salad fork is shorter than the luncheon or dinner (entrée) fork. The placement of the fork depends upon when the salad course will be served. When salad is served as a first course (typically American), the salad fork is placed on the outside, as it will be the first fork used. During formal meals, salad is served as a palate cleanser after the entrée, so the fork is placed closest to the plate. The separate salad course is typically leaf lettuce with perhaps one additional ingredient, tossed in light vinaigrette. Twirl leaf lettuce around your fork without cutting and lift it to your mouth. Before the 1920s, knives were made from silver or steel, which could not only affect the flavor of salads or fruit, their blades would also turn black from the acids. This gave rise to an old etiquette rule, "*Never cut salad with a knife*," but modern manufacturing with stainless steel has eliminated the problem, thankfully. Modern-day salads can contain iceberg lettuce or other ingredients of various sizes that must be cut to bite-size with your knife. Knife and Fork Manners below describes the proper utensil rest and finished positions.

THE DESSERT COURSE

Champagne is the traditional beverage that accompanies the dessert course. It is served in a tall, narrow flute to show off the rising bubbles. Also appropriate is the champagne coupe or saucer style. Even if you have refused wine throughout the meal, a good server may insist on pouring a little of the last wine offered because of toasts. Formal toasts (sometimes many) are usually proposed during the dessert course.

Your dessert utensils are a fork and a spoon. They may be above your plate as on page 263, in which case you pull them down into position while waiting for the server to bring you an individually plated dessert. Alternatively, dessert utensils may arrive with a fingerbowl (see next paragraph). The spoon is used like a knife, if you need it, perhaps for cutting a crust on a fruit tart. If you are served cake, you might only use the fork. If you are served ice cream, you will probably need only the spoon. However, even if you do not use one or the other of your dessert utensils, place them together in the finished position after eating, as on page 273, Finished Positions.

THE FINGERBOWL

Either before dessert or the cheese course, the fingerbowl (water, perhaps with flower petals floating) arrives if diners have needed to touch food such as artichokes, fruit, shrimp, or other shellfish. If a fingerbowl is presented to you, it may be atop a doily on a small plate with a fork on the left and a spoon on the right. You are supposed to reset your place by positioning the fork and spoon at their proper positions on either side before lifting the fingerbowl with one hand and its doily with the other to set them both on the upper left of your place setting (the bread plate will be gone), ready to be used later. That way the plate that the fingerbowl arrived on can be used to receive your dessert. The fingerbowl may also arrive without utensils, as a separate "course." Follow the host's lead for when to use a fingerbowl. There are many apocryphal stories of inexperienced guests picking up fingerbowls and drinking the contents. Instead, lightly dip the fingertips of one hand at a time and wipe them dry on the separate napkin (if not provided, dry your fingers on your lap napkin).

Q: How do I know when to eat American Style or when to use International Style?

A: Either style is acceptable, as long as you manipulate your utensils correctly. We urge you to master International Style, especially with multicultural groups, because Americans are the only people who eat in the conspicuous "zigzag style."

Q: Do I ask the senior officer or his spouse to be excused from the table?

A: Neither. It is rude to leave the table before hosts indicate that the meal is concluded. If you must depart temporarily, say "*Excuse me,*" place your napkin in the rest position, take care of your emergency, and return to your seat. You will know if a professional obligation demands your early departure, so inform your host ahead of time and ask if a guest of honor should also be told. When that time approaches, end any conversation with a comment that duty calls, make eye contact with the host, nod, and when he or she nods back, place your napkin in the finished position, excuse yourself quietly, and depart quickly so that the disturbance is minimized.

THE CHEESE COURSE

A cheese platter may be passed with bread and crackers as an accompaniment to the salad course (American), offered before dessert (French, because it goes well with any entrée wine left in your glass), or served as a separate course after dessert (with Port wine, as the English do), perhaps with a complement of fruit and nuts. Arrange a classic cheese tray with different textures, colors, and shapes—one each sharp, creamy, and veined. Sampling begins with the mildest and proceeds through the most robust. When helping yourself, the most important thing is to keep shapes intact. Do not lop off the pointed end from a wedge, for instance. When cheese is served with a salad, take a slice or two of your choice and put it directly on your salad plate, where it can be broken with a fork and eaten with the lettuce, or spread on a cracker.

AFTER-DINNER DRINKS

Your host knows the sequence of events for the evening, so keep your eye on him or her. Sometimes coffee or tea will be served as a separate course while still at the table. In a private home, you will most likely be invited into another room or onto the terrace for demitasse, chocolates, and *digestifs* (cognac, liqueurs). A brandy snifter is warmed to bring out the bouquet by cupping the bowl in your hand with the stem between your index and middle finger.

GUEST DEMEANOR

Subordinates and friends often look to your leadership as their role model at table. Do not lay personal items such as cell phones or keys on the table while being seated (see Chapter 17: Family Dining, Buffets, and Formal In-Home Meals for seating procedures). Females keep purses on the lap under their napkins or between their feet on the floor after they are seated. Nothing personal is ever added to the tabletop.

Pace yourself so that you are not finished eating too long before others, or still lingering over food well after everyone else. Taste all food—it is rude to leave food served to you untouched; you need not finish it. If food is not to your liking, make conversation.

Conversation

At formal meals, conversation is important. You are never invited simply to eat. Make a point to talk with guests seated on both sides of you and those across from you, if the table is not too wide. A male might begin with his dinner partner, the female on his right, but a monopolized or too-intimate conversation between partners is impolite. It is important to remain aware of what is going on at your table. Listen and contribute (if appropriate) as group conversations occur. Keep table talk pleasant with topics unlikely to cause offense. Safe and non-controversial subjects include the weather, the lovely decorations, leisure pursuits such as interesting travel, or a best seller you are currently reading. Be careful of controversial or unpleasant subjects, such as politics; avoid talking business or criticizing. Keep your voice at a moderate level; loud talk and laughter at the table can disturb others.

Toasts

Besides initiating pleasant conversation, your other guest duty is to know the appropriate behavior during toasts. Most toasts will be proposed during dessert with that course's traditional beverage, champagne. See Chapter 20: Toasts for the proper procedures.

HOW TO SPOT A SPY

During World War II when American pilots were shot down in Europe and tried to sneak across a border to safety, they were easily identified even though underground resistance movements were helping them. There are many reports that when the pilots stopped to eat a meal, they laid down their knives and switched their forks to their right hands to eat. This immediately identified them as Americans. Many spent the rest of the war in prison camps . . . all because they used their very best American-Style table manners.

Departure

Remember that no one departs a formal, seated meal until the host indicates that it is appropriate, unless there is an emergency. However, if you must leave the table for an emergency and return, if you are senior ranking or female, your dinner partner or table companion might make a half-rise to show respect. Junior ranking military personnel must *not* stand for superiors if both are attending a civilian formal dinner (for example, a wedding meal, corporate banquet, or diplomatic function), as other guests would consider the action quite rude and disruptive. Your final two actions at table before walking away are to place your napkin in the "finished" position after the host does (see Napkin Etiquette above) and push in your chair.

As with all hospitality extended to you, thank your hosts in person before departing and handwrite a note the following day (see Chapter 12: Correspondence and Stationery Essentials).

KNIFE AND FORK MANNERS

There are two gracious methods of eating with a knife and a fork—the American Style and the International Style. Today, only Americans eat in the style sometimes referred to as "zigzag" because the hand that holds the fork continually changes. All other cultures that eat with knives and forks advocate the International Style (sometimes called "European continental" even though it is used worldwide), keeping their utensils primarily in the hands that pick them up. You may use either way of eating—both techniques are correct—but you are urged to master the International Style as most versatile.

In the American Style, the non-dominant hand (usually the left) is kept resting on your lap as much as possible until you need both hands to cut food, butter bread, or pass items. Food is brought to your mouth mostly with the fork held tines up, in your dominant hand (usually the right). To cut food, switch the fork to your non-dominant hand and pick up the knife with your dominant hand, letting your index fingers point down the handles of both utensils. Pierce the food to be cut with your fork (hold tines down throughout the procedure), and cut up to three bite-size pieces—meat and or vegetable—and then lay your knife across the upper rim of your plate (centered or a bit to your dominant side) with the sharp edge toward the center of the plate. Transfer the fork to your dominant hand, holding it like a pencil, tines up, with the handle extending out between your thumb and index finger. Pierce or scoop one morsel, as necessary, and bring it to your mouth, remembering to rest the non-dominant hand in your lap until you need it to cut again.

In the International Style, both hands are used throughout the meal, with wrists resting on the table between courses instead of on your lap. It is often a revelation for those more familiar with American Style to discover when mastering the International Style that the forks have been conveniently and correctly placed on the left all along! Pick up utensils at the same time: fork with your left hand and knife with your right hand, pointing your index fingers down the handles. You will manipulate them in this arrangement throughout the course, only setting them down to "rest" or in the "finished" position (see next two sections). Spear one bite at a time, keeping your fork tines down. Use your knife to cut and to help place a small amount of vegetables on the back of the fork tines with the meat. Keep the knife in your right hand with the blade touching the plate as you swivel your left wrist slightly to place the food in your mouth, still with the fork tines facing down.

INTERNATIONAL STYLE LAUNCHED

Europeans were as right-handed with forks as Americans until the stylish upper class decided to differentiate themselves with the method we call *International Style:*
> If you wish to eat in the latest mode favored by fashionable people, you will not change your fork to your right hand after you have cut your meat, but raise it to your mouth in your left hand.

—French etiquette, *Manuel du Bonton et de la Politesse*, 1853

Rest Positions for Silverware

For both American and International Styles of eating you must lay down your utensils when you would like to talk, use your napkin, take a drink, or pass food items.

In the International Style, both hands are holding a utensil. Place your knife on your plate with the blade facing the middle and position the tines of your fork over the blade in a crossed position, forming an "X" in the center of the plate. If there is too much food in the center, cross your utensils where room allows, ready to be picked up again. Or carefully place your knife along the right rim (blade facing in) and your fork along the left rim (if the rim is flat enough), taking care that the handles do not touch the table; see page 273, International Rest Position.

AMERICAN STYLE MORE REFINED?

American table manners are, if anything, a more advanced form of civilized behavior because they are elaborate, time-consuming, and further removed from the practical result, always a sign of refinement.

—Judith Martin, *Miss Manners Guide to Excruciatingly Correct Behavior*, 1979

In the American Style, the rest position for the knife is along the upper edge of your plate, blade facing the center. Set your knife there between cutting maneuvers. The rest position for your fork is on the plate tines up, in any convenient location (but not touching the table) ready to be picked up again.

International Rest Position

American Rest Position

Finished Position

Finished Positions for Silverware

For both styles of eating, place your utensils *parallel together* to indicate that you are finished and would like the server to remove your plate. If you visualize your plate as a compass, the recommended position would have both handles aiming southeast, with the knife blade facing the middle for both styles, and the fork tines aptly up (American Style) or down (International Style). If you visualize your plate as a clock face, this recommended position would read 1550 hours (3:50 o'clock); see page 273, Finished Positions. Alternative, but less preferred locations, are at the 1800 hours (6:00 o'clock) position, or to lay the flatware beside each other on the dominant-hand side of the plate, handles perpendicular to the table edge.

SERVICE STYLES

There are four Forms of Service that wait staff use, commonly referred to by their French translations: Modern *Service à la Française* (French Service), *Service à L'Anglaise* (English Service), *Service à la Russe* (Russian Service), and *Service à L'Americaine* (American Service; also called Restaurant or Banquet Style).

French Service

In Modern *Service à la Française* the food is fully prepared in the kitchen and presented to guests on platters. Servers move counterclockwise (to the right) around the table, holding the platters at elbow height on the diner's left side for each person to serve him or herself. Turn your body toward the server and pick up the serving utensils with both hands (see how-to above in the Spoons and Serving Utensils paragraph). Place the serving utensils back together on the platter ready for the next person.

Traditional *Service à la Française* used to be more like what people now think of as family style, with all the platters and bowls of food (and they were many) on the table in an array of opulence before guests arrived, with sides called *hors d'oeuvres* ("outside" or "corner" dishes) surrounding the larger ones. After the first course of food was removed, so was the tablecloth, to reveal a clean one underneath ready to be piled high with more dishes, including the *pièces de résistance* (elaborate main dishes); and the procedure was repeated a third time for dessert.

English Service

Service à L'Anglaise also has the food fully prepared in the kitchen and arranged on platters or in baskets or bowls, but with this style the wait staff serves each diner, again from the guest's left side. It is easy to control portions in this style of service.

Russian Service

Service à la Russe is used when food is brought from the kitchen and finished by the server as you watch. Diners admire the process, such as tossing a Caesar salad, or flaming a crêpe Suzette on a portable stovetop near the table, before the food is plated and served. Another example is if the restaurant server offers to de-bone a whole fish at your table.

American Service

Service à L'Americaine (also called Restaurant or Banquet Style) has all food individually plated and garnished in the kitchen. Chefs are particularly fond of American Service, as it allows them to arrange the food, sauce, and garnishes in ever more creative ways to impress guests. Plates are presented to diners from their left sides; beverages are served from the right. In 1994, President Bill Clinton and Hillary Clinton instituted American Service at the White House.

USE YOUR NAPKIN

I can empathize with the old gentleman who took a bite of steaming-hot baked potato, spat it right out on the table, and said to his hostess, *"You know, some darned fools would've swallowed that."*

—Peg Bracken, "Perfect Dinner Party," *Family Circle* magazine, February 1979

CHAPTER 17

Family Dining, Buffets, and
Formal In-Home Meals

*G*overnment public servants, military and civilian—and their family members—normally have the opportunity to attend many social occasions throughout a career, from formal official, public, and state occasions to informal home and outdoor events. That gives them numerous opportunities to dine in a variety of different settings and locations. Civility should always be observed.

AT EASE KEY POINTS

❧ Take a host gift for in-home invitations (except large receptions).

❧ Greet hosts on arrival; reconnoiter. Sign guest book, read seating chart.

❧ Set glass down before going by receiving line, to buffet, or to dining table.

❧ Find and thank hosts before departing, unless event is very large.

❧ Write a thank-you note the following day.

FAMILY-STYLE DINING

People are most familiar with the family style of dining, since all our lives we have eaten with family and friends. It is the informal seating and serving of the food that makes it family style. Sometimes restaurants advertise their service as "family style" but usually people think of this style as most appropriate in someone's home. Since a dinner with a family is an intimate occasion, guests should consider it an honor to be invited. The hosts usually extend the invitation by telephone or e-mail, *"Melissa and I would like you to have supper with us on Saturday, at seven."* If you are the only guest, and if there are children in the family, the dinner hour may be as early as six o'clock.

During in-home family breakfasts, lunches, and dinners there is normally a special seat for mother and father, and each child has claimed a "favorite" seat and kept it throughout the years. In the United States, it is common for the father and mother to sit at opposite ends of the table. Friends are often told to "sit anywhere" but it is wise to avoid the head and foot of the table for this reason. If grandparents (parents-in-law) are visiting, they are given honored seats at table, and sometimes it is even a tradition for the parents to surrender their head places and "move down" symbolically in the family hierarchy.

Despite the fact that a written request may not be extended, invitations to dine in a family home require the same behaviors, courtesies, and respect that are given at any other dining venue. Indeed, family tables are daily training grounds for practicing good manners. Although there may be fewer items, all flatware, glassware, plates, and napkins are in the correct positions, even paper or plastic versions at barbecues and picnics. Chapter 16: Place Settings, Table Manners and Service Styles has table illustrations as well as overviews on American and International styles of eating. The only reminders here are to keep your arms as close to your body as possible while eating—especially watch elbows when cutting with your knife—and slow down; swallow each mouthful before taking another bite.

Family Customs
The goal of any host is to offer hospitality to congenial guests. Today's American family adapts the best of traditional dining styles to present-day modest incomes and fast pace, often with an international twist. The United States is a land of immigrant diversity with rich family traditions. Military Service and Foreign Service families often live briefly in several states and various countries all over the world. Many large American corporations send their employees and their families abroad to work. Therefore, it is only natural that citizens adopt and modify many customs and foods into their everyday living, perhaps some of the following:

- The host may prepare food, coffee, or tea in a ritual while guests observe.

- A host may share a particularly tasty morsel from his or her own plate.

- The sexes may eat separately, or may separate after dinner.

- The most common custom at the family table is to bless the food. The host, designated family member (perhaps in weekly rotation), or guest (if asked), says grace aloud for all (or the family may recite a prayer together). Blessings occur before anything is touched—including the napkin. If you are asked to pray, you need not attempt a blessing in an unfamiliar religion. Instead, use your own favorite grace and say it in your own sincere way. One that is acceptable to all faiths is: *"For what we are about to receive, God, make us truly thankful. Amen."*

- Sometimes a "secular grace" or welcome is said at family dinners in place of a prayer or following it, depending on the occasion and who has been invited. Especially if wine is being served, this welcome may be in the form of a *Toast*—a verbal salute to honor a guest or guests while holding aloft a glass. Toasts may be as simple as saying a single word or phrase, for example, *"Cheers"* or *"Bon Appétit."* (For information on toasting mechanics, see Chapter 20: Toasts.) After this formality, the meal begins.

Serving Food

Typically, all the food (except dessert) will be placed on the family table at one time. The mother or father (or both) starts by holding a bowl or platter for any guests of honor (who occupy the seats on their right sides) to take the first servings. Hosts ask that the bowl be passed on around (counterclockwise to the right). Hosts usually fill their plates only after everyone else has. Once the parents (or grandparents) pick up the first platter, other family members may start reaching for the platters or bowls directly in front of them, depending on family custom.

Diners hold the serving dish in their left or non-dominant hands while using their right or dominant hands to serve themselves moderate portions of food before passing the dish onwards (to the right, counterclockwise), including the salt and pepper (always passed together) and the bread and butter (passed one after the other). For informal family meals, only one butter spreader may be on the table and it is kept with the butter plate or dish being passed. Use it to remove the amount of butter desired and put it on the edge of your own plate. Return the butter spreader to the butter dish and pass both to the person on your right. Use a knife from your own place setting (there may be only one knife) to butter your bread or vegetables. If the bread is warm (for example biscuits, muffins, cornbread, or rolls) you may split it and place the butter inside to melt before breaking off a small portion to eat. Otherwise, tear a one-bite portion of bread; butter it only right before you eat the entire bite. If wine is served, the bottle or decanter may be set on the table, with hosts urging guests to serve themselves.

At a family dinner, or any informal meal, you may take a second helping when offered, or even a third if your hosts insist and if you really want the food. However, if you do not care for a second helping, you need not feel any obligation to take more. If passing your plate to the hosts for them to serve you more, leave your used knife and fork on it, the knife above and parallel across the top or at

Q: I spilled my drink off a lap tray at a buffet dinner. How do you juggle the lot gracefully?

A: As you discovered, it requires balancing and continual attention to a glass on a tray, but why do that to yourself? Wait to drink until after you have eaten. If nothing else, going for a drink gives you the perfect exit line to continue surfing the room at large functions. Otherwise, walk with one hand steadying it and set your glass on a nearby table once you are seated.

Q: What do I do if I get food on my clothes, or worse, on someone else's?

A: Blot inconspicuously at spots on your own clothing—do not call attention to your problem. If needed, excuse yourself and visit the bathroom for major repairs. Please never start dabbing at another's clothes. Apologize profusely, hand over your napkin, and get more clean ones.

Q: Is it proper to ask for seconds, and how should you ask?

A: Do not ask; you are never invited because you are hungry. It is a host's duty to offer more food. Only if an item is on the table may you say, *"Please pass the___."* Serve yourself, and pass it on to others, counterclockwise (to the right).

the right of the plate, the fork parallel right beneath it. Handles will be together so that they may be anchored with a thumb if necessary. Used utensils are never placed on the table.

Dessert may be served directly from the kitchen, after all plates and dishes have been removed from the table. When dessert is served at the table, a stack of plates, along with the dessert and serving fork or spoon, is set directly in front of one of the hosts to serve each person. Dessert silver is either in place on the table, or put on individual plates as they are passed. Coffee is frequently served throughout the family dinner, or with or after dessert while still at table. Cream and sugar are passed around the table.

Wait for the host to begin eating before beginning yourself (unless he or she asks you not to wait), and do not rise from the table until the host does. When something needs to be done during the meal, such as bringing in the coffee service or clearing the table, you may offer to assist, but most hosts prefer that guests not help; some use the opportunity to train their children to help serve guests. After dinner, leave within thirty to forty-five minutes unless the host invites you to stay for another planned activity, such as watching a movie or playing a game.

BUFFET-STYLE DINING

In keeping with the times, less formal dinners are the order of the day, with buffet meals favored. This serving method accommodates a flexible number of guests in a small space with or without help, and is the most popular for large events in a home setting, such as a dinner reception or a cocktails buffet. The host usually extends the invitation in written form (see Chapter 11: Invitations). Dress for these events may be *Casual* or *Informal*, which is only one step under *Formal* (see Chapter 22: Appropriate Attire). The host customarily greets guests at the front door or in the reception area. There may be a formal receiving line (see Chapter 18: Official Business Functions, Cocktails, and Receptions).

Q: Upper classmen laugh when I use good manners, *"Why do you eat like that now that you're not a Plebe?"* What can I do or say?

A: Smile and keep eating. Your peers have not internalized the proper behavior necessary for success (e.g., during job interview luncheons and workplace dinners). While they will be worrying about their table manners, you will be focusing on other professional goals. We commend your maturity and the leadership skills you are practicing during your school years. Rest assured that your tormentors (or others like them) will be working *for* you in the future.

Q: What if I am served something I don't want? I ask this because I am allergic to some things and picky about others. Last night I thought I was being discreet, but my host caught me hiding shrimp in my napkin.

A: If food is passed or served at table, you may say, *"No thank you."* If food that you cannot eat is on your plate already, make clever conversation as you salt it, cut it, and move it around while eating what you can. Place your utensils in the finished position at the end of the course; your plate will be removed. If asked, *"Don't you like it?"* simply reply with a smile that it is fine, thank you—no long explanations. Resist complimenting foods you do not eat—saying *"delicious"* almost guarantees that more will be happily piled onto your plate.

Buffet Lines

Start the buffet line when the host asks; normally the ranking guest or a spouse will be invited to go first. At the beginning of a buffet line, pick up a plate (and a napkin and flatware if they have not been more appropriately placed *after* the food items) before proceeding around the table. Wait your turn behind others (do not line-jump even if the buffet is long and there are gaps). Select food and place on your plate only the amount you wish to eat immediately, since it is appropriate to go back to a buffet table a second time if desired (only after all others have helped themselves once). Carry your plate into the living room or other room designated by the host. Wait for others to join you before starting to eat.

At *catered gatherings*, if you return for more food, take a clean plate, flatware, and napkin; used plates and utensils are left in the room where you have been eating. Wait staff will probably be circulating with trays and at your smiling nod they will come to relieve you of a used plate or glass. There may also be a "drop" table to leave items. Do not set anything down on polished furniture surfaces. For non-catered events follow your host's directions.

Seated Buffets

At a seated buffet, carry only your filled plate to a table that has been previously set with everything else: appropriate beverage glasses, flatware, and napkins. At very large buffets, the coffee service, water, wine, and glasses are placed in convenient areas, with guests helping themselves.

To locate your chair at this type of dinner, look for your rank/honorific/title and surname handwritten on a *place card* positioned above the place setting or atop your napkin (see Chapter 16: Place Settings, Table Manners, and Service Styles for details). For multiple tables there may be a *Seating Chart* displayed outside the dining area for you to consult (see Chapter 23: Seating Plans). Look to see where you will be seated and with whom you are sharing a table so that you can talk to someone else during cocktails and not exhaust all your conversation topics before coming to the table.

Unassigned or Open Seating Buffets

Most private homes lack the capacity for offering a formal seat to everyone in a large group. Guests will probably be urged to sit anywhere in a designated area—on couches, chairs, window seats, even raised hearths and stairs—as indicated by the protocol officer, aide, or hosts. Proper manners dictate that you manipulate your utensils properly, even when you are eating off your lap in a living room.

During official events, music may be played by a military band or ensemble of musicians. After eating, socialize with the other guests, enjoy the music, and if you wish, go to the bar for a beverage. A beverage area or bar is normally set up in a different room from the food. If you bring a date or guests, it is polite to go and get their drinks for them. It is also polite to offer to bring back drinks for senior ranking personnel, spouses, or anyone else in the immediate conversational group. The main course will probably be cleared and replaced with dessert (and perhaps coffee and tea) for you to again help yourself. Wait for hosts to invite you to do so.

FORMAL DINING

Formal dinners will have chairs at tables for everyone, seats indicated with place cards at full settings of china, silverware, goblets, and banquet napkins. Wait staff will serve food and wine in courses corresponding to the written *menu cards* (see Chapter 16: Place Settings, Table Manners, and Service Styles). There may be only one table for six in a private home or many tables in a large banquet hall, depending on the occasion. The hosts usually extend a formal invitation written in the third person with an R.s.v.p. deadline. Dress for these events will be *Informal* or *Formal*.

Guest Arrival

Guests arrive at the designated time—not early, not late. (Local customs overseas define "on time.") When the guest of honor is a dignitary attending a function at quarters on a military reservation, an aide or co-host will meet him or her at the base or station gate and escort the guest to the host's quarters. The hosts will be waiting in the hall to greet the honored guest, and to present other guests to him or her.

When the official event host is a married woman, if her husband is of lesser rank or without title, he is still in all respects treated as the event host—just as the wife of an official is treated as host. When the official is single, an aide may be assisting, or a co-host may have been asked to help with conversation and to sit opposite the host at table.

In quarters of officials of high rank, a military aide (or other help) will open the door for guests and direct them to the coatroom. (In homes of civilians with considerable means, this is the role of the butler.) The hosts stand just inside the living room door to greet guests. Guests greet the female of the couple first (or the host before a designated co-host) before greeting others. A guest of honor may be present, and the hosts will introduce other guests first to him or her (and spouse, if present) and see to it that guests are introduced into another group, if they do not know anyone. After that, it is up to the guest to meet and mingle. A choice of beverages will be offered before dinner; do not have more than two alcoholic drinks. Guests move from group to group for conversation, and remain standing unless invited to sit. In a large group, living room seats are for guests with disabilities. In smaller groups, the right side of the sofa as you sit is considered the seat of honor in a living room. If the honored guest is already seated, the sofa is available for anyone.

The Late Guest

When a guest other than the guest of honor is late, the general rule is to wait no more than ten or fifteen minutes after the cocktail hour before going in to dinner. The latecomer goes directly to his or her chair upon arrival. The female host remains seated, so that all the men at her table do not have to stand (only the man to the left of a late female guest rises to help seat her). The latecomer briefly says, "*I am very sorry to be late. It was unavoidable.*" He or she should give an explanation to the host privately after the meal.

If the guest calls to regret at the very last minute, the place setting and chair are removed and others further spaced out without re-ordering the seating plan.

Entering the Dining Room

When dinner is hosted by a couple, the host husband offers his arm to the highest-ranking woman guest as he says, "*Shall we go in to dinner?*" He leads the way into the dining room immediately after the announcement that dinner is served. The host wife takes the arm of the ranking male guest and they go in last, after all other diners. However, if the guest of honor is a man of very high position, or a dignitary of note, the host wife and guest of honor will enter the dining room first, with the host husband and ranking woman immediately following. All other guests follow, in no particular order. If it is a very formal occasion, escorts will have been assigned.

Taking Your Seat

A woman is seated as soon as she enters the dining room. She waits for a moment at a formal table to see if her dinner partner (the man on her left) will offer to help seat her. Men remain standing until the female host takes her place, with the second ranking male guest on her left seating her. (He has first helped the lady at the right of the guest of honor's chair, if present. See Escorting and Seating Partner in Chapter 23: Seating Plans). The guest of honor, who has walked in last with the female host, merely stands by his chair until she is seated, then all males sit down. If there is a butler, he will seat the female host.

When seating anyone, ask, "*May I help with your chair?*" and step behind to draw it back; then, as the person starts to sit down, slide the chair forward carefully. Remain in position to push again if necessary. A person being seated enters the chair from the right side, sits down, then lifts up (and helps pull the chair forward if needed) with the helper pushing in from behind, lifting a second time as necessary. When a female at a formal evening table or someone needing help rises, a dinner partner pulls the chair back without jerking, "*Let me help you.*"

Wait Staff for Formal Meals

A government or military person's household usually has little, if any, help, but a senior official may qualify for part-time help (called a Navy mess specialist, an Air Force airman aide, or an Army enlisted aide) depending on the official position and the assigned quarters. Examples are the Chief of Naval Operations, the Chiefs of Staff of the Army and Air Force, the Commandant of the Marine Corps, the superintendents and presidents of the various academies and military schools— and the President of the United States. Otherwise, when the occasion demands, hosts must hire help from a catering service or a military club to help them serve a formal meal.

The number one table server stands behind the female host's chair, directing the other servers. As soon as all guests are seated, the first course is placed on the plate, beginning with the woman at the right of the host. The female host is not served first unless she is the only woman at the table. Wine is poured as soon as the first course is served, unless glasses have been filled beforehand (the host may wish to open with a toast). Other food and wines will be served in separate courses. Do not thank the servers until the end of the meal, as it is disruptive to their work, necessitating constant *"You're Welcomes."* Guests do not start eating until the host (female, if present) begins. At large banquet dinners where waiting means that your food would get cold, you may start eating as soon as those at your individual table or nearest you have been served.

Conversation at Very Formal Tables

"Turning the table" means following the hosts' lead by talking with the person at your right to begin a formal meal, but changing conversation partners by talking to the person on your left after the first course. Feel free to talk to persons across from you also, if the formal table is narrow. Remember, especially if the table is large and the atmosphere formal, conversations will remain low-voiced.

DEPARTURES

The guest of honor makes the first move to depart, no later than forty-five minutes after dinner if no other entertainment has been planned. He or she must not keep everyone waiting when it is time to go. Other guests cannot leave a formal event until after the high-ranking guest leaves. If they absolutely must go, the departing guest makes his or her apology to the host first, then the guest of honor. If you know ahead of time that an early departure is necessary, explain it to the hosts beforehand, then briefly tell the ranking guest why you are leaving early and say goodbye.

When leaving, shake hands with your hosts and thank them for opening their home to you. The host wife (or non-principal event host) rises when guests stand to exit, but she stays with the other guests in the living room. The husband (or official event host) walks to the door with guests.

Although it is impossible to tell each guest good-bye after a large event, speak to your dinner partner before leaving, as well as to others with whom you were just talking. If an aide or butler opens the door for you, he or she will say, "*Good night, Sir* [or *Madam*]." You answer, "*Good night, and thank you.*"

Courtesy requires that guests write a thank-you note within two days for home hospitality. For exceptions to saying thank you, see Chapter 21: Guest and Visitor Civility. For couples, the guest wife normally writes the note to the host wife. For smaller informal gatherings, guests may telephone or e-mail.

CHAPTER 18

Official Business Functions, Cocktails, and Receptions

Official social functions are often arranged by organizations. They are best viewed as continuations of the employees' working day. It is considered good office politics for invited employees to attend as many of these events as possible.

AT EASE KEY POINTS

- ⚹ Learn invitation dress codes.
- ⚹ Arrive ten minutes early if you are co-host or facilitator.
- ⚹ Employees work the room alone (without spouse or date).
- ⚹ Stand and introduce yourself and others properly.
- ⚹ Principal (whoever host invited) goes first by receiving line; spouse follows.
- ⚹ Guest of honor leaves first so that others may depart.

OFFICIAL BUSINESS FUNCTIONS

An organized group social event for employees is designed to allow those who work together to become better acquainted with each other, and their spouses or dates (and sometimes entire families) to be introduced. A committee of employees may be appointed to make the arrangements. Frequently an informal flyer or internal e-mail invitation states the purpose of the gathering, R.s.v.p. information, date and time, location, and the dress requirement. If government-sponsored, the estimated cost for each person will be included. American civil servants do not use public funds to pay for their social occasions. Those more accustomed to corporation-hosted events may be surprised that when invited to a military or government function, they are often expected to fund their way. Explain this concept so that terms such as "make checks payable to" and "cash bar" do not confound them.

Parties may be at a military club, a government building, a tourist site, or a local restaurant, either casual (luncheons) or elaborate (an evening of cocktails, dinner, and dancing). They are usually designated *Uniform Required* for military venues. One example of a formal military gathering is the Dining In (see Chapter 4). Away from military posts and bases, service personnel may be required to dress in civilian attire so that they can blend into the community venue or the social scene comfortably. Through these social get-togethers, staff members develop rapport with each other in order to enhance working relationships.

Q: How do I do pass my business card with my right hand and shake hands at the same time while holding food and drink at a social gathering?

A: Mingle before eating! However, if you must carry food and drink, one procedure is to hold beverage and food with your *left* hand as follows: slip a cocktail napkin between your pinkie and ring fingers, balance your plate on your ring and middle fingers, keep your index finger and thumb above the plate rim and use them to grasp your glass close to one side of the plate, leaving room for food tidbits on the remainder of the plate. Eat from the plate with the fingertips of your right hand. When you are introduced, wipe your fingers on the napkin before shaking hands. Keep your cards at the ready in your right-hand pocket; put others' away in another pocket.

Q: For official workplace functions, what is expected in terms of gifts and thank you notes? Is there a difference if you know or don't know the host?

A: Some organizations have strict rules regarding gift-giving, especially to superiors. In government agencies, laws regulate gift acceptances. During gift-giving seasons, consider group ideas (e.g., food for breaks). If you bring back souvenirs from a business trip, strive to be inclusive or give them apart from the workplace. For very large receptions, no gift or thank-you note is necessary, but for in-home events, both are expected civility.

Official functions also commemorate organization successes, with attending employees representing the employer in interactions with community leaders and clients. If the event is for "outside people" then all employees are considered hosts and make every effort to talk to visitors. Key individuals may be designated as co-hosts and asked to arrive at least ten minutes early so that they are in place to greet and socialize as visiting guests arrive. This is especially important if the organization event is for international guests.

The organizers assign specific duties to official co-hosts. You may be called upon to act as an aide or announcer at a receiving line or as an escort for a Very Important Person/Distinguished Visitor (VIP/DV). Co-hosts do not take the best parking spaces, huddle up with their friends, or party as if they were ordinary guests. If you are a designated co-host, ask for and study guest lists beforehand. Your duties will include such things as guiding guests away from a receiving line, directing them to the guest book, bar, or food area, greeting lots of people, facilitating introductions, and making conversation (see Chapter 19: Introductions, Conversations, and Farewells). No high-ranking guest should be left unattended. You may be asked to usher them to the dining room at a specific time, or to help get guests to stand for toasts. Co-hosts always stay until an event is over.

When you are invited to business functions external to your organization, it is because of your title or position, not usually for your charming personality. In such cases, it is not a good idea to designate a substitute to attend in your place unless you get prior permission from the host. If a married couple has been invited to an official dinner and the principal is prevented from attending at the last minute, he or she informs the host immediately and asks whether the spouse should attend alone.

For most official government functions, it is a good idea to bring your invitation for passage through security checkpoints. Some invitations will include an admittance card with your name written above a sentence saying, *"Please present this card at the door,"* or similar wording may be printed on the bottom of the invitation itself.

Expect to exchange business cards during daytime business-related events. Gatherings with outside people are opportunities to develop new contacts and make appointments to discuss business, not merely to socialize. The best way a mannerly world citizen offers a business card is with the print facing the recipient (read more in Chapter 25: International Protocol and Civility).

Business Meals

Business meals facilitate the exchange of information in an informal social setting, usually a restaurant, but sometimes a residence. The host may have a seating plan in mind; ask where to sit if not directed. If the meal has not been prearranged, follow the host's lead to order food in keeping with his or her selection and number of courses. Do not order the most expensive menu item, food that is messy or that might stick to your teeth, or alcoholic beverages (the host may order wine).

It is not necessary for businessmen to help female colleagues with their chairs at daytime business meals if they would not offer a male the same courtesy. In business, people strive to be gender neutral. Either sex offers to help persons with disabilities or the encumbered whenever necessary.

During formal evening meals, a considerate male does extend the courtesy of offering to seat the female dinner companion on his right, followed by any other person near him needing help before taking his own seat. (Men seated at the left of the female host may need to assist her; see Escorting and Seating Partner, in Chapter 23: Seating Plans.)

To be of assistance to anyone, rise and offer, *"May I help with your chair?"* The diner sits down from the right side, lifts up, and the helper assists by pushing in the chair from behind. The helper waits to see if the chair needs to be a little closer by watching for the person to rise up a second time. When a female or someone needing help rises, an aware dinner partner stands to help with the chair, drawing it back without jerking it. When females return, courteous males rise or half-rise and dinner partners again assist with the seating. (At military hosted events it is customary to stand as the commanding officer departs the table or room. Military persons should *not* disrupt civilian events by standing for their commanders.)

Once everyone is seated, wait for your host to begin. Do not touch anything except your menu card, which you can read and set off to the side for later reference. Put it under your service plate if the table is crowded, but not under your napkin where it will likely fall to the floor. Menu cards list what food and beverages will be served and the order of courses. They may also contain a sentence or two in honor of a specific person or special occasion or have the date. If so, you may keep yours as a souvenir.

If a cleric is present at a public function, he or she will normally be asked to say grace or give a benediction. Remain seated unless asked by the host or clergy to rise. Following the benediction or in place of it, there may be a welcome toast by the host. The event's guest of honor has the duty of reciprocating. For detailed information on dining skills, please see Chapter 16: Place Settings, Table Manners, and Service Styles and Chapter 17: Family Dining, Buffets, and Formal In-Home Meals; for toasting, see Chapter 20: Toasts.

Females at Table

During formal dress evenings, females wait for a moment to see if male dinner partners will offer to help with chairs. A woman enters the chair from the right side, sits down, then lifts up (and helps pull the chair forward if needed) with assistance from behind, repeating the maneuver if necessary.

During business meals, there must be no gender bias. Females and males are treated alike according to workplace status, not chivalry. Businesswomen find that practicing civility is an effective form of self-promotion to ensure that equality. Always stand for introductions and shake hands (if distance is not too great) with a new arrival to your table. All diners with good manners will remain standing until the new arrival either sits down or departs. Do not "table hop" around a room, but sometimes it is appropriate to approach another table to greet or meet fellow business colleagues, even though you will not be eating with them.

A table host should begin each course, but sometimes that person will be oblivious about dining etiquette. Female businesspersons seated with them may be forced to act in their stead. One of your authors has several times experienced being the youngest or junior faculty member seated at business meals with senior PhD table co-hosts so intent on conversation that others grew frustrated waiting to eat. It was usually necessary to assume the leadership role by being first to pick up the utensils—to the collective sighs of relief by mannerly tablemates.

Spouses included in business functions need enough social confidence to maneuver the meal without using their mates as a buffer. They must bring something of themselves to the party without seeming put-upon. They also need to be aware that sometimes the employee will connect best by staying until the event's end (or be required to do so as a co-host). In any case, everyone must wait for the departure of the senior official or guest of honor of any nationality.

COCKTAIL PARTIES

The two-hour cocktail party varies in size from a handful to many people and is perhaps the easiest means of entertaining a large number of guests. The differences between cocktail parties and receptions are that cocktail parties are more casual, serve only appetizers and drinks, and have no receiving line. They are sometimes held immediately after the workday ends about 1700 (5:00 PM), as for TGIF Happy Hours, but are usually held just at the close of daylight hours. If the cocktail party begins at 1830 (6:30) or later, more substantial finger-food is provided. Cocktail parties are held in many locations, from art galleries to private homes to decks of ships.

Hosts stay near the entrance to welcome guests, but not in a receiving line. If hosts are not near the door, find and greet them when you arrive. They will introduce you to someone else nearby if you are new to the group—but after this, you are on your own. Introduce yourself, remember names, and spend no more than about eight minutes with any one person before moving on. Try to speak with *at least* three groups of people. Have a personal plan for circulating in large groups. You may decide always to move clockwise, or perhaps you and your date will go in different directions and meet after twenty minutes to compare notes. You and your spouse might stay together for the first fifteen minutes before separating for the duration, to meet up again only at the end of the party. The important thing is that dates and spouses not inhibit the employee from socializing separately—organization-hosted networking is considered a professional activity.

Q: As a junior service member, do I extend my hand first to a senior ranking person when I have initiated an office appointment or wait for the senior? What if I meet someone senior ranking socially when we are both in civilian clothes?

A: When in uniform, juniors defer to seniors to initiate handshakes. When in civilian clothes socially, extend a hand for all introductions. If you do recognize a senior, say, *"Good evening Sir/Ma'am* (or rank and name). *I serve with you at* ___." Continue with a short self-introduction and wait for the offer of a handshake.

Q: I am a Muslim male in the U.S. Army. I respect females by not touching them. My next assignment is to the embassy in Haiti, with a female Ambassador. How do I cope with this?

A: Your Imam can reassure you that the custom you mention is tradition or cultural, not against Islamic law. Since your assignment is to mingle with diplomats, it is proper to shake hands as a courtesy, recognized internationally. FYI, the diplomats at the Royal Embassy of Saudi Arabia tell us that they all shake hands, here in Washington and other Western countries, as a sign of respect.

Informal vs. Casual Cocktail Attire

Hosts must be careful when defining clothing requirements. If they write or say *informal* when they meant *casual* clothes, guests will show up in suit and tie, uniform of the day, or afternoon dresses. *Casual* on an invitation spans a wide variety also—it must always be further defined. "Cocktails on the terrace" probably means slacks and sports shirt, but a backyard barbecue might mean shorts and sandals or even bathing suits if there is a swimming pool. Guests should never hesitate to ask for clarification if hosts do not provide enough information.

Cocktail Food and Drink

A choice of drinks is offered at cocktail parties, including nonalcoholic beverages. The guest states a preference at the bar, where the choices may be displayed, or takes drinks from a server. An employee will ask a spouse or date, or an accompanying colleague, what he or she prefers, and then go to get drinks. Nondrinkers simply say *"No, thank you"* if a tray of alcoholic drinks is passed, which will cue the server to ask if a soft drink, water, or juice might be desired instead. If necessary, the guest asks for a nonalcoholic beverage.

The food at a cocktail party is not meant to be a full meal—you will not sit down to eat. The one- or two-bite morsels are offered after a guest has been served a drink. They are picked up and eaten with the fingers, except that some food, such as shrimp or meatballs, is served on or with toothpicks. Napkins are either handed to guests when the food is passed or are on the buffet table with or in lieu of small plates. Empty toothpicks are held in a fold of your napkin or discarded on your plate.

If servers are present, they will normally have one or two appetizer choices on their trays, which they offer while you are standing and talking with fellow guests. Take the offered cocktail napkin and only one item, as desired. (Sometimes a small bowl is also on the tray or held by the server for discarded toothpicks.) Before too long another server with new selections will come along. The snacks are designed to enhance the social atmosphere without inhibiting conversation. They are meant to help with metabolizing alcoholic drinks but are not designed to be a meal replacement.

If the host is going to feed you substantially, the invitation will read slightly differently. An invitation stating *Cocktails Buffet* informs guests that they need not make other plans for supper. Before you go to a buffet table for something to eat, set your glass down on a "drop" table or tray—do not leave your items on household furniture or take drinks with you to the buffet table. At the food station, pick up the small cocktail plate, a napkin, and a fork if provided. Select several of the offerings, and *go to another area to eat* and continue to make conversation. Cocktail parties are stand-up affairs. Do not go into a holding pattern around the food—it is rude to eat directly from a buffet table. You may return for more food if desired, picking up a clean plate each time. Sometimes there will be several food stations or a separate dessert area. You are expected to continue socializing throughout the event.

Departure from Cocktail Parties
Like open houses, cocktail parties (usually two hours in duration) allow great latitude in arrival and departure. You may arrive at any point within the first hour of a large party. Cocktail party invitations may not have a stated end time, but guests must be sensitive to local customs and watch for clues that the event is drawing to a close. The hosts may have made other plans for the remainder of the evening, perhaps planning to depart for dinner or a concert. The hosts may close the bar as a signal and servers may stop passing food and start collecting glasses instead. For the diehard guest, the host might be forced to say, "*Sorry, but Cheri and I are meeting the Fowlers in a few minutes*" or whatever the plans.

Before you leave, find your hosts to say thank you and good night (unless the event is very large), and tell the guest of honor that you are pleased to have met him or her. Thanking band members or vocalists (if present) may be accomplished with a smile and nod of appreciation as you stroll by them during the evening.

Write a note of thanks to your host within two days (see examples in Chapter 12: Correspondence and Stationery Essentials).

RECEPTIONS AND RECEIVING LINES

A reception is a "ceremony of receiving guests." There are many kinds of receptions: afternoon and evening, formal and informal, with a few or many people invited. Receptions differ from cocktail parties in that they honor a specific occasion or guest, there is a defined time frame on the invitation, the atmosphere is rather more formal, and there is always a receiving line. Receiving lines are the internationally accepted way to introduce someone to society, such as a newly married couple or a visiting dignitary. The senior official of a large government office or military command may designate a certain party as a "Hail and Farewell" for all recent newcomers and those about to depart. Receptions also mark special personal occasions, such as a golden wedding anniversary, a retirement, or the christening of an infant. Regardless of the occasion, a reception allows the host to invite as many friends and acquaintances as possible to meet the guest of honor or to celebrate the event. To ensure that everyone gets to meet a special guest, he or she stands beside the host in the receiving line.

Official receptions often have a period of toasting suitable to the occasion.

Reception Times
The hours of the reception are indicated on the invitation and usually span a two-hour interval (e.g., *at seven until nine o'clock*). Informal receptions might be held at eleven o'clock in the morning, two in the afternoon, or at five in the early evening. A formal American reception is usually from eight to ten or nine to eleven o'clock in the evening, but a similar formal reception abroad might not start until eleven or midnight. The times vary, but the principle remains the same: the later the event, the more formal.

Dress for Receptions
At daytime receptions, such as those in conjunction with a parade, garden parties in honor of a graduating class, or national day receptions, the dress most often is *Informal*. For evening receptions, *Formal* or *Black Tie* may be engraved or printed on the invitation or on small cards enclosed with them. (*White Tie* indicates the rare but most formal dress occasion.)

Reception Arrival and Departure

You may arrive at any time between the hours indicated on the invitation, but smart guests arrive before the receiving line disbands. A receiving line normally lasts for about half an hour or forty-five minutes after the stated beginning time; receivers then join the party. Guests who do not greet them in the line are expected to seek out, shake hands, and pay their respects to the hosts and the guests of honor—something of a challenge at large gatherings—hence the advantage of a receiving line. Latecomers may also miss the opportunity to have their pictures taken with dignitaries.

There are no rules about how long to stay at a reception. Thirty minutes at a large, crowded reception may be enough; the entire two hours may be desirable for a small reception. Do not arrive uncomfortably near the closing hour of an early evening reception—unless the host has invited you beforehand to stay on for supper or a follow-on event. When departing a large reception it is not expected that guests seek out the hosts to say good-bye, unless a "reverse" line is formed at the end of the reception for this purpose (perhaps as a hint that the event is concluding). If you need to depart a large reception and the guest of honor is still present, you need not wait, but it is not normally a hardship to delay until the senior ranking does leave. It may also be politic to seek out those above you in your hierarchy, if they are invited, to let them know that you are about to leave.

At smaller gatherings, do seek out your hosts to say goodbye. Good hosts will make saying goodbye easier for departing guests by staying near the door toward the end of an event. Thank your hosts as you shake hands again, express pleasure at meeting the guests of honor, and say good-bye. Do not monopolize a host at that point; the time for conversation has passed. Say goodnight and go.

Receiving Line Composition

For groups of fifty or more gathering to meet a special guest, always plan a receiving line so that everyone has a chance to shake hands with the important person. All receivers and social aides must be in place at least fifteen minutes before the start time on the invitation. At that time, hosts might want to initiate handshakes so that every receiver can shake every other receiver's hand, as the nine U.S. Supreme Court Justices do when they convene. If possible, position the receiving line to the right of entering guests. This keeps the honored guest on the host's right and helps guests who use a wheelchair or walking aid to shake hands easily while still moving forward. Consider using flags, seals, or emblems directly behind the line (see Chapter 7: Flag Etiquette for line and flag placement if pictures will be taken). Position the receiving line far enough from the door through which guests enter to allow them to get inside, remove coats, and check their appearance. Do not form it too near the cocktail area (where conversation, music, or the bar line may cause a distraction). Ideally, receivers' backs are against a wall because it is a pastime at receptions for guests to go get a drink and then watch the receiving line.

For very long events or events where guests are habitually late (common in the Middle East), a second receiving line may be formed after thirty to forty-five minutes, when the host and primary receivers are released to socialize and other employees of sufficient status take over so that latecomers are still welcomed by event representatives. For all-day events, such as a presidential inauguration or a celebrity wedding where everyone wants to greet the principals, a table behind the receiving line might hold water and glasses for the receivers, and breaks may be scheduled so that principals can sit down (out of sight).

For exceptionally large functions, there may be multiple receiving lines so that guests wait for as short a time as possible. Many officials can greet so that it is not a big responsibility for any one group. For example, at United States Naval Academy Plebe Formal Balls, it is common to run four simultaneous receiving lines to greet over 1,500 guests. A small number of people (four or five) stand in each line with a designated host or co-host and others beside them in precedence (rank) order.

There are variations in the manner in which receiving lines are conducted at various official, formal, and informal receptions, but always consider the following helpers:

GATEKEEPERS

Gatekeepers open doors, help with coats, and direct guests to the receiving line, which may be far from the door, perhaps in the garden behind a residence. Find space near the entry, but outside of the reception area, to position a gatekeeper's check-in table. Guests may need to pick up name tags or announcer cards there, sign a guest book, and leave (police and military) uniform hats. Arrange name tags alphabetically; they are helpful in gauging attendance. Protocol staffs assist guests in finding and perhaps putting on name tags (see Chapter 22: Appropriate Attire).

Queue time for a guest line (also called the reception line) should be no more than about fifteen minutes. Gatekeepers guide guests to refreshments and ask them to return later if the line is running long, reminding them to set down drinks before going through the line. They may also prompt guests on the procedure to use with an announcer.

ANNOUNCERS

Guests at small and informal receptions introduce themselves to the host, the first person in a receiving line. To help the host, an announcer stands a step away to relay guests' names at a formal receiving line. This protocol aide must listen for correct pronunciation of names and use the word "introduce" to most hosts (*"Colonel Sheridan, may I* introduce . . ."), but the word "present" for royalty, heads of state, religious hierarchy, or diplomats (*"Mr. Ambassador, may I* present . . ."). Announcer cards are helpful when multiple nationalities are invited with difficult–to-understand accents. Guest names and titles are printed on cards distributed at the door for guests to hand to the announcer. This method is used at the White House.

Colonel Peter Adkins
Commander Second Brigade
and Mrs. Ella Adkins

Sample Announcer Card

PHOTOGRAPHERS

A professional photographer may be placed at the end of a receiving line to take pictures of each guest and his or her escort, or in another location for a photo opportunity of each person with a very distinguished guest of honor. This serves to record memories and history, and facilitates personal relationships when the host provides the photos as mementos (*"thought you might enjoy a souvenir of our time together last week"*). If pictures are taken in another location, there will normally be a table for purses and drinks to be set down.

    If you are organizing a reception where a photographer will be working, he or she will appreciate a line that is not backlit in front of a bright window, or a location that does not make people squint. Be aware of the time that photographs will take. Most photographers will want to take two pictures of each couple to ensure that at least one is good. If the process takes as long as thirty seconds and there are two hundred guests, that means an hour and a half commitment at least.

FACILITATORS

Facilitators are additional helpers. They are perhaps assigned as co-hosts, one per room, to assist in hospitality throughout the evening. Position at least one about ten feet from the end of the receiving line to direct guests to the bar or food or to the next activity. Facilitators stay until the end of the function in order to be on hand to usher people out and say goodbye.

Q: A foreign 4-star came through the receiving line when I was the introducer and he extended his hand to me. I know better than to usurp the host's place, but what was I supposed to do, offend him by not shaking? (I shook.)

A: As you realize, an announcer's sole duty is to relay names of arriving guests to aid the host, who in theory knows everyone invited, but has so much to think about that movie stars wouldn't be recognized. Bravo for not embarrassing the guest, but next time try keeping your right hand behind your back (as if for parade rest) to discourage handshakes. If guests reach for your hand anyway, place your *left* hand *under* the guest's extended wrist, *smile,* and ask, *"Thank you, Sir; may I have your name to announce?"* When the name is provided, drop your hand, turn to the host, and relay the information. It is the host who welcomes guests with a handshake.

Q: How should we form a receiving line with joint American and international hosts?

A: The home turf will decide who is most appropriate to be first in line. Other hosts follow in precedence order (see Chapter 25: International Protocol and Civility). National flags can create an attractive background, especially if there is a photographer (see Chapter 7: Flag Etiquette).

THE RECEIVERS

The receiving line itself consists of as few people as possible. A piece of tape on the floor (a toe line) helps the protocol organizer position them, especially helpful if receivers will switch off during the function. It is very nice if the social aide also offers a bottle of quick-drying hand sanitizer for receivers to use when the line disbands.

The *host* stands first in line. The *host's spouse* may be next, if other spouses are receiving. The *guest of honor* and the *guest of honor's spouse* are next. Spouses of officials need not receive. Equally appropriate, especially if the host is translating for a non-English speaker, is to have the guest of honor beside the host. (Interpreters do not stand in receiving lines.) It is polite to end the line with an organization representative (male, if possible, for chivalry) appropriately connected to the occasion, but if the host feels strongly that the reception is to honor certain individuals only, it is not improper to have the last person be a guest (see the Receiving Lines diagram at the end of this chapter).

Once the announcer has presented a guest to the host, he or she shakes hands with a very brief greeting and introduces the guest to the next receiver,

"Mr. Guest, this is Chief Kennedy" or "Mrs. Guest, I'd like you to meet Public Figure Brown." That receiver listens carefully in order to relay the guest's name to the next receiver, and so on. Receivers may ask guests to re-introduce themselves.

Royalty are accustomed to conducting a sort of reverse receiving line at a formal function. Their invitees line up in family or country order and the royals pass by, greeting each group and chatting briefly.

Reception Lines (Guests)

There may be many helpers at a reception to open doors, take coats, and otherwise direct guests at large functions. Do not shake hands with them or the receiving line announcer. Guests never carry a drink while negotiating the receiving line, so if facilitators have urged you to go into the party and return to the line later, be sure to set glasses down. *The person invited* (most recognizable to the host) *goes down a receiving line first.*

Even if you are close friends with the announcer or think you are famous, state your honorific (Mr., Miss, Sergeant, Doctor, etc.) and name, pause, and add an identifier such as your position or affiliation, if applicable, such as, "*Ms. Alinda Lewis; International Association of Protocol Consultants and Officers.*" If the spouse or another person accompanies, then his or her name is also given. As couples approach the line, the principal person invited steps forward to give both their names to the announcer, as in, "*Major and Mrs. Peter Burtovoy; Pentagon staff*" (an example with rank), or "*Mayor Jones and Mr. Jones; Boston*" (official title), or "*Mr. and Mrs. Brown*" (civilian honorific).

If announcer cards are used, the principal guest still says the name(s) as he or she hands over the card so that the announcer can hear the pronunciation. The announcer keeps the cards.

Remember, guests do *not* shake hands with the announcer. The first person to shake your hand is the event host, who welcomes you to his party. Remove any large or sharp rings on your right hand before going by a receiving line, smile and make eye contact when you shake hands—lightly but completely, remembering that receivers have many hands to shake during the event. Greet each receiver with "*How do you do?*" or, in the case of a friend or acquaintance, "*It is good to see you, Gwen*" or "*Good evening, Reverend Yates.*" Never engage in extended conversation in a receiving line—you may talk to them after the line disbands. The goal is to keep the line moving. Be prepared to repeat your name if it gets lost along the way when the line is very busy or moving quickly.

If there is a photographer at the end of the receiving line, wait for your date or spouse to step up beside you, and pose with a smile while your picture is taken. Follow the guidance of the social aide or line facilitators at the end of a line.

Academy or School Receptions

Presidents and Superintendents of the various Service and Maritime academies and their spouses often give an afternoon or evening reception in honor of graduates, their family members, and guests. This tradition prevails not only at the academies, but also at the Officer Candidate and Officer Training Schools, Marine Corps Schools, and ROTC units in universities and colleges. As always, guests may arrive at any time between the hours stated on the invitation, but it is customary at large academy receptions for graduates to be assigned designated time frames for their battalions to attend.

Schools sometimes issue guidance requiring that a graduating student introduce all his or her guests prior to introducing himself or herself at a receiving line. This guidance may be as follows: Graduates step forward and clearly state the name of each person in their party for the announcer, for example: "*Mrs. Jones, Dr. Doe*, and *Miss Smith*." Family members are presented in this precedence order: mother, father, grandmother, grandfather, aunt, uncle, sister, and brother. Dates and guests are always introduced after family members. When each person in the party has been presented, the announcer turns once again to the graduate for a name and relays it, for example, "*Admiral Blank, Cadet Jones*." The superintendent, commandant, or school head (and spouse, if present) shakes hands with each guest as their names are said and they go by the line.

Guests say something appropriate to the receivers such as "*Good afternoon, Admiral Blank*," or "*How do you do, Mrs. Davis?*" and keep moving. They may wait for their graduate a few paces away from the line.

White House Invitations

To reply to a formal White House invitation, see Chapter 11: Invitations. Civilians wear clothing as requested on the invitation (*Formal* or *Informal*) and military personnel are in corresponding uniforms.

Bring photo identification and the invitation with you to assist gate guards and U.S. Secret Service security personnel. There will be more than one identification checkpoint. Arrive at the designated White House Gate about thirty minutes before the hour of invitation. Follow the social aides' directions for where and when to proceed, and where to leave your hat and coat.

Guests are expected to be in the reception room before the President or the President's spouse enters to receive them. The receiving line may take the form of a photo opportunity. A social aide either takes announcer cards from guests or they say their names so that the announcer can *present* guests to the President. Guests say, "*Good afternoon* [or *Good evening*], *Mr. President* [or *President Washington* or *Madam President*]" and then greet the spouse, "*How do you do, Mrs.* [or *Mr.*]

Washington" as they shake hands. Keep the line moving—do not open a conversation with either the President or spouse at this time.

If a photographer is taking pictures, follow the social aide's directions so that you will be facing the camera when your picture is taken with the President—there will be no second chances.

Always rise if you have been seated when the President or spouse enters or exits the room, unless *explicitly* directed otherwise. Do not sit while the President is standing (unless *specifically* advised otherwise) and do not depart the reception until after the President and spouse have left the room.

This is not the venue to exchange business cards; however, many times menu cards are passed for autographs among diners at individual tables during White House dinners because they make such good souvenirs.

RECEIVING LINES

<u>With Spouses</u>

➤ **(Gatekeeper)** *directs Guests to enter*

→ *Line is ideally positioned on guests' right, but Receivers should never have their backs to the party*

(Announcer) *stands a step away*   **(Photographer)**
from Host and presents Guests only—does not shake hands   **(Line Facilitator)**

Host [H]–H Spouse–Guest of Honor [GH]–GH Spouse–Others
[Equally appropriate: H–GH–GH Spouse–H Spouse–Others]
End the line with an event host, male if possible

<u>Without Spouses</u>

➤ **(Gatekeeper)**

→**(Announcer)**   **(Photographer)** *takes souvenir photos*

H–GH–Director–Supervisor–Senior Manager

                                      (Line Facilitator) *stands one meter
                                      from end; directs visitors to guest book,
                                      bar, or food area; helps introduce them
                                      to facilitate mingling*

<u>Traditional Wedding</u>

→ →   **(Photographer)**

Bride's Mother–Groom's Mother–(Maid of Honor)–Groom–Bride–(Attendants)

The one who gives the reception stands in the host position. Fathers traditionally stand in facilitator positions at line's end, but may receive following the mothers, if preferred. The Bride is always on the Groom's right. Maid/Matron of Honor and Bridesmaids may precede Groom and/or follow Bride, as desired. Best Man and Ushers never receive but serve as gatekeepers and facilitators. Elder female relatives may substitute for deceased parents, if desired.

CHAPTER 19

Introductions, Conversations, and Farewells

t is fortunate that the mechanics of making introductions are simple and natural, because you will be introducing yourself and other people for the rest of your life. A young boy who proudly brings a hero-worshiped older child over to a parent and announces, *"Mommy, this is Johnny,"* illustrates the simplest form of introduction that adheres to the rules of protocol. Courtesy gives honor to those who are older, higher in rank, titled, have a professional status, or are female (in social situations).

AT EASE KEY POINTS

- Stand for introductions.
- Bring juniors to seniors; say senior name first.
- Use "introduce" for most; "present" for dignitaries.
- Prominent persons, the elderly, and females initiate handshakes.
- Do not refer to yourself or your spouse by rank or honorific in conversation.

HANDSHAKES AND RESPONDING TO INTRODUCTIONS

The most typical greeting gesture for both men and women all over the world is to shake right hands. In the United States, the features that characterize a good handshake have been studied by the American Psychological Association (APA) and reported in the *Journal of Personality and Social Psychology* (Washington, D.C., 2000). They are: completeness of grip, vigor, strength, eye contact, and duration. Men and women in the United States shake right hands the same way with everyone. Anyone who might have a disability in a right hand or arm simply extends the left hand immediately and people will adapt. Do not squeeze another's hand, shake limply, hold too long, or pump it up and down in America.

(United States Naval Institute Photo Archives)

When introduced to anyone except a young child, stand and remain standing throughout the introduction. If at an inconvenient distance, or in a crowded, seated position (e.g., concerts, restaurant bench seats), half-rise and nod or bow slightly with a smile when introduced. Otherwise, step forward if possible for handshakes. The younger or junior waits for the senior to offer a handshake; socially males may also wait for females. An American woman does not hesitate to extend her hand first except to heads of state, members of royal families, and high-ranking religious dignitaries—these persons must always initiate. A military female also waits for a higher-ranking superior to offer a handshake.

When you are being introduced or presented, respect the rhythm or pace; wait for the introduction to be completed without interrupting. Assume a dignified posture (hands at sides is best), face the new person, and use good eye contact. Responses are *"How do you do?"* (a rhetorical question) or greetings according to the time of day, *"Good morning," "Good afternoon," "Good evening."*

Listen closely for honorifics and full names, then repeat the title/rank/honorific and last name as you shake hands with a nod and smile, *"How do you do, Chief Warrant Officer Delaney?"* or *"Good morning, Chaplain Ryan."* Check to be certain that you understood the name correctly, *"Good evening, Mr. Conetsco. Am I pronouncing that correctly?"* Most memory courses teach associating the name with an object, or repeating a name over and over in your mind to help remember it. When you have forgotten a name, but must introduce someone to others, admit your lapse, *"I'm sorry, I need to hear your name again,"* with poise and no embarrassment.

MAKING INTRODUCTIONS

An introduction, no matter how brief, should be an occasion of dignity for all concerned. It is best to keep introductions as direct as possible. If the persons are not near each other, the junior is brought to the senior, never the reverse. Do not touch individuals or broadly gesture as you introduce them. Stand with poise, body relaxed with good posture, arms down at your sides. Enunciate the names of all persons clearly and distinctly.

Look at the higher ranking or older person and say that name first, and then the name of the persons introduced, in precedence order, until all have been presented. For prominent individuals, provide titles so that they may be addressed correctly from the start. It is sabotage not to give this information because people will feel uncomfortable at having addressed her as "Krista," only to hear others later address her correctly as "Dr. Woodyard." If you use honorific and full name for one, use them for all. Adding a bit of information helps with conversation: *"Professor Patricia Samples, may I introduce Ms. Sondra Takacs from Ohio. Professor Samples is my favorite instructor."*

"Major McConville, this is Miss Simmons, from Graphics." Precedence order in the workplace is by leadership position, not chivalry. Say the ranking name before the junior name. Use "may I introduce" for most; "present" to dignitaries. Occasionally, as in our opening example, informal situations require only, "this is."

Whether professional or social, non-official persons (private citizens) regardless of age or gender are *presented* to religious dignitaries (such as bishops, Buddhist lamas, abbots), chiefs of state, royalty, diplomatic envoys (such as ambassadors and ministers in charge of legations), and other official persons (elected or appointed government and military leaders). Sometimes only the dignitary's position title is used:

"Mr. President, may I present Dr. Kent?"
"Your Holiness, may I present Admiral James?"
"Ambassador Leighton, allow me to present Miss Heuser."

If no other basis of precedence exists, it is courteous to present males to females (her name is spoken first). For peer introductions, start with the name of the one with whom you are better acquainted. Otherwise, young people are introduced to older people, regardless of sex:

> *"Aunt Cheri, this is my roommate, Nicholas Worley."*
> *"Mrs. Slotta, may I introduce my daughter, Anita?"*

Couples with different last names need both emphasized:

> *"May I introduce Captain Rachael Jones and her husband, Mr. Chad Smith."*
> *"This is Dr. Alexander Eaton and his wife, Sandra Ladda."*

Service Introductions

When introducing and addressing a military person, use the full rank or rating, as it is written; for example, use "Master Sergeant" if that is the rating. Cadets and midshipmen at the Service and Maritime academies and ROTC units are introduced with their student status, *"Cadet Randall Trent"* or *"Midshipman Megan Martin."*

Service chaplains are introduced by rank, and then their position and denomination may be mentioned. Military doctors and nurses are also introduced by rank, with the words doctor and nurse used in relation to patient care situations. However, if the officer is assigned as hospital commander or is flag rank, he or she is always referred to by rank. When introducing doctors or chaplains as speakers, give more complete information:

> *"Chaplain Paula Mayer, a colonel in the Air Force, is command chaplain at the Air Force Academy. She will be debating Colonel Colleen Boggs, a surgeon at Walter Reed Medical Center."*

A junior military person stands when any superior enters the room, and remains standing as long as the senior is standing, unless the superior instructs otherwise. Typically, the higher ranking offers a handshake first. The junior will stand again when the senior departs. When an aide presents you to a military person, allow the introduction to be completed without interruption so that you hear the complete rank or rating. Thereafter, the rank may be shortened during conversation: Lieutenant Colonel Walter Allen becomes simply "Colonel Allen"; Major General Leoma Short becomes "General Short." First Sergeant Charles Doe might be familiarly addressed as "Top."

When introducing or writing to armed forces married couples, use the military rank as follows:

> For a military male and a female civilian, it is Rank and Mrs.: *"Lieutenant Colonel and Mrs. Christopher Morris."*

> For a military female and male civilian, it is Rank Full Name and Mr. Full Name, *"Sergeant Elizabeth Walters and Mr. Harold Michaels."*

If both are military, it is Rank Full Name for both, *"Major Garry Dean and Captain Jeannine Burdette"* or if the same rank and service, make it plural, *"The Commanders Clay."*

Because military officer rank is a professional title of public service, it may be retained in retirement (specific levels are determined by particular Service branch regulations), just as a civilian governor, ambassador, or judge may retain his or her title. Officers who choose to use military ranks in civilian life, including those on the temporary disability retired list, are introduced using it, usually also mentioning the branch of Service, *"I would like to introduce Colonel Leslie Lowe. She served in the Marine Corps."*

FAMILY INTRODUCTIONS

When introducing a member of your family, omit his or her last name if it is the same as yours. If not, the last name is mentioned, *"Mary, this is Mr. Bradley Jones."* Then, turning to Mr. Jones, *"Miss White is my sister."* Otherwise, he will have no idea who "Mary" is.

When the person to whom you introduce your relative seems uncertain of your name, then add the last name. For example, *"Colonel Wilson, this is Amber Edwards, my wife."* After the customary courtesies are exchanged, you might add, *"Colonel Wilson is my group air officer, Amber."*

Spouses
Married persons refer to their partners as "my husband" or "my wife" to people who do not know them, and by first names to people who do. When you introduce your spouse to your colleague from work, for example, each may know the other's name well. Then all you need say is, *"Jenna, this is Chris."* Otherwise, *"Sergeant Smith, allow me to introduce my wife, Lee (or my husband, Ira)."* Do not use humorous references such as "the breadwinner" or "my better half." Never refer to your spouse by rank or as "Mr." or "Mrs." when speaking to others socially (except to an announcer at a receiving line). When talking with tradespeople or children, however, you do refer to your spouse by honorific.

In-Laws and Former In-Laws
When introducing them you may say "my mother-in-law" or "my father-in-law." If you prefer, say, *"Mother [or her name], may I introduce Lieutenant Paul Smith?"* Then, turning to Lieutenant Smith, you add, *"Mrs. Moore is Anne's [or Michael's] mother."*

Members of a family who have kept a warm relationship with former in-laws following a divorce or death may introduce them by referencing the association. A former father-in-law could say, *"I want you to know Renee, who was my son's wife* [or *is my son's widow*] *and is now married to Lieutenant Paul Smith."* She could introduce her former father-in-law as *"Colonel* [or Mr.] *Sloan, my first husband's father."*

Other Relations

A stepparent may be introduced as *"My stepfather, Mr. Morris,"* but the relationship need not be mentioned unless you care to.

Half-brothers or half-sisters are usually introduced as brothers and sisters, even though their last names may not be the same. You must give their names, however, when they are different from your own, *"Laura, may I introduce my sisters, Corporal Mia Lynn and Ms. Nichole Rasmussen. . . . Laura Moore works with me."*

Family members are introduced in this precedence order: husband or wife, mother, father, grandmother, grandfather, aunt, uncle, sister, brother, child, cousins. Dates and guests are always introduced after family members: *"Good Morning, Mrs. Brown. Thank you for inviting us. I am Gwen White. Let me introduce my brother, Aaron Black, and his girlfriend, Kaitlyn Green."*

Unmarried Couples

When an unmarried couple is living together, the best way to introduce them is simply, *"This is Jane Doe and John Smith."* If they are newcomers, your might add, *"They are living in Georgetown."* You do not need to explain their relationship—that is their privilege. In writing, the female name is again first, Miss [or Ms.] *Jane Doe and Mr. John Smith.*

FORGOTTEN INTRODUCTIONS

When you are presented to someone that you have met previously but who apparently has forgotten the introduction, you may reference it: *"Hello, Ms. Litton. We met at last year's holiday party."* Do not blurt out, *"You don't remember me, do you?"* It is obvious that she does not remember, and such a remark only causes embarrassment. If you are on the receiving end of such a question, smile and say, *"Please help me remember your name."*

Do not be quick to take offense at a forgotten introduction. Introductions made at large social functions, or made long ago, or to individuals who meet a great many people at many places are often difficult to recall. This momentary lapse of memory sometimes happens even between best friends.

When a person joins a group and you have forgotten his or her name, try re-introducing yourself by full name with a handshake. If he or she does not offer a name immediately in return, hold the hand a moment longer and raise your eye-brows with a look of interested inquiry. If that does not work, admit your lapse, *"Forgive me, I have momentarily forgotten your name and would like to introduce you."*

A: The Chief of Naval Operations (CNO) from Bahrain will be here meeting American leaders. Whose name is mentioned first?

A: If the American is the host, honor the CNO by saying his name first in both workplace and social venues, *"Admiral Visitor Guest, may I present Mrs. Home Team."* Introduce Americans to him, *unless* he will be presented to high-ranking government, diplomatic, or religious leaders. Between two foreign guests at a neutral venue (such as a restau-rant), the first name spoken is the ranking individual's: *"Senior Foreign Rank, may I introduce Junior Foreign Grade."* Verify and use proper titles and full military ranks.

INTRODUCTIONS IN GROUPS

In a theatre or auditorium, if introduced to the whole assembly, briefly rise with a smile and a nod, and then resume your seat. If newcomers join your group and you are already seated for a performance, stand to shake hands if not disruptive; other-wise, smile and nod.

Table hosts always stand when newcomers come to the table, in order to intro-duce them to others there, who also rise to acknowledge the new arrival unless doing so would inconvenience others. Similarly, all shake the newcomer's hand, if possible. Everyone remains standing while all introductions are made and the newcomer either sits down or departs.

At social gatherings of a dozen or so, a host introduces every guest. The easiest way to introduce a latecomer to a group is to announce, *"Everyone, this is Samuel Whitt."* Then the names of those present are stated in rotation around the room or table without worrying about precedence. At large functions, arrivals are intro-duced to those in closest proximity, left to converse, and later, when convenient, they are introduced to others. Guests must take the initiative to introduce them-selves as they mingle.

SELF-INTRODUCTIONS

It becomes your duty to initiate conversations with others when you are a stranger at a large reception or cocktail party and the hosts are busy elsewhere. Be prepared with a pleasant self-introduction as you join a likely looking threesome or more. Two people standing close together might not want to be interrupted (see Working Conversations below). Listen with a smile for at least two full minutes before commenting (unless asked a question). If that idea does not appeal, track the servers with trays of food. As refreshments are presented, people stop talking to make their choices and taste, giving you time to introduce yourself with a short, simple "elevator statement." This is a five- to ten-second positive comment that includes your name and what occupies your time or what you do, said in a way that makes strangers want to talk with you:

> "Hello, I'm Luke Woods. I met our host while fly-fishing. How about you?"
> "Good evening. I'm Donald Diplomat, your front man in Madrid."
> "Susan Civil Servant. I battle terrorism."
> "Sailor. Samuel Sailor. I navigate international waters."

The first duty of a man is to speak; that is his chief business in this world; and talk, which is the harmonious speech of two or more, is by far the most accessible of pleasures. It costs nothing in money; it is all profit; it completes our education, founds and fosters our friendships, and can be enjoyed at any age and in almost any state of health.

—Robert Louis Stevenson, *Memories and Portraits*

Your second sentence follow-on or answer to questions might include your job title or where you live. A longer "party prologue" or an "airplane overture" follows your opening statement with about twenty seconds of additional information (and an optional follow-on thirty seconds if asked another question). This more complete synopsis of yourself is thought through and prepared in advance to be appropriate, so that you never feel put on the spot when asked, *"Tell me a little about yourself."* When you have said what you intend, ask a question to turn the attention to the other person. Listen to their introductions with complete attention.

For professional networking, convey interest in the event as you connect: *"Hello, I'd like to introduce myself. I am Anna Hart, Social Director at the U.S. Naval Academy and this is my first conference this year."*

If offering a toast, always begin by introducing yourself, unless you are sure that everyone knows you and your relationship to the event. Lift the glass by the stem in your right hand: *"Ladies and Gentlemen, may I have your attention, please? I am Jerrod Michaels, the best man, and I would like to propose a toast."*

If you are a meeting escort or social event greeter, wait at the arrival point to shake hands and offer your full name, adding something that establishes why you are presenting yourself: *"Good Evening, General. I am John Delaney, your escort."*

If a Service member is not in uniform but wishes to identify himself or herself to a senior military member, it might be, *"Colonel, I'm Deborah Dean. I was the forward observing lieutenant in your battalion during the Alaskan maneuver."*

When you introduce yourself socially, never say your own rank, title, or honorific *except* to an intermediary, such as a receiving line announcer, an aide in an outer office, or to a receptionist answering the telephone. The standard for those who will relay the information is to give your name, pause, and then add a rank, title, or other applicable affiliation.

To a receiving line announcer (unless directed otherwise, e.g., for an academy dance it may be rank and last name only), say *"Katherine Boggs, Orthopedics Nurse, Rader Clinic, Fort Myer."* On the phone: *"This is Captain Boggs calling from Rader Clinic for Colonel Moore."* In an outer office to a receptionist or aide: *"Captain Boggs to see Colonel Moore."*

There are two other exceptions for using an honorific with your own name. If you are addressing a service provider or a child, state what they should call you.

Q: In conversations with children should one identify oneself as "Jeannine" or "Mrs. Queen?"

A: Mrs. Queen. Children and teenagers need to know an adult's honorific so that they can display good manners.

Q: How do I identify myself to contractors on the phone?

A: Honorific and last name keeps the relationship professional. Store managers, receptionists, and employees (including household help) wish you to explicitly state your preferences: *"Hello, I'm Sergeant Samuels."*

Q: How do you handle a senior officer consistently mispronouncing your spouse's name?

A: Tactfully . . . and give him a way to remember, *"Cherlynn rhymes with Caroline."*

The President of the United States

If you have the good fortune to introduce someone to the President of the United States, stand straight, look directly at the President, and say, *"Mr. President, may I present . . ."*

If you are the person presented, wait for the President to offer a handshake.

If called upon to make a formal introduction of the President at a banquet, give the full title: *"Ladies and Gentlemen—the President of the United States,"* adding *"of America"* if overseas or foreign nationals are present.

In conversation, use the position title, "Mr. President."

The Vice President is addressed and introduced in the same manner as the President. The spouses of presidents and vice presidents are introduced and addressed using "Mrs." or "Mr." (or other applicable honorific such as "Dr.") with the last name.

Though never called so while in office, a former president's courtesy title is "The Honorable," even if contemporary news media may refer to "President Clinton" or "President Bush." During conversation, a former president is properly called "Mr." with the last name.

The Art of Social Conversation

Many military personnel and government executives would rather work longer hours than go to social functions and make small talk. During daytime conversation, the subjects are generally work-related, but business talk is avoided at social gatherings, leaving workaholics with little to say. However, social events are opportunities to make "connecting" your principal mission. If you are a young adult, maneuvering the social hour is considered a professional skill set, an activity that you will perform many times in your career. Cocktail drinks, napkins, and hors d'oeuvres are powerful business tools if you have a strategy.

Conversational Topics

Recognize that social conversation, or "small talk," has as its objective an opportunity for relationships to develop without tension. All conversation starts with generic, non-intimate topics before becoming more personal or specific. Even with loved ones who have been away on a trip or temporary duty, after the initial hugs and kisses, conversation reverts to, *"How was your flight?" "Was the weather good?"* before getting more complicated, *"My parents are coming to visit."*

Topics for general conversation include compliments (delicious food, lovely decorations), "where are you from" questions, observational experiences

Q: When I don't want to talk any longer how do I politely break away from a person who has "attached" himself to me?

A: Never leave a shy person standing alone. Try saying, *"Time to mingle"* or *"Have you met__? Let me introduce you."* Say that you will check back later as you step away. Do so, making more introductions as necessary.

Q: In addition to politics and religion, are there conversation topics to avoid?

A: Controversial subjects (sex, religion, race, and politics) and any unpleasant subject (death, disasters, accidents, battle losses, or serious illness) should not be discussed at social functions, and are treated carefully at all times. In addition, both the very young and the very old are frequently sensitive about their age, and no one likes complaints.

(restaurants visited or sports/art/music events attended), and interesting (upbeat) information about the function or person being honored.

If you deal with classified or proprietary information during your workday, scan a newspaper or a favorite magazine before going to a social event. The latest movies or best sellers, people in the news, and current events will be fresh in your mind to fill any conversational lull.

Research the names and backgrounds of the conference participants or cocktail guests, if you can. Identify what you want to achieve *before* the event and you can truthfully say, *"I've been waiting all week to meet you."*

Cicero, the ancient Roman philosopher and politician, advised others above all to be eager to listen politely in conversation. Ask a person about him or herself and make little sounds of agreement, nods of encouragement, and ask follow-on questions. Most people wish to prolong the experience when they find a genuine listener.

The great gift of conversation lies less in displaying it ourselves than in drawing it out of others. He who leaves your company pleased with himself and his own cleverness is perfectly well pleased with you.

—Jean de la Bruyère, French philosopher, 1645–1696.

Operational Politics and Working Conversations

At large business-oriented gatherings, seek out those in your hierarchy and greet them. Let them know you are available in case they need assistance. You might be asked to facilitate a meeting between executive—and rival—decision makers.

This requires situational awareness, since who is brought to whom is important. Juniors are always brought to seniors, but if both executives consider themselves the ranking individual, you may be caught in a power play.

First of all, learn to recognize when not to intrude. If people are standing close together with heads tilted toward each other without smiles, and bodies positioned to eliminate space for others to stand with them, those individuals are "working." Do not disturb them. Such discussions will not last too long in a social atmosphere. When you feel the time is right, approach the person your superior wants to speak to, and with a smiling handshake, introduce yourself and ask for a moment of his or her time, gesturing to the side to encourage separation from the previous conversation. There will be less chance of posturing without witnesses. Also, try to position the high-ranking officer/diplomat/executive so that his or her back is toward your boss. Respectfully convey the request for a meeting by saying that your superior is "waiting to speak at your convenience this evening," and may you ask when that might be? If the other party indicates immediate availability, humbly indicate that you would be honored to escort him or her. If met with a display of arrogance, however, have in mind a neutral corner and time to suggest. If you can get agreement to that much, report back to your superior and let the principals deal with each other.

Disagreements

An effective way to disagree is to make no return comment at all about another's opinion and to change the subject away from the offensive statement. This does not mean that you refuse to state an opinion. If the group is composed of people of good will, intelligence, and tolerance, discussions will not turn into arguments. When you feel it necessary to disagree, say, with a pleasant smile, *"I have given the matter considerable thought and have come to an entirely different conclusion"* or *"My experience has been to the contrary."*

Exit Lines

Strive to spend between five to ten minutes with any one person or group before seeking a new conversation, because circulating and socializing is why you were invited. When you want to move on, have a strategy to close a conversation gracefully because your exit is as important as your self-introduction.

With a group, stop talking and wait for a natural break—someone walks up, a new topic is launched, there is a pause—before saying quietly, *"Excuse me"* and moving to another part of the room without shaking hands because that would interrupt the group's conversation.

As host, you can claim duties: *"I'm glad you are here tonight. Please excuse me now, I must see to my other guests"* or *"I enjoyed our talk. Please enjoy yourself while I check on the refreshments,"* shaking hands or not, as you feel appropriate.

With one-on-one conversations, always extend your hand. Honor the time you have spent with high-level persons by saying, *"I know there are people waiting to speak with you; thank you for your time"* or *"Thank you for our conversation. I know you need to circulate, so I'll excuse myself now."*

With anyone, go about your business with comments such as, *"Excuse me; I need to give my thanks to the host"* or *"I need another drink. May I bring you one?"* The answer will probably be "No," but if requested, deliver it promptly and depart again with a smile, *"Enjoy the party."* If you are bashful, ask for help, *"I don't know anyone here. Will you introduce me to someone so we can move on?"*

FAREWELLS

Say goodbye to all guests at a small gathering, such as a dinner. However, it is impossible to farewell every guest at a large party. Do so only to those with whom you were most recently talking and nod goodbye to anyone else who happens to be looking at you. Make no attempt to attract the attention of those who are apparently unaware that you are leaving. However, if you met someone earlier and had a nice conversation, you may want to say goodbye and shake hands, especially if you would like to meet again soon.

An American attending another nation's gathering shakes hands with the host first, then goes around the room to shake hands with others. When leaving a group of internationals, local custom may demand that everyone shake hands again to say goodbye to everyone else. As an American, you may consider this onerous enough that you will farewell the foreigners, but fail to do the same with attending American colleagues. If you do that, the internationals could misinterpret a lack of good feeling among you. Also, the international you meet and shake hands with at the beginning of the evening may kiss you when saying goodbye (see Chapter 25: International Protocol and Civility).

To say goodbye properly to someone who is departing, stand if you are seated. The guest of honor or ranking guest is usually the first to depart, unless they are houseguests. A departing guest makes some appreciative comment to the hosts, such as, *"It's been a very pleasant evening. Thank you so much."* Hosts might answer, *"Good night. So glad you could be with us."* Everyone shakes hands when saying goodbye. Do not continue in conversation or otherwise dawdle and delay. Just—go.

CHAPTER 20

Toasts

A toast is a verbal salute of goodwill with a beverage in honor of a person or celebratory gathering (informal); or a ceremonial tribute to a flag, country, organization, institution, or position (formal or official). The custom of "toasting" goes back to ancient times, when a piece of bread burnt in front of the fire was placed in a goblet with mead or another alcoholic brew, the charcoal reducing acidity and improving the flavor. When it became saturated, the toasted bread sank to the bottom of the goblet, and after some macho fellow challenged *"Toast!"* it was necessary to drain the goblet all the way to the bottom. In England during the 1700s gentlemen began saluting their lady loves, claiming their names alone could flavor cups of wine "like toast." Eventually, "to toast" became a call for a gathering of people to honor someone or something by raising glasses and drinking together. Another very old toasting ritual is "clinking" your mug or glass against your drinking partner's. It began as a way to assure mutual trust; beverages would slosh back and forth, deterring poisoning and treachery. If you wouldn't clink, you were highly suspect. Today, not raising your glass during a toast will still antagonize those around you.

AT EASE KEY POINTS

- ↝ Reserve some beverage in expectation of toasts at formal dinners and life milestones.
- ↝ All present stand and drink to all rulers and countries.
- ↝ Do not drink to yourself in the United States.
- ↝ If toasted you must reciprocate.
- ↝ Spouses of those toasted always participate in the ritual.
- ↝ Keep toasts short, simple, and sincere, with the spotlight on honorees.
- ↝ International Style: hold glass by stem with right hand, left hand supporting bottom.

Toasts at Table

At *formal dinners,* toasts are made with whatever table wine is in front of diners at the time of the toast, but clinking glasses together is no longer considered sophisticated. A "charged" glass is one ready for toasting, most probably containing wine. In the United States, sparkling wine (often champagne) is generally associated with celebrations, especially for life milestones and at certain times of the year (New Year's Eve, for instance). Formal toasts are not offered with mixed drinks at the table (never brought from the cocktail area) or liqueurs (after-dinner libations away from the table). In some cultures formal toasts are proposed with nonalcoholic beverages.

In *casual settings* touching glasses together helps reinforce the group's cohesion, and when initiated, the gesture is expected to be returned at least to those nearest you even if the gathering is so large that it precludes clinking with everyone. For more informal occasions almost any liquid at hand may be used to propose a toast: soft drinks, hot or cold tea or coffee, juice, or fruit punch—although some people persist in thinking that a toast proposed without alcohol is lackluster. Hosts always offer non-intoxicating beverages to those guests who prefer them.

Q: How do we entertain or toast when my wife and I are nondrinkers? We don't wish to cast judgment.

A: Many people avoid alcohol: because of health reasons, taste issues, religious prohibitions. Even American presidents have faced this problem. President Rutherford B. Hayes (from Ohio) served lemonade, coffee, and tea instead of liquor to his White House guests. President Jimmy Carter (Georgia) extended Southern hospitality by offering soft drinks and nonalcoholic beverages instead of hard liquor at cocktails (but at state dinners he showcased American wines). Use these leaders as role models. If you feel it necessary, inform guests who have not been in your home before that it will be a "dry" function, and provide a variety of attractive nonalcoholic drinks to permit choice.

Our forty-third President, George W. Bush (from Texas), routinely toasted other world leaders with water, tea, or a soft drink in his wine glass for eight years without provoking ill will. The Freemasons, among other American groups, ceased using alcohol for ceremonial toasts during Prohibition. An old U.S. Navy superstition was never to toast with water because it doomed all participants to a watery grave (death at sea); however, during an observance of the Fallen Comrade Ceremony water is *specifically* chosen for the toast. Speaking of solemn toasts, the collective verbal accord *"Cheers"* or *"Hear, Hear"* is inappropriate for toasts made in memory of anyone who has died, from uniformed members lost in the line of duty, civilians caught in a mine collapse, or any other tragedy. Instead, sad toasts are often made with glasses lifted *silently* in unison before drinking.

WHO PARTICIPATES

Etiquette calls for all present to take part in a toast; it is disrespectful not to participate. A teetotaler at table may lift and drink another beverage, or hold the wine glass aloft and bring it toward the lips before setting it down without drinking. If mingling at receptions without a glass in hand when a toast is proposed, feel free to copy diplomats the world over. When at crowded national day receptions without a hope of acquiring a drink in time for the obligatory toast, they will simply raise their arms and pretend to be holding a glass, go through the motions, and join their voices with others. The important thing is to participate in the honoring ritual itself.

Toasts are generally given by specific persons at various life events; for instance, by the engaged woman's father at an engagement party, by the best man at a wedding reception, and by the child's godparents at a christening. For life milestones there are often traditional phrases used, depending on the culture. At birthdays, for example, a conventional sentiment is *"Many happy returns"*; for anniversaries, *"To [X] years of marriage and continued happiness"*; at promotions or triumphs in business, *"Congratulations and repeated success."* Toasts may be proposed by anyone in private life, male or female, and tributes are generally welcomed when good wishes are presented with sincerity.

Q: I am invited to a Wetting Down party. Can I make a toast?

A: Congratulations will be offered all night long as the recently promoted service member (or several promotees if it is a joint event) celebrate, but a formal toast or two are probably also planned. If your friend is married, ask the spouse if your toast would be welcome; otherwise ask him or her directly. The answer will be yes (who doesn't like compliments?) and a time frame will be suggested. Give a dignified toast, such as, *"It is my very great pleasure to acknowledge Bill's success. Please stand and join me in toasting the newest [rank]. The [Service] is lucky to have his [bold/gallant/brave] leadership. To Bill."*

(United States Naval Institute Photo Archives)

CEREMONIAL TOASTS

Anyone working with local and national governments or uniformed organizations must be familiar with the customs observed when exchanging international or other important toasts. At diplomatic and formal dinners—no matter how small—at least two toasts are normally raised. The organization or agency host first presents a corporate welcome-to-the-table (or event) toast to all guests. At the event's conclusion the guest of honor must propose a thank-you-for-inviting-us toast to the host on behalf of everyone. The host may also propose one or more specific toasts recognizing the guest of honor (or reason for the function). Any guest so honored makes a reciprocal toast. Toasting can occur at the beginning of a meal or event, at its apex, or near its conclusion, but generally guest toasts are reserved for the dessert course at meals before any speeches are made. Always be careful to leave enough champagne or wine in your glass to be able to join in several toasts.

Guests may propose toasts after the host's welcome, but do not make spontaneous toasts at official events. Plan appropriate remarks in advance and ask permission of the ceremony's host before the gathering; also ask about when is most appropriate to offer your toast. At certain official occasions toasts must be made in strict protocol order by the senior country representatives present in order to pay proper homage to national leaders, celebrate friendships among countries, and to commemorate patriotic occasions. If relations are strained with a particular government, mention the good wishes of the American people for the prosperity of the country's people, and toast all present as "friends"—controversy is always avoided in toasts. Protocol planners work with foreign country counterparts to agree in advance on the number of toasts, their correct sequence, when they will be made, and often exchange the toasters' words so that translations can be made, especially if the event is covered by any media or interpreters are employed. The order and subjects of all toasts, once agreed upon, can be published so that everyone knows what is expected.

If you are in charge, be sure to confirm the proper spelling and complete position title (not just an honorific abbreviation) of any foreign leader, in addition to the full name, as governments and titles can change. For example, when a host—or the highest official of his country present—opens the toasting, he or she starts with the title of the guest of honor's ruler (the incumbent's name is not necessary). Most countries toast leaders of foreign guests first, but a few may start with their own sovereign. Toasts to any head of state (sovereign or president) are always made standing as a high honor. Sometimes guests must sit down between toasts to rulers, just so each can be separately and equally honored when all rise to toast once more.

CLUELESS AMERICANS

Toasting is a skill most Americans never hone, but at a dinner or a banquet, in less than a minute, a well-composed toast can convey more élan and diplomacy than a month of slick talk. But in the United States, more often than not, if the international guest rises at the dinner table to offer a warm and eloquent toast, most ill-prepared Americans will reciprocate by responding with a barely adequate "Cheers."

—Roger E. Axtell, *Dos and Taboos around the World*

DIPLOMATIC TOASTS

For important ceremonial events, the sovereign's toast is customarily followed by the national anthem of the country concerned. The foreign guest of honor then responds with a toast to the ruler of the host's country, followed by the host's national anthem. Americans in attendance stand silently and respectfully face the flags or music for all diplomatically recognized nations. When the United States is host, a foreign national anthem is followed, without pause, with "The Star Spangled Banner" unless two or more foreign anthems are played, then the U.S. national anthem is played once following the sequence. If you are working in another country, learn to recognize its national anthem as soon as possible. The U.S. attaché accredited to Romania throughout that country's struggle with their dictator erroneously gave the pre-revolution anthem to the visiting U.S. Navy, who hosted the *new* administration on board ship! If there is any question at all, double-check for the correct music and flag (the U.S. Department of State is one good source; the country's embassy is another).

When diplomatic guests are from more than one nation, the host may propose a collective toast to the heads of their several states, naming them in the order of the seniority of the representatives present. (U.S. representatives are commonly last at such times because diplomatic officials serve at the pleasure of our President, who is elected every four years.) To this collective toast the highest-ranking foreign official present will respond on behalf of all foreign guests by proposing a toast to the health of the host's head of state.

Formal toasts to sovereigns or leaders typically begin with the proposer saying something along the lines of: *"I have the honor to propose a toast to __"* or *"It is my great honor to propose a toast to __,"* and they end with (or the toast may consist entirely of) a ritual phrase. All repeat the appropriate response in unison, using the shorter response except when there are others with similar titles toasted at the same event:

King or Queen: *"To His [or Her] Majesty, the King [or Queen] of __."*
Response: *"To the King [or Queen],"* or *"To the King [or Queen] of __."*

Emperor: *"To His Imperial Majesty, the Emperor of __."*
Response: *"To the Emperor."*

Foreign President: *"To His [or Her] Excellency, the President of __."*
Response: *"To the President,"* or *"To the President of __."*

Prime Minister: *"To His [or Her] Excellency, the Prime Minister of __."*
Response: *"To the Prime Minister,"* or *"To the Prime Minister of __."*

Governor General: *"To His [or Her] Excellency, the Governor General of __."*
Response: *"To the Governor,"* or *"To the Governor of __."*

U.S. President: *"To the President of the United States."* (civilians)
"To the Commander in Chief, the President of the United States." (military)
Response: *"To the President,"* or *"To the President of the United States."*

All present drink to all rulers and countries, their own Services, agencies, or organizations, but they do not drink toasts proposed to themselves; for instance, the foreign guest of honor may be an ambassador. If he or she is toasted, the ambassador stays seated if others rise, and does not drink:

Foreign Ambassador: *"To His [or Her] Excellency, the Ambassador of __."*
Response: *"His [or Her] Excellency, the Ambassador of __."*

American Ambassador: *"To the Ambassador of the United States to __ [country]."*
Response: *"The Ambassador of the United States to __ [country]."*

Military Toasts

The toasts to sovereigns or leaders may be followed by toasts to military Services, government agencies, or business organizations, depending on the guest list. Here are basic military toasts, which can serve as models for others:

U.S. **Flag**: *"To the Flag of the United States of America."*
Response: *"To the Colors,"* or *"To the Colors of the United States."*

> Note: The colors toast is traditional in some U.S. military settings; if used it always opens the local toasting ceremonies.

U.S. **Army**: *"To the Chief of Staff of the United States Army."*
Response: *"To the Chief of Staff,"* or *"To the Chief of Staff of the Army."*

U.S. **Marine Corps**: *"To the Commandant of the Marine Corps."*
Response: *"To the Commandant,"* or *"To the Commandant of the Marine Corps."*

U.S. **Navy**: *"To the Chief of Naval Operations."*
Response: *"To the Chief of Naval Operations."*

U.S. **Air Force**: *"To the Chief of Staff of the United States Air Force."*
Response: *"To the Chief of Staff,"* or *"To the Chief of Staff of the Air Force."*

U.S. **Coast Guard**: *"To the Commandant of the Coast Guard."*
Response: *"To the Commandant,"* or *"To the Commandant of the Coast Guard."*

U.S. **Commissioned Corps of the Public Health Service**: *"To the Assistant Secretary of the Commissioned Corps of the Public Health Service."*
Response: *"To the Assistant Secretary."*

U.S. **National Oceanic and Atmospheric Administration Corps**: *"To the Director of the National Oceanic and Atmospheric Administration Corps."*
Response: *"To the Director."*

Toasting rituals occur with greater frequency outside the United States; please see Chapter 27: Manners at the Global Dinner Table for international gestures and more toasting examples.

Preparing to Toast

Proposing a toast is so important that it is often considered a social rite of passage to master the skill. The roles of host and guest of honor include toasting and they have time to prepare before an event, but any guest can be asked to propose a toast. Add to your leadership qualities by memorizing a short favorite quote appropriate for most occasions in case you are called upon to propose one extemporaneously. Ask permission of the host before giving a spontaneous toast at a formal event, because you do not want to upstage another guest. Lacking a program, only the host would know how many toasts were planned.

If your host requests ahead of time that you make a toast, write out your *brief* comments and practice. If you are stationed in another country, memorize a national song's chorus, a short poem, or a brilliant quote in the host language—closing with the favored local toasting words—to dazzle them. If the honoree is a close friend you may make personal remarks, but *never* tell a story or joke that might reflect adversely upon the person toasted, intentionally or otherwise. The main mistake novice toasters make is trying to be funny. A toast is not a speech. If you do include something meant to be amusing, do not laugh at it yourself. A smart host will never ask an unsuspecting person to toast, especially after a few drinks, because it could be embarrassing for both the unprepared toaster and the person he or she was meant to honor.

FAMOUS ONE-LINE TOASTS

"Here's lookin' at you, kid."
> —Rick's (Humphrey Bogart) toast to Ilse (Ingrid Bergman)
> with a glass of Veuve Clicquot in the movie *Casablanca*

"Live long and prosper."
> —Spock (Leonard Nimoy) in *Star Trek*, TV shows and movies

"God bless us every one!"
> —Tiny Tim in *A Christmas Carol*, novel by Charles Dickens

"Rose-lipped maidens, light foot lads."
> —Baroness Blixen (Meryl Streep) addressing the British Club
> in Muthaiga, Nairobi, in the movie *Out of Africa*

"In the little moment that remains to us between the crisis and the catastrophe, we may as well drink a glass of Champagne."
> —Paul Claudel (1868–1955), French poet and diplomat

"Hail the small sweet courtesies of life, for smooth do they make the road of it."
> —Laurence Sterne (1713–1768), English novelist and
> Anglican clergyman

"Three be the things I shall never attain: Envy, content, and sufficient champagne."
> —Dorothy Parker, American author,
> Algonquin Round Table, 1920s New York

THE MECHANICS OF A TOAST

Wise guests reserve a little beverage in their glasses in anticipation of multiple toasts at formal dinners and especially at social occasions marking life events. Give the toast-giver your full attention and raise the wine glass by the stem with your right hand when prompted. Join your voice with others and bring the goblet to your lips. Again, teetotalers need not drink; it is the motion that counts. Refusing to participate does not announce *"I don't drink, thank you,"* but instead *"I disapprove or disagree with this toast."* Guests do not stand unless the host or the toast-giver invites them to do so.

One does not propose a toast by raising an empty glass, so proposers must be sure to have some beverage remaining before beginning. More than one toast may be drunk with the same glass of wine. If the table is long, if there are multiple tables, or if the party is noisy, toast-givers stand up to command everyone's attention. Do not rap on glassware to gain notice, just repeat, *"May I have your attention, please."*

Unless you are sure that everyone knows you and your relationship to the event, always begin by introducing yourself and announcing to whom you are toasting (so that the honored person will know not to stand or drink to himself), with the complete honorific or title and name. Toast-givers in multinational settings lift the glass or cup formally with both hands approximately chest-high—the right hand holding the stem, bowl, or handle and the left hand with fingers flat to support the bottom. Always employ this international method, as it is appropriate anywhere and will be automatic to you when needed. Recap the reason for the event celebration and speak a few choice words maintaining the spirit of the occasion: best men at weddings speak of happiness, managers at their retirements reminisce and thank employees, heads of visiting delegations salute their hosts, consultants celebrate the signing of new contracts and business relationships, and so forth. Keep your toasts short, simple, and sincere with the spotlight on the honoree, not yourself.

When you have finished speaking, invite everyone to stand (if desired) and to raise his or her glass to join you. Lift the glass about shoulder high in your right hand to conclude. Gently gesture and look around the table or room, ending with eye contact between you and the honoree. The other guests might repeat whatever final words you say right before you take a sip of your beverage (e.g., *"To John and Mary"* or *"Go Army"*). You may salute with your glass again toward the honoree, if desired, but set your glass back on the table immediately and sit down if standing to signal the toast's conclusion.

When You Are Honored

When you are the one being toasted at table, remain seated if everyone else stands, and do not touch or sip your drink—or you will be drinking to yourself, an action considered self-congratulatory and inappropriate in the United States. Spouses of those being toasted, however, should always drink lest it appear either that they do not admire their mates or that they desire to claim the group's respect for themselves. The same applies for spouses during standing ovations or applause: join in the appreciation. The exception, of course, is if the couple is being honored together (for example, wedding anniversary toasts) when neither one participates.

After being honored with a toast, you offer a "thank you" toast in return, either immediately or shortly thereafter. If the proposer stood, you do likewise. At formal occasions with a toastmaster offering many toasts to the same individual (a very high-ranking military officer, a religious dignitary, or a state official), he or she does not always return every toast, but may make a slight bow in recognition of the honor instead.

CHAPTER 21

Guest and Visitor Civility

*A*wareness of protocol, etiquette, and civility is your key to navigating real-life situations. Knowing the accepted code of behavior actually simplifies matters.

AT EASE KEY POINTS

- ❧ Treat everyone with civility. Smile. Say please and thank you.
- ❧ Recognize VIP positions: in a car, living room, receiving line, at table, and through doors.
- ❧ Ranking guests start buffet lines, make toasts, and leave events first.
- ❧ Tip 15 percent or more.

APOLOGIES

No one likes to apologize, but you do when in the wrong. Be direct, look at the person, and do not fidget. A generous person will not make it difficult for someone apologizing, which may make all the difference in a future relationship. When it is desirable to renew the broken friendship, invite the person to lunch or to some occasion that is easy for both to enjoy.

Apologies are in order when you:

- step or pass in front of someone, or bump into him or her. The correct phrase is, *"Excuse me"* or *"I beg your pardon."*

- cannot grant a request. Add some explanation, such as *"I'm sorry, but I will lose my privileges if I shop for you at the PX,"* or *"Owing to the great sentimental value attached to the object, I cannot lend it for the exhibition."*

- fail to keep an appointment. Telephone or write a brief note explaining why.

- arrive late at a luncheon or dinner party. Go directly to your place and briefly apologize: "*I am very sorry to be late. It was unavoidable.*" Give an explanation to the hosts privately after the meal. If the meal has been held for you (the party has not gone into the dining room), explain to the host immediately and abjectly.

- break or damage something. Send flowers with an apology note saying you will replace the item. If you cannot replace it exactly, ask the owner if a substitute is acceptable.

- cause harm or hurt. In this case, you must do more than say "*sorry*"—you must ask, "*Please forgive me.*"

Q: What makes for a good houseguest at a weekend retreat?

A: Bring proper clothing, adhere to the schedule (rising, meal, and bed times), and take a book or PDA to amuse yourself when nothing is planned. Volunteer something specific to contribute: all the ingredients and labor to make pancakes one morning or a special happy hour drink. Automatically help carry anything, take out trash, and run errands. Knock and wait for approval before opening doors. Respect their wishes regarding help with food, group chores, and foraging for snacks. If the more-than-usual amount you consume depletes the host's supply (e.g., beverages), seek out a grocery store and replenish it. Do not use their toiletries, computer, or car. Do not discipline their children or pets. Never leave a mess behind: make your bed, wipe the bathroom sink, and hang your towel in your room for multiple use. Strip the bed before you depart; leave linens piled at the foot (do not fold them). Tip any household help unobtrusively (not in the host's presence) after a weekend visit or longer. Consult hosts on the amount, especially in overseas locations. Be punctual in arrival and departure. Always take a nice host gift and write a thank-you note.

ART GALLERY AND MUSEUM ETIQUETTE

Works on display are easily obstructed. Be mindful of others when having a good look or reading a long description. Speak softly to your friend in museums; tap his or her shoulder so that narration headsets can be lifted. Turn off your cell phone and other beeping devices or put them on vibrate; go outside to take any calls. If you must take young children, do not let them shout, run, or touch art or descriptions of art. Do not attach yourself to a private guided tour group.

At an open house, gallery show, or other exhibit, arrive on time. Wear subdued clothing (Informal or Formal, as requested), as the focus should remain on the artwork. Cocktail buffet rules apply if there are appetizers and drinks. The gallery owner may have an artist present to discuss the work with guests; he or she will probably not be at the entrance, but will stay near the exhibits. You are expected to admire the art, pay deference to the artist, and socialize with other guests throughout the event. The art will probably be for sale; see the gallery owner if you wish to purchase something. There may be a toast proposed. You will depart while the artist is still present—he or she stays until the end.

AUDIENCE CIVILITY

Audience attire will run the gamut depending on the venue, but avoid super-casual clothing at operas, concerts, and ballets. A sport coat is fine unless the event is designated *Informal* or *Formal* (see Chapter 22: Appropriate Attire). Colognes and perfumes can be troublesome in close quarters over long periods of time—minimize their use.

Attendees are at a live performance to enjoy themselves but personal restraint by all is required. It is very rude to enter or leave the theater or concert hall while the performance is ongoing. Check ahead of time if disability resources are needed (a courtesy wheelchair, accessible seating, audio-assistance or sign language, or companion-dog accommodation). Turn off personal devices. Put them on vibrate only if you are a doctor on call or have military duty; go outside to take emergency calls. Arrive about thirty minutes prior to the performance unless you are invited to a pre-reception. This gives you time to find your seat, organize your coat and handbag, and read your program. Face the person already seated as you maneuver past to and from your place so that your backside does not end up in his or her face.

The program contains a synopsis of the story and background information on the performers. Programs also list intermissions and their length (normally fifteen minutes), during which you may get a drink and snacks in the lobby. Sometimes there are warning chimes to signal the break's end, but regardless, do not be late or the doors may close, after which no one will be seated until the first convenient pause in the performance. Unwrap all candies and cough drops before the curtain rises or the music begins. Do not talk (or sing along or keep time or help direct) during performances.

It is appropriate to applaud at concerts, plays, operas, and ballets when the conductor appears, when the curtain rises or closes, as famous stars or principal dancers take the stage, and for curtain calls. Clapping is also permissible after an especially affecting aria, duet or chorus piece, oratorio, recitative, or a dancer's execution of a particularly difficult maneuver. Sometimes opera stars will stop performing long enough to bow in acknowledgment when the audience applauds their performances, at which time you may hear (or shout) *"Brava"* (for females) or *"Bravo"* (for males).

During operas, most companies use "supertitles"—translations projected above the stage so the audience knows what is being sung. Opera glasses are small binoculars used to get close-up views of the singers, their elaborate costumes, and dramatic staging.

BUSINESS TEA MANNERS

Tea has long been considered the drink of statesmen and diplomats. Afternoon tea is considered the least compromising male/female dining situation and is an increasingly attractive alternative to after-work happy hours. Normally teas begin at 1600 (4:00 PM) and last about an hour to an hour and a half. Teatime is convenient for businesspersons and military associates to gather before people have to fight traffic and disperse to their homes. If necessary, people can return to work (after alcohol at cocktails, minds are not sharp). It is both calming and stimulating to discuss the events of the day or plan strategy for the next over "cups that

---

Q: My officer friend said he usually gets the hot seat at military dinners. What does that mean?

A: At formal meals the host, co-host (or host spouse), guest of honor (GH), and second ranking guest all have important duties. If one does not know before coming to the table, he or she discovers the position immediately when seated. The right of the host is the place of honor; the left is for the second ranking guest. These positions face criticism if occupants do not "do their duty." GH duties include making a thank-you-for-inviting-us-all toast at dessert and leaving the function first because other guests are constrained to stay until he or she departs. If the GH forgets to toast, the second ranking must be prepared to cover. This can be sensitive as no one wants to usurp a superior. If you ever find yourself in the number two hot seat when the GH does not toast, say, *"I believe it is time to thank our host. Do you mind if I do the honors?"*

Q: What is protocol for assisting a senior official totally unaware of proper etiquette?

A: Good wait staff and servants correct others all the time, unobtrusively and with great courtesy: *"Sir, I do believe you would prefer . . . ," "Might I suggest this option . . ."* It is always good policy for any protocol assistant to inform the principal about an event: *"I need to review what will happen . . . ," "If we could role-play for a moment . . ."* Otherwise, guests do not correct each other's manners, and neither do staff members correct the superior's. Hire an outside protocol consultant to brief the entire group (use an important event as an excuse), then you can refer back to specifics, if necessary.

cheer but do not inebriate." Afternoon tea (or coffee) is an informal affair, not a full meal. This light repast may include finger sandwiches or savories, scones, and sweets (eaten in that order). The time to start discussing business is after the food has been served.

Tea foods may be buffet style or served by wait staff. Full pots of hot tea are delivered to the table, usually one per guest at restaurants. If provided, hold a tea strainer over the cup and lift the pot with the dominant hand. Add sugar, milk, or lemon if desired and stir noiselessly, returning the spoon to the saucer before drinking. Open smaller tea napkins completely on the lap. Anytime you eat, take small bites so that you can answer questions or join in conversation, and always swallow food before you take a sip of beverage.

If the room has a fireplace or nice window view, the chair or sofa (right side) facing it is reserved for the guest of honor. When leaning back in an armchair or sofa away from a table, lift the saucer together with the cup and hold them in the non-dominant hand at knee level. Lift the cup from that position with the dominant hand to drink.

HOSPITAL MANNERS

Nothing is more exhausting to a hospital patient than to have a visitor too soon after surgery or a serious illness, who stays too long, or who talks too loudly. Call for visiting hours, ask for patient's wishes, obey the rules regarding cell phones, and walk and talk quietly everywhere. Fifteen minutes is generally long enough to visit, unless you are a relative. Do not sit on the patient's bed and avoid jostling it. If you want to take the patient a small gift, flowers may not be the best choice if the patient has allergies. Consider a large box of candy or cookies that can be shared with the nursing staff, or a best seller or favorite magazine to read. Offer to run errands or supply a meal after the patient returns home.

LIBRARY ETIQUETTE

A library is a place of work as well as leisure. Speak softly; someone may be on a short deadline for research or homework. Turn off your personal devices or put them on vibrate; go outside for calls. Do not bring food or drink into a library—books are easily damaged by liquids or food smears and dropped crumbs attract insects that may spoil materials. Do not view salacious material on library computers; it is highly inappropriate in a public venue. Do not let children shout or run or pull items off a shelf without replacing them. Older children may browse unattended only if they can abide by the above rules. Queue quietly for check-out. Return borrowed materials on time and pay any fines you owe for missed due dates. Be respectful to librarians when asking for assistance.

OFFERING ASSISTANCE AND ACCOMMODATING OTHERS

Offer anyone who may appreciate it a hand or arm for assistance or escort. Hold the hand out, palm up to help someone in or out of a vehicle. Bend the right arm slightly at the elbow, with the forearm parallel to the floor to escort. The person being helped takes the hand or puts his or her hand under the elbow and on top of the escort's forearm, lightly but firmly, for balance. Helpers never grasp or take hold unless to prevent an accident.

When offering assistance to persons with a disability, wait until the offer is accepted, then listen to or ask for instructions. Do not assume the person always needs assistance, and do not be offended if offers of help are declined.

People exiting elevators, stairwells, rooms, buildings, and all vehicles (trains, buses, taxis) take precedence over people entering. Open doors and allow others to precede you—it is courteous for anyone, but required to stand aside for senior ranks. Following strict protocol (usually for the benefit of ceremonial onlookers), a high-ranking male official permits a young junior woman to open doors for him.

Start a revolving door or lead down steep stairs before a weaker person. When there is no waiter or usher to precede, an escort leads the way. When helping someone on with a coat, hold it open with the armholes at a comfortable height for arms to slip into them. Women with fur coats may prefer not to check them, in which case they are laid across a vacant chair back or seat.

HEROISM

Manners are based on an ideal of empathy, of imagining the impact of one's own actions on others. They involve doing something for the sake of other people that is not obligatory and attracts no reward. In the current climate of unrestrained solipsistic and aggressive self-interest, you can equate good manners not only with virtue but with positive heroism.

—Lynne Truss, *Talk to the Hand*

OFFICE CIVILITY

Mannerly executives walk out from behind a desk to greet announced visitors, and at the conclusion of a meeting the courteous executive will walk visitors back to the office door or to the elevator, and sometimes even to the lobby. Important note: women may misconstrue this for "male" courtesy when in fact it is done without reference to gender. See Chapter 1: Military and Government Protocol, under Office Calls for more information on entering an executive's office.

If a high-ranking officer or S.E.S. civilian visits your work area, stand up to greet him or her unless stopping by is a daily occurrence.

In some offices, it is common practice for many workers to share the same computer, or to allow a visitor to use another's workstation if it is empty for the day. If you must use another's desk, phone, or computer, leave a courtesy note saying what time you were there and what you used, ending with a thank you. Do not take anything (supplies) from another's office; leave it as you found it.

Do not spend any more time than necessary in someone's office or cubicle when he or she is not there. Even lingering to read cartoons or quotes posted on a bulletin board can be considered disrespectful. If you must leave something and there is no obvious in-box or the desk space is not clear enough to notice a "new" piece of paper, place your paperwork on the chair with a note: *"I didn't want to disturb your workspace, but wanted you to have the file we talked about."*

If your desk is in a cubicle surrounded by others, do not look over shoulder-high partitions into another's space, or try to have conversations over a divider. Instead, phone co-workers or walk over to their areas. Do not invade what little privacy exists in "bullpen" settings. Stop at the entrance and ask permission to enter; an individual's work area is personal territory. Do not set anything you are carrying (briefcase, coffee cup, purse) on another's desk—that is intrusive.

Arrive early enough to get settled and start work on time. Be punctual for staff meetings (see Chapter 1: Military and Government Protocol for conducting them). Smile and say hello to people. Do not listen to gossip or spread office rumors. Keep your own workspaces neat. Many government offices require securing materials in storage containers (safes) overnight, but even if you do not work with classified documents, it is a good habit to put everything away during the last ten minutes of your day and make a list of what you hope to accomplish the next day.

Take lunch breaks at different times from your immediate co-workers to gain a bit more privacy for you both. Do not eat strong-smelling food at your desk, store perishables there, or wear strong cologne. Sound also carries so play radios at a very low volume or use headphones. Keep your voice down on the phone. And please keep germs to yourself; stay home when you are sick.

SAYING THANK YOU

Some social occasions do not require a thank you. For another person's host gift to you or for his or her thank you note, you do nothing. At a large reception, it is not expected or desired that departing guests look up the hosts to shake hands again and say good-bye. Similarly, if many guests called after a very large party, the hosts would be on the phone for hours. When you are a frequent guest, you need not send a handwritten thank you after every visit. A sincere expression of thanks at the time of leaving is generally sufficient.

E-mails and telephone calls the next day suffice for small gestures (e.g., pastries sent to your office by a co-worker's spouse, a souvenir from a business trip, a tab picked up in the lunchroom). However, when someone has given you a substantial gift (theatre tickets, graduation cash), a wrapped gift (wedding, baby shower, birthday), performed an unexpected service (recommended you for a position, mowed your lawn), or opened their home to you in generosity (dinner, overnight guest, party in your honor), do not ever feel blasé about it.

Q: How do I shake hands with a person who has no use of his right hand? Do I reach for it anyway, or not offer to shake at all?

A: If you notice in time that a person cannot use (or does not have) a right hand, then offer your left hand to his left hand. If you do not notice until your right hand is hanging out there, *clasp* his left hand briefly with your right hand.

Q: I will be the date of an Army Colonel's daughter during his Black Tie retirement ceremony this June with S.E.S. civilians and senior officers from several Services. Not only will there be dancing and fine dining, I will be in the receiving line. *Help!*

A: Since you have a role in this military event, call the Colonel's office and ask for an official guest list with pronunciation guides to become comfortable with correct forms of address and titles of various leaders. Review forms of address, International Style dining skills, and receiving line etiquette. You will most likely meet your date at her residence, escort her to and from the event, and perhaps sit beside her at table. When you first arrive, get her a drink and circulate together for a bit before separating. Enjoy socializing with at least three high-level guests to polish your civility skills. Dance the first dance with your date and ask her mother and other family members to dance also. Write a note of congratulations to the retiree and a thank-you-for-including-me note to his wife the next day. If you exchange business cards with someone, add him or her to your contact group by writing an honored-to-meet-you note.

Most of the time you thank people in a handwritten note within forty-eight hours (see Chapter 12: Correspondence and Stationery Essentials). Anyone who has many social engagements or receives many gifts in a short period of time (a series of farewell parties or wedding presents) must keep a record of them in order not to overlook the obligation of a thank-you note (see Gift Log or Registry in Chapter 9: Military Wedding Etiquette).

If you feel the situation merits a more elaborate thank-you, send a gift (flowers are the automatic default) with mindful gratitude—someone thinks highly of you.

STANDING AND WALKING

Everyone rises when the President of the United States (and the President's ambassadors overseas) enters a room and remains standing in his or her presence unless told specifically to sit (e.g., the press corps). This is the same courtesy that junior service members render for higher ranks and prominent personages, and that everyone makes during introductions and farewells.

During *social* occasions such as a dinner party (not a business meal), men stand when a woman enters the room until she sits down, and rise again upon her departure from the room or table. Exceptions are for female hosts who come and go or if the woman remains standing.

On a bus or subway, offer your seat to anyone who looks obviously tired, is burdened, is much older than yourself, or is unsteady due to canes or crutches.

When walking down the sidewalk, hallways, or up or down stairs, always stay to the right in the United States so that others may pass on your left (this is reversed in countries that drive on the left). Walk facing traffic when there are no sidewalks.

When two persons are walking together, the junior keeps the senior on the right, with the senior setting the pace. When a junior military person passes a senior approaching from the opposite direction, he or she salutes well in advance, if in uniform. When overtaking a senior going in the same direction, pass to the left if possible (again salute in uniform) and say, "By your leave, Sir [or Ma'am]." The senior says, "Carry on."

When escorting a civilian outdoors, stay on the curbside or, if there is no curb, keep the honored individual on the right. When walking with two principals, walk between them if both might need assistance. When abroad, there may be a different local custom, usually with good reason; follow it.

Sleep not when others speak, sit not when others stand, speak not when you should hold your peace, walk not on when others stop.

—George Washington

TIPPING

Originally, tips were given to individuals for services better or beyond those expected. Nowadays, many working people depend on tips to make ends meet because they receive lower than minimum wages. They generally prefer cash (the local currency), even if you pay the bill by credit card. Standard wisdom is adding between 15 and 20 percent of your total bill as a tip, but always check to see if gratuities or "service charges" are already included. When overseas, if less than 15 percent is added automatically, leave a coin or two (round up) if you suspect that the servers may not benefit. When there is no bill to guide you (baggage handlers, package deliveries, door attendants, etc.) tip the equivalent of one to two dollars (per bag, package, or taxi hailed). For your regular service providers, tip generously during a yearly holiday by placing cash in envelopes with handwritten thank-you notes, or extend gratitude with gift cards, baked goods, candy, or bottles of liquor. Do not tip U.S. government employees because jurisdictional regulations bar them from receiving money or gifts (to allay the perception of bribery).

VISITING A HOUSE OF WORSHIP

Each religious denomination and individual sanctuary (church, synagogue, temple, mosque, etc.) will have its own protocol and etiquette rules. To ensure a pleasant and respectful visit, ask at the front entrance or office whether you may enter. If you are a tourist, ask permission before photographing religious festivals, cremation or burial grounds, or the inside of houses of worship—and never do so if services are ongoing.

If you would like to attend services or prayer meetings, seek permission ahead of time for unfamiliar religions and ask how to address the religious leader (see Chapter 15: Civilian Forms of Address). Do not be offended if you are prohibited from participating in certain portions of worship. Ask specific questions if information is not forthcoming, such as whether head coverings are required, or if removing shoes is necessary. Always dress modestly to visit religious sanctuaries.

Services may be on Friday, Saturday, or Sunday. There may be separate entrances and segregation by gender. There may be a requirement to wash your hands and feet before entering. People may sit on the floor. Monetary donations may be collected.

It is always wise not to handle religious artifacts and not to turn your back on religious leaders. Avoid pointing your feet (if seated) at any person or the altar or shrine. Be sure that personal electronics are turned completely off. Do not speak, or speak very quietly out of respect for the sacred space. Do not enter or leave the main worship space while services or prayers are ongoing.

CHAPTER 22

Appropriate Attire

*D*emonstrating proper etiquette necessitates being sensitive to your surroundings and this applies to dress as well as behavior. Clothing is a tool. Someone once said that humans are the only animals who make a daily choice in their fur and feathers. Dressing appropriately for the culture or occasion is a fundamental responsibility because your attire signals your status and respect for others. Your worth, identity, and potential in both business and private life may be determined by another's decision based solely on your appearance.

AT EASE KEY POINTS

- ⚙ Reality is that others judge your appearance.
- ⚙ Stand tall; posture counts.
- ⚙ Buy good quality basics first, then expand your wardrobe.
- ⚙ Adhere to invitation dress requirements.

MILITARY UNIFORMS

Clothes always look better on a person with erect posture. One of the bigger reasons is because dignified bearing broadcasts your confidence. Add a military uniform, properly worn, and the picture connotes authority.

Military uniform regulations differ depending upon climate and locale. Some uniforms are optional, seasonal, or required for specific pay grades only. Details will be found in the Uniform Regulations of each Service.

Uniform charts appear at the end of this chapter for the convenience of Service personnel and those who deal with them. These charts show the types of uniforms, with prescribed medals or ribbons, which are worn to *Formal*, *Informal*, and *Casual* occasions (see below, Dress Terms on Invitations).

Military Awards, Decorations, and Medals

Awards is an all-inclusive term covering any decoration, medal, ribbon, badge, or an attachment thereto that is bestowed on an individual.

A *decoration* is an award conferred on a person for an act of individual gallantry or for meritorious service or achievement, or bestowed corporately on units distinguished for gallantry in action against the enemy. Certain decorations carry the word "medal," for example the Distinguished Service Medal and the Medal of Honor. The Medal of Honor is worn from its neckband ribbon on both military and civilian dress.

A *ribbon* is a small piece of the colored suspension ribbon of a medal that is worn in lieu of the medal. The dimensions of all ribbons are 1⅜ inches by ⅜ inch (about 3.5 by 1 centimeters). When ribbons are worn, badges, such as the Navy command insignia, are worn immediately below the bottom row of ribbons.

A *badge* is a medallion awarded to an individual for a special proficiency. When large medals are worn, badges are placed directly below the bottom row of medals.

Decorations, medals, and ribbon bars are worn on the left breast pocket of the uniform coat or jacket, and are pinned or sewed from the wearer's right to the left in the order of official military precedence. In general, decorations and Service medals, regular size, are worn with Service dress uniforms in lieu of ribbons.

Miniature medals are one-half the size of the original large medal, with the

---

Q: What are the protocol rules about when and how civilians wear medals and ribbons?

A: Miniature medals (one-half original size) and replicas of ribbons in the form of lapel buttons or rosettes, honorable discharge, and service buttons may be worn on the left lapel of *Informal* (business suit) civilian clothes during special occasions. When wearing *Formal* evening clothes, miniature medals and decorations may be worn on the left lapel, with your own country's medals on top and foreign decorations below. The Medal of Honor is always worn full size.

Q: I will be in Choker Whites. All my groomsmen except Dad (best man) will be in uniform (including one in Army Blues). Is it OK for Dad to wear a tux with a pink vest and tie to match the bridesmaids' dresses? Does it matter if it is a long tie?

A: The correct tie with a tuxedo is the bowtie. The reason that Formal dress is also called "Black Tie" is because that is expected, along with a frilled or pleated white shirt. Ties and vests that match bridesmaids' dresses are fine, but the same effect is usually achieved with a boutonniere and cummerbund.

exception of the Medal of Honor, which is never miniaturized. Miniature medals are worn with formal uniforms. A holding bar is no longer than 2¾ inches (about 7 centimeters) in length. When four or fewer medals are worn, they are attached in a single row, fully exposed. When the number exceeds four, each medal may overlap the medal to its left, but not more than fifty percent. Thus, the maximum number worn in a single row is seven. If more than seven are worn, they are arranged in two rows; if more than fourteen, in three rows evenly divided. If this cannot be done, the top row will contain the lesser number of medals, with the center of the row placed over the center of the row below it.

Insignia of Service grade and specialty, such as aviator's wings or aiguillettes, are worn according to regulations and only when authorized.

Military Uniform Covers

Uniform covers—dress caps, hats, berets and other headgear—are worn out-of-doors when in uniform. It is a military custom to keep covers on even when greeting someone out-of-doors. Uniformed Service members greet each other with hand salutes, as appropriate, and nod to civilians. At some outdoor official ceremonies, such as military graduations or memorial services, local military guidance will dictate that personnel uncover.

As passengers in automobiles, taxis, buses, trains, or aircraft, military personnel in uniform may continue to wear covers, as comfort dictates, but headgear is removed indoors, except if reporting under arms.

Retired Military Personnel and the Uniform

Retired, reserve, and honorably separated personnel may wear the uniform of their highest grade held upon occasions such as inaugurals, memorial services, and military weddings, balls, or funerals, if they desire. Other appropriate occasions are military association meetings or functions, or when the membership of a group is predominantly veterans, honorably discharged or retired. Retiree uniforms are also authorized for such patriotic occasions as parades, national holidays, or ceremonies when any active or reserve U.S. military unit is taking part. The uniform may be worn when traveling to and from the place of the ceremony on the day of the occasion or within twenty-four hours of the time of the scheduled function.

Retired personnel may wear uniforms when engaged in a military activity, such as military instruction at educational institutions. If retired members ride in military aircraft, they may do so wearing civilian clothing, but must ensure that their attire reflects favorably on the military Service.

Do not wear the uniform when conducting personal or business matters, or in any demonstration or activity of a political, economic, or religious nature. These restrictions are in connection with commercial enterprises when such wearing, intentionally or not, gives rise to any appearance of sanction, endorsement, sponsorship, or approval by any Service or the Department of Defense.

Do not wear the uniform in retirement when visiting or living in a foreign country, except at a formal ceremony or social occasion as required in the invitation or the regulations or customs of the country. Under these circumstances, authority to wear the uniform may be granted by the Service secretary or the nearest military attaché.

Q: My mother is running for political office and wants me to show support and patriotism at her various functions and perhaps appear in a brief DVD information piece/campaign commercial. Can I wear my student Academy uniform?

A: No. The regulation in your case is Department of Defense Directive 1344.10, which prohibits active duty military members (including attendees at Service schools) from engaging in political activity while in uniform. This includes fund raising and campaign activities on radio, video, webcasts, or any other media. You may attend partisan and nonpartisan political activities as a spectator when not in uniform and when no inference or appearance of official sponsorship, approval, or endorsement by the government or any Service can be reasonably drawn.

Q: During the Academy Spring Formal, a young woman slipped into our dance wearing jeans and a midriff top. She was quite extroverted, in beautiful shape, and I asked her to dance. She started "dirty dancing," I got caught up in the excitement, and it was great. A small crowd gathered around us enjoying it all until the protocol officer, who acted like it was my fault, asked her to leave because she was improperly dressed. Was the protocol officer in the right?

A: Yes. If you had arrived in the wrong uniform, you would have been sent back to your room to change. Official events such as these are designed as venues for you to practice projecting the image of the leader you will become—one who adheres to appropriate dress and behavior. A person of refinement does not care to be conspicuous. There are times and places for casual dress and exhibitionism, but in uniform, your behavior is monitored and analyzed by the public.

CIVILIAN HATS AND CAPS

If a civilian man wears a hat or cap, it is polite to take it off when introduced to someone. This sign of respect evolved from medieval days when visors were lifted on helmets to reveal friend or foe.

Take off a hat or cap in a place of worship (unless the tradition requires covering the head). Remove them at a burial, an outdoor wedding, or dedication. Male U.S. citizens in civilian dress remove their hats or caps and hold them with their right hands over their hearts during the Pledge of Allegiance.

Males may continue to wear a hat or cap indoors in stores, lobbies, corridors, and in public buildings such as airport terminals, post offices, banks, or office buildings. Hats are removed when entering more private areas, such as offices, hotel rooms, or homes. Remove a hat before entering a theater or restaurant dining room as well (check it with your coat).

Men wearing hats or caps sometimes touch the bill or brim (a courtly custom) or tip the hat in acknowledgement to say "Hello," "Good-bye," "Thank you," or "Excuse me." Hats are also lifted as a sign of respect when passing a dignitary or elderly person (removed entirely when stopping to speak with them). To perform this informal salute, grasp the front bill or brim, then lift the hat slightly up and forward.

Civilian women wear hats with their outfits as a fashion statement and do not remove them. Women's hats are not usually worn after 1700 (5:00 PM) or in their own homes. However, if a female wears a baseball cap or cowboy hat, she follows the same rules as men in the above paragraphs.

GLOVES

In uniform, wear or carry gloves as prescribed. If you are introduced outdoors, remove your right uniform glove—if you have time. It is better to shake hands with your gloves on than to keep a person waiting, and you need not apologize for leaving them on. Remove uniform gloves indoors except when ushering at a wedding or funeral, or when on official guard duty. When introduced to someone during any of these occasions do not take off uniform gloves.

Civilian gloves include golf, riding, hunting, driving, work, and cold-weather gloves. These gloves are removed when the outdoor activities requiring them conclude. They are not worn inside.

Men and women may wear dress gloves to very formal evening events such as a White-Tie official function at the White House, royal court presentation, cotillion or debutante ball, opening night at the opera, or gala reception in honor of a celebrity. Brides may wear gloves with wedding gowns.

Male formal hats and gloves are not worn or carried indoors (check them with coats). Female guests and female members of a receiving line may keep formal dress gloves on throughout the greetings and during a dance. Never wear gloves to eat or drink anywhere.

Civilian fashion gloves are removed after arrival at informal luncheons, parties, or dinners.

Whether they are adorned with them or not, gloves for women are referred to by button-length. This is the measure of how far the glove extends beyond the wrist (one-inch spacing between buttons from the base of the thumb to the top edge). Eighteen- to 20-button (above the elbow) gloves are the most formal of all and are worn with bare-shouldered ball gowns. Sixteen-button (cover the elbow) "opera-length" gloves are worn with sleeveless formal dresses. If the dress has cap sleeves, 10- or 12-button (to the elbow) gloves are worn. If the sleeves are elbow length, the 8-button "mid-arm" or 4-button "bracelet" gloves are appropriate. Long sleeves limit length to 2-button "wrist" gloves. Black, white, and beige (from natural to brown) are traditional glove colors.

Q: I will wear a sleeveless gown and long gloves (which make me look so glamorous!) to a debutante ball. When do I take the gloves off?

A: You may keep your gloves on for the receiving line and dancing. Either turn your right glove back at the wrist (*Mousquetaire*-fashion) or remove both to do anything else— eat, drink, or apply makeup. Be sure your evening purse has room enough for your gloves. You may put them back on to depart.

Q: My friends say that I can't wear my lovely white dress to a debutante ball. Why not?

A: Just as knowledgeable women guests never wear white to weddings, which would compete with the bride, they also know that white is the color reserved for debutantes at their balls.

CIVILIAN WARDROBES

When Service personnel wear uniforms, they do so in accordance with published regulations governing which one is proper. In the civilian world, the most common "uniform" is the suit, and there are infinite varieties and colors. Navy blue is considered the most conservative color and is thought to symbolize honesty, integrity, and trustworthiness. Black is the ultimate power color because it is seen as sophisticated, assertive, and authoritarian, as is dark charcoal grey. White is viewed as fresh, clean, and hopeful—except in Far Eastern countries where it is the color of mourning. Camel, tan, and other brown shades are considered stable, secure, and persevering. Burgundy and maroon colors suggest classic refinement, elegance, and formality.

Research shows that a distinct "first impression" is made within seconds of an encounter. Lawyers know this and tell their clients how to dress to appear in the courtroom. It is amazing what is determined in those few brief seconds: age, marital status, economic and education level, personality, trustworthiness, social standing, level of sophistication, and even moral character. Over time, our society has developed specific rules, customs, standards, practices—whatever you want to call them—to coincide with different professions and lifestyles. What is appropriate in one setting may be outrageous in another, but everyone needs a conservative civilian wardrobe that can be worn for many occasions and seasons.

Basic Wardrobe Suggestions

Spend the largest amount of your money on the best quality dark suit you can afford. There are five points of suit fit whether you are male or female:

- shoulders (padded)
- body (lower cut armholes and boxier than military uniforms)
- length of sleeve (¼ inch or ¾ of a centimeter above the wrist so that ½ inch or 1¼ centimeters of the shirt sleeve will show)
- length of jacket (to the cupped hand for men, variable for women)
- length of trousers (must cover tops of shoes and break slightly)

In ties (and scarves), quality is everything. Buy silk. For shirts (or women's blouses), solid white cotton is the traditional and most sincere color. After white, choose pale solids first, then other choices. Shirt collars reflect the times; they are wider or narrower to match lapels and ties, as fashion dictates. For the right fit, make sure you can insert two (and only two) fingers between collar and neck. Long sleeves are professional.

Conservative colors for raincoats (trench coats) are dark or beige shades. Top coats are best in solid grey, black, or navy. Both fall to 2 inches (5 centimeters) below the knee (men) or longer (women). If Service personnel find that they cannot afford a raincoat or topcoat in the early years, the military raincoat without insignia is adequate, as belted trench coats are acceptable worldwide.

HOW TO TIE A TIE

Flip collar up before beginning. Illustrations are mirror reflections for a right-handed person.

The Four-in-Hand Knot: Ideal for small-spread collars like the tab, for heavy-weight silk, and to give a more streamlined look to a heavy face or neck.

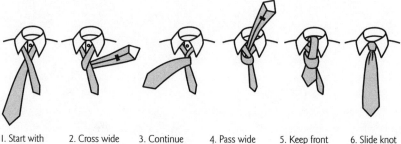

| 1. Start with wide end of tie on your right and extending a foot below narrow end. | 2. Cross wide end over narrow, and turn back underneath. | 3. Continue around, passing wide end across front of narrow end once again. | 4. Pass wide end up from behind. | 5. Keep front of loop loose with index finger. Pass the wide end down through loop in front. | 6. Slide knot up snug to collar, pressing right forefinger in center below knot to form a dimple as you tighten carefully. |

The Half-Windsor Knot: Appropriate for standard-spread shirt collars and to add bulk to lighter-weight foulard silk knots.

| 1. Start with wide end of tie on your right and extending a foot below narrow end. | 2. Cross wide end over narrow, and turn back underneath. | 3. Bring wide end up and pass down behind the left side. | 4. Pass wide end around front from left to right. | 5. Then up from behind. | 6. And down through loop in front. | 7. Slide knot up snug to collar, pressing right forefinger in center below knot to form a dimple as you tighten carefully. |

THE BOW-TIE KNOT:

1. Start with end in left hand extending 1½ inches (about 4 centimeters) below that in right hand.

2. Cross longer end over shorter end and pass up through loop.

3. Form front loop of bow by doubling up shorter hanging end and placing across collar points.

4. Hold this front loop with thumb and forefinger of left hand. Drop long end down over front.

5. Place right forefinger, pointing up, on bottom half of hanging part. Pass up behind front loop.

6. Poke resulting loop to the right through knot behind front loop. Even ends as you tighten knot.

Minimum Clothing List for Men

- One good quality solid color (black, navy, or grey) conservative suit, suitable for evening, in wool (worsted or tropical weight)
- One subtle pin-stripe suit
- One navy blue sports jacket
- One each grey and navy khaki pants (flannel for winter)
- Two belts in good quality leather (black or deep brown) without fancy buckles.

  Note: Braces (suspenders), if worn, are in a solid color with leather hardware, not metal clips. Do not wear a belt with them, even with belt loops on the pants.

- One white shirt, one light blue shirt, one striped or colored shirt
- Three ties. Red is the current power color. The three most conservative to buy are geometric designs, regimental stripes, and solid textured pattern. Ties should reach just between the top of the trousers and the bottom of the belt.
- One sweater or pullover
- One raincoat or all-purpose cold-weather coat

- *Shoes and Socks:* One each black dress (laced) and casual (slip-on with tassels). Positively no military shoes, such as Corfams, with civilian clothes. Keep shoes polished. Socks should be fine textured, never lighter in color than the trousers. Buy over-the-calf socks or use garters because bare skin ought never to show when you cross your legs.
- *Jewelry:* Confined to a simple watch with a leather strap, a wedding band, and perhaps a class ring
- *Optional:* Tuxedo for nonmilitary formal functions. Rental services suffice, but if worn more than twice a year, buy your own.

Minimum Clothing List for Women

The basic wardrobe is best built around a single dark color, so that the same accessories (jewelry, hosiery, shoes) can be worn with everything. Choose classics of such quality that they can be worn frequently and will remain in style.

- One classic 3-piece ensemble to include matching jacket, skirt, and pants in black, navy, or grey wool (crepe, gabardine, or light weight)
- One short cocktail suit (suitable for Formal/Black-Tie events)
- One formal long or tea length skirt (black) and an evening sweater set, evening blouse, or evening jacket
- One dress, street length, ¾ or long sleeves, with V-neck, scoop, or jewel neck, line in black, brown, or navy wool (suitable for evening and solemn occasions such as funerals)
- One cotton white shirt; one cotton or silk colored blouse
- One cotton or silk blend sweater set to coordinate with the 3-piece ensemble
- One black camisole
- One raincoat or all-purpose cold-weather coat
- *Handbags:* one black classic with handle (medium size, no ornaments), one black classic small evening with detachable shoulder strap, one casual in current fashion
- *Shoes:* One pair closed pumps (black), one pair sling back closed-toe (black or navy), one leather or black patent classic low or flat heel (black)
- *Jewelry:* One pearl necklace and pearl earrings. Choose either gold or silver classic earrings.

Dress Terms on Invitations

The decision as to guests' dress rests with the host. There are only three basic categories of dress: *Formal, Informal,* and *Casual.* If the invitation contains no indication, *Informal* is assumed, especially after 1800 (6:00 PM). *Informal* and *Casual* are often confused with each other, plus esoteric military terms (such as *Red Sea Rig*) or foreign terms (*Dunkler Anzug*) add further to guests' uncertainty about the type of dress expected. These and other well-known local terms such as *Island Casual* in Hawaii may need elaboration. When guests are uncertain, they ask for specific information from hosts when they R.s.v.p., and hosts can then further clarify *Casual*, if needed; for example, *"I am wearing a sports coat, open collar."*

The following are details of civilian attire terms. The reason only male dress requirements are given on invitations is because female fashions change constantly and women are more prone to dressing for effect. Check the uniform charts at the end of the chapter for military equivalents.

Formal Morning Dress

Very formal daytime attire, the black morning coat (cutaway or sack coat) is mainly worn at diplomatic or governmental state functions. A man participating in a formal daytime wedding party, or as pallbearer at a world leader's funeral, may wear such dress. It is worn with a grey or black waistcoat (vest), and a grey silk tie. Trousers are grey striped. The shirt must be white; the collar may be soft or starched with the points turned back with a grey ascot and pearl tiepin, or folded down with a black four-in-hand tie. Shoes and socks are black. The top hat is black or grey. The gloves are also grey. The topcoat is black or charcoal grey. For a formal wedding, the cutaway is worn; for the informal wedding, the sack coat. Boutonnieres are worn at various occasions, such as weddings, in the left buttonhole of a sack coat. A white, dress handkerchief is folded with an inch or two (2.5 to 5 centimeters) showing in the breast pocket.

Women wear Afternoon dress. Gloves are optional as is a hat, depending upon the occasion.

White Tie

This means full-dress eveningwear, or "tailcoat." The French term is *Tenue de soirée.* White Tie is not worn often except by men in the diplomatic service, senior officials, or at very formal weddings or ceremonial occasions. (President George W. Bush hosted the only White Tie event of his administration during the May 2007 visit of the Queen of England.)

Men wear evening jacket in black or midnight blue with tails open to the knee, and matching trousers. The lapels of the jacket are silk or satin. The trousers have a double row of satin or velvet braid extending from the waist to the bottom of each leg on the outside. The shirt may be starched or stitched; the collar is starched with points folded. The waistcoat (vest) is white. The tie is white starched piqué. Cufflinks are pearl or gold. Miniature medals may be worn. Shoes and socks are black. The top hat is black and gloves are white. For outdoors, a black overcoat or cape may be added.

Women wear floor-length ball gowns with gloves (see separate heading for lengths).

Formal (Dinner Jacket, Black Tie, Tuxedo, Cravat noir)

This term is the least often seen, but the best understood. Men wear the tuxedo, in black or midnight blue. The jacket is single- or double-breasted with satin lapels. The trousers, without cuffs, are trimmed with satin or velvet braid extending from the waist to the bottom of the leg on the outside. (For summertime, the jacket is white. Black trousers and black bow ties are worn with white jackets.) Waistcoats are not worn with a double-breasted jacket. With a single-breasted jacket, the waistcoat (vest) is white piqué or black plain, ribbed, or self-figured silk. Instead of a waistcoat, a cummerbund (pleated waist sash) of black, maroon, or midnight blue silk, velvet, or brocade may be worn (in the summertime a cummerbund is sometimes plaid or figured), with a black silk bow tie. The shirt is white, with attached fold collar and pleated or piqué bosom. Cufflinks are gold or silver, with or without precious stones. Miniature medals may be worn. Shoes are black (polished calf or patent leather) and socks match trousers. Fedora hats are rarely worn, but if so, grey goes with everything but White Tie. Gloves are grey. The topcoat is black, charcoal grey, or dark blue with an optional white scarf. A white handkerchief and studs are accessories.

Red Sea Rig (British), sometimes known as Gulf Rig (American) or Schooner Rig (U.S. Navy), originated in the days before air conditioning as a purely practical measure in the tropical heat and humidity of the Middle and Far East. It is now recognized as a formal evening option even if the tropical function is held indoors. It is simply tuxedo attire without the jacket, although local standards may dictate short-sleeved shirts and a red bow tie and matching red cummerbund.

Women wear floor length or tea length (¾-length) dresses, long skirts and blouses, short cocktail dresses, or cocktail suits, depending on current fashion. An evening bag of fine material (silk, satin, velvet, brocade, etc.) is carried. Best classic jewelry is worn.

National Dress is a costume or outfit representing your heritage country in an international forum. In all diplomatic circumstances, national ceremonial costumes may be considered both *Formal* and *Informal*. Out of courtesy to international guests, invitations usually state this option. For instance, *Scottish Highland* trews (close-fitting pants) or kilt (knee-length wraparound pleated garment) is an alternative for the tuxedo, as is the traditional Filipino *Barong Tagalog* (a finely embroidered long- or short-sleeved shirt, worn untucked).

Informal (Suit and Tie, Tenue de Ville, Lounge Suit)

When the invitation states *Informal* that means just one step under formal. *Informal* dress is appropriate for most receptions and dinners. This means that a man wears a dark, conservative business suit (trousers and jacket match) and tie. The more important the function, the darker the suit.

There are location variations, for instance, in some equatorial climates, the only time a suit jacket is worn is when calling on high government officials, and it would be light-colored. The embroidered white *guayabera* shirt in Latin America and the colorful *batik* shirt in the Far East are worn outside the trousers instead of a jacket. Both are lightweight, often with large pockets at the waist. The short-sleeved versions are *Informal*; the long-sleeved versions can be very elegant and are considered *Formal*.

Options for women include a street-length Afternoon dress with jacket, a dressy pants suit, or a business suit for luncheons, afternoon activities, and after-work receptions. This attire may also be worn for morning coffee parties, afternoon teas, garden parties, and outdoor receptions. For evening receptions, a cocktail dress or suit is worn. Special holidays such as Christmas affect cocktail party and reception attire colors and formality.

Casual

This term offers the broadest range of possibilities. Casual translates as lenient, permissive, and comfortably unrestricted. Casual does *not* mean sloppy—something contemporary Americans tend to forget. For instance, the French term is *Tenue décontractée*, which means slightly less than informal—a jacket or sports coat (that does not match pants) with or without a tie.

If the casual social event is among strangers, unless directed otherwise, civilian men would be wise to wear a sports coat (which they can remove if others do not). For women, any casual dress, slacks, pants suit, or skirt is appropriate (short skirt lengths and bare arms and legs can be considered offensive depending on the region or the country).

For invitation times of 1800 (6:00 PM) or earlier, dress will probably be open collars, sweaters, slacks, or walking shorts depending on the occasion. In the evening, however, dress for suppers or cocktail parties would lean more toward Informal (see above).

Casual may also indicate a more intimate gathering with friends and family in a relaxed atmosphere at home around a swimming pool, tennis court, or barbeque grill. The important point here is that guests need to come dressed in practical attire appropriate to the activities. If there is any doubt, guests ask hosts to further clarify.

Business Casual

This is a new term used in the United States. In Europe, the counterpart seems to be "Smart Casual" or *Tenue d'hivemage*. Unfortunately, there is no standard definition because what people wear to work on a day-to-day basis is extremely variable. Appropriate attire could range from short sleeves and jeans, to sweaters with slacks, to turtlenecks with sports coats or blazers. When the invitation indicates business casual in America, stick to pressed trousers and button-down collars or polo shirts.

> *The invitation to the 5:00 PM grand opening of the new U.S. Embassy said "smart casual" with no military uniform listed. R.s.v.p. was by return card with no phone number so I e-mailed the Defense Attaché Office to ask what that meant. They replied that the majority of local nationals and resident Americans had no clue, so most would probably wear coat and tie. The American attachés wore Dress Blues with four-in-hand tie (or their Service's equivalent) and the many ambassadors all wore suits, so I'm glad we decided on Informal (I wore a business suit and my wife wore a black linen dress with a matching sweater). "Why," wrote the frustrated D.C. government official, "can't you protocol people just stick to the basics? People were so confused that we saw everything from evening dresses to blue jeans."*

CIVILIAN DRESS IN AN ENVIRONMENT FOREIGN TO YOU

Regional and cultural sensitivity are powerful determiners of dress. Tailor your appearance to the culture, geographic region, or occasion. Dress that is appropriate in Los Angeles may be frowned upon in New Delhi (see Chapter 24: International Travel). To avoid offending people you are visiting or doing business with, it is wise to do a quick study of the culture, be it corporate or East Asian. A female American wrote from Latin America saying she was surprised to learn that *Casual* there meant, *"Wear only half your jewelry."*

Name Tags

Place them high on your right shoulder to allow the eye to flow from your hand-shake directly to your face. This is the same side that military persons wear names on uniforms. Name tags are appropriate at casual gatherings where many people do not know each other. They may be "write your first name" on peel-and-stick versions or be computer-generated and tailored to the event. If printed for a military or government gathering, include rank or honorific and full name; position or duty title is optional. Be sure that the name can be easily read from a distance. Do not let logos or emblems dominate. Name tags are properly placed on gatekeepers' tables (see Chapter 18: Official Business Functions, Cocktails, and Receptions).

ENLISTED

ARMY, Men

Uniform	Coat/Jacket	Trouser	Shirt	Cap/Cover
Blue Evening Mess Uniform	Jacket, Army Blue Mess	Army Blue	White, Formal w/wing collar w/vest, white w/white cuff links/studs	Not required
White Evening Mess Uniform	Jacket, Army White	Black high-waisted	White, Semiformal w/white vest w/white cuff links/studs	White Service Cap
Army Blue Mess Uniform	Jacket, Army Blue Mess	Army Blue	White, Semiformal w/gold cuff links/studs Dress	Not required
Army White Mess Uniform	Jacket, Army White	Black high-waisted	White, Semiformal w/gold cuff links/studs	White Service Cap
Army Blue Dress Uniform	Coat, Army Blue	Army Blue	White turn down collar, long sleeved w/gold cuff links/studs	Blue Service Cap
Army White Dress	Coat, Army White	Army White	White w/gold cuff links/studs	White Service Cap
Army Green Dress	Coat, Army Green	Army Green	White, Long Sleeved	Black Beret
Army Green Service "A"	Coat, Army Green	Army Green	Army Green (shade 415), Long/Short Sleeved	Black Beret
Army Green Service "B"		Army Green	Army Green (shade 415), long sleeved	Black Beret

See reference for further clarification: http://www.usapa.army.mil/pdffiles/r670_1.pdf

Necktie	Shoes/Socks	Gloves	Ribbons/Medals/ Cummerbund	Notes:
White Bow	Black/Black	White, when prescribed	Miniature Medals	Worn for White-Tie functions. Worn at general, formal social functions; private, formal social functions after retreat.
White Bow	Black/Black	White, when prescribed	Miniature Medals, Black Cummerbund	Optional Evening Mess Uniform. Worn at general, formal social functions; private, formal social functions after retreat.
Black Bow	Black/Black	White, when prescribed	Miniature Medals, Black Cummerbund	Worn for Black-Tie functions. Worn at general, formal social functions; private, formal social functions after retreat.
Black Bow	Black/Black	White, when prescribed	Miniature Medals, Black Cummerbund	Optional Mess Uniform. Worn at general, formal social functions; private, formal social functions after retreat.
Black Bow (before retreat) Black four-in-hand (on duty)	Black/Black	White	Ribbons	Optional uniform. Year-round wear. Worn on duty as prescribed by local commander and at general/ official social functions before or after retreat.
Black Bow, Formal (before retreat) Black Four-in-hand, Informal (on duty)	Black/Black	White	Ribbons	Optional Dress Uniform. Worn on duty when appropriate and authorized by local commander and off duty for social occasions. Corresponds to civilian summer tuxedo.
Black Four-in-hand (before retreat) Black Bow (after retreat)	Black/Black		Ribbons	Optional Uniform. Worn at private or official social functions.
Black Four-in-hand	Black Combat Leather Boots/Black	Black w/ outer garments	Ribbons	Year-round wear. Worn on/ off duty, during travel, at informal social functions. Acceptable at informal social functions unless host prescribes other uniform.
Black Four-in-hand	Black Combat Leather Boots/Black		Ribbons	Year-round wear. Worn on/ off duty, during travel, at informal social functions. Acceptable at informal social functions unless host prescribes other uniform.

ARMY, Women

Uniform	Coat/Jacket	Skirt/Slacks	Shirt/Blouse	Cap/Cover
Army Black Evening Mess	Jacket, Army Black Mess	Skirt, Black, Full-length	Blouse, White, Formal	None Authorized
Army Blue Evening Mess	Jacket, Army Blue Mess	Skirt, Blue, Full-length	Blouse, White, Formal	None Authorized
Army White Evening Mess	Jacket, Army White Mess	Skirt, Black, Full-length	Blouse, White, Formal	None Authorized
Army Black Mess	Jacket, Army Black Mess	Skirt, Black, Knee-length	Blouse, White, Formal	None Authorized
Army Blue Mess	Jacket, Army Blue Mess	Skirt, Blue, Knee-length	Blouse, White, Formal	None Authorized
Army White Mess	Jacket, Army White Mess	Skirt, Black, Knee-length	Blouse, White, Formal	None Authorized
Army All-White	Jacket, Army White Mess	Skirt, White, Knee-length	Blouse, White, Formal	Service Hat, Army Blue
Army Blue Dress	Coat, Army Blue	Slacks or Skirt, Army Blue	White, Short Sleeve	Service Hat, Army White
Army White Dress	Coat, Army White	Skirt, Army White	White, Short Sleeve	Black Beret
Army Green Dress	Coat, Army Green	Skirt, Army Green	Shirt, White	Black Beret
Army Green Service "A"	Coat, Army Green	Slacks or Skirt, Army Green	Shirt, Army Green (shade 415) Long Sleeve Tuck-in	Black Beret
Army Green Service "B"		Slacks or Skirt, Army Green	Shirt, Army Green (shade 415) Long Sleeve Tuck-in	Black Beret

See reference for further clarification: http://www.usapa.army.mil/pdffiles/r670_1.pdf

Necktie	Shoes/Socks/ Hosiery	Gloves	Ribbons/Medals/ Cummerbund	Notes:
Neck Tab, Black Dress	Pumps, Black w/sheer stockings	White, when prescribed	Miniature Medals, Black Cummerbund	Worn at general, formal social functions; private, formal social functions after retreat.
Neck Tab, Black Dress	Pumps, Black w/sheer stockings	White, when prescribed	Miniature Medals, Black Cummerbund	Worn at general, formal social functions; private, formal social functions after retreat.
Neck Tab, Black Dress	Pumps, Black w/sheer stockings	White, when prescribed	Miniature Medals, Black Cummerbund	Worn at general, formal social functions; private, formal social functions after retreat.
Neck Tab, Black Dress	Pumps, Black w/sheer stockings	White, when prescribed	Miniature Medals, Black Cummerbund	Worn at general, formal social functions; private, formal social functions after retreat.
Neck Tab, Black Dress	Pumps, Black w/sheer stockings	White, when prescribed	Miniature Medals, Black Cummerbund	Worn at general, formal social functions; private, formal social functions after retreat.
Neck Tab, Black Dress	Pumps, Black w/sheer stockings	White, when prescribed	Miniature Medals, Black Cummerbund	Worn at general, formal social functions; private, formal social functions after retreat.
Neck Tab, Black Dresst	Pumps, White w/sheer stockings	White, when prescribed	Miniature Medals, White Cummerbund	Wear at general, formal social functions; private, formal dinners/private or social functions.
Black Neck Tab	Pumps, Black w/sheer stockings	White	Ribbons	Optional uniform., Year-round wear. Worn on duty as prescribed by local commander and at general/ official social functions before or after retreat.
Black Neck Tab	Pumps, White w/sheer stockings	White	Ribbons	Optional Dress Uniform. Worn on duty when appropriate and authorized by local commander and off duty for social occasions.
Black Neck Tab	Pumps, Black w/sheer stockings	Black w/outer garments	Ribbons	Optional uniform. Worn at private or official social functions.
Black Neck Tab	Pumps, Black w/sheer stockings	Black w/outer garments	Ribbons	Year-round wear. Worn on/ off duty, during travel, at informal social functions. Acceptable at informal social functions unless host prescribes other uniform.
Black Neck Tab	Pumps, Black w/sheer stockings	Black w/outer garments	Ribbons	Year-round wear. Worn on/ off duty, during travel, at informal social functions. Acceptable at informal social functions unless host prescribes other uniform.

ENLISTED
NAVY, Men, CPO

Uniform	Coat/Jacket	Trouser	Shirt	Cap/Cover
Formal Dress (None designated)				
Dinner Dress Blue Jacket	Dinner Dress Blue Jacket	Blue Evening	White, Formal w/gold cuff links/studs	Required w/ outer garment
Dinner Dress White Jacket	Dinner Dress White Jacket	Blue Evening	White, Formal w/gold cuff links/stud	Required w/ outer garment
Dinner Dress Blue	Coat, Service Dress Blue	Dress Blue	White, Semiformal w/gold cuff links/studs	Cap, White, Combination
Dinner Dress White	Coat, Service Dress White	White		Cap, White, Combination
Full Dress Blue	Coat, Service Dress Blue	Dress Blue	Dress White	Cap, White, Combination
Full Dress White	Coat, Service Dress White	White		Cap, White, Combination
Service Dress Blue	Coat, Service Dress Blue	Dress Blue	Dress White	Cap, White, Combination
Service Dress White	Coat, Service Dress White	White		Cap, White, Combination

See reference for further clarification: http://buperscd.technology.navy.mil/bup_updt/
upd_cd/bupers/unireg/chapter3/chapter3.pdf

Necktie	Shoes/Socks	Gloves	Ribbons/Medals/Cummerbund	Notes:
Black, Bow	Black/Black	White, when prescribed	Miniature Medals, Gold Cummerbund	Worn to functions when civilians normally wear Black Tie. Prescribable Winter uniform.
Black, Bow	Black/Black	White, when prescribed	Miniature Medals, Gold Cummerbund	Worn to functions when civilians normally wear Black Tie. Prescribable Summer uniform.
Black, Bow	Black/Black	White, when prescribed	Miniature Medals	Worn to functions when civilians normally wear Black Tie. Prescribable Winter uniform.
	White/White	White, when prescribed	Miniature Medals	Worn to functions when civilians normally wear Black Tie. Prescribable Summer uniform.
Black, Four-in-hand	Black/Black	White	Large Medals Ribbons	Ceremonial Uniform. Worn on formal occasions.
	White/White	White	Large Medals Ribbons	Ceremonial Uniform. Worn on formal occasions.
Black, Four-in-hand	Black/Black		Ribbons	Year-round wear to official functions. Equivalent to civilian coat and tie.
	White/White	Black w/ outer garments	Ribbons	May be prescribed for summer wear when civilian wear is coat and tie.

NAVY, Women, CPO

Uniform	Coat/Jacket	Trouser	Shirt	Cap/Cover
Formal Dress (None designated)				
Dinner Dress Blue Jacket	Dinner Dress Blue Jacket	Blue Evening	White, Formal w/gold cuff links/studs	Required w/ outer garment
Dinner Dress White Jacket	Dinner Dress White Jacket	Blue Evening	White, Formal w/gold cuff links/studs	Required w/ outer garment
Dinner Dress Blue	Coat, Service Dress Blue	Dress Blue	White, Semiformal w/gold cuff links/studs	Cap, White, Combination
Dinner Dress White	Coat, Service Dress White	White		Cap, White, Combination
Full Dress Blue	Coat, Service Dress Bluet	Dress Blue	Dress White	Cap, White, Combination
Full Dress White	Coat, Service Dress White	White		Cap, White, Combination
Service Dress Blue	Coat, Service Dress Blue	Dress Blue	Dress White	Cap, White, Combination
Service Dress White	Coat, Service Dress White	White		Cap, White, Combination

See reference for further clarification: http://buperscd.technology.navy.mil/bup_updt/ upd_cd/bupers/unireg/chapter3/chapter3.pdf

Necktie	Shoes/Socks	Gloves	Ribbons/Medals/Cummerbund	Notes:
Black, Bow	Black/Black	White, when prescribed	Miniature Medals, Gold Cummerbund	Worn to functions when civilians normally wear Black Tie. Prescribable Winter uniform.
Black, Bow	Black/Black	White, when prescribed	Miniature Medals, Gold Cummerbund	Worn to functions when civilians normally wear Black Tie. Prescribable Summer uniform.
Black, Bow	Black/Black	White, when prescribed	Miniature Medals	Worn to functions when civilians normally wear Black Tie. Prescribable Winter uniform.
	White/White	White, when prescribed	Miniature Medals	Worn to functions when civilians normally wear Black Tie. Prescribable Summer uniform.
Black, Four-in-hand	Black/Black	White	Large Medals Ribbons	Ceremonial Uniform Worn on formal occasions.
	White/White	White	Large Medals Ribbons	Ceremonial Uniform. Worn on formal occasions.
Black, Four-in-hand	Black/Black		Ribbons	Year-round wear to official functions. Equivalent to civilian coat and tie.
	White/White	Black w/ outer garments	Ribbons	May be prescribed for summer wear when civilian wear is coat and tie.

NAVY, Men (E6 and below)

Uniform	Coat/Jacket	Trouser	Shirt	Cap/Cover
Formal Dress (None designated)				
Dinner Dress Blue Jacket	Dinner Dress Blue Jacket	Blue Evening	White, Formal w/black or silver cuff links/studs	White (w/outer garment)
Dinner Dress White Jacket	Dinner Dress White Jacket	Blue Evening	White, Formal w/black cuff links/studs	White (w/outer garment)
Dinner Dress Blue	Jumper, Blue Dress	Blue, Broadfall		Hat, White
Dinner Dress White	Jumper, White Dress	White Jumper		Hat, White
Full Dress Blue	Jumper, Blue Dress	Blue, Broadfall		Hat, White
Full Dress White	Jumper, White Dress	White Jumper		Hat, White
Service Dress Blue	Jumper, Blue Dress	Blue, Broadfall		Hat, White
Service Dress White	Jumper, White Dress	White Jumper		Hat, White
Service Uniform		Black, Poly/Wool w/Belt, Black, Cotton or Nylon web w/ Silver Clip and Buckle, Belt Silver	Khaki, Poly/Wool w/ Insignia, Collar	Cap Garrison, Black

See reference for further clarification http://buperscd.technology.navy.mil/bup_updt/ upd_cd/bupers/unireg/chapter3/chapter3.pdf

Necktie	Shoes/Socks	Gloves	Ribbons/Medals/ Cummerbund	Notes:
Black Bow	Black/Black	White (optional)	Miniature Medals Black Cummerbund	Worn to functions when civilians normally wear Black Tie. Optional winter uniform when dinner dress blue is prescribed.
Bow, Black	Black/Black	White (optional)	Miniature Medals, Black Cummerbund	Worn to functions when civilians normally wear Black Tie. Optional summer uniform when dinner dress white is prescribed.
Neckerchief	Black/Black	White (optional)	Miniature Medals	Worn to functions when civilians normally wear Black Tie. Prescribable Winter uniform.
Neckerchief	Black/Black	White (optional)	Miniature Medals	Worn to functions when civilians normally wear Black Tie. Prescribable Summer uniform.
Neckerchief	Black/Black	White (optional)	Large Medals Ribbons	Ceremonial Uniform. Worn on formal occasions.
Neckerchief	Black/Black	White (optional)	Large Medals Ribbons	Ceremonial Uniform. Worn on formal occasions.
Neckerchief	Black/Black		Ribbons	Year-round wear to official functions. Equivalent to civilian coat and tie.
Neckerchief	Black/Black		Ribbons	May be prescribed for summer wear when civilian wear is coat and tie.
	Black/Black		Ribbons	Worn year round for office work, watch-standing, liberty or business ashore when prescribed as uniform of the day

NAVY, Women (E6 and below)

Uniform	Coat/Jacket	Skirt/Slacks	Shirt/Blouse	Cap/Cover
Formal Dress				
Dinner Dress Blue Jacket	Coat, Dinner Dress Blue Jacket	Skirt, Blue, Formal	White, Formal w/black or silver cuff links/studs	Required w/ outer garment
Dinner Dress White Jacket	Coat, Dinner Dress White Jacket	Skirt, Blue, Formal	White, Formal w/black or silver cuff links/studs	Required w/ outer garment
Dinner Dress Blue	Coat, Service Dress Blue	Slacks, Blue, Unbelted	White, Dress	White, Cap, Combination
Dinner Dress White	Jumper, White Dress	Slacks, White, Unbelted		White, Cap, Combination
Full Dress Blue	Coat, Service Dress Blue	Slacks, Blue, Unbelted	White, Dress	White, Cap, Combination
Full Dress White	Jumper, White Dress	Slacks, White, Unbelted		White, Cap, Combination
Service Dress Blue	Coat, Service Dress Blue	Slacks, Blue, Unbelted	White, Dress	White, Cap, Combination
Service Dress White	Jumper, White Dress	Slacks, White Jumper		White, Cap, Combination
Service Uniform		Slacks, Beltless, Poly/Wool	Overblouse, Khaki, Poly/Wool w/ Insignia, Collar	Cap, Garrison Black

See reference for further clarification http://buperscd.technology.navy.mil/bup_updt/ upd_cd/bupers/unireg/chapter3/chapter3.pdf

Necktie	Shoes/Socks/ Hosiery	Gloves	Ribbons/Medals/ Cummerbund	Notes:
Dress, Black	Shoes, Formal, Black w/flesh tone hosiery	White (optional)	Miniature Medals, Black Cummerbund	Worn to functions when civilians normally wear Black Tie. Optional Winter uniform when Dinner Dress Blue is prescribed.
Dress, Black	Shoes, Formal, Black w/flesh tone hosiery	White (optional)	Miniature Medals, Black Cummerbund	Worn to functions when civilians normally wear Black Tie. Optional Summer uniform when Dinner Dress White is prescribed.
Black	Black/Black	White (optional)	Miniature Medals	Worn to functions when civilians normally wear Black Tie. Prescribable Winter uniform.
Neckerchief	Black/Black	White (optional)	Miniature Medals	Worn to functions when civilians normally wear Black Tie. Prescribable Summer uniform.
Black	Black/Black	White (optional)	Large Medals Ribbons	Ceremonial Uniform. Worn on formal occasions.
Neckerchief	Black/Black	White (optional)	Large Medals Ribbons	Ceremonial Uniform. Worn on formal occasions.
Black	Black/Black	White (optional)	Ribbons	Year-round wear to official functions. Equivalent to civilian coat and tie.
Neckerchief	Black/Black	White (optional)	Ribbons	May be prescribed for summer wear when civilian wear is coat and tie.
	Black/Black		Ribbons	Worn year round for office work, watch-standing, liberty or business ashore when prescribed as uniform of the day.

ENLISTED

USMC, Men

Uniform	Coat/Jacket	Trouser	Shirt	Cap/Cover
Evening Dress "A"	Jacket, Evening Dress	Blue Evening Dress	White, Soft Bosom w/cuff links/studs	White Dress Cap
Evening Dress "B"	Jacket, Evening Dress	Blue Evening Dress	White, Soft Bosom w/cuff links/studs	White Dress Cap
Dress Blue "A"	Coat, Blue Dress	Blue Dress	White, Soft Bosom w/cuff links/studs	White Dress Cap
Dress Blue "B"	Coat, Blue Dress	Blue Dress	White, Soft Bosom w/cuff links/studs	White Dress Cap
Dress Blue "C"		Blue Dress	Khaki, Long Sleeve	White Dress Cap
Dress Blue "D"		Blue Dress	Khaki, Short Sleeve	White Dress Cap
Blue-White Dress "A"	Coat, Blue Dress	White Dress	White, Soft Bosom w/cuff links/studs	White Dress Cap
Blue-White Dress "B"	Coat, Blue Dress	White Dress	White, Soft Bosom w/cuff links/studs	White Dress Cap
Service "A"	Coat, Service	Service	Khaki, Long Sleeve	Green Service or Garrison Cap
Service "B"		Service	Khaki Long Sleeve	Green Service or Garrison Cap
Service "C"		Service	Khaki, Short Sleeve	Green Service or Garrison Cap

See reference for further clarification http://www.tecom.usmc.mil/mcub/library/MCUR/ URTOC.htm

Necktie	Shoes/Socks	Gloves	Ribbons/Medals/ Cummerbund	Notes:
Collar, White Strip	Black/Black	White	Miniature Medals, White Waist Coat	Optional uniform. For official formal evening functions. White Tie events during summer and winter.
Collar, White Strip	Black/Black	White	Miniature Medals, Scarlet Cummerbund	Prescribed for official social Black Tie events during summer and winter.
Collar, White Strip	Black/Black	White	Large Medals	Prescribed for parades, ceremonies, formal/semiformal social functions. Not authorized for leave/liberty.
Collar, White Strip	Black/Black	White	Ribbons	Prescribed for parades, ceremonies, formal/semiformal social functions. Not authorized for leave/liberty.
Tie, Khaki	Black/Black		Ribbons	Prescribed for honors, parades, ceremonies on/off military activity. Authorized for leave/liberty.
	Black/Black		Ribbons	Prescribed for honors, parades, ceremonies on/off military activity. Authorized for leave/liberty.
Collar, White Strip	White/White	White	Large Medals	Prescribed for parades, ceremonies, formal/semiformal social functions. Not authorized for leave/liberty.
Collar, White Strip	White/White	White	Ribbons	Prescribed for parades, ceremonies, formal/semiformal social functions. Authorized for leave/liberty.
Tie, Khaki	Black/Black		Ribbons	Prescribed for formations at parades, ceremonies on/off the military activity. Authorized for leave/liberty.
Tie, Khaki	Black/Black		Ribbons	May be worn as uniform of the day. Authorized for leave/liberty. Not to be worn for formal/semiformal social events.
None	Black/Black		Ribbons	May be worn as uniform of the day. Authorized for leave/liberty. Not to be worn for formal/semiformal social events.

USMC, Women

Uniform	Coat/Jacket	Skirt/Slacks	Shirt/Blouse	Cap/Cover
Evening Dress "A"	Jacket, Evening Dress	Black Evening Dress, Long	White, Ruffled Tuck-in	
Evening Dress "B"	Jacket, Evening Dress	Black Evening Dress, Long or Short	White, Ruffled Tuck-in	
Dress Blue "A"	Coat, Blue Dress	Dress Blue Slacks or Dress Skirt	Shirt, White Dress	White Dress Cap
Dress Blue "B"	Coat, Blue Dress	Dress Blue Slacks or Dress Skirt	Shirt, White Dress	White Dress Cap
Dress Blue "C"		Dress Blue Slacks or Dress Skirt	Shirt, Khaki, Long Sleeve	White Dress Cap
Dress Blue "D"		Dress Blue Slacks or Dress Skirt	Shirt, Khaki, Short Sleeve	White Dress Cap
Blue-White Dress "A"	Coat, Blue Dress	White Dress Skirt or Slacks	Shirt, White Dress	White Dress Cap
Blue-White Dress "B"	Coat, Blue Dress	White Dress Skirt or Slacks	Shirt, White Dress	White Dress Cap
Service "A"	Coat, Service	Service Slacks or Skirt	Khaki, Long Sleeve	Green Service or Garrison Cap
Service "B"		Service Slacks or Skirt	Khaki, Long Sleeve	Green Service or Garrison Cap
Service "C"		Service Slacks or Skirt	Khaki, Short Sleeve	Green Service or Garrison Cap

Necktie	Shoes/Socks/ Hosiery	Gloves	Ribbons/Medals/ Cummerbund	Notes:
	Black Pumps w/dark/ grey/smoky hosiery	White	Miniature Medals, Scarlet Cummerbund	Prescribed for official formal evening functions. White Tie events during summer and winter.
	Black Pumps w/dark/ grey/smoky hosiery	White	Miniature Medals	Prescribed for official social Black Tie events during summer and winter.
Neck Tab, Scarlet	Black Dress or Pumps w/dark/grey/ smoky/skin tone hosiery	White	Large Medals	Prescribed for parades, ceremonies, formal/ semiformal social functions.
Neck Tab, Scarlet	Black Dress or Pumps w/dark/grey/ smoky/skin tone hosiery	White	Ribbons	Prescribed for parades, ceremonies, formal/ semiformal social functions.
Neck Tab, Black	Black Dress or Pumps w/dark/grey/ smoky/skin tone hosiery		Ribbons	Prescribed for honors, parades, ceremonies on/off military activity. Authorized for leave/liberty.
None	Black Dress or Pumps w/dark/grey/ smoky/skin tone hosiery		Ribbons	Prescribed for honors, parades, ceremonies on/off military activity. Authorized for leave/liberty.
Neck Tab, Scarlet	Black Dress w/dark/ grey/smoky/skin tone hosiery	White	Large Medals	Prescribed for parades, ceremonies, formal/ semiformal social functions. Not authorized for leave/ liberty.
Neck Tab, Scarlet	Black Dress or Pumps w/dark/grey/ smoky/skin tone hosiery	White	Ribbons	Prescribed for parades, ceremonies, formal/ semiformal social functions. Authorized for leave/liberty.
Neck Tab, Green	Black Dress w/dark/ grey/smoky/skin tone hosiery		Ribbons	Prescribed for formations at parades, ceremonies on/off military activity. Authorized for leave/liberty.
Neck Tab, Green	Black Dress w/dark/ grey/smoky/skin tone hosiery		Ribbons	May be worn as uniform of the day. Authorized for leave/liberty. Not to be worn for formal/semiformal social events.
None	Black Dress w/ dark/grey/smoky/ skin tone hosiery		Ribbons	May be worn as uniform of the day. Authorized for leave/liberty. Not to be worn for formal/semiformal social events.

AIR FORCE, Men

Uniform	Coat/Jacket	Trouser	Shirt	Cap/Cover
Mess Dress (optional)	Mess Dress Jacket w/chevron	High rise w/o cuffs	White, Formal Long Sleeve w/silver cuff links/ studs	Not worn
Formal Dress (Officers only)				
Semiformal Dress	Service Dress Coat w/chevrons	Dress Blue	White, Formal Long Sleeve	Not worn
Service Dress	Service Dress Coat w/chevrons	Dress Blue	Blue, Long Sleeve w/silver cuff links/ studs	Service Cap
Long Sleeved		Dress Blue	Blue, Long Sleeve w/silver cuff links/ studs	Service Cap
Short Sleeved		Dress Blue	Blue, Short Sleeve	Service Cap

See reference for further clarification: http://www.af.mil/shared/media/epubs/
afi36-2903.pdf

Necktie	Shoes/Socks	Gloves	Ribbons/Medals/ Cummerbund	Notes:
Satin Blue Bow	Black/Black		Miniature Medals Blue Satin Cummerbund	Worn for Black Tie affairs; tuxedo is civilian equivalent
Blue Herringbone Twill Tie	Black/Black		Ribbons	
Blue Herringbone Twill Tie	Black/Black		Ribbons Name tag	
Blue Herringbone Twill Tie	Black/Black		Ribbons (optional) Name tag	
Blue Herringbone Twill Tie (optional)	Black/Black		Ribbons (optional) Name tag	

AIR FORCE, Women

Uniform	Coat/Jacket	Skirt/Slacks	Shirt/Blouse	Cap/Cover
Mess Dress	Mess Dress Jacket w/ chevrons	Mess Dress Skirt	Mess Dress Blouse w/studs (cuff links optional)	Not worn
Formal Dress (Officers only)				
Semiformal Dress	Service Dress Coat w/ chevrons	Skirt or Slacks, Blue	Semi-formfitting White Blouse	Not worn
Service Dress	Service Dress Coat w/ chevrons	Skirt or Slacks, Blue	Tuck-in style Blouse w/studs (cuff links optional)	Service Cap
Long Sleeved		Skirt or Slacks, Blue	Tuck-in style Blouse w/shoulder mark insignia w/studs (cuff links optional)	Service Cap
Short Sleeved		Skirt or Slacks, Blue	Tuck-in style Blouse	Service Cap

See reference for further clarification: http://www.af.mil/shared/media/epubs/afi36-2903.pdf

Necktie	Shoes/Socks/Hosiery	Gloves	Ribbons/Medals/Cummerbund	Notes:
Blue Satin Inverted V Tie Tab	Black pumps w/sheer nylon neutral, dark brown, black, off-black hosiery		Miniature Medals Cummerbund	Optional uniform. Worn for Black Tie affairs; tuxedo is civilian equivalent.
Blue Satin Inverted V Tie Tab	Black pumps w/sheer nylon neutral, dark brown, black, off-black hosiery or Black slip-on w/black socks			
Blue Inverted V Tie Tab	Black pumps w/sheer nylon neutral, dark brown, black, off-black hosiery or Black slip-on w/black socks		Ribbons Name tag	
Blue Inverted V Tie Tab	Black pumps w/sheer nylon neutral, dark brown, black, off-black hosiery or Black slip-on w/black socks		Ribbons (optional) Name tag	
Blue Tie Tab (optional)	Black pumps w/ sheer nylon neutral, dark brown, black, off-black hosiery or Black slip-on w/black socks		Ribbons (optional) Name tag	

COAST GUARD, Men

Uniform	Coat/Jacket	Trouser	Shirt	Cap/Cover
Formal Dress Blue	Dinner Dress Blue Jacket w/ formal waistcoat	Blue Evening	White, Formal Wing Collar	Combination Cap
Dinner Dress Blue Jacket	Dinner Dress Blue Jacket	Blue Evening	White, Soft Front pleated	Combination Cap
Dinner Dress White Jacket	Dinner Dress White Jacket	Blue Evening	White, Soft Front pleated	Combination Cap
Dinner Dress Blue	Service Dress Blue Coat	Blue Evening	White Dress	Combination Cap
Dinner Dress White	Service Dress White Coat w/hard shoulder boards	White Dress		Combination Cap
Full Dress Blue	Service Dress Blue Coat	Blue Dress	White Dress	Combination Cap
Full Dress White	Service Dress White Coat w/hard shoulder boards	White Dress		Combination Cap
Service Dress Blue "A"	Service Dress Blue Coat	Blue Dress	White Dress	Combination Cap
Service Dress Blue "B"	Service Dress Blue Coat	Blue Dress	Air Force Light Blue	Combination Cap (prescribable)
Service Dress White	Service Dress White Coat w/hard shoulder boards	White Dress		Combination Cap

See reference for further clarification: http://www.pacom.mil/staff/j01p/docs/
Form%20of%20Uniform%Reg/USCG/uniform%20regs.pdf

Necktie	Shoes/Socks	Gloves	Ribbons/Medals/Cummerbund	Notes:
White Bow	Black/Black	White	Miniature Medals Gold Cummerbund	Worn at formal evening functions. Civilian is equivalent is White Tie.
Black Bow	Black/Black	White	Miniature Medals Gold Cummerbund	Worn for general or official social functions. Black Tie events.
Black Bow	Black/Black	White	Miniature Medals Gold Cummerbund	Worn for private formal dinners, dinner dances, and club affairs. Civilian equivalent is Black Tie.
Black Bow	Black/Black	White	Miniature Medals Gold Cummerbund	Worn for private dinners, dinner dances, and club affairs requiring more formality than the SDB "B."
	White/White	White	Miniature Medals	Worn for private dinners, dinner dances, and club affairs requiring more formality than the SDB.
Blue Four-in-hand	Black/Black	White	Large Medals Ribbons Sword	Worn for change of command, state ceremonies, formal occasions on ship, and personnel inspections when prescribed.
	White/White	White	Large Medals w/ Ribbons Sword	Worn for change of command, state ceremonies, formal occasions on ship and personnel inspections when prescribed.
Blue Four-in-hand	Black/Black		Ribbons Name tag	Worn for business and informal social occasions as correct for local custom.
Blue Four-in-hand	Black/Black		Ribbons Name tag	Basic uniform. Worn on all occasions as prescribed.
	White/White		Ribbons Name Tag	Worn for business and informal social occasions as correct for local custom.

COAST GUARD, Women

Uniform	Coat/Jacket	Skirt/Slacks	Shirt/Blouse	Cap/Cover
Formal Dress Blue	Dinner Dress Blue Jacket w/formal waistcoat	Formal Dress Skirt	White Dress	Black Tiara (optional)
Dinner Dress Blue Jacket	Dinner Dress Blue Jacket	Formal Dress Skirt	White Dress	Black Tiara (optional)
Dinner Dress White Jacket	Dinner Dress White Jacket w/ hard shoulder boards	Formal Dress Skirt	White Dress	Black Tiara (optional)
Dinner Dress Blue	Service Dress Blue Coat	Blue Dress Skirt	White Dress	Combination Cap
Dinner Dress White	Service Dress White Coat w/ hard shoulder boards	White Dress Skirt	White Dress	Combination Cap
Full Dress Blue	Service Dress Blue Coat	Blue Dress Skirt	White Dress	Combination Cap
Full Dress White	White Dress Coat w/hard shoulder boards	White Dress Skirt	White Dress	Combination Cap
Service Dress Blue "A"	Service Dress Blue Coat	Service Dress Blue Skirt	White Dress	Combination Cap
Service Dress Blue "B"	Service Dress Blue Coat	Service Dress Blue Skirt	Air Force Light Blue	Combination Cap, prescribable
Service Dress White	White Dress Coat w/hard shoulder boards	White Dress Skirt	White Dress	Combination Cap

See reference for further clarification: http://www.pacom.mil/staff/j01p/docs/
Form%20of%20Uniform%Reg/USCG/uniform%20regs.pdf

Necktie	Shoes/Socks/Hosiery	Gloves	Ribbons/Medals/Cummerbund	Notes:
Black Formal Necktie	Black Pumps w/ flesh tone hosiery	White	Miniature Medals, Gold Cummerbund	Worn at formal evening functions. Civilian is equivalent is White Tie. Worn for state occasions.
Black Formal Necktie	Black Pumps w/ flesh tone hosiery	White	Miniature Medals Gold Cummerbund	Worn for private formal dinners, dinner dances, and club affairs. Civilian equivalent is Black Tie.
Black Formal Necktie	White Pumps or Service Shoes w/ flesh tone hosiery	White	Miniature Medals Gold Cummerbund	Worn for private formal dinners, dinner dances, and club affairs. Civilian equivalent is black tie.
Black Overlapping Tab Tie	Black Pumps w/ flesh tone hosiery	White	Miniature Medals	Worn for private dinners, dinner dances, club affairs requiring more formality than the SDB "B."
Black Dress Tab	White Pumps w/ flesh tone hosiery	White	Miniature Medals	Worn for private dinners, dinner dances, club affairs requiring more formality than the SDB.
Blue Overlapping Tab Tie	Black Pumps w/ flesh tone hosiery	White	Large Medals Ribbons	Worn for change of command, state ceremonies, formal occasions on ship, and personnel inspections when prescribed.
Blue Overlapping Tab Tie	White Pumps /w flesh tone stockings	White	Large Medals Ribbons	Worn for change of command, state ceremonies, formal occasions on ships, and personnel inspections when prescribed.
Blue Overlapping Tab Tie	Black Pumps or Service Shoes w/ flesh tone hosiery		Ribbons Name tag	Worn for business and informal social occasions as correct for local custom.
Blue Overlapping Tab Tie	Black Pumps or Service Shoes w/ flesh tone hosiery		Ribbons Name tag	Basic uniform. Worn on all occasions as prescribed.
Blue Overlapping Tab Tie	White Pumps /w flesh tone stockings		Ribbons Name tag	Worn for business and informal social occasions as correct for local custom.

Uniform	Coat/Jacket	Trouser	Shirt	Cap/Cover
Blue Evening Mess	Jacket, Army Blue Mess	Army Blue	White, Formal w/wing collar w/vest, white w/white cuff links/studs	Not required
White Evening Mess	Jacket, Army White Mess	Black	White, Dress w/white vest w/white cuff links/studs	White Service Cap
Army Blue Mess	Jacket, Army Blue Mess	Army Blue	White, Semiformal w/gold cuff links/studs	Not required
Army White Mess	Jacket, Army White Mess	Black	White, Dress w/gold cuff links/studs	White Service Cap
Army Blue Dress	Coat, Army Blue	Army Blue	White	Blue Service Cap
Army White Dress	Coat, Army White	Army White	White	White Service Cap
Army Green Service "A"	Coat, Army Green	Army Green	Army Green (shade 415)	Black Beret
Army Green Service "B"		Army Green	Army Green (shade 415)	Black Beret

See reference for further clarification: http://www.usapa.army.mil/pdffiles/r670_1.pdf

Necktie	Shoes/Socks	Gloves	Ribbons/Medals/ Cummerbund	Notes:
Wing Bow	Black/Black	White, when prescribed	Miniature Medals, Black Cummerbund	Worn for Black Tie functions. Worn at general, formal social functions; private, formal social functions after retreat.
White Bow	Black/Black	White, when prescribed	Miniature Medals, Black Cummerbund	Optional Evening Mess Uniform. Worn at general, formal social functions; private, formal social functions after retreat.
Black Bow	Black/Black	White, when prescribed	Miniature Medals, Black Cummerbund	Worn for Black Tie functions. Worn at general, formal social functions; private, formal social functions after retreat.
Black Bow	Black/Black	White, when prescribed	Miniature Medals, Black Cummerbund	Optional Mess Uniform. Worn at general, formal social functions; private, formal social functions after retreat.
Black Bow (before retreat) Black Four-in-hand (on duty)	Black/Black	Black w/outer garments. White, when prescribed	Ribbons	Year-round wear. Worn on duty as prescribed by local commander and at general/ official social functions before or after retreat.
Black Bow (before retreat) Black Four-in-hand (on duty)	Black/Black	Black w/outer garment)	Ribbons	Optional Dress Uniform. Worn on duty when appropriate and authorized by local commander and off duty for social occasions.
Black Four-in-hand	Black Combat Leather Boots/Black	Black w/outer garments	Ribbons	Year-round wear. Worn on/ off duty, during travel, at informal social functions. Acceptable at informal social functions unless host prescribes other uniform.
Black Four-in-hand	Black Combat Leather Boots/Black	Black w/outer garments	Ribbons	Year-round wear. Worn on/ off duty, during travel, at informal social functions. Acceptable at informal social functions unless host prescribes other uniform.

ARMY, Women

Uniform	Coat/Jacket	Skirt/Slacks	Shirt/Blouse	Cap/Cover
Army Black Evening Mess	Jacket, Army Black Mess	Skirt, Black, Full-length	Blouse, White, Formal	None authorized
Army Blue Evening Mess	Jacket, Army Blue Mess	Skirt, Blue, Full-length	Blouse, White, Formal	None authorized
Army White Evening Mess	Jacket, Army White Mess w/ shoulder boards	Skirt, Black, Full-length	Blouse, White, Formal	None authorized
Army Black Mess	Jacket, Army Black Mess	Skirt, Black, Knee-length	Blouse, White, Formal	None Authorized
Army Blue Mess	Jacket, Army Blue Mess	Skirt, Blue, Knee-length	Blouse, White, Formal	None authorized
Army White Mess	Jacket, Army White Mess w/ shoulder boards	Skirt, Black, Knee-length	Blouse, White, Formal	None authorized
Army All-White	Jacket, Army White Mess w/ shoulder boards	Skirt, White, Knee-length	Blouse, White, Formal	None authorized
Army Blue Dress	Coat, Army Blue	Slacks or Skirt, Army Blue	White, Short Sleeve	Service Hat, Army Blue
Army White Dress	Coat, Army White	Skirt, Army White	White, Short Sleeve	Service Hat, Army White
Army Green Service "A"	Coat, Army Green	Slacks or Skirt, Army Green	Army Green (shade 415)	Black Beret
Army Green Service "B"		Slacks or Skirt, Army Green	Army Green (shade 415)	Black Beret

See reference for further clarification: http://www.usapa.army.mil/pdffiles/r670_1.pdf

Necktie	Shoes/Socks/ Hosiery	Gloves	Ribbons/Medals/ Cummerbund	Notes:
Neck Tab, Black Dress	Pumps, Black w/sheer stockings	White, when prescribed	Miniature Medals, Black Cummerbund	Worn at general, formal social functions; private, formal social functions after retreat.
Neck Tab, Black Dress	Pumps, Black w/sheer stockings	White, when prescribed	Miniature Medals, Black Cummerbund	Worn at general, formal social functions; private, formal social functions after retreat.
Neck Tab, Black Dress	Pumps, Black w/sheer stockings	White, when prescribed	Miniature Medals, Black Cummerbund	Worn at general, formal social functions; private, formal dinners/private or social functions.
Neck Tab, Black Dress	Pumps, Black w/sheer stockings	White, when prescribed	Miniature Medals, Black Cummerbund	Worn at general, formal social functions; private, formal social functions after retreat.
Neck Tab, Black Dress	Pumps, Black w/sheer stockings	White, when prescribed	Miniature Medals, Black Cummerbund	Worn at general, formal social functions; private, formal social functions after retreat.
Neck Tab, Black Dress	Pumps, Black w/sheer stockings	White, when prescribed	Miniature Medals, Black Cummerbund	Worn at general, formal social functions; private, formal social functions after retreat.
Neck Tab, Black Dress	Pumps, White w/sheer stockings	White, when prescribed	Miniature Medals, White Cummerbund	Worn at general, formal social functions; private, formal dinners/private or social functions.
Black Neck Tab	Pumps, Black w/sheer stockings	White, when prescribed	Ribbons	Year-round wear. Worn on duty as prescribed by local commander and at general/ official social functions before or after retreat.
Black Neck Tab	Pumps, White w/sheer stockings	White, when prescribed	Ribbons	Optional Dress Uniform. Worn on duty when appropriate and authorized by local commander and off duty for social occasions.
Black Neck Tab	Pumps, Black w/sheer stockings	Black w/outer garments	Ribbons	Year-round wear. Worn on/off duty, during travel, at informal social functions. Acceptable at informal social functions unless host prescribes other uniform.
Black Neck Tab	Pumps, Black w/sheer stockings	Black w/outer garments	Ribbons	Year-round wear. Worn on/off duty, during travel, at informal social functions. Acceptable at informal social functions unless host prescribes other uniform.

Uniform	Coat/Jacket	Trouser	Shirt	Cap/Cover
Formal Dress	Jacket, Dinner Dress Blue	Blue Evening	White, Formal w/mother-of-pearl cuff links/studs	Required w/outer garment
Dinner Dress Blue Jacket	Jacket, Dinner Dress Blue	Blue Evening	White, Formal w/gold cuff links/studs	Required w/outer garment
Dinner Dress White Jacket	Jacket, Dinner Dress White w/hard shoulder boards	Blue Evening	White, Formal w/gold cuff links/studs	Required w/outer garment
Dinner Dress Blue	Coat, Service Dress Blue	Dress Blue	Dress, White	Cap, White, Combination
Dinner Dress White	Coat, Service Dress White w/hard shoulder boards	White		Cap, White, Combination
Full Dress Blue	Coat, Service Dress Blue	Dress Blue	Dress, White	Cap, White, Combination
Full Dress White	Coat, Service Dress White w/hard shoulder boards	White		Cap, White, Combination
Service Dress Blue	Coat, Service Dress Blue	Dress Blue	Dress, White	Cap, White, Combination
Service Dress White	Coat, Service Dress White w/hard shoulder boards	White		Cap, White, Combination

See reference for further clarification http://buperscd.technology.navy.mil/bup_updt/upd_cd/bupers/unireg/chapter3/chapter3.pdf

Necktie	Shoes/Socks	Gloves	Ribbons/Medals/Cummerbund	Notes:
White Bow	Black/Black	White	Miniature Medals Waistcoat	Worn to official formal evening functions (White Tie events). May be prescribed for officers assigned to duty required by protocol.
Black Bow	Black/Black	White	Miniature Medals Gold Cummerbund	Worn to functions when civilians normally wear Black Tie. Prescribable Winter uniform.
Black Bow	Black/Black	White	Miniature Medals, Gold Cummerbund	Worn to functions when civilians normally wear Black Tie. Prescribable Summer uniform.
Black Bow	Black/Black	White	Miniature Medals	Worn to functions when civilians normally wear Black Tie. Prescribable Winter uniform.
	White/White	White	Miniature Medals	Worn to functions when civilians normally wear Black Tie. Prescribable Summer uniform.
Black, Four-in-hand	Black/Black	White	Large Medals Ribbons. Sword, prescribable (O-4 and above)	Ceremonial Uniform. Worn on formal occasions.
	White/White	White	Large Medals Ribbons. Sword prescribable (O-4 and above)	Ceremonial Uniform. Worn on formal occasions.
Black, Four-in-hand	Black/Black		Ribbons	Year-round wear to official functions. Equivalent to civilian coat and tie.
	White/White		Ribbons	May be prescribed for summer wear when civilian wear is coat and tie.

Uniform	Coat/Jacket	Skirt/Slacks	Shirt	Cap/Cover
Formal Dress	Coat, Dinner Dress Blue Jacket	Skirt, Blue, Formal	White, Formal w/mother-of-pearl cuff links and studs	Required w/outer garment
Dinner Dress Blue Jacket	Coat, Dinner Dress Blue Jacket	Skirt, Blue, Formal	White, Formal w/gold cuff links/ studs	Required w/outer garment
Dinner Dress White Jacket	Coat, Dinner Dress White Jacket	Skirt, Blue, Formal	White, formal w/gold cuff links/ studs	Required w/outer garment
Dinner Dress Blue	Coat, Service Dress Blue	Slacks, Blue, Unbelted	White, Dress	White, Cap, Combination
Dinner Dress White	Coat, Service Dress White	Slacks, White, Unbelted	White, Dress	White, Cap, Combination
Full Dress Blue	Coat, Service Dress Blue	Slacks, Blue, Unbelted	White, Dress	White, Cap, Combination
Full Dress White	Coat, Service Dress White	Slacks, White, Unbelted	White, Dress	White, Cap, Combination
Service Dress Blue	Coat Service Dress Blue	Slacks, Blue, Unbelted	White, Dress	White, Cap, Combination
Service Dress White	Coat Service Dress White	Slacks, White, Unbelted	White, Dress	White, Cap, Combination

See reference for further clarification http://buperscd.technology.navy.mil/bup_updt/
upd_cd/bupers/unireg/chapter3/chapter3.pdf

Necktie	Shoes/Socks/ Hosiery	Gloves	Ribbons/Medals/ Cummerbund	Notes:
Dress, Black	Shoes, Formal, Black w/flesh tone hosiery	White	Miniature Medals, Gold Cummerbund	Worn to official formal evening functions (White Tie events). May be prescribed for officers assigned to duty required by protocol.
Dress, Black	Shoes, Formal, Black w/flesh tone hosiery	White	Miniature Medals, Gold Cummerbund	Worn to functions when civilians normally wear Black Tie. Prescribable Winter uniform.
Dress, Black	Shoes, Formal, Black w/flesh tone hosiery	White	Miniature Medals, Gold Cummerbund	Worn to functions when civilians normally wear Black Tie. Prescribable Summer uniform.
Black	Black/Black	White	Miniature Medals	Worn to functions when civilians normally wear Black Tie. Prescribable Winter uniform.
Black	White/White	White	Miniature Medals	Worn to functions when civilians normally wear Black Tie. Prescribable Summer uniform.
Black	Black/Black	White	Large Medals Ribbons. Sword, prescribable (O-4 and above)	Ceremonial Uniform. Worn on formal occasions.
Black	White/White	White	Large Medals Ribbons. Sword, prescribable (O-4 and above)	Ceremonial Uniform. Worn on formal occasions.
Black	Black/Black		Ribbons	Year-round wear to official functions. Equivalent to civilian coat and tie.
Black	White/White		Ribbons	May be prescribed for summer wear when civilian wear is coat and tie.

OFFICERS
USMC, Men

Uniform	Coat/Jacket	Trouser	Shirt	Cap/Cover
Evening Dress "A"	Jacket, Evening Dress	Blue Evening Dress	White, Soft Bosom w/cuff links/studs	White Dress Cap
Evening Dress "B"	Jacket, Evening Dress	Blue Evening Dress	White, Soft Bosom w/cuff links/studs	White Dress Cap
Dress Blue "A"	Coat, Blue Dress	Blue Dress	White, Soft Bosom w/cuff links/studs	White Dress Cap
Dress Blue "B"	Coat, Blue Dress	Blue Dress	White, Soft Bosom w/cuff links/studs	White Dress Cap
Dress Blue "C"		Blue Dress	Khaki, Long Sleeve	White Dress Cap
Dress Blue "D"		Blue Dress	Khaki, Short Sleeve	White Dress Cap
Blue-White Dress "A"	Coat, Blue Dress	Dress White	White, Soft Bosom w/cuff links/studs	White Dress Cap
Blue-White Dress "B"	Coat, Blue Dress	Dress White	White, Soft Bosom w/cuff links/studs	White Dress Cap
Service "A"	Coat, Service	Service	Khaki, Long Sleeve	Green Service or Garrison Cap
Service "B"		Service	Khaki, Long Sleeve	Green Service or Garrison Cap
Service "C"		Service	Khaki, Short Sleeve	Green Service or Garrison Cap

See reference for further clarification http://www.tecom.usmc.mil/mcub/library/MCUR/URTOC.htm

Necktie	Shoes/Socks	Gloves	Ribbons/Medals/Cummerbund	Notes:
Collar, White Strip	Black/Black	White	Miniature Medals White Waist Coat	Prescribed for official formal evening functions. White Tie events during summer and winter.
Collar, White Strip	Black/Black	White	Miniature Medals Scarlet Cummerbund	Prescribed for official social Black Tie events during summer and winter.
Collar, White Strip	Black/Black	White	Large Medals	Prescribed for parades, ceremonies, formal/semiformal social functions. Not authorized for leave/liberty.
Collar, White Strip	Black/Black	White	Ribbons	Prescribed for parades, ceremonies, formal/semiformal social functions. Not authorized for leave/liberty.
Khaki	Black/Black		Ribbons	Prescribed for honors, parades, ceremonies on/off military activity. Authorized for leave/liberty.
	Black/Black		Ribbons	Prescribed for honors, parades, ceremonies on/off military activity. Authorized for leave/liberty.
Collar, White Strip	White/White	White	Large Medals	Prescribed for parades, ceremonies, formal/semiformal social functions. Not authorized for leave/liberty.
Collar, White Strip	White/White	White	Ribbons	Prescribed for parades, ceremonies, formal/semiformal social functions. Authorized for leave/liberty.
Khaki	Black/Black		Ribbons	Prescribed for formations at parades, ceremonies on/off military activity. Authorized for leave/liberty.
Khaki	Black/Black		Ribbons	May be worn as uniform of the day. Not to be worn for formal/semiformal social events. Authorized for leave/liberty.
None	Black/Black		Ribbons	May be worn as uniform of the day. Not to be worn for formal/semiformal social events. Authorized for leave/liberty.

OFFICERS
USMC, Women

Uniform	Coat/Jacket	Skirt/Slacks	Shirt/Blouse	Cap/Cover
Evening Dress "A"	Jacket, Evening Dress	Black Evening Dress, Long	White, Ruffled Tuck-in	Not required
Evening Dress "B"	Jacket, Evening Dress	Black Evening Dress, Long or Short	White, Ruffled Tuck-in	Not required
Dress Blue "A"	Coat, Blue Dress	Dress Blue Slacks or Dress Skirt	White Dress	White Dress Cap
Dress Blue "B"	Coat, Blue Dress	Dress Blue Slacks or Dress Skirt	White Dress	White Dress Cap
Dress Blue "C"		Dress Blue Slacks or Dress Skirt	Shirt, Khaki, Long Sleeve	White Dress Cap
Dress Blue "D"		Dress Blue Slacks or Dress Skirt	Shirt, Khaki, Short Sleeve	White Dress Cap
Blue-White Dress "A"	Coat, Blue Dress	White Dress Skirt or Slacks	Shirt, White Dress	White Dress Cap
Blue-White Dress "B"	Coat, Blue Dress	White Dress Skirt or Slacks	Shirt, White Dress	White Dress Cap
Service "A"	Coat, Service	Service Slacks or Skirt	Khaki, Long Sleeve	Green Service or Garrison Cap
Service "B"		Service Slacks or Skirt	Khaki, Long Sleeve	Green Service or Garrison Cap
Service "C"		Service Slacks or Skirt	Khaki, Short Sleeve	Green Service or Garrison Cap

Necktie	Shoes/Socks/Hosiery	Gloves	Ribbons/Medals/ Cummerbund	Notes:
	Black Pumps w/dark/ grey/smoky hosiery	White	Miniature Medals, Scarlet Cummerbund	Prescribed for official formal evening functions. White Tie events during summer and winter.
	Black Pumps w/dark/ grey/smoky hosiery	White	Miniature Medals	Prescribed for official social Black Tie events during summer and winter.
Neck Tab, Scarlet	Black Dress or Pumps w/dark/grey/smoky/ skin tone hosiery	White	Large Medals	Prescribed for parades, ceremonies, formal/semiformal social functions. Not authorized for leave/liberty.
Neck Tab, Scarlet	Black Dress or Pumps w/dark/grey/smoky/ skin tone hosiery	White	Ribbons	Prescribed for parades, ceremonies, formal/semiformal social functions. Not authorized for leave/liberty.
Neck Tab, Black	Black Dress or Pumps w/dark/grey/smoky/ skin tone hosiery		Ribbons	Prescribed for honors, parades, ceremonies on/off military activity. Authorized for leave/ liberty.
None	Black Dress or Pumps w/dark/grey/smoky/ skin tone hosiery		Ribbons	Prescribed for honors, parades, ceremonies on/off military activity. Authorized for leave/ liberty.
Neck Tab, Scarlet	Black Dress w/dark/ grey/smoky/skin tone hosiery	White	Large Medals	Prescribed for parades, ceremonies, formal/semiformal social functions. Not authorized for leave/liberty.
Neck Tab, Scarlet	Black Dress or Pumps w/dark/grey/smoky/ skin tone hosiery	White	Ribbons	Prescribed for parades, ceremonies, formal/semiformal social functions. Authorized for leave/liberty.
Neck Tab, Green	Black Dress w/dark/ grey/smoky/skin tone hosiery		Ribbons	Prescribed for formations at parades, ceremonies on/off military activity. Authorized for leave/liberty.
Neck Tab, Green	Black Dress w/dark/ grey/smoky/skin tone hosiery		Ribbons	May be worn as uniform of the day. Not to be worn for formal/semiformal social events. Authorized for leave/ liberty.
None	Black Dress w/dark/ grey/smoky/skin tone hosiery		Ribbons	May be worn as uniform of the day. Not to be worn for formal/semiformal social events. Authorized for leave/ liberty.

AIR FORCE, Men

Uniform	Coat/Jacket	Trouser	Shirt	Cap/Cover
Mess Dress	Mess Dress Jacket w/ shoulder boards	High rise w/o cuffs	White, Formal Long Sleeve w/silver cuff links/ studs	Not worn
Formal Dress	Mess Dress Jacket w/white single breasted vest	High rise w/o cuffs	White, Long Sleeved	Not worn
Service Dress	Service Dress Coat	Blue	Blue, Long Sleeve w/silver cuff links/ studs	Service Cap
Long Sleeved		Blue	Blue, Long Sleeve w/silver cuff links/ studs	Service Cap
Short Sleeved		Blue	Blue, Short Sleeve	Service Cap

See reference for further clarification: http://www.af.mil/shared/media/epubs/
afi36-2903.pdf

Necktie	Shoes/Socks	Gloves	Ribbons/Medals/Cummerbund	Notes:
Satin Blue Bow	Black/Black		Miniature Medals Blue Satin Cummerbund	Worn for Black Tie affairs; tuxedo is civilian equivalent
White Bow	Black/Black		Miniature Medals Blue Satin	Worn for White Tie affairs; tuxedo is civilian equivalent
Blue Herringbone Twill Tie	Black/Black		Ribbons Name tag	
Blue Herringbone Twill Tie	Black/Black		Ribbons (optional) Name tag	
Blue Herringbone Twill Tie (optional)	Black/Black		Ribbons (optional) Name tag	

Uniform	Coat/Jacket	Skirt/Slacks	Shirt/Blouse	Cap/Cover
Mess Dress	Mess Dress Jacket w/ shoulder boards	Mess Dress Skirt	Mess Dress Blouse w/studs (cuff links optional)	Not worn
Formal Dress	Mess Dress Jacket w/ shoulder boards	Mess Dress Skirt	Mess Dress Blouse w/studs (cuff links optional)	Not worn
Service Dress	Service Dress Coat	Skirt or Slacks, Blue	Tuck-in style Blouse w/studs (cuff links optional)	Service Cap
Long Sleeved		Skirt or Slacks, Blue	Tuck-in style Blouse w/shoulder mark insignia, w/studs (cuff links optional)	Service Cap
Short Sleeved		Skirt or Slacks, Blue	Tuck-in style Blouse	Service Cap

See reference for further clarification: http://www.af.mil/shared/media/epubs/
afi36-2903.pdf

Necktie	Shoes/Socks/ Hosiery	Gloves	Ribbons/Medals/ Cummerbund	Notes:
Blue Satin Inverted V Tie Tab	Black Pumps w/sheer nylon neutral, dark brown, black, off-black hosiery		Miniature Medals Cummerbund	Worn for Black Tie affairs; tuxedo is civilian equivalent.
Blue Satin Inverted V Tie Tab	Black Pumps w/sheer nylon neutral, dark brown, black, off-black hosiery		Miniature Medals Cummerbund	Worn for formal evening functions and state occasions (White Tie affairs); evening gown is civilian equivalent.
Blue Satin Inverted V Tie Tab	Black Pumps w/sheer nylon neutral, dark brown, black, off-black hosiery or Black Slip-on w/black socks		Ribbons Name tag	
Blue Satin Inverted V Tie Tab	Black Pumps w/sheer nylon neutral, dark brown, black, off-black hosiery or Black Slip-on w/black socks		Ribbons (optional) Name tag	
Tie Tab (optional)	Black Pumps w/sheer nylon neutral, dark brown, black, off-black hosiery or Black Slip-on w/black socks		Ribbons (optional) Name tag	

Uniform	Coat/Jacket	Trouser	Shirt	Cap/Cover
Formal Dress Blue	Dinner Dress Blue Jacket w/formal waistcoat	Blue Evening	Formal White Wing Collar	Combination Cap
Dinner Dress Blue Jacket	Dinner Dress Blue Jacket	Blue Evening	White Soft Front pleated	Combination Cap
Dinner Dress White Jacket	Dinner Dress White Jacket	Blue Evening	White Soft Front pleated	Combination Cap
Dinner Dress Blue	Service Dress Blue Coat	Blue Evening	White Dress	Combination Cap
Dinner Dress White	Service Dress White Coat w/hard shoulder boards	White Dress		Combination Cap
Full Dress Blue	Service Dress Blue Coat	Blue Dress	White Dress	Combination Cap
Full Dress White	Service Dress White Coat w/hard shoulder boards	White Dress		Combination Cap
Service Dress Blue "A"	Service Dress Blue Coat	Blue Dress	White Dress	Combination Cap
Service Dress Blue "B"	Service Dress Blue Coat	Blue Dress	Air Force Light Blue	Combination Cap (prescribable)
Service Dress White	Service Dress White Coat w/hard shoulder boards	White Dress		Combination Cap

See reference for further clarification: http://www.pacom.mil/staff/j01p/docs/Form%20 of%20Uniform%Reg/USCG/uniform%20regs.pdf

Necktie	Shoes/Socks	Gloves	Ribbons/Medals/ Cummerbund	Notes:
White Bow	Black/Black	White	Miniature Medals Gold Cummerbund	Worn at formal evening functions. Civilian is equivalent is White Tie.
Black Bow	Black/Black	White	Miniature Medals Gold Cummerbund	Worn for general or official social functions. Black Tie events.
Black Bow	Black/Black	White	Miniature Medals Gold Cummerbund	Worn for private formal dinners, dinner dances, and club affairs. Civilian equivalent is Black Tie.
Black Bow	Black/Black	White	Miniature Medals Gold Cummerbund	Worn for private dinners, dinner dances, and club affairs requiring more formality than the SDB "B."
	White/White	White	Miniature Medals	Worn for private dinners, dinner dances, and club affairs requiring more formality than the SDB .
Blue Four-in-hand	Black/Black	White	Large Medals Ribbons Sword	Worn for change of command, state ceremonies, formal occasions on ship, and personnel inspections when prescribed.
	White/White	White	Large Medals Ribbons Sword	Worn for change of command, state ceremonies, formal occasions on ship, and personnel inspections when prescribed.
Blue Four-in-hand	Black/Black		Ribbons Name tag	Worn for business and informal social occasions as correct for local custom.
Blue Four-in-hand	Black/Black		Ribbons Name tag	Basic uniform. Worn on all occasions as prescribed.
	White/White		Ribbons Name Tag	Worn for business and informal social occasions as correct for local custom.

COAST GUARD, Women

Uniform	Coat/Jacket	Skirt/Slacks	Shirt/Blouse	Cap/Cover
Formal Dress Blue	Dinner Dress Blue Jacket w/formal waistcoat	Formal Dress Skirt	White Dress	Black Tiara (optional)
Dinner Dress Blue Jacket	Dinner Dress Blue Jacket	Formal Dress Skirt	White Dress	Black Tiara (optional)
Dinner Dress White Jacket	Dinner Dress White Jacket w/hard shoulder boards	Formal Dress Skirt	White Dress	Black Tiara (optional)
Dinner Dress Blue	Service Dress Blue Coat	Blue Dress Skirt	White Dress	Combination Cap
Dinner Dress White	Service Dress White Coat w/hard shoulder boards	White Dress Skirt	White Dress	Combination Cap
Full Dress Blue	Service Dress Blue Coat	Blue Dress Skirt	White Dress	Combination Cap
Full Dress White	White Dress Coat w/hard shoulder boards	White Dress Skirt	White Dress	Combination Cap
Service Dress Blue "A"	Service Dress Blue Coat	Service Dress Blue Skirt	White Dress	Combination Cap
Service Dress Blue "B"	Service Dress Blue Coat	Service Dress Blue Skirt	Air Force Light Blue	Combination Cap, prescribable
Service Dress White	White Dress Coat w/hard shoulder boards	White Dress Skirt	White Dress	Combination Cap

See reference for further clarification: http://www.pacom.mil/staff/j01p/docs/Form%20 of%20Uniform%20Reg/USCG/uniform%20regs.pdf

Necktie	Shoes/Socks/ Hosiery	Gloves	Ribbons/Medals/ Cummerbund	Notes:
Black Formal Necktie	Black Pumps w/flesh tone hosiery	White	Miniature Medals, Gold Cummerbund	Worn at formal evening functions. Civilian is equivalent is White Tie. Worn for state occasions.
Black Formal Necktie	Black Pumps w/flesh tone hosiery	White	Miniature Medals, Gold Cummerbund	Worn for private formal dinners, dinner dances, and club affairs. Civilian equivalent is Black Tie.
Black Formal Necktie	White Pumps or Service Shoes w/flesh tone hosiery	White	Miniature Medals, Gold Cummerbund	Worn for private formal dinners, dinner dances, and club affairs. Civilian equivalent is Black Tie.
Black Overlapping Tab Tie	Black Pumps w/flesh tone hosiery	White	Miniature Medals	Worn for private dinners, dinner dances, and club affairs requiring more formality than the SDB "B."
Black Dress Tab	White Pumps w/flesh tone hosiery	White	Miniature Medals	Worn for private dinners, dinner dances, and club affairs requiring more formality than the SDB.
Blue Overlapping Tab Tie	Black Pumps w/flesh tone hosiery	White	Large Medals Ribbons	Worn for change of command, state ceremonies, formal occasions on ship and personnel inspections when prescribed.
Blue Overlapping Tab Tie	White Pumps /w flesh tone stockings	White	Large Medals Ribbons	Worn for change of command, state ceremonies, formal occasions on ship and personnel inspections when prescribed.
Blue Overlapping Tab Tie	Black Pumps or Service Shoes w/flesh tone hosiery		Ribbons Name tag	Worn for business and informal social occasions as correct for local custom.
Blue Overlapping Tab Tie	Black Pumps or Service Shoes w/flesh tone hosiery		Ribbons Name tag	Basic uniform. Worn on all occasions as prescribed.
Blue Overlapping Tab Tie	White Pumps /w flesh tone stockings		Ribbons Name tag	Worn for business and informal social occasions as correct for local custom.

CHAPTER 23

Seating Plans

*W*here people are seated is powerfully political, and everyone knows it. Hosts from diplomats to wedding planners agonize over seating charts. The main purpose of a seating plan is to ensure that guests know the host appreciates their status and organized things to please them.

The right side is the position of honor for most of the world. In heraldry, for example, flags on home ground are positioned on the right of other flags. In the military, "right of the line" in ancient battle formations was critical because the strongest swordsman's arm was unhampered in that position. In religious traditions, the right side of the deity is the honored position. Therefore, the right side of the host is the best seat at most tables; the host's left side is next, then back to the right side, then left, and so forth.

People are honored in precedence order at social functions so that all can observe who they are, based on their proximity to the host. Are you the organization or people's leader? Mother's favorite? The birthday boy's best friend? Your position in life is reflected in your placement at table.

AT EASE KEY POINTS

- ✂ Separate guest list by gender before rank ordering.
- ✂ Ensure all tables have an event host and a guest of honor.
- ✂ Position principals to face middle of room and each other.
- ✂ Escort VIPs to their seats.
- ✂ Brief captain of servers so that ranking guests are served first.

UNDERSTANDING PRECEDENCE

Webster's Dictionary defines precedence as the act, right, privilege, or fact of being first in time, place, order, rank, or importance. Customs differ by locality, but the following are fundamental international principles.

Public precedence order is based on power:
- Officials in authority (uniformed Services, government public servants, diplomatic envoys, royalty, religious hierarchies) outrank "regular" people.
- Great wealth is respected (millionaires have more status than those on food stamps).
- Professional status is usually ranked by the salary commanded (lawyers are more prestigious than cashiers; scientists are more esteemed than cabdrivers).
- Position level or seniority within organizations is important (managers are above staff in business; doctorates outrank masters' degrees in academia).
- Spouses are ranked the same as the officials or professionals they married when attending organization-hosted *social* events (unless both work for the same employer, in which case the spouse has his or her own precedence ranking).

Most cultures also accord respect to:
- Age (adults have standing over children). An older, well-respected person is often seated higher than his or her position alone would require.
- Kinship (immediate family, extended family, and honorary family members).
- Gender *in social situations* (females are accorded more honor than males of equal precedence: doors and chairs are held for them). Within the workplace, females and males are treated according to their business status, not chivalry.
- Persons with disabilities are accommodated with accessibility considerations.

If clearly defined differences do not exist, people accord status as best they can. It is not always possible to determine a person's wealth, for example, and it is difficult to compare persons from different occupations, but a person's proper place in the hierarchy must be recognized or the individual as well as the population he or she represents will take insult.

LIVING-ROOM SEATING

The right side of the sofa (as you sit) is considered the place of honor in a living room or salon. If there are two or more couches, the ranking one normally faces the door with its back against a wall. Invite the guest of honor to sit there. The host normally sits facing the senior guest, across from, perpendicular, or alongside to facilitate conversation. If there are no sofas, the largest or "best" chair is the place of honor. In other cultures, the honored seat may be nearest the fireplace, family art treasure, or religious display. When hosting a group more in number than places available (e.g., cocktail party), living room seats are normally reserved for elderly or frail guests with most people standing and moving from group to group.

Q: What I need desperately (before Monday AM) is guidance on seating VIPs in an audience when it is just rows of chairs with a podium front and center.

A: Official precedence begins in the first row in front of the podium; seat the head VIP there. Alternate right, left, right, and so on until you run out of VIPs. If there are multiple nationalities of similar rank attending, front-row seating can be decided by host country alphabetical order. Escort VIPs to correct seats or line them up in order and lead them in two minutes before your event begins. If the event is televised, provide a VIP guest list to the media so that they can announce names as VIPs enter.

AUDIENCE SEATING

In spaces you control, label chairs if the Very Important Person (VIP) will be seated as part of the audience in an auditorium, a tiered lecture hall, and so on. If spouses attend an official event honoring their mate and both are in the audience, seat them together. For other family members, age, relationship, and available seating will determine placement (precedence after spouses is usually children, mother, father, grandmother, grandfather, sister, brother, aunt, uncle, cousins).

For auditoriums with a central aisle, the ranking person sits in the front row, first seat off the right side as you face the stage or podium, the second-ranking sits in the first seat to the left of the aisle. The third-ranking sits to the right of person #1, the fourth-ranking sits to the left of person #2, and so on, back and forth. If ranking persons number more than seats in the first rows, seat the next ranking person in the second row, first seat off the right of the aisle, the next ranking in the second row, first seat off the left of the aisle, and continue alternating.

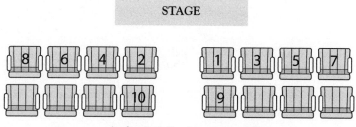

Auditorium Seating, center aisle

For auditoriums without a center aisle, seat the ranking individual in the center of the first row, with the second-ranking person on the right, the third-ranking on the left, and so on back and forth. If ranking persons number more than seats in the first row, the next ranking person starts in the center of the second row, and continue alternating.

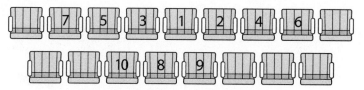

Auditorium Seating, no center aisle

Reserved Seats at a Performance

If you want to reserve a block of seats for a large group to attend a performance and observing protocol is important, choose the most desirable section (generally the center one) and reserve three or four rows deep (depending on the size of your party) instead of one long row. The most honored guests sit to the right and left of the host, but the next three ranking guests generally sit directly behind the host in order to stay in the preferred center, right to left as you face the stage. Other guests are seated up to six places on either side of the host and up to four rows behind him or her; precedence decreases as distance from the host increases. If the reserved rows are not in the center section, the first echelon of your guests may be seated in the front six to eight seats (ranked right to left as you face the stage), the next echelon behind them, and so on until all special guests are seated. Arrange for your group to meet in an anteroom so that you can share the seating arrangement. Line them up in the correct order and lead the way, walking together through the auditorium or conservatory to the reserved seats.

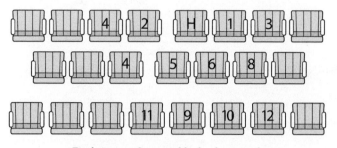

Performance Seating, block of reserved seats

CONFERENCE ROOMS

Seating precedence is important at meetings, especially if they are international. You may wish to pre-position name placards on a conference table beforehand. If the table does not accommodate everyone, the lowest-ranking persons ring the room in chairs against the wall. The ends of conference tables are normally for the senior hosting official or meeting chairperson. They sit facing any screen or podium (if there are formal presentations) with any high-ranking visitors on the right and left. Alternatively, senior hosts may sit in the middle of one long side with all visitors directly opposite them (facing the best view), if this will not appear too confrontational. The hosting official's aide sits near to and faces the door to deal with interruptions.

Observe seating precedence even for impromptu high-ranking meetings. An assistant can collect the business cards of important visitors in the lobby or anteroom, determine participants' protocol order, and quickly position their business

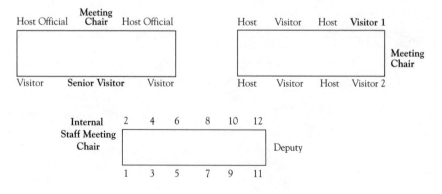

Conference Table Options

cards as place cards on the conference table before the party is admitted. If you arrange many such impromptu meetings, obtain place card holders for this purpose, and blank business-size cards for writing the names of those who do not bring cards. Store co-workers' cards with the place card holders so that they will always be on hand.

Q: During recent negotiations, I did what my reading of the culture's protocol suggested and seated foreign businessmen together on the conference table's right side, but they were not pleased. Our company president sat at the head with other executives down the left side, his deputy on the other end. How would you have seated them?

A: Your plan had the visiting executives facing underlings. The principals should have been seated across from one another for good face-to-face discussion. In addition, visitors are always given the "window" or best view, regardless of table side.

DIGNITARIES AND THEIR ALTERNATES

In official life (government, military, ecclesiastical, and diplomatic events), strict published protocol lists determine seating; not age, kinship, gender, or reputation. It is the *position* that is honored. For instance, a young male official in a higher echelon will precede an older female official who is lower ranking.

When senior dignitaries are unable to attend, they may ask to send a formal representative. If so, the designate is seated "first" within his or her rank, not at the rank of the represented official. For example, an O-6 military person representing an O-9 would be given the first precedence seat in a group of other O-6s. If the designate actively participates at meetings, conferences, and business seminars on behalf of his superior, however, he or she is seated with the same precedence as the dignitary.

An exception is a designated representative sent to a function in the United States by the President; that person is accorded VIP/DV Code 1 courtesies (see Chapter 8: Order of Precedence and Military Forms of Address).

LIMOUSINES AND CARS WITH DRIVERS

When a male escorts a female socially, he practices chivalry by opening the car door for her, waiting until she is seated, and closing her door. If he is driving, he

gets out of the car first, opens her door, offers her a hand to assist (especially helpful out of low cars parked near high curbs), and closes her car door.

In a taxi or a car with a driver, the chauffeur may open car doors. The VIP seat
is backseat curbside, the second ranking seat is the other backseat window. The
third ranking seat is the front passenger seat (beside the driver). Younger or junior
individuals enter vehicles first and sit where they will least inconvenience seniors.
See Chapter 25: International Protocol and Civility for a detailed explanation of
seating dignitaries for arrival ceremonies.

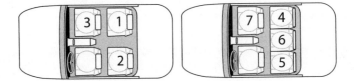

Precedence seating in U.S. cars with drivers.
For arrival ceremonies, 6 and 5 switch places.

AIRCRAFT

If a group is boarding a chartered aircraft, the senior member will enter first to
select a seat, followed by the next ranking, and so on. However, when a government aircraft has been assigned to transport a senior official, all junior-ranking
personnel board first and take their seats before the VIP arrives at the plane or
helicopter. Do not ever make a VIP wait on you. Normally, either the crew or the
senior official's aide will ensure the proper seat is reserved for the dignitary.

VIP seat locations vary, depending on the size of the plane. In Air Force One,
the U.S. President's plane, there is a private suite in the nose of the 747 jet that
includes an office. Top advisers sit nearest the office door, and then come seats for
less senior staff. VIP guests are farther back with the Secret Service behind them,
and the news media are in the very rear of the plane. In smaller aircraft with rows
of seats, the honored position is usually on the left side so that the dignitary can
see the welcoming committee upon landing.

All passengers remain in their seats while the VIP deplanes first.

ON STAGE

Escort VIPs to their chairs or be sure they know exactly where to sit. The best way
to do this for something public, like before a live audience or for TV cameras, is to

handle introductions behind the scenes (use full honorifics and names), and line speakers up in the correct order to walk on. For example, at an interview after a sports competition, the principals might line up and walk in as follows: the agent, the star players, the coach, and the team owner—this keeps the coach and stars seated at the center of the table for the cameras.

A panel of government officials must enter in order, following rules of precedence, such as: Prime Minister, Deputy President, Major General, and lower ranks last. As officials enter, newscasters may name them for the cameras; they stop at the middle chairs and lower ranks pass behind them. Only when all are in position does everyone sit down, the ranking VIP making the first move.

Multiple seating on a stage is normally behind one long oblong table, but unique seating configurations may also be appropriate. Place water pitchers with glasses between every two people.

CHANGE OF COMMAND SEATING

The time-honored military Change of Command Ceremony marks the formal passing of responsibility from one commander to another. Events may include a full parade of personnel *Marching in Review* or an *Inspection of the Troops* or the *Passing of the Guidon* (regimental flag). The outgoing commander may be retiring or the incoming commander may be receiving a promotion. Either could be receiving awards.

The reviewing stand (dais or raised platform) is positioned so that the audience can see the ceremony, but the principals face and speak to the troops on the parade field, with the audience as guests at their back. Principals are seated on the stand according to rank and position, with the departing commander (host) in the center and relieving commander (co-host) at his left. The Guest Speaker and Chaplain may be on either side of the principals between two lecterns, one for the Master of Ceremonies (MC) and the other for the speakers. The MC also sits on the platform, but off to the side near a lectern. Members of an official party arrive in inverse order of precedence with the senior entering last, except that the outgoing officer will generally precede the relieving officer, although the latter may be junior.

If high-ranking personnel attend, they may also be seated on the reviewing stand, behind the principals, right to left as they face the parade field. Military personnel rank higher than civilian guests do at these events unless the civilians are very high-level dignitaries. Local civilian dignitaries whom the commander deals with on a daily basis receive preferred seating over civilian officials coming from another city, whether on the dais or in the audience. Overseas at American events, reserve a few seats for important persons who may decide to attend at the last moment.

The audience seats directly in front of the ceremony area are reserved for honored guests and family members, as applicable. If there is an aisle, spouses and children of the outgoing commander are seated to the right, and the family of the incoming commander is seated to the left as you face the dais, with their guests beside them (see Audience Seating above). The spouses of dignitaries, speakers, and chaplain (if attending) are seated next to the relieving officer's spouse or immediately behind depending on the number of front-row seats available.

Local civilian officials are often invited to attend Changes of Command. If a local official has not visited the installation before, make every effort to honor him or her with escorts and preferential seating. See Chapter 1: Military and Government Protocol for explanation of audience manners.

The Change of Command Reception following the ceremony is the first opportunity for the relieving officer (and spouse) to meet local community leaders. Always have a receiving line with an announcer (see Chapter 18: Official Business Functions, Cocktails, and Receptions for illustration). During the reception, the new commander (and spouse) acts as host with the departing commander (and spouse) next in line as guest of honor/co-host.

Q: What is the proper music when the official military or government party enters to be seated at the head table?

A: It helps to have music or the official party tends to appear self-conscious or too solemn as they walk. If there is a band, they will be playing music while guests gather. The important thing is to change tempo to emphasize that the event is beginning. The band leader will help you make an appropriate choice from among their selections to match your occasion or a particular VIP; for instance, the President gets "Hail to the Chief," the Secretary of Defense rates the "Honor's March," a diplomat hears his own national anthem, and so forth.

HEAD TABLES

A head table is usually a long, single table at one end of the room with chairs only on one side. No one sits at the short edges of a head table. Only distinguished members of the community concerned sit at a head table and they are seated strictly according to protocol rank order, not gender (although spouses may be included; see below). The host (the presiding officer, club president, council chair-person, etc.) is always at the central seat with the senior honored guest to the right, the second-ranking person to the left, third to the right, fourth to the left, and so forth. Place cards are always used on the head table for clarity.

Do not crowd a head table; give everyone plenty of elbow room, as they are the focus of attention. The number of people is increased or decreased as needed. Strive for an even number so that guests may pair off for conversation. Event hosts should anchor the ends of head tables so that visiting guests have companions on each side. For instance, at a university banquet, the students might be hosts anchoring the ends with school officials and their spouses between. It is desirable at all schools of higher learning for young people to learn how to host. See below, left, this page, the Military Academy Banquet Head Table illustration, for one way a head table at a school might be arranged.

Spouses of the official host and guest of honor often sit at a head table, but not beside their mates (except for horseshoe-shaped tables). In the Host and Hostess Head Table illustration, note that the host's spouse is seated in the #3 position, and the spouse of the senior ranking is seated in the #2 chair. When other spouses are present, they are seated between guest officials and members.

No one is ever seated on the other side of a head table facing the principals, or on the short edges of a head table—that would turn it into just another long banquet table. If desired, oblong side tables may be placed against the front of a head table in a "U" (horseshoe) or "E" or "T" shape.

9	**Student**
7	Commandant
5	Dean's Spouse
3	Principal Speaker
1	Superintendent's Spouse
H	**Student Host**
2	**Host's Date**
4	Superintendent
6	Speaker's Spouse
8	Dean
10	Commandant's Spouse
11	**Student**

Audience

**Military Academy Banquet
Head Table (students are in bold)**

7	Distinguished event member
5	Master of Ceremonies
3	**Host's Spouse**
1	Guest of Honor
H	Host
X	Interpreter (if necessary)
2	**Guest of Honor's Spouse**
4	Principal Speaker
6	Clergy

**Host and Hostess
Head Table (spouses are in bold)**

Dining In Head Table

The President of the Mess, regardless of gender, sits in the center host position with the guest of honor, usually the speaker, on the right; the second ranking guest is on the host's left. Event co-hosts sit at the ends so that guests do not feel marginalized. Because of directing responsibilities, the Dining In Vice President is never seated at the head table. See Chapter 4: Organizing a Dining In and Dining Out for an illustration and various ways head table occupants might enter a room formally.

Dining Out Head Table

The host president's spouse is seated to the right of the guest of honor, and the guest of honor's spouse is seated to the left of the host president (see above, right side, Host and Hostess Head Table).

Speaker Head Table

When a table for speakers is needed at a banquet or other event, there is normally a central podium. Seating is essentially the same as any head table, except the host is always seated to his or her own right with the podium on the left (facing the audience). The first ranking guest is beside the host, but the second-ranking guest is seated on the podium's other side in seat #2. A principal speaker (a lecturer, a master of ceremonies or toastmaster) may be seated on the podium's left, if desired for ease of access, even if someone else is higher ranking. If the #2 individual is not an organization dignitary, always seat an event co-host beside him or her. Continue alternating distinguished guests right and left to the ends of the table, striving for even numbers on both sides of the podium and event hosts at the ends.

The head table normally faces multiple smaller tables, which may be round, square, or rectangular in any stand-alone formation. Designate appropriate organization co-hosts and guests of honor for each stand-alone table.

Speaker's Table with Podium

Anniversary or Wedding Head Table

When a couple is honored because they are married, seat them beside each other at the center of a head table with the female to the right of the male. At a wedding for instance, the bridal pair are centered, with the bride to the right of the groom and the maid (or matron) of honor on his left. The best man sits on the bride's right. It is nice to have males anchor the ends of a wedding head table, if possible.

If the number of wedding attendants is large, or the newlyweds or anniversary couple want their children to sit with them, two round tables may be designated as "head" tables. At weddings, if young flower girls and ring bearers sit at a head table, their parents should be with them. Having two tables also allows more room for spouses of older children or wedding attendants to sit together.

6	Male
4	Bridesmaid
2	Best Man
HS	Bride
H	Groom
1	Maid of Honor
3	*Bridesmaid
5	*Male Attendant

Bridal Party Head Table
*avoids placing female at end

DINING TABLES

Interpreters and Security Personnel

Interpreters must be strategically placed at useful intervals to translate for principals; therefore, their own grade is not relevant and they are "passed over" or "not noticed" as relative precedence continues around them. They are never seated in the guest of honor position or between a dignitary and host, but on the principal's other side at formal dinners. Interpreters do not eat during official meals as they are there to work.

Bodyguards or security personnel are never seated between principals either, and though they do not usually sit at table, they may need to, depending on the circumstances. If so, they will want their backs to a wall. If your chosen public venue is not secure, do not hesitate to arrange seating to protect the physical safety of a dignitary, even if it is not in accordance with accepted protocol guidance. Also, be sensitive to international customs and other unusual circumstances (e.g., an obligatory "royal-chair-puller-out" for a country leader, or a diplomat who is deaf in one ear).

Place Cards and Menu Cards
See Chapter 16: Place Settings, Table Manners, and Service Styles.

Table Placards
To expedite the seating of guests at a large function, it is helpful to label multiple tables prominently. Table placards are uniform in size, color, lettering, and so forth. They may be numbers, but since everyone would prefer to be at table #1 instead of #15, use names appropriate to the event instead of numerical hierarchy. For example, Academy Award–winning movies would be appropriate table names for a dinner in Hollywood, Hall of Fame names for a sports event, or space shuttles for a NASA-hosted occasion. Table numbers or names may be removed after the first course is served. "YASA" cards (see below), with an accompanying seating chart showing table locations, assist guests in finding their chairs.

YASA Cards and Escort Cards
At a large dinner when there is no assigned seating beyond the head table, *You-Are-Seated-At* (YASA) Cards are provided to guests as they arrive at a check-in table outside the dining area. They are used instead of place cards to sort guests into individual tables, if not chairs at those tables. At the check-in table, two cross-referenced lists, one alphabetical and one by table name, are helpful.

YASA Cards may be folded cards or flat cards in envelopes. The individual's name (or couple's name) is on the front of the envelope or folded card, and the seating information is on the inside.

Escort Cards are similar, and are used for very formal dinners. A male guest finds a small envelope or folded card in a tray on a hall table, with the name of his female dinner partner inside. A table diagram will be displayed to enable the man to check the seating arrangement, or an enclosed small diagram card will show the correct table. If he does not know her, he arranges to be introduced during the cocktail hour so that he can escort her into the dining room. At large official dinners, aides introduce dinner partners when necessary; otherwise, the host or a friend makes necessary introductions. The male lets his dinner partner know that he will escort her, because this information is not provided to her.

When labeling YASA cards or Escort cards, use the "conversational" or "salutation name," that is, *Major and Mrs. Jones*, or *Mr. Smith*.

Mr. and Mrs. Martin

You are seated at Table 12

entrance

Midshipman Boggs
Dot indicates seat

You are seated at Table 3

You Are Seated at (YASA) Cards

Mr. Davidson

Folded Escort Card

Ms. Rasmussen

Seating Boards and Charts

Display neat, easily understood, properly oriented seating diagrams prominently in a central location (or multiple locations if the group is very large) of the cocktail area or foyer. YASA boards have an alphabetical list of all guests with their table numbers and another sheet with a diagram of the room layout. For smaller events, there is room on the table schematic for guest names to be written in the correct positions.

Who Escorts and Seats Whom

The Host always leads the ranking guest who will be seated on his or her right into the dining room. Other guests follow in no particular order to find their place cards (except at very formal dinners when escorts are assigned; see Escort Cards above). During formal meals, a female waits to see if her dinner partner will offer to help seat her. The host spouse (or co-host) enters last with the guest who will be seated on his or her right.

For a married couples example, the host husband (H) escorts the senior guest wife (1L) in first and seats her (see Chapter 17: Family Dining, Buffets, and Formal In-Home Meals for the procedure). The host wife (HS) escorts the senior guest husband (1G) in last. A male guest of honor escorted in by a hostess does not help seat anyone; the gentleman on the hostess' right (2G) has that duty.

In case of a guest governor within his own state, or those higher on the Order of Precedence list, the example couple would reverse their positions—in other words, the hostess would escort a male governor in first and the host would follow immediately with the governor's wife. In that case, the governor might offer to seat the hostess as others are arriving at table, but the responsibility remains with the second ranking man.

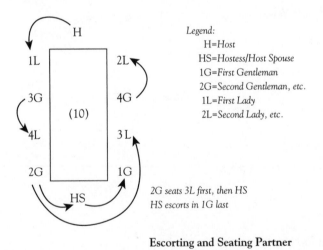

Legend:
H=Host
HS=Hostess/Host Spouse
1G=First Gentleman
2G=Second Gentleman, etc.
1L=First Lady
2L=Second Lady, etc.

2G seats 3L first, then HS
HS escorts in 1G last

Escorting and Seating Partner

The Single Host

If desired, a single host may ask a guest (ahead of time) to act as co-host. The host and co-host sit opposite each other either at the ends or center sides of a table. In the latter case, no one sits on the short ends. The invited co-host is usually a senior ranking person from the same organization as the host. For example, the co-host would be the ranking American guest at an American-hosted meal that includes guests from foreign countries, or the ranking military guest when the host is military and the guests include nonmilitary civilians. Since the traditional male-female alternating plan works best, the co-host may be male for a female host or vice versa, if all guests are couples or equal numbers of each gender are invited.

If the event is without spouses ("stag"), a co-host is not necessary and seating may be determined by rank alone, especially if there are wide differences in rank. The highest-ranking guest from a visiting group may sit opposite the host. If so, it may be more congenial if members of the hosting headquarters sit beside the ranking guest, and members of the visiting party occupy positions next to the host. Otherwise, a strict precedence arrangement may end up looking like a table of arbitration, with all Americans on one side and all foreign guests on the other, for example, or all uniforms on one side and all civilians on the other.

```
   6    2    H    3    7
 ┌────────────────────────┐
 │      (10 people)       │
 └────────────────────────┘
   9    5    1    4    8
```

Stag (without spouses) Seating

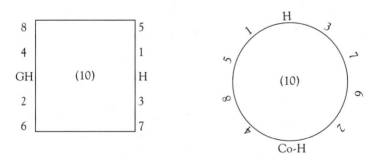

Separate Tables

It may be convenient or necessary to seat guests at two tables. If so, husband and wife hosts sit separately, positioned to maintain line of sight with each other. Do not follow order of precedence so precisely that you end up with all organization members at one table.

Multiple round tables are popular for both formal and informal meals. There is a friendliness about round tables that appeals to young and old, as King Arthur's

Knights of the Round Table popularized. Several tables may be arranged for six (larger tables may be used, but six is the number that can be accommodated using card tables covered with the portable table tops often available from rental agencies), with the host at one table, the host spouse at another, and co-hosts designated for any others.

Table Hosts

At large events with separate tables, there are more potential positions of honor. Designate a co-host for every table and seat a guest of honor on the co-host's right. Inform co-hosts that they have this duty so they will be extra welcoming and gracious to guests at their tables, preparing conversation topics if they feel the need. Spreading out the senior attendees gives junior guests the opportunity for social interaction with them.

Position co-hosts to maintain line of sight with each other and the host. This helps them see how things are going at their respective tables; they can also help cue each other for proceedings. Table co-hosts make sure that everyone is introduced and otherwise act to facilitate conversation. The event host informs the

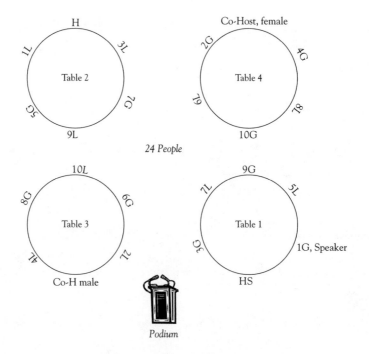

24 People

Podium

Round Tables, Guest Speaker

head waiter or banquet manager where the guests of honor are seated at each table so that servers can do their job properly. Table co-hosts monitor servers, ensuring the ranking guest is served first; however, if the wrong person is served (the plate touches the table), *do not* make the server move it—it is too late!

Guest Speakers and Distinguished Guests at Round Tables

Seat anyone making remarks as close to the podium as possible and facing the middle of the room. Being near the podium makes getting up and returning easier, especially for a Master of Ceremonies or a Toastmaster. Event co-hosts may be positioned with their backs to the podium, allowing the other guests a better view of the speaker.

Position distinguished guests at their respective tables so that a majority of guests can see them and, more importantly, so that they can see the audience. This also facilitates toasts; when they stand to address the room, they will not have their backs to some listeners.

The "U" or "E" or "T" Shaped Tables

Oblong side tables may be placed against the front of a head table in a "U" or "E" or "T" shape. When a "U" or horseshoe-shaped table is used at official banquets, try to limit seating to the outside edges. Married hosts sit together (female to the right)

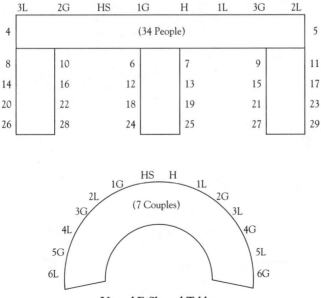

U- and E-Shaped Tables

on the outside "U" center with their honored guests beside them. The other guests alternate in descending order of precedence down both sides. If additional places are needed, the inside seats begin at the lower third section of the horseshoe table, or guests are seated each side of the "E" or "T" arms, with the seats inside but nearer the host higher in precedence than those farther away and outside.

Forfeiture of Host Status

Hosts relinquish the foremost positions at their own tables *only* when their guest is the Chief of State or Head of Government of any country. (The Chief of State and Head of Government might be the same person, but not always. In the United Kingdom, for instance, the Queen is the Chief of State, but the Prime Minister is the Head of Government.) The country leader sits at the head of a table, and his or her spouse sits at the opposite end. In order not to "give honor to themselves," the host and spouse sit to the *left* of the president, royalty, or country leader and spouse, with the high-ranking male and female guests sitting at the *right* of the leaders.

The exception is when leaders of countries host one another. Being equal in standing to each other, for instance, the hosting President of the United States simply seats visiting monarchs or leaders as guests of honor at the right and left in the White House.

Ranking Attending Guest Spouses

International protocol accords spouses of government officials equal precedence with their mate's rank or grade or position *for protocol purposes*. In countries practicing polygamy, only one wife at a time is invited to official luncheons and dinners.

When any organization is hosting a function for married couples, spouses take the same rank as the principal employee unless both of them work for an invited organization, in which case they are each placed where their official position dictates.

Married couples do not sit next to each other at formal meals (the exceptions are the "U" shaped table and wedding or anniversary head tables). Most spouses will be separated the entire table length from each other when following strict seating protocol. However, for lively conversation at informal tables, try placing spouses across from one another. They will have the opportunity to get to know new people on either side of them, while admiring the view of their significant other.

To avoid seating a female spouse at the outer end of a table, it may be necessary to seat two women or two men next to each other, violating the alternating male-female rule when the genders are equal in number. When genders are not equal in number, space them as equally as possible.

The Unmarried Couple

Unmarried couples invited to official occasions are treated as individuals. International protocol recognizes only marital status. Dates or accompanying guests are seated based on their own merits; they cannot claim equality to each other's rank.

Seating Relatives at Table

When parents (grandparents) are guests at a formal meal, the husband's mother or mother-in-law is seated to his right at the table, and his father or father-in-law is to the right of the wife. When both sets of in-laws are on hand, the wife's mother is seated to the husband's right, and his mother is seated to his left. The husband's father is seated to the wife's right, and her father is to her left. If many in-laws are eating together, perhaps for a holiday dinner, then the rule of seniority may be followed. When children are present, alternate them and the grandparents. Precedence order is usually: mother, father, grandmother, grandfather, aunt, uncle, sister, brother, adult cousins, and eldest to youngest children.

CREATING SEATING DIAGRAMS

Work out the various seating arrangements possible at your government facilities of choice (commercial venues can provide options for their spaces). Develop diagrams and templates to make planning easier. When guest lists are complete, work with applicable protocol offices of the agency, the foreign country, military unit, university, and so forth regarding order of precedence for their officials. Double-check all titles, ranks, positions, and spelling of names to help with place cards and relative status comparisons across disciplines. Even then, the guest list is just names and positions, unless background context is known.

The new wife of a longtime ambassador in Venezuela tells what happened when he delegated a seating plan to her shortly after she arrived as he was called out of town: *"I sat one man beside his former mistress, another beside his political rival, a woman beside her ex-husband. . . . At least two guests left in tears because someone was mean to them. It was a disaster because they were just names to me."*

If you are a protocol professional working for the host with high-ranking or international guests, coordinate seating charts with your organization's foreign relations and political sections; they are familiar with local politics and issues of the day. The host will also review the seat assignments in advance and inform you if accommodations are needed for any reason, such as rivals or persons with physical limitations.

Dining Table Arrangement Rules

- A male-female alternating plan has proven best for social conversation. If genders are equal in number, two males or two females do not sit beside each other.
- The positions of honor are beside hosts, who sit opposite each other at the ends or the center sides of a table.
- Spouses do not sit beside each other (see the Head Tables section above for exceptions).

Following the above rules at a seated dinner for five couples, this would mean that the gentleman guest of honor (1G) is seated at the right of the hostess (HS) and the lady guest of honor (1L) at the right of the host (H). The second-ranking couple (2G & 2L) is similarly seated, this time to the left of hosts. The third-ranking guest couple (3G & 3L) sits beside the guest of honor couple, alternating gender. The fourth-ranking couple (4G & 4L) sits beside the second-ranking couple, alternating gender.

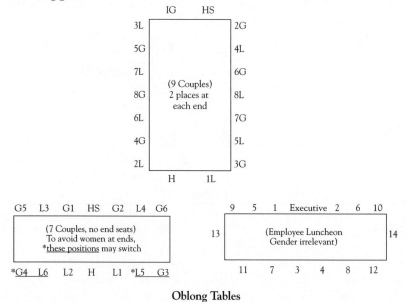

Oblong Tables

Multiples of Four

Dinners for odd numbers and six, ten, fourteen or eighteen guests, and so forth, are easily arranged, whether or not all are couples. Husband and wife hosts sit in the head positions opposite each other. However, when the genders are equal in number, any multiple of four—eight, twelve, sixteen, and so forth—creates a problem. No matter how many times you try, two men or two women end up beside each other. The solution is for the non-principal host to relinquish his or her position and move one seat to the left, which allows the ranking guest of honor (same sex as the principal host) to sit at the head to balance the table.

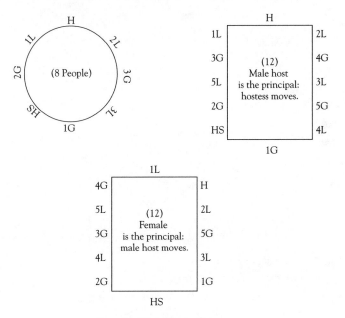

Couples Divisible by Four

Other Standard Practices

Outside (visiting) guests are seated between event insiders. For example, a military officer might host a dinner that includes civilian dignitaries. Seating should be alternated so that the civilians are interspersed with the uniformed personnel.

When both foreign and U.S. military are guests, members of like grade are ranked the same; military personnel in uniform must always be seated according to protocol.

There must be no unoccupied seats at formally set tables. In the event of last minute cancellations, remove entire place settings and chairs.

Seating protocol is most important for the first three or four ranking guests. One way to honor equal ranks is to seat them each at separate small tables, creating more positions of honor because a host and a guest of honor are designated for each.

Seat the two most talkative guests in the middle of a long table to focus conversation and forestall guests' thinking that the other end is having a better time.

Violate any of the preceding rules, if it makes sense to do so. For instance, language limitations with international guests may dictate a modified precedence arrangement to facilitate conversation.

Q: The hosting college president is unmarried, the round table seats seven, the female guest of honor's husband is the only spouse attending. Where does the husband sit?

A: Spouses are protocol-ranked the same as their principals and usually sit opposite them. A guest of honor always sits on the host's right. Since there is no hostess or co-host, the honoree's husband may be seated on the host's left in this instance.

Q: What is the international sandwich method of seating?

A: For seated dinners or luncheons with a diplomatic purpose, care is taken to seat official guests between event hosts. For instance, visiting internationals are interspersed with hosting U.S. officials in descending rank order.

Lower-Ranking Guests of Honor

To avoid problems, try to ensure that the event's guest of honor is the one with the highest rank. If lower ranking, a guest of honor is not seated beside the host at an official dinner unless the senior guest relinquishes that position (ask the ranking person well ahead of time and do not object if he or she refuses). For example, if a military couple has a civilian older brother visiting and it is the brother's birthday, he may be the stated honoree at dinner, but they could not seat him in a guest of honor position next to either host if a Vice Admiral, a General, and their spouses were also guests.

Beyond seating the lower ranking guest of honor farther down the table or asking a ranking guest to waive his precedence (pushing the highest-ranking guest down one level affects everyone else's relative position also), the host could ask the senior person to co-host a second table.

Similarly, a host may honor two or more high-ranking guests of equal status by utilizing separate tables to allow each a prominent position. For example, at a White House state dinner, three tables were arranged side by side. The President was host at one table with the Chief Justice seated across from him, the First Lady hosted the second table with the Speaker of the House beside her, and the Vice President was host at the third table.

Rank Ordering Guests

When a spouse (or date) will not accompany every guest, the best way to rank individuals is to separate your guest list into two columns, male and female, then list principals in descending rank order with their mates opposite. Once the list is made, number each side for proper placement on your model templates:

Gentlemen	Ladies
1G Mr. Senior Diplomat	—— (unaccompanied)
2G Admiral Military	1L Mrs. Military
3G Bishop Religious	2L Mrs. Religious
——	3L Dr. Scientist
4G Commander Police Chief	4L Mrs. Chief
——	5L Ms. Ballerina
5G Mr. Basketball Star	——
6G Mr. Business	6L Ms. Local Business

Then all you need do is double-check for problems such as spouses seated next to each other or language barriers. Using the seating plan for seven couples on page above, you find no problems with this sample guest list, and could proceed quickly to writing place cards or other chores.

When seating has been properly handled, dignitaries are pleased by their official recognition, others are flattered to be seated beside them, and everyone is impressed with the hosts' leadership skill.

Section 5

INTERNATIONAL CONSIDERATIONS

CHAPTER 24

International Travel

$\mathcal{T}$he focus of this chapter is to keep your travels abroad hassle-free and to give you every possible advantage so that you are ready to work and socialize. Most likely you are inclined to international travel, whether navigating exchange study programs, leisure pursuits, or working in a foreign country. You probably feel more adept than the average American at navigating cross-culturally, or think that successfully blending in overseas will not be your problem. However, each time you travel abroad, the subtle local manners and etiquette are just as important to research as the current monetary exchange rate and what vaccinations are required for entry by the country you visit.

AT EASE KEY POINTS

- ⚘ Research your destination. You will be under public scrutiny after arrival.
- ⚘ Attend security briefings.
- ⚘ Create a trip file/checklist for ease over a lifetime of travel.
- ⚘ Implement a *Will* and *Power of Attorney*.
- ⚘ Identify memento and gift ideas that represent your hometown.
- ⚘ Pack business and correspondence cards.

You will need clear country-specific information on local civility customs such as proper personal space (standing too close or far apart in conversation or in queues), information about the dominant religion (courtesies and faux pas), and advice on when and how much to tip during likely interactions. Military sites, the interiors of houses of worship, and poverty-stricken areas are usually restricted (photos discouraged), and travelers should be aware that many peoples do not like their pictures taken. Before filming individuals, always ask their permission and respect the response if it is "no." In some cases they might ask for money (one sign is rubbing the thumb and fingers together on an outstretched hand), but do not offer it automatically because doing so may be even more offensive than taking the picture without permission. A newly arrived American in the Third World wrote to us: "*Poverty is traumatic to witness as a daily experience. At the airport while loading bags into the car, a little girl begged me for money, a pen, candy, or anything else. Her mother stood right beside her encouraging this. It was hard to know what to do.*" You cannot concentrate on business or enjoy being a tourist if you are unsure about how to interact with the people you meet.

Behaving in the locally approved manner is just one part of the equation. Another part is whether or not your host country's populace respects the U.S. government or American corporations, because those opinions will surely color how you are treated. Many of you have experienced firsthand that our world image is not always a positive one. Culture clashes, political resentment, economic envy, "Ugly American" travel predecessors . . . there are many explanations. Being an American abroad today is both an opportunity and a challenge. You have the tacit responsibility and honor of representing the United States; act accordingly.

Q: There are too many security problems lately for my family to be comfortable with my upcoming overseas deployment. What can I do for their peace of mind?

A: Let your family know that you are taking safety issues seriously. Attend any available predeparture briefings on personal security. Reassure loved ones that you are conscientious by designating a trusted relative to oversee your fiscal responsibilities while you are gone. Make an appointment with a lawyer to prepare a *Will* and a *Durable Power of Attorney* with a clause similar to this one:

"Notwithstanding my insertion of a specific expiration date herein, if on the above-specified expiration date I shall be, or have been incapacitated and unable to act because of circumstances beyond my control by virtue of my having been taken Prisoner of War (POW), been made a victim of civil strife as a detainee (hostage), kidnapped, held incommunicado, or am otherwise Missing in Action (MIA), then this Power of Attorney shall automatically remain valid and in full effect until thirty (30) days after I have returned to the United States following termination of such status."

If you work for the military or government you are undoubtedly patriotic and interested in strengthening international relations because you know that it is likely you will be dispatched one day to the front lines in support of U.S. policy. However, any American traveling abroad, official or tourist, will *always* make a challenging target for someone. It is a sad truth of our times that visitors from the most affluent countries can suffer more from local street crime, be held accountable for behavior that would be ignored in a host country citizen, or feel victimized by a foreign national's verbal slings and arrows. The following suggestions will help you arrive at vacation or business destinations in a confident frame of mind.

WEB SITES AND RESEARCH

If you will be traveling as a lone tourist (not part of an organized group) in a region prone to natural disasters or political instability, consider getting trip insurance and be sure to register with the local American embassy (always in the capital city) or American consulate (in other selected major foreign cities) so that they can find you in case of emergency. The U.S. Department of State accepts online registration from its citizens traveling abroad at www.travel.state.gov. Embassy staff can provide the latest Security/Force Protection Condition (FPCON) and advise in other ways. On a trip to Panama, for instance, the U.S. embassy told one of your authors that carrying a white tote bag downtown (which she was innocently using as a combination briefcase and purse) might get her into trouble, as the minority party was using the color white as a political statement to incite rebellion.

If you are going on business, ask your destination office for an itinerary and "welcome packet" to review *before* you depart. Beyond basic advice such as whether or not to drink the local water and information on who will participate in your meetings, these packets usually include an event schedule for clues about after-hour activities. Research your travel location via the Internet by country and city location. There are world newspapers available in English for additional local insights, and links to government-published travel information and background notes. The U.S. Department of State's Citizens' Emergency Center (www.state.gov) will have up-to-date information on health conditions, crime, and dates that travel will be disrupted due to planned demonstrations or high-ranking official motorcades. You can compare the U.S. warnings with other English government information sites, such as Canada (www.voyage.gc.ca) and the United Kingdom (www.fco.gov.uk). Visit weather Web sites for average daily temperatures and forecasts by National Meteorological and Hydrological Services (NMHSs) worldwide, world calendar Web sites for dates of heavily traveled host country holidays to avoid, and travel Web sites to calculate the conversion of dollars into any currency.

You will need enough local money immediately (in small denominations) for a taxi, newspaper, fast food, and the like in case no one meets you or your plane is delayed until after the local money exchange closes. Most international currency can be easily ordered through your bank with a few days' notice. Be sure that your credit card is accepted at your destination. Double-check this! During one TDY/

TAD (government temporary duty), your author had a credit card from a company endorsed by the U.S. government that two of the four countries visited refused to accept! Also, double-check to be sure that your credit limit is high enough to cover trip expenses. Call your credit card companies in advance to inform them of travel plans, as many will automatically suspend a card if they see unusual activity abroad. Double-check that their toll-free telephone numbers (as well as your airline's and health care provider's numbers) will work from your overseas locations, or get alternate contact numbers.

Value Added Tax (VAT), also called Goods and Services Tax (GST), is a point-of-sale tax levied by many countries on almost everything, but the percentage varies from country to country. Tourists may claim VAT reimbursement on significant purchases when they depart the country. Major airports have a reclamation system, such as a special envelope and drop box. Refunds may be mailed to your home address, adjusted on your credit card balance, or refunded in cash at the airport. If you plan to make major purchases, seek out VAT reimbursement information at the airport as you enter a country so that you will know what to request from the merchants. One more money caution: many more businesses overseas automatically add a gratuity to their bills than you are used to in America, so examine charges before calculating the tip.

Trip File/Checklist

You will undoubtedly go abroad many times. Make the rest of your travel life easier by creating a secure *Trip File/Checklist* on your computer now. It will prove an indispensable future reference. Your checklist would include toiletry and clothes essentials, notification phone numbers (for stopping mail, newspapers), and other actions to accomplish before you leave, such as the advice in this chapter.

International travelers are urged to photocopy (or scan into their computers) personal documents such as passports, visas, immunization records, airline tickets, itineraries, driver's licenses, medical insurance cards, and credit cards. Enlarge the backs of cards in order to easily read phone numbers, or enter numbers immediately into your cell phone's memory. If a wallet or passport is lost or stolen, pertinent information is at hand. If you scan your photocopies into a document file, keep them on a separate computer disk or flash drive (so that personal information is secure from computer hackers). Right before your trip, encrypt the document and "secure e-mail it" to yourself *and* to a family member or trusted friend. If necessary, you can visit the nearest Internet café while abroad and retrieve data.

Before leaving on an international trip, be sure that your home office and family members have your itinerary, and that the home office knows how to contact your family members and vice versa, in case of emergency. Be sure to obtain relevant contact information, including both the cell and home phone numbers of your sponsor or in-country point of contact (if there is one). If your flights are delayed to the point of affecting connecting flights, you will be able to communicate details after business hours.

TRAVEL ENSEMBLES

Dress "internationally" during travel. Depending upon your position and trip purpose, that means dressed well enough to conduct business. Long flights and long connecting times do require comfortable clothes, with elastic in the waists, and slip-on shoes, but that does not mean "weekend sloppy." Take a sport coat as part of your ensemble; it can be stowed in the overhead bin until landing. In many nations how you dress is a sign of respect for those around you, is the visible indication of your social status, and directly affects how others will treat you.

Nothing will make you more uncomfortable than being dressed inappropriately at the start of a business trip or tour of duty. You just might be greeted formally by a local counterpart at plane-side or in the terminal—the smaller the country, the higher the probability (see Chapter 25: International Protocol and Civility). If you are high-ranking (or escorting a dignitary) the local media could be recording the arrival. *"Your advice to dress professionally when arriving at the airport came in handy. I was met by a parade of people which surprised me. Tell others it's possible that the first contact may be with a host country liaison,"* wrote one of our clients. Americans can feel markedly underdressed next to the beautiful yards and yards of fabric used to make clothing in some parts of the world—picture an African diplomat in an elaborately pleated, flowing garment, perhaps accompanied with a turban or headdress, next to a conservative Western business suit. Do not compound the problem by dressing too casually during business travel.

Be mindful not to draw special attention to yourself while traveling overseas because not everyone you meet will have the best intentions. Try to behave quietly and inconspicuously, keeping a low profile. This is hard to do if you are wearing eye-catching neon colors, cowboy boots, or high-fashion belts. People who stand out in any crowd make the easiest targets for harassment or worse. Expensive jewelry could attract thieves; patriotic or religious items may incite heated political discussion. Why wear them while traveling? Strive for an "international" look by choosing dark-colored, conservative clothes. Cover your chest and back completely, arms to the elbow, and legs to mid-calf (minimum). Females must be especially mindful to wear very conservative apparel in some cultures. Slacks or pantsuits (not jeans or tight-fitting) are the most popular travel attire for women of all ages because they are the most comfortable; loose skirts and tops tend to fly up when walking across tarmacs or parking lots or past forced-air security detection devices.

Q: I am a woman flying alone to two developing countries. What are your recommendations?

A: To be left alone on aircraft, put on the airline headset or listen to an iPod. Try to arrive in daylight hours. At your hotel, make sure the staff does not call out your room number or name. Observe proper female decorum, *as defined locally*, to avoid unwanted attention. Take only reputable (recommended by your hotel) tours; avoid playing tourist alone. In many countries women are not respected if they ride in the front seat of taxis or put their purses on restaurant floors (pick-up signals), sit at coffee shops/cafés (bastions for men only), or go about without a male escort (especially in the evenings). It is not about how an independent American defines her role that is important now, but the impact that local customs and assumptions of proper female behavior will have on you. When in doubt, ask someone who has been there.

After arrival in a foreign environment, continue to dress modestly and neatly. Roger Axtell in his book series, *Dos and Taboos around the World*, suggests wearing items of clothing that are valued by the culture in which you are traveling, such as silk scarves when in France. In other cultures, keeping a scarf in your bag at all times gives you the option of covering your arms or head as needed; for example, when visiting houses of worship. Even when exercising, men do not wear shorts or go without a shirt in public in many parts of the world. Women must not wear tight or revealing clothing or dress like men in tank tops or shorts, especially in the Islamic world.

The world is a book, and those who do not travel read only a page.

—St. Augustine

CHECKED LUGGAGE

Many airlines charge for checked bags. Excess baggage fees will apply if suitcases weigh above a certain limit, or number more than allowed. International carry-on limits are often only 19 inches and 20 pounds (approximately 45 centimeters and 9 kilograms). The U.S. domestic flight maximum for years has been 22 by 16 by 9 inches and 40 pounds, but individual airlines vary. Double-check the rule limits for your carrier, and if changing planes during your trip, the size of a connecting plane or a different airline may affect what and how you pack, as will international security checks, border crossings, and border customs.

Mark your bags so that you can easily recognize them. When you are suffering from jet lag, all bags really do look alike. The author has traveled the world with bright-colored yarn pom-poms on the handles of her bags. No one ever mistakes her bags for theirs and the pom-poms are very easy to spot on conveyors. Also, pack self-contained bags—each suitcase complete for a week, with all accessories, underwear, and so forth together—or that one bag lost will contain vital parts of your wardrobe and you might be stuck with only your travel shoes. As one of our clients said, *"Plan for the airlines to lose your luggage. Don't make a big stink about it—the luggage will show up. If you get upset, you'll be the only one upset."* Put clothes in clear plastic or mesh bags (especially small items, like underwear and socks) for easy re-packing after security or customs searches. Split toiletries and put them in different suitcases so you will always have at least half your supplies, or put them in your carry-on. To preclude permanently lost bags, put your U.S. address and dates of travel *inside* your checked luggage. Use only plain luggage tags for your international destinations (American flags or U.S. business logos can invite unwanted attention); tags with flaps that hide the address are even more secure.

If you are traveling abroad for the first time, you may not realize that your destination will probably operate on a different electrical system (50 Hz, 220 volts) from the United States (60 Hz, 110 volts). American plugs will not work in most outlets of the world either. Do a Web search for the electrical systems in use at your destination. If you travel abroad frequently, a reliable battery or wind-up travel alarm is a worthwhile investment, as are dual-voltage or "convertible" personal appliances (hair dryers, curling irons, electric shavers) that you use every day, along with a set of international adapter plugs. Check with your laptop computer and personal digital assistant (PDA) manufacturers for advice on how to recharge on 220 volts while abroad. Final packing tips are to be prepared in case of fire or emergency—take a set of quick pull-on clothes (sweats) and a small flashlight (power outages are more common in some locations than others).

Q: I will be TDY to several nations with histories of instability and labor strikes. What is your advice?

A: Smile and be polite to everyone—ticket-counter workers, security personnel, and flight attendants—delays are not their fault. Keep your voice calm and speak slowly as a sign of respect. A loud, fast voice can be seen as threatening or aggressive in many cultures. Reconfirm your travel arrangements and hotel reservations at *every* stop. In developing nations, overbooking is a frequent occurrence and a common ploy is to have the flight leave earlier than published, especially if strikes are imminent.

Q: My friend got the zippers on his luggage cut off, even though he bought Department of Homeland Security–approved locks. What should I use?

A: The locks you mention work well in the "homeland" but are not guaranteed beyond our borders. To deter petty thieves, consider luggage straps to wrap your bags, use plastic zip-ties instead of locks, or see if your airport offers plastic wrapping for luggage (there may be a nominal charge). If overseas security forces need to look inside bags, they can unbuckle straps, cut (and hopefully replace) zip ties, or peel away plastic, but must break and discard conventional locks. Check with the airline.

Just before you leave home, line up your entire luggage ensemble and take a picture or two. Store them in your computer and carry hard copies with you. Jet-lag headaches and language barriers will not matter if a photo of your lost suitcase can aid in filling out forms or talking with airline personnel. Insurance companies want you to make a list of each bag's contents, but since that is a painful chore most of us avoid, simply take a picture of everything laid out on the bed just before you put it all in and close the suitcase for the last time. The pictures will be sufficient to jog your memory if bags are permanently lost and will be useful for supporting insurance claims.

CARRY-ON BAGS

Double-check the latest information on what can be carried on board aircraft. Of course, passports, immunization and medical records, and travel documents (ticket, car rental, hotel information) always stay with you. Be sure that the name on your ticket reads *exactly* the same as the name on your passport so that security personnel will not challenge you. Consider memorizing your passport number so you will not need to keep pulling it out to fill in forms. Carry enough prescription medicines *in the original bottles* (again making sure the name on your prescriptions match your ticket) to last for several days in case disaster grounds your plane or diverts it. If you are moving abroad, school and employment records are also hand-carried. Smart travelers take extra eyeglasses, a change of clothes (at least under-wear), and daily-used toiletry items on board "just in case" (liquids such as contact lens solution or anti-diarrhea medicine may be banned in large quantities). If non-original containers are used, label the bottles with their contents. Airline and air-port food can be unreliable, so carry on high-protein snacks such as trail mix or power bars. Even if you do not need them in transit or for travel delays, snacks are often welcome in your hotel room or while sightseeing. Other useful items to carry on are stain remover packets, hand-sanitizer wipes, travel umbrella, and business cards. Hand-carry high-theft items such as jewelry and cuff links also.

The shared camaraderie of overseas travel, along with an exchange of business cards, has begun more than one profitable relationship in a destination city. Carry a handful of your cards. You will be expected to provide your card when meet-ing most local businesspersons and government officials, or when presenting your company's or government agency's publications, brochures, or magazines. If a PCS (permanent change of station) or long-term business contract in another country is upcoming, you might pursue business cards with the local language translation on the back (see Chapter 25: International Protocol and Civility for exchang-ing cards with local nationals). Treat cards as valuable items. Not everyone has a card in the United States; fewer people may own them in your destination coun-try. Please see Chapter 12: Correspondence and Stationery Essentials for more on business, social, and correspondence cards.

HOTEL TIPS

When giving reservation dates, please be very specific. When Americans request a room from June 2 to 4 they mean three nights; however, other countries would understand two nights only, believing that June 4 is the departure date. Clearly state your arrival time (after six or seven PM your room may be given to another unless you confirm otherwise), the number of lodging nights desired, and the departure date to avoid confusion. Verify the type of room (single or double), style of bath (tub or shower), the price (and whether it includes breakfast), and check-in time (may be as late as four o'clock). Local laws vary; hotels may charge one night's lodging if your reservation is not cancelled with a minimum of twenty-four hours' notice.

Request rooms between the third and fifth floors so that you will be above entry by street criminals, but hot water pressure and local fire ladders can still reach you.

Building floors are counted differently in other countries. Street level is ground floor, followed by first floor (called the second floor in the United States), and so on. Elevator doors in older buildings might not open automatically. Americans (including your authors) have stood staring at elevator doors for as long as five minutes, waiting for them to open before figuring this out.

As you enter hotel rooms, you might think that the porter goes through a routine simply to qualify for a tip, but please view the process as a security check instead. Here is the procedure in well-run hotels: The porter props open your room door with a bag, opens any closet doors and the shower curtain (assuring that no one lurks there), and turns on the TV, heat or air conditioning, lights, and water to show that they work. While he is present, open any balcony doors to check locks, and the drapes to check for access into the room from that direction. Your author once had a flat roof right outside a hotel window and asked for a different room. The porter insisted that no one could get onto the roof. She calmly pointed to the pair of shoes and cigarette butts in plain view. No one should be shy about ensuring his or her own safety. Also, call the front desk to ask for a time check before the porter collects his gratuity (usually $1.00 per bag) and departs. What you are really doing is making sure that the phone works. Once the porter leaves, the land line phone could be your only connection to the outside world.

If you understand the language, tune in the hotel radio to a local news station and listen as you get dressed every morning. It is easier than setting aside time to surf the net or buy and read a newspaper. If you do not speak the local language, Voice of America (VOA), British Broadcast Corporation (BBC), and Cable Network News (CNN) broadcast regularly in English to keep travelers informed of *international* news (ask the front desk for stations and times).

SETTLING IN

One of the first things a traveler consumes locally is water. If germs are a concern, ask at hotel check-in for bottled water to drink and to use for brushing your teeth (check to be sure that seals are unbroken). Be aware that getting hot water in bathrooms might prove challenging. Weary travelers wrestling with how to cope in a foreign bathroom might find the tap for hot water on the "wrong" side, or confusingly marked with a "C" (the first letter for the word "hot" in French, Italian, and Spanish).

When preparing to leave your hotel for the first time, take a sheet of stationery from the desk in your room, a pack of matches from the lobby, a card from the concierge, or anything with the hotel's local street address. This will be a comfort if you need to take a taxi, especially in large cities with more than one hotel of the same name. Speaking of taxi drivers, they ought to drop passengers close to entrances, not across the street or from a corner.

Some twenty-first century items to consider for peace of mind are GSM (Global System for Mobile) phones that work in many countries, prepaid SIM (Subscriber Identity Module) cards to insert into a GSM cell phone for international roaming, voice and text mail, and GPS (Global Positioning System) units that tell you where you are and help locate addresses. Check to see if they are available for local rent but it may be more inexpensive to buy them if you travel overseas frequently.

If you will be working in or moving to the capital city, get a local street map upon arrival and locate the nearest friendly embassies: the United States and another where your native language is spoken. Be sure that you can recognize the host country flag because it marks official buildings like courthouses and police stations. If you become a victim of crime or accident, the flags can help you find the authorities.

TRADE SECRETS

The protection of trade secrets and the desire to obtain them are as old as travel itself. American government and military personnel and business travelers are high priority targets for technological, proprietary, and other privileged information. An unaware person will happily share personal information about themselves, their colleagues, and their work during normal conversation in social or travel settings. Stay security-conscious even if you are on holiday. If you do not have a security office to brief you, pay close attention to the following.

It is usually impossible to detect a well trained and skilled "spy," as his or her line of questioning will probably seem like harmless banter, no different than any other conversation with a stranger. *"The greatest compliment that was ever paid me was when one asked me what I thought, and attended to my answer,"* wrote Henry David Thoreau. However, former CIA director Richard Helms reminds us how dangerous such compliments can be: *"Were I an industrial spy given the task of penetrating a highly secure computer communications system and extracting its secrets . . . I would seek to suborn someone with access to the information I need to permit me to enter the system as a legitimate user."*

This is not to imply that you avoid establishing new professional contacts or making friends. Just give forethought to what you will say when sensitive questions come up in conversation. Be ready to tactfully deflect questions that are intrusive regarding your job, private life, and coworkers. Do not feel compelled to directly answer any question that makes you uncomfortable. A simple ploy is to start asking questions about them and their way of life and listen at least as much as you talk.

In some instances, it will be impossible to avoid scrutiny. Sometimes American government or business representatives are always assigned to specific rooms because they are electronically monitored or routinely searched with cooperative collusion between host government officials and hotel personnel. Keep sensitive documents (including passports) with you and maintain control of your unwanted personal or proprietary papers until you can dispose of them away from your hotel. Upscale hotels often keep files on guests so that they can anticipate future needs. Analyzing your trash is one way they acquire information.

FIRST IMPRESSIONS

Pay attention to daily courtesies such as how people move down sidewalks, how they greet each other socially and in a business context, the appropriate speaking distance between persons, conversation volume and speech rate, and so on, so that you can blend in. You may be surprised to learn that you can be an affront despite your best efforts.

Olfactics refers to the smell response, from food fragrances to body odor issues. Even though you bathe daily you may still offend the noses of overseas contacts. People who seldom eat some spices or animal products are extremely sensitive to the body odor exuded by those who do. For instance, the Japanese initially referred to Koreans as "garlic eaters" and called the first Europeans they met "butter-stinkers." A Chinese woman (who rarely ate dairy products) once explained that Americans smelled of "baby spit-up" to her and her friends. Since your author is a big cheese lover, she gained a completely new appreciation of first impressions after that conversation.

CULTURE STRESS

If you, or children traveling with you, have blond or red hair, another culture stress is that you might draw a crowd in countries where all locals have dark hair. They will stare and may touch your hair "for good luck" without asking permission. Even in nations with a strong preference for saving face and non-confrontation your author has felt unnerved many times by hands touching her from behind, but when she turned around no one would meet her eyes and she never knew who it was.

Visiting a local restroom, toilet, or water closet (WC) may make a deep first impression on travelers. One of the more interesting is a "squat" toilet instead of a "sitting" one. This style is popular in many parts of the world; the author has even encountered them in Paris. Depending on the location, it can be a literal hole in the floor (think outhouse; no flush) or a flat porcelain commode with molded foot rests on both sides and automatic flush (sometimes only after several users). You do not sit or lean on anything when availing yourself, so Westerners with physical challenges might find them very difficult. Cultures that use this design of commode prefer them as more sanitary because it is not necessary to touch anything. Public toilets may be used by both men and women at the same time— quite startling when you come out of the stall to find the other sex washing up at the sink. Public water closets may charge a small fee, either through coin slots in the stall doors or by tipping a human attendant who may be the sole dispenser of tissue, soap, and towels—no tip, no amenities. Toilet tissue varies to an astonishing degree in size, texture, and availability; smart travelers carry Kleenex and personal wipes for public restrooms without soap or tissue.

Learn key social phrases: *"Hello," "Goodbye," "Please,"* and *"Thank you."* Everyone makes mistakes, and a very smart thing to learn is the local-language equivalent of the phrase, *"Please forgive an outsider."* Also, realize that benefactors will gladly offer further insights if you ask them after they have pointed out your mistakes. They would not bother if they did not want you to succeed. View them as volunteer mentors who can show you the ropes and share insights. Finally, do not think that speaking in English makes your conversations private in another country. English, the language of computers, is widely understood even if it is not spoken.

When you travel, remember that a foreign country is not designed to make you comfortable. It is designed to make its own people comfortable.

—Clifton Fadiman, American author and radio personality

INTRUSIVE QUESTIONS

When you travel abroad it is common to hear, *"We like Americans, but not your government"* in countries that you might privately suspect of having corrupt governments themselves. You have a unique opportunity to correct any misconceptions of the United States that internationals have been taught by television and movies. Other cultures might feel very free to ask personal questions of strangers or delve into topics that could embarrass you, such as:

"How much money do you make?"
"Can you help me get a visa to study in the United States?"
"Why are there so many addicts [or guns, divorces, unemployed] in the U.S.?"
"Why aren't you married?" . . . *"Why is a young woman traveling [or living] alone?"*
"Why don't you have children?" . . . *"Don't you want a son?"*

Remember that local nationals will define you based upon their own cultural assumptions. Develop a global mind-set and a gracious coping strategy for "rude" conversations by practicing diplomatic responses to the questions above and similar others. For requests, be polite but do not commit yourself unless you can deliver. Being a citizen ambassador requires as much civility as being an official representative. Please, pick one aspect of the host country—its medieval history, the local dance or music, their handcrafted wares, the food—something respectful and *positive* to comment upon when anyone asks how you like it there.

GIFTS AND SOUVENIRS

Please see Chapter 25: International Protocol and Civility for courtesies involved in official gift-giving. This section deals with personal token gifts. Even if you are lower ranking or meeting primarily American compatriots while overseas, carry a few small gift items from home along with your correspondence cards. Writing an individual thank-you note to especially helpful people or mentioning their names in notes to their superiors is always one of the nicest gifts you can give. In addition, small farewell gifts are appropriate for local escorts, translators, or others who are especially helpful—even drivers assigned for the duration of your business trip. This type of gift is generally appreciated because it is understood that the recipient has no obligation to reciprocate, as you are leaving the country. If you plan to buy the very latest issues of magazines to read while on the plane, do not discard them; save them to give to interested associates (American or foreign) as they may not be available locally. Staple your business card on the cover with a note such as, *"Thought you might enjoy the cover article"* (see page 208 in Chapter 12: Correspondence and Stationery Essentials). Remember to be gracious and present gifts with both hands.

It is a good idea to consider inexpensive gift items even for American *expatriates* (citizens resident in another country) with whom you will be working.

Although some cultures disapprove of food gifts being brought into the country (check on customs regulations), usually small sealed containers from the United States are acceptable (check airline regulations regarding volume of liquids allowable in hand luggage if considering something like maple syrup). An alternative is to purchase two or three boxes of imported chocolates or bottles of liquor from the airport duty-free shop to ensure that you have gifts on hand. Your authors like to take gifts pertaining to the next U.S. holiday, especially if we know that a business associate has children. American expatriates yearn for symbols from home, and secular Easter and Christmas items often intrigue even foreign contacts. It can give locals "status" in the eyes of their friends to display or share a gift from you along with a story of "my American friend's childhood memories." For example, tell them about Thanksgiving gatherings around bowls of whole nuts if giving a nutcracker and pick set with a bag of pecans (considered the American nut), or give an Easter bunny nestled in cellophane grass or jelly beans and tell them about hunting colored eggs, or give a Christmas stocking filled with candy canes. Pack flat gift bags and tissue paper (research country-appropriate colors) to wrap items after arrival, because airport security might tear open pre-wrapped gifts.

The final international gift suggestion pertains to the traveler's daily associates. Consider buying small, inexpensive mementos for folks in your office (as well as immediate family members). The Japanese call it *omiyage*; Indonesians call it *oleh-oley*; other cultures also have special words to refer to a custom that has more significance than mere souvenirs. In mountainous Japan and the tropical jungles of Indonesia, for example, journeys away from one's own close-knit circle were historically arduous and risky. A returning traveler presented everyone with gifts reflecting the journey so that the unity of the group could be re-cemented and everyone could be included vicariously. Everyone can take this tradition as helpful guidance. Keep this idea in mind when someone from another culture visits you in the United States also. Offer ideas for low-cost mementos for *their* family and friends and help them acquire them, such as patches representing the local university or your military Service branch; sample products that local businesses produce; or items from museums, historic landmarks, or gift shops in your area. It is the well-mannered inclusion of others that counts, and counts, and counts.

CHAPTER 25

International Protocol and Civility

When meeting someone of another culture, especially if you are a guest in their country, it is important to convey respect for their customs. Many societies place much greater value on civility (respectful demeanor, a controlled face, a pleasant voice, good posture, and restrained gestures) than does the United States. Always err on the side of formality to show that you have good manners. Americans can appear arrogant or threatening when they use loud voices, frown or employ skeptical expressions, stand with hands on hips, or point with fingers or shoe tips. These actions are likely to be interpreted as anger or boorishness and may cause others to view you as untrustworthy.

AT EASE KEY POINTS

- Find a host country mentor. Research local practices.
- Shake hands to match: gently, firmly, or with further gestures.
- If locals restrict eye contact, look them right in the neck.
- Do not criticize religions, local dress, or attitudes toward women.
- Look at the principal, not an interpreter.
- Follow *Seating* and *Introductions* precedence.

In multicultural environments, professionalism is paramount to ensure that our personal opinion, the organization point of view, or the U.S. position is presented in the most favorable light. In the global village, this primarily means the dignified and respectful use of language—verbal language, written language, and body language—so that we do not discredit our organization, our country, or ourselves. International standards are presented throughout this book, but this chapter explicitly states courtesy codes for everyday interactions across cultures to help avoid misunderstandings, confusion, possibly even hostility. If you follow well-accepted guidelines, it will greatly reduce the possibility that someone from another culture will feel slighted or threatened in your company. *However, the concepts presented here do not negate the necessity for your personal research into locally acceptable practices.*

PROTOCOL AND PRECEDENCE

International protocol can be described as the global code of civility. Accepted practices have grown among nations in the course of their associations with one another. Adhering to these practices creates an environment that facilitates courteous dialogue, which in turn builds mutual trust and strengthens relationships. Picture a sports field: One country arrives prepared to play football, another rugby, and others soccer. To get them all working together requires one playbook. The accepted one for worldwide civility is based largely on the official etiquette of Europe as formalized by the diplomatic Congress of Vienna in 1815. Governments, businesses, and special interest groups have referenced it ever since. If you master the concepts summarized here you will be more welcome onto the international playing field, because the informality of private life in the United States does not always prepare us to resolve social problems in an international venue.

In America, common sense and good manners might lead us "logically" to defer to an older, distinguished looking woman from a prominent country at the expense of a young man who appears junior in experience from a very small, emerging nation. Such genuine regard for age, females, and influence will not make anyone happy if the latter individual is *the* ranking diplomat, scientist, business executive, or academician representing his country.

When you deal with foreign representatives, they will be most concerned with their sense of entitlement and *precedence*. In the United States, citizens acquire status mostly through personal achievement, but in many societies it is granted by birth to the right parents, with those individuals boldly expecting deferential treatment and due honor. American emphasis on equality and working to achieve our own rank, status, or position is considered dangerous to the natural order for people who have been raised in such cultures; acceptance of one's lot in life keeps the peace. You may have an aversion to *inherited* hierarchies, but rank order is highly valued in the United States also; in the military for instance, so precedence is an easily grasped concept. In every arena, there is an established "pecking" order where deference is demanded of juniors. A group of chickens illustrates this. The top bird eats or drinks first and enforces supremacy by pecking on any bird in its way. The second ranking bird does the same, except always gives way to the dominant bird. The third bird submits to the first two, but not to any others.

The lowest ranking bird gives way every time and submits to being pecked on by every other bird in its flock.

Because Order of Precedence rules have been codified for two hundred years (adopted by more than 150 modern nations since the 1815 Congress of Vienna), ignorance is no excuse and deviations are viewed as deliberate insults to other nationalities. In short, every government representative yields to an international pecking order, but every government sets its own internal precedence and maintains its own diplomatic list. The Department of State maintains the official U.S. Government Order of Precedence, with the President being first, then other federal posts, down through diplomatic envoys, military ranks, and state governors (see one list in Chapter 8: Order of Precedence and Military Forms of Address). When the United States hosts foreign dignitaries, there is another precedence order for all official functions: first come Chiefs of State, followed by Heads of Government, then Foreign Ministers, next are Chiefs of Mission (ambassadors), and so on. The Chief of State and Head of Government might be the same person, but not always. In the United Kingdom, for instance, the Queen is the Chief of State, but the Prime Minister is the Head of Government.

A rank order list works very well, except when two or more representatives of equal rank attend the same official function. In that case, precedence is further broken down. Within the United States, it is usually by the date: that departments or agencies were established, of a state's admission into the Union, or when an official began service. Alphabetical lists are also used. But sometimes even simple decisions such as ordering by date or alphabet can create problems. Alaska is the forty-ninth state by date of admission to the Union but is the second alphabetically. Internationally, whose alphabet should be used for country names? The *United States* is low on an English list, but much higher on a French list, as *États-Unis d'Amérique*. Countries without alphabets rank order names based on the number of lines in their pictogram.

To keep nations from fighting, the Congress of Vienna determined that precedence of all diplomatic envoys of equal title will always be by the date and hour they arrive in country instead of by alphabet, physical size, the importance of the representative, or the relative influence of the nation they represent. When one nation sends a *Chief of Mission* to another country, he or she presents credentials to the hosting nation's head of government and is accredited (recognized) as *Ambassador Extraordinary and Plenipotentiary* by the host country on that date (like academic date of tenure or military date of rank). It does not matter if the ambassador is a young dot.com millionaire, a retired four-star general, or part of a royal family—it is first arrived, first recognized. The dates of accreditation for all ambassadors are published on the hosting country's Diplomatic List, and becomes their basis for ranking everyone else within that embassy (or legation) as compared to other countries' diplomats of the same position.

As a matter of interest, host governments issue distinctive, coded diplomatic license plates to help track accredited representatives. Usually, the lower the tag number, the higher internal precedence that diplomat has within his own embassy. Often the list of codes is public record or readily available to fellow diplomats.

Americans, with our emphasis on self-made reputations, are always surprised that nothing an individual does can move him or her higher in an order of precedence queue. It is the important position that is invited to official functions, no matter who the current title-holder may be, because diplomats change assignments as often as the military. The change of an embassy's ambassador or a legation's minister changes the relative positions of the entire staff. For example, if the Ambassador of Estonia arrived in London before the U.S. Ambassador, Estonia's only Military Attaché (who might be a Lieutenant Colonel) ranks higher than the American Defense Attaché (who is an Admiral) *the entire time Estonia's Chief of Mission serves* in the United Kingdom. The list is fluid; when the Estonian Ambassador departs, everyone moves up in the list with newcomers starting at the bottom—with the possible exception of some Catholic countries that prefer to honor the Vatican representative (papal nuncio) as ranking diplomat, no matter when he arrives. If the Estonian diplomats in our example are in town longer than any others of similar positions, they become the doyen or dean of the diplomatic corps and the attaché corps, respectively.

International finance, Olympic committees, worldwide media bureaus, academic associations, or any other international group interested in avoiding insult will consult the local Diplomatic List, as necessary, as the best unbiased source for settling multinational precedence questions. Outside of governmental and international organizations, the "rules of engagement" can vary even within the same country. Therefore, ask a host country mentor for specific guidance prior to public and private events.

American Embassy Precedence
American diplomatic missions are delegations, commissions, embassies, consulates, or legations led by diplomatic agents. Ambassadors head embassies, also called missions (hence "Chief of Mission"). Consuls General lead consulates; Ministers head legations; both follow ambassadors in rank. An American ambassador is the personal representative of the President of the United States when serving abroad, and embodies the sovereignty of our entire nation. By virtue of their Presidential appointments, ambassadors are afforded all diplomatic courtesy. They are addressed as Ambassador [last name] or Mr./Madam Ambassador.

Everyone but the chief of state is presented to him or her (*"Mr. Ambassador, may I present . . ."*). For more courtesies that high-ranking individuals merit, see Key Government Officials below. If the ambassador is away temporarily, his second-in-command takes charge and is called *chargé d'affaires ad interim.* An embassy without an ambassador is led full-time by a *chargé d'affaires (de missi).* When an ambassador is on a trip home, he or she is still high ranking, but does not represent the President until returning to post.

The mission staff is posted abroad to support the ambassador. When invited to a function but unable to attend, the ambassador may send a representative from the embassy in his or her place, but that person is not accorded more precedence than his own rank and title merits. The embassy may have a Defense Attaché Office. Military attachés take precedence among themselves according to their respective grades (e.g., Colonel before Major) and seniority of Service (Army, Marine Corps, Navy, Air Force, and Coast Guard in that order). Military attachés rank after the counselors of the embassy or legation. At a post where the Department of State has not assigned a counselor, they rank after the senior secretary. Assistant military attachés take precedence after the lowest-ranking second secretary of the embassy.

VERBAL FAUX PAS

The United States' freewheeling democratic outlook breeds egocentric language that can be insulting to internationals. Our fellow citizens make four frequent faux pas when talking with those from other cultures. First, we commonly think of ourselves and refer to ourselves as "Americans" when dealing with persons from North, Central, and South America. *All* persons living in these places are Americans, so claiming exclusive rights to the title will not build goodwill with them. On the other hand, in Asia everyone refers to us as Americans. Keep your correspondents in mind when referring to your nationality. Related to this egocentric worldview is to say *"the rest of the world"* in reference to any place outside U.S. borders. If you want to understand how dismissive or belittling this can be, recall how you felt when first seeing that wildly skewed tourist map of Texas taking up most of the space (as a joke) on a map of the continental United States. Assuming you are not Texan, your likely perception was that they had a disdainful view of your state and an aloof attitude toward you simply because you were not born Texan.

Equally inconsiderate (or lazy) is failing to enunciate local place names correctly. Lima, Ohio, and Lima, Peru, are not pronounced the same. A colleague living in the Athens suburb of Kefalari consistently mispronounced it Kelafari *for three years*, to his detriment. He did not care that Greeks and American expatriates alike were always irritated.

The second blunder is to assume that the American way is the better way of doing something. The United States is very definitely a junior "greenhorn" country from a worldwide perspective. Some cultures are thousands of years old and their citizens view decision-making, for instance, from the perspective of its likely impact on many future generations. Their methods have stood the test of time and they do work. Never criticize them by attitude, body language, or speech. It is easy to check yourself for a critical, impatient spirit: How many times do you say (or want to say), *"That's not the way we do it in the United States"*? Instead, speak quietly, with respect, at all times. Many of us get louder when frustrated, but shouting will not be considered forceful, just extremely poor manners, especially for women. Slow down. Most cultures do not hurry when they eat, converse, or work. Try to learn the metric system. Clothing and shoe sizes, temperature and distance—everything will be easier to understand if you master the international system of measurement.

If you learn from your mistakes, locals may be very tolerant of your lack of manners, even when your repeated errors create an uncomfortable, negative atmosphere for them. Please be respectful, dignified, and seek advice from a host national mentor whom you respect, and consensus from local leaders or elders (if appropriate) and *listen*, so that you discover the "proper" way to get things done. Even with a mentor, you will sometimes become frustrated when they simply do not appreciate that *your* way is so obviously the *best* way. For instance, it is natural for most Americans to single out a productive individual for public praise, but to do so will probably have the opposite effect you are trying to achieve. To be seen as a nonconformist is often to disrupt the group's harmony and mutual security. Your natural inclinations can create conditions (or reputations) that live on long after you leave.

The third transgression is failing to conform to local social greeting customs. Most cultures have long histories and traditions of civility. Learn the polite host-country language phrases to use during introductions, with the correct time-of-day greetings, such as good morning or good afternoon. Always make time for greetings—they are important. If you walk up to a group of people, greet everyone according to *local* custom, which may include far more basic courtesy than a quick smile and group hello before you turn to speak with one person. Listen completely to introductions before shaking hands or engaging in other greeting gestures (see Body Language Faux Pas below). Display proper respect by using correct forms of address (titles and honorifics such as Doctor, Professor, or Mr. and Mrs.) and last names. Do not employ the everyday American custom of addressing a person by first name immediately after initial introductions. Far from indicating immediate acceptance or friendliness to foreign colleagues, the presumption of using the given name of someone just met is insultingly familiar or disruptive to the highly valued harmony in most societies. In addition, try to greet internationals in their own language, even if you will never learn more. You will be surprised at how well you will be accepted just by changing "hello" to the local phrase, such as *"konnichiwa"* (Japanese) or *"hola"* (Spanish).

Finally, Americans love emphatic language, humor, and teasing, but these do not cross boundaries well. Words have different connotations; personal subjects are not regarded in the same ways. Learn how to say, *"I am sorry"* or other appropriate ways to apologize in the local language, along with basic civility phrases such as *"Please"* and *"Thank you"* if you do not speak it fluently. As discussed in Chapter 24: International Travel, if someone points out your mistakes it is because they want you to succeed. Ask them for more insights and treat them as volunteer mentors. Do not be overly defensive about others' personal remarks (excepting any type of harassment, such as sexual harassment). It might not be rude locally to inquire into your marital status or why you do not have (more) sons, how much you weigh, or what your clothes cost. As long as you are not divulging information affecting your personal or professional security, try to take it as a compliment that foreigners are interested in you. When you are newly arrived or meet locals and they ask what you will be doing in country, always say something like, *"I hope to have many varied experiences; what do you suggest I include?"* You will gain wonderful insights and friends if you focus on avoiding verbal unpleasantness at all times.

WRITTEN FAUX PAS

"You are what you write."

Written communications are considered an extension of the person composing them, especially in international forums. Precision is important. Materials must be translated, and if needed, verified for accuracy. It is a matter of respect to exchange written materials—speeches and toasts, gift-presentation remarks, briefing handouts, letters and contracts, even invitations—in as complete a manner and with as much lead time as possible. For instance, if it is important to receive a prompt response to an agenda or event invitation, be sure to explicitly request, *"Please reply by* [day, date]." Include a contact person and phone number in addition to the address (e-mail, facsimile, or street address) that you use to convey the papers.

Always remember that anything you provide might be made public. Be formal in language (no slang, spell out acronyms, do not abbreviate), use correct honorifics, titles, and ranks, and double-check the spelling of foreign names. Correctly address envelopes by using the official's title (perhaps by itself on the first line) and full name, followed by the street address, and so forth. In the United States, type the name of the country in capital letters on the bottom line of international addresses. Begin business letters or cover documents with the recipient's address again and polite salutations (Dear Honorific and Last name: or Dear Sir or Madame:) and end with formal expressions of thanks and closings (Sincerely, Very respectfully). Date your communications in the international fashion (day/month/year), spelling out the month to avoid confusion (10 January 2012). Employ the twenty-four hour clock (19.00 instead of 7:00 PM) as it is in universal use outside the United States. "Cross" your sevens (7), "slash" your zeros (∅), and spell out the words with the numerals in parentheses immediately following, as in: sixty (6∅). List enclosures in your cover document and include your contact information on each page (headers or footers work well) in case pages become separated.

Personal data are sacred. Do not transfer private information across borders by e-mail, facsimile, telephone, and so forth, if you do not know that the recipients will safeguard it. In the U.S. government, the *Privacy Act of 1974* protects American personal data. However, other countries may not consider your privacy a priority. For example, you may need to make online or phone reservations for an American delegation at a foreign hotel that requires names, passport numbers, charge account numbers, and the like. In confirmation, they may send you a transmission with names and a room list. It is the originator's responsibility to exercise due diligence by requesting the hotel's privacy policy before giving out anyone else's personal information (i.e., I may do as I like with my own data, but not yours). If you fear the receiving office does not have an adequate level of protection or confidential information guidelines, refer to United States Department of Commerce Web site, www.export.gov/SafeHarbor, for policies regarding collecting and handling private data. If you determine that there are not reasonable precautions in place you must at a minimum inform the delegation that the country (or company) does not ensure an adequate level of protection *before you make the reservations*. To protect yourself, obtain delegates' written permission to pass personal information before proceeding. (See Chapter 14: Personal Electronics Etiquette, for e-mail manners.)

Social correspondence can also hold more significance overseas. Please be aware that anything sent out by your office or yourself may be retained for souvenir value. Local nationals may greatly prefer a hard-copy invitation card and a dated menu card to computer-generated versions. These do not need to be translated. Invitations the world over use the same format (see Chapter 11: Invitations), and a dated menu card with American foods listed in English may be appreciated as reminders of meaningful social connections.

Q: I am an American working overseas. Is it OK to send fill-in-the-blank invitations in English to the locals? If so, can I use numbers for the date and time?

A: Yes to both questions. An invitation can be almost completely understood even in an unknown language, because all the components appear in the same internationally accepted order: the *host* requests *your company* at an *event* on *date* at *time*. All words except those in the address and phone number are most properly spelled out, but, like you, foreign diplomats have long resigned themselves to using numerals for the date because guests find it hard to recognize *tizennegydik, čtrnácty, neljästoista, fjortonde,* or *décimocuarto* as *fourteenth.* Send your English language invitations to nonnative speakers with the time in 24-hour clock numerals—in near-universal use with a period instead of a colon (i.e., 19.30 for seven thirty).

Q: Here at my overseas post their customs do not seem to include thank-you notes. Should I still do them?

A: Yes. Americans with good manners stand out in the United States also. Handwriting a thank-you note is often overlooked as a simple method for fostering relationships and personal connections, always important abroad. You probably have at least one language in common with your hosts, but if not, keep the reason for your note understandable by starting off with the local word for "Thank You" (e.g., *Gracias, Merci, Danke*) before continuing in a few short English sentences. It might behoove you to have several useful phrases translated (*"Thank you for your hospitality," "Thank you for your time," "Thank you for your generosity"*) because good manners ensure that you will be remembered (and included) in future.

International Business Cards and Exchanges

No matter if you are lower ranking, or working primarily with American compatriots while overseas, carry a good supply of business cards, since people exchange them even in non-business situations. Order business cards in a clear, plain typeface so that nonnative readers do not need to struggle with modern exotic or antique gothic English script. In addition, a "clean" card has much more presence than a crowded one; less is more. If you will be conducting frequent business in a foreign country, consider having the reverse side of your business cards printed in the host country language in a font similar to the front, or ordering separate host language cards. "*My bilingual business cards have proven invaluable, particularly for spelling my name and e-mail address correctly. FYI: Contacts seem to regard the mere receipt of my cards as an honor,"* said a diplomat client of ours working in Egypt. Obviously, the simple act of bestowing such an "honor" often pays handsome dividends in future business dealings with the same people. Please see Chapter12: Correspondence and Stationery Essentials for the proper format for business, social, and correspondence cards.

If you want their business cards but international acquaintances have not asked for yours, ask for theirs only as the conversation concludes, and offer yours in return. A level of rapport needs to be developed prior to the exchange. Wait for VIPs to initiate a card exchange—after all, there are always ways to contact public figures. An ambassador's wife told us about asking for someone's card at a host country social event. Even though she was careful to receive it properly, it changed the entire tone of their personal interaction because the local national felt reduced to the level of trade. If someone presses you to take his card as you are introduced, and you know that the present circumstances are not the time or place, simply accept it quietly and put it away immediately (one does not comment on others' manners). Keep your own business cards in a single pocket and designate another for cards received so that you do not give out someone else's card by mistake—doubly embarrassing overseas. Female executives without pockets in evening clothes make sure to carry a purse with enough room for business cards.

Q: During the Cherry Blossom Ball in Washington, D.C., I met a Japanese CEO. He presented his business card but I don't own cards and I didn't know what to do. I have now generated some on my computer. Should I mail him one?

A: Since you have his address, this is a perfect opportunity to do some "personal connecting" by sending a handwritten note saying how honored you were to have been introduced, where you met, and your hope to meet again. If you do not yet have personalized correspondence cards, use a commercial one, being sure to legibly print your name, address, phone number, and e-mail address under your signature. Do not enclose a social or business card—it is too late for that exchange. FYI for the next time: the Japanese present and accept business cards with both hands, print facing the recipient. Pause to read cards you receive, and do not write on them in front of the giver.

Citizens of the world make every effort to present and accept items properly in an international forum. To offer and receive business cards with foreign nationals it is courteous first to put down anything you are holding. Sometimes it will be acceptable to use your right hand only, or your right hand supported by the left (culture-dependent) along with a nod (bow). However, the best way is to offer your business card with both hands, the thumbs and forefingers holding each top corner, the print facing the recipient. Accept another's card by taking it with the thumb and forefinger of both hands at each bottom corner. A joke that circulates in the Peace Corps has local nationals asking, *"What do even Americans respect? A peanut, because they must hold it in both hands to open!"*

Spend a moment holding another's card and reading it respectfully. If you are at a conference table with many new faces, place their cards in front of you in their seating order for quick reference so that you can address them respectfully by honorific and name. Put cards away at the conclusion of the conversation or meeting, in a card case or a breast-pocket or front jacket pocket, as foreign nationals may be offended if you put their cards in your hip pocket and sit on them. If you do not own a card case, consider buying one if they are a status symbol in your country of business.

BODY LANGUAGE FAUX PAS

Avoid any actions that disrupt the social order or call attention to yourself. For instance, avoid crossing your legs because it points your foot at others and may aim the bottom of your shoe at them—both are rude in many countries. Staring with an expressionless face after making eye contact, without making any attempt at a polite greeting, is also rude. In most places, it is ill bred to eat while walking on a downtown street (the exceptions being in front of market stalls, food vendors, or during street fairs). Proxemics (use of space) can be an issue, depending on the culture. People may stand closer in conversation than you find comfortable, or you may find yourself continually taking another step forward trying to close the gap that makes you feel insecure.

Most citizens of the United States learn to claim about a three-foot bubble of restricted space around themselves, especially in a daytime, business context. Americans reach forward to shake hands, but carefully maintain this comfortable barrier and avoid touching in any other manner. Some nationalities touch each other often in conversation, but a stranger intruding past someone's "safety perimeter" makes him or her startle and jerk back, particularly if the stranger reaches toward the head—that is a privilege granted only to intimate friends and family. The only unfamiliar people allowed to touch strangers freely are those we employ, such as hairdressers, dentists, masseuses . . . and even then, people may be ill at ease until they have enough experience to relax, as any preschooler in a doctor's office can tell you. As a male military diplomat tells it, *"When the Korean gentleman*

seated beside me put his hand all over my leg it could have been an international inci-
dent! I'm not used to people touching me like that in conversation."

Grit your teeth if you have to, but do not move when someone from a foreign culture invades your perimeter to stand close to you or touches you often during conversation (haptics), because he or she is only obeying the local courtesy "comfort" zone. Keep your appearance approachable by standing poised and relaxed with good posture, head up, torso facing the speaker, and arms casually at your sides instead of the very uninviting postures of crossing your arms tightly in front of your body or clasping hands behind your back in the "at ease" position. If you are feeling crowded, gesture with your arms while talking (this requires physical space and widens the circle), invite a third person to join your conversation (bodies will naturally shift equidistant), or invite your conversation partner to sit down (be sure to choose chairs instead of the sofa).

Body movement and gestures (kinesics) are not easy to read across cultures. Nods do not consistently mean agreement, but can simply mean "I'm listening." Smiles and laughter do not always mean happiness or amusement, but instead are often signs of embarrassment. Handholding and linking arms are simple signs of family kinship or uncomplicated friendship. Males all over the world hold hands with each other to convey nothing more than respect and alliance, as Prince Abdullah, Kingdom of Saudi Arabia, did at the White House with American President George Bush on April 25, 2005, before global TV cameras. Only Americans were startled by the sight. Males carry small handbags (normally with a wrist strap) for money and accessories in cultures as close to ours as Canada; but American males object to "purses." Cross-cultural disorientation can occur when a "ladies-first" American culture meets a "gentlemen-first" culture while all are attempting to make a graceful entrance or exit through the same door.

Both males and females need to be aware that their eye behavior (oculesics) might be considered rude, challenging, or sexually provocative. Eye contact between conversation partners is only acceptable for specific (variable) lengths of time before stress levels rise and locals deem it "staring" or "rude." If the person seems uncomfortable, keep eyes directed away (usually down) while conversing and glance only occasionally at the person's shoulder or collarbone. On the other hand, locals may walk right up and stare at a stranger (you) without feeling at all rude, especially if by appearance you stand out in the crowd. International body language is such a nuanced subject that only greeting behaviors are discussed below.

Handshakes and Greetings

In multinational diplomatic, government, and military circles worldwide, the handshake is the socially correct greeting and the most typical for both men and women (see Chapter 19: Introductions, Conversations, and Farewells). In local business and social settings, however, the traditional greeting of the host country (if different) will probably be more common. In tribute to you, the outsider, an initial body language greeting may be a "Western-style" handshake (probably much gentler than you are used to), but it will almost certainly be followed by something else in cultures not rooted in Greco-Roman traditions. Reciprocate the local gestures to show respect for time-honored customs. This can be an adventure.

In New Zealand, when you encounter a Maori (the indigenous people) warrior at a first nation/native community event, he might be wearing a grass skirt and looking fierce with bulging eyes, spear and tongue thrust out by way of a challenge. You may advance when he moves his tongue to the right side of his mouth. You may even end up rubbing noses and saying *"Tena Koe"* (*"How do you do?"*). Other cultures also touch in greeting. A *salam* (Malaysia) is a two-handed maneuver. An individual's clasped hands will lightly touch your outstretched hands before his hands are brought to his chest, expressing *"I greet you from my heart."* The *mano* (Philippines) is a gesture in which you lift an elder's hand to your forehead. The international may pat you on the right forearm, the right shoulder, your back, or embrace you with or without an accompanying handshake. Others will greet you by clasping your extended hand with both hands along with a slight bow (lowering the head somewhat).

Some indigenous body language greetings involve no physical contact at all. A *namaste* or *namskar* (India) or *wei* (Thailand) is done with hands pressed together palm-to-palm (as if praying), and held chest high or under the chin with a nod, meaning *"I honor the sacred in you."* In other cultures a bow (Japan) from the waist is practiced. The lower ranking person holds his pressed-together palms higher or bows deeper and/or longer. (These gestures also express thanks and apology. Do not turn away while locals are performing these maneuvers!)

A Muslim may acknowledge an introduction with only a nod of the head and a smile, especially between genders. An unsophisticated man from a culture that separates the sexes socially might make a rude point of refusing a female handshake. A client in multicultural Rome wrote to us, *"I learned the hard way—ugh!— not to extend my hand to the Iranian attaché."* The best way for the Western female to deal with this situation gracefully is to put her refused right hand over her heart, bow her head slightly and say *"How do you do?"* or the local equivalent when introduced. If the male extends his hand for a handshake, however, the American female should reciprocate.

Social Kissing

In some cultures, you must expect a social kiss. In Latin America, for example, everyone greets and says good-bye to everyone else at a social function with kisses on both cheeks in place of or following a handshake. When an international friend introduces you to his or her group, you are automatically accepted and the others will include you in their ritual greetings and farewells. If the occasion is social, the very same stranger you meet and shake hands with at the beginning of the evening may try to kiss you when saying goodbye. If a person of the same sex attempts to kiss your cheek(s) after a brief introduction or after a short social function, it may violate a cultural bias of your own that you will not fully appreciate until you are confronted with it. A client writing from Egypt reported, *"I took the new American Naval Attaché to meet some close office contacts in Port Said. After two years in the Middle East, I didn't think a thing of it as we greeted each other with the check-to-cheek kiss. The Naval Attaché had not seen this before and was quite taken aback. I could tell that he was in shock and praying hard that these guys would not try to kiss him! He made sure of this by extending his hand and arm WAY OUT FRONT to make sure a good old American handshake was all that was exchanged."*

In cultures practicing social kissing, the usual procedure is for the right cheeks to touch during the handshake or in place of it, accompanied by a soft but audible inhalation through the nostrils, or a kissing noise. Actual lip contact is usually avoided. In some countries, just the one cheek-to-cheek will be common (as in the United States), in others it is both (in Venezuela, for example) and in others it will be customary to do right-left-right, or three touches (common in Belgium); rarely it will be four or more. Just remember that the sequence is right cheek first (lean to your left) and then the other (pull back from the neck to turn your head to the right as they turn theirs). Readers may observe extensive social kissing between teammates during TV coverage of the Olympics and other international sports.

SOCIAL KISSING

Actually, kissing people hello takes some skill. First, you have to establish who is going to be the kisser and who is going to be the kissee. There should be no indecision once the kisser has decided to plant one on. He or she should grab the kissee by either the hands or the shoulders and kiss from the left (only vampires approach from the right).

—Erma Bombeck

Hand Kissing

Females may encounter men wishing to kiss their hands instead of exchanging a handshake. A gentleman entrenched in this tradition may raise the hand of a married woman as he bows over it. He will get close enough to breathe on the back of it, but will not actually press his lips to anything but his own thumb—germ protection for both of them and any other like-minded fellow who follows him. It is improper to kiss the hand of an unmarried woman unless she is older. Hands of leaders high in religious hierarchies (or the rings they wear to signify their rank) are routinely kissed by any adherent of the particular faith represented; non-parishioners simply shake hands. Other group loyalty gestures sometimes include a hand kiss also (*Godfather* movies, anyone?). American men should *not* kiss the hands of women, as they tend to look either awkward or give off unconscious sexual vibes.

KEY GOVERNMENT OFFICIALS

Royalty, government officials, religious hierarchies, and the diplomatic corps take precedence over public citizenry, as do uniformed personnel (military, police, firefighters) on duty. If you are lucky enough to meet the President of the United States, stand up when the President (or an official representative overseas, such as an ambassador) walks into the room and remain standing as long as the President is standing. Junior military personnel offer this same courtesy to higher-ranking superiors. For persons of consequence, however, standing to greet also extends to their spouses. Other high courtesies are to keep important people on your right side when walking, allow them to precede you through doorways, refrain from riding in elevators with them unless invited (you may be the official escort), usher them to their seats, and offer to help with their chairs, as needed. Key officials sit in the backseat, curbside, in a car with a driver, and their cars precede all others. During shipboard ceremonies, high-ranking officials are the first to step on deck and the first to step off; at airport ceremonies, they are last to board and the first to disembark. Always defer to the precedence of key government officials.

To do any of the following is to show that you have no appreciation for the nature of an official event or the offensiveness of your actions: Do not walk in front of escorted dignitaries, even if you are the advance person. Do not "work the room" before joining them at table, even if you are locally famous. Do not arrive fashionably late, dress inappropriately, or talk on your cell phone, even if you do so at all other venues.

Incumbent officials rank higher than do former officials; they are often referred to properly by title alone. For instance, U.S. Presidents are addressed as "Mr. President" while in office. Some government positions confer the rank or honorific for life, if the person chooses to use it. When greeting retired officials, use the title and last name together at all times so that there is no confusion about who currently holds the position, for example, "President Washington." An official's spouse is referred to by honorific and surname, no matter if actively serving or not, as in "Mrs. Washington." When referring to retired officials in writing or speaking about them to others, the correct form is *Former* President George Bush, *Former* Governor Arnold Schwartzenegger, *Former* Judge Roy Bean, and so on. For someone who has held many official jobs, call the secretary or assistant to ask what title the official prefers.

You may rarely entertain governmental officials or diplomats (or royalty or religious dignitaries), but you may meet them in receiving lines, be introduced to them, or attend functions where they are present. Mastering the proper courtesies will always serve you well as models for deference in every arena.

Introducing Foreign Leaders

For key government officials, royalty, and religious hierarchies use the phrase, *"May I present"* instead of *"May I introduce."* When you are introduced, wait for the complete introduction and for foreign dignitaries to offer a handshake first. Respond to introductions with the traditional *"How do you do?"* (For how-to-introduce formulas, see Chapter 19: Introductions, Conversations, and Farewells.) Internationally, check your assumptions that surnames or family names are always the same and always last in the spoken sequence. It could be that the surname is first, that spouses keep and are referred to by their own names, or that there are male and female forms of the same surname in the local language. Not every culture makes it as clear as some Asian ones, which underline the family name in print, or Francophone countries where the convention is to write surnames in capital letters.

Most of the time, you will need to research the country practice. President William Clinton learned the lesson of names the hard way. In July 1993 on a state visit to Seoul, President Clinton referred repeatedly and publicly to the wife of Korean President Kim Young Sam as Mrs. Kim, correctly remembering that surnames there are first in the sequence, but forgetting that Koreans keep their maiden names and her name was actually Sohn Myong Suk, or Mrs. Sohn. In many South American countries, double surnames (paternal and maternal) are used; the father's surname is listed first and is the one used with the honorific in conversation. In English-speaking countries, hyphenated surnames (such as Smith-

Jones) are used to honor both parents, but the paternal name is usually listed last and the entire combination is used with the honorific. In addition to being careful with titles and honorifics when addressing people who have high social status, be aware that sometimes a respectful honorific for elders in general society may be the local word for grandfather/grandmother, mother/father, or aunt/uncle.

Working with Interpreters

Depending on the participants and their status, the location, and the agenda level, you may need to locate interpreters for speakers of other languages (including sign language for the deaf). It is possible to hire fluent English/multilingual interpreters for verbal work, and translators for written document translation, nearly everywhere. Prior to the arrival of a foreign leader and delegation, negotiate with them concerning the leader's requirements, as well as the needs of other delegation members. Depending on the volume and intensity of the work, two or more interpreters may be needed for each language.

Consecutive Interpreters convert several sentences or phrases at a time from one language into another. They need paper and pencil to make notes. Speakers need to know if this method will be used so that they can adjust their delivery. Planners need to know because pauses to allow for translation will double the program time.

Simultaneous Interpreters normally wear headphones linked to the dignitary's microphone (or to a video broadcast monitor) and translate into a microphone connected to personal receivers worn by essential staff and press (as at the United Nations), along with a sound system so that members who understand the principal's language can hear. Simultaneous interpretation obviously requires much more in the way of technical support and advance planning, for example, each language needs an interpreter (or two).

All interpreters need to be in the presence of, or be able to see and hear the principals. Interpreters hold coveted positions because they sit or stand at leaders' elbows. Foreign leaders usually bring their own interpreters to important meetings. For instance, only U.S. interpreters are used to articulate the President's words. Normally the same few career staff personnel are vetted to accompany government leaders. These interpreters get to know leaders and their speech patterns really well. Interpreters are always used for international technical contracts, diplomatic state visits, and for such topics as arms negotiations, but not always for ordinary office meetings. Interpreting can take up to half the meeting time (because everything must be repeated), so executives often prefer not to bother for informal matters. High-ranking individuals in the international arena usually have a second and even a third language sufficient for most conversations.

Meet with the interpreter ahead of time to explain the schedule and essentials, such as dress requirements. Introduce him or her to the official for whom they will be interpreting ahead of time, if possible, to let them identify mannerisms or speaking idiosyncrasies and to discuss any technical terms to be used during the session. If possible, provide interpreters with scripts in advance, including any *PowerPoint Slides* or *Handouts* for meetings or press conferences, and any formal *Toasts* scheduled for meals. For important toasts, the host and guest of honor exchange written remarks a few days beforehand so that comments are pre-approved. Be prepared to record the actual toasts for the media, or to provide written translations if good press is desired. When printed *Speeches* are provided to event guests, they are in the original language as well as translated. The speaker must not omit or add wording so that what the interpreter is saying can be followed along on paper.

Accord an interpreter the proper respect by including him or her as part of the official party with a guest name tag indicating his or her position. The best seat for the host's interpreter is behind the host official (at the left elbow if the DV is at the right); second-best is beside the official (again probably on the left), for instance during a formal dinner. Interpreters never eat during official meals. Only those that have not worked with interpreters before will make the mistake of urging them to eat. If the interpreter's mouth is full at a crucial moment, it is very bad form and no one will be pleased.

If photographers or media are present, interpreters always step away during filming or picture-taking. They never appear between the principals. For heads of state, it is a breach of protocol for anyone to stand between them (except perhaps their spouses in a receiving line). Regarding receiving lines, if a guest of honor does not speak the local language and the host does, the guest of honor is placed beside the host (in the second position) so that the host can interpret for him or her as reception guests are introduced (see Receiving Line illustration in Chapter 18: Official Business Functions, Cocktails, and Receptions). Interpreters are not necessary in receiving lines.

DIPLOMACY IN ACTION

President Truman's Middle Eastern guest landed by helicopter on the south lawn behind the White House and was escorted through the closest door under the Truman balcony. He was so sullen at dinner that the President asked what was wrong. The interpreter explained that in the Emir's country only servants enter a house by its back door. President Truman immediately responded, "Sir, please tell the Emir that the White House has no back door. He entered the South Front." The Emir's status thus restored, his mood improved at once and so did international relations.

If you are the one communicating through an intermediary, look at the principal, not the interpreter, during discussions. Acknowledge the interpreter's presence at the beginning of discussions and thank them at the end, but otherwise, treat them as invisible unless they must ask you a direct question.

Limousine Protocol and Arrival Ceremonies

Drivers or chauffeurs defer to the person seated in their vehicles' place of honor and tend to do so automatically, even if a junior person mistakenly sits there. Most senior executives and ranking officials intuitively take the "VIP" seat—backseat curbside in any automobile with a driver (including taxis). The second seat of status is directly behind the driver. The middle of the back seat (and jump seats in limousines) is considered the lowest ranking unless there is to be an arrival ceremony.

For arrival ceremonies, the highest-ranking individual retains the back seat curbside, but the second ranking person must sit beside him in the middle, with the third ranking nearest the other back seat window. When the VIP car door is opened, dignitaries must exit in rank order to be greeted and escorted inside, observed for media reports, or their arrival announced to the crowd (for instance at Hollywood's Academy Awards or a military parade). If there is a fourth principal in the car, he or she sits in the front passenger seat and waits until the others have exited the back seat—the driver (or door attendant, escort, bodyguard) will close the back door and open the front passenger door, allowing the fourth principal to disembark last. The ranking dignitary *must* be the first person publicly greeted by the host as he or she arrives.

If you are a protocol officer or an accompanying escort, it is your responsibility to ensure that VIPs are seated properly for an arrival ceremony. If you are assisting at the arrival point, be prepared *not* to open the car door if you observe, for example, that a spouse or subordinate has been inadvertently seated backseat curbside instead of the principal. In that case, you (or the door attendant or military guard) must step up close to the spouse's door handle to delay matters while another escort or protocol aide steps smartly around the vehicle to the VIP's car door, opens it, and ushers the dignitary around the end of the car toward the host or the official greeting party. A Navy admiral finds it easier to exit from the driver's side because of an injury. His wife reports that sometimes, if she opens her car door too early at curbside, the Marines almost take her head off slamming it closed to make sure her husband exits first!

When VIPs depart in a car with spouses, the driver will open the back door curbside so that the spouse can enter first and slide over to sit behind the driver. Then the principal enters and the driver closes the door. The spouse who objects to sliding across the seat may lag behind until the dignitary is seated before moving to the traffic side of the vehicle for the driver to open the other passenger door, but this option is strongly discouraged because of safety concerns in cities with heavy traffic.

Another word about safety you may not have considered. In the United States, cars drive on the right-hand side of the road, which conditions Americans over a lifetime to look left when crossing the street. In some countries (e.g., the United Kingdom or Indonesia), cars drive on the left-hand side of the road. You will need to remember the distinction so that you do not step into traffic or head for the wrong side of the car in those countries; there, the VIP seat is the *left* rear (still curbside).

(In drive-left societies, people also move down the left side of hallways, sidewalks, and so on, which is why you will keep walking into people unless you are culturally aware. For more information on business travel and safety, see Chapter 24: International Travel.)

Make reservations for a commercial car and driver at least twenty-four hours in advance and determine payment method to avoid disruption at the conclusion of the trip. A non-refundable deposit may be required. Inform the service provider of the status level of the passengers so that you do not get a stretch limousine with flashing laser lights more appropriate for prom nights than VIPs. Limousines are customarily stocked with complimentary beverages (sodas, bottled water, and ice) and champagne can be ordered. Food is not consumed in limousines as a rule. Ask for limousines with privacy dividers, GPS tracking systems, and uniformed drivers with cellular phones, at a minimum. Other amenities include an intercom, television and DVD player, and stereo system. Chauffeurs ought to be on time, courteous, and professional. They pull their cars up as close as possible to pick up and drop off patrons. Allow them to open and close the car doors respectfully and to assist you in and out of a vehicle, if necessary. They also take care of packages, a walker, wheelchair, luggage, and so forth without drawing undue attention.

Brief drivers with explicit directions so that they can operate independently if they become separated from other vehicles in an official convoy. Prepare a list of key phone numbers, outline routes to be taken, and provide a map of any government facility noting stops 1, 2, 3, and so on, with directions on where to wait and when to return. At each drop-off point, the driver waits for the escort officer to escort VIPs to the door and return to the car, and confirms the next meeting point before driving away. It is customary to tip a commercial chauffeur at the conclusion of the evening (15 to 20 percent may be automatically added to the bill, so double-check paperwork). A government or military driver is prohibited from accepting a tip but would appreciate a note of thanks routed through his or her supervisor.

INTERNATIONAL BUSINESS MEETING ETIQUETTE

Initial meetings are for establishing trust via conversation, observing manners, and reading body language nuance. For instance, in time-conscious societies (the U.S is one) schedules are rigidly adhered to, but other cultures do not get upset or consider time "wasted" when people are late or digress to non-business discussions. If you go to their venue, make an early day appointment and arrive on time. Sometimes you will be kept waiting to judge your true interest in doing business, and locals are often free to interrupt your meeting once it has begun, but delays may be less in the mornings.

Speak the language of commerce or science or government in business meetings without using slang, especially sports and hunting slang—pervasive in America—or abbreviations and acronyms. Often the acronym is used so regularly that government personnel must pause to remember that TDY, PCS, and CONUS, for instance, are meaningless outside specific arenas. It takes but a moment to ensure there is no confusion by saying temporary duty, permanent change of station, and continental United States.

Greeting someone with a desk or table between you is an unnecessary barrier. If the meeting is in your office, walk to the door to greet foreign nationals. At the very least, team members stand up when the other group enters the boardroom and do not sit until the international visitors are offered seats. Greet the foreign leader or manager first, then others. Extend hospitality by offering water, coffee, or tea, and perhaps a pastry.

Negotiation tactics and decision-making styles differ across cultures. The process might begin by focusing on something you view as unimportant or best left to subordinates. It will actually be very important because personalities are being assessed. Pay special attention to the body language of the potential partners and be aware that they are carefully evaluating your nonverbal communication. Be patient. Wait for the foreign national to change the topic back to the business matter at hand, if he or she digresses.

Do not challenge or criticize individuals—it could seriously jeopardize another's *face* (dignity or reputation in front of others). Many cultures value group harmony and try to save face by avoiding the word "no." Therefore, remember that "yes" does not necessarily indicate agreement any more than a nod does. Both may simply mean "I hear you" or "I understand you." Avoid closed questions that require a yes or no answer (*"Will you attend the function?"*) Instead, ask open-ended questions (*"When do you think we can sign the contract?"*)

Be comfortable with the idea that no decisions may be reached; the first couple of meetings may be for checking you out and gathering facts. Are you trustworthy?

Are you respectful? Do you stick with decisions? Are you logical or emotional? There must be a confidence-building platform on which further serious discussions will build. Nothing will be accomplished internationally without this building of trust and personal relationships. See Chapter 1: Military and Government Protocol for more on meetings and conferences.

CHAPTER 26

International Guest and Host Duties

*I*f you are sensitive to cultural differences, you may join a distinguished group of peers whose demeanor and attitude have had a very real impact on global relations. Catherine the Great of Russia appointed *"handsome men with good complexions able to consume vast quantities of liquor"* to support her international relations. Napoleon of France instructed his representatives to *"look after the ladies."* As an American in another country, you have an obligation to represent your own nation with pride.

AT EASE KEY POINTS

- ✧ Ascertain American reputation in the chosen society.
- ✧ Eat International Style. If hosting, review menu for religious sensitivities.
- ✧ Develop signature gift and meal ideas. Receive and present with both hands.
- ✧ Determine local social season cycle.

Although Americans become quite accustomed to participating in all types of social events during our professional careers, an international function places a different emphasis on our conduct. We must be doubly conscious of being socially correct because the shorthand way people evaluate us (and those we represent) in new situations is through our social skills.

Many societies are so hospitable that you will be included in a social occasion after only a few meetings. If you are serving in any official capacity, you will definitely be "noticed twice." American military stationed overseas are often invited to national day celebrations where their uniformed presence adds "color." American public servants stationed abroad attend counterpart government-hosted events, sometimes as trophy guests, especially if the United States has been in the local news recently. Visits by American business and government leaders are often considered "high profile," and social events are always planned to take advantage of their newsworthiness; usually local media are invited.

Accept as many local invitations as possible during the first six months of an overseas assignment. In most countries, if you refuse an initial offer it will not be extended again. Some invitations will come your way because locals assume that you are interested in host country customs and rituals and they want to share their cultural heritage. Other invitations will be command performances because of your job title or your boss's job title. You are always invited for what you can contribute to the event; therefore mastering multicultural civility is essential.

AMERICAN REPUTATION

Everyone cherishes his own culture, sometimes to the point of rejecting foreign influences because of fears that traditional values are threatened (xenophobia). Sometimes local nationals will closely observe your manners, fully expecting Americans to be culturally offensive. Surprise them by being sensitive. If you think for a moment, you can see why the United States does not have the best international reputation. Media reports focus on bad news, so greedy, violent, dishonest, disrespectful Americans are in newsprint and film every day. Hollywood films and television shows also depict less-than-admirable American lifestyles.

Encourage mutual trust among American and foreign business associates by becoming comfortable in local surroundings and living conditions. If ignorant of your host culture, do research, especially to ascertain how Americans are viewed. Find a mentor and ask questions. (Use great care in choosing a knowledgeable person, as your tendency will be to default to them as authorities.) If you discover that Americans have a disadvantageous reputation locally, actively work to counteract the negatives. If Americans are seen as disrespectful, dress conservatively and behave formally while listening carefully to everyone in the room. If Americans are perceived as always in a hurry, have your first business meeting over tea or coffee without pursuing your business agenda; be calm and relaxed as you develop a relationship.

Ask a foreign national ahead of time what order of events to expect during a specific occasion. Show that you are a well-mannered guest who can adapt to local social circumstances, no matter if the local dignitary you came to meet does not appear or the event does not proceed according to plan. Be sure to ask if it is likely that you will become the center of attention in some way (perhaps through a toast) so that you can prepare to represent your organization and your country with dignity.

Excellent Multicultural Guest Manners

R.s.v.p. properly (within forty-eight hours) and with enthusiasm so that local hosts feel confident and pleased to have included you. Dress conservatively to present yourself well (women must avoid form-fitting and scanty clothing). Learn the local dress terms, such as Red Sea Rig (tropical tuxedo without jacket) or National Dress (outfit representing your country).

Bring a small hospitality gift (preferably from your home country; see International Gift-Giving below) for an invitation to a private home. In some cultures, a well-intentioned gift of an American food item might indicate to hosts that you do not think they will feed you sufficiently or that the local food is not good enough. Insult is not taken if the food is a common local gift such as a box of chocolates. Present your gift with both hands to whoever greets you at the door.

When you arrive in an international social gathering, pay your respects in the accepted manner: first to the host, then the guest of honor or elders of the household, if identifiable, followed by greeting each individual present (unless the gathering is very large). Local nationals may never approach you, believing that it is your duty to make the first move. A diplomat spouse in Cote d'Ivoire reports her success: "*I was invited to participate in African tribal dance lessons because of my persistence in trying to communicate. I give the language my best shot with the promise that the next time I see them I will have learned ten new words to try out on them.*"

Look for a guest book, name tags, seating chart, and receiving line. Sign a guest book by printing your name, wear the name tag on your right shoulder, talk to other than your future dinner companions during cocktails, and remember that the position invited goes first down the receiving line, followed by the spouse or date. (See Chapter 18: Official Business Functions, Cocktails, and Receptions for dealing with an announcer or photographer.)

Have a plan for connecting in large groups. It might be to circle the room once before getting something to drink, because the local custom is to exchange business cards during all introductions. It might be to agree on a time and place to meet later before socializing separately without your date, spouse, or colleagues. Dates or spouses must not inhibit the employee from working at business functions. Organization-hosted functions require staff members to "sing for their supper" because these events are continuations of the workday.

Introduce yourself properly. Always stand and step forward to meet someone, and shake hands (hold food and drinks in your left hand so that your right one remains available). Use honorifics or titles and pronounce names correctly. When you are new in a culture, you may be able to request a guest list if you let it be known that you want to practice pronunciation and memorize names.

America is now a land of minorities, familiar with diverse names; still, *Yannis Papazacariou, Pricha Cleauplodtook,* and *Sivasilim Tiagarajen* do not come trippingly off the tongue.

Talk graciously with other guests regardless of rank or status. Sophisticated people do not ignore each other simply because they do not speak each other's language(s). Smiles need no translation, and simply standing with someone for a while after you have introduced yourself will be greatly appreciated. Most international guests will at least know Host Country Language Lesson 101 ("*Hello.*" "*How are you?*" "*Fine, thank you.*" "*How is your spouse?*"). Using such simple ploys can fill quite a bit of time and make someone feel included who might otherwise have spent the evening staring at her shoes.

Do not sit down in a private home until invited. Always avoid the sofa's right-hand side as that is a common guest-of-honor seat. There may be a place of honor not obvious to Americans, such as beside the family religious shrine. Just as all show respect for all national anthems and flags, so too does everyone respect all religious symbols.

Many cultures equate food with hospitality. When food or drink is *offered* to you in a local home, you may decline respectfully or accept as desired. However, if it is *served* to you, never refuse and sample it at least. Declining provisions can be a personal affront, especially in more humble homes (guard your facial expressions). If you are a ranking guest, or married to one, you may be asked to start buffet lines or sit beside hosts. At table, do not eat or drink until the host indicates that you may. Pass food with both hands. Keep some liquid in your glass for toasts. (See Chapter 27: Manners at the Global Dinner Table for toasting mechanics.)

Join in planned activities—acquiesce with a song, a poem, or funny story if you are asked to contribute. Prepare something ahead of time, if colleagues warn you that such can occur. One Air Force attaché memorized an appropriate country western song, which he could recite as an epic poem; it got him through three overseas tours. Another attaché wrote, "*When we first got here we were asked to dance or sing something American at parties. I don't dance, so we sing* 'Home on the Range' *or* 'Deep in the Heart of Texas' (*our state*) *and the* 'Halls of Montezuma' (*my branch*)."

Before departure in some cultures, it is important that everyone say goodbye to everyone else. Guests of honor may be required to leave a party first, or stay until all others leave. Normally, hosts must open the door before guests can leave a home. International hosts may expect you to declare repeatedly your intention to depart before they allow you to go, if it is good manners to insist that guests stay.

Write thank-you notes. Always write thank-you notes. Americans must show appreciation of courtesies received. They must also reciprocate social invitations.

Hosting Internationals

"If you want to get your point across, entertain."

Many Americans may live abroad for weeks or years in support of foreign relations, politics, or commerce. Others aid visits to and from the United States involving international business officials (chief executive officers, boards of directors, city representatives), government dignitaries (congressional and governor delegations), diplomatic personnel (current and former heads of state and ambassadors), or military flag officers and their delegations. Whenever people get together internationally, no matter the arena, they often socialize together also.

Americans are assumed to have money and resources, and therefore able to extend hospitality and to reciprocate social or business entertaining. Funds may be authorized for hosting if it directly promotes your employer's interests. This is called *representational entertaining*. Most organizations wanting respect in a foreign country learn quickly that one of the better ways to foster friendships and further relationships despite different nationalities or governmental philosophies is by hosting a social event. Also, scientists, photographers, ballet dancers, religious group members, sports aficionados, sorority and fraternity affiliates, professional guild members, hobbyists—all have something in common, regardless of nationality. Americans abroad have the privilege of connecting with similar others, whether or not it is an official duty. So re-evaluate the ritual of social events to discover their value to your transnational government, business, or personal objectives.

Extending Invitations Abroad

Whether you plan functions for business or pleasure overseas, be sure that you understand the local social cycle. If you arrive during the slowest social time of the year, you will meet fewer people and this could affect your visit success or adjustment to living there. Let's take northern Europe as an example, since their social cycle is similar to mainland United States. The season begins in September, when children are in school and the weather grows more comfortable. It builds to the yearly social peak at Christmas and New Year's, then dies back down. There is a smaller peak at Easter, and during warmer weather there may be some increase in social activity, but there are no parties at all in July and August during the hottest weather when people traditionally take thirty-day out-of-town vacations.

Climate, important local holidays, and differing concepts of time and punctuality also affect social activities. The southern hemisphere enjoys summertime in December and January. Religious observances dominate social activity in the Middle East. Guests might leave your home at the stroke of eleven in northern European countries, yet not even arrive until that hour in many South American nations. Those who routinely battle heavy traffic in any number of congested cap-ital cities have learned not to be unduly concerned with arriving late.

Some cultures do not consider an invitation issued during conversation as genuine. It is as if you had said, *"Let's get together for lunch sometime."* They may answer *"yes"* to be polite, but you must follow up. Many will feel under no obliga-tion to respond to the R.s.v.p. on a mailed invitation either. If you are hosting a social event with internationals, it would be a good idea to contact every person by phone to invite them (this is even done by the White House), then send a printed *p.m.* (To Remind) *card* (see Chapter 11: Invitations). Strategy in the host country may also require another phone call close to the day of your event—inter-national etiquette accepts that all hosts need definite answers in order to plan a function. However, hosts in societies where buffet meals or communal platters are the norm might find themselves making room for more people than invited—indeed, it is an honor for extra people to show up. Guests invited to your event in these places might feel free to bring along friends whom you do not know. If this happens, receive them graciously because your invitee is advertising his close rela-tionship with you.

Q: A South Korean businessman was invited to visit our company headquarters in Illinois, but when he arrived no one met him at the airport. When he got himself to our building no one from the company seemed to know about him. What can we do for damage control to repair our international corporate relations?

A: A sincere apology letter written by your Chief Executive Officer (CEO) should be *hand-carried* from your satellite office in Korea directly to the businessman with an offer to reimburse him for his travel costs immediately. A local protocol advisor from your satellite office (or the American embassy) will be able to provide further ideas, perhaps recommending that a substantial "company" or "engraved" gift item might further assuage the situation; or that another headquarters invitation be issued, this time with a named escort who will meet him at the airport with a limousine.

Q: What is American protocol about when to curtsy or bow?

A: In the United States, only performers or honorees on stage acknowledge the applause of an audience with these gestures. Men bow from the waist, women bow or curtsy (bend the knees with one foot behind the other). Americans do neither before their own leaders nor to foreign royalty. Instead, we deeply nod our heads in formal respect.

Remember that in many places an offer of hospitality (invitation extended, food or drink offered) needs repeating at least three times to be considered sin-cere. Be aware that there is a possibility that invitees will not show up even after agreeing to be there, because saying yes was a ploy to save face for both of you at the time (culture-dependent). However, the local population will most likely attend your gatherings simply because you are American and they want to check you out. They will view you as reflecting an accurate image of your family, your profession, and all Americans in your age range. You will be a "goodwill ambassador."

Hosting Internationals for Business

Some cultures insist that social relationships precede or accompany business discussions. A degree of trust and friendship must be developed informally; therefore, time spent together in conversation over food (possibly with wine at both lunch and dinner) is part of the learning process. Hosting such events is not the same as holding a party in Suburbia, U.S.A. Your demeanor is under evaluation and it will establish your personal status as well as your employer's reputation.

Whether you are (or are simply married to) a military person, business agent, spokesperson, academic representative, or government diplomat, if you host an international social affair you would be wise to practice civility. In addition to the multicultural guest manners listed above, make every effort to honor high-ranking invitees who have earned deference in their own countries, because they will be thin-skinned when it comes to their status in a multinational forum. Greet people properly with honorifics; introduce and seat them according to precedence. (See Chapter 23: Seating Plans for comprehensive seating information, and Chapter 1: Military and Government Protocol for developing agendas, programs, and briefing papers.)

Ideas, Techniques, and Tools

Multicultural business or social events need to appear seamless and smoothly run. Invited guests could be military, diplomatic, international, business, social, or a combination. The goal of business entertaining is to ensure that information is exchanged with your organization's point of view presented in the most favorable light. That involves lots of planning. Smart Americans take social roles seriously and plan carefully.

Develop master checklists and databases to serve as your private "yellow pages" with such information as neighborhood service providers' hours and shopkeepers' names. The planner in digital format allows you to easily update and share information. Your records can include correct pronunciation of guest names (including spouses), who has lived in the United States, whose son just went off to an American college, and the last time they were officially hosted by your organization. As you work with your database, it will become annotated with a record of how well the events went, caterers' menu successes, and future suggestions for improvement.

Put out a guest book in the reception foyer or in a corner of the cocktail area. Head each new event page with the day's date. If international guests seem leery of this practice, buy a large host country picture book with room to write directly on the pictures or around edges of the pages, and ask them to *print* their names and their organization's name. Tell guests that the picture book is a souvenir or memory book and will be retained for that reason as well as a record of official visitors and business social events.

Develop seating charts and place cards. Precedence order is important and these tools let everyone know that you have taken care to honor the highest-ranking people in the room. Planning committees may need to guard place cards so that no one re-organizes them to gain better access to the host or guest of honor. Policies should be considered for dealing with arrivals who are not on the guest list, and how long the event or dinner will be held for late guests.

Assign greeter, facilitator, and gatekeeper roles from among your colleagues. American flag lapel pins on the left lapel of civilian clothes (not uniforms) help identify them at large functions. Every important function requires a rehearsal or walk-through with everyone involved: hosts, co-hosts, protocol officers, escorts, security personnel, photographers, and wait staff. The dry run gives participants confidence; everyone becomes familiar with their responsibilities and can anticipate possible problems. A ranking official or executive—not a junior person—greets all foreign delegations at their car door (best practice for diplomats and high-ranking officials) or at the lobby (front) door so that they will feel warmly welcomed. Escort delegations into the venue, usher them to their seats for meetings, or offer a drink at cocktails and introduce them to others. Make introductions clearly and slowly so that honorifics and full names can be absorbed. Hosts and facilitators stay until the end of the function in order to be on hand to say goodbye and escort people out. See Chapter 1: Military and Government Protocol for more information on escorting Very Important Persons/Distinguished Visitors and Chapter 18: Official Business Functions, Cocktails, and Receptions for Receiving Line diagrams.

Menu Planning is necessary in order to accommodate religious dietary laws (consult Chapter 30: Food and Drink Preferences of Various Religious Groups, for taboos). International hospitality has been defined as the ability to pour cold water warmly, which is the very least you ought to do.

- **For office meetings**, put beverages (tea, coffee, juice, water, soft drinks), and snacks on a table in front of seated visitors who will not be served a meal (otherwise review Chapter 27: Manners at the Global Dinner Table). In business and social settings, it is the responsibility of the host to take the initiative to start the program, make opening remarks, and offer guests some refreshment. Be prepared for guests to ignore the food while business conversation proceeds until you specifically invite them to partake. Guests may politely refuse your first offer of food or drink; keep offering it to internationals as many as three times (culture-dependent). After three tries, if the guest still declines, you may stop offering. If they take refreshments, they will politely compliment them. Be aware that in many cultures a host's invitation to eat or drink is a signal that the call or visit is drawing to a close, so your guests may think that you are urging them to leave. Also, the first office visit in many countries might more appropriately be deemed a short social or courtesy call. Visitors are introduced in protocol order, and will perhaps present the office host with a small token gift, partake of offered beverages, make polite conversation, and depart fairly quickly. Subsequent visits will be business-oriented. (See Chapter 1: Military and Government Protocol for more on Office Calls.)

- **For business dinners**, the focus remains on relationship cultivation, which means putting your guests at ease. For internationals unfamiliar to you, always request information about what they cannot eat or drink and record it for future reference. (Do not say "allergy." President Bush senior was not allergic to broccoli—he just hated it, as everyone in Washington knew.) Individual menu cards at a dinner table are useful for informing guests about food ingredients. For buffet tables, a pig carved from a lemon or brussels sprout is a great nonverbal garnish to label pork dishes. It is a thoughtful gesture to provide fruit juice or flavored waters for nondrinkers; unopened individual bottles at their place settings will reassure guests who avoid alcohol.

HOSTING INTERNATIONALS AT HOME

Tailor your entertaining efforts to what the locals find comfortable. Some cultures socialize before eating and leave immediately after dinner. Other countries reverse it. You can see the problem if a "socialize after" host invites "socialize before" guests and serves a meal very soon after the guests arrive—they may feel that they are being rushed away. Invite at least two foreign nationals so one person alone will not feel insecure. Be very specific about time, place, dress, and travel directions. Know the position and status of your guest in his or her own country and invite other American guests who are similar.

Wait staff serving formally at table is preferred in many societies because it allows hosts to relax with guests without running in and out of the kitchen, checking on food, or acting as servers. Americans entertaining in cultures accustomed to formal dining will want to consider hiring help, even for very casual events, because hosts are expected to stay with guests. Although your local friends may remain quite formal in their own entertaining, remember that everyone likes variety and they will be interested in how social events are typically hosted in the United States. Feel free to invite guests to a breakfast, barbecue lunch, or tea instead of evening events.

In other international settings, food is always offered buffet-style to accommodate choice (dietary diversity, portion control, religious restrictions) and lavish displays will be expected—a problem if your budget is tight. Another consideration with buffets is seating. Internationally, do your best to provide tables and chairs for everyone, as eating while standing or balancing plates on laps makes many nationalities uncomfortable. At the Washington home of an American rear admiral who was hosting a buffet dinner, a Ukrainian general was eating from a lap tray when a U.S. official walked over to meet him. The polite Ukrainian immediately stood up and spilled his entire meal all over the host's floor. For casual events, it helps if hosts enclose an explanation sheet (as you might maps and directions) with their invitations for concepts such as Open House or Brunch that might be locally unknown. Be sure to give "how to proceed" directions before guests navigate your buffet line. It may be obvious to you that Eggs Goldenrod goes over the toast points, but not to everyone.

Signature Meals

Invest time in perfecting a "signature" food to serve to foreign guests. Serving U.S. regional cuisine or your family's specialties helps make your guests feel especially honored. Limit your choice of American food to one course only; guests might find the novel taste combinations a bit overwhelming otherwise. For example, celebrate some aspect of your home state in menu form: Midwest Johnny Appleseed Celebration or New England Clam Bake. A host might develop a menu card complete with an outline map of Texas marked with a star on his hometown to highlight his family's authentic, handed-down recipe for chili or barbecue. Another host from Minnesota might feature wild rice harvested by Indian ancestors in the time-honored manner from the lake near his birthplace, and someone else might celebrate his heritage by sharing curry with all the condiments "just like Mother used to make."

If this idea appeals to you, plan to serve the chosen dish as your standard "house special" to make entertaining easy. Always share a short explanation (between courses or at dessert) about why you have chosen it for your guests. Tell them where you were brought up or have lived, of family heritage traditions, or about convincing your aunt to share her secret recipe. U.S. Secretary of State Colin Powell regularly hosted all the Chiefs of Mission (ambassadors) and their spouses at the ultimate American theme party—a July 4th barbecue on the top floor of the Department of State building because it provided a great view of fireworks around the Washington Monument. His menu was mini hot dogs and burgers, popcorn, mini apple pies, cookies, and lemonade.

Serve the kind of food you usually do in order to share your real life, but look for the nexus between the cuisine of your guests and regional American foods. For example, spicy Louisiana recipes would most likely appeal to your friend, the Indonesian, whereas simple New England cuisine would be a safer choice for an unknown Scandinavian. Since America is an immigrant nation, *anything* you grew up eating, or like to cook and serve, will probably be appropriate. The only caution is to consider not serving Italian food to the Italians or Chinese food to the Chinese, and so forth, since they would probably find no joy in eating what is likely to be imitations of their ordinary, everyday fare. Serve food instead that is unusual for your guests. Even turkey and mashed potatoes are exotic in Japan.

When inviting foreign nationals to your home, be mindful of local manners. Hosts may need to pass snacks repeatedly, even at informal gatherings, if guests consider it improper to help themselves. National cultural habits also affect the type of hospitality you extend. A long luncheon is not the best idea in a country known for afternoon siestas. A male-dominant culture may prefer "stag" events, so that their wives may be left at home.

Unfamiliar international guests might be silently reserved and formal, for instance, waiting for your proper introductions before they will speak to each other, or only answering your direct questions because English is difficult for them. Anything that takes time to accomplish allows conversation to develop. A military spouse wrote, *"We use hot stones to cook the meal at the dinner table, similar to the fondue pot idea. This is very useful when people can't communicate well with each other because it gives us something to do."* An Army major general's wife taught one of your authors to serve "cantaloupe soup"—half of a very ripe melon with a jigger of port in the hollow; eaten with a spoon to get some port with each bite. This course takes awhile with plenty of time to chat. The signature food itself can help inspire conversation with strangers—one of the reasons it is suggested. *"They were always astonished by homemade desserts, no matter how easy, since they always buy theirs,"* wrote a military wife in France. Another couple had great success by serving recipes from the White House Web site and said that the President's favorite cookies were a big hit. The more personal touches the better for representation.

No Common Languages

Prepare in advance to host internationals. Language barriers will be less awkward if you display picture books of the United States or family photo albums. It is very easy to establish rapport by sitting on the sofa looking at pictures with guests, without much need for words. Use a world map or globe to share where you have lived or traveled. Guests may like a tour of your backyard garden, or enjoy the view out a picture window—if you remain beside them for company. Organizational plaques or awards, and artwork or souvenirs from previous assignments, might spark common interest with your guests, providing opportunities for follow-up and closer friendship. A military spouse wrote, *"I wish I had more photos of my hometown and family. My sister was 'Employee of the Month' at her store and sent me a picture that I put in my living room. It generated lots of interest and conversation among my foreign guests."*

There are some problem-solving games that can be played without a common language, such as Sudoku (numbers 1–9 are used to fill in a grid without repeating; no math skills needed) or Tangoes (seven puzzle pieces combine to duplicate pictures; endless combinations). Short programs (no more than fifteen minutes) of singing or playing instruments can also help fill time pleasantly. Talented expatriate children who entertain their parents' friends sometimes find, much to their delight, that guests hire them for future performances. However, sometimes the presence of children and pets can be culturally inappropriate. Your children can greet foreign guests in your home, but excuse them immediately afterward, as their activity and conversation can be a great distraction when language fluency is an issue, or for cultures where children are commonly cared for out of the public eye. And never expect foreign guests to appreciate that you have a creature with claws and fangs living inside your home—always sequester pets in another room.

Interior Design as Representation

When you live overseas, your entryway or foyer ought to say United States of America, not another port of call. It welcomes you home after a stressful day and shares a little about who you are with your guests. A diplomat client wrote, *"We display the American flag and our state flag proudly and properly in our entryway. We also have some artifacts (tractor seat, scythe, maple tree topper, handsaw) and large photos of farm country from my home state, Minnesota, in the reception area."*

The media has popularized U.S. history for you, from pilgrims to astronauts. If you are from west of the Mississippi, Hollywood has led your host country to think that you wear spurs. Although you may never decorate this way in the United States, consider hanging a ten-gallon hat, lariat, or something "cowboy" on your wall. Every state has an association with an American Indian tribe. Display their artifacts or pictures, as does the U.S. Department of State in their Diplomatic

Reception Rooms. They report that foreign guests are drawn more to them than any other artwork on display.

An American overseas may be lucky enough to be living in a country where he or she can claim family roots (check for your family names in a local phone book). If so, be sure to "advertise" it somehow. An old marriage certificate, letter, birth or death certificate, or family bible record can be photocopied and framed. It would be quite a nice compliment to say that it gives you a thrill to walk down the local street looking at faces of people with whom you share ancestral bloodlines. Any physical genealogy object bolsters your "wholeness" and makes you approachable and memorable, especially if you tell a quirky or poignant story about a family tree relative. An old map or picture of the family farm gives you the chance to tell the story of how great-grandpa used to name his registered Herefords after his family members, some of whom did not consider it an honor, and how his haystacks looked exactly like the ones you saw on your travels through Slovenia. Even such a normally touchy subject as a criminal in the family is "colorful" if you can cite a connection to a pirate or notorious gunslinger.

A representational area need not be large. Designer calendars have beautiful pictures of America, from national parks to distinctive North American animals or endangered species, which can be framed for display at year's end. You can talk about the "exotic wildlife" that roams the woods behind your house at home, or the family vacation at Yellowstone. A corner table can routinely display a vignette of the latest American holiday, which leads to discussions about how you celebrated Valentine's Day as a child. Frame an appropriate holiday greeting card or a picture of your kids in costumes, and add a holiday-specific item (jack-o'-lantern, reindeer figurine, a bunny, or a small banner flag). Your family's favorite little-known celebrations may be even more meaningful, from Juneteenth (the day Texas slaves learned of freedom), to the Woolly Worm Festival (Ohio celebration). Everybody will have a collection of local souvenirs, but American things can be real conversation pieces. Be sure to save an area to display the gifts your guests will give to you (they will look for them when they visit again). In addition, you may want to incorporate gift ideas you plan to give to others, because if you like them and are seen using them, so will your recipients.

If your host country is desert or tropical, take silk spring flowers and preserved colored leaves and put them out at appropriate seasons for your guests to "see what my yard [or home state] looks like at this time of year." Even a basket of pinecones is striking in places where evergreens do not grow.

Smoking

Many of your foreign guests will smoke. If you want them to come to your home, you will have to designate one area for smoking, and try to limit it to that room if you do not like the smell. Encourage them to go there by putting out coffee-table ashtrays, American cigarettes and cigars, and a collection of souvenir matches from your travels in the States.

Miscellaneous

Before scheduling your major event in a foreign location, consult world calendars on the Internet such as www.interfaithcalendar.org or www.earthcalendar.net to avoid having to contend with local holiday observances celebrated publicly with parades, office closures, or street entertainment. Some religious festivals are observed at home with immediate family only, which might make your guest quota difficult to fill. On the other hand, community events are good to piggyback onto; use them as the evening's focus by inviting guests home for drinks and nibbles before or dessert and coffee afterward.

THANKSGIVING TRADITION

As usual, I gave a little talk between the first and second course of my Thanksgiving dinner for foreign guests, explaining, "Everything tonight is typically American." I had a cornucopia centerpiece and candles. The dinner lasted long and the candles burned low. With perfect timing during the final toast, the whole thing caught fire, and now they think that a flaming table is U.S. tradition!

—U.S. Military Attaché wife

Hospitality and respect are very important in most cultures. Consider hosting an event for all your host country neighbor families early on in an overseas assignment. It is good security to know and become known in good times so if there are any bad times you can reach out for help. Besides, chances are good that someone in the neighborhood would make a good professional connection. The idea is to welcome them into your apartment (or backyard) to take the mystery out of "the outsider" in their midst. Locals will be willing to make allowances based on your desire to connect, but it will help them feel welcome if you follow basic multicultural manners. It has been said of us: *"You Americans have it backwards. In your houses, you say 'make yourself at home' and you are very casual to guests. Yet in public you expect total strangers to be very polite to you."* It should be the other way around. An American in Oman wrote, *"I've had to adapt my personality to the locals. They are extremely polite and gracious. For example, it is customary to walk guests the whole way to their car, open the car door, wait till they are seated, and only then say goodbye. One visitor wouldn't park her dirty car with the other guests, saying she didn't want to embarrass them or me. I am trying to emulate their thoughtful graciousness."*

INTERNATIONAL GIFT-GIVING

The best international gift serves as a material reminder of an occasion when an individual was privileged to interact with someone from another culture. Gifts establish (and help maintain) both personal and business relationships. Gift exchanges abroad seem to cause as much anxiety as do our personal table manners and clothing choices. Everyone wants to give suitable gifts at the appropriate times in the locally acceptable manner, and to show cross-cultural awareness, especially if in a foreign country during its local gift-giving seasons. The advice in this section will help polish your public gift-giving interactions; however, it does not negate your personal research into host country customs. For instance, it is impolite everywhere to refuse a gift, but accepting one can sometimes cause unanticipated distress. Local recipients may have been raised with manners that insist all gifts must be reciprocated; therefore, host nationals may consider it rude of you to give them a gift that would be a hardship to reciprocate. U.S. law may affect whether an American accepting a gift may keep it (see Official Gift Presentations and VIP Gift Exchanges below).

It is universally advisable to present and accept a gift with both hands. If the gift is presented as part of a ceremony, it will be accepted immediately with formality and opened in front of the assembled group. Wrap a gift to reflect the value that you place on giving it. Be sure to research paper colors, patterns, and textures, as well as ribbon preferences for specific cultures. Wrap the top and bottom of the box separately so that the top lifts off smoothly to reveal the contents if the gift must pass through customs or if it will be opened before an audience. No one wants to fumble, especially a VIP during an official gift exchange (see below). If this is not possible, leave boxes unsealed or unwrapped until right before presentation to comply with local security practices, because guards just love making you open packages. Be sure to insert your business or social card inside a wrapped gift so that it will not become detached before the recipient can send a thank-you. (If you ever receive a diplomat's social card with mysterious initials, look them up in Chapter13: Abbreviations in Social Correspondence.)

Q: I will visit my sister, a Fulbright scholar teaching elementary school English overseas, for spring break. She suggested that I bring gifts to her class. What should
I consider?

A: Create small paper "goodie" bags so the gifts become a personal reflection of you.
Assemble them after arrival to make packing easier. Strive for American items. Include
pencils and notepads with your civilian company logo or military service seal. Add
a digital picture of yourself and your sister as kids, or buy some postcards from your
family's hometown. Youngsters like stickers (Disney cartoons); older kids might prefer water-applied tattoos (perhaps of current movie heroes). Add individually wrapped
items: bubble gum, drink straws that turn milk into flavors, red shoestring licorice,
Pixie Stix (sugar straws), wax Coke bottles (filled with sugar water) and tell them
stories about enjoying them when you were their ages. Kool-Aid and popcorn can
be made on site or sent home to share. Ask your sister if these suggestions will
work locally before investing in them. Enjoy the opportunity to nurture international
relationships.

Q: How should I present a gift to my female Chinese friend?

A: Present the wrapped gift (red is a good color in her culture) with both hands privately
unless you have gifts for everyone. If you give gifts to more than one person, start
with the senior or elder and proceed in rank order. Chinese manners teach declining a
gift initially and not opening it in the giver's presence lest the resulting reactions dis-
appoint. Continue offering your gift if it is politely refused (as many as three times). If
you really want it opened immediately, you will have to insist. You might want to reassure her that it is not necessary to reciprocate, as she may be uncomfortable at having
nothing to give you.

Q: What host gifts are expected for third-country government functions (not U.S. or
host country)? Is there a difference if you know or do not know the host?

A: For in-home functions, always take a small gift. If *any* event is held in your honor,
send the host a nice gift later. No gifts are needed for official receptions, unless the
country has very limited representational funds, the event repays an entire year's social
obligations, and you want your counterpart to have something American. For a reception host you know well, it is never wrong to be more gracious, but send your token
the next day, along with a thank-you note.

Personal Gifts

Even if you are lower ranking, or meeting primarily American compatriots during a short business trip overseas, carry a few small gift items and correspondence
cards (useful for any social note that may be needed, from happy birthday to thank
you). Small, flat, and easily wrapped choices are key if you need to pack gifts in a

suitcase for traveling. One idea is picture frames to fit your camera's digital photos. When you take pictures of locals you meet (perhaps with you so that they will remember you) and give them their picture in a frame, it guarantees smiles. For additional thoughts on personal travel gifts and souvenir ideas, please see Chapter 24: International Travel.

Always bring a "bread and butter" hospitality gift when invited to a local's home. You are being given the invaluable gift of personal hospitality and most cultures consider expressing appreciation one of the most important rules of protocol and etiquette. Remember that in many countries it may be customary to refuse a personal gift as many as three times for politeness' sake before finally accepting it. Keep insisting that you would like your host to accept it, but *do not* insist that the receiver open the gift in front of you. It is a matter of saving face for both of you in case the gift does not meet expectations. Conversely, your gift will be opened immediately in some countries and put on display. In addition, in male-dominant societies it is wise to give hospitality gifts to the same sex—that is, to the host if you are male, or to the hostess if you are female.

An appropriate gift is one that can be shared with all living there, such as a beautiful basket of fruit or box of professionally made pastries. Please review Chapter 30: Food and Drink Preferences of Various Religious Groups before considering alcohol or products containing meat. If considering flowers (not the best choice for a male host or in cultures that only use flowers at weddings and funerals) be aware that colors may have particular local connotations. White flowers often suggest mourning, red roses usually indicate courtship. Sometimes good choices for flowers are the colors of the recipient's country flag. No matter what culture, if you desire to give flowers, always send them in advance, as it is difficult for hosts to cope with them at the door when their focus is on greeting guests.

Find out what items are either unavailable locally or heavily taxed to give you ideas for what would be especially appreciated. Chef tools may not make good gifts. Many times your authors have heard from Americans serving abroad: "*Host*

REPRESENTATIONAL FLOWERS

Between My Country
and the Others
There is a Sea
But Flowers
negotiate between us
As Ministry.

—Emily Dickinson

---

*country people we see don't do cooking or housework because of servants. The people
who came here with house or kitchen-type host gifts are annoyed."*

Just as a meal featuring your home state is suggested, another recommendation
is to research appropriate gift ideas from your region of the United States. Ideally
all your gifts are "Made in America" or educate about our country because international gifts reflect the status of the donor. Flowers, candy, or wine might work,
but the flowers die, the candy is eaten, and the wine will not last once opened.
How much nicer it would be if foreign recipients could point to your gift item and
say, *"My American friend gave me that. It's from the United States."*

Official Gift Presentations and VIP Gift Exchanges

It is important that your organization have an official policy on giving as well as
receiving gifts. It must be fluid enough to cope with cross-cultural exchanges. For
instance, if the policy states that only one gift for presentation may be given or
accepted per person, what will happen when the local greeting ritual includes
providing mementos, and the departure ritual entails presenting official guests
with a more expensive gift such as a silver tray with commemorative engraving?
Are principals expected to deduct the cost of gifts given as a business expense,
or should there be a specific directive or a supply of gifts for this purpose? At the
least, the organizational policy ought to state that all official gifts for presentation must be pre-approved by headquarters before purchase, and someone in the
approval chain must be tasked with doing culture-specific research, such as region-
ally objectionable colors, numbers, or items to avoid.

There are always local courtesies involved in official gift presentations: the
proper timing (before or after business is conducted in the host country), which
delegation members will receive gifts (and who needs to reciprocate), the appropriate value of gifts exchanged, and if seals or corporate "branding" or the recipient's name and title may be affixed to the item.

Most official gift exchanges will be part of the public record and must follow
locally proper protocol. Many are recorded on video for posterity, and finesse in the
ritual procedure is likely to be considered more important than the actual items
exchanged. Participants must be briefed on appropriate gift acceptance language
(verbal and non-verbal). As previously mentioned, it is important to present and
accept gifts using both hands to indicate respect and appreciation; never use only
the left hand. Formal wording during a presentation will include statements such
as, *"On behalf of the Secretary,* [federal department], *The Honorable* [full name]; *and
our Director,* [your specific office], [honorific and full name], *I am pleased to present*
[or accept] . . ."

VIP gift presentations, whether leader-to-leader (publicly or privately) or between the leaders' protocol offices (most often in private), must be done with mutually agreed-upon formality. Negotiate gift exchanges well ahead of time so that appropriate gifts can be purchased and wrapped for presentation or shipping. Develop a detailed time line for gift presentations. Even a five-minute exchange is a lot of time out of a thirty-minute meeting.

Another reason to coordinate official gift exchanges ahead of time, protocol office to protocol office, is so there are no surprises. An unexpected gift can embarrass an official if he or she is not prepared to reciprocate or is prohibited from accepting because of business directives or government regulations. U.S. government employees are prohibited from accepting gifts from certain sources or gifts that are valued higher than Federal Regulation 5 CFR § 2635 stipulates. These threshold amounts are adjusted periodically for inflation (see U.S. Office of Government Ethics, www.usoge.gov). The burden is on the employee to seek guidance. Similarly, U.S. businesspersons are subject to the tenets of the Foreign Corrupt Practices Act of 1977, 15 U.S.C. §§ 78dd-1, et seq. (see Department of Justice, www.usdoj.gov/criminal/fraud/fcpa).

If accepting expensive gifts is deemed unavoidable, employees are usually advised to "save face for the giver" by receiving them on behalf of the United States or business organization. The gift subsequently will be displayed at headquarters, donated to a charitable cause, or sent to the U.S. National Archives, as appropriate.

There are specific times for gifts that certain countries consider proper; do not try to go against tradition. Many cultures, such as the Japanese, like to give gifts both when they first meet and again when they part. Latin Americans and citizens of the People's Republic of China usually prefer to wait until business matters are concluded before presenting gifts. It may be wise (especially in the Middle East) to present organization gifts before a group—never privately—to prevent any perception of a bribe, even if the gift is meant for a particular individual such as the company head.

International Gift Suggestions

Gifts are given for the same reasons all over the world: birthdays or name days (saint's days), religious holidays or New Year's, milestones such as anniversaries and retirements, as ritual to cement official ties, and to acknowledge in-home hospitality.

Research the recipients' culture for anything that may be objectionable. For instance, it is considered bad luck in many countries to present an even number, so odd numbers of items are better (except for thirteen, which many Americans regard with superstition also). Sharp items (scissors, knives, letter openers) can be misconstrued as a desire to sever the relationship, and a potted plant given during an illness or troubled time may be considered a suggestion that the evil take root. Certain colors or combinations may not be appropriate; purple, white, or black may be regarded as mourning colors. Someone in the Third World could misconstrue a gift of host soaps in pretty shapes as an inference that they are not clean enough to suit you.

American companies and citizens overseas would be wise to purchase gifts that are "Made in the USA." Items manufactured by your company, or objects that reflect your unique job within an organization may make appropriate gifts. Collect a variety of gifts, in several cost categories, to stock a gift closet. Most importantly, develop a method to document who received the gift, what it was, when and why it was given, and where and how it was presented.

The following ideas, in no particular order, will help you get started compiling your own list of appropriate American representational gifts.

- Christmas ornaments from the White House, or souvenirs from the homes of Presidents Washington, Lincoln, and the current President make good gifts, especially if they come nicely boxed with little explanation sheets. (Note: other U.S. Presidents are *not* appropriate unless you are positive that they will have name recognition overseas.)

- Calendars, coffee-table books, or appointment diaries are available with pictures of internationally known U.S. parks, unique wildlife, and endangered American species.

- The pineapple was the Colonial American symbol of hospitality and still appears on many items suitable for host gifts.

- Native Americans (Indians) always intrigue foreign nationals and there is a tribe associated with every state. The Smithsonian's American Indian Museum (www.nmai.si.edu) sells Indian art.

- Typically, American scenes such as those painted by Norman Rockwell, Grandma Moses, or Winslow Homer might generate positive interest if displayed in your home. If a guest comments positively, a miniature replica would be especially meaningful.

- The United States is one of the first nations with a space program. Give astronaut pens that write upside down, freeze-dried ice cream, miniature space shuttles, space patches, or desk accessories. Satellite photo close-ups, Google Earth style, of the recipient's hometown or the view of space from his location might be welcome.

- Do some research: Is your hometown a trade partner or "sister city" with any international location? Have host country immigrants settled there in large numbers? Ask for ideas that others familiar with the overseas location already know will be especially welcome.

- Call your elected representatives (local, state, and federal) to ask what internationals appreciate about your home state. What do the officials themselves give as gifts, serve at dinners, and display in their offices?

- If possible, tie into a special interest or experience of the person receiving the gift to make it meaningful. If the recipient previously visited a particular area of the United States and enjoyed it, that may inspire gift-giving ideas. A framed picture taken during an official visit and signed by a local dignitary is always popular for display.

- If recipients are military or law enforcement, take a supply of uniform buttons and "unit commemorative coins" to exchange. If your host country does inexpensive jewelry work, have them mounted as key rings, money clips, or lapel pins.

- Adorn useful items—such as umbrellas, small (5 by 8 inch) imitation leather covers for notepads, coffee mugs, or pocket calculators—with appropriate seals, crests, or logos.

- The United States Mint (www.usmint.gov/50states) has gift items made from the individual state quarters, dollar coins, and presidential coins (double-check the name recognition in your host country).

- The United States Postal Service (www.usps.gov) promotes distinctive plants and animals from North America, American icons, and other special topics. Stamps may be added to enhance a framed artifact. One example is a Virginia stamp matted with an anonymous quote in calligraphy: *"To be a Virginian, either by Birth, Marriage, Adoption, or even on one's Mother's side, is an Introduction to any State in the Union, a Passport to any Foreign Country, and a Benediction from Almighty God."* Use the saying or something similar for your own state and "adopt" the recipient via a presentation.

- Nonperishable and nonbreakable are best for a gift closet, but if you do give food, consider the following: Pecans are regarded as the "American" nut. Cranberries, blueberries, and Concord grapes are native to our shores. Sweets appropriate to the nearest American holiday (jellybeans at Easter, candy corn at Halloween, saltwater taffy in summer) are more interesting than another box of chocolates.

- Be creative in the wrapping. Put an American wine in a red, white, and blue bag, or emulate this military officer: *"I made color labels in Burmese on my home computer:* 'Compliments of the Air Attaché, Embassy of the United States of America, Yangon, Union of Myanmar' *to fit over a standard size* Hershey Bar. *They love chocolate and I'm from Pennsylvania, so this is a great representational gift from me and Hershey, PA."*

THE GLOBAL VILLAGE

I am neither an Athenian nor a Greek, but a citizen of the world.

—Socrates

CHAPTER 27

Manners at the Global Dinner Table

$\mathcal{A}$ tourist, exchange student, visiting worker, or sojourner in another country is a de facto goodwill ambassador for his or her own nation. Your demeanor while dining overseas is often the most visible characteristic foreign nationals have to judge your personal sophistication and trustworthiness, and they will generalize from your behavior the manner in which all other Americans accept and understand their culture. You have a responsibility to practice civility by welcoming the food served and the regional styles of eating as acceptance of a local host, his country, and other guests. When invited to dine in another country, you will probably join your host in a restaurant, but you may be invited to his or her home. Please do not decline home invitations as they are signs of great honor, not to mention fascinating experiences, no matter how humble the dwelling or meal. Show your appreciation for such generous hospitality by reciprocating with a meal before you leave the country: at a restaurant if you are staying in a hotel, or in your temporary living quarters.

AT EASE KEY POINTS

- ⚘ Master the three most prevalent styles of eating.
- ⚘ Defer to host and family elders.
- ⚘ Find a local mentor for guidance on:
  - Toasts (when to respond, toasting words)
  - Food (passing, finishing, second helpings)
  - Beverages (how to refuse more)
  - Arrival/Departure (how and when)

Invariably societies agree to the patterns of behavior in this section: Hospitality means sharing food and friendship. Guests recognize that hosts have gone to extra effort in order to serve local delicacies or specialties, and in appreciation, good guests wait to be shown to their places. Honored guests are given choice seats, most often on the right side of hosts, but sometimes a culture chooses the *left* of hosts (e.g., India and Sweden) as the honored position. Everywhere, guests wait for host permission before eating. Many times there is an abundance of food when guests are present in order to demonstrate generosity. It is not necessary to eat everything you see in a foreign country, but please be polite enough to taste the food, especially if you are offered the best (prized) morsels of food before other guests. In the Middle East it is common for the guest of honor to be served a sheep's eye or gonad. A friend with the U.S. Agency for International Development had this happen to her in Yemen. Knowing it would be dishonorable to turn down such a delicacy, she tried a gonad and reports that it was not bad, and her one-bite taste made everyone happy.

Guests are often urged to eat more, but to eat as if starving is disrespectful to others; guests share more or less equally, deferring to each other. Talking with a full mouth or putting more food into a full mouth is considered bad manners. Wasting food is frowned upon. Adding extra salt, pepper, or seasonings to food might rudely suggest that it is not tolerable as prepared. It is equally bad manners to drop any food on the table or your body as it is lifted to your mouth.

If there is a special guest of honor, there may be some activity after dinner—a cultural presentation of dance or singing, movies, or games. No matter how badly guests may wish not to participate, it is universally expected that persons with good manners join in the entertainment provided. Guests must always be polite and gracious. Just as hosts open the door for guests to arrive, they must also open doors for guests to depart.

Tell me what you eat and I'll tell you who you are.

—Jean Anthelme Brillat-Savarin (1755–1826),
French epicure and gastronome

Other traditions vary widely; look for your own norms in this paragraph: In many cultures, it is considered unhygienic and therefore bad manners to wear "outside" shoes in the house or dining area. In other societies, only muddy or snowy boots are left by the door. Some cultures eat separated by sex or age; for instance, when outsiders are invited to a home in Saudi Arabia or Yemen, women and men go to separate rooms immediately to socialize and eat. (Many Americans have experienced similar meals taken on a ranch or farm where children are served dinner earlier than adults, the hungry men are served as soon as they come in from working, and the women eat together more leisurely after the men have left the table.)

In one location, small talk will take place primarily before the meal. In another, lengthy mealtimes provide an opportunity to hear details about family and friends while savoring food and drink. In yet other countries meals may be consumed rather quickly in relative quiet and concentration so that socializing can occur afterward when guests are relaxed. Some societies indicate generosity by offering food or drink once and accept the guest's first stated preference. Good manners in other cultures say that hosts must offer refreshments at least three times; guest refusals will be ignored as polite gestures until after that magic number. Various peoples of the world express appreciation for food by audibly burping to indicate that they are now satiated and enjoyed the meal, but others consider it good manners to stifle burps. Some cultures leave a little food on their plates to indicate that the host served an abundance of food and they cannot eat more, but "clean-plate club" societies consider leaving any food a signal of dissatisfaction or wastefulness. Some hosts insist at least three times that guests stay before permitting them to leave, which would confound guests brought up to leave promptly after dining. People with different cultural expectations at the same function can confuse if not insult each other inadvertently if they do not realize what is going on.

ADAPT YOUR MANNERS

Adapt your manners to your hosts: speak softly if they do, hold your glass or cup with two hands, use your knife and fork to eat pizza, pick up your asparagus with your fingers, whatever. The best way to enjoy local foods is to eat them in the manner intended. If you do not blend in with the residents, you risk looking self-important, comical, or rude. Accept manners that differ from yours without comment even if you cannot bring yourself to join in, such as using a toothpick at table (note: toothpick manners dictate mouths be shielded with the other hand).

When platters of food are passed around the table, almost universally it is acceptable to use both hands to offer and receive them. Guests do not touch the eating utensils (fork, spoon, glass) or food of others (no shared chips or dips). Any food that someone else touched or was on a personal plate is considered unsanitary; some cultures refer to it as "polluted" and are ritually forbidden from eating it. An exception to this rule (in some cultures) might be for the host to share a particularly tasty morsel with the honored guest, or for diners to place a select bite of food in another person's mouth during a meal to convey affection. Sharing a taste of the most succulent piece of lobster claw or bite of chocolate dessert with a close friend or family member beside us at table strengthens interpersonal bonds.

Just as there are those with varying degrees of language ability, people have different levels of food ability. Some do well in diverse food cultures from the beginning (neophilia means "love of the new") and some never do well (neophobia means "fear of the new"). If you are lucky enough to be fed in the home of someone from another culture, please demonstrate your sophistication with willingness to master appropriate manners and eat in traditional ways. Populations eating with flatware (knifes and forks) use primarily International Style table manners (see Chapter 16: Place Settings, Table Manners, and Service Styles). Practice eating with your hands (Chapter 28: Communal Platter Dining) and learn to wield chopsticks (Chapter 29: Chopstick Protocol) to enjoy the hospitality prevalent in the Middle and Far East.

Toasting rituals are also important to understand, as toasts occur with great frequency outside the United States.

INTERNATIONAL TOASTING RITUALS

Public blessings are expected in many countries, including the United States, for instance during wedding dinners, for American Thanksgiving dinners, to salute a religious guest of honor, or if a member of the clergy is present to deliver a benediction. Diners may be asked to stand for grace or prayer. As a substitute for a blessing or in addition to it, the host may offer a nonreligious injunction: *Bon Appétit* or *Guten Appetit,* sometimes as the last words of a welcome toast.

Wherever you go, toasting rituals are significant and it is a grave insult not to participate. Think of them as you would think of shaking hands—it is offensive to refuse. Russians and the cultures they have influenced have a history of great dramatic flair in "Bottoms up!" toasts and smashing empty glasses after an especially important one so that no less worthy toast will ever be given with that goblet.

Some drinking salutes will not start until everybody is served the special local alcoholic beverage, such as Greek *retsina* or Japanese *saké*. Juice, sparkling cider, carbonated soft drinks, tea, even goats' milk may be substituted in places where drinking alcohol is not appropriate. In those societies, a toast may be in the form of a blessing, speech, song, or other honoring tradition such as greeting each person by name around the table, probably in protocol order. If groups are separated by sex, each will be proposing appropriate toasts within their own rooms, proceeding by hierarchy. The most important person, who is often the eldest, stands (holding his or her glass in both hands about waist high), speaks a few words about the honored person, and sips—but without a salute of the glass, and without inviting others to join in, although they may. When that person sits down, the next highest ranking stands and offers comments, then the third in status, and so on. For example, the father (not the grandfather) of a bride would give the first toast at a wedding, and people close to the couple in descending order of importance would then give subsequent toasts.

Q: I don't drink but everyone in this country seems to. I hate the "why not" questions. What should I say when offered alcohol?

A: The worst thing to say is, *"I don't drink."* That is a challenge to serve a host nation or personal favorite libation (which they believe you would just *love* if you only tried it). Ask for something specific, such as a local soft drink. If someone offers to get you another drink during a party, try: *"I believe I'd like mineral water* [or *juice* or *tonic*] *this time"* to avoid discussion. If a drink is forced on you, remember: no one can fill up an already full glass. Just carry it around at cocktails or ignore it in favor of water at table. Also, never refuse to toast—that is a political statement against the honoree. Lift your glass as the toast is proposed, and bring it toward your lips with a smile before setting it down (you needn't pretend to sip).

Q: I know it is OK to turn my wine glass over or put my place card on top so the waiter will not serve me alcohol in the United States. Is this proper etiquette internationally?

A: When you do not desire wine at formal Western-style tables, touch the glass rim with your first two fingertips as the server approaches and he will not fill (or refill) it. It may be locally appropriate to waggle a cup back and forth or wave your hand over a glass overseas. *Never turn a glass or cup over* or set anything on top of it in the United States or abroad unless specifically directed by your host.

Nondrinkers

It is not *usually* remarked upon when non-imbibers do not actually drink from a glass of alcohol; merely holding the glass aloft with a smile and perhaps miming a sip is sufficient because it is the gesture that counts. Guests who do not drink alcohol simply set down their full cups or glasses. However, sometimes not to drink translates as questionable personal virility—many toasting words literally mean "Bottoms up!" or "Empty glass!" If your rejection of alcohol might cause loss of face, be ready with a *locally acceptable* reason given with sorrowful regret for abstaining, for instance, medication you are taking or religious observance. Keep in mind that locals will watch in future to see if your actions are consistent. Not to drink in societies such as Korea, Japan, or China will be especially noticed. Polite persons in the Far East do not drink alcohol at table unless others do, and one after another around a table they will toast any guests.

IN THE LINE OF DUTY

The Defense Intelligence Agency director did not drink alcohol for religious reasons. This major general went on an official trip to Russia, where public "Bottoms up!" toasts are frequently performed with the national beverage. He recognized the affront of publicly refusing to participate with host country leaders and solved his diplomatic dilemma by delegating toasts to his American attaché escort, who happened to be a young female lieutenant. She drank *a lot* of vodka for her country. *Na Zdorovia!*

International Toasting Protocol

Internationally, toasts proceed via local formula including at least some of the following:

- The host's welcome (before or during the meal)
- Recognition of any honored guests (and their spouses) in precedence order
- Salutes to the honored guest's head of government (in which case the guest must return a formal toast to the host's sovereign leader)
- Relationships between military or business organizations celebrated
- World peace and fellowship of compatriots from both countries extolled
- Past heroes and future generations praised
- The guest of honor's thank-you-for-inviting-us-all toast

All present drink to all rulers and countries. Join in for toasts proposed to the United States, our President, your commanding officer, director or company chief executive officer (CEO), and so forth, even if they are not present. Americans do not toast to themselves but other cultures may, usually after a humble bow or nod. Check beforehand to find out what locals expect.

If you are the guest of honor, prepare and practice a toast befitting the event because it is your duty to reciprocate. Ask a mentor for proper local etiquette so that you will know when to offer a return toast: immediately, at the apex of the meal, at dessert, with port, or some combination. For instance, in Hong Kong and China, toasts might be offered during the shark's fin soup course because it is regarded as a festive luxury. Celebratory gatherings might feature official toastmasters who are responsible for making occasions memorable, as in Georgia, one of the oldest countries of the world, where they are called *tamadas*. In many cultures, dinner guests never sip without being toasted or offering a toast, so all diners propose toasts often.

International Toasting Procedures

Toasters in multinational settings lift the glass or cup formally with both hands approximately chest high—the right one holding the stem, bowl, or handle and the left hand with fingers flat to support the bottom. Make eye contact with the honoree and offer a toast ending with the local sentiment to urge others to join in. For example, British-influenced nations say *"Cheers," "Bottoms up,"* or *"To your health"*; Germanic countries say *"Prôst"*; Latin states use *"Salud"* or *"Salute"*; French influenced cultures say *"A votre santé"*; in the Far East it is *"Kampai"* or *"Gambei"*; Georgia's word is *"Gaumarjos"*; and in Ireland they say *"Slainte"*. Learning the local toasting word or phrase may be all that is needed to respond graciously, along with the appropriate body language, which may include linking arms, making eye contact before drinking, looking around at everyone present both before and after a toast, or showing that your glass is empty before the next toast is proposed. Toasters set glasses back on tables immediately and sit down to signal the conclusion of their comments. In societies that lift their beverages in formal salute there is normally no clinking of glasses together; but if it does happen, younger or lower-ranking people should be careful that the edge of their glass hits below the edge of any elder or superior in order to show respect.

Unless you have coordinated with your host ahead of time, do not initiate official toasts overseas. In fact, do not touch your wine goblet, glass, or cup until the host has welcomed you to his table and lifted his own glass—and never propose a toast to yourself. For more on toasting, see Chapter 20: Toasts.

Scandinavian Skoal

Toasting customs are deep-seated and most ritualized in the Scandinavian skoal (toast). No one drinks any wine until after the host has made a general skoal welcoming all guests. Throughout dinner, hosts skoal everyone around the table; guests drink with them. Each skoal should be returned within a few minutes. Males initiate individual skoals to their female dinner partners at least once during a formal meal. They will wait for the female to return her glass to the table before setting down their own glasses. At the end of the meal, the guest of honor (seated at the *left* in Scandinavian countries) makes a short speech of thanks, and skoals the hosts on behalf of all the guests, who join in this final skoal. The traditional procedure described next is a good formal toasting model:

Lift your glass from the table by the stem in your right hand, moving it near your body and the table edge (the Swedes say even with the third button of your shirt). Face the person you wish to salute (or turn your entire upper body toward the person beside you). Lift your goblet about nose high, extending your arm a bit. Look directly into your partner's eyes (he or she will be making unblinking eye contact with you also). Nod, say *skoal*, draw your glass down and toward your body, lifting it smoothly back to your lips (sort of a J-swoop), and maintain eye contact *the entire time* you sip. Salute with your glass (short gesture upward) before returning it to the table.

One final note about alcohol: It is easy to drink too much wine or unfamiliar intoxicating beverages when international hosts keep filling your glass, especially in hot weather with no air conditioning. Watch your consumption or you will be surprised and possibly embarrassed when you try to stand up.

INTERNATIONAL TOASTS

"May every patriot love his native country, whether he is born in it or not." AMERICAN

"Happy are we met, happy have we been. Happy may we part, and happy meet again." IRISH

"It is around a table that friends understand best the warmth of being together." ITALIAN

"Eat, drink, and be merry." MANY CULTURES

"To love, wealth, and the time to enjoy them." SPANISH

"May you live in interesting times." CHINESE, YIDDISH, AND OTHER LANGUAGES

"Who knows but that we were born for such a time as this." ESTHER 4:14, THE BIBLE (paraphrase)

"America—half-brother of the world!—with something good and bad of every land." PHILIP BAYLEY
(Note: Add a 'good' host-country acquisition to this quote to make it a memorable toast.)

CHAPTER 28

Communal Platter Dining

*T*he first word in the expression "table manners" does not apply if you dine at floor level instead of on a raised flat surface, but "minding your manners" is consistently important no matter where or how you eat. The custom of consuming food directly with the hands is as old as mankind. Eating with the fingers is like having another tongue—the pleasure of the meal is extended by enjoying the temperature and texture of the food.

In early Hawaii, diners ate poi (a thick, pasty pudding of taro root) by dipping in one, two, or three fingers (depending on its consistency) from the same bowl. Modern Americans eat at table with their hands all the time: fried chicken and corn-on-the-cob at picnics or barbecues; hamburgers, French fries, and tacos at fast-food restaurants; or dainty sandwiches and pastries at afternoon tea. But most Americans eat from individual plates. They no longer share food from their personal bowl with others (parents feeding young children are an exception).

AT EASE KEY POINTS

- ❧ Wear loose clothing suitable for sitting at floor level.
- ❧ Eat with right hand only; limit fingers used.
- ❧ Do not point feet at anyone or the food.
- ❧ Drink coffee or tea prepared in your honor.

Many societies, thousands of years old, still dine communally from shared platters or bowls using their fingers. Cutlery might be offered to an American guest even though everyone else is eating by hand, but do not miss the opportunity to enjoy their food the way it was meant to be eaten. Expand your table skills and build multicultural relationships by learning to dine as the locals do. Examples of cultures that routinely eat from a communal platter without forks, knives, or spoons are as diverse as Saudi Arabia, Ethiopia, Nepal, and Indonesia.

The American custom is to reach for food presented in a communal serving dish (such as a bread basket) with either hand, using the forefinger and thumb like tongs or a pincer, with the other fingers held out of the way. Just as it is polite in the American Style of dining to keep your left hand in your lap for the most part, cultures eating entire meals with their fingers from communal platters or bowls consistently employ only the right hand—the thumb and tip of one, two, or three fingers, depending on the country. The left hand, reserved for personal body care, never comes into contact with plated food. The use of both hands is usually acceptable only to cope with a larger piece of food that is to be entirely consumed by the guest, such as meat clinging to a bone. Pull meat from bones into *small* pieces with your right hand; it is bad manners to hold a bone with both hands at your mouth. You may use both hands to tear the piece of bread or food you have taken from the communal plate onto your napkin or lap (if individual plates are not provided), but use only your right hand to bring food to your mouth.

Each culture decides how many fingers must remain unused and either curled against the palm or held aloft to stay clean. Copy the graceful hand movements and body language of your hosts. Some societies permit all four fingers and thumb to be used for eating, as long as only the fingertips are used and the palm of the hand remains untouched by food. Others use only the thumb and three (or two) fingers of the right hand, keeping the smallest finger(s) curled into the palm away from food. In addition to limiting the number of fingers employed, it is usually also impolite to dirty them above the second knuckle. Take small amounts because the entire quantity should be consumed in one bite. Licking the fingers is considered impolite as well as unsanitary. It takes practice to keep requisite portions of your hand clean. The goal is to perform the maneuvers with grace and without conscious effort. It will only take one complete meal to get past the awkward stage, where you are concentrating so hard on "minding your manners" that it is hard to eat and carry on a conversation simultaneously.

Q: During a social banquet, our hosts wanted us to eat a rice dish "communally" with our hands. We felt so awkward that they were embarrassed. We felt awful. What key things are important so we don't make anyone uncomfortable again?

A: Participate in the hand-washing ritual. A prayer may begin and end the meal. Emulate the graceful motions of your hosts, employing only the right hand. The entire bite goes into your mouth at once but not the fingers. Smile and ask for pointers. Compliment the food. Enjoy eating in the manner intended, along with your growing sophistication.

COMMUNAL GUEST MANNERS

Although cultures do differ, in general the following applies. Dress conservatively in clothing that will allow you to sit comfortably on a pillow or the floor with sleeves and jewelry that will not dangle into food platters. Modest dress is required for both men and women in most dining situations. This means to cover legs well past the knee, arms at least to the elbow, and no bare torsos (or necklines that reveal cleavage). Arrive promptly so that you may be introduced to elders and honored guests. Take a small gift when invited to someone's home. Stay strictly in the public guest areas unless you are escorted into other rooms; these cultures do not give house tours.

All the food platters are laid out together (family style), sometimes well before guests arrive, sometimes just before eating. Guests approach the food only when invited to do so by the host who will tell you where to sit. It is rude to have your back to an elder or honored guest. Therefore, they will be seated as far from the door as possible or with their backs to the wall in whatever location is deemed

Floor-level Communal Dining

the place of honor: perhaps next to the host, or beside the fireplace, or nearest the family art treasure. Everyone sits around the displayed food, ready to partake from the common central bowls or plates.

In some places, guests sit on chairs, benches, or sofas around low tables (typically round and coffee-table height). If local traditions dictate floor level, food platters will be on the floorboards or ground spread with a rug, blanket, or other special covering rather like a picnic. To sit down on the floor, males most often sit cross-legged but sometimes are permitted to recline on one arm with legs extended away from the "table" cloth and other guests. Women kneel or keep legs tucked to one side. It is very rude for the lowest part of your body (feet or the soles of shoes) to point at anyone or toward the food.

Eating by hand from the same plate as others requires considerate manners. Guests are assumed to have washed their hands well before the meal. Still, because other diners need to be reassured about hygiene, the host, designated family member, or servant makes a small ceremony of providing a public opportunity for cleanliness just as everyone gathers around for the meal (and sometimes after). Guests are approached in local precedence order with a jug of water to pour over hands while a basin for catching used water is held underneath. Wash without splashing and if a communal towel is provided, be careful to leave some dry areas for the next guest. Once hands are clean, be attentive to keep them that way. Now is not the time to use a tissue or rummage through a pocket.

Wait for the host to offer some words to explain the reason for the gathering, to give a

Hand Washing Ritual

benediction, to salute the ranking guests, and so on. Your host will begin eating or direct the guest of honor to take the first morsel, piece of bread, portion of rice, or something else. As in the American Style of eating (see Chapter 16: Place Settings, Table Manners, and Service Styles) remember to keep the left hand in your lap away from food. If a bowl or basket is passed to you, accept it with both hands, the right hand alone, or with your left hand supporting the right wrist instead of touching the platter with your left hand (if the host culture so stipulates). Serve yourself with your right hand only.

If the bowl or platter comes from your right instead of your left, continue passing it in the same direction. Food may be spicy hot, fire hot, or served at room temperature. Hands are sensitive to heat, so if food is too hot simply wait for it to cool down. Cooked food will be vegetables in sauces, stews made with meat, fried or baked meat (with bones), and plain vegetables cut in bite-sized pieces. Meals will most often be served with rice, couscous, potatoes, or bread. If personal plates are provided (rare), take a small amount of food of each type onto your dish before beginning to eat, but do not automatically assume that small plates are for individual use. They may instead be discard plates for bones, seeds, and such. If there are no receptacles, place bones directly in front of you on the "table." If utensils are available, they may be used only for serving, not for eating. Napkins may or may not be provided. If they are, they may be in unfamiliar fabrics and sizes.

Separating Your Portion

If individual flatware is provided, it will probably be only a tablespoon. Sometimes a fork (held in the left hand as a helper to push food into the spoon) will be offered but not a knife. You may eat with either your hands or utensils, but not both at the same time. If spoons are provided for a particular course, such as with couscous in Morocco, use yours to separate out the portion you intend to eat (directly in front of you—like cutting a wedge of cake) on the communal platter before putting the spoon into your mouth. Eat only from your area without touching another diner's section of the platter with your utensil. If bread is provided, select an individual serving and hold it on your lap or napkin. Using your right thumb and fingers (amateurs use both hands) break off a small piece from what you have just taken. If the bread is thin or flat, such as Ethiopian *injera*, use only your right hand to wrap it around your choice of food and lift the morsel directly from the communal platter to your mouth. If the bread is a thicker loaf such as Moroccan *kesra*, the action will be more like bracing the food as you lift it, or using a piece as a scoop.

The entire bite goes into your mouth at once. Use your right index finger and thumb as if they were pincers or tongs (together with the culturally approved number of other fingers) to take a single bite. Turn your hand slightly palm up and lift it to your mouth. Place your fingers near the lower lip and use your thumb to push (flick) the bite of food up and into your mouth. Do not tilt your head back and drop food into your mouth. Do not put fingers into your mouth. Finish chewing and swallowing one bite before reaching for another or it will appear that you are trying to beat everyone else at table to the choicest bits. As always, it is bad manners to double dip, put fingers in your mouth, or lick them. It is also rude to talk with your mouth full, put more food into an already full mouth, to chew with your mouth open, to touch food and put it back, or to stare at someone else's food.

Cups and glasses may also be shared with the group. Be prepared to fill the drinking vessel with the table beverage (such as beer), drink it all at once, and pass it on to the next person. (American colonists drank from *possit* or *tyg* cups with several handles to facilitate many people passing and sharing the same vessel. Still common are doubled-handled consommé cups that allow you to drink soup at the formal Western table.) If individual beverages are provided, they may be served to you in original containers (soft drink cans or juice bottles) or in vessels you would not expect, for instance hot tea and coffee may be served in small glasses instead of cups, or in cups without handles (see next sections on coffee and tea). Sometimes beverages are not provided until after eating is finished.

When everyone eats from a communal platter or pot, it is polite to finish the meal at the same time, so pay attention to the host's pace. If you are the guest of honor, everyone will watch you and stop eating when you do, so ask beforehand to determine if good manners dictate finishing everything or accepting more helpings. If the latter is the case, take care over the amount of food you take initially. A host may share a particularly tasty morsel or two from his or her own plate, perhaps even placing a select bite in the honored guest's mouth. Everyone will watch for your reaction to that transaction.

Depending on the customs of the household, a prayer may end the meal. Also after eating, hands may be rinsed again, either with the pitcher and catch basin system or by dipping fingers into large cups of scented water. Observe others' behavior; the authors have heard stories of guests mistakenly drinking from these "finger bowls," particularly in very hot climates or in countries that do not provide beverages during the meal.

Do not expect Western-style desserts, but there may be a coffee or tea ritual after a meal.

COFFEE AND TEA CEREMONIES IN COMMUNAL DINING SOCIETIES

Coffee or tea is often served after a meal just as in the United States. However, since many cultures do not drink alcohol, coffee or tea becomes the main social beverage. Service may take the form of a traditional or special ritual whenever there are visitors, which should be viewed by the Western guest as a tribute to them and to the importance of the occasion. A critical component may be serving the coffee or tea from a special pot, poured into special glasses or cups, in a particular manner. Making the beverage and serving it properly is an important ceremony of hospitality and may be done from start to finish in front of visitors. For example, in Ethiopia, women grind the coffee just before brewing, which takes a long time. In Uzbekistan, the traditional male host steeps tea and pours it back and forth from pot to cup three times before presenting it to the guest of honor. He cradles the cup in his right hand supported by his left and hands it to the guest with a slight bow. In Morocco, presweetened mint tea is also poured back and forth several times before hosts (or servants) serve guests by holding the teapot high in the air (two or more feet) and making long streams to fill small glasses.

The coffee and tea may be brewed very strong for guests as an indicator of host hospitality. The resulting brews could be bitter, and if so, are generally offered with milk and sweetener (honey, jam, or sugar). Instead of granulated sugar, rock sugar may be served, which does not dissolve well. Locals may hold pieces between the front teeth while the beverage is sipped, which sweetens each mouthful, or keep a rock in the bottom of a cup to sweeten multiple servings. Spices may be added to coffee or tea, for instance, Indian *masala chai* is highly spiced black tea brewed with both milk and sweetener.

Learn the local cultural gestures for appreciation during a coffee or tea service. Sometimes it is inappropriate to comment directly on the host's preparation of a beverage, but locals smack their lips in approval. Also, acquire the proper gestures to say that you have had enough to drink, such as wagging the cup back and forth as the pourer approaches to refill.

COMMUNAL MEAL'S END

There may be well-known local indications that the evening is at an end, such as the arrival of fruits, sweets, or glasses of water. Guests may be expected to depart quite quickly after coffee or tea. If you are the guest of honor, your departure will probably be necessary before others can leave. Your host may insist several (usually three) times that you remain, but good manners demand that you depart as expected. Say goodbye to everyone, perhaps singling out elders and guests of honor. Thank the host as he or she opens the door for you.

CHAPTER 29

Chopstick Protocol

*I*t is clear that if the United States wants to maintain its place in the world, Americans must learn multicultural adaptation. Some of us are not very attuned to body language, ritual, or nuance, important aspects of good manners in East Asian countries. Cultures strongly influenced by China and Japan include Taiwan, Mongolia, Korea, Tibet, Nepal, Singapore, and Vietnam, among others.

Good manners at East Asian tables are very similar to those at most others. Sit with good posture; keep your elbows in toward the body and off the table. Wait on the host's welcome toast to all guests. The senior guest replies immediately and thanks the host on everyone's behalf. Throughout dinner, individual toasts can be given. Someone will pick up his cup, catch your eye, say the local toasting word, and both of you will drink together. Delay eating until the host directs the beginning of each new course. Sample each dish offered. Avoid any actions that are considered wasteful, such as taking more food than you need.

AT EASE KEY POINTS

- ✤ Wear clothing with pockets; carry a handkerchief.
- ✤ Pace yourself; food and drink may be abundant.
- ✤ Keep chopsticks together at all times; never leave them upright in a bowl.
- ✤ Drink coffee or tea prepared in your honor.

Asian cultures consider it uncivilized to have knives at table, as if asking diners to dissect something. Everything will be cut in bite-sized pieces in the kitchen for ease in using chopsticks, those "perfect extensions of the fingers." Chopsticks are a pair of even-length sticks that are held together in one hand and used when cooking and eating East Asian food. The first evidence of chopsticks dates back to about 2000 BC in China and to the early AD centuries in Japan. (In contrast, the fork and spoon first joined the knife on European tables in the seventeenth cen-tury.) Chopsticks are made of a variety of materials: bamboo, unfinished or lac-quered wood, bone, ivory, and in modern times, metal and plastic as well. They have narrowed tips (pointed tips are more common in Japanese-influenced cul-tures) indicating the end that goes into your mouth.

If you eat with chopsticks there is no need to worry about which fork goes with what food because the same utensils are used throughout the meal. While principles of etiquette are similar, the finer points may differ from region to region. Generally, chopsticks etiquette equates to general Western flatware etiquette. If you would not do it with your knife and fork, do not do it with chopsticks. Never tap, play, or make noise with them; do not point with them or with the index finger holding them; never lick them; do not put them back on the table once used. Do not use them to push or pull bowls or plates; do not pick up a serving dish while still hold-ing personal chopsticks. If there are no serving utensils and you have already begun eating, it is considered acceptable to reverse your personal chopsticks to the clean ends in order to help yourself from a communal dish. This shows respect for oth-ers at the table. Do not dither or poke around searching for tasty morsels. Flip your chopsticks back to their original position before eating again.

What is different in East Asian Dining Etiquette is that belching and slurping soup are considered appropriate table behavior, all the more obvious because silent contemplation is considered a virtue—expect long pauses in conversation. Talking with the mouth full may also be acceptable. Toothpicks are often on the table and it is acceptable to use them publicly after a meal as long as your other hand dis-creetly covers your mouth. In some cultures, communal platters are not passed; guests offer their plates or bowls to receive food from the host (or other person act-ing as server), passing each other's along if the distance is great. Another differ-ence is that eating utensils are never separated; keep your chopsticks together in one hand as a set, even while stirring. If you drop one, request another pair; do not ask for a single chopstick.

It is *very offensive* to pass food from your chopsticks directly to somebody else's. The bones of cremated Buddhist bodies are passed from person to person in that way as they are put into an urn. Equally offensive is to leave chopsticks standing upright in your rice bowl—the universally offensive dining faux pas.

Standing chopsticks call to mind funerary rites throughout Asia. The deceased's personal chopsticks may be positioned in a full bowl of rice as an offer-ing of sustenance for the journey to the afterlife. In addition, any stick-like object facing upward resembles the incense sticks left burning in front of tombs.

Funerary Chopsticks

CHOPSTICK MANNERS

Hold your chopsticks just past the middle, closer to the eating ends. Cradle the bottom chopstick against the web of your thumb, resting the tip on your fourth (ring) finger. Anchor it by pushing against it from the outside with your thumb between the thumb's first and second knuckle. This chopstick never moves, but serves as a base to clamp food against. Hold the upper chopstick as you would a pencil, about one inch (2.54 centimeters) above and parallel to the bottom chopstick. The tips of the thumb, middle, and forefingers control the movement as a fulcrum for the upper chopstick to pinch morsels, as if with tongs. Novices find the top chopstick creeps backward as they maneuver; it helps if you loosen your grip and "realign" them against your eating surface occasionally. Do not make a tapping noise when you do this, because it broadcasts your amateur status. It is rude to use chopsticks to stab or spear food; they are for lifting only. When a piece of food is too large to fit into your mouth, experienced diners can exert controlled pressure on their chopsticks while moving them apart from each other with one hand—effectively "cutting" the piece of food in two—but it is perfectly acceptable to lift larger morsels from your own bowl to your mouth with chopsticks and bite off a piece, lowering the uneaten portion back into your bowl.

Anchor First Chopstick

Add Second Chopstick

Maneuvering Chopsticks

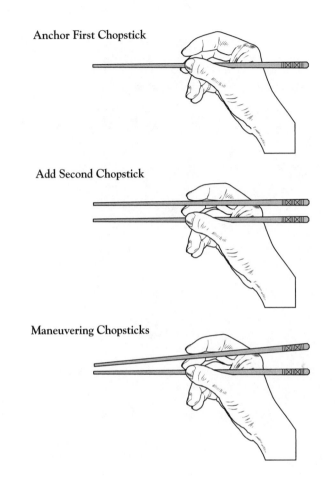

Rest and Finished Positions for Chopsticks

As with Western flatware, put your chopsticks down when you would like to talk, use your napkin, take a drink, or pass food items. When you set your chopsticks down, do not cross them or place them in a "V" shape (both are bad omens). Never rest the ends of your chopsticks on the table like a gangway either; lay them down *parallel together* in the locally accepted position, described next.

In *Japanese-influenced* homes and formal restaurants, a small ceramic rectangle or flat figurine may be provided as part of the place setting. The pointed ends of your chopsticks go on it for both the Rest and Finished positions. If there are no chopstick rests, place your utensils horizontally across the plate edge closest to you (front) with the tips pointing left for both Rest and Finished positions. (Chopstick

Chopstick Rests

Rest and Finished Position, front

cultures are predominantly right-handed, but if you are left-handed, lay your chopsticks down in confidence with the tips pointing right.)

Chinese-influenced cultures believe that putting chopsticks down heedlessly brings bad luck to all eating with you. Place your utensils in the Rest and Finished positions by setting them down horizontally along the top of your plate or bowl to keep them off the table entirely (or vertically on the right side of your bowl or plate, as in Korea). Never rest your chopsticks across the middle of your bowl like a bridge.

Rest and Finished Position, back

Rest and Finished Position, side

Far Eastern Guest Manners

It is an honor to be the guest in these cultures. Always set aside an entire evening for a social event, arrive promptly or slightly early, and pace yourself when consuming food and drink. It is common to provide an overabundance of food. For invitations to a private home take a small gift (see Chapter 25: International Protocol and Civility). There will most probably be a place to leave your shoes before entering a house or dining room. Sometimes slippers will be provided for guests, but it is wise to wear nice socks in case there are none. In some cases, there may be special toilet slippers outside the bathroom or lavatory. If so, change into them, leaving the other slippers outside the door and then change back when you leave the lavatory. In private homes, remain in the public guest areas unless you are invited into other rooms. Bedrooms and kitchens are private.

Watch hosts carefully as examples and follow their guidance. You will be presented to elders and other guests with great politeness (Confucius taught respect for seniors). Approach the table only when invited to do so by the host. There may be Western-height dining tables or lower-than-coffee-table style surfaces and cushions on the floor. If the latter, as explained in Communal Dining above, you may kneel on your legs (everyone), shift your bottom onto the floor keeping both legs to one side (females), or sit cross-legged (males). Seating locations are of great consequence. The most important guests are seated in places of honor, which might be at the head of the room facing the door, nearest the family heritage art or religious display, or facing east. Napkins have not traditionally been a part of Asian table manners; take a handkerchief with you just in case. The elderly first and then ranking guests (or perhaps vice versa) are offered food as a sign of respect before other diners take any. Honored guests are usually presented with local delicacies, which might not appeal to you, but please take some and make every effort to taste the offerings.

Please refrain from ever asking for a knife or fork. Expand your table skills in order to help build multicultural relationships. Once you have eaten an entire meal as the international host does, you will be past the awkward stage. In Thailand, spoons are the primary table utensil, held in the right hand. Forks, if available, serve to push food onto the spoons. They do use chopsticks, but not as often as other Asian countries since the introduction of Western utensils by King Rama V in the nineteenth century.

In most other Asian countries, however, chopsticks are the table utensils of choice. In a home setting, each family member may have his or her own personal set. You will be provided with a "guest" pair. Disposable, lightweight wooden chopsticks are seen in Japanese restaurants, attached at one end to reassure the customer that they are new. Split them apart but do not rub them together as if suspecting splinters. If your set has rough edges, request a new pair. In restaurants, disposable chopsticks come in paper envelopes. It is customary to fold the paper to use as a chopstick rest if none has been provided—copy your host's behavior.

The rice bowl is usually placed on the left of your place setting. Lift it and hold it in your left hand to make it easier to eat from. Rice grains typically stick together and chopsticks can easily lift a mouthful. Some cultures find it offensive to eat rice with anything other than chopsticks. However, Koreans eat both rice and soup with a spoon. Koreans also consider it as rude as Western cultures do to pick up and eat from a bowl. The Chinese, on the other hand, say that they pick up their bowls to be different from animals that eat with lowered heads.

Use the serving utensils to take food from a communal platter and place it in your own bowl or plate. When eating food in a sauce from your plate, pick up the food morsel with your chopsticks and place it on top of your rice so that the juices help flavor it (sauces are not poured directly onto rice). If you dip a piece of food from your own plate (tempura for instance) into sauce, you may convey it directly to your mouth, but using the rice bowl as a way station helps amateurs because it corrals drips, and the lifted bowl gets food closer to your mouth, thus limiting the likelihood of spills. Use your chopsticks, never fingers, to remove bones, gristle, seeds, and such from your mouth. Place the discarded item to the right side of your own plate or Bento box, or on the table, never in your rice bowl.

Tea is the beverage of choice during meals throughout the region. Rice wine and beer are also traditional table beverages, but polite Asians do not drink alcohol at table without toasting others. (See sections on Tea Ceremonies and International Toasting Rituals in Chapter 27.)

The soup bowl is typically on the right side of your place setting, if soup is not served as a separate course. Japanese-style soups are sometimes served in lacquer bowls with lids. If steam causes the lid to stick, squeeze both sides of the bowl gently with one hand and it will pop loose. You may lift soup bowls as if they were cups and sip the broth. A ceramic soup spoon with a flat bottom can be set down periodically in order to pick up chopsticks for capturing solid ingredients. People around you may eat long noodles in soup by holding the bowl high to avoid splashes, lifting some noodles by chopsticks, and feeding them inch by inch into their mouths, sucking in with a controlled slurping sound. Many believe that inhaling air when eating improves the flavor. Try it and see if you agree.

Eating every bite of food could cause your host to "lose face" (to feel shame in front of others) because he or she did not serve enough to satisfy you. It may be locally good manners to leave some food on your plate during each course of a meal to honor the generosity of your host. Do not take the last piece of food from a serving platter in a private home. In some cultures, it is called "the piece of shame" because to take it shows personal greed. On the other hand, most Asian cultures consider it good manners to eat every grain of rice to show respect to this staple of life and to the host for providing it to you.

Observe your hosts to determine if the chopstick Finished position is vertically on the right side of your bowl, horizontally across the top or bottom (never the middle), or return to the chopstick rests.

Specific Chinese Etiquette

In Chinese-influenced cultures, the host begins each course by serving the guest of honor and one or two other nearby guests. Dinner and drinking can last many hours. Twelve-course banquets with frequent toasts are a Chinese trademark with up to four appetizer dishes, six to eight main courses, soup, and fruit. Unaware Americans have been known to fill up on the first few courses and then have to force themselves to continue eating through the rest of the meal because it is rude to refuse food.

At Chinese-style banquets, in addition to teacups, you may find three glasses at your place setting. The largest is for beer, cola, or water, the smaller glass is for wine, and a stemmed shot glass is for toasting with clear, very potent alcohol. Drink to yourself along with others with a slight bow (nod of the head and shoulders) of appreciation. The Chinese toasting word is *Gambei*—meaning "Bottoms up." The host will strive to keep guest glasses full as a sign of generous hospitality; pace yourself.

Round tables are traditional so that everyone faces each other. Each person is provided an individual bowl of rice. If a bowl of rice or a serving platter is passed to you, accept it respectfully with both hands, perhaps with a bow. Use the serving chopsticks or spoons provided to transfer a portion from the serving platter to your own rice bowl (there may not be any other personal plates). If the dish is too large or too hot to pick up, leave it in place and restrict yourself to taking from the side of the dish more or less facing you. Otherwise, offer food to those on either side before helping yourself and setting the platter down. Do not overload your bowl. Lift your rice bowl with the non-dominant hand (traditionally chopsticks were always held in the right hand) to heart level and hold it close under the chin while using your chopsticks to put or push food into your mouth.

At formal meals, a good host makes every effort to ensure that the guest of honor gets the choicest morsels. He or she may take some food from his or her own plate and place it on the plate of the guest. This is not necessarily done *before* the host has begun eating. Allow the host to start each course. In a home, all the food will be served at the same time, probably one dish for every person present and perhaps one "for the table" in addition to rice or noodles. Always leave a little food—a mannerly gesture. It is not considered wasteful, but is a sign of a generous host who has provided more than enough to eat. Soup may be served near the end of the meal, a reverse of the Western custom. Do not expect a sweet dessert, but fruit may be served. Guests are expected to leave the table within twenty minutes after the last course is served, but individual Chinese guests might leave the table earlier without offense. The guest of honor, like the host, must stay at table until everyone has finished. If your host encourages guests to take uneaten food home, take it.

Specific Japanese Etiquette

Japanese tables are typically set with the rice bowl on the left, the soup bowl on the right, all other plates and dishes in the middle, often corralled in individual Bento boxes. Bento boxes may also be one piece in clever little sections—an aristocratic version of the old-style divided cafeteria tray. Bento boxes are not communal. The small containers may be covered; remove the lids and place them on the table. If provided, lift the bowl of soup (primarily broth) first with your right hand and balance it on the outstretched fingers or palm of your left hand; take a sip or two before setting it down. Chopsticks are found parallel with the edge of the table in front of a Japanese place setting, or resting on the tiny ceramic platforms on the right (chopstick rests). Lift your rice bowl in the same manner as the soup bowl, on your left palm held chest high, and transfer a small bite of rice the short distance to your mouth with your chopsticks. Other bowls remain in the Bento box at all times. Choose food with your chopsticks from each section in rotation, as desired, taking a bite of rice every few mouthfuls. Traditionally the rice bowl remains in your left palm throughout the meal unless you would like more soup or a drink. (In Korea, do *not* cradle your rice bowl; leave it on the table when eating as you would a bowl on a Western table.)

Soup and rice are meant to last throughout the meal. Do not waste food, especially rice; eat every grain. Put bones, seeds, and such on the table or back in the Bento box, never in your rice bowl. When finished, replace the covers of your Bento bowls. See Chopstick Finished Positions above.

Politeness is everything in Japanese table etiquette. To indicate the beginning and the ending of a meal there are standard phrases. In place of grace before eating, diners say *"Itadakimasu"* (I gratefully receive). Wait to begin eating until all are served and the most honored guest begins. *"Dozo"* (Please, or After you) is an all-purpose word used at the dinner table when passing food or utensils to someone. At the meal's conclusion they say *"Gochisosama deshita"* (Thank you for the meal). If you are the guest of honor at a dinner, leave shortly after the meal is finished, as no one will leave before you. If you are not the guest of honor, wait for the highest-ranking person to leave so that you avoid causing offense.

Guests may be given a small wet towel (heated in winter and chilled in summer) to wash hands (and face if desired) before and sometimes after eating. It may arrive in its own basket or tray, where it is returned after use. If it is handed to you with chopsticks, servers will probably wait while you use it and then collect it before you need worry about where to set it down; if not, drape it loosely and lay it on the table. Since napkins are not common, carry a handkerchief or request to keep the wet towel, if desired.

The youngest adult present should pour alcohol for the senior person first, then all other members of the party before placing the *saké* (rice wine) carafe, beer, or wine bottle back on the table or bar to wait on one of the guests to serve him. Diners never pour their own drinks; rather they keep their attention on refilling the cups of others. Politely pour tea for others and allow them to pour for you rather than fill your own cup. Teapots are much smaller than Western ones, as are the handleless cups. When you finish all the liquid in your cup or glass, you will be served more; leave it full to show that you do not care for more. *"Kampai"* ("Bottoms up") is the polite way to toast in Japanese influenced societies.

Experienced diners dip sushi (bite-sized portions of cold rice flavored with vinegar and one or two other ingredients wrapped in seaweed), or sashimi (bite-sized portions of raw fish atop cold rice) into soy sauce with the rice side up. That way it does not soak up too much and disintegrate; inexperienced eaters find this maneuver difficult without the fish falling off. It is correct, though more casual, to eat sushi (originally a street-vendor food) with your fingers. Copy your hosts; if acceptable, it is done by holding each piece gently between the thumb and first two fingers. Place only a little soy sauce in the tiny dish provided for it, and replenish as needed. It is considered wasteful to fill it. Wasabi (bright green, very hot mustard) is mixed a bit at a time into the salty soy sauce until you are pleased with the taste. There is always more than enough and you may keep adding soy and wasabi as needed before dipping. The pink or orange shavings are pickled ginger, used as a palate cleanser between bites. Just as at Western tables, sauces and palate cleansers are not taken with every bite of food; too much will drown out other flavors and make everything taste the same.

At a Japanese-style restaurant, sitting at the bar is popular if you want primarily sushi or sashimi. The bar staff will automatically bring you a wet towel and a complimentary cup of hot green or oolong tea. Place your order with the sushi chef (who has celebrity status) behind the counter, but ask the wait staff for menu items such as drinks, soups, salads, desserts, or anything else such as more soy sauce. Tell the sushi chef when you have finished, as he has been keeping track of your order and will have the wait staff total your bill. It is perfectly acceptable to tell the chef your budget for the evening, if desired.

FAR EASTERN TEA CEREMONIES

Tea is part of every aspect of East Asian cultural life, both high and low. It is considered common courtesy to offer guests tea, and a sign of ill-breeding for guests to refuse a cup. Since ancient times, tea has been regarded as divine, used in religious offerings because of its purity, simplicity, and as a symbol of humbly serving others. Looking at its connection with Zen Buddhism, tea is an example of finding spiritual enlightenment from appreciating everyday things. For many cultures, drinking tea is not only refreshment—it is a dialogue between the body and the spirit. So is tea preparation, a ritual that many believe can only be done with grace and harmony if the heart is at peace. Formal and informal tea ceremonies have become cultural representations of the Asian spirit. *"Please be seated. Please have a cup of tea."* These words extend the warmest of welcomes.

Chinese Tea Etiquette
The Chinese *gaiwan* is a teapot and cup all in one (in use since about AD 1350). It has three pieces that stay together: a saucer, small handleless bowl, and lid. Your skill in manipulating it will be considered by others in Chinese cultures as a mark of your sophistication. Place a single serving of black or oolong tea in the bowl, pour a small amount of boiling water over the leaves, and use the cover to immediately drain off the rinsing water into the discard bowl on the table. Bring the gaiwan to your nose and uncover it to breathe in the freshly released aroma of the tealeaf (similar to enjoying the bouquet of wine or brandy). Pour in boiling water again, down one side of the bowl to produce a swirl in the cup. Cover and steep for two minutes or less. If drinking green or white tea, omit rinsing and steep *without replacing the lid* or the more delicate leaves may cook or "stew."

It is a sign of refinement to drink silently with no rattling. Pick up the entire gaiwan, rest it on your left palm, and take hold of the lid's knob with your right thumb and index finger, letting the other fingers drape naturally over the edge of the lid against the cup. Tilt the lid slightly away from you, leaving a small gap to allow sipping. Males, with their larger physiques, often manage this process with a single hand. If leaves are floating, use the lid as a filter to push them gently out of your way before drinking. The moment you taste a trace of bitterness, add more hot water.

There is much auspicious symbolism ascribed to tea. To celebrate a Chinese engagement, the bride's family accepts gifts from the groom's family during a ceremony in which the bride must offer tea to elders from the groom's family, followed by her own elders. It is a popular sentiment that a marriage contracted with tea will be eternal and will produce many descendants.

Japanese Tea Ceremony

Tea appreciation has been raised to a fine art in the Japanese Tea Ceremony. Dress conservatively in loose clothing that will allow you to sit comfortably on the floor, with at least one pocket but no voluminous sleeves that might be a nuisance. Do not wear dangling bracelets or jewelry that might make noise. Arrive promptly so that you may be introduced to other guests. You will be invited into a special tea room with tatami (straw mats) on the floor. Leave your shoes or slippers at the door as only socks or bare feet are appropriate. You will be asked to kneel on the tatami the entire time you participate in the ceremony.

Guests first observe the ritual of the host purifying the tea utensils. When he or she bows to you, bow back (nod of the head and shoulders). Antique cups may be passed around for you to admire; hold them close to the mat so that if you drop the heirloom it will not break. With both hands, take the serving tray with sweets made of powdered rice (like a cookie). Put the tray directly in front of you. With your right hand pick up the sweet, put it on the piece of paper provided (it serves as your plate) and set both down in front of you. With both hands pass the tray to the guest on your right. If you are last, set the tray down by lining it up on the binding joining the tatami on your right side. Pick up your paper, rest it on your left palm, and eat the entire sweet with your right hand. The reason for this tidbit is that the powdered tea used in the ceremony is rather bitter. You are supposed to finish the sweet before the host makes tea, because it is important to do one thing at a time in this ceremony. After you finish, fold the paper so that no crumbs fall on the mat and put it in your pocket. The host will now whip the powdered, bright green tea into foam, ladle it into individual cups, and pass it to you. Set it directly in front of yourself and bow (to say thank you). Pick up the cup with your right hand, put it on your left palm, and bow again (the second bow is like a grace). Turn the cup to the right twice, and then drink the entire amount with an odd number of sips. When it comes to the last sip, slurp it to finish the tea. This sound indicates not only that you enjoyed it, but also that you are making the effort to finish the foamy tea thoroughly.

CHAPTER 30

Food and Drink Preferences of Various Religious Groups

*R*eligious beliefs often include dietary laws for purposes of spiritual health and usually describe forbidden food or drink, when to fast, and the approved preparation of animals for food. Despite religious dietary laws, *adherence will vary widely even among those who practice the same faith.* Variations may be due to branches or denominations within the religion, national variations, or individual conformity. The best practice is to ask if there is anything a guest cannot eat or drink in advance of your event.

During some parts of the year (Lent, Ramadan) it may be rude to offer refreshments as simple as coffee and donuts during a meeting, and insensitive to eat or drink in front of others. On buffet tables for international guests, a "non-verbal" garnish (such as a pig carved from a lemon or Brussels sprout on foods containing pork) helps guests decide what to eat. If you are planning a toast, offer fruit juice in addition to wine or champagne for those who do not drink alcohol.

AT EASE KEY POINTS

- ✦ Alcohol, beef, pork, and shellfish are problematic to many.
- ✦ Vegetarian dishes, lamb, and chicken are widely accepted.
- ✦ Observance varies even among people of the same faith.
- ✦ Always ask if there is anything a guest cannot eat.
- ✦ Serve juice, water, and soft drinks in addition to alcohol.

BUDDHISM

Since Buddhism is a personal and individualistic religion, no dietary restrictions are enforced, but limitations may be self-imposed. Many followers of Buddhism are vegetarians, in part because of a doctrine of non-injury or nonviolence.

Abstinence from eating any meat stems from the desire to avoid harming other living creatures. Some do not drink alcoholic beverages.

Some countries where Buddhism is practiced are Burma (Myanmar), Cambodia, Japan, Korea, Laos, Nepal, Sri Lanka, Thailand, and Vietnam. Buddhism practiced in Southeast Asia (*Mahayana*) is different from that in Northeast Asia (*Theravada*).

CATHOLICISM

Many Catholics abstain from eating meat on given holy days, particularly in the Lenten season (before Easter). As customs vary widely, it is best to inquire about a guest's preferences. Many countries host large populations of Catholics, for instance Brazil, Italy, Mexico, Portugal, Spain, and the United States.

HINDUISM

Dietary restrictions will vary widely among Hindus according to local custom, caste, and their acceptance of outside practices. Many followers of Hinduism and Jainism are vegetarians because they desire to avoid harming other living creatures. Most (not all) Hindus do not eat meat, fish, or fowl. Others will also refrain from eggs. Some (especially Jains) will not eat root vegetables (e.g., onions, carrots, garlic, beets).

Milk and milk products are normally acceptable. Most Hindus do not drink alcoholic beverages, but fruit juice or cola beverages may be offered as a substitute.

The Hindu religion is practiced widely in India, Nepal, and Sri Lanka. Many large concentrations of Indians are found in other countries as well.

ISLAM

Food (especially meat) that Muslims are allowed to eat is called *halal* and food that should not be eaten is called *haram*. Due to religious laws, no pork (bacon, ham, sausage, etc.) is served to Muslims, nor any food prepared by using pork products (e.g., bacon grease, broth, lard).

Religious law also forbids alcoholic beverages. Usually, a Muslim guest of honor will not drink, but has no objection if others do. Saudi Arabians are more orthodox in this respect and do not drink alcohol, while Pakistanis are more liberal and frequently do take alcoholic drinks.

Devout Muslims fast during the entire month of Ramadan, believed to be the month during which God gave the Qur'an (Koran), the Islamic holy book, to the Prophet Muhammad. During Ramadan, eating, drinking, and smoking are done only before dawn and after sunset.

Some countries considered predominately Muslim are: Afghanistan, Egypt, Ethiopia, Indonesia, Iran, Iraq, Ghana, Jordan, Lebanon, Libya, Malaysia, Morocco, Pakistan, Saudi Arabia, Syria, Tunisia, and Turkey. Although India has a majority of Hindus, it also has a substantial minority of Muslims. Large Islamic populations are found in other countries as well.

JUDAISM

The system of Jewish dietary laws discussed in Jewish scripture is called *kashrut*, and those who observe it are said to be "keeping kosher." Kosher foods include all fresh fruits and vegetables, any fish with fins and scales, most dairy products, and certain types of meat and poultry (when slaughtered by a kosher butcher). Jews who keep strictly kosher will eat even kosher meat only when it is prepared with kosher utensils in a kosher kitchen. Others will observe one or more, but not all, Jewish dietary laws. They may avoid shellfish, or not eat any pork, or they may not eat meat and milk products together (such as a cheeseburger).

During the week of Passover, which usually occurs in or near April, an additional set of restrictions is in effect, and further planning may be required to accommodate them. Israel has a growing majority of Jews, but it also has a substantial minority of Muslims. Large Jewish populations are in many other countries, including the United States.

MORMONISM

The Church of the Latter Day Saints abstains from alcoholic beverages by religious law. Fruit juices are an acceptable alternative. They may also avoid any caffeine product (coffee, tea, cocoa, and cola beverages), but many Mormons take exception to this restriction. The United States hosts the largest population of Mormons.

WHAT WOULD YOU SERVE IF ALL RELIGIONS WERE AT THE SAME TABLE?

The largest group of world leaders in history gathered for a meal celebrating the fiftieth anniversary of the United Nations on October 21, 1995. Everything from flower colors to serving order to food ingredients accommodated the many religious and cultural sensitivities. They could not serve shellfish, pork, beef, or sauces that contained alcohol. Here is the chosen American-style menu as published in the *New York Times*:

Hors d'oeuvres
Wild Mushroom Risotto Cakes
Four-Cheese Polenta Diamonds
Sweet Potato Pancakes

First course
Salad topped with a Goat Cheese Crouton

Main course
Rack of Lamb and Roast Chicken Breast
with Wild Rice and Wheatberry Pilaf

Dessert
Ice Cream with Chocolate Sauce

Sources: Overseas Briefing Center, U.S. Department of State; Joint Military Attaché School, U.S. Department of Defense; Hampton Road Fleet Reserve Center, U.S. Navy; and the *New York Times* newspaper.

INDEX

Index

A

abbreviations: on business and social cards, 16, 207, 208; electronic correspondence, 224; jargon, military, 7; rank, 127–37, 163; in social correspondence, 7, 127–37, 221–22; written communication and, 7

address, forms of: Air Force officers and personnel, 127, 136–37; Army officers and personnel, 127, 134–35; Cabinet officers, 241–42; city officials, 247–48; Coast Guard officers and personnel, 127, 132–33; Congress, 245–46; diplomats, 243–45; divorcées, 163, 253; doctors, 253; Federal agency heads, 248; federal dignitaries, 238–46, 248; first names, 15, 239, 442; foreign dignitaries, 238; grade equivalency chart, 18–19; international protocol, 441–42; introductions and use of titles, 9, 14–15, 123; Marine Corps officers and personnel, 127, 130–31; Navy officers and personnel, 127, 128–29; President and White House officials, 238, 240–41, 242–43; professors, 253; rank charts, 127–37; religious dignitaries, 249–52; state officials, 247–48; Supreme Court justices, 238, 241; widows, 253

Air Force Academy Cadet Chapel, 146–47

Air Force, U.S., 4; address, forms of, 127, 136–37; birthday, 110; color guard ceremonies, 118; parade formation order of precedence, 126; rank chart, 127, 136–37; Service song, 75; toast to, 320; uniforms and headgear, men, 366–67, 386–87; uniforms and headgear, women, 368–69, 388–89; VIP/DV visitor codes, 122–25

air travel: carry-on bags, 428–29; checked luggage, 427–28; gifts and, 435; meeting businessmen, 463; professional dress, 425; seating arrangements, 400; snacks, 429; VIP/DIV arrivals, 49–50; VIP/DIV departures, 55; women flying alone, 426

American embassy precedence, 439–40

American-Style table manners, 269, 270, 271–74

apologies, 324–25; apology letters, 214, 463

appreciation, letters of, 41

arch of swords/arch of sabres, 150–53, 158

Army, U.S., 4; address, forms of, 127, 134–35; birthday, 110; color guard ceremonies, 116, 118; parade formation order of precedence, 126; rank chart, 127, 134–35; Service song, 75; toast to, 320; uniforms and headgear, men, 350–51, 374–75; uniforms and headgear, women, 352–53, 376–77; VIP/DV visitor codes, 122–25

art gallery etiquette, 325–26

Asian cultures and manners, 496; alcoholic beverages, 485; Bento boxes, 505; Chinese-influenced cultures, 501, 504–5, 507–8; chopsticks, 496–501, 502–3, 504, 505; communal platters, 497, 503; dining etiquette, 497; drinks, pouring, 506; funerary chopsticks, 497–98; guest manners, 502–7; guest of honor, 504, 505–6; Japanese-influenced cultures, 499–501, 505–7, 508; knives at table, 496; leaving food on your plate, 503–4, 505; napkins, 502, 506; offensive behaviors, 497; rice and rice bowls, 503, 505; round tables, 504; shoes, 502; soup and soup bowls, 497, 503, 505; sushi, 506–7; tea, 503, 506; tea ceremonies, 507–8; toasts, 487, 504; toothpicks, 497; wet towel, 506

assistance to others: chairs, assistance with, 283, 288–89, 408; coat, helping on with, 329; exiting elevators, stairwells, rooms, buildings, 329; hand or arm for assistance, 329; persons with disabilities, 329; revolving doors, 329; steep stairs, 329

audience civility, 326–27

auditoriums and audience seating, 396–98

aviation participation at funerals, 98

award ceremonies, 24–25

awards, 336

B

badges, 336

baggage, 426–28

ballets, audience civility for, 326–27

Barong Tagalog, 347

Belgium, 449

Bento boxes, 505

Bierce, Ambrose, 10

biographical sketch, 8–9

birth or adoption announcements, 218–19

birthdays, 110

blessings and prayers, 258, 277–78, 289, 483, 489, 494

body movement and gestures, 10, 303, 447

bodyguards and security personnel, 42, 145–46, 405–6

briefings. See meetings and briefings

Buddhism: dietary laws, 509–10; forms of address, 250

buffet-style dining, 280–81, 467

bugle calls, 5, 91–92, 112–13

building dedications, 25

bunting, 106

burial at sea, 98–99

Bush, George W., 99, 315, 345, 447, 451

business cards: abbreviations on, 16, 207, 208; diplomatic attaché cards, 204–5; exchange of, 12, 204, 287, 288; exchange of in international/foreign locations, 429, 444–46; format and lettering, 203; information on, 203; introductory calls, 12; letters of introduction and, 16; meetings and briefings, 9; need and uses for, 200; writing notes on, 16, 207–8

Business Casual dress, 348

business functions, 286; business meals, 288–90; chairs, assistance with, 288–89; cocktail parties, 290–93; conversations, 311–12; farewells, 313; gender bias, 289; gifts, 287; handshakes, 204, 287, 291, 298, 301–2, 313, 331; international social occasions, 464; invitations/admittance cards, 288; menu cards, 289; official business functions, 286–90; prayers and blessings, 289; receptions and receiving lines, 293–300; spouses at, 290; tea manners, 327–28; thank-you notes, 287; uniform requirements, 287. See also Dining In

C

Cabinet officers: address, forms of, 241–42; music for, 402

Canadian government Web site, 423

cannon salutes. See gun and cannon salutes

cantaloupe soup, 468

caps and hats, civilian, 339

cars with drivers, 399–400, 450, 454–55

Carter, Jimmy, 315

Casual dress, 347–48

Catholicism: dietary laws, 510; forms of address, 250

cell phones: audience civility, 326; etiquette, 231–33, 234; GSM (Global System for Mobile), 431; international/foreign locations, 431; meetings and, 8; pollution,

231; speakerphones, 236. *See also* telephone etiquette

ceremonies: award ceremonies, 24–25; building dedications, 25; changes of command, 26–27; decoration ceremonies, 25; document signings, 27; escorts, 21–22; Fallen Comrade Observance, 81–87; flag retirement, 110–11; format for, 20–21; frockings, 29; generic checklist, 23–24; groundbreakings, 25; gun and cannon salutes, 5, 25–26, 90–91; honors, 28–29; host of, 20; Navy vessels, 31–33; presentation of medals, 24–25; promotions and re-enlistments, 29–30; purpose of, 20; ribbon cuttings, 25; sequence of events, 21–23; Silent Drill Platoons, 30; wreath layings, 33

chairs, assistance with, 283, 288–89, 408

Change of Command Ceremony, 401–2

Change of Command Reception, 402

changes of command ceremonies, 26–27

chapels: fee or donation for using, 102, 143, 146; memorial service honors, 99; military chapel funerals, 94–95, 96, 97; Service academy chapel weddings, 146–50

chaplains, 102, 143, 304

children: gifts for, 435, 473; international social occasions and, 469; at weddings, 179

China: alcoholic beverages, 485; chopsticks, 501; gifts, 473, 476; invitations, 193; table etiquette, 503, 504–5; tea ceremonies, 507–8; toasts, 485, 487, 504

chopsticks, 496–501, 502–3, 504, 505

Church Pennant, 109

city officials, 247–48

civility. *See* protocol, etiquette, and civility

civil/public servants: grade equivalency chart, 18–19; occupations of, 4; pay grade charts, 121; precedence order, 18–19, 121

Clinton, William, 451

clothing: appearance, importance of, 334, 341; colors for, 340–41; dress terms on

invitations, 345–48; first impressions, 341; gloves, civilian, 339–40; hats and caps, civilian, 339; improper dress, 338; for international travel, 425–26; jewelry, 344; men's clothing list, 343–44; raincoats, 341; regional and cultural sensitivity, 348; shirts, 341; shoes, 344; for social occasions, 338; socks, 344; suits, 340–41; ties, 341, 342–43; wardrobes, civilian, 340–44; for wedding guests, 144; women's clothing list, 344. *See also* uniforms and headgear

Coast Guard, U.S., 4; address, forms of, 127, 132–33; birthday, 110; color guard ceremonies, 118; parade formation order of precedence, 126; rank chart, 127, 132–33; Service song, 75; toast to, 320; uniforms and headgear, men, 370–71, 390–91; uniforms and headgear, women, 372–73, 392–93; VIP/DV visitor codes, 122–25

cocktail parties, 290–93

coffee ceremonies, 494–95

color guard: ceremonies, 116–18; Dining In, 66–67; at funerals, 93, 99; Joint Armed Forces Color Guard, 116, 118

Commissioned Corps of the Public Health Service, U.S., 4; birthday, 110; Service song, 75; toast to, 320; VIP/DV visitor codes, 122–25

communal platter dining, 497; Asian cultures and manners, 497, 503; beverages, 493; bread and, 493; coffee ceremonies, 494–95; eating with fingers, 488–89, 492–93; end-of-meal signals, 495; guest manners, 490–94; hand-washing ritual, 489, 491; offensive behaviors, 489; separating portions, 492–93; tea ceremonies, 494–95; utensils, 492–93

concerts, audience civility for, 326–27

condolence letters, 215

conference panel, questioning from audience, 46

conference room seating arrangements, 9–10, 398–99

Congress of Vienna, 437, 438

conversations: art of, 310–13; disagreements, 312; exit lines, 312–13; international social occasions, 461; ranks and names, 14–15; social occasions, 270, 310–13; spies, 431–32; terms of respect, 14–15; topics to avoid, 311. *See also* address, forms of; introductions

corporate and business world: first name use, 15; gift regulations, 476; precedence order, 120, 395

covers, 6, 337

crime, 422–23, 429–30

cubicle civility, 330

D

decision-making styles, 456–57

decoration ceremonies, 25

decorations, 336

dedications, 25

dignitaries: address, forms of, 238; designated representatives, 399; host status and, 412; international protocol, 450–55; seating plans and arrangements, 399; special military funerals, 100–101

dining facilities, military: behavior at meals, 6–7; invitations to guests, 6–7; seating at, 7

Dining In: committees, 59; departing, 58; fines and reports, 57–58; guest of honor, 64; guest speakers, 57, 61, 63, 64; head tables, 63, 64, 404; invitations, 59–61; menu and service, 61–62; music, 59; participants, 57; penalties, 57–58, 68–70; preparation, 58–64; printed program, 58; recognition of missing compatriots, 62, 78, 81–87; Rules, 58; seating plans and arrangements, 63–64; sequence of events, 57–58, 65–72; toasts, 58, 71–72, 73–78

Dining Out, 57, 79–80, 81, 404

dining tables, 405–13, 414–17

diplomatic attaché cards, 204–5

diplomatic officials: American embassy precedence, 439–40; designated representatives, 440; diplomatic calls, 13; license plates, 439; precedence order, 438–40; special military funerals, 100–101

document signings, 27

Dos and Taboos around the World (Axtell), 258, 318, 426

dress. *See* clothing

drive-left societies, 455

drum or fife procession, 66

Durable Power of Attorney, 422

E

Egypt, 449

electronic correspondence, 223–24; abbreviations, 224; automatic replies, 224; caller ID, 235; e-mail, 224–29; e-mail invitations, 230–31; interruptions, 234; liability caveat, 229; security issues, 230; text messages, 225, 231, 232, 235; thank-you messages, 331; voice mail, 235–36. *See also* cell phones; telephone etiquette

elevator statements, 9

elevators, 430

engagement parties, 157

enlisted personnel: Air Force uniforms and headgear, 366–69; Army uniforms and headgear, 350–53; Coast Guard uniforms and headgear, 370–73; Marine Corps uniforms and headgear, 362–65; Navy uniforms and headgear, 354–61; oath of office, 30; promotions and re-enlistments, 29–30; staff as, 4

escort cards, 406–7

escorts, 38, 41–46, 51, 52, 55

etiquette. *See* protocol, etiquette, and civility

executives, 4. *See also* officers

expatriates, gifts for, 434–35

eye behavior and contact, 447

F

Fallen Comrade Observance: at Dining in or Dining out, 62, 78, 81; preparation, 81–84; script, 84–87; silent toasts, 82; toasts, 86, 315

family introductions, 305–6

farewell calls, 12–13

Federal agency heads, 248

federal employees, occupations of, 3

fife or drum procession, 66

first impressions, 12, 341, 432

fixity and silence, 10

flag, United Nations (UN), 118–19

flag, United States: approved flag customs, 109; burial at sea, 98–99; color guard, 66–67, 93, 99, 116–18; dates for display of, 110; designations, 107; dipping, 102, 107, 116; display of, 104–6, 109; disposal of, 110–11; funeral protocol, folding. and presentation, 92–93, 98–99, 102, 107–9; half-staff and mourning flags, 102, 108–9; history of, 103–4; honors ceremonies, 28; at military reservations, 6; miniature flags, 107; ordering flags, 106–7; parade review, 115–16; Pledge of Allegiance, 111; posting the colors, 21, 22, 119; precedence order, 106, 114–15, 119; respect for, 6; retirement ceremony, 110–11; retiring the colors, 119; reveille and retreat ceremonies, 112–13; saluting, 116; toast to, 320

flag rank officers, 7, 8

flags, international: display of, 114; etiquette, 119; precedence order, 114–15, 119; respect for, 6, 113–14

flags, personal, 23, 28, 99, 102, 106

flowers: at funerals, 90; international social occasions, 474, 475; for weddings, 144, 147

food and drink: after-dinner drinks, 269; both hands to offer and receive, 40, 461, 482, 504, 508; both hands to serve, 266, 274; buffet-style dining, 280–81, 467; cantaloupe soup, 468; cheese course,

269; cocktail parties, 291–92; coffee ceremonies, 494–95; dessert course, 268; Dining In menu and service, 61–62; drinks, pouring, 506; family-style dining, 276–79; fish course, 266; food gifts, 435, 460, 474, 475, 478–79; formal dining, 282–84; holiday-themed food, 468, 471; international social occasions, 461, 465–66, 467; main course, 267; at meetings and briefings, 10–11; menu cards, 180, 258, 259, 282, 289, 443–44; at military dining facilities, 6–7; religious beliefs and dietary laws, 509–12; removal of objectionable food, 261; rice and rice bowls, 503, 505; salad course, 267–68; seconds, requests for, 279; service styles, 274–75; signature meals, 467–68; snacks, 429; sorbet course, 267; soup and soup bowls, 265, 497, 503, 505; spills, 279; sushi, 506–7; tea and tea ceremonies, 327–28, 494–95, 503, 506, 507–8; VIP/DV visit meals and menus, 37–38; at wedding receptions, 154, 155–57, 180. See also table manners; wine

Force Protection Conditions (FPCON), 36–37, 423

foreign service, 18–19

Formal dress, 346–47

Formal Morning dress, 345

fraternal or military organizations, 98

frockings, 29, 127

funerals, military: attire for, 90, 94, 101; authorization for, 88; aviation participation, 98; burial at sea, 98–99; caisson, 100; casket, 94; chapel service, 94–95, 96, 97; color guard, 93, 99; cremation, 95; flag protocol, folding, and presentation, 92–93, 98–99, 102, 107–8; fraternal or military organizations, 98; graveside service, 96; gun and cannon salutes, 25–26, 90–91, 97; Honors Detail, 88–89, 92, 94, 102; memorial service honors, 99; military honors, sequence for, 89–93; national anthem, 89–90; pallbearers, 93–94; protocol notes, 101–2;

special military funerals, 100–101; taps, 91–92, 99

G

gifts: acceptances of, 476; for associates, 434–35, 473–74; both hands to offer and receive, 258, 434, 460, 472, 473, 475; business functions, 287; for children, 435, 473; coordination and negotiation of exchange, 476; cultural customs and, 476–77; for family members, 435; food gifts, 435, 460, 478–79; at funerals, 90; gift ceremonies for VIPs/DVs, 40, 475–76; holiday-themed gifts, 435; hospitality gifts, 474–75; international gift suggestions, 473–75, 476–79; international social occasions, 460, 472–79; log or registry, 160–61, 332; Made-in-America gifts, 475, 477; for new spouse, 160; personal and token, 434–35, 473–75; presentation of, 40, 475–76; regulations for accepting, 476; table favors, 159; for wedding attendants, 159; wedding gift registry, 160; wrapping, 472. See also thank-you notes

gloves, 339–40

Goods and Services Tax (GST), 424

government order of preference, 121–25, 438, 450, 451

grade equivalency chart, 15, 18–19

greeting cards, 216–17

greetings: hand kissing, 450; handshakes, 204, 287, 291, 298, 301–2, 313, 331, 447–48; international protocol, 447–50; social kissing, 449. See also address, forms of

grog ceremony/penalty grog bowl, 68–69

groundbreakings, 25

guest of honor: Asian cultures and manners, 504, 505–6; communal eating, 490–94; departures, 284–85; diplomatic toasts, 318–19; duties at dinners, 327, 495; introductions, 282; invitations, 195–96; precedence order, 123; seating plans and arrangements, 64, 327, 394, 408, 415, 481; at tea, 328; toasts, 327, 485–86

guest speakers: Dining In, 57, 61, 63, 64;

escort for, 46; head table, 404; letters of invitation, 193–94; seating plans and arrangements, 63, 64, 400–401, 411

guidon exchange, formal, 26–27

Gulf Rig dress, 346

gun and cannon salutes: at ceremonies, 5, 25–26; at funerals, 25–26, 90–91, 97; saluting, 116; three rifle-volley salutes, 26, 90–91, 97; twenty-one-gun salutes, 25–26

H

hair color, 432

hands: both hands to offer and receive business cards, 445–46; both hands to offer and receive food, 40, 461, 482, 504, 508; both hands to offer and receive gifts, 258, 434, 460, 472, 473, 475; both hands to serve food, 266, 274; eating styles, 270, 271–72, 489, 492, 493; gesturing with, 303, 447; hand kissing, 450; handshakes, 204, 287, 291, 298, 301–2, 313, 331, 447–48; holding hands, 447; left hands, 204, 489, 492; toasting and, 74–75, 157, 322, 483, 486

handwriting, improving, 212

hats and caps, civilian, 339

Hayes, Rutherford B., 315

Helms, Richard, 431

heroism, 329

hierarchy, 120–21

high-profile visits. See VIPs/DVs

Hinduism, 251, 510

holiday-themed food, 468, 471

holiday-themed gifts, 435

honor guard: cordon at weddings and receptions, 150, 152–53, 158; Fallen Comrade Observance, 83–84; funerals and memorial services, 99, 100, 102

honors, military: ceremonies, 28–29; dignity of, 3–4; flags, 28; full honors, 28–29; funerals, sequence for, 89–93; honor cordon, 29; music, 21

Honors Detail, 88–89, 92, 94, 102

hospital manners, 328

hospitality gifts, 474–75

host and co-host duties, 258, 279, 287–88, 327, 408–9, 465

host status, forfeiture of, 412

hotels: address of, 430–31; privacy of information and, 432, 443; room assignments, 432; security issues, 429–30; tips, 429–30; VIP/DV arrival, 51–52

houseguests, 325

I

India, 448, 481

Indonesia, 435, 455

Informal dress, 347

in-law welcome letter, 163, 213

in-laws, introducing, 305–6

insignia of Service grade, 337

interior design of homes, 469–70

international business meeting etiquette, 456–57

international protocol: address, forms of, 441–42; body language faux pas, 446–50; bows and curtsies, 463; business card exchanges, 444–46; Congress of Vienna, 437, 438; dignitaries and officials, 450–55; eye behavior and contact, 447; flags, international, 6, 113–15, 119; formality and manners, 436; gift ceremonies, 40; greetings, 447–50; hand holding, 447; invitations, 443–44; meeting businessmen, 463; mentors, host-country, 433, 439, 441, 442, 459, 485; precedence order, 437–39; professional behavior, 436; souvenir value of social correspondence, 443–44; thank-you notes, 444; touching and personal space, 432, 446–47; verbal faux pas, 440–42; written faux pas, 442–44

international social occasions: behavior during, 458, 459; buffet-style dining, 467; business functions, 464; checklists and databases, 464–65; children and, 469; conversations, 461; cultural customs, 468; departures, 461, 471–72; flowers, 474, 475;

food and drink, 461, 465–66, 467; food gifts, 474, 475, 478–79; gift suggestions, 473–75, 476–79; gifts, 460, 472–79; guest books, 460, 465; guest manners, 460–61; holiday-themed food, 468, 471; hospitality and respect, 471–72; host and co-host duties, 465; hosting internationals, 462–66; hosting internationals at home, 466–72; interior design of homes, 469–70; introductions, 460–61; invitations, 458–59, 462–64; language skills and barriers, 469; menu cards, 466; planned activities, 461, 469, 481; reciprocating invitations, 461; representational entertaining, 462; scheduling considerations, 471; seating plans and arrangements, 465; signature meals, 467–68; smoking, 471; table manners, 258, 480–83; thank-you notes, 461; toasts, 483–87

international/foreign locations: behavior in, 421–23, 425, 428, 446–50; business card exchanges, 429, 444–46; cell phones, 431; civilian dress, 348; climate, 462; clothing for, 425–26; country-specific customs and behaviors, 421–23, 441; credit cards, 423–24; crime in, 422–23, 429–30; culture stress, 432–33; currency, 423; documents, scanning or copying, 424–25; Durable Power of Attorney preparation, 422; electrical systems, 427; English, understanding of, 433; females, suggestions for, 425–26; filming individuals, 421–22; first impressions, 432; Force Protection Conditions (FPCON), 423; gifts, personal and token, 434–35, 473–75; Goods and Services Tax (GST), 424; guest duties, 199; hair color, 432; handshakes, 313; hot water, 429, 430; hotel address, 430–31; hotel rooms, 429–30, 432; introductory calls, 12; intrusive questions, 433–34, 442; itinerary, 425; language skills and barriers, 433, 440–42, 469; maps, 431; names, enunciation of, 440–41; national anthems, 6, 113–14; news broadcasts, 430; olfactics, 432; opinions toward U.S. and treatment of travelers, 422, 433–34; phrases to learn, 433, 442; radio broadcasts, 430;

registration for traveling abroad, 423; research and Web sites, 423; restrooms, 433; security issues, 422; social times, 462; spies, 270, 431–32; table manners, 258, 480–83; taxis, 431; telephones, 430, 431; time and punctuality, 462–63; toilets, 433; toll-free numbers, 424; trade secrets, 431–32; travel to, 421–23; trip file/checklist, 424–25; Value Added Tax (VAT), 424; water, 430; weather information, 423; Will preparation, 422

international/foreign officials: address, forms of, 238; conference room seating arrangements, 399; diplomatic toasts, 318–19; introductions, 451–52; precedence order, 437–39; protocol, 450–55; seating plans and arrangements, 399, 416; special military funerals, 100–101

International-Style table manners, 269, 271–74

interpreters, 38, 42, 405, 452–54

introduction letters, 15–17

introductions, 301; elevator statements, 9; family introductions, 305–6; forgotten introductions, 306–7; in groups, 307; handshakes, 301–2; international protocol, 441–42; international social occasions, 460–61; international/foreign officials, 451–52; letters of, 15–17; making, 303–5; at meetings and briefings, 9, 11; mispronounced names, 309; of newly married couple, 153; office calls, 14–15; party prologues, 9; precedence order, 303–4, 307; responding to, 301–3; self-introductions, 9, 308–9; service introductions, 304–5; surnames, 451–52; title mentioned during, 9, 14–15, 123; VIP/DV visits, 44–45

introductory calls, 11–12

invitations: address, forms of, 127–37; advancing, 194; to ceremonies, 23; changing answer to, 197; Chinese, 193; components of, 188–91; dining facility guests, 6–7; Dining In, 59–61; dress terms on, 345–48; e-mail invitations, 230–31; face-to-face invitations, 197, 198; family-

style dining, 277; guest of honor, 195–96; handwritten, 193, 213–14; international protocol, 443–44; international social occasions, 458–59, 462–64; letters of invitation, 193–94; luncheon, 163; methods for extending, 187; official social events, 192–93, 220; p.m. (To Remind) cards, 196, 197, 198; postponing, 194; printing of, 187–88; ranking spouses, 192–93; recalling, 194–95; reciprocating invitations, 461; reply cards, 192; responding to, 199; "save the date" cards, 198–99; social (non-official events), 193; style of, 187–88; verbal and telephone, 196, 197–98, 235–36, 463; White House invitations, 196, 197. See also wedding invitations

Iran, 448

Islam, 251, 510–11

J

Japan: alcoholic beverages, 485; chopsticks, 499–501; gifts, 435; greetings, 448; table etiquette, 505–7; tea ceremonies, 508

jargon, 7

Judaism, 251, 511

K

kissing: hands, 450; social, 449

Korea, 451, 463, 485

L

language skills and barriers, 433, 440–42, 469

Latin America, 449, 476

left hands, 204, 489, 492

left-drive societies, 455

letterhead, government, 200

letters and written correspondence: abbreviations, 7, 127–37, 221–22; address, forms of, 127–37; addressing envelopes, 219–20; apology letters, 214, 463; of appreciation, 41; birth or adoption announcements, 218–19; "compliments," 212; condolence letters, 215; greeting cards, 216–17; handwritten, 163, 211, 212, 213–14; in-law welcome letter, 163, 213; international protocol, 442–44; introduction letters, 15–17; mourning cards, 216; personal letters, 213–16; recommendation letters, 15–16; reference letters, 217–18; "respects," 212; return address, 207, 220; self-introductions, 16–17; social letters, 211–12, 213; souvenir value of social correspondence, 443–44; written faux pas, 442–44. *See also* stationery, personal; thank-you notes

library etiquette, 328–29

limousines, 399–400, 454–55

luggage, 426–28

M

Malaysia, 448

Maori, 448

Marine Barracks, Washington, D.C., 30

Marine Corps, U.S., 4; address, forms of, 127, 130–31; birthday, 110; color guard ceremonies, 118; parade formation order of precedence, 126; rank chart, 127, 130–31; Service song, 75; toast to, 320; uniforms and headgear, men, 362–63, 382–83; uniforms and headgear, women, 364–65, 384–85; VIP/DV visitor codes, 122–25

marriage: at-home cards (change of address cards), 182–83; to foreign national, 161; housing allowance, 162; in-law welcome letter, 163, 213; military lifestyle, 164; name changes, 162–63; official marriage status, 161–62; permission for, 161; personnel department, notification of, 162; professional and social names, 162–63. *See also* wedding, military; wedding receptions

marriage announcements, 180–81

medals, presentation of, 24–25, 336–37

media: VIP/DV visits and, 39; at weddings, 146

meetings and briefings, 7–9; access to

workplace locations, 8; agenda for, 8; business cards, 9; cell phones, 8; conference room seating arrangements, 9–10, 398–99; folders and papers, 10; food at, 10–11; formality during, 11; information about attendees, 8; international business meeting etiquette, 456–57; introductions at, 9, 11; mixed meetings, 11; notepads and pens, 10; place cards, 399; thank you notes, 10; walking briefs, 45

memorial service honors, 99

menu cards, 180, 258, 259, 282, 289, 443–44, 466

Merchant Marine, 110

Middle East: diplomacy in action, 453; social kissing, 449; social occasions and receiving lines, 295

military lifestyle: misconceptions about, 41; moving, 164; service members, everyday business of, 4; spouses, challenges for, 164

military members: occupations of, 4. *See also* enlisted personnel; noncommissioned officers; officers

military reservations: amenities available, 5; American flag at, 6; meals at, 6–7; security at, 5; sights and sounds, 5–6; speed limit, 5; visits to, 5–7

miniature flags, 107

Missing Man Table and Honors. *See* Fallen Comrade Observance

Mormonism, 251, 511

mourning bands, 101

mourning cards, 216

museum etiquette, 325–26

music: Dining In, 59; for entering an event, 402; honors at ceremonies, 21; mourning bands, 101; patriotic, 112; for weddings, 147

Muslims: dietary laws, 510–11; forms of address, 251; greetings, 448; handshakes, 291

N

name tags, 349

napkins: Asian cultures and manners, 502, 506; etiquette, 258, 260–62

national anthem: at ceremonies, 21; at funerals, 89–90; reveille and retreat ceremonies, 112–13

national anthems, foreign, 6, 113–14

national ceremonies, 3–4

National Dress, 347

National Guard, 110

national march, 112

National Military Family Association (NMFA), 164

National Oceanic and Atmospheric Administration Corps, U.S., 4; birthday, 110; Service song, 75; toast to, 320; VIP/ DV visitor codes, 123–25

Navy, U.S., 4; address, forms of, 127, 128–29; birthday, 110; color guard ceremonies, 118; parade formation order of precedence, 126; rank chart, 127, 128–29; Service song, 75; toast to, 320; uniforms and headgear, men, 354–55, 358–59, 378–79; uniforms and headgear, women, 356–57, 360–61, 380–81; VIP/ DV visitor codes, 122–25

Navy vessels: boarding, 31; burial at sea, 98–99; captain, 31; christening, 31; construction and fitting out, 31; disembarking, 33; etiquette aboard, 32–33; flag customs, 109; naming, 31; piping aboard, 32; side boys and tending the side, 31–32

negotiation tactics, 456–57

noncommissioned officers, 4

O

office calls, 11; agenda for, 15; diplomatic calls, 13; ending, 14; farewell calls, 12–13; introductions, 14–15; introductory calls, 11–12; planning for, 14–15; private in-office visits, 13–14; rank and terms of respect, 14–15

office civility, 330

officers: address, forms of, 127–37; Air Force uniforms and headgear, 386–89; Army uniforms and headgear, 374–77; Coast Guard uniforms and headgear, 390–93; executives as, 4; Marine Corps uniforms and headgear, 382–85; Navy uniforms and headgear, 378–81; oath of office, 30; postgraduate education of, 3; promotions, 29–30, 127; responsibility toward other and, 4

olfactics, 432

"One More Roll" (U.S. service members), 87

operas, audience civility for, 326–27

P

parade formation, 126

parade review, 115–16

Partnership for Public Service, 3

party prologues, 9

"passing the buck," 32–33

pay grade charts, 121

Pentagon, 6

personal and token gifts, 434–35, 473–75

personal honors, 116

personal letters, 213–16

Philippines, 448

photos and photographers: at ceremonies, 22, 25; head and should shot for bio, 8; hosting internationals at home, 469; interpreters, 453; at receptions and receiving lines, 296, 298, 300; VIP/DV visits, 39–40, 54

place cards, 127, 154, 156, 258, 259–60, 399

plays, audience civility for, 326–27

Pledge of Allegiance, 111

p.m. (To Remind) cards, 463

points of order, 69–70

political activity while wearing uniform, 338

port wine ceremony, 70

posting the colors, 21, 22

Powell, Colin, 468

POW/MIA Recognition. *See* Fallen Comrade Observance

prayers and blessings, 258, 277–78, 289, 483, 489, 494

precedence order: American embassy precedence, 439–40; civil/public servants, 121; corporate and business world, 120, 395; cultural customs, 395; diplomatic officials, 438–40; flag, United States, 106, 114–15, 119; flags, international, 114–15, 119; flags, personal, 106; foreign officials, 122; foreign service, 18–19; government order of preference, 121–25, 438, 450, 451; guest of honor, 123; international protocol, 437–39; military, 18–19, 120, 122, 127–37; panel of government officials, 401; parade formation, 126; principles of, 395; public precedence order, 395; seating plans and arrangements, 63–64, 327, 394, 403, 408–9, 412, 413, 414, 415–17; visitor codes, 122–25

prescription medications, 428–29

President and White House officials: address, forms of, 238, 240–41, 242–43; host status and, 412; introductions, 310; music for, 402; precedence order, 438, 451; South Front of White House, 453; state dinner seating arrangements, 416; White House invitations, 196, 197, 299–300

Privacy Act of 1974, 443

private information, 432, 443

private in-office visits, 13–14

promotions: ceremonies, 29–30; frockings, 29, 127

Protestant faiths, 252

protocol, etiquette, and civility: civilians' preconception of, 4; correcting the manners of others, 327; importance of, 3–4, 199; manners, basis for, 329; office civility, 330; real men, 4; respect, 121–22; silence and fixity, 10

Public Health Service. *See* Commissioned Corps of the Public Health Service, U.S.

punch bowl ceremony, 68

R

rank: abbreviations, 127–37, 163; charts, 127–37; conference room seating arrangements and, 9–10; grade equivalency chart, 15, 18–19; introductions, 304–5; precedence order, 18–19, 120, 122, 127–37; professional and social names, 162–63; rank flags, 109; respect for, 122–23; responsibility toward other and, 4; royalty and, 4; self-introductions and, 9; stationery, personal, 202–3; wedding invitations, 167–68, 195

rank devices, 5

real men, 4

receptions and receiving lines, 293–300, 402, 453. *See also* wedding receptions

recommendation letters, 15–16

Red Sea Rig dress, 345, 346

re-enlistment ceremonies, 29–30

reference letters, 217–18

rehearsal, wedding, 145

rehearsal dinner, wedding, 145, 157

religious beliefs and dietary laws, 509–12

religious pennants, 109

religious services or meetings, 333–34

representational entertaining, 462

reputation of Americans, 459

reserve personnel, 202

restrooms, 433

retired military personnel: introductions, 305; stationery, personal, 202–3; uniforms and, 337–38

retirement ceremony and dinner, 331

retreats, weekend, 325

reveille and retreat ceremonies, 112–13

ribbon cuttings, 25

ribbons, 336

round tables, 409–10, 411, 504

royalty, rank and, 4

R.s.v.p., 60, 169, 171, 178, 190, 192, 199, 221, 463

rum punch ceremony, 70–71

S

salutes and saluting: to colors, 116; at funerals, 102; gun salutes, 116; personal honors, 116. *See also* gun and cannon salutes

Schooner Rig dress, 346

Scottish Highland trews, 347

seating plans and arrangements: aircraft, 400; auditoriums and audience seating, 396–98; cars with drivers, 399–400, 454–55; Change of Command Ceremony, 401–2; conference room seating arrangements, 9–10, 398–99; diagrams, 408, 409, 410, 411, 413, 414, 415; dignitaries, 399; Dining In, 63–64; dining tables, 405–13, 414–17; escort cards, 406–7; escort precedence list, 408; E-shaped tables, 411–12; guest of honor, 64, 327, 394, 408, 415, 481; guest speakers, 63, 64, 400–401, 411; head tables, 63, 64, 156, 402–5; honored seat, 13, 277, 282, 396; international sandwich method, 416; international social occasions, 465; international/foreign officials, 399, 416; interpreters, 453; limousines, 399–400, 454–55; living-room seating, 282, 395–96; male-female alternating plan, 156, 409, 412, 414, 415; married couples, 412; place cards, 127, 154, 156, 258, 259–60, 399; precedence order, 63–64, 327, 394, 403, 408–9, 412, 413, 414, 415–17; private in-office visits, 13; protocol office assistance to plan, 413; relatives, 413; reserved seat at a performance, 397–98; round tables, 409–10, 411; seating boards and charts, 407; second ranking guest, 327; separate tables, 409–11; on a sofa, 13, 282, 395; spouses, 64, 80, 408, 411–12, 414–15; stag events, 409; on stage, 400–401; state dinners, 416; table hosts, 410–11; table placards, 406; talkative guests,

416; T-shaped tables, 411–12; unmarried couples, 413; unoccupied seats, 415; U-shaped tables, 411–12; VIPs/DVs, 145–46, 149, 161, 396, 400–401; weddings and receptions, 145–46, 149, 155–56, 161, 404–5; You-Are-Seated-At (YASA) cards, 64, 127, 406–7

security issues: bodyguards and security personnel, 42, 145–46, 405–6; electronic correspondence, 230; Force Protection Conditions (FPCON), 36–37, 423; hotels, 429–30; international/foreign locations, 422; luggage, 427, 428; materials and documents in workplace, 330; at military reservations, 5; private information, 443; spies, 270, 431–32; threat assessments, 36–37; VIP/DV visits, 36–37, 51–52; wedding party, arrival and departure of, 145; White House receptions, 299

self-introductions, 9; letters, 16–17

Senior Executive Service (SES) officials, 7, 8

Service academies: receptions, 299; weddings at chapels, 146–50

Service grade insignia, 337

service members, everyday business of, 4

Service songs: at ceremonies, 21; at Dining in, 75

ships. *See* Navy vessels

side boys and tending the side, 31–32

signature meals, 467–68

signatures, 212

silence and fixity, 10

Silent Drill Platoons, 30

silent toasts, 82

Skoal, 486–87

Smart Casual dress, 348

smoking, foreign guests and, 471

smoking lamp, 61, 71

social cards: abbreviations on, 16, 207, 208; civilian cards, 209; format for, 206, 207; information on, 206, 207; joint cards, 209; "leave cards," 206; letters of introduction and, 16; need and uses for, 200, 206; printing, 207; spouses, 209; writing notes on, 16

social occasions: buffet-style dining, 280–81; chairs, assistance with, 283, 288–89, 408; civility, 276; cocktail parties, 290–93; conversations, 270, 310–13; departures and farewells, 284–85, 313; dress for, proper, 338; escort cards, 406–7; family-style dining, 276–79; formal dining, 258, 282–84, 315; guest demeanor, 270–71; guest of honor duties, 327; handshakes, 204, 287, 291, 298, 301–2, 313, 331; host and co-host duties, 258, 279, 287–88, 327, 408–9, 410–12; host status, forfeiture of, 412; hot seat, 327; interpreters, 453; invitations, 192–93, 220; late guests, 283; napkin etiquette, 258, 260–62; official business functions, 286–90; place cards, 127, 154, 156, 258, 259–60; prayers and blessings, 258, 277–78, 289, 483, 489, 494; receptions and receiving lines, 293–300, 402, 453; retirement ceremony and dinner, 331; second ranking guest, 327; service styles, 274–75; skills, social and diplomacy, 3; standing, 304, 332; thank-you following, 285, 331; "turning the table," 284; wait staff, 284. See also Dining In; international social occasions; seating plans and arrangements; table manners; toasts; wedding, military; wedding receptions

soup and soup bowls, 265, 497, 503, 505

South America, 451–52

speakerphones, 236

spies, 270, 431–32

sporting events, audience civility for, 326–27

spouses: at business functions, 290; challenges of military liefstyle, 164; gifts for new spouse, 160; introductions, 305; invitations for ranking spouses, 192–93; names and name changes, 162–63, 451; rank ordering, 412, 416–17; seating plans and arrangements, 64, 80, 408, 411–12, 414–15; social cards, 209; of VIPs/DVs, 52–54

staff, 4. See also enlisted personnel; noncommissioned officers

standing, 9–10, 304, 332, 450

state dinners, 416

stationery, personal: color and styles of, 200–201; correspondence cards, 210–11; embossed flags, insignia, seals, and coats of arms, 201; envelopes, 200; informals, 211; names and suffixes, 201–2; need and uses for, 200; printing choices, 201; titles and rank, 202–3. See also business cards; social cards

Supreme Court justices, 238, 241

Sweden, 481, 486–87

sword ceremony, 67

swords: arch of swords/arch of sabres, 150–53, 158; cake-cutting ceremony, 145, 156, 158–59; at funerals, 90; uniform of bearers, 144; at weddings, 144, 150–53, 158

T

table manners, 257–59, 280; after-dinner drinks, 269; American-Style, 269, 270, 271–74; appetizer fork, 265; bread and butter plate, 264; cheese course, 269; dessert course, 268; fingerbowl, 268; fish course, 266; for foreign locations, 258; formal place setting, 257–58, 263–64; goblets, 264, 266; guest demeanor, 270–71; international/foreign locations, 258, 480–83; International-Style, 269, 271–74; leaving the table, 261–62, 269, 271; main course, 267; napkin etiquette, 258, 260–62, 275; salad course, 267–68; sorbet course, 267; soup course, 265; spoons and serving utensils, 265–66; table rules, 258–59; table traditions, 262–64

table placards, 406

taps, 91–92, 99

tea and tea ceremonies, 327–28, 494–95, 503, 506, 507–8

telephone etiquette: business telephones, 233–34; caller ID, 235; conference calls, 236–37; identification of self, 309; invitations, 196, 197–98; phone style, improving, 236; service or help, calling for, 236; speakerphones, 236; thank-you messages, 331; voice mail, 235–36. *See also* cell phones

telephones in international/foreign locations, 430, 431

tending the side and side boys, 31–32

text messages, 225, 231, 232, 235

Thailand, 448

Thanksgiving, 471

thank-you notes: business functions, 287; handwritten, 10, 160, 213, 214; importance of, 199; international protocol, 444; international social occasions, 461; meetings and briefings, 10; replies to sympathy messages, 216; situations that merit, 331–32; social occasions, 285; time frame for sending, 161, 332; VIP/DV visits, 56; for wedding presents, 160–61; wording of, 214–15

three rifle-volley salutes, 90–91

tipping, 333, 455

toasts, 270, 314; being honored with, 323; casual settings, 315; ceremonial toasts, 317–18; Chinese, 485, 487, 504; Dining In, 58, 71–72, 73–78; diplomatic toasts, 318–19; engagement parties, 157; Fallen Comrade Observance, 86, 315; formal dining, 315; guest of honor duties, 327, 485–86; history of custom of, 314; international social occasions, 483–87; interpreters, 453; mechanics of, 322; military toasts, 320; nonalcoholic beverages for, 78, 82, 86, 157, 315, 316; nondrinkers, 484–85; one-line toasts, 321; preparing to, 320–21; second ranking guest, 327; silent toasts, 82; Skoal, 486–87; solemn toasts in memory of anyone, 82, 315–16; at table, 315–16; toasting, hands to use, 74–75, 157, 322, 483, 486; VIP/DV visits, 38; wedding receptions, 156, 157–58; Wetting Down party, 316; who participates, 316

toilets, 433

toothpicks, 482, 497

tour guides, 38

training, military, 5–6

troop formations, 5

Truman, Harry S., 453

Two-Bell Ceremony. *See* Fallen Comrade Observance

U

uniformed Services. *See also specific Services*

uniformed services, 4

uniforms and headgear, 5; Air Force men, enlisted, 366–67; Air Force men, officers, 386–87; Air Force women, enlisted, 368–69; Air Force women, officers, 388–89; Army men, enlisted, 350–51; Army men, officers, 374–75; Army women, enlisted, 352–53; Army women, officers, 376–77; awards, decorations, and medals, 336–37; behavior while wearing, 338; Coast Guard men, enlisted, 370–71; Coast Guard men, officers, 390–91; Coast Guard women, enlisted, 372–73; Coast Guard women, officers, 392–93; covers, 6, 337; at funerals, 90, 94, 101; gloves, 339–40; Marine Corps men, enlisted, 362–63; Marine Corps men, officers, 382–83; Marine Corps women, enlisted, 364–65; Marine Corps women, officers, 384–85; Navy men, enlisted, 354–55, 358–59; Navy men, officers, 378–79; Navy women, enlisted, 356–57, 360–61; Navy women, officers, 380–81; political activity while wearing, 338; posture and, 335; regulations for, 335, 340; rules and regulations for, 5–6; sword bearers, 144; swords, 90; for weddings, 144, 336

United Kingdom, 423, 455

United Nations (UN): flag, 118–19; menu for anniversary celebration, 512; Universal Declaration of Human Rights, 121

United States Department of Commerce, 443

United States Department of Defense Directive, 35

United States Department of Justice, 476

United States Department of State: Chief of Protocol, 36; Citizens' Emergency Center, 423; duty-free entry to U.S., 36; precedence order, 121–25, 438, 450, 451; registration for traveling abroad, 423

United States government order of preference, 121–25, 438, 450, 451

United States Mint, 478

United States Office of Government Ethics, 476

United States Postal Service, 478

unmarried couples, 306, 413

V

Value Added Tax (VAT), 424

Venezuela, 449

VIPs/DVs: accommodating desires of, 38–39; after-action reports and records of visit, 55–56; agenda for, 46–49; air travel, 49–50, 55; chronicle visits, 39–40, 54; codes and orders of precedence, 122–25; departures, 55; duty-free entry to U.S., 36; education about mission, 41; escorts, 38, 41–46, 51, 52, 55; flight-line arrival, 49–50; funds for hosting, 35; gift ceremonies, 40, 475–76; hotel arrivals, 51–52; international VIPs, 34–35; interpretors, 38; interpretors, escorts, and tour guides, 41; introductions, 44–45; letters of appreciation, 41; letters of invitation, 193–94; meals and menus, 37–38; media and, 39; music for, 402; photos, 39–40, 54; planning for visit, 34–36, 42–43; private discussions, 40–41; seating plans and arrangements, 145–46, 149, 161, 396, 400–401; security issues, 36–37, 51–52; spouse itineraries, 52–54; support for, 35; thank you notes, 56; threat assessments, 36–37; toasting, 38; tour guides, 38; transportation for, 35, 38, 50–51, 400, 454–55; walking briefs, 45; wedding and reception seating plans and arrangements,

145–46, 149, 161; wedding attendance, 141–42, 149; welcome packets, 37

visitor codes, 122–25

voice mail, 235–36

W

walking, 332, 450

wardroom etiquette, 6–7, 32–33

water, toasting with, 78, 82, 86, 315

water in international locations, 429, 430

weather information, 423

wedding, military: arch of swords/arch of sabres, 150–53, 158; attendants, dress of, 144; attendants, gifts for, 159; bride, dress of, 144; clergy, 143; criteria for including military traditions, 141; elements of military weddings, 141–42; flowers, boutonnieres, and corsages, 144, 147; formality of, 142, 144; guests, dress of, 144; introduction of newly married couple, 153; location, 142; media at, 146; music, 147; pew cards, 146; processional, 147, 148; program, 163, 179–80; recessional, 147, 148, 149, 152; rehearsal, 145; rehearsal dinner, 145, 157; reserved pews, 148–49; "save the date" requests, 143; scheduling considerations, 142–43; seating plans and arrangements, 145–46, 149, 161; at Service academy chapels, 146–50; swords at, 144, 150–53, 158; VIPs/DVs, 141–42, 145–46, 149, 161; wedding party, arrival and departure of, 145; wedding party, dress of, 144

wedding anniversary announcements or invitations, 183–84

wedding gifts, 160–61

wedding invitations: acceptances and refusals, 178–79; addressing envelopes, 170–71; children as guests, 179; guest list, 165, 168, 179; handwritten, 174, 177, 213–14; letters of invitation and replies, 177–78; mailing, 165; ordering, 165; postponing a wedding, 182; rank and honorifics, 163, 195; recalling, 181–82; reception invitations, 176–77; reply cards

and other inserts, 169–70; return address,
171; service and rank, 167–68; traditional,
165–67; wording variations, 172–75

wedding receptions: announcers, 154;
attendants, gifts for, 159; cake-cutting
ceremony, 145, 156, 158–59; food and
drink, 154, 155–57; gift for new spouse,
160; head table, 156, 404–5; invitations,
176–77; location, 154; menu cards, 180;
place cards, 154, 156; program, 157;
receiving lines, 154–55, 156, 300; seating
plans and arrangements, 145–46, 155–56,
404–5; table favors, 159; toasts, 156,
157–58

White House invitations, 196, 197, 299–300

White Tie dress, 345–46

Will, 422

wine: declining, 484; Dining In, 61–62;
family-style dining, 278; formal dining,
264, 266, 267, 268, 269, 284, 315; port
wine ceremony, 70; toasting, 73, 315, 317;
wine-pouring ceremony, 67–68, 70, 73

wreath layings, 33

Y

Yemen, 481

You-Are-Seated-At (YASA) cards, 64, 127,
406–7

About the Authors

Cherlynn Conetsco began a public service career with high visibility embassy postings to Indonesia and Greece. In addition to her six years of overseas residency, numerous business trips have taken her to over twenty-five countries to practice cross-cultural etiquette. She appreciates now more than ever the unparalleled experiences gained during more than twenty-seven years of government and diplomatic service.

Conetsco is the first to create, present and direct subsequently accredited protocol and multi-cultural awareness programs that continue to train American diplomats. She is highly acclaimed for her legacy in curriculum design and instructor expertise with the Joint Military Attaché School.

Conetsco delivers eye-opening, content-rich keynotes and seminars on interacting correctly and confidently. Her innovative briefings to individuals and groups worldwide ease transition from one milieu to another, one culture to another, and from one set of responsibilities to another, thus contributing immensely to the social and professional success of her corporate, diplomatic, military, and private clients. In addition to holding a Masters in Public Administration, she is a Certified Protocol Consultant®, CPC® and current President, International Association of Protocol Consultants and Officers (IAPC) based in metropolitan Washington, D.C.

Anna Hart is a corporate and international protocol consultant and lecturer with over 25 years experience. Her clients include corporate executives, businesses, government agencies, universities and the diplomatic community.

Most recently, Ms. Hart serves as the Social Director to the Brigade of Midshipmen and the Protocol Adviser to the Commandant at the United States Naval Academy in Annapolis, Maryland. A Certified Protocol Officer (CPO), she is the first to develop and present the Academy's four-year training curriculum in protocol, etiquette, and civility for a student population of 4,300 Midshipmen. Her programs prepare Midshipmen to represent the naval services in any future assignment.